2/5/19

Flo,

while I was
ordering a copy
for WHLS;
thought you
should have
your own copy.

Your friend,
Patrick

SIMONE LADWIG-WINTERS

# LAWYERS WITHOUT RIGHTS

## THE FATE OF JEWISH LAWYERS IN BERLIN AFTER 1933

WITH FOREWORDS BY
THE HONORABLE STEPHEN G. BREYER,
BENJAMIN B. FERENCZ
AND RONALD D. ABRAMSON

Cover design by Elmarie Jara/ABA Design.
Interior design by Betsy Kulak/ABA Design.

Printed in the United States of America.

22 21 20 19 18   5 4 3 2 1

Discounts are available for books ordered in bulk. Special consideration is given to state bars, CLE programs, and other bar-related organizations. Inquire at Book Publishing, ABA Publishing, American Bar Association, 321 N. Clark Street, Chicago, Illinois 60654-7598.

www.shopABA.org

# Contents

# Introduction

The publication of the English translation of this book, *Lawyers Without Rights: The Fate of Jewish Lawyers in Berlin after 1933*, marks an exciting new step for a joint project of the American Bar Association and the Bundesrechtsanwaltskammer (German Federal Bar) that has focused on the tragic fate of Jewish lawyers in Nazi Germany and the meaning of the rule of law.

The partnership evolved after the German Federal Bar in late 2011 asked the ABA for assistance to bring to the nation's capital for the first time a compelling exhibit of 25 panels depicting the humiliation, degradation and purge from the German legal profession of roughly 5,000 lawyers from 1933 to 1938 simply because they were Jewish or had Jewish ancestry.

The exhibit, Lawyers Without Rights: Jewish Lawyers in Germany under the Third Reich, debuted in the United States in 2004 with a display at the Leo Baeck Institute in New York. Over the next eight years, the German Federal Bar arranged for the exhibit to travel to nine additional cities, and in 2012, with ABA assistance, the exhibit was shown at three Washington-area venues. (To see the exhibition program, go to https://lawyerswithoutrights.com/pdf/LWR-Booklet_orig.pdf.)

In the fall of 2012, the two bar groups formalized an arrangement to work together to display the exhibit in the United States and to explore other projects. Since then, more than 50 U.S. venues have hosted the exhibit without charge, from New York City to Los Angeles, in addition to Mexico City and Toronto. Host venues have run the gamut from federal courthouses to state supreme courts, public libraries, law schools, Jewish community centers, synagogues and private venues.

This book on the fate of Jewish lawyers in Berlin after 1933 evolved from that agreement and our shared interest in passing on to future generations the horrors of the Holocaust as well as fostering a better understanding of the rule of law.

The occupational bans on Jewish lawyers in Berlin, the capital city and home to the largest bar in Germany, was first detailed 20 years ago and updated in 2007. This English translation comes 85 years after the National Socialist regime in Germany began its step-by-step exclusion of Jewish lawyers and jurists, beginning with a partial occupational ban in 1933. By 1938, Nazi law had eliminated all but a handful of Jewish legal "consultants" from the profession. Hundreds subsequently died in concentration camps or committed suicide; scores fled the Nazi regime, emigrating across the world, including to the United States. A few earned U.S. law degrees, like lawyer Hanna Katz, one of 19 Jewish women lawyers in Berlin whose biography in this book notes she became a member of the American Bar Association.

The ground-breaking research by German author and historian Simone Ladwig-Winters began when Joel Levi, an Israeli lawyer from Tel Aviv, asked the regional bar in Berlin for a list of Jewish lawyers whose licenses had been revoked by the Nazis because of their Jewish background. Other regional bars subsequently began their own research, forming a more complete picture of the humiliation, degradation and occupational bans Jewish lawyers experienced from 1933 to 1938.

In numbers and depth of research, the Berlin book represents the most significant look at this systematic exclusion of German lawyers of Jewish origin from the legal profession. The author determined that the Berlin bar had by far the largest number of lawyers in the entire country, and of the 3,890 in the Berlin Court of Appeal district, nearly half—or 1,835 lawyers—were members of Jewish origin. The fate of 1,807 of them are detailed in the biographical section of this book.

The English-translation of *Lawyers Without Rights: The Fate of Jewish Lawyers in Berlin after 1933* includes three significant additions—forewords from the Honorable Stephen G. Breyer, associate justice of the U.S. Supreme Court and one of three sitting Jewish justices; Benjamin B. Ferencz, the sole surviving prosecutor from the Nuremberg trials; and Ronald D. Abramson, a Jewish lawyer and philanthropist whose family foundation, the Anne and Ronald Abramson Family

Foundation, provided support for this book. With minor exceptions, the second edition of Ladwig-Winters' book has been presented in its entirety, including prefaces from the Berlin bar, the author's insights into her research, notes and abbreviations.

The American Bar Association, a voluntary bar with more than 400,000 members, and the German Federal Bar, which represents all 166,000 German lawyers, are pleased to bring this book to the American public. It is presented as a tribute to those German-Jewish lawyers and their families whose fates were sealed starting in 1933 and as a way for all Americans to better understand and appreciate the meaning of "the rule of law" and how cruel, totalitarian regimes can dismantle it.

We invite you to be part of this remembrance and educational effort. At www.lawyerswithoutrights.com, you can find opportunities to support the Lawyers Without Rights project or arrange to bring the exhibit or a member of our speakers' bureau to your community for a "book talk."

We thank you again for your interest in our project and your commitment to the rule of law.

—The American Bar Association and the German Federal Bar

# Acknowledgments

project of this magnitude involves a host of contributors, from the authors who generously wrote our forewords to the American Bar Association employees who diligently managed the actual production of this book, *Lawyers Without Rights: The Fate of Jewish Lawyers in Berlin after 1933*. Coupled with our exhibit of 25 panels that has been touring the United States since 2012, our challenge is to make sure we appropriately acknowledge all who contributed in so many ways to these efforts.

It begins with the German Federal Bar, which not only developed the exhibit but made the necessary agreements in Germany to bring this English translation to the United States. Special thanks to Presidents Axel Filges (2007–15) and Ekkehart Schäfer (2015–18) for their assistance and commitment to the broader Lawyers Without Rights project, as well as to Executive Director Stephan Göcken, who since the beginning has steadily steered the exhibit and this translation project into reality.

Project support has come from the Federal Republic of Germany's embassy in Washington, D.C., and particularly from current legal advisor Holger Scherf and his predecessor Knut Abraham. German author and historian Simone Ladwig-Winters provided the excellent research and writing of this book in German some years ago and remains receptive today to the inquiries of U.S. relatives of German Jewish lawyers and jurists who seek more information on their forebears. Our gratitude also goes to the Berlin Bar Association and Bebra Verlag, the German publishing house, for their willingness and assistance in bringing the *Lawyers Without Rights* book to the United States.

As noted in the Introduction, this book translates the second edition of Ladwig-Winters work largely in its entirety. But we are honored to provide three original, compelling forewords by The Honorable Justice Stephen G. Breyer, an associate justice of the U.S. Supreme Court since 1994; Benjamin B. Ferencz, the sole surviving prosecutor at the Nuremberg trials; and Ronald D. Abramson, a Washington, D.C., lawyer whose generosity includes both a foreword as well as providing underwriting for this book from the Anne and Ronald Abramson Family Foundation. We thank all three for their valuable, distinctive contributions to this book and the effort and time it took.

As the U.S. partner, the ABA appreciates the contributions of many in support of both the Lawyers Without Rights exhibit and book and would like to single out a few volunteers and staff members for their special assistance. Then-President Stephen Zack (2010–11) provided strong guidance early in our partnership, as did the late Wm. T. (Bill) Robinson III (2011–12), who on Holocaust Remembrance Day in 2012 brought the exhibit to Washington, D.C., for the first time, hosting it at the ABA offices. Later Presidents Linda Klein (2016–17) and Hilarie Bass (2017–18) gave their support to expanding the project to include publication of this book, and ABA Executive Director Jack Rives has been a strong advocate throughout the project.

Other staff members who have played a critical role in the development of the exhibit and this book have been Bill Choyke, project coordinator; Thomas Susman, the director of the ABA Governmental Affairs Office; Jackie Casey, director of the ABA Fund for Justice and Education; ABA Publishing, including Director Donna Gollmer, Editorial Director Bryan Kay and Production Services Director Marisa L'Heureux; Center for Human Rights Director Michael Pates, whose group oversees the Lawyers Without Rights project; and colleagues Mark Florkowski, Mitch Higgins and Priscilla Totten, who over the years have provided assistance when called upon. And we appreciate the diligent efforts of translator Thomas Irwin, who spent months doing the difficult work of converting the text from German to English.

Many more both at the ABA and at the German Federal Bar contributed in some way to our projects. To all, we appreciate your work and thank you for your efforts.

—The German Federal Bar and the American Bar Association

The American Bar Association and the German Federal Bar offer special thanks to the Anne and Ronald Abramson Family Foundation for its generous support for *Lawyers Without Rights: The Fate of Jewish Lawyers in Berlin after 1933.*

# Foreword
## The Honorable Stephen G. Breyer

As Nazi atrocities fall further into the past, direct recollection becomes more difficult. But recollection does not become less important. The Bible frightens us when it speaks of a King, perhaps an entire new generation, "who knew not Joseph." And the French writer Albert Camus elaborates the thought in his book *The Plague*, an allegory of the Nazi occupation of France. His hero, Dr. Rieux, explains (in a way that I find moving) why he has written down the story:

> the *bacillus de la peste*, the plague germ (a symbol for the evil in human nature), never dies; it never entirely disappears; it simply goes into remission, perhaps for decades, but all the while lurking: in the furniture, in linen cupboards, in bedrooms, in cellars, in trunks, in handkerchiefs, in file folders, perhaps one day to reawaken its rats, and then, to the misfortune or for the education of mankind, to send them forth once again to die in some once-happy city.

By helping us recollect, law can help us guard against the day when that perpetual evil, analogous to the plague germ, might re-awaken.

This book, *Lawyers Without Rights: The Fate of Jewish Lawyers in Berlin after 1933*, helps us recollect. It recounts the early days of the Holocaust from the perspective of the law and Jewish lawyers in Ger-

many, and Berlin specifically. It is important that we and future generations remember the misuse of laws in Germany and how it permitted a
society to effectively purge a significant group of lawyers solely because
of their religion, sending many in exile or to their deaths. It is about the
misuse of law.

The book also reminds us that law can play a positive role in the
task of recollection. Those who work with the law can engage in certain classic legal tasks, such as gathering and preserving evidence and
creating legal precedent. One man who engaged in just those tasks was
Justice Robert Jackson, once a member of the U.S. Supreme Court on
which I sit.

Nearly 75 years ago, Jackson put aside his work in Washington
to serve as the chief prosecutor at Nuremberg. He later described his
Nuremberg work as the most important experience of his life, "infinitely
more important than my work on the Supreme Court or . . . anything
that I did as attorney general." His object was to make "explicit and
unambiguous" in law "that to persecute, oppress or do violence to individuals or minorities on political, racial or religious grounds . . . is an
international crime . . . (and individuals) can, and will be punished."

Jackson began by telling the Nuremberg tribunal:

The wrongs we seek to condemn and punish have been so calculated, so malignant and so devastating, that civilization cannot
tolerate their being ignored because it cannot survive their being
repeated. That four great nations, flushed with victory and stung
with injury, stay the hand of vengeance and voluntarily submit
their captive enemies to the judgment of the law is one of the
most significant tributes that Power has ever paid to Reason.

And then he built what he called a "drab case." He did not try, he
said, to "appeal to the press" or public. He understood his role as collecting hard evidence largely built on the Nazis' own documents "the
authenticity of which" could not be "challenged." And the evidence was
largely unchallenged. Nineteen convicted defendants could not answer
that evidence (three were acquitted). There was nothing to say.

Jackson collected evidence, not simply to convict the war criminals,
but also to document the facts for history to remember. "We must establish incredible events by credible evidence," he said. The evidence must
be presented "with such authenticity and in such detail that there can

be no responsible denial of these crimes in the future and no tradition of martyrdom of the Nazi leaders can arise among informed people."

Prosecutors brought to Nuremberg 100,000 captured German documents. They examined millions of feet of captured film. They produced 25,000 still photographs, a large majority from Hitler's personal photographer. Month after month, detailed by 17,000 transcript pages, the prosecutors assembled a mountain of evidence. History was revealed and remains revealed for all to see. Like the work of Jackson's team at Nuremberg, this book provides overwhelming evidence and documentation of how a Nazi regime through statute undermined the rule of law and why vicious regimes cannot be allowed to try again.

Like this book, trials can tell stories that help produce emotional, as well as factual, understanding of just what occurred. Doing so was a significant part of another historical trial that took place more than a half century ago in Jerusalem. That was the trial of Adolf Eichmann, the man in charge of transporting millions of Jews to death camps.

In prosecuting the case against Eichmann, Israel's Attorney General Gideon Hausner provided documentation. But he did something more. He sought out survivors of the Holocaust to bear witness. About 100 took the stand. They told their own stories about what they saw, what they endured, what they survived and how they remembered those who did not survive.

The audience was different from that of Nuremberg. The trial was televised both in Israel and around the world. Millions in the United States watched the proceedings. For the first time, many people heard Holocaust survivors tell their stories with their own voices. Hannah Arendt described how the trial not just told us—but showed us—the banality of evil. Historian Deborah Lipstadt tells us that the human stories "changed our perception of the victims of genocide."

Seen from the perspective of remembrance, both trials played an important role. We remember through facts, figures and rational argument; we also remember through human stories that carry emotion and implant feeling. The documented record prevents history from doubting what was done; the compelling personal stories help prevent the future from forgetting the victims themselves, their stories and their humanity.

The example of Nuremberg has helped to inspire the establishment of tribunals, often international tribunals, with authority to protect basic human rights and to pursue those who violate them. But like Penelope's tapestry, the legal cloth that we weave in the day is often unraveled during the night. This provides even more reason to continue the work—to substitute, as Justice Jackson reminded us, the power of Reason for the force of Power. The Talmud teaches us, "it is not incumbent upon you to complete the work. But neither are you free to evade it."

Nuremberg reminds us that the Holocaust story ended with a fair trial. That trial, along with other ways in which law furthers the work of remembrance, fuels our eternal aspiration for justice. As this book so stirringly shows, the road to justice begins with a sound legal system. And as the Book of Exodus tells us, we cannot allow future generations to forget historical tragedies like the Holocaust and what can happen when there is no rule of law.

# Foreword

## Ronald D. Abramson

" I do not say that art is my aim; art is my means," so said Poland-born illustrator Arthur Szyk (1894–1951), one of the greatest artists and political satirists of the Holocaust era who immigrated to the United States in 1940. Today, Szyk's popular traveling exhibit includes 25 reproductions of political caricatures that protested Nazi and fascist tyranny during World War II and advocated for the rescue of European Jewry.

The exhibit Lawyers Without Rights: Jewish Lawyers in Germany under the Third Reich, also 25 panels, depicts how the legal structure of the Weimer Republic dissolved beginning in 1933 and how the *rule of law* was systematically displaced by a statutory *rule by law*. The changes led to the expulsion of several thousand Jewish lawyers and jurists and raised the specter of whether the National Socialist state of Germany needed lawyers at all.

I first became acquainted with the Lawyers Without Rights exhibit when it was on display at The George Washington University Law School in early fall of 2012 in my hometown of Washington, DC. I was moved and impressed and extremely elated to learn that the American Bar Association and the German Federal Bar would be sponsoring this traveling exhibit throughout the United States. In doing so, they expanded a little-known project highlighting the plight of Jewish lawyers in Germany during the Nazi era. The joint commitment by these

two bar associations has since brought greater awareness of the Holocaust and the rule of law to thousands of people throughout the United
States and parts of Canada and Mexico.

The English translation of *Lawyers Without Rights: The Fate of
Jewish Lawyers in Berlin after 1933* represents an even more ambitious
step to broaden awareness of how the Nazis misused the principle of law
to lay plans for a "Final Solution" that would eventually send six million
Jews to their deaths and millions of others fleeing their homelands. Simone Ladwig-Winters' historical account of how this systematic attack on
the legal profession steadily weakened resistance provides an important
message that today's legal profession must stand strong to resist any
temptations that could—and will—undermine the values of a society
and its allegiance to the rule of law.

As an attorney for nearly a half a century, these issues are very personal to me. As a Jewish attorney, I am even more troubled that the non-
Jewish lawyers in Berlin and Germany at the time largely stepped aside
and offered little resistance to the dismantling of their profession as well
as to the substitution of jurisprudence in Germany with Hitler's law.

Even more personal to me is that the Lawyers Without Rights project affords an opportunity to continue the Abramson family's commitment to educate future generations of the tragedy and lessons of
the Holocaust. My father, Albert Abramson, who died in 2012 at the
age of 94, is widely credited as the principal force in the creation of the
U.S. Holocaust Memorial Museum in Washington, DC. A successful
apartment developer, he followed the same pragmatic approach in the
mid-1980s to move this American memorial ahead when the effort was
stalling and the aging and deaths of survivors created a special sense of
urgency.

As his obituary in *The New York Times* recounted, my father, who
was chairman of the museum development committee, argued fiercely
with the famed Romanian-born Jewish-American writer and Holocaust
survivor Elie Wiesel regarding planning of the museum. After years of
disagreement, Mr. Wiesel stepped aside, and my father's responsibilities
grew, assuming more oversight of programming, fundraising and cul-
tivating support in Congress for the Holocaust museum. As the *Times*
pointed out, he won over survivors loyal to Mr. Wiesel by praising them
as the "spiritual leaders" who kept the project alive. "Building a project
of this complexity was something beyond their experience—just like

writing a book would be beyond mine," he told *The Washington Post* in a 1987 interview.

Our family's continuing commitment to this principle is evidenced by our support of the U.S. Holocaust Memorial Museum through the funding of a number of graduate student research fellowships at the museum's Jack, Joseph and Morton Mandel Center for Advanced Holocaust Studies. This program provides graduate students the opportunity to begin their thesis or dissertation research projects in a setting of intellectual stimulation and support.

The Anne and Ronald Abramson Family Foundation is honored to have the opportunity to underwrite this book. It stands as a tribute to the Jewish attorneys in Berlin and throughout Nazi-controlled Europe who were brutally segregated and expelled from the practice of law. Of the 1,404 Jewish lawyers in Berlin alone whose fate is known, 28 committed suicide, more than 500 died during this time, 107 survived the camps or went underground and 703 emigrated to new and usually lesser lives abroad. About five dozen left Germany and returned. Their stories collectively provide a painful reminder of why lawyers must lead the resistance when fair justice and the rule of law come under attack.

As Szyk said of his art, the Lawyers Without Rights project is not the aim but a means. We must all work together to keep the memory of the Holocaust current and the meaning of the rule of law relevant and alive.

# Foreword

## Benjamin B. Ferencz

That a book published in 2018 by the American Bar Association should focus on the persecution of lawyers in Germany during the Third Reich—which collapsed almost 75 years ago—reminds us that the bleak lessons of such an ignominious past are as relevant as ever. The failure to enforce law and time-honored principles of justice still poses increasing threats to people everywhere.

As soon as Hitler's Nazi government took control of Germany in 1933, numerous discriminatory new German laws were enacted to assure that "Aryan blood" would no longer be contaminated by Jews, Gypsies and other "inferior" groups, all of whom had to be removed from power. Among such laws were prohibitions on the practice of law by Jews and a broad-ranging exclusion of Jews and other "undesirables" from the professional, social and economic life of Germany. They were excluded from schools and subject to an array of legal prohibitions designed to make living conditions unbearable. Virulent Nazi anti-Semitism led to specific plans for "The Final Solution" that called for total annihilation of all the Jews in Europe. Other perceived adversaries of the regime faced a similar fate.

The quadripartite war crimes trial by the International Military Tribunal at Nuremberg, established by the victorious Allied powers and led by the United States, confirmed only part of the sorry story. The trial transcripts and judgment offer irrefutable proof of mass atrocity crimes that have been meticulously recorded in undeniable historical archives.

After receiving my law degree from Harvard in 1943, I joined the U.S. Army as a combat soldier, participating in every major battle in Europe. My last assignments included gathering evidence in Nazi concentration camps as they were being liberated. The scenes of horror were indescribable. The trauma has never left me. I had peered into hell.

When the war was over I was invited by the Pentagon to return to Germany to assist in a dozen subsequent war crimes trials. I was appointed chief prosecutor in the "*Einsatzgruppen* case." All 22 high-ranking and well-educated commanders were promptly convicted of murdering over a million innocent Jewish men, women and children. Victims were slaughtered simply because they did not share the race, religion or ideology of their executioners. It was my first case. I was then 27 years old.

Although I knew that each of the 22 defendants was certainly guilty of outrageous crimes against humanity, I did not ask for the death penalty. I felt the scales of justice could never be balanced by hanging only a handful of the 3,000 other mass murderers. If I could encourage a rule of law that would prevent such genocides in the future it might have some permanent humanitarian significance. It was my "plea of humanity to law."

I stayed on in Germany to set up new programs for restitution and compensation to all victims of Nazi persecution. I was guided by the elementary principle of justice: That those responsible for illegal harms should be required to repair injuries and compensate their victims. Victims of Nazi persecution were the beneficiaries of these programs, regardless of their race or creed.

In 1952, encouraged by German Chancellor Konrad Adenauer, an unprecedented treaty was signed among West Germany, Israel and the "Claims Conference" representing leading Jewish charities. I set up legal aid offices in 19 countries to help claimants with complicated indemnification claims. Of course, all of this could not have been done without the help of German lawyers.

Former German Jewish lawyers who had been forced to flee Nazi Germany became the key staff members for the three restitution organizations. Many of them had served as translators, advisors or researchers during the Nuremberg trials. Since most of them could not be qualified to practice law in their countries of refuge, they had to depend upon menial employment to survive. Despite modest salaries, many were glad to return to their native Germany in hopes of being able to resume their shattered lives.

One former Berlin Jewish lawyer deserves special note. Herbert Schoenfeldt, a respected Jewish lawyer in Berlin, had to carry his aged mother on his back to escape over the Pyrenees Mountains to France. In New York he worked as a shoe salesman.

We became friends when he was hired as a legal consultant for the subsequent Nuremberg trials. When those proceedings neared conclusion, I hired him to direct the restitution office I had set up in Stuttgart. He later directed a new office in Bonn, where he could have closer contact with politicians who had to approve new restitution laws.

He became a key player in the Claims Conference efforts to obtain compensation on behalf of concentration camp survivors forced to serve as slave laborers for leading German industries. Schoenfeldt died in 1956, as the final compensation law was being passed. He received a state funeral from the German government in recognition of the respect he had earned.

For those lawyers who were persecuted or had to flee Nazi tyranny because of their religion, *Lawyers Without Rights: The Fate of Jewish Lawyers in Berlin after 1933* demonstrates that their suffering has not been forgotten. Nor has it been in vain.

I have just started my 99th year, having spent most of my life striving for a more humane and peaceful world where all humans—whatever their race, creed or gender—are entitled to live in peace and human dignity. I appreciate the new German generation's efforts to overcome the evil deeds of their ancestors. My slogans remain "Law not war" and "Never give up!"

# About the Second Edition

When the first edition of *Lawyers Without Rights* appeared in 1998, it was the 60th anniversary of the general occupational ban on Jewish attorneys. In 1938 the National Socialist government—before the pogrom in November—felt that the time had come when it was no longer necessary to allow their Jewish colleagues membership in the bar. Prior to this was gradual exclusion by means of terroristic attacks on individuals in the first months after the National Socialist seizure of power and the 1933 occupational ban, which at that time still granted exceptions, as well as the undermining of their economic interests. The second stage after 1933 was undertaken by the National Socialist state in 1938, which involved another wide-ranging occupational ban. Afterward only a few attorneys of Jewish origin were admitted as "consultants," who were legal advisers and representatives with limited powers.

The 1998 presentation was the first to systematically document exclusion from the growing profession and focus on the victims. The book was accompanied by an exhibition that was financed by the Berlin Bar Association and individual sponsors. It premiered at the "New synagogues—Center Judaicum" foundation. In the meantime the project that originated in Berlin developed further. Based on the 1998 exhibit, the author developed a concept for an exhibition by the Federal German Bar Association to be displayed in various cities and regions in conjunction with the Association of German Jurists, each with regional research results and biographies. The traveling exhibit has since been shown in more than 35 cities.[1] The exhibit was also presented in English translation in Israel (Jerusalem, Tel Aviv and Haifa); in the United States (in New York and Los Angeles), in Mexico, as well as in Canada (in

Montreal, Toronto and Ontario, in both English and French). In June 1999 the International Association of Jewish Lawyers and Jurists held a conference in Berlin on the subject of Jewish attorneys. This gave rise to the opportunity to talk with participants from all over the world about their personal relationship to Berlin.[2]

This broad manner of presentation has attracted an interested public, as well as relatives of former attorneys. Information about further life histories that were virtually unavailable for lawyers who left Germany were able to be filled out with help from family members. The book *Lawyers Without Rights* had also made its way in the world. People from Norway and Tasmania, Chile and South Africa, Königs Wusterhausen, Berlin-Wilmersdorf and Schöneberg, got in touch with the author, in order to help complete the life histories in the biographical directory. Many surviving family members are grateful to see that their father, grandfather or aunt has not been completely forgotten. They sought to round out the individual biographies with documents and other materials. On the other hand, objections were raised that the investigation did not go deep enough, did not always take the right approach, or contained incorrect information. In individual instances the criticism was often justified, yet there was an abundance of material and data to evaluate which could not always be sufficiently checked in every case. This has now been taken into account in this second edition.

*Lawyers Without Rights* was and is a work in progress. It constitutes a scholarly investigation, on the one hand, designed to provide the names and—to the extent possible—the fates of excluded and persecuted attorneys and, on the other hand, to present and analyze the results of the discriminatory measures these attorneys were confronted with. The criteria for incorporation into the documentation are clearly outlined below.

Included in this work are people who worked as attorneys in 1933, who were based in Berlin, and who were of Jewish origin based on National Socialist criteria. The requirements put forth above have been strictly adhered to. As a result, in comparison to the first edition, numerous people are no longer included in the documentation because, after meticulous examination of the sources, it became clear that one of the three requirements could not be met.[3] In most cases it turned out that, while these people were jurists, they were not admitted to the bar as attorneys in 1933.

The notice of departure to New York of Hanna Katz, dated June 6, 1941

For example, the first edition of the book provides information about prominent personalities, such as the jurist and photographer, Eric Salomon, who was forced to endure bitter persecution. However, detailed research has meanwhile shown that he was not admitted to the bar as an attorney in 1933.[4] The reexamination undertaken for the new edition has had the result that about 50 people have been removed from the directory. On the other hand, around 175 additional persons could be included.

The focus of the documentation is on measures taken to effect exclusion from the legal profession. At the same time, to the extent it was possible, the further life story of those affected was also included. The newest results from research were taken into account in this regard.[5] Because the documentation could not be based on a finalized list that was handed down, various sources of information had to be carefully gathered together for each person. A typical example of the difficulties encountered during the course of research was when two attorneys had the same name. In such cases proper assignment of information was not always easy, often even impossible. For example, in each case there were two attorneys with the names Paul Casper, Siegfried Bergmann, Julian Jacobsohn, Willy Landsberg, Fritz Kalischer and Arthur Levy, and even three attorneys named Fritz Strauß (one of which was not of Jewish origin). Because some sources only mention people without their first name and the dates of birth were almost always missing, in the case of namesakes, reliable identification was often only possible through the critical comparison of various sources. Nevertheless, one cannot be certain whether or not inaccuracies or mistakes have crept into these or other short biographies. The author would be thankful for corrections and additions from readers of this book.

It must also be noted that the research was made difficult because important materials no longer exist. In a city where so much is collected and preserved, there is not a single signboard of even one "consultant," there is not a single stamp of even one excluded notary. Enormous gaps crop up everywhere in the materials that have been passed on. Up to now only one complete attorney's file has been found, which contains many important documents. Just one, although there should be files for over 1,800 people. This one file has only survived by chance, because it found its way to Norway over a labyrinthine path. The discovery of this file is unique; the radical fashion in which it was sought to erase the existence of the Jewish attorneys is reflected in the missing documents. It must also be assumed that even after the war such documents "disappeared" or were destroyed on purpose. Nevertheless, the bureaucrats and professional colleagues acting at that time could not succeed in erasing all testimonials. The secure and preserved materials convey important information to us today. This is what the present documentation is based on.

It's really not a matter of lost files. It is not just files that disappeared, but also human beings. For many persons who were murdered, the only thing that could be determined with certainty is the day of their deportation. This book is especially devoted to the memory of these abducted and murdered attorneys.

# A Book That Serves as a Sign of Hope:

## Berlin Bar Association Preface to the Second Edition

S hame, joy and hope—these were the feelings of Dr. Bernhard Dombek, president of the Berlin Bar Association, when he presented the first edition of this book in 1998. Meanwhile the volume that chronicles the sad fate of our Jewish colleagues, including several female attorneys in Berlin, has itself become a catalyst for the process of coming to terms with history. The book was followed by a highly respected exhibition that was on display, among other locations, in Israel, New York, Los Angeles, Canada and Mexico. This exhibition, in turn, initiated a series of publications that shed light on the fate of Jewish colleagues in various German cities.

The response generated by the first publication brought additional and new findings back to Berlin from all over the world. As a result the biographical index of Berlin attorneys of Jewish origin, which remains the very heart of the book, was able to be expanded to include 175 names and destinies. It was and remains our intention to establish a memorial for the stories of these ostracized and persecuted colleagues.

The introductory chapters that place the fate of these individuals in the context of their systematic exclusion under National Socialism have been expanded and revised. Here mention will only be made of the activities of the "legal advisers." After October 1938, Jewish attorneys who had been excluded from the legal profession due to the occupational ban could apply to be admitted as legal advisers after a disclosure of their financial circumstances and a statement of their political views. The fate of 91 legal "consultants" has been researched for this book—91 of what were previously 1,835 attorneys of Jewish origin.

As the first female president of the Berlin Bar Association, I find the chapter concerning the occupational ban on Jewish attorneys especially interesting. It was only in 1922 that women were allowed to study law. At the beginning of 1933, 19 women of Jewish origin were admitted to practice law in Berlin. However, they were all disbarred in the same year—with one exception—due to the occupational ban.

I was also troubled by the question of just why the Berlin Bar apparently passively acquiesced to the systematic exclusion of their Jewish colleagues.

From January 9 to 13, 1933—therefore still before Hitler's "seizure of power"—bar association elections were held at regular intervals for the 16 board positions that became free. For the first time politics played a role in these elections, because the NSDAP (National Socialist German Workers' Party) presented its own list. Altogether, 1,292 members of the bar cast their votes. In the first round of voting eight Jewish colleagues were elected with an absolute majority, including the chairman Ernst Wolff with over 1,000 votes. The National Socialist candidate Reinhard Neubert did not even have a chance with just 324 votes. During the by-election on February 11, 1933—and therefore already under Hitler's rule—the Jewish colleague Stern received 306 votes, while the National Socialist candidates, having received 26 and 21 votes respectively, once again were confronted with a crushing defeat.

It was only after the beginning of the Nazi reign of terror, which led to the resignation of the entire bar association board "in light of political developments," that National Socialists could take it over. That they were unable to trust the Berlin legal community is shown by the way the election was carried out. Prussian Minister of Justice Hanns Kerrl issued an administrative circular that the "election" would take place on April 22, 1933 "without discussion by ballot through acclamation" and would take place in a "public session." These "members of the public" consisted of 300 members of the SA and the NSDAP, who sat in closed ranks between the approximately 700 attorneys who were present. Reinhard Neubert, who had run unsuccessfully in January, appeared wearing a party uniform and was now officially chosen as chairman. Within half an hour 33 board members were "elected" through acclamation—without discussion and with two opposing votes. From this point on National Socialists dominated the Berlin Bar Association.

Up to 1935 German bar associations were directed by board members. The new version of the Reich Attorney's Code of December 13, 1935, deprived bar associations of their legal capacity. The chairmen were made subject to the instructions of the president of the Reich Bar Association and were given the official title of "president." It is indeed characteristic of the mood of the postwar era that it was apparently not regarded as self-evident that this designation should be revoked upon introduction of the Federal Attorney's Code. Perhaps this book will have the effect of causing this matter to once again be taken under review.

The response to this book in the past years is an encouraging sign of hope that there will never again be attorneys without rights in this country.

Dr. Margarete von Galen
President of the Berlin Bar Association
June 2007

# Shame, Joy and Hope:

## Berlin Bar Association
## Preface to the First Edition

It was supposed to be a list, nothing more than a list. This was the wish of the board of the Tel Aviv Bar Association. It was expressed during a 1995 visit to the Berlin Bar Association and inspired by Gerhard Jungfer's lecture about the expulsion of Jewish attorneys from the Berlin Bar. A list of excluded attorneys with their names and their last addresses, if known. An indication of their individual fates—in order to show that neither they nor what they had suffered has been forgotten.

The board of the Berlin Bar Association can only feel shame that there was still no such list almost 60 years after the expulsion of the last Jewish attorneys. Why hadn't the board already created a list? Why was it necessary for the Tel Aviv Bar Association to encourage the 1995 board to take action?

Those who had already dealt with this topic in a scholarly fashion told us that the wish of the Tel Aviv Bar Association could not be fulfilled. The files of the Berlin Bar Association had been burnt; a list would be riddled with numerous omissions. Moreover, in November 1998 a highly respected memorial service had been held by the Berlin Bar Association in remembrance of the expulsion of Jewish attorneys.

Despite these concerns confidence prevailed, as well as the desire to erase the shame over previous failure. This confidence was justified, because we found Simone Ladwig-Winters. She undertook the mission we entrusted her with a high level of commitment and a great deal of expertise. Ever recurring skepticism on our part about the success of our and her project was always—to our utmost gratification—cogently disproved by her. The list of attorneys subjected to anti-Semitic persecution after 1933 is virtually complete. This lessens our shame that the list has been created at such a late date. It is not just the list. It is accompanied by extensive documentation concerning the events that led to the expulsion. Simone Ladwig-Winters has presented the exclusion of attorneys of Jewish origin after 1933 and the stories of many individuals caught up therein in a sober scholarly fashion that is nonetheless deeply moving.

However, consternation and sorrow concerning the human suffering that speaks forth from this documentation is not enough. Neither is the rage felt toward our colleagues of non-Jewish origin from whom not a single word of protest against the fate of their Jewish colleagues has been passed on. We need the hope, better yet the certainty, that all German attorneys will watchfully ensure that human rights are respected everywhere. Never again must there be attorneys without rights.

Dr. Bernhard Dombek
President of the Berlin Bar Association
September 1998

# Lawyers Without Rights: A Documentation of Exclusion

Immediately after the seizure of power, which was really more of a transfer of power to the National Socialists, the charged atmosphere of anti-Semitism unleashed itself in its full vehemence against Jewish attorneys. Together with doctors, as well as the proprietors of businesses and department stores, they were targeted to be excluded from their established professions. In 1933 radical National Socialists intended to quickly implement an occupational ban on Jewish attorneys. Yet contrary to the expectations of the backers of this initiative, the 1933 division into Jewish and non-Jewish attorneys did not yet lead to comprehensive and complete segregation. This measure only took place five years later in 1938.

With 3,400 attorneys Berlin had by far the largest bar in the entire Reich. In the district of the Berlin Court of Appeal, which extended well beyond the borders of Berlin, there were actually 3,890 attorneys.[6] These circumstances were due to the fact that many public officials of the Reich and Prussia, as well as of major banks and almost all important associations, had their headquarters in the city. Nowhere near all attorneys were members of the bar. Many worked as an in-house counsel for large businesses or associations.[7] The proportion of attorneys of Jewish origin in Berlin should be placed at 1,835.[8] Given a total of 3,400 attorneys who belonged to the Berlin bar on December 31, 1932, 43 percent of the members were of Jewish origin.[9] This high proportion of colleagues of Jewish origin clearly set Berlin apart from other cities.[10]

In 1933 Berlin was not just the capital of the Reich, but also the German city with the largest Jewish community—it had 160,565 members. About a third of all German Jews lived there.[11] The Jews of Berlin were especially represented in the mercantile community and the independent professions, as well artists. This specific choice of professions was of long standing. The Jewish minority had been discriminated against for centuries and excluded from the production of material goods and thereby also prohibited from owning land (up to the beginning of the nineteenth century). At the same time they were denied access to public service.[12] It was only during the course of the nineteenth century that these limitations were gradually abolished and that Jews could thereby make inroads into these previously inaccessible areas. With the opening up of the universities many chose to pursue legal studies. The inclination to deal with legal issues immediately suggested itself to those interested in education. For example, Heinrich Heine also studied law. Jurisprudence, due to its basic normative structures and philosophical principles, was something that many students were acquainted with from traditional Jewish disputation. The practice of law therefore became a major field of activity for Jewish jurists, because for many years they had been denied access to positions as public officials in the administration of government or as judges, as well as at universities. While as of 1869 they had de jure equality with other German citizens, something that was also confirmed by the Equality Act of 1871 after the formation of the German Reich, they were nonetheless held back de facto in the appointment and promotion as public servants.[13] Informal practices led to a subtle and lasting exclusion from public service. The indeterminate time allotted for classification as a new entrant into the administrative grade of the civil service[14] ensured that there would be an additional social selection process in regard to candidates for judges, because the status as candidate for judicial office was without remuneration.[15]

The practice of law emerged in 1878/1879, inseparably linked to the development of civil society. Those who did not wish to be baptized and yet still wanted to work as jurists were well advised to set up a law practice.[16] Many Jews therefore chose the insecurity of a law practice over the uncertain prospect of a judicial office that might never be attained.

Even before the end of the German Imperial Era the proportion of Jews that were members of the Berlin Bar was substantial for this reason. This development received new impetus as sons (and also daughters, beginning in the 1920s) took over their father's law firm. Uncertainties regarding retirement and provision for old age or concerning income were offset by opportunities in material terms, which were not factors, for example, in judicial office. The judge knew what sort of career opportunities awaited him and what he had to expect at the end of his professional career, regardless of whether he had been a good or a mediocre jurist. This is something that an attorney could not know, yet if he was fortunate and prepared to take on his cases with a high degree of commitment, then he could attain a comfortable standard of living, as well as considerable social recognition.

The change of power in January 1933 completely altered this situation. The National Socialists, supported by their German nationalist conservative coalition partners, immediately implemented their anti-Semitic program through political measures. The racist categories of "Jew" or "non-Aryan" (the latter included more than simply "Jews") were at once transformed into legal structures that created a different reality.

The new regulations affected a group that was completely unprepared for them. It was certainly not a group that was in any way homogeneous in terms of politics and religion. Within the bar anti-Semitic exclusion was implemented in just a few years. Both the structural and the individual consequences thereof, when investigated in terms of the Berlin bar, constitute a microcosm for the entire Reich.[17]

## Research Methods

The first wave of exclusion and the final occupational ban occurred decades ago. Through this documentation the Berlin Bar Association is seeking to bring back a general awareness of the events affecting and the fate of the excluded attorneys.

The goal was to create a list of those subjected to anti-Semitic discrimination by National Socialist policy. The criteria for including people in this documentation were:

- admitted to the bar as an attorney in 1933,
- regarded as Jewish and/or "non-Aryan" as defined under National Socialism,
- located in Berlin, that is, in the municipality of Berlin.[18]

The definition of who was to be defined as "non-Aryan"[19] was to be found in Ordinance 1 to Implement the Law for the Reestablishment of Lifelong Civil Service of April 7, 1933:[20]

A person is not Aryan if he is the descendant of non-Aryan, especially Jewish, parents or grandparents. It is sufficient if one parent or one grandparent is not Aryan. In particular, this is to be assumed if one parent or one grandparent was an adherent of the Jewish religion.

The definition was not based on current religious affiliation, but rather on descent in relation to grandparents. As a result, the circle of those affected extended far beyond members of Jewish congregations. It encompassed all people regardless of their religious affiliation or worldview who had a grandparent who once belonged to a Jewish congregation. It therefore also included a group of people who were now deemed "mixed-blood Jews," as well as all dissidents who had left Jewish congregations or Jews who had converted to Christianity.

For the creation of a directory as to who was and who was not a member of the bar in 1933 and thereafter, there was no material available associated with the Berlin Bar Association from that time.[21] Therefore existing printed primary sources, archive collections and relevant secondary literature had to be analyzed. This consisted primarily of: judicial sources,[22] such as the file cards and personal files of the Reich Ministry of Justice, which are safeguarded in the German Federal Archive,[23] the "1933 Trial Docket for Prussian Judicial Officials" and the Judicial Ministerial Gazette for Prussian Legislation and Administration of Justice (JMBl.), the lists of prohibition on representation,[24] which appeared irregularly and were separately bound—and in the meantime are safely stored in the Berlin State Archive. Apart from the printed sources none of these collections are complete. Regarding the card files, which consist of a collection of about 55,000 cards, many are missing, as is also the case with personnel files. These sources are nevertheless invaluable, because they provide extensive information.[25] The Trial Docket for Prussian Judicial Officials has also proven indispensable, although it is a little cumbersome to work with, because the names have been listed in accordance with admission to the respective courts, usually without mention of the first name.[26] In addition, use was made of publicly accessible directories such as address books, industry directories and telephone books. For some of the persons identified the records of the 1939 Census were also used, in which each had to provide his "racial" lineage back to his grandparents. Here one finds abbreviations such as "JJJJ" (four Jewish grandparents) or "JJNN" (two Jewish grandparents, two non-Jewish grandparents), which provide information about classification according to NS criteria. This study was also supplemented with biographical data obtained from a research project on the Reich Flight Tax and tax warrants of apprehension.[27]

Through the combined evaluation of primary and secondary sources it was finally possible to obtain 1,807 names of attorneys who were admitted to the Berlin Bar and defined as Jews after the seizure of power in January 1933.

In order to determine the further course of the lives of these persons, the names were matched with recent data collections. In essence this consisted of the entire data of the Berlin Memorial Book,[28] as well as the Theresianstadt Memorial Book, the Book of Remembrance of Victims of the Deportations to the Baltics and the second edition of the comprehensive memorial book "Victims of the Persecution of the Jews Under the National Socialist Tyranny in Germany, 1933–1945," edited by the German Federal Archives.

In addition, particular attention was given to individual fates during the course of emigration. To this purpose the memoirs available at the Leo Baeck Institute in New York, were evaluated.[29] Another important source was applications of immigrants to the American Committee for the Guidance of the Professional Personnel, an institution which made decisions regarding the award of scholarships for American law schools. In the applications the persons concerned had to provide information on their previous life history. Of the approximately 500 applicants, a not inconsiderable part thereof came from Berlin and was also taken into consideration for the awarding of scholarships.

In regard to the situation of those attorneys who survived in Berlin and/or returned there after 1945 and applied to be readmitted to the bar, the few personnel files of the Bar Association from this time were able to provide information. In the meantime, these have been added to the collection of the Berlin State Archives.

Contemporary witnesses, who could make a subjective contribution to this investigation on the basis of oral history, were only rarely available. Frequently, during the course of research, the author encountered the remark: "Unfortunately you came too late."[30] The conversations that the author held repeatedly with Werner Wolff, who had been a young attorney in 1933, were quite helpful. His memories were very exact, and they provided a very vivid impression of the structures that shaped the work of an attorney in the early 1930s—how older attorneys dealt with younger ones or who was valued for his legal talents or his human stature. In a similar fashion the husband of the attorney Käthe Loewy, the attorney Fritz Manasse—who was still practicing in 2003, but has since passed away—was able to supplement the picture with important information. At this time, I wish to extend my heartfelt thanks to both of them.

The biographical directory that has been produced in this way extends, to the extent information could be ascertained, beyond information over a person's legal activities and professional career. The short and sometimes longer information concerning individuals should give the reader a personal feel for the exclusion and persecution. In addition to this, the overall statistical analysis should provide an insight into the quantitative dimensions of exclusion.

## A Unique Document: The Album of Willy Naatz

The Berlin Bar Association does not have any documents of its own from the Nazi era. It must remain an open question whether these were completely destroyed as a result of the war or also due to later intentional acts. Here too personal continuity has contributed to the fact that after 1945 there was no impulse to look more closely into these matters. Nothing has been passed on. As a result, the album of Willy Naatz, the Law Clerk of the Bar Association of the District Court, in which about seventy photographs of Jewish attorneys have been preserved, constitutes a unique document.[31] Willy Naatz (March 16, 1879, Berlin–December 30, 1955, Berlin), who started his work with the Bar

Association as a simple employee at the age of 14, acted as a central information and communication exchange within the District Court.

Willy Naatz at his workplace in the attorneys' office of the Berlin District Court on March 16, 1955, his 76th birthday

Naatz ensured that attorneys who had appointments at two different courts at the same time would have corresponding arrangements made for appropriate representation, procured robes for them if they had forgotten their own, supplied attorneys with sandwiches and once persuaded two attorneys who were soon to appear in court as adversaries to engage in a chess game (which was received with some surprise by clients who happened to pass by).[32] Naatz also took part with great success in performances of the musical society that was associated with the Court. During his more than 60 years of service in the Court Bar Association, he gained the recognition, friendship and trust of many lawyers. During National Socialism Naatz and other law clerks undertook the task of examining the political views of an unknown attorney. Such an attorney "was involved in casual conversation, during which one was cautiously able to get a feel for the newcomer. By means of jokes, which tentatively hinted at or even contained strong political content, the newcomer was cautiously sized up. Depending on his reaction, the law clerks passed judgment upon the lawyer who had then been made subject to this clever form of test. The evaluation that was passed on was both acknowledged and determinative. It was then immediately made clear whether the newcomer was 'warm,' 'lukewarm' or 'cold'—which was then passed on as a signal to alert or reassure others."[33] Naatz kept his integrity; he did not differentiate between Jewish and non-Jewish attorneys. This is also shown by the heartfelt congratulations sent to him by some survivors on the occasion of commemorative days (his 50th and 60th work anniversaries, as well as his 70th, 75th and 76th birthdays).

In his album, in which Naatz kept the many congratulations, there is also a worn-out card. The place and date is marked "Theresienstadt, August 28, 1944." It is the card of a deportee, Judicial Councillor Dr. Siegmann, with whom Naatz had obviously maintained contact. Siegmann was taken to Auschwitz shortly after sending the card from Theresienstadt and murdered there. His postcard to Naatz is apparently the last that was heard from him. It is the only letter of this nature from the 299 Berlin attorneys who perished that has been passed on. Surely there must have been more—it is just that nobody kept them. In addition to formalized procedure, the profession had also developed a very lively social life for its members as well as its own—even if still young—tradition, there was apparently little room for "sentimentality," such as that cultivated by Naatz. The major positions of the bar were held by National Socialists. There was no resistance in the face of the "segregation" of Jewish colleagues. Those who continued to work without interference could apparently not allow themselves to dwell on melancholy feelings about them and the bygone times for which they stood. Apparently even after the end of the Nazi era this behavior was slow to change. It was only after a change of generations that certain questions could be raised at all.

Missing files and the lack of contemporary witnesses may have well led to the fact that the results of research are not satisfactory in certain individual short biographies. One could also criticize the terminology employed. For example, the term "occupational ban" was not used at that time to designate that one was prevented from practicing one's profession due to prohibitions on representation (1933) and/or disbarment (1933, 1938). Yet the concept describes the circumstances with the most accuracy. Nevertheless almost none of the affected parties would have made use of such a drastic term. Many examples of this kind can be found, which would serve well as the subject of further research.

Language is certainly the area in which it is easiest to take measure of injuries and taboos, as well as of developments. If, for example, in the following text terms like "mixed-race" or "Aryan" recur, this is not the result of a thoughtless adoption of Nazi terminology, but rather use of the definitional classification that had claim to absolute validity during National Socialism and was thereby the expression of discrimination.

The powerful effect of this oppression on language is shown by the personal files that arose after 1945 of those who sought readmission to the bar as attorneys. Individuals who had lived "undercover" described their experience in an extremely abbreviated form. In part the term "illegal survivor" was used—as if survival could be illegal. It was already in 1947 that Victor Klemperer, with his book *LTI, lingua tertii imperii*,[34] brought attention to the consequences that were the result of language that had been mutated through the NS reign of terror. These consequences continue.

Here it must be noted that no disrespect to the contribution of female attorneys is intended if this documentation does not generally make specific reference to female attorneys. While there was only a small number of women, they nonetheless constitute 19 of the 1,807 persons ascertained. However, constant reference in the text to attorneys using both the male and female pronouns would prove cumbersome.

The documentation of the fate of Berlin lawyers of Jewish origin is not just a controversy that involves the past. One person I spoke with on the condition of not being mentioned by name, because he feared that after publication he would be known as a "Jewish oaf." A family member of several Jewish attorneys expressed the view that everything occurred so long ago that it would be best not to once again dredge up "the old stuff" and added that he was well aware of what happened to "his people," but didn't want to talk about it . . . because otherwise life would be unbearable."[35]

In psychoanalysis there exists the principle of the triad "remembering, repeating, working through," that at least with the instruction to remember, takes up a central point of Jewish tradition: "Zachor!—Remember!"[36] If one deals with these individual destinies, one can't help but feel the loss of intellectual greatness, linguistic brilliance and human diversity caused by the violent segregation, fragmentation, expulsion and destruction of this minority. In the 1990s Wolf Jobst Siedler made the observation: "In Auschwitz Eichmann physically murdered the Jews, while doing the same to the German spirit."[37] As questionable as it is to style oneself as a victim, the bold polarization into "Germans" and "Jews" is yet more problematic. Max Alsberg, Erich Frey, as well as other prominent personalities, as for example Alfred Kerr or even Victor Klemperer, always felt themselves to be members of the former group and then, if at all, the latter. At the same time regret at the loss of spiritual greatness is too limited. Even the persecution or expulsion of a single attorney, burdened with all the usual human strengths and weaknesses, constitutes a fundamental violation of human rights. Therefore this documentation attempts to portray the fates of all attorneys of Jewish origin and not just those of the luminaries. The exclusion of Jewish attorneys structurally altered the profession as a whole. Vigorous proponents of the legal system and the culture that it was based on were lost, who would have taken action to defend human and basic rights such as the inviolability of the private sphere, as well as also for other central legal doctrines such as the presumption of innocence. They were passionate spokesmen for the rationality of law. Many of them promoted democratic principles through their work.

The knowledge of the enormous capacities and mental abilities that were lost constitutes the positive impression, if one were to use the image of a printing block. The "negative impression" constitutes the sufferings endured through persecution by all of those affected, regardless of whether they were prominent or less well known.

—Simone Ladwig-Winters

# Jurisprudence
## in the
## Weimar Republic

The Constitution of the Republic remained in Weimar. The corridors of power, whether in the bureaucracy or in businesses and associations, were all to be found in Berlin—as was the Reichstag, which housed the German Parliament. Berlin was not just the capital of Prussia—which no longer existed after 1945—but was also the capital and the seat of government of the entire Reich,[38] which thereby gave it a central position. The city brought forth various superlatives: the largest population, the most wretched tenements, the most attractive department stores, the fastest traffic, the most noble villas, the most intense social conflicts, the most elegant cafés and the most bizarre cabarets. Music, the fine arts, theater, literature—those in search of greatness made the pilgrimage to Berlin. There was constant change, especially in the field of the arts. Many of the works that were created at that time still possess charisma. Bert Brecht, Käthe Kollwitz, Max Liebermann, Otto Nagel, Lesser Ury, and Alfred Döblin created major works at the beginning of the century in Berlin. One person who enjoyed modest fame at that time was Rideamus. The libretto of the operetta *Der Vetter aus Dingsda* (*The Cousin from Whatchamacallit*) was primarily written by him, as well as many cheerful stories written in verse that were scattered with caricatures. Behind the nom de plume Rideamus ("Let's laugh") was hidden the mischievous, somewhat short-sighted lawyer, Fritz Oliven. Driven into exile because he was a Jew, he is only known to a few antiquarians today.[39]

Fritz Oliven, 1931

Jurisprudence was confronted with a special challenge in the nervous atmosphere of this city and the new conditions of the Republic. Contemporary publications, which primarily dealt with criminal cases, gave the impression that all important legal proceedings took place in Berlin, even though the Reichsgericht, the highest German court, was located in Leipzig. Spurred on by intense press coverage, there were trials that caused a downright sensation, which were closely followed by the public. When the opportunity presented itself, throngs of curious onlookers gathered at the Moabit Criminal Court, drawn by the prospect of being directly presented with part of another person's private life. Numerous political trials gave the impression that justice was meted out according to the motto "Mild to the right, hard on the left."[40] In the wake of numerous attacks against republican politicians, for which, inter alia, the "Organization Consul" was responsible, in part the reality was that the punishments were either very halfhearted or did not occur at all.[41] The infamous "Brigade Ehrhardt," for example, played a decisive role in the Kapp Putsch (March 13, 1920–March 16, 1920). This caused the German government to flee from Berlin and democracy was to a great extent saved by means of a general strike. The members of the "Brigade Ehrhardt" later surfaced in the "Organization Consul."[42]

### Political murders[43]

| Committed by the | Right | Left |
|---|---|---|
| Unpunished murders | 326 | 4 |
| Partly punished murders | 27 | 1 |
| Punished murders | 1 | 1 |
| Total murders | 354 | 22 |

It was only when the victim was prominent that the perpetrator was proceeded against without tolerant benevolence. Even in cases where a sentence had been pronounced, this did not mean that the convicted criminal would have to serve it. A total of 25 general amnesties and numerous individual amnesties created the impression that in the case of political crimes no real responsibility for criminal acts should be assumed.

One such an attack from the "right" was the prussic acid assassination attempt on the Social Democratic Party (SPD) politician Philipp Schneidemann, who was then mayor of Kassel. On June 4, 1922, on Pentecost, Scheidemann was taking a walk in the woods with his daughter and his granddaughter when a young man sprayed prussic acid in his face three times, using a rubber ball he carried with him. Before Scheidemann lost consciousness, he was able to get off two shots at the fleeing perpetrator.[44] The attack did not result in death, only because it was very windy at the time and the acid quickly dissipated. It was especially perfidious that later the victim was transformed into the perpetrator in press reports, because Scheidemann had been carrying a weapon upon the advice of the police and he had also used it against his attacker.

Only three weeks later, on June 24, 1922, Foreign Minister Walther Rathenau was fatally shot in his car during his morning trip to the Ministry on Königsallee in Berlin-Grünewald. In both cases the perpetrators were very young men who in part had grown up in middle class circumstances. Both were punished as individuals. Yet it was apparent but not provable that the "Organization Consul," which was supported by influential and wealthy persons, lurked in the background and sought to fight against the Republic with acts such as these. Rathenau stood for a policy of conciliation with German's former opponents in war, which was contemptuously abused by some as a "policy of appeasement." The corresponding newspapers agitated against Rathenau; the saying went around: "Shoot down Walther Rathenau, that goddamned Jewish sow!" The ground was thereby laid for an attack on his life. Rathenau was fully aware of the threat, but this did not keep him from pursuing the interests of Germany. However, he did not undertake any excessive efforts to protect himself, because the Scheidemann attack had shown him how many random factors survival depended on. Due to his political views Rathenau attracted influential people such as the German Nationalist Helfferich as enemies.

Karl Helfferich was born in 1872 to an industrial family in the Pfalz. After a career in the foreign service (as of 1901) and his appointment as a director of Deutsche Bank (1908), he increasingly developed ambitions for an important office in the area of the national economy. During the First World War, he became Secretary of State in the Reich Department of the Treasury. From 1918 he also nursed deep animosity[45] against the Reich Minister of Finance Matthias Erzberger (center). When Erzberger undertook to defend himself against attacks by Helfferich through a libel suit, various prominent attorneys stood against one another as representatives of the parties. Helfferich retained the universally acclaimed Prof. Dr. Max Alsberg, while Erzberger had sought, among others, the representation of Dr. Eugen Friedlaender. Erzberger won the trial, but the fine that Helfferich was subjected to was so ridiculously low that the victory left a bitter aftertaste. The press coverage of the trial did more to damage than to help Erzberger's reputation. On the final day of the trial a young man rushed at him with a drawn weapon with the intent of shooting him. The war veteran Friedlaender boldly took action and prevented the worst. A year later, on August 26, 1921, Erzberger was assassinated by two members of the "Brigade Ehrhardt." The perpetrators escaped abroad with official help and thereby avoided criminal prosecution. The attorneys in the Helfferich trial, Alsberg und Friedlaender, were both robbed of their status as lawyers after 1933 because they were Jews.[46] As the number cited above of 354 murders committed by right-wing perpetrators clearly demonstrates, though such acts were possibly also regarded as a relic of the war years, they were also a thoroughly established means of conducting politics. As chairman of the German National People's Party (DNVP), Helfferich encouraged these tendencies with his polemical outbursts. He died on April 3, 1924 at Bellinzona.[47]

It is difficult to judge the judiciary based on the number of convictions, because the law is often victorious precisely when a deed goes unpunished. An example is presented by the presumption of innocence imputed to the person whose guilt is alleged. However, the examples put forth here highlight the development of the judiciary and its attitudes in the Weimar Republic.

The societal change was also reflected in apparently "unpolitical" trials. Extraordinary criminal acts and those involved in the trials concerning them found themselves at the center of public attention. The board member of the Berlin Bar Association, Dr. Dr. Erich Frey, had a special place in the spotlight. He used his exquisite appearance, diabolical look, reinforced by a monocle, to turn himself into a real attraction. His life was also dazzling. When, after a turbulent night, he bolted directly into the courthouse, wearing his tailcoat, the Law Clerk Naatz, the office manager of the Court Bar Association, had to quickly help to make him appear presentable.[48] In his memoirs,[49] Frey gives a so-called schoolboy murder trial against the high school student Krantz special attention. This trial also offered everything that the public hungered for: titillating details, gentle shudders in the face of untamed youth, whose apparent recklessness ended in death for two of them. Even "hardened" trial observers such as the well-known Sling (Paul Schlesinger), who was a reporter for *Vossische Zeitung*, were fascinated.[50]

Erich Frey (right) during the "Student Murder Trial"
with the defendant Paul Krantz (middle, 1928)

In 1927 two 19-year-old young men, Günther und Hans, were found shot dead in their Steglitz apartment. The classmate of one of them, Paul Krantz, 18 years old, who came from humble origins, was accused of the crime. Based on the investigation, it was determined that Krantz had stayed in Günther's parental home, as did Günther's 16-year-old sister Hilde. Hilde's and Günther's parents lived in modest prosperity and were away at the time of the crime. Apparently, Hilde spent the night before the crime with Hans, who was later killed. Her brother Günther was said to harbor homosexual longings for Hans. During that evening the accused, Krantz, had to content himself with the role of an infatuated, rejected lover, although a day before the drama he himself had slept with Hilde. His motive was seen as jealousy. Frey mounted a defense of Paul Krantz that was both forceful and lively. Frey was cool and deliberate, yet at the same time used theatrical effects tactically in that he occasionally let the defense rest, while he exerted himself to obtain an acquittal. During this time, he developed a close, fatherly relationship to Krantz. As a result, the judgment of acquittal that was later announced in regard to the key count in the indictment filled him with a special sense of relief and joy. The opinion of one of the many experts maintained that it was highly likely that Günther first shot Hans and them himself with the weapon of Krantz.[51]

Another big trial involved the infamous "Immertreu" ("Always True") "Ringverein" ("Ring Club") (main proceedings February 4–9, 1928), the only collaboration between Frey and Max Alsberg, an equally famous criminal defense attorney of that time. The trial involved the death of a carpenter after a fight between members of the Ringverein "Immertreu," who were coming from a burial in tailcoats and top hats, and a group of carpenters who were gathered together in a tavern frequented by their guild. The interconnected sports and social clubs to which "Immertreu" belonged, based on their by-laws, offered their mostly previously convicted members support in finding work and the opportunity to engage in sport and take part in social gatherings. In fact, they were alliances for members of the Berlin underworld. Eighty clubs that had quaint names such as "Heimatklänge" ("Echoes of Home"), "Hand in Hand" or "Deutsche Kraft" ("German Power") had organized themselves into about 1,000 members, whereby it was an open secret that they financed themselves partially through extortion through the protection racket.

At the same time the members followed a strict code of ethics. They served as the basis for Fritz Lang's famous film *M—eine Stadt sucht einen Mörder* (*M—a City Seeks a Murderer*—1931). Brecht's Dreigroschenoper (*Three Penny Opera*—1928) also oriented itself on their appearance. In the actual trial, Frey toyed with public opinion much more strongly than Alsberg, in that he purposely informed the press and created the image of "nice criminals" or "tough kids," who had nicknames like "Muskel-Adolf" ("Muscles Adolf"), "Klamotten-Ede" ("Dapper Ede") or "Mollen-Albert" ("Beer Bottle Albert"), but who, according to Frey, had a natural instinct for what is right. This honorable criminal lived off the earnings of prostitutes who were devoted to him and who once again had such cute names as "Aktien-Mieze" ("Stock Kitty"). The Court sentenced the main accused, Adolf Leib ("Muskel-Adolf") to 10 months in prison, while the other accused parties were acquitted.

The schoolboy murder trial was about moral decay. In the "Immertreu" trial dubious racketeering took center stage—both trials were concerned with the change in or loss of social values, with the press taking an active role in forming and personalizing opinion. Frey himself enjoyed the public prestige or, better said, sensation. He basked in characterizations such as "charming,"[52] but was always consistent in pursuing the actual goal—success in court. When necessary, he could speak impromptu for an hour, only looking at his notes once in order to cite a case of the Reichsgericht. "Otherwise I always kept my eyes on the judge and jurors."[53] Frey, who had been baptized, left Germany in October 1933 and went to Chile. He was regarded as "non-Aryan" and was warned of his impending arrest. Even he described himself as "politically undesirable."

Alsberg, who had a much more reserved manner, suffered a similar fate. He too was very soon put at risk due to his exposed position after January 1933. Alsberg, with his sophisticated approach, was the model of an elegant, eloquent and rational intellectual.[54] He had a wide variety of clients, but they came primarily from the economic and political elite. The industrial magnate Hugo Stinnes was one of his clients. Alsberg's colleague Frey, a competitor, could not help but pay him tribute: "His final speech for the defense (in the "Immertreu" trial) would have been a credit to any academy."[55]

Alsberg worked in a large law firm at Nollendorfplatz 1 with three (non-Jewish) colleagues, Dr. Kurt Poschke, Dr. Kurt Gollnick and Dr. Lothar Welt. In addition to his work as an attorney, he published numerous articles on a wide variety of legal issues. He was an honorary professor at the Handelshochschule (Commercial College) in Berlin.[56] He did not just use language as a tool in trials, but also applied his linguistic brilliance on the artistic level. In 1930 he wrote the play *Die Voruntersuchung* (*The Preliminary Investigation*), which premiered in the Berlin Renaissance (later it was made into a film). The drama *Konflikt* (*Conflict*) was completed in 1933, but is no longer performed in Germany. Alsberg, whose qualities in analysis, conception, as well as in rhetoric were given the highest praise, was criticized by another well-known defense attorney, Alfred Apfel, in *Weltbühnen* because he was not an explicitly political lawyer.[57] In fact, his judgment in the run-up to the *Weltbühnen* trial showed a certain political naïveté. In this trial, Alsberg, together with Rudolf Olden, Kurt Rosenfeld and Alfred Apfel, was one of the defenders of Ossietzky. On the way to the trial, at the Reichsgericht in Leipzig, Alsberg was full of confidence in the persuasiveness of his arguments. It was a bitter experience for him to confront the mood that surrounded him as a defense attorney who was an "advocate of the left."[58] Alsberg was not accustomed to political justice of this nature.

In the *Weltbühnen* trial in November 1931 Ossietzky was found guilty by the Reichsgericht (up to the pronouncement of judgment) in a hearing that was closed to the public. As editor of *Weltbühnen* he was held responsible for the publication of military secrets. An article by Walter Kreiser (pseudonym: Heinz Jäger) titled "Windiges aus der deutschen Luftfahrt" ("A Gust of Wind from German Aviation") made reference to a mysterious Department "M" and an "Erprobungsabteilung Albatros" ("Albatros Test Department"). "Both departments possess around thirty to forty airplanes each, sometimes even more. But not all the airplanes are always in Germany."[59]

This seemingly innocuous concluding sentence alludes to a secret military cooperation between the Reichswehr and the armed forces of the Weimar Republic and the Soviet Union, which would have been a way of thwarting the Treaty of Versailles. The Court found Ossietzky guilty of treason and sentenced him to a year and six months of imprisonment. In May 1932 three of his defense attorneys accompanied him to the gate of the Tegel Penitentiary. Alsberg was not there. He was probably not at home in the climate of the "left," because it was so dissimilar with that associated with his customary clients, who generally ranged from German nationalists to conservative in their political views. Yet it cannot be overlooked that Alsberg had already made a political choice by his unconditional commitment to a legal system that was based on equality and freedom and that had no place for the abuse of power and arbitrariness. Yet, he was not a socialist and definitely not a communist. Alsberg fled Germany for Switzerland in early 1933. He shot himself during the fall of the same year.

In another explicitly political trial, the so-called Eden-Tanzpalast ("Eden Dance Hall") trial, the young attorney Hans Litten called Adolf Hitler to the witness stand in 1931. Clarification was sought concerning the occurrence of an SA attack on a gathering of the workers' hiking club "Falke" that took place in the Eden Dance Hall in November 1930. "Stief und Genossen" ("Stieff and His Comrades") were accused of three counts of attempted manslaughter, as well as of breach of the public peace and assault. During the trial Litten wanted to know if "Storm 33" was a so-called raiding party and if its use included killing people. He asked Hitler extremely uncomfortable questions on the relationship between the National Socialist German Workers' Party (NSDAP) and violence:[60]

*Litten:* Are you aware that in SA circles there is talk of a certain type of "raiding gear"?

*Hitler:* I have never heard of raiding gear. . . .

*Litten:* You said that the National Socialist Party never undertakes acts of violence. Didn't Goebbels make the statement that the enemy had to be stamped into pulp?

*Hitler:* That should be understood to mean that opposing organizations have to be defeated and destroyed. . . .

*The Chief Judge reads aloud a question that had been formulated by Litten:*
> Was Hitler, when he appointed Goebbels as Reich Propaganda Director, aware of the passage in his book where Goebbels states that one shouldn't recoil from upheaval, that Parliament should be blown up and that the government should be chased to the devil and where the call to revolution is printed in spaced letters?

*Hitler:* Today I can't say under oath whether or not I knew about Goebbels's book. The statement . . . is completely without significance to the Party . . . because the booklet has not been officially sanctioned by the party . . .

*Litten:* Based on Goebbels's example, doesn't this give the impression that the program is not very far-reaching unless you reprove or expel a man like Goebbels instead of appointing him as Reich Propaganda Director?

*Hitler:* The entire party operates strictly on a legal basis and Goebbels as well . . . He is in Berlin and can be called here as a witness any time.

*Litten:* Has Mr. Goebbels been prohibited from circulating this writing of his?

*Hitler:* I don't know.

On the afternoon of the trial Litten once more returned to this theme:

> *Litten: Is it true that "Das Bekenntnis zur Illegalität" ('The Avowal of Illegality"), the revolutionary magazine of Goebbels, has been taken over by the party publishing house and has reached a circulation of 120,000? . . . I have been able to establish that the booklet has been sanctioned by the party.*

> *Chief Judge: Mister Hitler, in the morning hearing you actually stated that Goebbels's booklet was not an official party one.*

> *Hitler: It isn't. An official document of the party becomes so in that it bears the emblem of the party. Moreover, in regard to these matters it is the head of propaganda himself who has to be examined and above all [Hitler screams with a red face]—Mr. Attorney, how can you come to say that this is a call to illegality? That is a statement that cannot be proven!*

> *Litten: How is it possible for the party publishing house to print materials that are in clear opposition to party policy?*

> *Chief Judge: That doesn't have anything to do with the trial.*

Hitler had not made a good impression and his efforts to whitewash the actions of the Nazi Party as in accordance with law had failed. He lost control of himself in full public view. In that instance he was not purposefully speaking in anger, as was the case in later public appearances, in which his entire body language and shifting voice demonstrated passion and total commitment, but had rather been "led on" by Litten. Up to then only the attorney Kurt Rosenfeld had achieved this in 1932 during the "Meineid-Prozess Abel" ("Abel Perjury Trial").[61] Rosenfeld, an equally prominent defense lawyer, a Social Democrat and a Jew, had, like Litten, drawn the personal hatred of Hitler upon himself through his examination of him as a witness.

Examples could be given of a number of many important trials that reflected the social conflicts of the Weimar Republic. One trial of especial importance was the trial against the artist George Grosz and his publisher Wieland Herzfelde, the brother of John Heartfield. Blasphemy charges were brought against both after the publication of a graphic.

The incriminating art print showed Jesus Christ on the cross wearing a gas mask. The caption below it stated: "Shut up and continue." The court reporter in the Office of the Judge of the General Criminal Division for Appeals in Moabit was the aspiring jurist Adolf Arndt, who was just 26.

Previously Arndt was employed, after completing his second state legal examination and entering the law profession, in the law firm of Alsberg, but then switched to a judicial office. In the blasphemy trial Alfred Apfel was the defense attorney for Grosz and Herzfelde. Apfel, a burly man who radiated vital energy, zeroed in on Chief Justice Siegert. In the appeals proceedings on questions of law and fact Siegert even himself declared that he felt self-conscious. On the day of the oral proceedings socially prominent citizens packed themselves into the courtroom: testimony was given by representatives of both Christian denominations, the Reich Art Protector Redslob and the renowned pacifist and patron of the arts Harry Graf Kessler.[62] In his preliminary assessment Arndt was of the opinion that Grosz's intention to oppose war with his image gave him good chances. He therefore did not subjectively fulfill the legal elements of blasphemy and was acquitted. In the following appeal on questions of law only the Reichsgericht had to confirm this judgment, however, it ordered the destruction of the print plates, because they objectively fulfilled the elements of the legal offense of blasphemy.[63] In the *Vossische Zeitung* the acquittal was received with great enthusiasm and was greeted as a "sign" of how, in the middle of this turbulent time, a better future was being prepared by a few courageous men.[64] In 1933 Arndt left the judicial office because of his classification as a Christian "non-Aryan"; however, he was able to tentatively become an attorney and join the bar.

The drawing that gave rise to the politically important "Blasphemy Trial": George Grosz's portrayal of Christ, titled "Shut up and keep doing your duty"

That this development would lead all the way to exclusion and persecution could not yet be foreseen at the beginning of the 1930s. The exemplary cases cited above show that the changes in society also left their effect in the courtroom. In the Weimar Republic the old structures that had dominated imperial Germany were in the process of dissolution. This development took place successively; restorative forces collided with those new impulses that embraced the republic. However, the desire of the old elite for authoritarian structures that would facilitate the management of social development had not been abandoned. Numerous lawyers of Jewish origin felt that they had a commitment to democratic development and worked to oppose these forces of reaction.

These structural changes were also felt by those studying law. With the end of the authoritarian state the points of main emphasis in terms of content had changed, but at the same time there were still outspoken representatives teaching who rejected the Republic and in their doctrinal concepts insisted on the blind recognition of authority. Regardless of the content, the legal socialization continued to be based on the seemingly objective observation of the regulatory framework, leaving little room for the development of independent personalities. This tendency was reinforced by strict tutoring that likewise did not promote independent cognitive processes, but rather employed drilling for the narrow reception of legal norms. For this reason, many German attorneys were more likely to turn a cold shoulder to persons or phenomena giving expression to the criticism of social norms. Nevertheless, it would be simplistic to maintain that the power of the old elite was able to continually advance and finally led to the ascension of National Socialism.

The well-known attorneys of Jewish origin had acquired their reputation in the Weimar Republic and graced many trials with their brilliance. They had entered the public limelight apparently without any worries about "Risches" (Yiddish term for anti-Semitic reactions), although it is true that the agitation against social democratic and communist attorneys was deeply imbued with anti-Semitism by political opponents (for example against Kurt Rosenfeld). Anti-Semitism was still alive, indeed even more threatening than in imperial Germany. This is because that, while "before 1914 anti-Semitism was permitted and considered socially acceptable by the authoritarian upper class, brutal outbursts such as calls for murder and bloody excesses, were not tolerated. . . . While German Jews found themselves at the very peak of their success in the Weimar Republic, they were also endangered as never before.[65]

Their integration into various professional boards and committees seemed suited to doing away with the prejudices of the past. Lawyers who were Jews were elected by their colleagues to various bodies of this nature. Through professional and conscientious work, they sought to increase the prestige of the practice of law. Positions on the boards of bar associations—as well as on disciplinary courts—were held by attorneys who were Jewish on the basis of their religion and their background. Those holding such positions took the risk that a lawyer who was disbarred based on the decision of a disciplinary court, would take the matter personally and react with anti-Semitic feelings.[66]

Many less prominent attorneys of Jewish origin wanted to rid themselves of the stigma that was often associated with certain names. As early as 1920 Sammy Gronemann, a self-employed attorney and a staunch Zionist, commented in his book *Tohuwabohu (Tohubohu/ Chaos),* on the great number of Cohns and Kahns at the District Court and he took umbrage at the name changes that were often undertaken: "Siegmund Kahn?—that just can't be!—He is released from serving further time for his name through the highest decree as an act of grace."[67]

The broad class of Jewish lawyers did not fear discrimination; many believed, for example, that they had sufficiently demonstrated their German patriotism by taking part in the First World War. Their professional work and the position they held thereby was enough to make them feel close to the bourgeois middle class. Many attorneys were also admitted as notaries so that, through the authentication of documents pertaining to property and wills, they constantly had social contact. The Eastern European Jews, who were stylized into a problem in Berlin and stood out due to their clothing, language and social position and usually were not German citizens, did not play any role as clients for Berlin lawyers, regardless of whether they were Jewish or not.[68] The attorneys themselves had become part of the middle class and, through their choice of profession, had clearly decided in favor of a lasting future in Germany since the profession of attorney is bound to the circumstances of a political system.

During the Weimar Republic the number of people entering the legal profession increased. Rudolf Dix, who was a board member of the Berlin Bar Association and who was not a Jew, expressed his concern in 1927 at the Bar Association convention about the development of the profession.[69] The increase in the number of lawyers, combined with an intensifying competitive pressure, placed at risk his concept of a lawyer as "a man who pursued a broader, more comfortable lifestyle."[70] In his view, restriction of access into the profession with a numerus clausus— or an enrollment limit—was a sensible measure that could be taken against the "proletarianization and demise" of the legal profession. The position he took gave rise to strong reactions. Nonetheless, in 1928 the assembly of representatives of the German Lawyers' Association (DAV) resolved to impose restrictions on licensing, but did not go into further details. Berlin Judicial Councillor Julius Magnus, who was editor of the *Juristische Wochenschrift (The Weekly Legal Journal)* (JW), expressed fear that there would also be clandestine limits to access for Jewish jurists.[71]

The danger was quite real, as access to a career as a judicial official in the Wilhelminian era showed. Anti-Semitic discrimination also had to be feared because of intensified political agitation. Critics of the numerus clausus proposal, such as Ernst Fraenkel, who analyzed processes with precision, saw the danger of a selection principle that would be linked to a restriction on admission, whereby Fraenkel did not wish to transfer the power of selection either to the state or to the legal profession itself.[72] The debate about the numerus clausus continued until 1933. Further debate was made irrelevant by political events.

With the transfer of power to the National Socialists, the development wherein the society of the majority of Germans and the Jewish minority were being increasingly fused with one another was broken off. Up to that point the Jewish minority had no longer been excluded from the social sphere and only limited itself sectorally. For many, during the course of their studies they developed a wish to belong to some type of fraternity, generally a dueling one. There was just one Jewish student fraternity, which also kept up the tradition of dueling. For a young man who, on the one hand, wanted to prove himself physically and, on the other hand, to build up a network of conventional relations, this usually resulted in a conversion. Most felt that they were increasingly becoming part of the German community. The consciousness of being a Jew was pushed further into the background. Under National Socialist criteria, the term "Jewish attorney" referred to a group that was not homogeneous in many areas.

While the requirements for a legal education were uniform, of course results of the state legal examinations differed greatly. It hardly needs saying that the competence of lawyers ranged from excellent to average to bad, both for Jews and non-Jews.[73] It was striking just how many Jewish lawyers obtained an additional qualification in the form of a doctorate. There were 1,187 lawyers of Jewish origin who had a doctorate (some even several). Deserving lawyers were granted the honorary title of Judicial Councillor; 203 Jewish attorneys were entitled to use this title.[74]

Due to limitations on admissions conditions, women could only first take the state legal examination in the 1920s. The proportion of women in the legal profession was correspondingly small. Through their more open and more education-oriented family structures, Jewish women were more likely to make their way in the legal profession. Yet women only constituted 19 of the 1,807.[75] Yet this ensured that these women could be independent and make a living for themselves.

As a rule, income did not only depend on the area in which an attorney worked, but also how long his practice had been established. As a result, women were not able to bring in as much income as older, longer established colleagues, yet even for the latter it was not always their fees that were the basis of their livelihood. For some, it was the wealth of their wives that provided for their affluence. This was the case with Judicial Councillor Sandberg, who could devote himself to indigent clients at his leisure and sometimes even worked on a pro bono basis.[76] The generally tense economic situation was noticeable in all spheres of life—and also in the case of attorneys' fees. Manek Riegelhaupt, for example, who had been admitted since the beginning of the 1930s, had to endure such difficult times that he was forced to send a debt reminder to the Red Cross, which he had as one of his clients.[77] Many attorneys fell upon hard times. On the other hand, large law firms, such as those of Max Alsberg and Erich Frey, or those that had large companies as regular clients, were quite successful economically. The range of income between attorneys was quite large. It ranged from several thousand Reichsmark (RM) per year up to over 50,000 Reichsmark. Of course, the costs of operating a large law firm was significantly higher than those of a more modest one. The available documents show that in almost all law firms there was an office manager (in most of the known cases, a man) and at least one female secretary, in order to organize the business internally. Since there weren't any technical means of transmission, many docu-

Erich Frey (third from right) as a legal adviser at a contest

ments had to be transported by messenger. Often several law firms that were located in the vicinity pooled their resources in order to employ such services.

As Jews received growing recognition from German society, the process of assimilation also proceeded more rapidly.[78] In the meantime, one could confidently point out ancestors who had been Prussian Jews for generations.[79] As one would expect, most lawyers of Jewish origin were also adherents to the Jewish religion. Attorneys such as Alfred Klee and Julius Seligsohn were involved in the Berlin Jewish community. Reformed Judaism in Berlin was more liberal and thereby in ongoing contrast to the main community. The attorney Moritz Galliner was active as a board member there. The attorney Max Naumann was another member of this Jewish community. He was a controversial figure because of his German nationalist activities.[80] Members of the orthodox Jewish community also practiced law. One of these was Dr. Marcus Birnbaum, who was a member of the Adass Jisroel Synagogue. In addition, there was a small number of attorneys who supported Zionism. For most Zionism was more of an ideal project; only very few had ever considered permanently settling in Palestine. Some had acquainted themselves with the circumstances there from their own experience and then returned to Berlin. In the early 1930s, one such attorney, Hermann Jalowicz, took part in the Maccabiade Games (a sports event of the Maccabi World Union, which first took place in 1932 in Palestine, then every three years thereafter).[81] Yet Prussian Jewry was generally skeptical of Zionism: "A son who left Judaism in favor of Zionism was more likely to be excluded from the family than one who left it for communism."[82]

Many attorneys of Jewish origin changed their faith from Judaism to Christianity, in Berlin primarily to Protestantism. There were marriages between Jewish and Christian partners, who were drawn together by their mutual affiliation with a church congregation. In 1933 there were a total of 80 lawyers of Jewish origin who were Protestants and 12 who were Catholic. A little later some of them belonged to the Reich Association of non-Aryan Christians.

At least twelve attorneys had completely disassociated themselves from religion and were regarded as dissidents. Often this attitude was associated with socialist or communist views. For them religion was simply unnecessary to achieve a more just society; God was therefore unnecessary.

However, there were only a few proponents of this view; otherwise there were many political viewpoints represented in the group of lawyers of Jewish origin. Those openly committed to communism were in a minority. The spectrum ranged from left-wing liberals, such as Alfred Apfel and Rudolf Olden, to German nationalists, like Max Naumann, co-founder and chairman of the Association of German National Jews. Based on today's finding, the majority seemed to have been politically liberal.

# Exclusion After the Seizure of Power

# The First Wave of Exclusion:
# Terroristic Attacks Against Jewish Attorneys

After Hitler was appointed Reich Chancellor and a coalition government was formed that included German nationalists, the National Socialists increased the level of national terror. The Reichstag fire during the night of February 28, 1933 served as a signal to act. It provided the motive to arrest more than 5,000 political opponents, especially Communist officials and members of the Reichstag, as well as Social Democrats and other opponents of the Nazis. The Dutch Communist Marinus van der Lubbe, who was arrested at the scene of the crime, was later sentenced to death and executed. It was for this reason that, on March 29, 1933— afterward—a special law was enacted that increased criminal penalties, because up to then the maximum punishment for arson had been penal servitude. The other four accused, three Bulgarian Communists (among them the well-known Georgi Dimitroff) and a German Communist, Ernst Torgler, were acquitted by the Reichsgericht, the Weimar Republic's highest court, in Leipzig.

On the day of the Reichstag fire, Reich President von Hindenburg signed the emergency decree "For the Protection of the People and the State." This so-called Reichstag fire decree suspended key basic civil rights: personal freedom, freedom of speech, of the press, of association and assembly, the confidentiality of postal correspondence and telephone communication, the inviolability of property and the home. At the beginning of February another emergency decree was promulgated that legalized "protective custody," which then proceeded to be used as an arbitrary instrument of terror. In Berlin the wave of arrests following the Reichstag fire caught up the attorneys Alfred Apfel, Ludwig Barbasch and Hans Litten. Apfel was released after eleven days, Barbasch after six months. Litten remained in prison until his suicide.[83]

Carl von Ossietzky together with his defense attorneys
Rudolf Olden (left) and Alfred Apfel (right, 1932)

Alfred Apfel fled to France after he was set free. His photo was published in 1933, together with those of many others, on a poster under the caption "Traitors to the German people." At the same time his German citizenship was revoked. Apfel died in 1940 at the age of 58 in Versailles under unknown circumstances.

Another lawyer who was imprisoned after the Reichstag fire was the rather inconspicuous attorney Fritz Ball. He was still arrested at the end of March 1933. He recorded his experience and impressions together in a haunting report. Fritz Ball relates:

> Frightening rumors about a torture chamber are circulating . . . One hears about these things with increasing frequency. Colleagues who have vanished are sought after. Sometimes they are found alive, sometimes dead. Those who were politically active against the Nazis and are able to, flee.[84]

On March 30, 1933 Fritz Ball was arrested at his law firm on Viktoria-Luise-Platz in Schöneberg, which he ran together with his brother. It was at four o'clock during office hours that the SA men arrived. Ball heard the noise and came out of his consulting room. He reports:

*Illustrierter Beobachter*, supplement of the Völkischer Beobachter 1933, part 3b, p. 1176. The Berlin attorneys Bernhard Weiß, Johannes Werthauer and Alfred Apfel are in the second row.

The office secretaries immediately whisper to him: "Your brother has been arrested." My brother is a member of the board of the bar association and this exposes him more than me. I enter the hall. It is also full of SS men. A Sturmführer (SA rank equivalent to a second lieutenant in the army), as was apparent from his uniform, is engaged in a conversation with my brother. "Get dressed and come with me," he tells my brother. My brother responds with: "Do you have an arrest warrant?" The gruff Nazi then issues the order: "Shut up and put on your coat." My brother reaches for his coat and hat. Then I say to him: "There are two attorneys named Ball here, Kurt and Fritz Ball. Who are you looking for?" He pauses, takes a small slip of paper out of his pocket and then says: "Fritz." I grab my coat and hat. I say, "That's me." I can hear my office secretaries sobbing behind me. At that moment, a client appears who seems shocked at the sight of the SA and the weeping women.

My wife emerges from our private apartment. I kiss her good-bye, but we don't say a word. . . . While standing in the door-way I call out to my office manager: "Immediately call Minister Hugenberg to tell him that I have been arrested." An open van is waiting outside the house. It is the type the SA uses to transport prisoners.

Ball is brought to one of the improvised concentration camps and placed in the basement of the barracks on General-Pape-Straße.

I am immediately surrounded by a dozen of quite young SA people. I am interrogated as to what my name is, where I live, what political party I belong to and how I voted in the elections. Questions pop out from everywhere. "What did you do to try and prevent the fact that so many Eastern European Jews have come to Germany since the last war?" This question is posed by the person who seems to be in charge in the office. "Are you a Jew?"—"Yes."—"Your profession?"—"Attorney at the Berlin Court of Appeals and Notary." "That's something you have been for a long time," someone screams out behind me in front of the crowd. "Tomorrow you Jewish pigs will all be driven out of the courts. You have our Führer to thank that you are still alive today." "We will say," someone behind me replies, "that he lived up to today"—speaking with a very serious voice. "We could have done away with you long ago." Then question after question comes for half an hour. Confused, disconnected, totally senseless questions. I answer as well as I can.

Ball is thrown into a basement room further down below.

A wooden door slams shut behind me. It is as black as night around me. I slowly feel my way forward, then I feel a bench. From behind my left side four little glowing lights shine on me. They look like lightning bugs. I suddenly become totally calm and just have one thought: if they would just simply shoot me in the chest with a pistol and not subject me to long torture. It is strange how calm I feel in this eerie situation. Then I hear a human voice: "Don't be afraid. We are four officers of the Ehrhardt Guard.[85] We have been sitting here for 36 hours. I've got matches with me, I'll light one for you, so that you will be able to orient yourself. . . ." On the bench there is room for three people to sit. They bring me over there to sit, then offer me water. They ask me questions and then they speak about themselves. I tell them what I already have said ten times in the office, that I have never been politically active, that I am an attorney and notary and that I spend my free time in the appreciation of good art. I tell them that I don't have any idea why I have been arrested and that there has to be some mistake.

Later on, the four confide the addresses of their families to Ball. During the course of a new interrogation Ball is asked about his car. However, because he did not own a car and because his law office was not located, as had been assumed, on Bendlerstraße, it then is apparent that he has been confused with another person of the same name. He is then informed that he is to be released on the next day. He once again returns to the dark basement cell and attempts to sleep while sitting. Fritz Ball continues:

I am really able to nod off a little. I wake up in shock. It becomes louder in the hall. Apparently, the officers are away and the rank and file are now left to their own devices. The door is flung open. The SA storm into our partition. The hall is suddenly brightly lit. They grab me and pull me out. The door of the cell slams shut behind me. They drag me into a corner. I see a big bull whip, they bend me over, but they don't strike me, they raise me back up and let me fall back on a chair. They tie my arms behind my back. They scream and howl like they are extremely drunk. One encounters many intelligent faces among them. I even think I know some of them. All of them are young fellows between eighteen and twenty-five years of age. They call out to me, ask questions, crack jokes, scream at me. Then one of them places himself before me and says: "At 6 am you will be shot." My response is: "I don't believe that. I think that I will be released tomorrow morning. You wouldn't shoot someone who is innocent." "What a fine suit the young man has on." They touch the fabric of my jacket, my pants. One of them attempts to touch me in an unseemly fashion. He asks, "Are you also gay?" "No, I am married, I have a wife and three children," I answer. And then I think, but most of you beasts are gay. Suddenly I hear the word "hello." A giant pair of scissors is brought in and then things get going. They tug at and cut my hair, which is fairly long. They attempt to cut a swastika on my head. They cut me, I bleed. They push and shove me back and forth in order to get a better look. The noise and yelling becomes increasingly worse . . . "He's got to look at himself in the mirror." They hold a mirror in front of me. I see my mutilated hair and say, although I can barely speak after this virtual scalping: "I thank you, sirs, that you have given me a haircut for free, otherwise I would have to go to the barber, who charges me double because of my thick hair."

Then Ball is once again left alone. At some point the SA man shows up, who threatens him with a bull whip. A man is brought into the cell. He is bleeding and his teeth have been knocked out. A gunshot goes off in the neighboring cell. There are recurrent screams; at one point, Ball thinks he recognizes a female voice. Later an SA guard tells him of the death of the attorney Günther Joachim. The Social Democrat, who acted as a defense attorney for the Red Cross and who was a Jew, had been tortured and mistreated for so long in another SA prison (on Jüdenstraße) that he died of his injuries.[86] Fritz Ball continues to record his experiences:

Then suddenly somewhere in the compound music is being played. They are playing hymns on accordions and concertinas. We can only hear the music faintly in the basement we are locked up in, but I can clearly make out each sound . . . an eerie and tense mood holds sway in our chamber. Everyone listens with horrified expressions. My young neighbor and I are the only ones who don't know what is happening. However, this is soon explained to us. Whenever they are beating a man to death above, they play hymns as an accompaniment in order to drown out his screams.

Ball loses his sense of time. It is only due to the light that enters the cell that he becomes aware that morning is approaching.

Finally, my name is called out. One of the two officers who had interrogated me in the corridor during the night in regard to my car and many other matters is standing before me . . . "I can release you," he says in a manner that is not unfriendly. "You have to wait until 11 am, until the second lieutenant is here. You really caused us a lot of work. Because of you six cars waited in front of the door until late in the night. The telephone was ringing off its hook. My boys had a little bit of fun with you. They do that here with everyone when we are not here. I am glad to see that you are still in a good mood. The remarks about the haircut really pleased me." . . . Finally, the clock chimes 11 am and I am called up. The second lieutenant is standing before me. "I had to make a lot of phone calls because of you. Never before have I received similar responses about someone from everyone questioned. Everyone said that you have never been involved in politics and that you are a respectable fellow. This is certainly no Hotel Adlon, but I hope you didn't have too bad of a time."

Ball was in fact released, but only after the three gold pieces he had among his valuables were taken away from him. At home he was confronted with the fact that one of his stenographers had been arrested. She had become extremely upset over the arrest of her boss, which then caused the 16-year-old apprentice to report it to the police. The same SA troop that had arrested Ball came back again later to pick her up. It was her screams that he had heard during the night.

In April 1933 Ball lost his license as both an attorney and as a notary. In order to support his family, he became a soap salesman. Shortly before the war broke out he fled to Great Britain and later went to the United States. His brother Kurt managed to reach Palestine. After the founding of the state of Israel he helped build the national memorial Yad Veshem under the name Kurt-Jacob Ball-Kaduri.

Just like Joachim, Apfel, Barbasch and Litten, the attorney Arthur Brandt was also arrested in 1933. They were first and foremost political opponents of National Socialists. Above all, the fact that they were also Jews was given emphasis in the propaganda relating thereto. These attorneys had made personal enemies, who were now cruelly testing out their newly found power. As members of an organized resistance, they were to be put out of action.

The young attorney Hans Litten also became a victim of such "personal settling of scores." Hitler was unforgiving and after being summoned to appear in the Eden Trial, Hitler became irascible just at the mention of Litten's name. Litten, the son of a Christian mother, was classified as a "half-Jew." This

Dr. Kurt Ball, 1931

rage was not only directed against him as an attorney, but especially against him as a "Jewish attorney." Nazi propaganda had generally settled upon this formula even before the seizure of power. In 1933 the agitation became completely unrestrained and did not hold back from sinking to the lowest level. For example, Kurt Rosenfeld was accused of having mocked the German judiciary, because it was said that at the end of March he had hung a picture in his reception room showing the rape of Justitia by a judge. Rosenfeld avoided arrest by fleeing to Prague, and then later fled to the United States, where he died in 1943.

Another person who nearly escaped arrest was Rudolf Olden. In contrast to Litten, who was more of a Franciscan ascetic, Olden loved people and sought out their company. For him the struggle for social justice was always associated with the emphatic feeling of being uplifted by a group of like-minded people. Whereas Litten took his commitment to an ideal with deep seriousness, Olden instead had a tendency toward playful lightheartedness, although he nonetheless kept his eye on the goal. Humor and charm accompanied Olden's nonetheless sincere and constant political commitment. For example, he was one of the organizers of the gathering of 900 politicians and intellectuals under the slogan "free speech" that took place on February 19, 1933 at the Kroll Opera House— therefore only a few days before the Reichstag fire. The rally was broken up by police after three hours. It was the Kroll Opera House that would function, just a little later, as the replacement building for the Reichstag that had been burnt down.

"Judge and justice,"
contemporary graphic art

Olden was warned of his impending arrest and was able to escape across the Czechoslovakian border. After a temporary stay in Paris he made his way to Great Britain. In 1936 his German citizenship was revoked (on the same list as Thomas Mann).[87] After the beginning of the war the British government declared him, as a stateless person, to be a "dangerous foreigner" and had him interned. Without income and without nationality he rather reluctantly accepted an appointment at the New School of Social Research in New York—he would have rather stayed in England. In 1940, during the trip to North America, the boat he was on was torpedoed by a German U-boat; Olden and his wife Ika died together with many others during the attack.

Rudolf Olden (right) in conversation with attorney Gerhard Wilk, 1931

# The Second Wave of Exclusion: Statutory and Bureaucratic Measures

In the first weeks after the 1933 seizure of power, individual acts of terror were carried out against attorneys of Jewish origin. As brutal as the violence may have been in a specific case, it was equally ineffective from the National Socialist perspective in regard to the comprehensive exclusion of Jews from the legal profession and all of society.

After the parliamentary elections of March 1933 that had already—after the Reichstag fires—taken place under a state of emergency, the National Socialists increased their pressure. The results of the election had been disappointing for the NSDAP. Although, with almost 44 per cent of the votes, they were the strongest faction in parliament, they were still only able to attain a parliamentary majority with their coalition partner, Alfred Hugenberg's German National People's Party (DNVP). The attempt of the National Socialists to achieve a majority in a more or less legal fashion had met with failure. Hitler and his party now took recourse to a dual strategy: they increased the "terror from below," in order to push through their political interests "from above." With staged "spontaneous acts of the people's will," which included open violence, seemingly unavoidable circumstances were created that required the state to undertake political policies that were appropriate "for the maintenance of public law and order."

One target of these attacks was the judiciary. Beginning with an attack on the Görlitz District Court on March 9, a wave of violence rolled through Prussia and other provinces of the Reich. The methods employed were similar in all places. SA men and other "angry fellow Germans" rushed into courthouses and forced those officials and attorneys of Jewish origin (and those they held to be so) to leave the courthouse through threats and acts of violence, often humiliating and mistreating them, as well as taking individual jurists into "protective custody." At the same time, they threatened to return if "the Jews" came back to the courts.

The mood was further inflamed when the NSDAP declared a boycott on April 1 of Jewish shops, businesses, doctors' offices and law firms. On the day before the boycott, on March 31, Nazi hordes forced their way into the courts of Berlin. After the attack on District Court 1 and the Central Municipal Court, both located on Neue Friedrichstraße (today Littenstraße) in the vicinity of Alexanderplatz, an attorney issued an urgent report.

James Yaakov Rosenthal remembers:

On the day before the Shabbat Boycott, i.e. on March 31, 1933, I was a young attorney who was busy running from one appointment to another at the Central Civil Courthouse [District Court] in the vicinity of the train station at Alexanderplatz [today Littenstraße]. I was keeping appointments for myself and naturally for a few other colleagues who I was filling in for. Then all at once, at 10:15 am, freshly accoutered SA people, who had been gathered there by their superiors, suddenly came into the courthouse all at the same time in droves and shouted out: "Jews and those of Jewish descent assemble in the Lichthof!" We gathered there together. One couldn't help but wonder about some of them. Yet the Nazi authorities had never been mistaken in compiling their lists; they knew exactly where a grandmother or a grandfather created a snag. We found ourselves gathered together in the commendable presence of the presiding judge of Berlin District Court I, Mr. Soelling, née Seligsohn, whose father was a leading member of the Jewish congregation in Bromberg. His brother Seligsohn worked as an attorney in Berlin; he himself belonged to the Stahlhelmbund der Frontsoldaten [paramilitary organization of WWI frontline soldiers in the Weimar Republic] and behaved like a big-time National Socialist and, we could say, the very antithesis of a friend of the Jew. But none of that helped, they were already informed and we gathered together. Some secretaries from the Court, judges, attorneys, practical trainees who had passed the first state bar examination, new entrants into the civil service who had passed the second one, indeed all the levels of rank and various professions relating to the administration of justice were gathered together there by the hundreds. Many of us, I have to say, lost our nerve. There were very, very sad scenes. For me and for my colleagues. After a while, SA people appeared at Lichthof and said: "Whoever leaves this building without causing trouble and promises never to enter it again will have nothing happen to them. We wish to warn you all against any protests or resistance." One could read this on the same day in the Berlin newspaper *8-Uhr-Abendblatt*: "This morning a large crowd of people thronged into the Berlin Central Municipal Court and into District Court I and loudly demanded the immediate dismissal of Jewish judges. At the same time, Jewish attorneys were asked to leave the courts. Thereupon Sunday duty was called for the Courts. Other judges were appointed in place of the Jewish judges and for District Court I it was decreed that new entrants to the civil service would preliminarily hold office in place of the Jewish judges. Afterward, the Jewish judges and attorneys left the courthouse, also among them the presiding judge of the District Court, Soelling."—One already knew from rumors what was going on in the basements of police headquarters and from SA cellars in other parts of the city. I had already decided that my life had come to an end. Yet, as I started walking down the street and still didn't feel a single shot in the back, I then told myself, and this was purely instinctive, I am not speaking here from any moral high ground, but rather it was pure instinct: it's come to an end. If I reach home safely, to my mother, then tomorrow we will begin making preparations to emigrate.

On his way home Rosenthal passed buildings where other lawyers had hung out their shingles:

I knew some of the attorneys; with some I had no acquaintance. I quickly ran up into the offices. "Where is the boss?" Usually they didn't know and said: "He is in court." "Notify him immediately that he must no longer go to court, if he values his life. I can confirm and certify this!" They looked at me as if I had lost my mind. I got home safely. I was in a state of mind that I wouldn't wish on anyone. And my mother, trembling and weeping, had already heard the rumor about what had happened in courts and was certain that she had already lost me. She told me that at the moment she had heard the rumors she had instinctively said, "We have our roots here. We have not damaged this country in any way, but instead our families were among the most loyal sons and citizens of this state and of this city. But that is now at an end. We are going to Jerusalem."[88]

On the same day, in the evening, the provisional secretary of the Prussian Ministry of Justice, Hanns Kerrl,[89] issued a decree that would have serious consequences. Kerrl had been appointed as Secretary of the

Ministry only a few days before, on March 27. He had not completed any legal studies, but had been a Prussian judicial civil servant in his role as judicial administrator. On April 20, Kerrl he was to be officially appointed Secretary of the Prussian Ministry of Justice because of his long-standing membership in the NSDAP. Son of a Protestant headmaster and a lieutenant in World War I, he had already joined the NSDAP in 1923. From 1929 to 1933 he had been a member of the Prussian Parliament. The Kassel attorney Roland Freisler, who had recently been appointed Undersecretary, stood at his side in the Prussian Ministry of Justice. "Kerrl's Decree" of March 31, directed at the presiding judges of the Superior Courts of justice, the presiding judges of higher regional courts, the chief public prosecutors, and the directors of prosecuting authorities, promulgated that:

> The uproar of the people concerning the arrogant demeanor of currently practicing Jewish attorneys and Jewish doctors has reached such an extent that we are compelled to take into account the possibility that—especially during a time of the legitimate defensive actions of the German people against the universal Jewish hate propaganda—that the people take matters into their own hands. This would constitute a danger for the maintenance of justice and its administration . . . I hereby request that all Jewish judges currently holding office promptly submit a request for leave of absence with immediate effect . . . Particular agitation has been caused by the arrogant demeanor of Jewish attorneys; I therefore request that an agreement be reached today with the bar associations or local associations of lawyers or other appropriate authorities that as of 10 am tomorrow morning only certain Jewish attorneys are to practice law and to do so in a ratio that represents the proportion of the Jewish population to that of the rest of the nation. I also wish to undertake the appropriate negotiations to arrange for the full resignation of the board of the bar association.[90]

Inimitable in its language, completely unambiguous in its content, this meant a house ban for all Jewish jurists. This decree constituted the first targeted intervention of National Socialists "from above" into the Prussian judicial system. It took the conditions created by the attacks on

April 1, 1933: As in the case of the business shown above, posters were also displayed in front of "Jewish" law offices. The initial public labeling began simply with the pasting of a notice stating "Jew" on the office sign.

the courts themselves "from below" as an excuse in the absence of any legal reason therefor. Nevertheless, the measure was diligently implemented by the presiding judges.

On the next day, April 1, a Saturday, normally an ordinary working day at that time, Jewish lawyers were confronted with another concern. There was a staged boycott that was expressly directed at law firms of Jewish lawyers. How would the boycott proceed? Would it lead to violent attacks? Yaakov Rosenthal describes his experiences:

> On April 1, early in the morning, somewhat unsuspecting, in accordance with my usual habits, at six-thirty in the morning I went into the little neighboring synagogue of a Talmud Torah for devotions. Then suddenly I saw: an SA man in full uniform was standing before our front door. And I also saw my small lawyer's sign at the entrance to the building, lo and behold; it was smeared over in brown, marked with a large swastika. It became clear to me . . . that I was seeing the demise of generations of an old and time-honored world.

Upon returning after an hour and a half, the SA man was still at his place, standing straight as a column, as if he were waiting in a sentry box to be able to present himself to the Kaiser. I went up to my mother and told her what had happened. After a little snack, well-prepared but not tasting as good as usual, as one might easily imagine, my mother said: "We are now going to take our customary Shabbat walk." I said: "What are you thinking about? Do you really want to take a walk today?" She replied: "Do you know anything you should feel guilty about?" She was a true Prussian puritanical woman. "If you don't, then show the world that you are a man! Put on your best tailcoat again! Today we Jews have our Shabbat. We are not going to allow it to be spoiled!" So, we took a walk. Along Unter den Linden to the Hackescher Markt, along Rosenthaler Straße, to the Börse train station—all these were areas that were filled with Jewish attorneys, doctors, small Jewish shops, and large businesses. Everywhere one was confronted with the same view. The poster: Don't buy from Jews! There were SA men in front of every office building. The signs of companies, attorneys, doctors, all painted over with the swastika.[91]

Another attorney, Bruno Blau, recalled in the 1950s what the situation was like in the courts on the day after "Kerrl's Decree":

Of course, those affected by the decree in question heard no further announcements during the few hours of the night that were still available. It was simply not possible for the Secretary to implement the desired measures in this amount of time. Yet this was not even intended; instead, on the morning of April 1, a large number of SA men were ordered to go to the courts—both with and without uniform—in the role of representatives of the "people" and who were there to carry out the alleged wishes thereof. They were assigned to all rooms in which legal proceedings were taking place and there demanded that all Jewish judges and attorneys present immediately stop what they were doing and then leave the courthouse. In almost every instance this bullying had its effect. Individual judges, who refused to comply based on their official duties and responsibilities of office, were actually thrown out of the courthouse by means of physical force. This happened in Berlin to a judge who had

Schöneberger Ufer at the beginning of April 1933. Waiting attorneys line up to gain access to No. 36, the headquarters of the Berlin Bar Association, in order to request further admission. The building, the address of which was Groß Admiral-von-Köster-Ufer 67 since 1936, no longer exists today. The entrance leads to the inside of the block in which Elisabeth Hospital is located. SA guards regulate the advance.

been seriously wounded in World War I and crippled as a result of his injuries.

The brown shirts also showed up in the waiting room that had been designed for attorneys in order to remove the Jewish attorneys there. In Berlin they encountered Dr. Wilhelm Liebknecht there, the brother of Dr. Karl Liebknecht, who had been murdered together with Rosa Luxemburg. After they had asked him if he was a Jew, he responded: "No, but this is a moment during which I regret being German."[92]

The press informed the public about the new developments. The *Vossische Zeitung*, in its April 1, 1933 morning edition, reported as follows:

Today the courts are back to functioning as usual. . . . By order of the Prussian Ministry of Justice all courts are to resume proceedings as of noon today, . . . Jewish judges who have refused to submit a request for leave of absence are prevented from trespassing and entering the courthouse due to the house rules . . . Jewish officials working in the area of corrections are immediately to be put on leave of absence. In regard to the bar associations . . . it is to be agreed that, as of early Saturday [and therefore the same day, the author] at 10 am only certain Jewish attorneys are to continue in the practice of their profession. These attorneys are to be chosen in consultation with the N.S.D.A.P. district director of legal affairs or with the chairman of the district group of the Association of National Socialist German Jurists. When it is not possible to reach agreement in this regard, then all Jewish attorneys are to be denied entry into court.

Within two days the situation had profoundly changed. All at once a house ban had been imposed and with a single stroke it had become uncertain for Jewish attorneys whether they would be able to continue to practice their profession.

In order to continue to work as attorneys, those affected thereby reacted promptly and applied for their further admission to the bar. The Prussian Ministry of Justice was surprised by the throng of applicants. On April 6 Kerrl sent a supplementary order to the presiding court of appeals judges for implementation, which then replaced the order of March 31. The original states:

Increasing numbers of Jewish attorneys and notaries are directly applying to the Ministry of Justice to be readmitted to the bar and the office of notary. I wish to point out that such applications cannot be decided on a local basis for reasons of equality of treatment. On the other hand, I have not overlooked that there are particularly pressing cases that require special processing and a special decision. A condition for dealing with requests of this nature on my part must however be the complete and unconditional recognition by the party making the request that the currently existing situation created by the agreement in question, is acknowledged by the individual petitioner as legally binding upon him. The government of national elevation in Prussia and I myself as a Reich Commissioner of this government for the administration of justice in Prussia can only take individual requests for processing when the loyalty of the petitioner to the government of national elevation has been demonstrated and confirmed through such an acknowledgement.

I therefore request that, on the day of receipt of this letter, under specification of the wording of this letter's content, all Jewish attorneys who are no longer admitted to the bar and/or who are no longer active as attorneys and notaries, make a new petition for admission to the bar that meets the stated requirements and that is to be submitted to the presiding judges of higher regional courts . . . All requests must arrive at my office with the morning mail, at the latest by Tuesday, April 11."[93]

On the basis of these instructions the presiding judge of the Berlin Court of Appeals and his colleagues at the other Prussian higher regional courts issued a general order[94] that all Jewish attorneys were to make an application for admission to the bar together with a statement of allegiance to the government. This trick put Jewish attorneys on the spot: if they insisted that this requirement was illegitimate and illegal and did not apply, they would no longer be able to practice law. If they made their declaration of allegiance, then they were indicating their acceptance of the legal situation and at the same time kowtowing before the government that was discriminating against them. They had no choice in the matter. The personnel files of the Reich Ministry of

Justice, as they have been passed on to us, show that in most cases the required declaration had been made.

For example, Bruno Mendelsohn, an attorney at the German Court of Appeals since 1919, 45 years of age, wrote on April 8, 1933:

> On the basis of the order of April 6, 1933, I request new admission to the bar as attorney and notary . . . I have never been politically active and have never belonged to a political party with Marxist affiliations. I hereby acknowledge my complete and unconditional recognition of the basis of the agreement in question that the currently existing situation is legally binding on me. If a statute of the Reich regulates my admission, then I also base this petition on the conditions of the Reich statute.[95]

Bruno Blau comments on the confusing situation:

> [It] . . . then became known that in Berlin only 30 attorneys were to be admitted to make appearances in court and that applications therefor had to be submitted personally in the afternoon in the business offices of the bar association. Although the number was so limited and though there was little chance of being taken into consideration, everyone thought that they couldn't pass up the opportunity and made their way to the bar association—the most of them long before the appointed time, so that they could submit their application as early as possible.
>
> We had to wait in front of the building for hours and did so in the rain and under the supervision of young SA fellows, until we were allowed into the building one by one. This process was humiliating to us in the highest degree and was also intended to be so, although it was known that there were quite a few older people among us, as well as gentlemen who were well known due to their academic achievements and who, up to then, had enjoyed a high level of general prestige.
>
> A few days later after the worthy candidates had been chosen, the exercise of their profession was made virtually impossible for the other attorneys. This was because, in regard to court proceedings, they were compelled to seek out the representation of other attorneys for their clients, attorneys who were insufficiently informed about the matter and who also did not have the

trust of the client. Often it was also not even possible to find a somewhat suitable representative, so that there was nothing left to do but postpone the proceedings.[96]

Meanwhile, in the Ministry of Justice, a statutory regulation of the matter was being prepared. On the morning of April 7, 1933, provincial ministers of justice (some of whom had been appointed provisionally) met at the Reich Ministry of Justice with

At the beginning of April 1933, applications of Jewish attorneys for the further practice of law were submitted to the Bar Association

the Reich Secretary of Justice Franz Gürtner and his undersecretary Schlegelberger.[97] A detailed discussion took place over limitations on admission to the bar for Jewish attorneys. Reports from Breslau, Berlin and Bavaria stated that in the wake of Kerrl's decree (a similar decree was issued in Bavaria) all Jewish attorneys [had been] caused to refrain from the "exercise of their profession."[98] The threat of independent actions ("on one's own initiative") on the part of the SA hovered over the meeting; consequently, no clear limitation on the attorneys' activities was achieved.[99] There was a request for a clear sign that would show that government action was being taken. By granting the statutorily unauthorized measures a seemingly legal character, on the one hand, any resistance against exclusion could be eliminated from discussion. On the other hand, the most radical factions of the party were able to be brought to a more moderate position. The intention was to proceed publicly by taking clear steps that demonstrated governmental authority and at the same time to restrain radical NS factions from uncontrolled excesses.

After diligent work over the weekend on Monday, April 10, the Reich Ministry of Justice published the "Statute Concerning Admittance to the Legal Profession" that was backdated to April 7. It contained—analogous to the "Law for the Restoration of the Professional

Civil Service" of April 7 for civil servants—an occupational ban for all "non-Aryan" attorneys. Two general exceptions were provided for, which were likewise analogous to the "Professional Civil Service Statute." Attorneys who had already been admitted before August 1, 1914 ("elderly attorneys") and—if Reich President von Hindenburg[100] intervened—"combat veterans" or direct relatives of those who fell in World War I were to be once again admitted to the legal profession. An important difference in content between the two statutes was that the exclusionary rule for civil servants (which also applied to attorneys in their role as notary) had a provision that contained the word "must," while that for attorneys had a provision that contained the word "can." Yet this margin of discretion in favor of attorneys—based on available documents—was actually never used.

With the passage of the statutes there was still one issue that had not been cleared up. Who should now be regarded as "non-Aryan"? This was dealt with a few days later, on August 11, through "Ordinance 1 for Implementation of the Law on Restoration of the Professional Civil Service." The matter was resolved there:

> A person is not Aryan if he is a descendant of a non-Aryan, especially Jewish parents or grandparents. It is sufficient if one parent or one grandparent is not Aryan. In particular, this is to be assumed if one parent or one grandparent was an adherent of the Jewish religion.[101]

A nationalist and racist definition had thereby prevailed. It gained absolute validity as National Socialist doctrine and was also used for the legal profession and in all areas of society. The circle surrounding those to be excluded was thus quite widely drawn. It included all people who were adherents of the Jewish religion or, regardless of their religious beliefs, had parents or grandparents who at some time had been the member of a Jewish congregation.

## The Process of Readmission

The competent authorities in the Ministry of Justice worked diligently. Undersecretary Freisler stated:

The results of the preliminary examination have shown that the measures provided for in the statute of the Reich in part go significantly further than the provisional ordinances I issued.

The preliminary work necessary for the implementation of the statute is extraordinarily voluminous and difficult. It required substantial preliminary work that I carried out rapidly but also with the necessary amount of deliberation. The examination of individual cases that numbered in the thousands will, if possible, be completed in the first week after Easter.

I expect all attorneys, especially all Jewish attorneys, regardless of whether they are currently admitted to practice or not, to show the competence in classification that is necessary to properly examine the important question of admission or non-admission to practice for individual attorneys. I believe that such an expectation is legitimate, especially in light of the enormous number of declarations of acknowledgement that my office has received from Jewish attorneys.

The question of retention of Jewish attorneys over the next two weeks and the actual continuation of the current state of affairs caused by the recent measures during this time of examination will depend on whether the final determination can be made at an earlier or a later date.[102]

It seems strange that the amount of administrative work required in a case of this nature was stated in terms of the amount of paperwork involved. For Freisler it was simply of no significance that the matter concerned the very existence of the attorneys being affected by this measure.

In implementing the statute, in regard to the readmission of an individual attorney, the following exceptional circumstances gave rise to an exemption from the occupational ban: admission before August 1, 1914 or having been a "frontline soldier" in World War I or being the direct relative of one who fell in battle. During the examination process, the files were in part dealt with in a very routine fashion: the same colored pencil markings are used again and again—"green" for frontline fighter, if this person received an Iron Cross, then with a green cross; "red" as the mark designating "non-Aryan," "blue" for elderly attorneys and, in some cases, "brown" for "mixed race." The red marks piled up too, at the same time as the green and the blue.

One person who was not willing to take a submissive attitude to the violations of law that were given the appearance of legal measures was Ernst Fraenkel, an attorney at the Berlin Court of Appeals, who was 35 years of age. His request of April 8, 1933 states:

> If I should also be admitted to the practice of law in the future, I will, true to my oath as an attorney, conscientiously fulfill my duties as a lawyer in accordance with the statutes currently in effect. A declaration to the effect that I acknowledge the agreements that currently prevent me from practicing law as valid, is something that I cannot do because I am not familiar with such an agreement.[103]

This statement was also designated with a colored pencil as an "unsatisfactory declaration." Fraenkel was considered a "non-Aryan." Moreover, he was suspected of Communist activities. The examination process dragged on, but finally the earlier "frontline fighter" was nonetheless admitted to practice.

In fact, the application of the statutory rules also did not leave any room for discretion in the case of attorneys, but rather essentially constituted an occupational ban.[104] The designated exemptions applied—one would suspect that this turned out differently than NS bureaucrats had expected—to quite a number of lawyers.

The application for readmission was subject to strict criteria. The examination process got under way when, on April 25, 1933, the general principles for a ban on representation were issued in Prussia, one would suspect in order to formalize the procedures: the Implementation Ordinance (AV) for the Reich Statute Concerning Admission to the Practice of Law.[105]

## § 1.

The Higher Regional Court (OLG) presiding judges are to submit a list by May 5, 1933 designating those attorneys in their court district for whom an examination is necessary to determine whether they are to be disbarred based on the Reich Statute of April 7, 1933. In doing so, to be taken into account are the views of the OLG presiding judge himself or of a District Court (LG) presiding judge or of a presiding Municipal Court judge or of the chairman of a bar association board or of the Gau (region) chairman of the respective Gau of the Association of National Socialist Jurists (NSDJ) or of other authorities deemed appropriate therefor in the opinion of the OLG presiding judge. For the attorneys listed in this group report it is to be noted:

a) if they were members of the bar on August 1, 1914,

b) if their admission to the bar has ever been interrupted,

c) if the court to which they were admitted has been changed since August 1, 1914,

d) if the attorney, during the time of his admission to the bar, has continuously been practicing law, whereby it is to be noted if for a time he was exclusively or primarily employed as the in-house counsel of certain companies or in similar positions, or if, apart from that, his practice of law has been interrupted through military service or illness—which are not to be viewed as actual interruptions for the purpose of this inquiry.

## § 2.

Those attorneys of "non-Aryan" origin who base their admission to practice law on the conditions of § 1 Paragraph 2 of the Reich Statute Concerning Admission to the Practice of Law are to do so in writing, with provision of the reasons therefor, the facts pertaining thereto, including the submission of supporting documents, all of which are to be provided in triplicate to the office of the competent OLG presiding judge. This statement of the applicant's case must be in possession of the office of the competent OLG presiding judge by May 4, 1933.

The competent OLG presiding judge will then submit this statement, as well as any appendices thereto, to the Ministry of Justice, at the latest by May 6.

## § 3.

The OLG presiding judge is to make, at the latest, by May 5, 1933, written inquiries to:

a) the competent police officials and public prosecuting agencies,

b) the board of the bar association,

c) the district Gau representatives for the respective Gau of the Association of National Socialist German Attorneys (BNSDJ) and

d) other organizations that seem suitable in order to obtain the view of these authorities as to whether attorneys have had past involvement in Communist activities.

The authorities inquired of are to provide the relevant facts and, to the extent possible, to provide evidence in support of their viewpoint.

The competent OLG presiding judge is to submit all of these responses together with any appendices to the Ministry of Justice, at the latest by May 20, 1933.

The Ministry of Justice reserves the right to itself examine the aforementioned materials in a suitable manner and to itself take measures to also collect information concerning the question of which attorneys have been involved in Communist activities.

## § 4.

In cases in which the submitted material provides sufficient grounds for further examination of the issue as to whether the attorney in question has indeed been involved in Communist activities, then the attorney will be informed of the evidence that has come forward against him and, within a time period of one week, be given the opportunity to make a statement and provide ameliorating evidence.

## § 5.

In terms of §4 of the Reich Statute Concerning Admission to the Practice of Law, I will issue a ban on representation in individual cases. I will not issue bans on representation before May 2, 1933.

Any attorney who believes that he has been banned from representation under § 4 Paragraph 2 of the Reich Statute Concerning Admission to the Practice of Law without justification, is entitled to present his legal views in writing and in triplicate in a timely fashion, with the inclusion of a certificate of good standing from the following:

a) the competent OLG presiding judge,
b) from the competent chief public prosecutor,
c) the board of the competent bar association, all of which are to be submitted to the Ministry.

*In cases in which all three certificates of good standing have been submitted, if there are not other reasons preventing me from doing so, in making my decision about the issuance of a ban on representation, I will assume that the party in question is not entitled to practice law. Service of the bans on representation that I have issued will take place through the OLG presiding judge at my request.*

## § 6.

In all cases I reserve the right to make the final decision regarding the future disbarment of attorneys who have up to now been admitted to the practice of law—doing so on the basis of the Reich Statute of April 7, 1933. I will issue the decision as quickly as possible while taking care to undertake a correct and conscientious verification.

## § 7.

The currently existing situation is to be maintained everywhere until May 8, 1933, because, even while working with the utmost speed, I require this period of time to examine those cases constituting exemptions to the ban on representation.

## § 8.

Prior requests submitted, regardless of the authorities they were submitted to, in matters concerning the Reich Statute of April 7, 1933 are not to be considered as applications in the sense of these Implementation Provisions (Ausf. Best. = Ausführungsbestimmungen), but are rather to be regarded as rendered inapplicable by the Implementation Provisions.

This Implementation Ordinance, dated Tuesday, April 25, has been published in a special issue of the Judiciary and Ministerial Gazette. All applications already submitted were thereby made invalid.

The attorneys affected thereby informed one another about the declarations to be made, as a transcript of a confidential telephone communication of "Councillor Meschelsohn" shows:

> Councillor M. received a circular with the request to continue to pass it on in secret: the issuance of certificates of good standing only have a chance of success if an attestation is included that the attorney in question never engaged in Communist activities, in particular that he never supported Communist organizations, associations and causes and that he has also never, of his own free will, offered to undertake the defense of Communists. Such an attestation will better serve its purpose if it comes from a regimental association, from a person who is a German nationalist, or someone else suitable.

> Berlin, April 29, 1933[106]

At this point those who were affected had to obtain three certificates of good standing if they were interested in maintaining their admission to the bar. The time periods therefor were short, just seven work days were granted in order to submit everything. On Saturday, May 6, the presiding judge of the Berlin Court of Appeals was to forward the corresponding applications to the Ministry of Justice. At the same time investigations were initiated regarding any Communist activities. The wide circle of institutions and persons who could now make allegations encouraged unsupported denunciations.

After May 8, 1933 a representation ban was issued against at least 619 attorneys of "non-Aryan" origin.[107] Practically speaking, such a ban on representation was not just a hindrance to appearing in court, but it also generally reduced opportunities to take on clients, because it was no longer possible to guarantee reliability to a client for an unlimited period of time.

In their applications for readmission that were now to take place on the basis of "legal" principles, the attorneys affected thereby demonstrated in detail to what extent the rules for exceptions applied to them. It was mainly service on behalf of Germany during World War I that was cited. Those who had taken part in World War I presented their military ID. However, the term "frontline soldier" was interpreted extremely narrowly. If a person worked in the commissary procuring supplies this was not acknowledged. This came as a profound shock to those affected. It was a difficult situation for those who, despite their patriotism, were still found to be unacceptable.

The personal files of the Reich Ministry of Justice that exist today reflect the entire drama. The appendices to the over 1,700 applications received (for Berlin alone) contain numerous letters from satisfied clients, who spoke out in favor of the continued admission of "their" attorney. As requested, there were also many letters from NSDAP members. Comrades from World War I praised the patriotic and brave behavior of the attorneys when they had been soldiers. Clients often emphasized the nationalist viewpoint of their attorneys. They did not want to accept the fact that Jews, when they had risked their lives for Germany, were now no longer allowed to work unless they had done something wrong to deserve it and that the anti-Semitic policies of National Socialism essentially sought exclusion of Jews as a whole and were not willing to take individual cases into account. In some instances, the opportunity was also

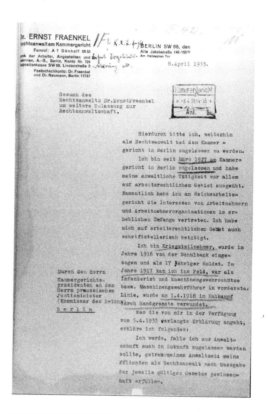

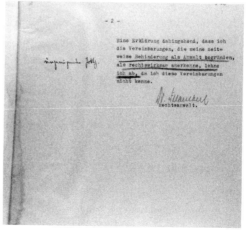

used to get back at an attorney who had not won legal proceedings he had been engaged in. Immoderate in tone, in part factually incorrect, even the vilest formulations of clients were given written form.[108]

Those upon whom a representational ban had been placed were generally young. Women of Jewish origin were also affected. For a small portion of these the ban was once again suspended until October 1933. However, generally the ban on representation was the first official step to an occupational ban. The attorneys of Jewish origin who were once again admitted to the bar received a special pass that entitled them to appear in court.[109]

Official sources state that in May 1933, 1,761 attorneys who were classified as "non-Aryan" made application for readmission.[110] Based on the total number of 1,835 attorneys affected, only 74 did not submit an application for their continued admission to the bar.[111] Some were dead or in jail or had fled in the face of political persecution. It must have been clear to many applicants that they had virtually no chance of being readmitted.

Among those who lost their admission as an attorney and a notary after April 1933, was Dr. Ludwig Bendix.[112] Bendix was imprisoned on June 2, 1933, after he caught the attention of authorities due to his defense of a member of the German Communist Party. He was released in October. Dur-

Ludwig Bendix, 1933 and 1937

ing his incarceration, it was made fully clear to him "that he was being taught a lesson."[113] Nonetheless, he had no intention of leaving Germany, "because Germany was his home and he would seem like a traitor if he abandoned his country."[114] Bendix sent the following circular to his clients after the Gestapo made it clear to him that he was to call himself a "legal consultant."

> . . . Dear Clients, I have been compelled to give up my practice as an attorney and a notary.—However, after a life-long practical and theoretical concern with German law, I feel such a close

relation to it that I must continue my work within the limits prescribed for me under currently applicable law, due to subjective and idealistic reasons.[115]

As a legal consultant he dealt, inter alia, with the advising of those seeking to leave the country in order to earn their living. Through his circular many people became acquainted with his difficult situation. In many cases the response was not sympathy, but rather they attempted to exploit his predicament in that they put pressure on him to reimburse them for attorney fees they had paid him. Despite all this, Bendix strove to keep a dignified bearing.

> Despite all the disappointments and intimidation, I am not going to let myself be beaten down. . . . It may seem crazy, but I insist on another viewpoint. I fight for every inch of ground and cling to it with every fiber of my being. I won't let myself be uprooted . . . My undying struggle to regain the life that has been taken from me has created an inner necessity that drives me forward, despite all differentiations and discrimination, to affirm a shared heritage with those who now hold sway over the country and people and to leave it to personal disputes with them to draw the line in individual instances. I regard it as a duty to myself to maintain my personal dignity by making use of every possibility offered by the laws currently in place. In any case, I have repeatedly had the impression that this attitude of unconditional solidarity has had a strong effect. . . . When it came down to it, figuratively speaking, I took a thousand different paths, all of which I knew led into the desert. But this knowledge could not hold me back from taking them. I wanted the full fruitlessness of my endeavor to be reported in my files in black and white.[116]

After Bendix was taken into "protective custody" for the first time in 1933, he was once again arrested in 1935. From July 1935 to May 1937 he was once again imprisoned—in the Dachau concentration camp. The 22 months in a concentration camp profoundly changed him and his relationship with his family. He was released under the condition that he immigrate to a country outside of Europe. Bendix went to Palestine, in 1947 he followed his son, who would become a renowned sociologist, to the United States. Ludwig Bendix was able to save his life, yet his roots were cut. He died in 1954 at the age of seventy-six in Oakland, California.

The Law for the Restoration of the Professional Civil Service was applied to a large number of lawyers, because they were also notaries. As notaries they were civil servants and therefore subject to especially strict examination. Someone who had been admitted to the bar because he had been a "frontline fighter," could certainly not rely on the fact that he would also be admitted as a notary. A special relationship of trust to the state was required of civil servants; on the other hand, the state no longer showed trust to its civil servants if they were of Jewish origin.

At the beginning of 1933 1,149 attorneys of Jewish origin were also admitted as notaries, almost two thirds of this group. After the examinations that took place in 1933, 524 of these were no longer permitted to act as notaries. This reduction in their practice proved extremely serious for those who were affected, because in many law firms it was work as a notary that was the material basis of the practice. It can be shown that the loss of their status as a notary caused many attorneys to give up their practice entirely and also to terminate their admission to the bar. In this manner those in political authority came one step closer to their goal—a "Jew-free bar."

While the documents were still being proofed, it quickly became foreseeable that the majority of those applying should have been readmitted, because they fell under an exception. In early summer it then appeared that the procedure underwent a radicalization. In individual files it could be demonstrated that the attorney affected could formally meet the qualifications of an exemption. Yet then a search was undertaken to find other reasons to refuse readmission. One of the reasons found was the consolidation of the three Berlin district courts that was undertaken in the fall of 1933. In the case of some judges and public prosecutors, this was used as a way to facilitate the denial of further admission. This possibility of exclusion was also used at the beginning of 1934, as shown by the files of various attorneys: for example, Georg Gerson, born 1887, attorney since 1913, or Karl Hirschland, born 1881, attorney since 1914, or Arnold Kurtzig, born 1898, a "frontline fighter." Although his bar membership was acknowledged after 1933, it was taken away in 1934 upon the consolidation of the district courts.

The Implementation Provision of April 25, 1933 had opened up the possibility of consulting other offices concerning their knowledge of "Communist" activities in the past. There was no way to legally proceed against this reason for exclusion. In the case of the attorney Heinrich Benda it can be shown that he—having lost an eye during World War I—had to be recognized without question as a "frontline fighter." Yet it was alleged that before the vote, in March 1933, together with a student, he had posted a handwritten piece of paper upon which was written: "Get rid of Hitler. Fight for the dictatorship of the proletariat." The process of readmission was terminated, because there was now sufficient information in the files to deny him readmission to the practice of law.

Another method was information from the registration offices that was obtained through the bar association. In this matter it was determined who was, for whatever reason, abroad. In the case of the attorney Dr. Werner Steinitz this was used as the reason not to readmit him to the bar.[117]

Admissions to the bar were rigorously denied to those for whom the exemptions did not apply. This thereby eliminated a great deal of the competition "from the marketplace." The remaining attorneys, primarily those who were not Jewish, benefited regardless of whether they approved or disapproved of the measures in individual cases. Despite the serious consequences raised by the exclusion on those affected attorneys as well as on the administration of justice, their absence immediately led to noticeable positive material benefits for those remaining. This appreciable improvement in income boded well for an increasing recognition of party policy by "Aryan" attorneys. Service on behalf of jurisprudence or the German state was no longer of any concern; only "racial classifications" were relevant. The goal was to separate the individuals by definition from society. The definition was the first step of exclusion. The consequences that later arose were only first detectable later.

The situation was exacerbated by the forced resignation of the board of the bar association. As in other areas, for example in the retail trade, the leaders of the respective associations were targeted in order to replace them with new leadership, which mostly consisted of National Socialists or at least those who sympathized with them. On March 28, 1933, the board of the Berlin Bar Association resigned, although the 33 members had only been elected a few weeks before. During the election (January 9–13, as well as February 11, 1933) 3,400 members of the bar had voted for whom was to occupy the 16 seats that would be unoc-

cupied. The first list, which also included the previous chairman Ernst
Wolff as a candidate, had been put together by the Berlin Bar Association. The second consisted of District Court attorneys, whose primary
issue was simultaneous admission to the Berlin Court of Appeals, the
third had an explicitly political orientation and consisted exclusively of
National Socialist attorneys. The previous board was confirmed, due
to the contribution it had made to professional policies and its credibil-
ity. Nineteen members of the board were of Jewish origin,[118] this proportion reflected the demographic make-up of the bar. The individual
candidates had proven themselves in terms of professional policy. They
did not represent any clear political direction. The top candidate of the
National Socialist list, Reinhard Neubert (324 votes) and the attorney
Richard Frost (283), had the worst results.[119]

This board had reacted indignantly to the arrest of the lawyers
Apfel, Barbash and Litten. The chairman, Ernst Wolff, wrote to the
Prussian Ministry of the Interior on March 3, 1933, asking for information on when the persons concerned would be free again.[120] On March
28, 1933 the board of the Berlin Bar Association unanimously resigned.
What precisely caused the board members to take this step is unknown,
just as is the motive.

On March 31, 1933, three days after the resignation of the regular
board, the attorney Neubert was provisionally entrusted with the task
of managing the board—the same person who had failed so miserably
in January.

On April 11, a general decree ordered new elections. The "election"
had to take place on April 22, 1933 "without debate in a ballot that
took place through acclamation" and "in a public session." The "public" consisted primarily of a delegation of the SA. According to the rec-
ollections of an eyewitness every other row of chairs was occupied with
uniformed men.[121] The "election" of 33 board members only took half
an hour with the following result: 24 NSDAP members, six members
of the Stahlhelm (paramilitary organization of World War I frontline
soldiers in the Weimar Republic) or DNVP (German National People's
Party), and 3 who could be generally regarded as having right-wing
views."[122] Neubert became the chairman; later he became the chairman
of the Reich Bar Association.

At this point, there was no longer any real spokesman for the interests of Jewish colleagues on the board of the Bar Association. As with
the case of the resignation of the board of the Bar Association, it is not

known whether clients were pressured or if Jewish attorneys were forced to give up clients. In any case, there was little need for them. An eyewitness reported that her father, Dr. Georg Cohn-Lempert, had an established representation in the Tempelhof Municipal Court up to 1933, with his own board in the room for attorneys, on which one could see which room he was in at the moment. After April 1933, a younger attorney was now sitting in the room for attorneys and was ready to undertake representation. This colleague was considered "Aryan"; all at once he was being employed where otherwise Dr. Cohn-Lempert would have been engaged. Non-Jewish attorneys quietly profited from the waves of economic and social discrimination of their Jewish colleagues. No-one spoke out against the exclusion.[123]

The attorney Tillmann Krach, who has intensively dealt with these events since the beginning of the 1990s, was unable to identify either "sympathizers with the new rulers nor a selfish grasping for profit." Walter Oppenhoff, an attorney from Cologne, views the simple matter of "playing along"[124]—in contrast to "saying no"—as an attempt to exert influence by the responsible part of the bar, who were still caught up in traditional manners of thought and behavior of the profession and the sense of a decent and civilized political system. They were trapped in a false optimism, in that they acknowledged statutes as law. Acknowledging current statutes as law, the attorneys were of the view that by remaining in the system they would still be able to mitigate negative measures. Yet to do so it would be necessary to organize or to undertake extremely brave measures. Even later, as the exclusionary measures were relentlessly intensified, no influence of any note was brought to bear. This raises doubts about the assessment of the matter by Krachs and Oppenhoffs. After the war, Adolf Arndt has stated that there were people who conducted themselves "decently."[125] In doing so he was not referring to courageous deeds, but rather, for example, the continuation of a personal, respectful manner of social intercourse, greeting a person upon encountering him, an indication of sympathy, possibly even concrete support in matters involving representation. While you wouldn't be punished for such behavior, it would require backbone under the prevailing social conditions. It was simpler to simply refer to existing regulations and to accept the material advantages they provided. That was precisely the intent of those who initiated these measures.

The examination of 1,761 applications (all in Berlin) for readmission to the bar continued to drag on until September. On October 15,

1933, a list containing all attorneys admitted to the bar was published. It listed 1,168 attorneys who were considered to be Jewish. Based on existing knowledge, the admission of altogether 588 attorneys was revoked. In 1933 a third of all Jewish attorneys had thereby been permanently disbarred and driven from their profession.

Around two thirds of the original number of 1,835 attorneys continued to practice their profession.

## The Occupational Ban on Young Attorneys

For those who had not taken part in World War I, perhaps because at this time they were still children or had been decommissioned because they were unsuitable, there was no exemption rule available as a reason for readmission to the bar. Generally, all younger attorneys were therefore excluded from the bar—here we are referring to those born in 1902 and thereafter.

One person who was affected thereby was Dr. Ludwig Elkeles. His personal files contain a letter from his mother to Reich President Hindenburg that emphasized her son's patriotic commitment to Germany.[126] She pointed out the financial hardship the family was suffering, because her other son was also without work, because as a Jew he was no longer able to work as a doctor in a hospital. The financing of studies for the children had already put a great financial burden on the family and now it was confronted with the fact that the second son was also to lose the opportunity to practice his profession. This had all put the Elkeles in a desperate economic situation. Just like this mother many others of those affected described their existential need due to the absence of income to the judicial authorities. Many had only gotten through their studies by doing without, their law firms were not yet established and nonetheless there were often several family members who were dependent on the income. None of the letters made reference to the insufficient legal basis created by the occupational ban, as one would have expected in the case of jurists; apparently most of them had quickly seen that the power of the government could structure the law in any matter it wished. They therefore limited themselves to the attempt to obtain an exemption, yet otherwise they were standing before an abyss.

In the case of Oswald Ahrweiler, who was Catholic, even the Bishop of Osnabrück wrote a letter on his behalf to the Minister of Justice. The answer was without ambiguity:

> ... As a consequence of the extraordinary number of Jews that have flooded the Prussian legal profession, virtually no exceptions can be made. Even today there are about 1,500 Jews as opposed to about 1,800 German attorneys in the Berlin Court of Appeals district. Certainly, you can understand that the legal profession and especially the Berlin Bar, is energetically opposed to the readmission of attorneys of Jewish origin. They put forth the argument that this type of jurist may no longer be a civil servant, due to the Professional Civil Service Statute and that therefore their admission to the bar would undoubtedly create the impression that the legal profession has lower standards of quality than those put forth for civil servants, which could only result in a lower opinion of those engaged in the practice of law.[127]

Rules were created, and these rules were used for purposes of argumentation. For those affected it was a vicious circle. Jewish jurists were prohibited from setting up a new practice, thereby ensuring that the entire new generation of attorneys consisted only of non-Jewish applicants. For those young attorneys who had been admitted to the bar in March 1933, as well as those receiving practical training in judicial or other legal work after having passed the first state examination—not to mention new entrants to the administrative grade of the civil service who had passed the second state examination—the occupational ban profoundly altered their career prospects: they had completed their studies, perhaps also their practical training, then suddenly it was all over—no further prospects. In this situation involving an absence of professional prospects, many decided to leave Germany. Most were unattached and summoned the necessary courage to start over. Some of them were sent abroad by their families, in order to scout out the conditions and to prepare for the rest of their family to join them.

One of the few (as far as is known only two) jurists of Jewish origin who were still admitted to the bar during this stage, was Adolf Arndt, who has already been mentioned. After he had left his position as a judge, he was allowed to be an attorney. Presumably in his case the determinative factor was that he had already at one time been in practice as an attorney before 1933.

## The Occupational Ban on Women

At the beginning of 1933 there were 19 women of Jewish origin admitted to the bar as attorneys in Berlin, a proportion of just about 1 percent. These circumstances primarily resulted from the fact that women were only first allowed to obtain law degrees in 1922.

The oldest of them was Edith Speer, née Klausner, who was born in 1879.[128] She must have been significantly older than her male colleagues at the time she completed her degree, but was not the first woman to be admitted as an attorney in Prussia. This honor goes to Margarete Berent, who was born in 1887. She too was admitted as an attorney for the first time in 1925 at the comparatively advanced age of 38. In 1928 it was considered newsworthy by the *Frankfurter Zeitung* to report that Ella Auerbach became the first woman to be admitted as an attorney at the Court of Appeals.

The youngest attorney who was threatened by the 1933 occupational ban was Hilde Kirchheimer, née Rosenfeld, who later took on the name Neumann, who was 28 years old. In 1933 she had been practicing law for a year.

With only two exceptions, all these attorneys were born in large cities. There one could find better opportunities for girls to receive a quality education during their school years and more tolerance was granted to the idea of women entering professions that were not typically associated with them. Some of those affected, like Hilde Kirchheimer, came from a family where the father was already an attorney. They were acquainted with the work of an attorney and could depend on later taking over the father's law firm. Others, on the other hand, had married colleagues and expanded their relationship to a partnership on the professional level; an example thereof was Ella Auerbach, née Levi. Nevertheless, the absolute number of women practicing law was still always incredibly small. The later attorney Erna Proskauer reported that at that time the presence of women was downright "exotic" at the universities: "I think that I know everyone there, who is more or less my age."[129]

With the occupational ban of early 1933 the professional existence of women was at risk. They were not "frontline fighters." They couldn't have obtained their admissions to the bar before 1914, because they were only allowed to earn a law degree at the beginning of 1922. The personal files reflect the misfortune that was conjured up by the occupational ban in individual instances. Despite intensive individual efforts to obtain classification as an exemption under the rules, the occupational ban against female Jewish attorneys was thoroughly applied—with one exception. One woman was allowed to continue with her admission to the bar despite her inability to meet the conditions for an exception: Hanna Katz.

In Hanna Katz's case, consideration was given to her international prominence and this was the determinative criterion for continued admission to the bar, because she was the only German representative with a seat on the board of the International Law Association—in this case the Trademark Committee. In addition to her activities as an attorney, Katz was an interpreter, something that made her participation in international matters easier, if she hadn't been already qualified in the first place. Because her work for the Association was conditioned on the fact that she maintained a practice as an attorney and the British delegation had already expressed interest in taking over her position, she retained her admission, because it was imperative that an English representative should be prevented from replacing her. Apparently, Katz was still trusted to pursue German interests in regard to Association policy. This viewpoint was not shared by all governmental departments, for example, Hanna Katz had great difficulties in attending a 1936 conference that was held abroad, because she had difficulties in obtaining appropriate travel documents. For reasons of foreign policy, in 1938 she was the only Jewish woman to be admitted as a "legal consultant." In 1941 Katz was still able to immigrate to the United States.

Half of the female Jewish attorneys, for which sufficient information is available, were solo practitioners. Those who were married were often partners with their husbands, as was the case with Ella Auerbach. She had a law firm in the Burgstraße with her husband Richard. Some of the men, like Richard Auerbach, could continue to practice law, because they had been acknowledged as "frontline fighters." Because younger attorneys who could no longer work in Germany frequently went to live abroad, the female attorneys married to them generally made their decision on whether or not to remain in Germany based on the views of their husbands. They most certainly, after they themselves had been disbarred, supported their husbands in their work, although of course they could not make appearances in court. In 1939 Ella and Richard Auerbach immigrated to the United States, but only after Richard Auerbach had his reputation besmirched in 1937 due to proceedings brought by a legal disciplinary court and was then also finally disbarred in 1938.

Due to the occupational ban, after 1933 only 15 women in Berlin were practicing law and only one of them, Hanna Katz, was Jewish. Working from anti-Semitic premises, another goal of the National Socialists was thereby attained, namely to force women out of what was originally a profession that was restricted to men.

## The Situation up to October 1933

The result of the first two waves of segregation—the terrorist and the bureaucratic—became evident on October 15, 1933, when a list of those lawyers admitted to practice law was published, which was published in three versions. A complete list was issued by the board of the Berlin Bar Association, which included all attorneys admitted in the district of the Berlin Court of Appeals. Another list appeared in the same printing type on the same day with the remark "only for official use." In it, without being noted in a legend, all Jewish lawyers were designated by means of a small star before their name.[130] A third list was also published by the BNSDJ. It only included "Aryan" attorneys. The existence of the "star list," which only appeared in this form in Berlin, is an interesting phenomenon that has not yet been given the treatment it deserves in literature on the Third Reich. After the enormous amount of agitation, baiting and persecution that had purportedly taken place, it had become so peaceful in the fall of 1933 that the competent authorities did not deem it expedient to publicly take discriminatory measures. This also matches the approach that was taken in other areas, such as the retail trade. In the middle of 1933, after department stores had been initially targeted for intensive attacks, the wave of propaganda subsided as it became apparent that the implementation of political goals had palpable economic effects.[131]

On the basis of a list of 1,835 attorneys of Jewish origin in Berlin at the beginning of 1933, according to the "star list," in October 1933 there were still 1,168 persons (63.7 percent) continuing to practice law in Berlin. Apparently, the political authorities had to take into consideration the proper administration of justice to a far greater extent than was either foreseeable or desirable in the spring of 1933. All this being said, it still meant that a third of the attorneys who had been classified as Jewish were not able to attend to their practice for three quarters of the year after the National Socialist seizure of power—all due to the outbreak of anti-Semitism.

In the meantime, attempts had been made to install a second level of justice.[132] The "Will of the Führer" had entered into effect along with formally maintained legislative procedures,[133] party institutions were endowed with sovereign powers and the Gestapo was allowed to issue arbitrary sanctions. However, during the first few years of the Third Reich economic interests were able to prevail over the basic policy of segregation of Jews. It was essential to continue to allow more than 1,000 Jewish attorneys in Berlin to practice law for various reasons:

- The role played by foreign policy considerations is not to be underestimated. Many foreign companies were not prepared to automatically comply with the requirement that they entrust their affairs to "Aryan" attorneys.
- For the most part Jewish lawyers had non-Jewish employees. If a law firm went under, then this was always accompanied by the loss of jobs. Since it was vital that unemployment not be further increased, consideration was given to the importance of keeping these people employed.
- The agitation against Jews had created a number of issues in private law that at least required legal consultation, and perhaps also the authentication of documents by a notary. Such issues included the transfer of companies that were now regarded as Jewish, as well as the transfer of land to non-Jewish buyers, the division of property between spouses in the case of divorce and the administration of estates.
- There was an increase in labor court proceedings, because here too the formal examination of termination of employment for anti-Semitic reasons remained without limitations. Beginning at the end of 1933 there were increasingly more labor law decisions that did not accept "racial classification" as a reason for dismissal.[134]

- Criminal law proceedings gained a completely new aspect, not only because of political denunciation, but also because of actual opposition to the system—all of which made representation in court necessary, which still had not been dispensed with in the first years of the National Socialist dictatorship.

The division into "Jewish" and "non-Jewish" had essentially created an entirely new area of disputes, which would only increase in the course of time. The reassessment of conflicts that were now all at once to be reevaluated in terms of "racial criteria," reached all the way into the private sphere and thereby included disputes between tenants, businessmen and their unsatisfied customers and estranged married couples. This all led to an increase in litigation. Even under a government in which arbitrary actions were becoming more and more part of daily life, people still sought to clarify the legal nature of their situation. As propaganda continued to whip up hostility against Jewish attorneys, they increasingly found themselves put at the mercy of the goodwill of their clients. Many clients exerted pressure in order to reduce bills, behind which always lurked the risk of a complaint against the attorney. Accusations that were the fallout of unsuccessful legal proceedings brought an increasing number of cases before disciplinary courts for lawyers.[135] Such disciplinary courts were held when an attorney was accused of committing a violation against the bar's code of professional conduct. As anti-Semitic rules expanded this gave rise to innumerable new fact situations, for example, an error over one's own ("Aryan") descent or simple statements of opinion that, when expressed by Jews, were immediately regarded as a cause for disciplinary action.[136] In the legal disciplinary hearings general developments were reflected in legal disciplinary hearings with the result that numerous such proceedings ended with disbarment. Arthur Aron Lenk met such a fate due to "corruption."[137]

The facts of the case: Mrs. Mellis (of Jewish origin, with an "Aryan" husband) went into a tirade during a radio broadcast of one of Hitler's speeches, using the words: "Christian sons of bitches." A complaint was brought against her; the Gau Propaganda Office, Dept. of Concentration (dealt with those making statements against the regime], requested that she make a response by November 8, 1934. At first the married couple Mellis sought the advice of a friend, then they engaged Lenk to represent them as an attorney. The proceedings against Ms. Mellis were terminated. Lenk maintained that he had reached an acceptable conclusion of the matter and requested at least 400 to 500 Reichsmark. It cannot be precisely reconstructed from the facts whether or not Lenk had a hand in stopping the proceedings against Mrs. Mellis. His fee request at the instigation of Mrs. Mellis was interpreted as corruption. Based on the Reich Code of Professional Conduct for Attorneys he was disbarred. His appeal was dismissed in 1936.

Although not every proceeding ended with an occupational ban for the accused attorney, the attacks grew in intensity. Usually one of the National Socialist offices was involved, including the Reich Office for Business Ethics, as in the proceedings against the attorneys Richard Auerbach und Wilhelm Goldberg.[138] In the National Socialist publication *The Attack* of November 28, 1936 (late edition), the behavior of Goldberg before the court was attacked under the headings "Brazen as ever" and "Outrageous tone taken by Jewish attorney." Legal disciplinary proceedings against Goldberg were sought merely for his appearance before the court but not just against him, but also against his Jewish partner. About a year later matters had developed up to the point of the main proceedings before the legal disciplinary court. The accusations apparently had so little substance that Auerbach had to be acquitted while Goldberg received a reprimand.

For the remaining Jewish attorneys who had managed to sail around the cliffs of the admission process, it appeared that matters had settled down. They were in all likelihood busy enough in exerting themselves to recover their financial losses through taking on more cases, to the degree this opportunity offered itself. Yet this stage of apparent peace only created a sense of false security.

Not everyone was deceived by appearances. This is given expression by the assessment provided by the Berlin attorney Friedrich Solon, who was an aspiring poet:[139]

> *1933*
> *Should I be patient and live on sufferance?*
> *Feeling sorry for myself and bemoaning my fate?*
> *That which is due to me from life,*
> *The bill therefor is long overdue.*
> *The weak are threatened by a dark destiny,*

*Those who do not want to understand the struggle,*
*Will be forced to endure*
*What these times make out of them.*
*In order to live I must struggle,*
*Imperious, taking action, never passive.*
*And: how will I master these times?*
*Everything is and remains undecided.*

# The Third Wave of Exclusion: Undermining of the Economic Foundations

In the legal area the exclusionary measures were not limited to attorneys; instead this exclusion was associated with a targeted "segregation" and transfer of Jewish judges and prosecuting attorneys.[140] One can only assume that this method of proceeding was undertaken in a calculated fashion. On the one hand, the appropriate stacking of the court with judges impeded the criminalization of National Socialists who committed acts of violence; on the other hand, the judicial examination of exclusionary measures in individual instances was prevented. At the same time efforts were made to increase the degree to which young jurists were educated in terms of National Socialist ideology.[141] Renowned figures reinterpreted their own teachings. For example, the expert in constitutional law Carl Schmitt observed: "All of today's German law must exclusively and solely be infused with the spirit of National Socialism . . . Every interpretation must be an interpretation in the sense of National Socialism." And it must be added: "this is because we are working in terms of a bond that is more reliable, more alive and deeper than the deceptive attachment to the easily manipulated phrases of thousands of paragraphs."[142]

In addition to the well-known personalities who gave luster and recognition to National Socialism by associating their names and their ideas with it, an intentional practice of appointing young National Socialists at the universities sought to disseminate teachings that were infused with its ideology. Among those so appointed, just to name some of the best known, were the 30-year-old Karl Larenz and Ernst

Forsthoff, a student of Carl Schmitt, who was only one year older. At that time Larenz specialized in civil law, while Forsthoff put more of an emphasis on administrative law. Both presented their teachings in a convincing fashion and wove National Socialist ideas into their fields of work. In this fashion, National Socialist legal doctrine, which up to then had been on rather shaky grounds, was given a reputedly firm scholarly basis. For example, Forsthoff classified Jews as "a foreign people" who were residing in the German nation.[143] In the case of a person so otherwise committed to rationality, it is difficult to dismiss such statements as being the result of a "youthful and idealistic perspective," as just an "error," as one biography suggests.[144] Forsthoff later fell into disagreement with the responsible authorities, which caused him to be prohibited from teaching from 1941 to 1943, but then he was finally once again allowed to do so. The reputations of Larenz and Forsthoff continued almost unabated in the Federal Republic of Germany. Their services in the development of law after 1945 should not be belittled, although a public and scholarly treatment of their respective contributions in the support of National Socialism is still lacking.[145] The contemporary effect of the contributions of intelligent legal scholars should not be underestimated. It contributed to enriching the hollow, emotionally based tendencies of National Socialism, by providing reputedly objec-

The Prussian Minister of Justice Kerrl (under the gallows) at a training camp for law students doing their internship in August 1933 at Jüterbog

tive facets. This was necessary to perform a flanking maneuver, where actions such as those taken by the Prussian Minister of Justice Kerrl, who allowed pictures to be taken of himself under gallows to which a section of a statute was attached. The theorists created a scholarly system that worked to enable the deprivation of justice.

The separation of Jewish and non-Jewish lawyers was also further extended in the Berlin bar. On May 23, 1933, it was decreed that law firms involving legal partnerships in which the partners were regarded as "different" in accordance with racial criteria, were to be dissolved.[146] Bruno Blau described what this meant in one specific instance.[147]

> For a number of years, I ran my office together with a non-Jewish colleague, by sharing the general expenses of the business equally. We got along wonderfully and neither of us ever had the intention of changing the existing arrangement. . . . My colleague therefore rented another office. Since all the rooms together were too large for me, I was also compelled to look for another office. Indeed, because I couldn't find suitable premises in the vicinity of my old office, I didn't have any other choice but to move to another part of Berlin. I incurred significant expenses during the move and also suffered a loss in that I had to reorganize my whole business and, in part, start over again in a new locality. As a result of this move it also became necessary for me to engage in litigation, the details of which are of some interest. I had entered into a contract with a private telephone company, which provided me with a telephone system that was intended for me, as well as for my former partner. After the partnership had to be dissolved due to an official decree, the system was no longer of use for me as a solo practitioner and I could simply not make use of it in my new, much smaller office. I therefore had the company pick up the five phones that belonged to the system. They nonetheless requested the full fees for the system for the entire duration of the contract—and this was for several more years. I refused to pay with the justification that, as a result of the official decree, for which I bore no responsibility, the basis on which the transaction had been entered into no longer existed and that as a result the contract no longer had to be fulfilled. This

viewpoint was later acknowledged by the courts as being correct. However, at this time there had not yet been any decisions to this effect. Because I felt that I clearly had the law on my side, I brought suit. In this regard I had the misfortune that my case came before a Jewish associate judge who, as a result of the already mentioned "Law for the Restoration of the Professional Civil Service" had been transferred to a much lower position as an associate judge at the district court. The judge was the head of the division handling my case and the outcome would predominantly depend on his decision. I now had to learn through bitter personal experience what I already knew sufficiently from my own prior practice of law—that Jewish lawyers, due to an excess of objectivity, took a perspective that worked to the detriment of Jewish litigants. In other words, they wanted to even avoid the very appearance that, as Jews, they were unjustly intervening on behalf of a Jewish party. As a result I lost the trial; I am convinced that I would have won if a non-Jewish judge had been in charge of the proceedings, unless this judge happened to be a fanatical Nazi.

*Völkischer Beobachter,* March 29, 1933

While admission to practice was being reviewed, most attorneys were virtually unable to appear in court, which of course had its effect on income. In addition, loss of notary status was a serious blow to law firms. As a result of the prohibition on representation, many clients began to feel uncertain about "their" attorneys and turned to other lawyers to represent their interests. If a partnership broke up, it was often not the Jewish attorney that retained its former clients, but rather his non-Jewish colleagues. This behavior should not cause one to rush to the conclusion that clients were motivated by anti-Semitism. An attorney was sought out in order to better represent one's interest. The client's choice was not based on political affiliations, but rather on the desire for a reliable and permanent ability to represent interests. Yet this was precisely what Jewish attorneys were not able to guarantee. As a result, the income of Jewish law firms was further reduced. Yet another blow was the fact that Jewish attorneys were no longer able to undertake legal aid representation. Siegfried Neumann, an attorney who had a law firm not far from Berlin, suspected that a secret decree had been the cause of these measures.[148] To top things off, the courts only appointed non-Jewish attorneys for opinions and reports.

As if that was not enough, the major economic associations and numerous companies also promptly terminated their contracts with Jewish attorneys who served as consultants. These were completely "apolitical" measures that were supposedly undertaken in order to avoid damage to the respective organizations. Based on the biographies of Berlin attorneys of Jewish origin, it is not possible to quantify the effect of these encroachments, yet the reality was that the income of Jewish lawyers was continuously being reduced. On the other hand, expenses generally remained the same. While one could do without individual employees, the cuts became increasingly noticeable. Siegfried Neumann, who has already been mentioned, summed matters up sarcastically: "the racial question has turned out to be a financial one."[149]

The various biographies give testimony that there were nonetheless many clients, even National Socialists, who remained loyal to their attorneys, even though the question of further representation had been placed into question. At the same time, this was rarely sufficient to provide a counterbalance for the various clients that have been lost, especially the big ones. The economic deterioration was the equivalent to another wave of exclusion.

## The Worsening of the Situation in 1935

Change was taking place at all levels of society; trade unions had been banned in 1933, as well as all parties. In addition to the governmental administration, party departments were set up. No clear hierarchy was established between the two, which gave rise to a chaotic situation in terms of who was competent for what. This nourished the hope that under these conditions no fundamental policies would be able to be developed against the Jews. In addition, the massive power disputes taking place within the NSDAP and its branches were coming to a head. At the height of this internal conflict came the bloody settlement of matters at the end of June/beginning of July 1934, during which SA Chief of Staff Ernst Röhm and some 85 other Nazis were arrested and killed by the Gestapo and the SS. In this way, Hitler and the leaders surrounding him were able to secure their claim to power as against the SA, as well as against conservative opponents.[150] During this time the pressure exerted by party authorities on both the economy and the judiciary diminished.

Yet this state of affairs did not last long. By 1935, at the latest, the repression of Jews once again intensified. Acts of violence against them increased to such an extent that these outbursts needed to be challenged in some way. It was announced that a general regulation of the legal situation of Jews would be announced at the Nuremberg Party Congress in September 1935. On August 20 intensive negotiations took place between representatives of high finance and high-ranking members of the government and the party.[151] The direct result of these discussions was a decree by Frick, the Secretary of the Interior of Prussia and the Reich, which banned all individual actions against Jews by the members of the NSDAP and its branches.[152] The regulation of the "Jewish question" called for by the economic sector, among others, continued to remain unresolved. At the same time the economic condition of the persons concerned continued to steadily deteriorate. This had the result that they were increasingly forced to depend on the allegedly well-meaning intervention of well-informed people, whether from banking circles or accounting firms or colleagues. The "elimination of Jews from public life" took place on a case-by-case basis.

The Nuremberg Congress (September 10–16, 1935) began without a fully formulated draft of regulations against Jews. Various drafts were drawn up during the course of hectic consultations between Secretary of the Interior Frick, Assistant Secretaries Stuckart and Pfundtner and the Deputy Assistant Secretaries Medicus, Seel, Sommer and Lösener, as well as various representatives of the local police and the Reich Doctors' Leader Wagner.[153] Lösener was responsible for the final definition of the term "Jewish" in the draft that was adopted.[154] On September 15, 1935 the "Statute for the Protection of German Blood and German Honor" Reich Law Gazette (RGBl. I, 1146) presented a conceptual classification of who was to be deemed a Jew from now on. The superordinate concept was "non-Aryan," which contained the subcategories "Jew" (with three Jewish grandparents) and "Mixed Race," whereas this group was divided once again into "Mixed Race in the First Degree" (with two Jewish grandparents) and "Mixed Race in the Second Degree" (with one Jewish grandparent).[155] The determinative factor for descent was the religious status of the grandparents. Systematic deficiencies in logic were overlooked.[156] The so-called Nuremberg laws were enacted by acclamation. Hitler had given the following phrase currency: "The Party commands the State."[157]

Various interventions in the legal sector followed thereupon. The situation of lawyers had already been generally discussed since 1933, now the principle of freedom to provide legal advice was abolished. In place of the attorney as a representative of the client's interests, the new role of "servant of the law" was established by the "Law for Prevention of Abuses in the Area of the Provision of Legal Advice" (December 13, 1935, RGBl. I, p. 1475). This law opened up further intervention possibilities—now it was possible also to proceed against the provision of legal counsel by attorneys who had already been excluded by the occupational ban, as well as against tax consultants and other professional groups, who dealt with legal issues.[158]

> Whoever now wanted to provide legal assistance, needed authorization, which in return required that he be a member of the National Socialist Legal Protection Association and that there were not already a "sufficient" number of attorneys admitted locally and that the person not only be suitable in terms of professional training, but also politically in the sense of the National Socialist state . . .[159]

The statute was not directed against Jewish attorneys who were still admitted to practice law, but primarily against "former ones," who had been robbed of their membership in the bar. At the same time the circle of those "Aryan" attorneys who were allowed to take on people as clients who had "less than 75 percent Aryan blood"—and were therefore "non-Aryans"—was further limited. A member of the BNSDJ was not allowed to take on a "non-Aryan" in a controversy against "a fellow member of the German nation or a German company."[160] At the end of 1934, 9,147 attorneys in Germany belonged to the BNSDJ, the entire German "legal front" included around 140,000 people.[161] With the prohibition on accepting Jews as clients, the separation into Jewish and non-Jewish clients was successfully being carried out and ultimately the legal status of Jews would be undermined.

The action of the Berlin Bar Association took a similar approach, when it brought charges based on unfair competition in 1935 against Ludwig Bendix, who has already been mentioned, on the basis of the circular cited that he sent to his clients.[162] The extra-procedural consultation and representation activities of former attorneys were regarded by the professional organization as a disturbance that took away business from their "Aryan" colleagues. The presumption seems likely that despite the eagerness to act displayed here the parties affected hardly earned large amounts through this type of work and thus the "Aryan" attorneys were hardly suffering any losses. Bendix was acquitted in the proceedings that followed (in which he was defended by Councillor Aronsohn, who lost his life in Theresienstadt and was the father of the attorney

Erna Proskauer, who practiced all the way up into the 1980s), although the presiding judge did not seem very well disposed toward him.[163]

The BNSDJ, which had been a subdivision of the NSDAP since 1934, was renamed in 1936 as the "National Socialist Association for the Protection of Law" (NSRB). As "protectors of the law"

German jurists, as was now clear, were released from their obligation in regard to a free development of the law and instead bound by their allegiance to the protection of the National Socialist system.[164]

Although most of the Jewish notaries had already lost their admission as notaries in 1933 due to the "Law for the Restoration of the Professional Civil Service" the statutes now enacted in 1935 in the wake of the Nuremberg Rally, prohibited those still remaining from practice.[165] Bruno Blau noted in his memoirs:[166]

> In 1935 the Jewish notaries, without prior notice and without a legal basis, were prohibited by the Secretary from exercising their office. We were required to deliver up our seals, registers and other official documents immediately. One notary—Dr. Hans Kaufmann—refused to comply with what he regarded as an unlawful demand. This was a man who had been seriously wounded in World War I and been promoted to the rank of first lieutenant. However, in the end he had no other option but to comply with the order issued by a superior authority.

In the biographical index, the removal of admission as notary is noted as December 31, 1935.[167] The attorney Berthold Haase gave up his admission as an attorney after the enactment of this law. In his memoirs, he wrote:

> Thus, in the 62nd year of my life, my career came to an end, one in which I had devoted myself to the interests of justice with seriousness and pleasure and in which I had exerted my best efforts for the maintenance and strengthening of German culture.[168]

An anti-Semitic mood prevailed in all of the associations. At the same time the matter was made subject to discussion, as to whether the National Socialist state needed lawyers at all. Therefore, the wearing of insignias on the robes was rejected, although it had been desired by some Nazis and would have generally enhanced the status of attorneys.[169] Jewish attorneys had still not been banned from the practice of law in principle. They were still needed by innumerable familiar clients who were preparing to emigrate in the face of the worsening situation in Germany, as well as for consultation concerning transfers of property, even if "Aryan" colleagues were also needed, who could still be active as notaries, in order to authenticate the transfers. In fact, the attorneys who were still in practice found themselves in a conflicting situation: they were trustworthy, those seeking advice from them believed them, if they were told that when they were put in a situation where they were forced to sell that they had no effective legal means of defense at their disposal. In this manner the remaining Jewish attorneys, in many cases, facilitated the carrying out of transactions that made "Aryanization" possible and became unwilling collaborators with the National Socialist system.

# The Final Wave of Exclusion: The General Ban on Practicing Law in 1938

The material situation of Jewish attorneys had deteriorated to such an extent that many who still practiced in 1938 had moved their offices to their private residences. One of these was Kurt Liepmann—he gave up his office in a central location, in the immediate vicinity of Alexanderplatz, and instead continued his practice in his apartment in Wilmersdorf. In 1939 Liepmann immigrated to Belgium, which was occupied by German troops in 1940. From his final signs of life one can only conclude that before 1942 the attorney Kurt Liepmann was placed in the detention center Camp de la Plage in Argelès sur Mer in France, close to the Spanish border, and died there.

Within many families, the husband still clung to his traditional understanding of his role as provider for his family. There are reports from various families that reflect the desolate economic situation. For example, the grandchildren of Councillor Sandmann were always sent to a certain baker, who was grateful to Sandmann for various reasons. They had to show up at the bakery and then received a certain bag filled with bread and baked goods.[170] In another family a fight broke out because the wife had given away her expensive fur coat. The husband insisted that things were not yet quite so bad for the family; the wife had to go back and retrieve her coat.[171]

Even without tightened prohibitions, enumerable law firms would had to be abandoned. In this regard, Bruno Blau notes:

. . . even if the complete occupational ban feared by me had not been sanctioned by law, then one still would have reached this goal in a de facto manner, at least for me and many of my colleagues. Even Jewish clients engaged non-Jewish attorneys, as long as they were allowed to, even those who belonged to the Nazi party and were known as opponents of the Jews. Later, initially party members and then all non-Jewish attorneys were prohibited from representing Jews.[172]

Those so affected were confronted with the irreconcilable contradiction that they still understood themselves as officers of the court and that they still trusted in the principle of the rule of law, yet individually they had long been victims. It was not apparent to all that as Jews they had long since suffered their demise as members of civil society, something that was formulated with the utmost clarity in 1936 by the Supreme Court of the German Reich:

The earlier (liberal) idea of the legal content of personality does not make any basic differentiation in value between similarity or difference in blood. . . . By contrast, in accordance with the National Socialist worldview in the German Reich only those of German ancestry (and those given statutory equivalence with them) are to be treated as in possession of full legal rights. In this regard, basic delineations derived from the earlier law of aliens have been revived and thoughts once again introduced that were previously acknowledged through the differentiation between those of full legal capacity and persons with diminished rights. In prior times the level of complete absence of rights was introduced because the legal personality had been completely eradicated, something equivalent to physical death; the figure of speech "civil law death" and the idea of dying to the world by entering a monastery are derived precisely from this comparison.[173]

At the 1936 Olympic Games in Berlin efforts were made to create an atmosphere that concealed these circumstances. The appearance was created of an open community that was receptive to new international relationships. During this year, for the first time, the level of industrial production of 1929 was reached—inclusive of the armament industry.[174] This short-term revival of the economy was primarily due to preparation for war. Twenty-seven and a half billion Reichsmark was made available for the additional promotion of economic development; of that, 21 billion went to support rearmament. The authorities responsible for the four-year plan, which was directed by Hermann Göring and had been set up outside the network of ministries, pursued the same goal: to make the economy ready for war.[175] As these events unfolded, further measures were undertaken against Jews. The reallocation of property and ownership improved the situation of those individuals who were not classified as Jews. In 1937 there was increased work toward creating the organizational framework for a complete elimination of Jews (in Nazi parlance: "dejudaization") from all walks of life.

In 1938, during a time of increased rearmament, segregation had already increased to such a degree that Jews were no longer necessary as economic agents. Reinhard Neubert, who in the meantime had advanced to become president of the Reich Bar Association, warned repeatedly of a "comprehensive solution of the Jewish solution."[176] Ordinance 5 concerning the Reich Citizenship Law of September 27, 1938 (RGBl. I, 1403) then promulgated that all Jews would lose their admission to practice law as of November 30, 1938.

In Berlin at least 674 Jewish attorneys who were still practicing law[177] were thereby banned from continuing to do so. Siegfried Neumann, who has already been mentioned and who wrote about his experiences in 1939, observed:

It seems strange that, based on a statute dated before the time of the Munich Convention [September 29, 1938], the final excision of Jewish attorneys from the German bar would only be announced in the Reich Statute Gazette after the Munich Convention had been concluded.[178]

Indeed it doesn't seem like it was the best time to take openly exclusionary measures applying to an entire profession, in the middle of the cozy climate of such an important international conference as that taking part in Munich, during which the decision was made to give Germany the Sudetenland. The reasons for the delay in publication will have to remain unresolved. In any case, the ordinance against Jewish attorneys belonged to a whole collection of measures by which the ministerial bureaucracy eradicated the remaining structures underlying Jewish business operations and self-employment.[179] The momentary climax of this development was the staged pogrom that took place from November 9–10, 1938.

Prior to these events, in October 1938, between 15,000 and 18,000 Jews living in Germany, but who did not possess German citizenship, had been expelled from Germany and forced to cross the Polish border.[180] Among them were the parents of Herschel Grynszpan, who assassinated the Legation Councillor von Rath in Paris at the beginning of November and whose actions were used as the reason for the pogrom in November. Yet this circle of people are not part of the group being researched here, as almost all Berlin attorneys were German citizens.

After the pogrom many Jews in Germany had the impression that things couldn't get any worse:

> 91 murdered, numerous wounded, mistreated and raped, 191 synagogues destroyed through arson; around 7,500 destroyed (and plundered) Jewish businesses; devastation of many Jewish homes and almost all cemeteries. Material damages amounted to at least 25 billion Reichsmark. Thirty thousand Jews were arrested. On November 12 a special tax of 1.12 billion RM was placed upon German Jews. In addition, the state seized the insurance benefits paid out for the damages.[181]

After these results, measures were taken to extort the last penny out of those who had been damaged through a payment of "reparations," a decision that was made during a discussion at the Reich Air Ministry on November 12, 1938.[182] Today these events have been evaluated as follows:

> The pogrom against the Jews during November 1938 has been quite properly regarded as a devastating blow that was the culmination of the humiliations they had been undergoing in tems if legal rights through a public demonstration designed to destroy the identity of German Jews.[183]

Even attorneys who had their signs vandalized, their law offices devastated or who had been arrested, as for example the attorneys Alfred Traube or Dr. Erich Nelson, were forced to pay reparations. After the pogrom untold thousands of men between 18 and 65 years of age were imprisoned; those taken into custody in Berlin were generally sent to the Sachsenhausen concentration camp. A large number of them were once again released, after they had signed a written declaration committing them to emigrate from Germany; as was the case for the two aforementioned lawyers. Quite a few died after being made subject to unspeakable torture.

Here we will take a moment to look at individual attorneys who, while they do not strictly belong to those being researched in this text, also had to suffer oppression: men married to Jewish women. In 1936 every attorney admitted to the bar had to make a declaration that he was "not married to a Jew in the sense of the Ordinance of November 14, 1935 RGBl. p. 1333."[184] Two years later, in 1938, the rules for divorce due to "racial grounds" were made easier and the concerned parties were often "advised" to get divorced by institutions or radicalized individuals.[185] Many nonetheless remained loyal to their wives. One of these attorneys was Alfred Puhlmann.[186] After his wife had been imprisoned, he took part in demonstrations (presumably in 1943), together with a group of Christian husbands, for so long in front of the collection point on Levetzowstraße—just as women in 1943 spoke out on behalf of their husbands on Rosenstraße[187]—until the women were finally released.[188]

## The Work of "Legal Consultants"

Chicanery against the spouses of Jews was commonplace, yet most of those affected thereby still had to work. During the course of "dejudaization" the German business world and community still needed professional consultation and representation; the plundering of the Jews was to be smoothly brought to its conclusion. It is for this reason that a new profession was established, that of the "legal consultant." "Legal consultants" were the Jewish representatives of Jews. A previously existing term was used to designate this profession, one which had a pejorative ring in legal circles, the German term "Konsulent" [legal consultant], with more or less the same derogatory meaning as the term "quack" when used in regard to a doctor.[189]

In order to be licensed as a "legal consultant," the applicant had to be Jewish, as put forth in the "Nuremberg laws" and to have been employed as an attorney up to the time of admission. The first consideration was given to "frontline fighters" who had been injured in the war.[190] The provision concerning admission of legal consultants was published on October 17, 1938. An application for admission had to be submitted to the presiding judge of the Berlin Court of Appeals within one month. The presiding judge of the Berlin Court of Appeals was to prepare a list of suggested candidates after first consulting with the chairman of the Berlin Bar Association and national police authorities. The application was required to put forth individual financial circumstances and one's political orientation, information concerning one's own ancestry and that of one's wife was also to be included.[191] Even though the status of "frontline fighter" had already been established in 1933, the matter now had to be gone into again, including the provision of information about injuries and decorations.

While the exact selection procedure can be reconstructed with precision for Hamburg,[192] in Berlin it can merely be said that during 1938 and 1939 282 persons applied to be "legal consultants," 40 of whom were put on the list of suggested candidates. One hundred and thirty-seven of the applicants were "frontline fighters," but were nonetheless not accepted; 105 who were not "frontline fighters" had applied.[193]

After admission, the "legal consultant" was advised of his duties. Every document signed by him had to include the following phrase: "Admitted only for purposes of the legal consultation and representation of Jews,"[194] something that also had to be placed on the sign designating the law office as such.[195] The first and last names were always to be given, as well as the compulsory name[196] that had meanwhile been introduced for Jews. Most had generally let matters stand with the customarily used name "Israel" (for women "Sara"). Dr. Alexander Coper had instead chosen to call himself Berl. Next to the name, the number of the identification card, which Jews always had to carry with them, had to be given. Appearances made it clear that the "legal consultant" was a jurist of low rank; in court he was not allowed to wear any robes and he was not allowed to enter the room reserved for attorneys.[197] Any absence of over a week had to be reported to the presiding judge of the district court that had supervision. Authorization was required for every aspect of legal work, something the incurred additional fees. Something that really cut into the work life of legal consultants was the requirement that a significant portion of their fees had to be paid to the Reich Bar Association.

A so-called equalization office was set up at the Reich Bar Association that administered the fees that were to be paid in by the "legal consultants." The amount to be paid in was based on the amount of the fee received. For amounts up to 300 RM the "legal consultant" retained 90 percent, for amounts from 300 RM, 70 percent was retained, for amounts from 500 to 1,000 RM, 50 percent was retained, and for amounts over 1,000 RM the "legal consultant" retained 30 percent. Costs for expenses such as document fees and a lump sum fee for office costs were taken into account.[198] The table of amounts levied by the Reich Bar Association created a situation where, for example, in the case of a fee in the amount of 400 RM the "legal consultant" doing the work retained 280 RM, while in the case of a fee of 1,100 RM, which generally involved more work, 330 RM was retained. The rest had to be paid into the "equalization office." A certain basic level of security in terms of earning a living was thereby created, yet "legal consultants" with bigger clients didn't have it better than those with smaller ones— quite the opposite. Precisely what the income of a "legal consultation" practice really was, cannot be given with certainty today.[199]

At the equalization office anyone who had been banned from practicing as a notary in 1935 and from practicing as an attorney in 1938 could make a request for support.[200] After an examination of "need and merit" by the chairman of the Bar Association, a supplement could be granted in the amount of 200 RM per month for a single person and of 250 RM per month for those who were married, widowed or divorced. An additional supplement of 10 RM per child under 16 years could also be applied for. The equalization office was established on the assumption that its costs would also be met by the fees that were syphoned into it. Those former attorneys who had now taken up practice as "legal consultants" were able to maintain a minimum standard of living in comparison to their colleagues who had already been completely excluded from the legal community.

In the district of the Berlin Court of Appeals there were to be 40 "legal consultants" admitted. For a transition period it was possible to employ twice as many, therefore 80. Based on the research undertaken in this study, 91 persons had been identified who worked as "legal consultants," some of them only part-time. With 91 legal consultants (from a previous number of 1,835 attorneys) the proposed number of 80 had been exceeded, yet one was well on the way to the goal formulated in 1933 of only having 35 Jewish attorneys admitted to the practice of law in Berlin. The overwhelming majority of "legal consultants" consisted of former "frontline fighters," or of "attorneys admitted before 1914." The only woman admitted among them was Hanna Katz.[201]

By March 1939, therefore in a period of five months, the number of "finally" admitted "legal consultants" had been reduced to 40 for the city of Berlin, six for Berlin and associated districts, as well as Hanna Katz (who had a special status).[202]

The former attorneys, now "legal consultants," were forced to adapt to the new situation. Their client base was severely diminished, yet they still had to struggle to eke out a living. Dr. Georg Hamburger was one of those who worked as a "legal consultant," beginning in 1938. Up to 1932 he had still been chairman of the board of the bar association; he was a Protestant. His photograph is included in the album of the legal clerk Naatz. Hamburger was extremely conscientious in managing the affairs of his clients, most of whom had already emigrated.[203] Since August 1938 he had supplemented his name with the addition "Israel." After 1941 many of his former colleagues "disappeared," they were deported. Hamburger continued to deal with the cases entrusted to him until he had to sign a declaration of income on June 21, 1943. He was taken to the collection point at Große Hamburger Straße 26. On June 30, 1943, he was deported to Theresienstadt as part of Elderly Shipment 93. He died in Theresienstadt a year later of tuberculosis.

Hamburger's fate was shared by more than a third of all "legal consultants": they worked up to the last moment and were then suddenly "picked up," then first placed at a Berlin collection point, afterward in a concentration camp. Many died from enfeeblement or from a disease that their constitution could not resist in their weakened condition, others wound up in the gas chambers.

Of the 91 persons who had been identified as "legal consultants," there is no information available for the further fate of 7, for the other 83 further details are available. Thirty-three (40 percent) thereof were murdered. Two "legal consultants," Dr. Walter Grau and Dr. Richard Kann, committed suicide. Richard Kann had made the decision to do so with his wife Susanne at the beginning of December 1942. They therefore probably avoided the next transport, scheduled to leave Berlin on December 9, 1942 with 994 people; it was going to Auschwitz.

One, Dr. Max May, died a natural death. Fifteen "legal consultants" (12.5 percent) survived in Germany, partially in camps, partially by "going underground," partially also through the protection of their non-Jewish wives. In the applications that the survivors had to make after 1945 for readmission to the bar, one often finds only very sparse information over the actual living conditions during that dark time. As with the situation in the camps, one can only imagine that the living conditions involved in "going underground" were of the worst nature imaginable.

Five "legal consultants" (6 percent) emigrated and returned back to Germany after 1945; 27 (32.5 percent) remained in the countries to which they had been able to emigrate or flee. More than two-fifths of the "legal consultants" died due to persecution.

One person should be mentioned in this connection who, though not an attorney, served the administration of justice with her work: the "clerk for legal consultants," Dorothea Schram, née. Klar (born July 24, 1902 in Berlin). She was Jewish, was later deported and was killed in Auschwitz on March 2, 1943.

More than a good third, namely 32, who had been admitted as "legal consultants," were able to flee Germany by 1942. One of the most famous of them was Dr. Julius Fliess. He was able to be smuggled into Switzerland in September 1942 through the secret rescue mission "Operation Seven." This case was an exception. Generally those who were able to go abroad only worked for a short time as "legal consultants" and had, for example, while imprisoned during the November 1938 pogrom, signed a declaration obligating them to emigrate. This was the case with Dr. Erich Nelson, whom we have already mentioned, who was released after making this declaration of obligation to emigrate and who finally made his way to Great Britain. The other emigrants also mostly applied for admission as a "legal consultant" with the idea of working for a short period of time while they were waiting for approval to immigrate to a country that would grant them refuge.

Some "legal consultants" employed, due to the initially high workload, other former attorneys as "legal consultant assistants." Work of this nature was only allowed upon approval by the presiding judge of the competent district court.[204] For those employed as "assistants," this was often their only opportunity to obtain paid work. For these attorneys who could not even get admission as "legal consultants," the drop in social status must have been a profound social and psychological burden: up to the general occupational ban of 1938 they had been practicing attorneys, now suddenly they were legal assistants. Yet these people were driven to such work by sheer necessity. At least they were being paid. Among those who took up work of this nature, were: Herbert Fuchs, Bruno Marwitz, Felix Rosenthal and Dr. Paul Schidwigowski, who at times himself had been admitted as a "legal consultant."[205] Schidwigowski dealt with the affairs of his colleague Hanna Katz; in 1943 he was deported and shortly thereafter was murdered in Auschwitz. Most of the other persons mentioned suffered the same fate. Their religious beliefs did not play a role. For example, Dr. Herbert Fuchs was a Protestant.

Generally speaking, one could say of the "legal consultants" that they were attorneys of Jewish origin, that their work allowed them to be the Jews most incorporated into the National Socialist system. They were generally older and had taken part in World War I, their viewpoint was Prussian and dutiful in the most positive sense. Their civil rights were constantly being reduced, yet they nonetheless sought to support themselves through their work and thereby also helped to support the system. It is not appropriate for the generations that have come after them to judge them in a negative fashion, because it was most certainly other organizations and institutions that had created the conditions that put them in such a difficult situation in the first place.[206]

## The Example of Alexander Coper

One person who survived the camps after the National Socialists came to power was the attorney Dr. Alexander Coper, 42 years of age. His wife was Protestant and had been classified as "Aryan" on the basis of National Socialist racial criteria; the marriage had been categorized as "privileged" Because they had two chil-

dren together. After 1933 the number of clients for his law firm rapidly diminished, yet he was not prepared to give his practice up. Following the 1938 general occupational ban, Coper took on the name "Berl" and was admitted as a "legal consultant" under the name of Dr. Berl Coper. His income level decreased even further, "i.e., Jewish clients really don't have anything to pay with."[207] Insult was added to injury in that a significant portion from his fees was syphoned off by the government. His wife had war duty at a publishing house. The

Dr. Alexander Coper

family sought to fight its way forward, regardless of how well (or how poorly) things were going. The children also had to leave school and were conscripted into the workforce, although in a more restrictive manner than the mother, since they bore the "mixed race" classification. In November 1943 Coper was arrested based on the charge of falsifying food ration cards. His son assumed that this was the result of a malicious accusation. "Whoever is acquainted with him knows that he is not the type of man to do this."[208] From November 1943 to early 1944 Coper remained in prison. Then, to the complete surprise of the family, he was released on April 21, 1944. This was a time of the massive bombing attacks in Berlin; Mrs. Coper lost her life during one of them. As tragic as this incident already was, it had consequences: the protective effect of the "privileged marriage" expired. In October 1944 Coper, now widowed and having lost a leg during World War I, was arrested and deported to Theresienstadt. He has attempted to capture his life in Theresienstadt in a poem, thereby passing them on to subsequent generations. Four stanzas are quoted below:

> *15.–21. III. (presumably 1945)*
> *The mother is dead and in a cold grave.*
> *I am left alone with the children.*
> *And as my reward*
> *I was mercilessly shipped away.*
>
> *My poor, sad Berlin,*
> *I too have to leave you now.*
> *You are disheveled and completely slashed up*
> *Bleeding from thousands of wounds.*
>
> *And yet and yet and nonetheless yet,*
> *I love you still.*
> *If I were to see the last of you,*
> *My heart would be filled with heaviness.*
>
> *You have done so much harm to me,*
> *Yet I am still not in revenge's grip.*
> *You are a part of the whole of my life,*
> *Yet for the time being I'll speak the more thereof.*

Coper survived his time in the camp. His children, 19 and 20 years of age, also successfully survived their time of conscription into the Todt Organization (OT). In early summer of 1945 Coper returned from Theresienstadt back to Berlin. In the vicinity of Rüdesheimer Platz, where the family had lived, the family members reunited in the ruins. Soon thereafter Coper hung out his shingle on one of the houses, in order to let the world know that he had taken up his law practice again. In the years just after the war this was not especially lucrative, then he started to get more cases after 1952. In 1958 the 67-year-old Coper retired and died soon thereafter.[209]

## The Special Status of Those Who Had Been Classified as of "Mixed Race"

The other group of attorneys of Jewish origin that was still allowed to work after the 1938 general occupational ban was those who had been classified as of "mixed race."[210] After 1938 they were not subject to the same restrictions as "legal consultants." As already noted, religious views did not play any role into whether one was classified as a "non-Aryan." Yet religion was used as a frame of reference for the classification of "ancestry." For this reason, National Socialist categories were inconsistent, because they mingled "racial" ancestry and religious affiliation with one another. The determinative factor was the religious affiliation of parents and grandparents. At the latest, this information had been gathered at the time of the 1939 census. In order to prove "Aryan" status, one had to demonstrate four grandparents who were not regarded as Jews (census code: NNNN). The subcategories of the classification "non-Aryan" essentially consisted of: "Mixed Race 1st Degree"—which applied to persons who were not of Jewish religious affiliation, but had two grandparents who were regarded as Jews; "Mixed Race 2nd Degree"—likewise not of Jewish religious affiliation, but with only one grandparent who was deemed a Jew. However, when

Dr. Ferdinand Bang

a person classified as "mixed race" married a "full-blooded Jew," then his status was changed into that of a "full-blooded Jew."

There were 73 attorneys in Berlin who had been demonstrated to be of "mixed race." In 1936, 69 of them were still active and had been given their special status.[211] Four of these attorneys had either lost or given up their admission to the bar: an occupational ban had been imposed on Dr. Fritz Faß and Hans Frankfurter in 1933. Dr. Willy Landsberg lost his license as a notary, whereupon he closed down his law firm, while Dr. Werner Steinitz apparently was no longer living in Berlin. Since he was no longer registered as living there, he lost his admission to the Berlin Bar. The foregoing shows that in 1933 those classified as being of "mixed race" were treated the same as so-called full-blooded Jews, in terms of their mutual classification as "non-Aryan" and therefore made subject to the same segregation measures. They had to reapply for admission and, in order to continue the practice of law, they had to qualify for one of the exemptions. Yet for those of "mixed race" who were able to secure readmission in 1933, they at least had a much more unrestricted sphere of action for the next seven years than "full-blooded Jews."

In the case of some of those affected their "ancestry" only came out in the course of time or when it was no longer possible to hold back the relevant information. For example, this was the case for Edgar von Fragstein und Niemsdorff. In his case, in 1933 it remained unknown that two of his grandparents were to be regarded as Jews. Of the 69 attorneys classified as of "mixed race," 51 thereof fell into the classification "Mixed Race 1st Degree" (two Jewish grandparents), 18 as "Mixed Race 2nd Degree" (one Jewish grandparent). Not one of these people was affiliated with Judaism in the religious sense. Four were dissidents, without any particular religious beliefs, the rest of them were overwhelmingly Protestant (56), seven were Catholic, one was Calvinist, while no information is available for one person. A significant portion of the people in this group were married to non-Jewish women. The effect on internal family structures was significant. In personal files one encounters letters from mothers or fathers of the attorneys affected that give the impression that the parents were ashamed of the problems that they had caused for their children through "ancestry issues."

The compilation of a specific list in 1936 documents the potential dangers that those of "mixed race" were exposed to. Those affected thereby were in part not fully aware of the danger of more extensive persecution. In 1939 a total of 18,145 persons belonging to the category "Mixed Race 1st Degree" and 8,971 belonging to the category "Mixed Race 2nd Degree" lived in Berlin.[212] Attorneys belonging to this group of people were in part active all the way into the war.[213] For example, they only lost their telephone connection after 1941, while Jews had to give theirs up in August 1940.[214]

At the Wannsee Conference on January 20, 1942, those of "mixed race" were also the subject of discussion; the issue was discussed as to whether they should be included in deportations or instead sterilized.[215] No further, more precise method of dealing with them was arrived at during the Conference. Perhaps the assumption of Hilberg is accurate: "Those of 'mixed race' were saved because they had more German than Jewish blood."[216] The attorneys affected could still practice without hindrance for a longer period of time, because at least after the war broke out there was a significant lack of jurists. Apparently, it had not been possible to provide a sufficient number of upcoming young non-Jewish attorneys or perhaps these young attorneys had been made subject to conscription because of the war.

Just how "German" a person who had been classified as of "mixed race" could feel is shown by the circumstance that two of them (attorneys Bang and Broecker) took over the function of a National Socialist Block Warden ("Blockwart").[217] One of them was also a member of the National Socialist German Social Service (NSV) that took up monthly collections for, among other things, the financing of their healthcare facilities. The reasons for which the person concerned joined must remain a matter of speculation. Another attorney was a member of the Stahlhelm until its prohibition and then later a member of the NSDAP, which he then, however, had to leave. During denazification proceedings after 1945 he was classified as a "nominal Nazi."

Some persons who were classified as being of "mixed race" were taken into custody by the Gestapo and made available to the Todt Organization. This organization was named after its founder, Fritz Todt (September 4, 1891–February 8, 1942).[218] In June 1933 Hitler made him responsible for German road construction and engineering. Bearing in mind the preparations that were being made for war, Todt kept up the construction of the Reich highway system in a determined and energetic fashion. In 1938 he was made responsible for, among other things, building the so-called Siegfried Line. In order to attain this objective in the shortest possible amount of time, he created strictly organized troops of workers, who primarily consisted out of "foreign workers" (workers of foreign nationality), concentration camp inmates and even of "non-Aryans" who had not yet been imprisoned. The compulsory workers were placed in work camps outside of Berlin. In another project of the Todt Organization, at the special work camp Zerbst Airport, the attorney Georg Graul was among those put to work. Graul, who had voted as a German nationalist in the last three elections, had been active as a Freemason. His only son had already fallen in battle in 1939. Graul felt himself driven to "go underground."[219] He survived and was readmitted to the bar after 1945.

Adolf Arndt

Four other attorneys were employed at the end of October 1944 by the Todt Organization for the purpose of rubble clearance. Adolf Arndt was forced to work for the Todt Organization in Paris during the closing of the Gestapo headquarters there. He was not a very strong man and soon found that he was being stretched to his very limits.

> Other prisoners pushed him aside saying "Let us do that for you Adolf!" And then they would carry down the "painting chests." If one of them happened to fall to the ground—then cognac flowed on the street.[220]

There was cooperation on all levels between the party, the judiciary and administration up to the last stages of the war. For example, in the middle of 1943, the presiding judge of the Berlin Court of Appeals identified all attorneys who were not members of the National Socialist Legal Protection Association—something that almost all attorneys belonged to at this time. He then gave their names to the Employment Office, describing their legal work as "not necessary for the war effort." "Non-Aryans" could not join the National Socialist Legal Protection Association and were therefore correspondingly reported to the Employment Office. The attorney Hermann Gustav Scheer thought that things had turned out well for him with the position he had been given as the in-house counsel for the Hertling Transport Company.[221] Another, Hans Richter, who had taken part in World War I, practiced law up to the end of the war. Then finally, based on information he had himself provided, he nonetheless had his admission revoked "due to racial grounds." For him, after 1942, "as Hitler's retreat began," he once again started to get more clients, because it seemed that open anti-Semitic agitation had reduced in intensity. This statement seems ironic in light of the fact that at the same time the deportations of Jews were moving on full steam ahead.

# The Fate of
# Jewish Attorneys

After the pogrom and the general occupational ban of 1938, attorneys of Jewish origin were confronted with circumstances that were even more trying. The differentiation between Jews and non-Jews had now been essentially completed. The compulsory Hebrew names and the identity cards demonstrated in black and white that those affected thereby were of Jewish origin. In 1941 an external form of identification, the yellow star, was introduced. It had to be worn on clothing in a clearly visible fashion. Jews had to surrender their valuables and radios. Their telephones were disconnected, and their house pets were taken away. The regime's anti-Jewish measures invaded the most private spheres of personal life.[222]

The biographical directory of this book provides information about the individual destinies of Berlin attorneys of Jewish origin. In the following text, they have been divided up into four groups in order to provide an overview of their fates:

- "Those who met with death"—this category also includes those who committed suicide in the face of the threat of being put to death. In this group one primarily encounters people who chose to take their own lives after having been sent away for internment.
- Those who died from causes other than those involving violence or as a result of the general wartime conditions.
- Those who survived in Germany or during confinement at a camp.
- Those who either emigrated or fled; in this case the category is subdivided according to the various countries to which they fled.

The further or final life's journey was able to be retraced for a total of 1,404 attorneys of Jewish origin.

# "Those Who Met with Death"

It was already in March 1933 that the attorney Günther Joachim met with a violent end; he was beaten to death during his internment by the SA. At that time, Joachim's fate was regarded as an extraordinary occurrence. In 1933 no one would have held it possible that—only a few years later—people, including numerous attorneys, would be murdered on an industrial scale.

There is proof that eight Jewish attorneys died in Berlin as a result of violent attacks against each of them, all in the context of the general National Socialist policy of persecution. One of them was Julius Blumenthal. He was already made subject to an occupational ban in April 1933. He thereafter took an active role in the Jewish community and became director of its legal department in 1939, as well as acting as the legal correspondent of the newspaper *The Jewish Informer* (*Jüdisches Nachrichtenblatt*). In 1942 the Jewish community was requested to designate a group of employees who were to be transported away for internment. Those who had been picked out were able to flee. In retaliation Blumenthal and several others were taken hostage. According to an eyewitness report, the hostages were chosen in the representatives' hall of the Oranienburger Straße synagogue, today's Centrum Judaicum. All of the hostages were shot soon thereafter in December 1942.

A total of 299 Berlin attorneys[223] perished as a result of National Socialist persecution. No exact date of death is available for 162 of them: 118 people died in concentration camps, during internment, or in ghettos; 11 were arrested in European countries they had immigrated to and then finally died during internment or in a concentration camp.

# Transport to the Camps and Death

On October 18, 1941, the first train, which contained 1,013 people, left the Grunewald train station, moving in the direction of Littzmannstadt/Lodz. There were seven attorneys among the human cargo, including Bernhard Goldschmidt and Julius Grau, who had both been attorneys at the Berlin Court of Appeals. Goldschmidt was 40 years old and therefore significantly younger than Grau. Goldschmidt had already been disbarred in 1933, because he was a Jew. Grau had been admitted as a "legal consultant" in 1938/1939. No one knows if they knew one another, if they had run into one another at the courthouse, or if the younger attorney had at some time taken over a court appointment for Grau. Even less is known about whether they met one another at the destination to which they were transported. For both of them, either Litzmannstadt or Lodz was the place they met their death. That is all that is known with certainty. There is no date of death, no cause of death.

"The death occurred in the Sachsenhausen concentration camp on December 3, 1942" and "shot during an act of resistance against the authorities" are the statements contained in the December 3, 1942 death certificate of Julius Blumenthal.

The term "those who met with death" is merely an approximate formulation and is not a concept meant to correspond to the requirements of scholarship. Of the attorneys listed in the biographical directory who perished in the concentration camps, the death camps or the ghettos, an exact date of death is only known for 118.[224] One hundred and sixty-two people were transported away for detention and lost their lives thereby for whom there is no exact date of death. In the meantime, further research concerning Theresienstadt and the Baltic[225] has made it possible to provide information as to the camp or ghetto they had been transported to. Up to a few years ago, the only information available was the general statement of "to the East." In the short biographies that are to follow the point in time used to indicate the fates of these people is information concerning the date of transport, which constituted the final breaking off of the life that they had lived in their native city of

Berlin.[226] Of these people who were transported the only thing that is known is when they left Berlin and for what destination. What is unknown is just what happened to them once they reached their point of arrival, or whether they died even before they reached their destination. Did they die in a concentration camp or were they murdered by mobile death squads? Were they gassed or shot? Did they starve to death or die from typhus? Were they strangled to death by guards or did they drop dead during the course of forced labor ("death through work")? The debasement, humiliation and psychic damage to other human beings, all of which were a prelude to death, can only be left to conjecture.

Without seeking to undertake a classification of the victims, it can be said that precisely the (Berlin) attorneys were under the most serious threat of death, due to their age, their health and their social position. Those who were still to be found in Germany in 1941 were often old, frequently in bad health or disabled veterans. They belonged to the bourgeois middle class and due to the type of work they pursued were hardly suited for physical exertion. For this reason alone, only very few survived their time in the camps.

In the biographical information, the date on which a declaration of property was made is often provided. During the first period of transportation for purposes of internment, this form was provided to those concerned several days before they were to report to the collection point. The requirement to fill out the form was the first step in undertaking officially ordered transport to a protectorate.[227] Later on, those chosen for transport had to fill out and sign the declaration of property at the time they were "picked up." The declaration of property included all moveable belongings, from a collar to a shoehorn. It also included a list of all known outstanding debts, whether to the dentist or the plumber. In some cases, the declaration of property is the last sign of life from the person who was shipped away.[228]

The internment transports began in October 1941. This was before the Wannsee Conference, which was not, as has frequently been assumed, the point at which the "final solution" was decided upon. Up to the last human shipment in April 1945 over 180 transports left Berlin for various destinations.

Information concerning seven murdered Berlin attorneys is provided below for illustrative purposes:

Dr. Jacques Abraham was an extremely well-liked attorney and notary; up to 1933 he was also editor of the *Journal for Civil Service*

*Law* (*Zeitschrift für das Beamtenrecht*). In the fall of 1933 he continued to retain his admission to practice law, however his notary license was revoked. He was able to practice law up until the 1939 occupational ban. Thereafter he seems to have worked as an unskilled laborer, presumably against his will. In the meantime, he sought to obtain a visa for South America, but was never successful in this endeavor. Apparently, he still tried to escape; he was arrested at the Dutch border during the course of an escape attempt. He signed his declaration of property on October 14, 1942. Five days later, on October 19, 1942, he was shipped off to Riga as a part of Transport 21. Thereafter there were no further signs of life from him. His official date of death was recorded as December 31, 1942; Dr. Jacques Abraham was 62 years old.

Fritz Hammerschmidt was admitted as an attorney to the Berlin Court of Appeals. His law firm was located on Kantstraße 19 in Charlottenburg, where he practiced law in a partnership with his brother Walter. In April 1933 Fritz Hammerschmidt was made subject to a prohibition on representation. It was then lifted and in the fall of 1933 he was once again admitted to the bar. He practiced his profession until the 1938 general occupational ban. Fritz Hammerschmidt became father of a son sometime between 1935 and 1936. The only other fact known is that he later worked as a laborer. On February 29, 1944 Fritz Hammerschmidt signed his dec-

Fritz and Erna Hammerschmidt

laration of property; he was then taken to the collection point at Schulstraße 78. Several days later, on March 9, 1944, he was shipped out to Auschwitz as a part of Transport 50, together with his wife Erna, her mother Martha Frischmann and their son Anselm, who had meanwhile turned eight. The exact date on which Hammerschmidt died cannot be determined; he was about 52 years old. The only person who survived was Erna Hammerschmidt. She was transferred to the Ravensbrück concentration camp, where she was later freed by Allied troops.[229]

Walter Hammerschmidt, the brother and partner of Fritz Hammerschmidt, was already made subject to an occupational ban in 1933 and was arrested in the course of the November 1938 pogrom. He was placed in the Sachsenhausen concentration camp, but was released at the end of December "as a seriously ill man." He died shortly thereafter from septicemia.[230] Professor Sauerbruch recommended to the widow that she have an autopsy performed on the corpse, but the Gestapo refused to release the body. The widow was sent an urn containing his ashes. She was later deported to Auschwitz with her second husband, where both of them were murdered.[231] It was not just the Hammerschmidts, but also the Selten family and other families of attorneys who were wiped out during the persecution.

Georg Siegmann

Councillor Dr. Georg Siegmann can be seen on one of the little photos that were kept in the album of Willy Naatz, the legal administrator for attorneys admitted to the District Court. The photo shows a jovial man with a love for life—yet that was another life, another time, when he still had a law firm on Lindenstraße in close proximity to Belle Alliance Platz (today Mehringplatz) and was working as an attorney and notary. That all changed once the National Socialists took power. While, as an "elderly attorney," he retained his law license up to the 1938 general occupational ban, his law firm suffered one setback after another. Siegmann, who was born in 1869, was picked up in Berlin, after which he signed his declaration of property, on July 2, 1942. Two weeks later he was shipped to Theresienstadt.

On August 28, 1944, he was still able to send a postcard to Willy Naatz:

*Theresienstadt, 08/28/1944*

*Dear Mr. Naatz!*

*After being separated for more than two years I am writing to say hello as a sign that I am still among the living. Please greet Miss Wilhelmine Schickmer [?] for me, who resides at Kluckstr. 25 bei Sommer. Tell her that we are surprised that we have not heard from her for so long.*

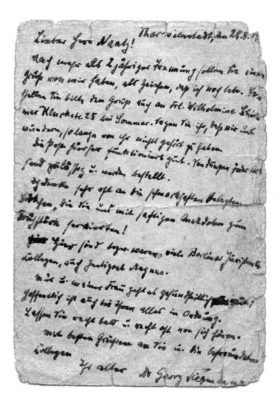

*The mail functions well here. Mailings of all types are reliable and properly processed.*

*I often think of the tasty sandwiches that you served us for break-fast together with your entertaining anecdotes!*

*Here in Theresienstadt there are and/or were many Berlin jurists and colleagues, including Councillor Magnus.*

*My wife and I are in good health; hopefully everything is going well with you.*

*Please write me soon and often.*

*I give you and the colleagues I am friends with my warmest greetings*

*Your dear friend Dr. Georg Siegmann*

Naatz was apparently a go-between for information. He was to make inquiries concerning the whereabouts of Miss Wilhelmine Sch. and to inform the circle of attorneys interested therein about the death of Julius Magnus, who died in Theresienstadt on May 15, 1944. In

October 1944 Siegmann was moved to Auschwitz, after which he left no further traces. At this time, he was 75 years old.[232]

Councillor Dr. Julius Magnus, born in 1867, was an attorney who specialized in copyright and patent law. He was also a notary. He received special recognition as editor and publisher of the *Legal Weekly* (*Juristische Wochenschrift*), from 1915 to 1933. Magnus worked as an attorney until the 1938 occupational ban; he had already lost his admission as a notary in 1933. On August 25, 1939, he fled to the Netherlands. There he was captured by German troops and sent to the Westerbork concentration camp. At the beginning of 1944 he was sent to Theresienstadt by way of Bergen-Belsen, where he died of starvation.[233]

Julius Magnus

In April 1933 Dr. Ernst Wachsner was made subject to an occupational ban as attorney and notary. It is unknown how he was able to eke out a living afterward. Later he was conscripted into forced labor. He was arrested on June 25, 1943. His declaration of property bears this date. He was then brought to the collection point Große Hamburger Straße 26 and three days later he was sent to Auschwitz with Transport 39. Afterward there was no further sign of him. He was 55 years old.

Dr. Kurt Zarinzansky was an attorney and notary, whose law offices and residence were located at Ansbacher Straße 10 a in the Bavarian Quarter. He was allowed to work as a notary until the 1935 general occupational ban on Jewish notaries. He worked as an attorney until the 1938 general occupational ban in this regard. Zarinzansky was a Catholic. After the occupational ban he worked as an executor of wills. In March 1943, he filled out his declaration of property. Two days later he was shipped to Auschwitz. Apparently at this point the 53-year-old man was strong enough to survive until 1945. On March 11, two years after he had been shipped out of Berlin and shortly before the end of the war, he died in Mauthausen.[234]

# Suicide

As has already been shown through the example of the "legal consultants," some attorneys, when faced with the gathering crisis for those of Jewish origin, reached their own conclusions concerning the hopeless situation and chose to take their life (28 people, 2 percent).

We have already discussed the fate of the attorney Hans Litten, a political activist who opposed National Socialism. Already in 1940, his mother sought to acquaint readers with the last years of his life through the book, *The Struggles of a Mother* (*Eine Mutter kämpft*). In his preface to the book, Rudolf Olden wrote: "If you can't get rid of a person who is causing problems based on that fact alone, then one seeks out minor matters that can be used as a trap for him."[235] Litten's life and death certainly have its striking aspects: his mother was a Christian, his father also converted to Christianity. Litten gave the impression of youth and at the same time sternness. He not only confined himself to the essentials in terms of his austere outward appearance, but also in his dealings with other people. For this reason, his work allowed him, much more than in the ordinary case, to be "a champion of justice" (Olden).[236] Olden used the emotional phrase to describe this prim personality, who was always so clear and unemotional, qualities which enabled him to analyze things in an absolutely devoted and dry fashion. Litten was dedicated to seeking the truth, whether it was in law or in art. Because of his inflexible, classical canon of values, he was a provocation for the Nazis, who themselves posed as guardians of values. Because Litten always concentrated on content, his presence alone served to unmask Nazi propaganda. In return he was made subject to a harsh retribution. Litten was mistreated and finally could not stand the suffering anymore. However, his letters and the lectures that he held in the concentration camp on topics related to art showed that he could not be broken despite everything that had been done to him. Hans Litten took his own life in February 1938 in Dachau concentration camp.[237]

In the face of the massive wave of encroachments and attacks that already took place during 1933/1934, many people took the step of committing suicide, such as Prof. Dr. Max Alsberg. Yet most only took this step once transport to the camps was imminent. The word "suicide" does not seem quite appropriate in this context; on the other hand, there is no adequate word that describes the choice of a self-designated time of death that would perhaps involve less suffering in comparison to life in a concentration camp.

The religious dimension of this phenomenon is dealt with by the *Philo Encyclopedia (Philo Lexikon)*, the handbook of Jewish knowledge. The 1936 edition states in simple words: "Suicide is forbidden in Judaism; God's warning to the patriarch Noah and his descendants: 'And surely the blood of your lives I will require' (Genesis 9:5) is considered the basis of the prohibition." Historical instances involving a heroic death can be judged more mildly. No one takes the decision to commit suicide lightly. Yet many took this option into consideration. On September 29, 1941, the "legal consultant" Georg Hamburger—mentioned previously—who was a Protestant and a member of the Confessing Church (which stood in opposition to National Socialism), wrote the Protestant theologian Helmut Gollwitzer, expressing the bitterness he felt after his effort to flee had failed: "[Because] I don't have any relatives or any people close to me who can help me bear this, because I have truly been left behind all alone here." In 1942, as more and more people were taken into custody, the number of suicides increased. Hamburger sought out Gollwitzer's advice as to whether one was allowed to avoid being transported "to the East" through suicide; he himself viewed this step as justified in exceptional situations. Gollwitzer strove to give him theological support and rejected suicide in general.[238] Hamburger was not part of the first transport in October 1942. On June 21, 1943, he signed his declaration of property, which listed all of his remaining possessions. The documents that have survived include a gas bill for a small amount. He was then brought to the collection point at Große Hamburger Straße 26 in the Mitte district of Berlin. Hamburger was sent away to Theresienstadt on June 30, 1943. He died there of tuberculosis at the beginning of 1944.

Many did not want to give themselves up, as examples thereof we give the following names: Dr. Fritz Dalen, Dr. Hans Michaelis, Dr. Julius Schoenfeld. Councillor Hermann Kolsen committed suicide in August 1942 at the age of 83. In December of the same year, Dr. Richard Kann committed suicide together with his wife.

It must also be said that the number of suicides listed here must be regarded as clearly too small. The survivors often didn't want "suicide" named as the cause of death. In 1933, a considerable number of men younger than 60 years old died.

## "Natural Death" and Death Due to General Wartime Conditions

A person who was admitted to the bar in 1933 had to be older than 26. The conditions were a period of study that lasted years, the passing of two bar examinations and a corresponding preparation period. The average age of attorneys admitted to the bar was relatively high. As a result, the correspondingly high number of attorneys deemed Jewish died of natural causes after 1933 (206 persons or 14.7%). It is possible that the actual number is smaller than that given here, due to uncertainties as to whether some deaths were not really the result of suicide. However, for the most part, it must be assumed that the cause of death was age or an incurable illness, which means that the death was limited in its direct connection to National Socialist persecution. For example, Erna Proskauer[239] tells of an acquaintance, Councillor Leopold Silberstein, who suffered greatly because the fact that he was a Jew prevented him from practicing his profession. Yet his death was not caused by any outside influences. He had a close and intense relationship with his wife, the daughter of his former landlady. During his legal studies, she copied his examination paper by hand. They both only got married after his law practice could provide sufficient security to support both of them. This meant that she waited 19 years for him. In 1934 they were running errands; while Ms. Silberstein went into a store, her husband waited on a bench in the vicinity. When she came back, her 64-year-old husband was dead. In later years, looking at matters objectively, the descendants often came to the conclusion reached by the grandson of Councillor Gustav Sandberg, Prof. Grenville,[240] that was expressed regarding the death of his grandfather in a Jewish hospital located on Iranische Straße: "He died at just the right time." It has been said of the seventy-year-old Bruno Marwitz that he died in 1940 "of a broken heart."[241] In this he was certainly not alone.

Five people (0.4 percent) died directly as a result of general war conditions.

# Survival in Germany or in the Concentration Camps

The group of survivors, either in Berlin or in a concentration camp, includes 107 people (7.6 percent). Some of them have already been mentioned, such as Dr. Alexander Coper, who came back from Theresienstadt. For this group, it is essentially their application for readmission to the bar after 1945 that provides relevant information. The photographs included with the applications show completely emaciated people with a weight—at between five foot nine inches and six feet —that only amounted to 132 pounds. Their faces also show scars that are evidence that long ago they had belonged to a dueling fraternity.

A significant proportion of those who were able to survive in Berlin were married to non-Jewish wives. Persecution was a hard test for any relationship. It was of course not self-evident that the married couple would also stay together during this period. Julius Tasse was among those who were supported by their wives when he was imprisoned on Rosenstraße. The stubborn campaign of his and other wives in the same circumstances was in part responsible for the fact that the prisoners were released.[242] At the latest, beginning in 1943, being a partner in a "mixed-race marriage" no longer offered security. While there was really in any case no real security in a system that was so arbitrary, yet for persons who were regarded as Jews based on the racial laws, the situation was even more threatening.[243]

In Berlin the chances of going underground were greater than in smaller cities. However, this did not solve a person's problem in finding a way to obtain sufficient food, because a person living illegally had no access to the necessary food ration cards. In addition, provision of food to the population was already based on rationing, so that it was hard to find support in this regard, even from persons of good will who were ready to take risks. In the personnel files of the bar association applications made after 1945 are descriptions of the fate of some of those who went underground that illustrate the actual need during this time in a restrained fashion. Names of non-Jewish colleagues and acquaintances who actively helped those subject to persecution only appear very sporadically. In some cases, the situation was made yet more difficult by the fact that a colleague was pursuing legal disciplinary proceedings against a Jewish colleague, as in the case of Dr. Max Lustig. This was how he lost his admission as a notary, as well as an attorney. in 1935. The bar association seemed to be actively participating in the exclusion of

Dr. Georg Cohn-Lempert at the beginning of the 1930s

Jews. For example, Dr. Werner Windscheid was notified of a complaint brought against him.[244] He was then charged with "demoralization of the armed forces and giving aid and comfort to the enemy." A judgment against him followed, but he was still able to later go underground.

Dr. Georg Cohn-Lempert could depend on the support of his wife. In 1933, the couple already undertook separation of property and Ms. Cohn-Lempert, who was regarded as "Aryan," bought a house in the Sudeten Mountains in Krummhübel. Else Ury, the author of the famous "Nestling" books ("Nesthäkchen"-Bände) owned a house there. She was later killed in Auschwitz. Ms. Cohn-Lempert took care to see that the house she had purchased was enlarged. After their Berlin apartment was destroyed by bombs on November 22, 1943, the family moved to Krummhübel with their two grown daughters and a grandchild.

In 1940 Cohn-Lempert had himself baptized by a friend he had gone to school with, who had become a pastor. Even though this was no longer allowed, Cohn-Lempert did it in the hope of helping his two daughters. In the 1940s, in Berlin, he was conscripted to work for a company that manufactured canteens. During the confusion of the war, Georg Cohn-Lempert was able to follow his wife and daughters to Krummhübel. The family was able to live there undiscovered. Georg Cohn-Lempert was simply referred to as "the professor." Because of the official confirmation that the family had been bombed, they did not need to show any papers; they seemed to have been forgotten. Beginning in 1943, Georg Cohn-Lempert received a monthly support payment of 100 RM from the bar association. In his daughter's opinion it was primarily her mother who exerted efforts to receive this money.[245] Georg Cohn-Lempert was only able to return to Berlin with his wife in the 1950s. According to his daughter, he always regretted that no one took an interest in his fate or that of the others who had returned. After his return, he was particularly surprised by the personnel in the ministries: "Globke? What the? Is he still around? He threw us all out."[246]

One of the few women who went underground to avoid being sent to a concentration camp was Anita Eisner. She had been able to maintain a certain level of income through asset and property administration up to the time of the intensive persecution measures. During the course of her work she had regular contact with NS officials.

Anita Elsner

She writes:

> For example, I remember . . . that in the course of one week I had five summons before the customs investigations office and the Gestapo, summons during which one never knew if one would leave with one's freedom or be held there for some reason. . . . It wasn't just that all of my relatives, including my mother of almost 80 years old and my only sister, but also my friends who remained in Germany were shipped off and relentlessly killed by the Nazis, but I also had to live through the experience of seeing dozens of my clients, as well as the dependents of friends and clients who had been entrusted to me, be forced to take the path into oblivion. . . . From March 1943 until the capture of Berlin, for over two years, I had to survive illegally, received no food rationing cards and generally didn't know what I would live on and where I would be spending the next night.[247]

Letters that she sent to a friend in Alsace through an intermediary[248] show how Anita Eisner tried to strengthen herself mentally with philosophical writings. She turned out to be the only member of her immediate family who survived. The consequences of such a fate were often a constant feeling of grief and serious psychological problems, because the survivor or survivors could not find an explanation for why he or she had survived and the others had not.

Whether or not the attorney Dr. Alfred Köhler was plagued by such feelings remains unknown. Only the bare facts remain. In 1942 he had to report to a collection point for transport. He was released without explanation, but his mother and his sisters were murdered in a concentration camp.

While some were able to save themselves in that they went underground and therefore lived in a sphere not open to public scrutiny, others made an effort to continue their previous life by concealing or keeping secret parts of their family history that would have led to their persecution. Such a deception was difficult to maintain on a long-term basis.

A more frequent fate was that of Dr. Walter Schindler, who managed to survive by living under a false name. Dr. Ernst Schindler—probably his brother—was also able to do this. Up to April 22, 1945, he was held in an ordinary prison and was freed at the end of the war.

Another notable case was that of the attorney Mr. Pollack, who escaped persecution through the personal intervention of his wife, a renowned vocalist in operas and operettas. His wife had to pay for her efforts through a ban on performance. Another husband of a prominent actress was Dr. Hermann Eisner, who was married to the popular Camilla Spira, who was known especially for her role as the landlady in *The White Horse Inn* (*Weißen Röss'l*). Eisner was a member of the board of the Engelhardt Group up to 1934. His family immigrated to the Netherlands

Attorney Hermann Eisner with his wife Camilla Spira at Bad Gastein, 1932

and were taken into custody there, like so many others, after the German occupation. Eisner was sent to the Westerbork concentration camp and survived. After liberation, the couple returned to Berlin. Dr. Eisner would still be able to take up his practice of law for several years.

## Emigration and Flight

The large majority of Berlin attorneys of Jewish origin were able to leave Germany in time. A total of 759 went abroad, of which 56 (4 percent of 1,404) returned to Germany, the remaining 703 (50 percent), generally together with their relatives, remained abroad.

After 1933, a third of all Berlin attorneys of Jewish origin no longer had a viable future in Germany due to the occupational ban. It was especially highly motivated and well-educated young people who went elsewhere to seek a better life after Germany had denied them the opportunity to take equal part in its society. Once discriminatory measures had begun, the Jewish community also exerted itself by undertaking various investigations concerning suitable conditions for emigration, as well as in regard to advice for those seeking to leave the country and training programs designed to prepare them to do so.[249] The key goal thereby was seen as finding appropriate professional activity in the country targeted for emigration. However, for most the question was not where to find favorable conditions for resettlement, but where to find any refuge at all.

Numerous emigrants met with failure, others succeeded in a brilliant career. Based on available data, it is not always possible to reconstruct just what they later made out of their lives.

The exodus from Germany accelerated up to the beginning of the war in 1939. In his memoirs, Bruno Blau later came to the conclusion that those who had been made subject to an immediate exclusion had, without knowing it, "drawn the better lot."[250] They were more likely to be able to immigrate to a country of their choice because they could fulfill the restrictive immigration requirements that were to be found in many places. Once there, they were able to adapt to the specific circumstances of the country, well before the great waves of emigration began and, above all, to learn the language—perhaps even going on to establish a new professional career in law. Blau's bitter assessment fails to take proper note of the fact that those who left Germany early on were generally younger than those who followed later. This fact alone made them able to react more flexibly to the option of emigration and allow them a more favorable start. For many of these younger people forced emigration coincided with a stage of individual self-determination. Instead of mourning for the loss of what they had achieved and for their homeland, they instead took up the task of building up a new life with a certain defiant boldness. They were thereby often enabled to distance themselves from a father who had played a formative role in their lives, one who would have allowed them to comfortably settle in to the day-to-day work routine of the family law firm, but who would nonetheless always have been felt as a dominant presence.[251] Even though in some cases forced independence in a foreign country might have meant a new chance, one must not forget that emigration did mean leaving relatives, friends and those close to you behind.

Although the interest of the Third Reich in driving people out of the country was great, those responsible wanted to benefit from the process. Numerous measures designed to exact the very last dime from those willing to leave were enacted. Here we will only mention the Reich Tax on Exported Property (Reichsfluchtsteuer), a restriction on the export of foreign exchange that was already in effect before 1933, but that was gradually increased thereafter. In the final analysis, there were levies undertaken based on a whole bundle of measures that forced emigrants to leave their property in Germany. Siegfried Neumann, who has been quoted numerous times in this work, summed the matter up: "It didn't constitute emigration, but rather expulsion."[252]

The Conference of Evian had already shown[253] that no serious solution was being sought on the international level concerning the plight of the many people seeking to leave Germany. It should therefore come as no surprise that those individuals who were able to get abroad still encountered anti-Semitic feelings. In addition, the financial situation of the refugees was exacerbated. Asylum abroad was only available to those who had sufficient foreign exchange. Those seeking to leave were, however, rarely able to demonstrate this, since before their departure they had to pay a variety of levies to various administrative authorities, ranging from the Reich tax on Exported Property to advance payments of income tax. In the end, they often only had the money for passage by ship. Moreover, their dramatic situation was ruthlessly exploited, for example, by the purchasers of their homes or their household effects. It was only occasionally that colleagues rallied to the support of those in distress. Furthermore, the two major Christian denominations in Germany, whose members had been among those persecuted for years, acted with noticeable restraint. While it is true that the employees of the office of Pastor Grüber (for "non-Aryan" Protestants) and the St. Raphael Association (for "non-Aryan" Catholics) acted fairly, yet in the final analysis Germany's major churches failed to provide support. In addition to these two institutions, it was mainly the Quakers who strove to provide support for those "non-Aryans" unaffiliated with any religion.

A poem by the Berlin attorney Friedrich Solon highlights the plight of those resolved to emigrate:[254]

> S.O.S. (1938)
> The dam has broken, unleashed and wild,
> The flood pours forth, the water rises.
> Move on, ferryman, move on!
>
> The horror grows, the distress grows.
> The water comes, death is coming!
> Move on, ferryman, move on!
>
> "There! Take the little ones aboard!"
> Then you've done the first, the best thing!
> Move on, ferryman, move on!
>
> A final kiss—the flood is raging—
> Dear God, take them into your protection!
> Move on, ferryman, move on!
> Now speed on and pick up the elderly
> And everyone who is in misery, sick and weak!
> Move on, ferryman, move on!
>
> And even if the way is still difficult and far—
> You don't have much time any longer!
> Move on, ferryman, move on!

*O father and mother, he's picking you up now.*
*Farewell, farewell! We—will go last!*
*Move on, ferryman, move on!*

*Dawn is breaking—and over the foaming sea*
*The storm is accompanied by a mighty roar!*
*Move on, ferryman, move on!*
*The beams are breaking, the house is crashing—*
*Be strong and believe and stand firm!*
*Move on, ferryman, move on!*

*The earth is shaking, the sky is rumbling, the heavens*
*   crackling—*
*Hey, ferryman! Arrive before nightfall!*
*Move on, ferryman, move on!*
*Move on!*
*Move on!*

Solon, who was still admitted as a "legal consultant" after the general occupational ban, immigrated together with his family to Great Britain in 1939. After 1933 it was in fact the highest priority of the National Representative Agency for German Jews (Reichsvertretung der deutschen Juden),[255] to bring children into security. At least 18,000 children and young people left Germany without the accompaniment of their parents.[256] The parting—that for many would be a final farewell—frequently took place at the Anhalter train station in Berlin. Among them were also children from Berlin attorneys. One of them, who travelled to England alone, was the son of Moritz Galliner. He never saw his parents again.

Those able to emigrate together with their families could count their lucky stars.

## Emigration Within Europe

A total of 227 attorneys (34.7 percent of 655 people for whom information is available), therefore almost a third of all those who fled, found refuge within Europe. Due to linguistic preferences and family relations—and despite completely different legal systems—the overwhelming majority chose to travel abroad to an English-speaking country, that is, the emigrants went to Great Britain. At least 113 people, half of all emigrants within Europe, moved there. After the war broke out, a great number of them sought to move to the United States. Those who remained in Great Britain who were unable to obtain British citizenship, something that was a rare occurrence, were interned as "enemy aliens." Some of the camps were located on the islands off the coast of England (Isle of Man). However, some of those interned were shipped off to Australia or Canada.[257] Dr. Heinrich Freund was one of those who, after having just escaped persecution in Germany, then found himself placed in a British camp. He was forced to spend four years in Australia and finally became sick and destitute. He was finally able to reach the United States, but died two months after his arrival.

Dr. Theodor Alexander was another one of those who was interned by the British government. He was released after three months in 1940, due to the exertions of his wife. Mrs. Alexander was the provider for the family. She worked for the Quakers. In 1941 Alexander also received a work permit and was employed successively as a road, factory and subway worker. Later he became a waiter and, shortly before he was to be promoted to head waiter, took work as a counter clerk with British Railways. He turned 65 in 1952 and, having reached retirement age, was released from service. He didn't receive any retirement because he lacked a few months before reaching a 10-year period of employment. Subsequently Alexander worked for the Office of the United Restitution Organization (URO) in London as a legal consultant. After 1953 he lived primarily in Berlin. On March 2, 1955, he was once again admitted as an attorney there and specialized in compensation proceedings. A half year later, in September 1955, he died in Berlin.

Ernst Goldschmidt wanted to stay in Germany, even though he had abandoned his law practice in 1935 or 1936, due to insufficient income. His wife had built up one of the most important private schools for Jewish students in Roseneck in Berlin, and Goldschmidt helped her after he gave up his own profession. He was to be arrested in the wake of the Crystal Night pogrom of November 9–10, 1938. Yet, because he had been warned, he could flee by taking the night train to Denmark. From there he traveled to Great Britain, where he stayed for four months. Meanwhile his wife had sought to obtain a guarantee that he would not be arrested if he came back to Germany. Once this was granted, Goldschmidt returned to Berlin in March 1939. He was indeed not arrested, but the school had to be closed. In July 1939, the married couple immigrated to Great Britain, where they promptly set up a new school in Folkstone, which was near the coast. In 1940, as England was threatened by German air attacks, the school had to be relocated. Prior to this Ernst Goldschmidt had been interned on the Isle of Man for a year. After his

Ernst Goldschmidt

release, he set up a small business as a sales representative. In 1947 the couple moved to London. Two years later, in 1949, Goldschmidt died at the age of 64.

Even the highly respected Ernst Wolff barely made it abroad—to Great Britain—in time. Wolff's wife died during a German bombing attack on London. After the war, he returned to Germany and became a judge in Cologne.

Various biographies show that a number of emigrants wanted to stay as close as possible to the German border.[258]

In many places the best choice seemed to be to settle in the Netherlands, since it was relatively easy to obtain a residence permit there. Of course, it was not foreseeable that the refugees would be caught up with there by their persecutors. To this extent information relating to "emigration to the Netherlands" that is found in the biographical directory is fraught with some uncertainty, since individuals could be shipped out of the Netherlands to death camps without later having their fate included in one of the various memorial books. The same applies for those who chose to live in France or Czechoslovakia; some people were arrested there[259] and often sent off to camps.

Apart from Great Britain, in Europe it was Switzerland and Sweden that offered the most security from National Socialist persecution. Only very few were able to reach Switzerland. One of them was the seriously injured war veteran Julius Fleiss,[260] who escaped to Switzerland in a dramatic rescue mission in the 1940s.

At least six Berlin attorneys went to Italy and were able to survive there, because the exclusion of the Jewish minority was not pursued with the same fanaticism with which it was in the countries occupied by Germany.

Within Europe, Portugal was the place of flight furthest away from Germany. Most emigrants only regarded it as a transit point on the way overseas. However, two Berlin attorneys settled there permanently: one was Dr. Albert Arons. He had chosen Portugal because the "typical emigration" countries were already filled up and he wanted to remain in Europe. In addition, a year earlier Aron's mother-in-law had met a woman on the crossing to Argentina who was originally from Germany, but now lived in Portugal.[261] Armed with the business card of this lady the family set off. The four members of the family celebrated the 1935/1936 Christmas and New Year's season in Switzerland. It was during this time that their parents informed their adolescent daughters that they would not be returning to Berlin. The sisters reacted with joy and relief. They were too alert and informed to ignore the fact that they had been cut off and excluded at school. The woman they met in Portugal, whose name remains unknown, provided the family with support and made it easier for them to begin their lives anew. The sisters settled into their new homeland, quickly learning the language and making friends. Matters stood differently in Portugal for Albert Arons. He was unable to work as an attorney because he did not know the language, and, in addition, his degrees were not recognized. Moreover, he did not move in the corresponding social circles. He was forced to work in the area of business, something he had not been well disposed to up to then. He tried his hand at the sardine export business. His wife had learned photography, but because the materials required were so expensive, her efforts to establish a profession in this regard soon proved impractical. Albert Arons's business failed, and he became ill. This man, who had volunteered for World War I still held conservative political views, which led to disputes with one of his daughters concerning the political situation in Portugal. In 1948, only three weeks before his fiftieth birthday, Arons died from emphysema during a stay at a health spa in Grenoble. Although Albert Arons did not grow old, he did survive National Socialism.

## Immigration to the United States

For most emigrants, the United States was the dream destination, but only a few of them actually reached it. Two hundred former lawyers succeeded in escaping to the United States (30.5 percent, almost one third of all emigrants for whom the destination is known). Once they arrived in the United States, only a minority of them still wanted to continue to work in the area of law.[262] Those few who still wanted to continue working in this area were confronted with the problem that their degrees were not recognized in the United States. The most therefore strove to earn corresponding American qualifications and made an application for a scholarship to attend an American law school with the American Committee for the Guidance of Personnel Professionel.[263] This Committee was founded in 1938 to provide support for journalists and attorneys who had fled Germany. The documents of the Committee indicate that the United States offered sufficient security against the Nazis, but also made it clear to the new arrivals that the United States had not been waiting for them to emigrate.

The older attorneys struggled with various difficulties. They had to provide for the livelihood of their family, generally through unfamiliar, low-skilled work. As a result, they only had limited opportunities to learn the language, let alone legal terminology, and certainly did not have the opportunity to focus on American law. There was a formal age limit of 35 years for scholarships, which was exceeded by most of those making applications. Moreover, unwritten rules existed for awarding them. The applicant had to be in good health (a large number of the immigrants had fought in World War I and had lost an arm or a leg, but even those who had escaped unscathed, often suffered from psychological scars that had been left behind due to persecution). Applicants also had to be able to present a convincing CV (something that was hardly possible within the framework of the age limit). Moreover, above average achievements had to be demonstrated—and the applicant was not to appear "Jewish." For all those involved it was clear that the immigrants were always Jews, but they were expected not to manifest the external characteristics that corresponded to the usual stereotypes.[264] In the documents one encounters the moving application of Werner Meyer, which he later withdrew, because he only regarded himself as an "average attorney."[265] Fred Levy, who had an arm amputated and who was having difficulty in supporting his family, was rejected.[266]

Two Berlin attorneys received one of the 29 scholarships. Among them was Ernst Fraenkel, who was certainly a man of exceptional talent. In his case, he was accepted even though he exceeded the age limit, because of his convincing biography. He included a manuscript of his major work *The Dual State (Der Doppelstaat).*[267] Fraenkel, who could

Ernst Fraenkel with his wife in exile, the United States, 1941

work as an attorney up to 1938 due to his status as a frontline soldier, sought American citizenship. He served as a consultant to the American government in Korea, in the early 1950s he was a lecturer in Berlin at the German Academy for Politics (Deutsche Hochschule für Politik). Later he was appointed as a professor at the Free University of Berlin (Freie Universität Berlin), then later to the its Otto Suhr Institute of Political Science. Although Fraenkel once again lived and worked primarily in Germany, he didn't want to seem ungrateful to the American government and the nation that had offered him refuge during his time of persecution. Fraenkel was a man whose personality had many aspects: a German in terms of culture, a jurist by education, a Jew due to persecution, a political scientist by profession, an American by conviction.

Like many others who, based on their age in 1933, could have become parents, Fraenkel and his wife had apparently decided against having children of their own. This phenomenon is just one of the many results of this research, yet is not one that allows itself to be pursued in greater depth. Yet it seems to have been an exceptional case if members of the group being researched here had children after 1933, even though most of them lived in established relationships. If they did have children, these generally had been born before 1933. Apparently, the existential uncertainty of a world that seemed to have lost its bearings caused most of them to shy away from starting a family.

Wilhelm Dickmann (later William Dickman), born in 1900 (and thereby two years younger than Fraenkel) was a Protestant. He also received one of the coveted scholarships for law school. He later became an American citizen and after the war worked in the staff of the American High Commissioner General Clay, where he was instrumental in helping to draft the law for the dissolution of Prussia.[268] It is said of him that, after the war, he visited former acquaintances, still wearing an American uniform, and provided care packages as a personal contribution to giving support to the Germans, even though his mother and his sister had been killed. He sought to identify fully as an American because his achievements were appreciated in the United States. In the 1940s he had married the daughter of a former Prague rabbi. The couple did not have children.

William Dickman in U.S. uniform in London in 1945

Others, such as Dr. Adolf Hamburger, wanted to return to Berlin after the end of the war. However, they found that they were unable to establish any links with the period before they had emigrated. After a short period of time in Germany, Hamburger returned to the United States.[269]

## Immigration to Palestine

A large number of emigrants, who had initially gone to France or Italy, sought to go from there to South America or Palestine after the war broke out. Palestine was "the promised land" for only a few. Zionism had not been widely acknowledged among the circle of middle-class attorneys.[270] In addition to the territorial and political problems there, the civilization hardly seemed developed in comparison to Western European standards and the climate was inhospitable.

Nevertheless, around a sixth of all those attorneys who emigrated went to Palestine (111 or 17 percent of 655). Despite the careful preparation for agricultural activities by institutions of the Jewish community in the first years after 1933, the work situation was very complicated. The transfer of capital that seemed to have been generally secured through the Havaara Agreement[271] apparently did not offer sufficient opportunities for earning a livelihood. Many immigrants had to reorient themselves.[272] For example, in Israel it is still reported today that the Berlin jurists were particularly active in the Haifa ice trade: "and then came Mr. Councillor and the attorney Dr. Such-and-Such, in order to sell the yekkes ice [for cooling purposes]."[273]

Only very few were able to find legal work, because it was difficult to become familiar with the legal system that had been prescribed by the British Mandate of Palestine administration. That is why, besides the trade in ice, every job was sought after. Dr. Gottfried Samter emigrated from Berlin and made his way as a taxi driver. Yet as soon as an opportunity offered itself after the end of the war, Samter, like many others, went back to Germany, something most of his acquaintances advised him against.[274] Many of the emigrants played a leading role in building the state of Israel.[275] Some remained active in the area of law, for example, the former Berlin attorney Felix Rosenblüth,[276] who became Israel's first Minister of Justice, or Prof. Dr. Wolfgang Zeltner, who became the presiding judge of the Tel Aviv District Court. Dr. Joseph Münz became a legal official in the Department of Transportation.[277] Kurt-Jacob Ball-Kaduri, who has already been mentioned, no longer worked in a legal capacity but was instead behind the initiative the built the Yad Vashem memorial.

The great majority of the emigrants was able to build a life in Israel. The nickname "yekkes" was attached to them and they kept many of their peculiarities. Many a former attorney could not keep himself from wearing a tie, even in the most sweltering heat. Many were, however, completely unable to adapt permanently to the conditions of the country. After a certain period of time they regarded Palestine only as a temporary place of exile. Most of these exiles returned to Germany after the end of the war. Many attempted to move to the United States.

## Flight to South America and Shanghai

As of 1938 and most certainly after the war broke out, those who wanted to leave Germany and even Europe hardly had a choice: they had to flee to the country of refuge for which they could get hold of passage on a ship. In some cases, political problems in the countries of exile led to a situation where the ships were not allowed to dock. As early as 1939, numerous refugee ships reported that they were denied permission to enter their port of destination. Among them was the *St. Louis*, whose 937 passengers were not allowed to go ashore and therefore had to be transported back to Europe. In such cases, the passengers could count themselves lucky if, after weeks of wandering at sea, they could, for example, be taken to the UK after their arrival in Belgium. A total of 5,000 refugees crossed the sea in their ships without reaching their destination and were forced to return to Europe. Often, they were shipped off to Nazi death camps after their arrival back.[278]

A considerable number of Berlin attorneys (82 or 12.5 percent of 655 emigrants) went to South America, South Africa, or Shanghai. As in every country they fled to, the refugees had to go through the most trying situations. It can be shown that five Berlin attorneys went to South Africa, among them Dr. Erwin Spiro und Dr. Willi Bachwitz.

Shanghai was one of the few places in the world that Jews could travel to without a visa or without major financial resources.[279] Yet Shanghai was so foreign, the living conditions so onerous, that from the very beginning a stay there was only viewed as a temporary solution. Nevertheless, Shanghai is specified as the city of refuge for 18 Berlin lawyers. These included Felix Latte and Dr. Paul Remak. Other "safe" countries of refuge such as Australia could rarely be reached directly. One generally was sent there on a compulsory basis by Great Britain. Australia, like South Africa, was very much in demand, but entry was difficult because limits on immigration precluded a large number of arrivals.

For someone accustomed to Western European standards, the climactic and cultural conditions in South America could prove oppressive. At the same time, the political structures of the individual countries, which were not so firmly established, offered opportunities for professional areas of employment,[280] but rarely in the field of law. However, emigrants had to deal with virulent anti-Semitism that made it more difficult for the refugees to obtain a secure resident status. Despite this,

Chodziesner family, August 1937. On the left, the daughter Gertrud (Kolmar), who was murdered in Auschwitz, on the her right her daughter Hilde Wenzel, née Chodziesner, with her daughter, behind her stands her husband Peter Wenzel; in the center on the bench is Ludwig Chodziesner, behind him stands his daughter Margot Chodziesner, who died in 1942 in Australia; front right Dorothea Chodziesner, née Galliner, who died in 1943, with her son, behind her stands her husband Georg Chodziesner.

it has been determined that those who found refuge in South America, especially in Chile, Argentina and Uruguay, adapted to their new homes and lived there permanently.

Dorothea Chodziesner was stranded with her child in Chile. Born in 1904 as the daughter of the liberal Rabbi Galliner, she had married at the age of 25 and set up practice a little later as a lawyer. She married into a larger family group. Her father-in-law, Ludwig Chodziesner and all his brothers were lawyers. Her sister-in-law Gertrud Kolmar was a lyric poet. Dorothea Chodziesner gave birth to a child in 1935, at a time she had already been made subject to the occupational ban. The fact that she became a mother under these circumstances seems to be unique, no other female attorney in the same circumstances is known. In August 1939, a month before the war broke out, her husband fled to Great Britain, where he was interned and shipped to Australia. He was released in 1942 in order to join the Australian army. In the meantime, his wife Dorothea had traveled to Great Britain with her child. After arriving, she decided not to stay permanently and traveled to Chile in 1939/1940. She died there in Concepción in November 1943 at the age of 39 from a gastric ulcer. Her eight-year-old child could only move to Australia to be with the father two years later. Ludwig Chodziesner, the father-in-law and/or the grandfather, had been sent to Theresienstadt. While packing his things, he was supported by a distant relative (by marriage), Hilde Benjamin, who later became Minister of Justice in the German Democratic Republic (DDR). Ludwig Chodziesner died in Theresienstadt, his daughter Gertrud Kolmar in Auschwitz. Only a few of what had once been a large family group survived.

Willi Althertum, who had been managing director of the Berlin Bar Association up to 1933, immigrated to Sao Paulo, Brazil. On November 7, 1944, he concluded his memoirs with the following words:

> We found a home but not a native land in Brazil. Our native land is the entire world, with all its light and life. Filled with awe, love and thanks we embrace it with our view. We had the good fortune to become citizens of the world.[281]

Not all emigrants would have been able to agree.

## The Fate of Jewish Attorneys in Numbers

During the course of the research for this documentation, the names of 1,807 people could be ascertained. Based on a number of 1,835 Berlin attorneys of Jewish origin who were admitted to practice law, this means that 98.5 percent of all attorneys persecuted after 1933 for anti-Semitic reasons have been included. In the case of 403 people the information available was essentially limited to their names, their law firm address in 1933 and events related to the practice of law itself after 1933. For 1,404 people, additional information about their fate was available.

The key findings of this investigation are listed below:

- At least 664 attorneys of Jewish origin, therefore more than a third, had been excluded by October 1933. This means that they had been made subject to a prohibition on representation or that they had fled. The 1933 exclusion primarily affected young attorneys who were born in 1902 and thereafter, as well as all women—with one exception.
- At the same time the number of Jewish attorneys admitted to practice in October 1933 were 1,168, a number well over that of 35, which was the political goal sought after by the Nazi regime.
- Most Jewish attorneys already lost their licenses as a notary in 1933.
- In 1935, in the wake of the "Nuremberg Laws," all attorneys regarded as Jews lost their license as notaries.
- In 1938 a general occupational ban on all Jewish attorneys who were still in practice (at least 671) went into effect. At this point their contribution to the German administration of justice was no longer necessary.
- Around 90 of those who had been attorneys were admitted on a limited basis and/or "permanently" as "legal consultants."

The further fate of Jewish attorneys in numbers:

**(Total number 1,404)**

| | | |
|---|---|---|
| Natural death | 206 | 14.7% |
| Suicide | 28 | 2.0% |
| Death due to wartime conditions | 5 | 0.4% |
| "Died" | 299 | 21.3% |
| Survived in the camps or went underground | 107 | 7.6% |
| Emigration | 703 | 50.0% |
| Exile and return | 56 | 4.0% |

# Summary

The segregation and exclusion of the Jewish minority took place in waves. While the first (up to March 1933) can be characterized as terror against individuals, the second (from April to October 1933) is characterized by its "orderly," bureaucratic nature. In this wave those affected were identified and classified, after which a third of them was made subject to an occupational ban. The third wave (taking place on a parallel basis as from April 1933) destroyed the economic foundations necessary for the further pursuit of the profession of those affected. During the fourth wave (at the end of 1938) all attorneys of Jewish origin were made subject to an occupational ban. The various exceptions made for "legal consultants" and those of "mixed race" were linked to a corresponding special status.

Exclusion and persecution led to the murder of enumerable people and to an "expulsion" of massive proportions. Yet nonetheless, 163 Berlin attorneys of Jewish origin, who were admitted in 1933, either stayed in Germany or came back to it. Dramatic and decisive moments that were apparent to everyone were April 1, 1933 and November 9–10, 1938. At the same time "the increase of statutorily sanctioned injustice . . . that finally entered into a phase where questions regarding justice and injustice had become obsolete and where the creeping terror of the absence of individual rights had replaced life-extinguishing, individual acts of terror"[282] was taking place in a more pedestrian fashion.

Regardless of whether one describes the developments as "creeping" or as a series of waves, they were always experienced openly and painfully; in every instance, it was an exclusion that became more and more comprehensive.

For attorneys, in their role as "officers of the court," the arbitrary exclusion of many of their professional colleagues must be regarded as a significant development, for now these tasks had to be assumed by other attorneys. A profession based on individual self-sufficiency is not one that is well-suited at any time to actions demonstrating solidarity. The dismantling of the self-governing bodies, which were based on democratic principles, further contributed to this "failure to act." Nonetheless there could have at least been vehement expressions of opposition in professional journals. Any joint actions failed due to the bar association itself, which was dominated by National Socialists beginning in April 1933. For example, a boycott of work in the courts could not be organized, because there were no structures throughout Germany through which one could undertake meaningful opposition in the public sphere. This gives rise to questions concerning the behavior of bar associations and other legal organizations. Judgment of behavior of individual board members can only be undertaken with reservations. While it is known that in some associations of other sectors the top officials exerted personal pressure,[283] one must bear in mind that these were trade associations in which other interests and power factors were at play than was the case, for example, with bar associations and legal organizations. Only the German Legal Association (Deutsche Juristentag e.V.) sought to resist being taken over.

Regardless of this the question arises as to whether there was any will at all in the legal profession to exert opposition against anti-Semitic exclusion that was actually necessary to suppress. There were some who did not agree with the new system, even though they themselves had not been affected by its measures. Adolf Arndt used the term "decent" for those colleagues who continued to express their opinion. Today this term is no longer in use, but it still very precisely describes what constituted a sound moral position. There were people who were "decent" and remained so. Others changed their views and adapted; the environment of constant propaganda had its effect. In addition, another factor that certainly came into play for non-Jewish attorneys was that they could take on numerous new clients. This brought financial benefits with it and as a result did not promote a commitment to disenfranchised colleagues—but rather had the opposite effect. Today it can no longer be reconstructed just who took on how many former clients of Jewish colleagues and "maliciously" profited therefrom (often Jewish attorneys recommended trustworthy clients to their colleagues), or just who had an established law firm transferred over to them. However, in many cases an advantage was derived from the exclusion. Yet the massive tomes of statutory injustice put forth by the state do not constitute a release from individual responsibility. An attorney was a "servant of the law"—yet what law? In Germany, after 1933, the principles of human rights were simply ignored. In April 1933 and in the following years the most absurd and uncivilized measures were given statutory form. Non-Jewish colleagues hardly had any doubts about such measures, based on the motto: "law is law." It seems like no one took steps to prevent this development. It was only in the early stage that clients stood up for their attorneys, yet this was a matter that always concerned concrete individuals. Legal colleagues remained reserved. Well-known attorneys were accustomed to having enough spokesmen for their merit. As to their ordinary colleagues, it was thought that there were too many to permanently exclude them. Nobody wanted to take risks on their behalf. Moreover, in some cases personal animosity may have skewed one's view.

Siegfried Neumann, who has already been quoted, writes in his memoirs that "even the next generation of attorneys had not been profoundly influenced by Nazism."[284] This statement should not be allowed to hide the fact that younger colleagues at the universities had been made subject to the usual indoctrination that followed the declaration that the Treaty of Versailles was a national disgrace. Reactionary student fraternities created a social network that continued to exert influence well beyond the university years. As a result, a critical examination of factual and ethical issues was not encouraged or viewed as an aspect of scholarly discourse. The role of tutors in promoting an aspect of education that encouraged the blind belief in authority has not been properly dealt with in this context.

In general, the National Socialist system exploited the administration of justice. Jurists were used as tools and not as professionals.[285] In that they let themselves be used, they worked together with this system as it was built. They were not just assistants, but rather made an active contribution to a legal system based on injustice that led to the exclusion of entire population groups. In the foreground there stood the short-term positive benefits that accrued to individuals. Human or legal concerns regarding segregation were not made vocal.

The following biographical directory describes the fate of those who had been excluded because they were defined as Jews. Among the Berlin attorneys were exceptional personalities. Yet the overwhelming majority of the persons named were simply average jurists. Regardless of their standing, their profession, homeland—often their language and health—in many cases, even life itself, was taken from them.

# After 1945

The year 1945 was not just zero hour, but also a time of new beginnings. The Allies strove to set up a legal system that had been cleansed of National Socialism. A priority was the reintroduction of an independent judiciary, which led to a search for suitable prosecutors and judges. Those who had spent years abroad or who had gone underground in their own country showed little interest in taking on the role of prosecutor or judge. According to the personal files created after 1945, those concerned refused—almost without exception—to give up their role as attorneys. Presumably the experience of their own persecution still lingered too vividly for them to feel themselves able to distance themselves sufficiently in making decisions of such a nature. The web of National Socialist attitudes and tendencies still seemed too tightly woven for them to be able to unravel it.

That the tendency to shy away from entering the judiciary was well justified, is shown in the example of Botho Laserstein.[286] Laserstein had fled to France and survived there, in contrast to his wife, his daughter and other close family members. In 1951 he returned to Germany and became a public prosecutor in North Rhine-Westphalia. After he had associated himself with various causes, such not introducing the death penalty, a campaign of defamation broke out against him. He felt himself compelled to show that he did not personally resent Nazi crimes. The best way that he could have shown that would have been by consistently adapting to the circumstances of the Federal Republic of Germany. Yet Laserstein had his own, democratically legitimate views on important social issues. It remains an open question as to whether Laserstein constituted a complicated and difficult personality for those who dealt with him directly. What is certain is that he did not meet with sympathetic understanding from those around him. He was made subject to investigations on various levels. For example, it was said of him that he moved in homosexual circles. Laserstein was suspended from service without proof of official misconduct. He committed suicide in 1955.

Another person who made his way back to Germany was Dagobert Pincus. He had fled to France and taken part in a Résistance group there. As soon as he had the opportunity, he returned and applied in Berlin for readmission to the bar. Acquaintances could not understand his decision to return to Berlin, a city that most people "would rather leave today than tomorrow." Nevertheless, he was intensively striving to obtain his admission. He had to close the first law office he opened in Köpenick after difficulties with the authorities there. He then moved his law office to Halensee. Unlike Laserstein, Pincus was able to accommodate himself to the circumstances in Germany. He continued to keep up contact with those who had also suffered persecution, such as Max and Erna Proskauer. They had immigrated to Palestine and returned to Germany in the 1950s. Max Proskauer established his own law firm in Wedding, which was taken over by his former wife after his death.

Adolf Arndt was an impressive person. Having been persecuted as a person of "mixed race," after the collapse of National Socialism, he was searching for a political home that would offer the guarantee of a new beginning. He decided to work actively for the SPD. Although his origins were in the bourgeois middle class, he took attentive notice of Kurt Schumacher's "offer to the intelligentsia" in the summer of 1945. Arndt was caught up in Schumacher's effort to involve all liberal and democratic oriented forces in social justice. Arndt's statements examining the direct National Socialist past have a depth and precision rarely found at that time. Those who shared his commitment marveled at a "factual authority and personal persuasive power"[287] that must have exercised its own special fascination on others.

Dagobert Pincus (right),
Max and Erna Proskauer

In one of his most important contributions he quotes a saying of Jean Jaurès[287]: "Preserving tradition does not mean picking up the ashes thereof, but rather keeping its flame alight."

# Biographical Directory of Berlin Attorneys of Jewish Origin

# A

## Abraham, Hans Fritz Dr.
*Date and place of birth and death:*
12/21/1880 — no information
*Home address:* Hugo-Vogel-Str. 42, Wannsee
*Law firm address:* Friedrichstr. 182, W 8
*Additional information:* Attorney at the KG
and notary; was a board member of the RAK
up to 1932. Applied and was readmitted
as an attorney after the National Socialist
seizure of power in 1933, but license as notary
was revoked. Emigration to Cambridge,
Massachusetts, USA.
*Sources:* Br.B. 32; TK 33; *li; Verz.; JMBl. 33,
S. 220; BArch, R 3001 PAK; BG

## Abraham, Jacob, Judicial Councillor
*Date and place of birth and death:*
02/23/1866 Schroda - no information
*Home address:* Rügener Str. 21
*Law firm address:* Bergstr.125, Neukölln
*Additional information:* Attorney at the
Neukölln AG, at the LG II and notary; after
the National Socialist seizure of power in fall
1933 he was disbarred and his license as a
notary was revoked.
*Sources:* Jüd.Adr.B; Br.B. 32; TK 33; *li; LAB
Liste 15.10.33; Pr.J. 33, S. 807; BArch, R
3001 PAK; BG

## Abraham, Jacques Dr.
*Date and place of birth and death:*
09/10/1880 Berlin - internment 1942
*Home address:* Passauer Str. 14, W 50
*Law firm address:* Kanonierstr. 37, W 8
*Additional information:* Attorney at the LG
I-III and notary, editor of "Zeitschrift für das
Beamtenrecht" (Journal for Civil Service Law)
up to 1933. After the National Socialist seizure
of power in 1933 his license as a notary was
revoked; was admitted as an attorney until the
1938 general occupational ban; then worked
as an unskilled laborer. Date of declaration
of property: 10/14/1942, transported to Riga
on 10/19/1942, officially established date
of death: 12/31/1942. An earlier attempt to
flee ended in failure at the Dutch border, an
attempt to emigrate to South America was also
unsuccessful, because he had not received a visa.
*Sources:* Br.B. 32; TK 33; JMBl. 33, S. 208; *li;
BG; BArch, R 3001 PAK; Philo-Lexikon, S.
604; MRRAK; VZ 39; BdE; GB II; Göpp., S.
237

## Abraham, Rudolf
*Date and place of birth and death:*
07/01/1901 Berlin - March 1943 Auschwitz
*Home address:* Rankestr. 17, W 50
*Law firm address:* Belle-Alliance-Platz 17,
SW 61
*Additional information:* Attorney at the KG.
After the National Socialist seizure of power
he was made subject to an occupational ban
on 06/17/1933. Transported to Auschwitz
on 03/03/1943, was murdered there during
March 1943.
*Sources:* Br.B. 32; TK 33; Liste d. nichtzugel.
RA, 25.4.33; JMBl. 33, S. 209; BArch, R
3001 PAK; BG; GB II

## Abraham, Siegfried Dr.
*Date and place of birth and death:*
02/05/1893 Berlin - no information
*Home address:* Am Hirschsprung 31,
Zehlendorf-Dahlem
*Law firm address:* Krausenstr. 9/10, W 8
*Additional information:* Attorney at the LG
I-III and notary. After the National Socialist
seizure of power in 1933 he was readmitted
as an attorney; his license as a notary was
revoked at the end of 1935; he worked as an
attorney until the 1939 general occupational
ban. He presumably emigrated after
01/16/1939.
*Sources:* Br.B. 32; TK 33; *li; Liste 36; DJ 36,
S. 314; BArch, R 3001 PAK; MRRAK; BG

## Abraham, Theodor Dr., Judicial Councillor
*Date and place of birth and death:*
08/21/1869 - 01/27/1935 Berlin
*Home address:* Grunewaldstr. 42, Schöneberg
*Law firm address:* Grunewaldstr. 42,
Schöneberg
*Additional information:* Attorney at the
LG I-III, at the AG Berlin Mitte and notary.
After the National Socialist seizure of power
in 1933, his license as a notary was revoked;
upon request he was readmitted as an
attorney; he died in 1935 at the age of 65.
*Sources:* Br.B. 32; JMBl. 7.7.33; *li; LAB,
Liste, 15.10.33; BArch, R 3001 PAK; BG

## Abrahamsohn, Hermann Dr.
04/19/1885 Berlin - no information
*Home address:* Bismarckstr. 80,
Charlottenburg
*Law firm address:* Bismarckstr. 80,
Charlottenburg

*Additional information:* Attorney at the AG Charlottenburg, at the LG I-III, and notary. After the National Socialist seizure of power he was readmitted to the practice of law; his license as a notary was revoked at the end of 1935; he continued to work as an attorney up to the 1938 general occupational ban.
*Sources:* Br.B. 32; TK 1933; *li; Liste 36; DJ 36, S. 314; BArch, R 3001 PAK; Tel.B. 38; MRRAK

**Abrahamsohn, Ludwig Dr.**
05/01/1883 Berlin - no information
*Home address:* Wittelsbacher Str. 25, Wilmersdorf
*Law firm address:* Linkstr. 13 and/or 42, W 9
*Additional information:* Attorney at the LG I-III and notary. After the National Socialist seizure of power in 1933 his license as a notary was revoked, upon making application therefor he was readmitted as an attorney; he continued to be listed as an attorney until at least the beginning of 1935; he emigrated to London, Great Britain.
*Sources:* Br.B. 32; TK 33; TK 36; JMBl. 7.7.33, S. 208; *li; LAB, Liste 15.10.33; BArch, R 3001 PAK; BG

**Abrahamsohn, Max Dr.**
04/16/1884 Frankfurt/Oder - 11/22/1943
*Home address:* Aschaffenburger Str. 16, W 30
*Law firm address:* Aschaffenburger Str. 16, W 30
*Additional information:* Attorney at the LG I-III, at the AG Berlin Mitte, and notary; after the National Socialist seizure of power in 1933 his license as a notary was revoked, upon making application therefor he was readmitted as an attorney; he continued to be listed as an attorney until at least the beginning of 1936. He died in November 1943 as a result of an "air raid."
*Sources:* Br.B. 32; TK 33; JMBl. 7.7.33; *li; Liste 36; BArch, R 3001 PAK; BG

**Abramczyk, Wilhelm, Judicial Councillor**
07/09/1864 Potsdam - 12/19/1942 Theresienstadt
*Home address:* Schlüterstr. 54, Charlottenburg
*Law firm address:* Hohenzollerndamm 207, W 15
*Additional information:* Attorney at the LG I-III, at the AG Berlin Mitte and notary,

in-house counsel for the Berliner Lehrerverein (Berlin Teacher's Association); after the National Socialist seizure of power in 1933 his license as a notary was revoked, upon making application he was readmitted as an attorney; he was made subject to the 1938 occupational ban for attorneys of Jewish origin; in 1934 he planned to emigrate to Switzerland. Date of declaration of property: 09/25/1942, interned at the collection point Artilleriestr. 31; transported to Theresienstadt on 10/03/1942, he died there several weeks later.
*Sources:* Br.B. 32; JMBl. 7.7.33, S. 208; *li; Tel.B. 38; BArch, R 3001 PAK; MRRAK; BG; ThG; GB II

**Adams, Paul Dr.**
No information
*Home address:* Schönhauser Allee 129, N 58
*Law firm address:* Gleimstr. 62, N 31
*Additional information:* Attorney at the LG I-III, avoided the first wave of exclusion that followed seizure of power by the National Socialists; he could still practice law until 1940, because he had been classified as "mixed race."
*Sources:* TK 1933; *li; LAB, Liste Mschlg. 36; Tel.B. 38; Tel.B. 41; BArch, R 3001 PAK

**Adler, Fritz Dr.**
11/01/1899 Stettin - no information
*Home address:* no information
*Law firm address:* Tauentzienstr. 20, W 50
*Additional information:* Had been an attorney in Berlin since 1927, admitted to the LG I-III; after the National Socialist seizure of power he was made subject to an occupational ban in June 1933, after which all attempts to be readmitted to the Berlin Bar ended in failure.
*Sources:* Br.B. 32; TK 1933; Liste d. nichtzugel. RA, 25.4.33; JMBl. 33, S. 234; BArch, R 3001 PAK, PA

**Adler, Waldemar Dr.**
07/24/1894 Böhmen - 04/28/1982
*Home address:* Fennstr. 30, N 65, Wedding
*Law firm address:* Wolframstr. 77, Tempelhof
*Additional information:* After the National Socialist seizure of power, he had been classified as "mixed race first degree," because two of his grandparents were of Jewish origin. He was married to a non-Jewish wife. In April 1933 he was made subject to a general occupational ban,

which was then suspended. After 1938 he was one of the few "non-Aryans" who were allowed to continue working as attorneys (1940 at his private residence), although he was not able to realize significant income from his practice. In 1940 he was conscripted by the Todt Organization as a forced laborer, but was able to flee and lived "underground" in the vicinity of Berlin until the end of the war. In 1945 he was readmitted as an attorney and notary. At the end of September 1981, at the age of 87, he terminated his membership in the Berlin Bar; he died six months later.
*Sources:* *li; BArch, R 3001 PAK; LAB; Liste Mschlg. 36; Tel.B. 41; Ausk. B. Dombek nach LAB, RAK PA; BG

**Ahrweiler, Oswald**
08/29/1900 - no information
*Home address:* no information
*Law firm address:* Sächsische Str. 70, W 15
*Additional information:* Attorney since 1930; his mother was not Jewish; he was a Catholic; after the National Socialist seizure of power, he was disbarred despite intensive efforts to avoid this outcome, he was made subject to the occupational ban, because he was considered to be a "non-Aryan." The Bishop of Osnabrück had intervened on his behalf to obtain readmission to the Bar. Up until then the administrative authorities had been diligently searching for political reasons with which they could justify his disbarment, yet the Chief of Police could not uncover any prejudicial evidence. The Bishop was provided with the following explanation for disbarment on 12/12/1933: "Due to the extraordinarily large foreign infiltration of Jews in the Prussian legal profession it is not possible to make any exceptions. In the district of the Berlin Court of Appeals even today there are still about 1,500 Jewish attorneys as opposed to 1,800 German attorneys. It is quite understandable that the legal profession itself, in particular that of Berlin, has energetically opposed the readmission of attorneys of Jewish origin. They base their view on the fact that such jurists are no longer permitted to be civil servants on the basis of the Law for the Restoration of the Professional Civil Service (BBG) and would therefore, upon being admitted, give the impression that the legal profession has lower qualitative requirements than those put forth for civil servants, which would then perforce lead to

a lessening of esteem for the legal profession."
*Sources:* JMBl. 33, S. 234; BArch R 3001 PAK, PA

**Albu, Curt**
08/16/1885 - no information
*Home address:* no information
*Law firm address:* Charlottenstr. 56, W 8
*Additional information:* Attorney at the LG I-III and notary; after the National Socialist seizure of power in 1933 his license as a notary was revoked, he was still admitted as an attorney until at least fall 1935; he emigrated to New York, USA.
*Sources:* Br.B. 32; TK 33; *li; JMBl. 33, S. 208; TK 36; BArch, R 3001 PAK; BG

**Alexander, Alfons Dr., Judicial Councillor**
06/08/1863 Berlin - 10/28/1942 Theresienstadt
*Home address:* Bülowstr. 20, Schöneberg
*Law firm address:* Bülowstr. 20, Schöneberg
*Additional information:* Attorney at the LG I-III, at the AG Berlin Mitte and notary. After the National Socialist seizure of power his license as a notary was revoked, he was temporarily made subject to a ban on representation, but was then readmitted to the bar up to the final 1938 occupational ban. Date of declaration of property: 09/18/1942, interned at collection point Große Hamburger Str. 26; transported to Theresienstadt on 09/23/1942, died there a month later.
*Sources:* Br.B. 32; TK 33; *li; JMBl. 33, S. 208; Naatz-Album; BArch, R 3001 PAK; MRRAK; BG: GB II

**Alexander, Eduard Dr.**
03/14/1881 Essen - 03/01/1945 while being transported to Bergen-Belsen
*Home address:* Cimbernstr. 13, Zehlendorf-Nikolassee
*Law firm address:* Lützowplatz 27, Schöneberg
*Additional information:* Member of the German Communist Party (KPD), for a time editor-in-chief of "Die Rote Fahne" (The Red Flag) (business editor up to 1929); 1921-25 served as a representative of the KPD on the

Berlin City Council; admitted as an attorney since 1913 at the LG I-III and the Schöneberg Municipal Court, at the same time he was admitted as a notary. After the National Socialist seizure of power in 1933 he was made subject to an occupational ban as both an attorney and a notary; he was classified as "half-Jewish"; arbitrator for the German-Soviet trading company until 1940; arrested during the course of the "Thunderstorm" campaign (Aktion "Gewitter") [following the failed assassination attempt on Adolf Hitler on 07/22/1944] and transported to Sachsenhausen on 08/22/1944, then died during the last days of the war while being transported from the Sachsenhausen to the Bergen-Belsen concentration camp.
*Sources:* Br.B. 32; TK 33; JMBl. 33, S. 209; GStA, Rep. 84 a, Nr. 20363; BArch, R 3001 PAK; BG; GB II; Verfolgte Berl. Stadtverordnete u. Magis-tratsmitgl.

**Alexander, Kurt Dr.**
No information
*Home address:* no information
*Law firm address:* Potsdamer Str. 23 a, W 9
*Additional information:* Attorney at the LG I-III, at the AG Berlin Mitte and notary. After the National Socialist seizure of power in 1933 his license as a notary was revoked; he was no longer listed as a member of the Berlin Bar as of early 1936.
*Sources:* Br.B. 32;TK 33; *li; JMBl. 33, S.220; LAB, Liste 15.10.33; DJ 36, S. 360; BArch, R 3001 PAK; BG

**Alexander, Theodor Dr.**
06/13/1887 Königsberg - 09/11/1955 Berlin
*Home address:* Bismarckstr. 68, Charlottenburg
*Law firm address:* Neue Grünstr. 17, SW 19
*Additional information:*
He was already baptized as a child; since 1913 he was admitted as an attorney at the Berlin LG; he fought in the First World War, he received the EK I. Kl.; in-house counsel for the German Iron Trade Association (Deutscher Eisenhandel AG). After the National Socialist seizure of power he was readmitted as an attorney and as a notary upon request, because he was recognized as a "frontline fighter;" his license as a notary was

revoked at the end of 1935. As a consequence of the Night of Broken Glass he was arrested and interned at Sachsenhausen Concentration Camp on November 10, 1938; he was released on 12/23/1938 on the condition that he would immediately emigrate. He wanted to emigrate together with his wife to the USA via Cuba. After arriving in Cuba (February 1939), both were incarcerated for three months due to a change in government that had taken place there. With the help of the Quakers they were able to get back to England shortly before the outbreak of war, as foreigners they did not initially receive work permits. In June 1940 he was interned for three months as an "alien enemy." In the meantime his wife was allowed to work and obtained employment as a clerical assistant for the Quakers. In 1941, he also received a work permit and earned his living as a street, factory and station worker. Later he became a waiter, shortly before he was promoted to head waiter he switched employment to the British Railroad and became a clerk there. At the age of 65, he was dismissed from service in 1952 on reaching the age limit, but he did not receive a pension because he was short of ten months' employment. Subsequently, he initially worked at the URO (United Restitution Organization) in London as a legal consultant, then from 1953 he was largely active in Berlin. On April 2, 1955 he was readmitted as an attorney and put the main focus of his activity on reparation cases. He died in September 1955 in Berlin.
*Sources:* Br.B. 32; TK 33; *li; DJ 36, S. 314; BArch, R 3001 PAK; LAB, RAK, PA; Ausk. RA Achelis

**Alexander-Katz, Ernst**
10/17/1891 - 01/01/1968 Haifa, Israel
*Home address:* Kaiserdamm 30, Charlottenburg
*Law firm address:* Wilhelmstr. 44, W 8
*Additional information:* He adopted the Catholic faith in 1912; married in 1914; in the same year volunteered for military service. He studied law at Cambridge, Munich and Halle. After the First World War had ended he completed his clerkship in Berlin; he completed his doctorate in Freiburg in 1922. In 1923 he became an attorney in Berlin and was finally admitted to the LG I-III. At that time he was already a member of the Centre

and was a member of the municipal council. The "baptized Jew" He was mocked as a zealous new convert for his commitment to Catholic institutions. After the failure of a second marriage and a brief stay in Vienna, he returned to Berlin. In October, 1932, he set off on a trip to the Far East. After the seizure of power by the National Socialists, he remained in Palestine, where he married for the third time. In the spring of 1933 he was disbarred. He found a position at the Technical University in Haifa. After the end of the war, he traveled frequently to Europe and campaigned among Jews for immigration to Israel. His first wife had been murdered in Auschwitz.

He had been a senior lecturer at the Technion in Haifa and a specialist in finance. Together with Wilhelm Gerhoff and Fritz Neumark, he published the "Handbook of Finance."
*Sources:* TK 33; Liste d. nichtzugel. RA, 25.4.33; JMBl. 33, S. 253; BArch, R 3001 PAK; BG; Verfolgte Berl.

### Alexander-Katz, Günther Dr.

11/14/1891 Berlin - no information
*Home address:* Darmstädter Str. 7, W 15
*Law firm address:* Leipziger Str. 105, W 8
*Additional information:* Attorney at the LG I-III and notary, after the National Socialist seizure of power in spring of 1933 he was disbarred; at the end of April he was readmitted to the Bar; at the end of 1935 his license as a notary was revoked; he was admitted to the Bar until the general occupational ban in 1938; he was a member of the Paul's Covenant Union of Non-Aryan Christians; later he was listed as "residence unknown." His wife Elisabeth was regarded as "Aryan;" he survived and moved to Rhineland-Palatinate.
*Sources:* Br.B. 32; TK 33; Liste der nichtzugel. RA, 25.4.33 (Nachtrag); *li; DJ 36, S. 314; MRRAK; BArch, R 3001 PAK; Mitt. bl. Reichsverband nichtarischer Christen, 6.12.1934; BG ; Ausk. Flechtmann

### Alexander-Katz, Heinrich Dr.

01/04/1897 Görlitz - no information
*Home address:* Ithweg 16, Zehlendorf
*Law firm address:* Wilhelmstr. 139, SW 48
*Additional information:* He had participated in the First World War, and had been awarded the EK II. Kl. He had been established as an

attorney since 1925, most recently admitted to the LG I-III. After the National Socialist seizure of power he was admitted as an attorney upon request. His wife Hildegard was considered non-Jewish, the couple had two children. According to the police of the RJM, he emigrated to London, Great Britain, on 01/18/1938. His house in Zehlendorf was sold, his law firm address was taken over by the attorney Dr. Wagner.
*Sources:* Br.B. 32; TK 33; *li; BArch, R 3001 PAK, PA; BG

### Alexander-Katz, Richard Dr., Judicial Councillor

No information - 1934
*Home address:* no further information available
*Law firm address:* Belle-Alliance-Str. 46 a, SW 29
*Additional information:* After the National Socialist seizure of power he was admitted again as an attorney to the KG upon request; according to the entry in the personnel files of the RJM A. died in 1934.
*Sources:* Adr.B. 32; TK 33; *li; BArch, R 3001 PAK

### Alsberg, Max Prof. Dr.

10/16/1877 Bonn - 09/11/1933 Samaden, Schweiz
*Home address:* Jagowstr. 22, Grunewald
*Law firm address:* Nollendorfplatz 1, W 30
*Additional information:* Attorney from 1906-1933, most recently at the LG I-III, and notary in Berlin; established a law firm together with Kurt Poschke, Dr. Kurt Gollnick and Dr. Lothar Welt; the law firm was located at Nollendorfplatz. He was one of the most prominent defenders of the Weimar Republic (for example, in the process against the "Ringverein Immertreu"), also in political trials (for example against Carl von Ossietzky). Lecturer at the University of Berlin, as of 1931 an honorary professor, member of the Board of Trustees for Legal training and Professional Training and the Criminal Law Association of Berlin Lawyers. After the National Socialist seizure of power, the RAK Berlin on 5/11/1933 had placed him on a list of attorneys who were not to

be admitted for political reasons. The reason
for this was listed as the "Verteidigung im
Landesverratsprozess Ossietzky, Material:
Zeitungsnachrichten" ("Defense in the
Ossietzky court proceedings, material:
newspaper news"). His license as a notary
was suspended at the beginning of July 1933.
He fled to Baden-Baden, then to Switzerland,
stayed briefly in Zurich and then went to
a sanatorium in Samaden, where he shot
himself.

Numerous publications, including:
Justizirrtum und Wiederaufnahme
[Miscarriage of justice and revision of
judgments], 1913; Der Prozeß des Sokrates
im Lichte moderner Psychologie [The trial of
Socrates in the light of modern psychology],
1926; Große Prozesse der Weltgeschichte
[Great trials of world history], 1928;
Drama: Voruntersuchung [Drama: the
pre-trial investigation], 1930; Philosophie
der Verteidigung [The philosophy of legal
defense], 1930; Editor of Zeitschrift für
die gesamte Strafrechtswissenschaft [The
journal for criminal law], Kriminalistischen
Monatshefte [Criminology monthly]; a
number of works have been published
about him, e.g. Jungfer, G.: Max Alsberg.
Verteidigung als ethische Mission [Defense
as a moral undertaking]; in: KJ (Editor):
Streitbare Juristen [Polemical jurists]. Eine
andere Tradition [A different tradition].
Baden-Baden 1988; Riess, Curt: Der Mann
in der schwarzen Robe [The man in the black
robe]. Hamburg 1965.
*Sources:* Br.B. 32; TK 33; GStA, Rep. 84 a,
Nr. 20363; JMBl. 7.7.33, S. 208; Pr.J. 33,
S. 442; LAB, Unterlagen zum versteigerten
Eigentum [Documents concerning property
sold by auction]; Walk; Göpp. (with numerous
references); 1965; corrections together with
his daughter Renate (USA)

### Altenberg, Bruno Dr.

09/04/1889 Berlin -no information
*Home address:* Stübbenstr. 10, W 30
*Law firm address:* Roonstr. 2, A 1
*Additional information:* He had worked
for the Prussian Ministry of War during the
First World War. He was unable to fight in
the war because of health reasons, attorney
at the KG and notary. After the National
Socialist seizure of power in spring of 1933
occupational ban, his service during the First

World War was not acknowledged despite
numerous intercessions. His law firm, which
was in the immediate vicinity of the Reichstag
and the law partnership with Jakob Auerbach
was dissolved.
*Sources:* Jüd.Adr.B.; Br.B. 32: TK 33; Liste
d. nichtzugel. RA, 25.4.33; JMBl. 4.8.33, S.
253; BArch, R 3001 PAK

### Altenberg, Oskar Dr.

12/20/1893 Berlin - Deportation 1943
*Home address:* Bregenzer Str. 3, W 15
*Law firm address:* Potsdamer Str. 40,
Spandau
*Additional information:* He took part in
the First World War from June 1915 to
November 1918, most recently as a NCO
and was awarded the EK II.Kl. Attorney
at the KG (since 1924) and notary (since
1930) in partnership with Alfons Loewe;
after the National Socialist seizure of power
in 1933 he was readmitted. In 1935, based
on groundless accusations, disciplinary
proceedings were initiated at the instigation
of the Gestapo, but then later abandoned.
In 1935 his license as a notary was revoked.
Because of his difficult economic situation,
he applied for a subsidy with the Judge of the
Court of Appeals in Berlin. Since there were
no grounds for political doubts, this was
granted in the amount of RM 70. He worked
as an attorney until the general occupational
ban in 1938, after which he was admitted as a
"consultant." The last letter in his personnel
files dates back to 09/16/1941, he outlines
his duties as a Jewish consultant, which he
undertook for the consultant Dr. Alfred
"Israel" Karpen. Transported on 06/28/1943
to Auschwitz.
*Sources:* Br.B. 32; *li; DJ 36, S. 314; BArch, R
3001 PAK, PA; BG; GB II

### Alterthum, Willy Dr.

12/05/1879 Berlin - no information
*Home address:* Waldseestr. 8, Reinickendorf
*Law firm address:* Wilhelmstr. 44, W 8
*Additional information:* He was born at
Spandauer Brücke Street no. 14; on the
maternal side, he came from the Blumenthal
family from Oranienburg (Havel), which
resided at Louisenplatz 5. He obtained his
doctorate in 1903. After the completion of
his legal studies he established himself as an
attorney. Since 1930 he was full-time director

of the RAK. After the National Socialist seizure of power he was suspended as of 03/31/1933 and had to sign a dissolution contract on 10/25/1933. His admittance was granted upon request, since he was considered an "elderly attorney," but his subsequent attempts to establish himself as an attorney failed. That is why he decided to emigrate together with his family. He was disbarred on 09/04/1934. On 10/29/1934 he arrived with his family in Brazil and settled down in Sao Paulo. Last sentences of his memoirs, 11/07/1944: "We found a home but not a native land in Brazil. Our native land is the entire world, with all its light and life. Filled with awe, love and thanks we embrace it with our view. We had the good fortune to become citizens of the world." Numerous publications, amongst others in Berliner Anwaltsblatt.
*Sources:* Br.B. 32; TK 33; *li; Verz.; LAB, Liste 15.10.33; BArch, R 3001 PAK; LBI, NY, Memoirs; BG

**Altmann, Franz Dr.**
05/26/1900 Breslau - no information
*Home address:* Jägerstr. 11, W 8
*Law firm address:* Frankfurter Allee 50, O 112 (Adr.B. 32: Jägerstr. 11)
*Additional information:* Attorney at the LG I-III and the AG Berlin-Mitte. After the National Socialist seizure of power in the spring of 1933, he emigrated to New York, USA on 01/01/1934.
*Sources:* TK 33; Liste d. nichtzugel. RA, 25.4.33; Verz.; JMBl. 33, S. 253; BArch, R 3001 PAK; BG

**Altmann, Paul Dr.**
07/29/1901 Berlin - 1954 Kfar Witkin, Israel
*Home address:* Herkomerstr. 12, Treptow
*Law firm address:* Wilhelminenhof 82 a, Oberschöneweide
*Additional information:* Attorney at the AG Köpenick and the LG I-III. After the National Socialist seizure of power he was made subject to an occupational ban in July 1933; 1937-39 at the Palestine Office in Berlin; 1939 emigration to Palestine; after 1945 he was involved in the drafting of the reparation laws.
*Sources:* Adr.B. 32; TK 33; Verz.; JMBl. 33, S. 209; BArch, R 3001 PAK; BG; Walk

**Amberg, Dr. Carl (Karl)**
01/20/1884 - no information

*Home address:* no information
*Law firm address:* Dircksenstr. 26/27, C 25
*Additional information:* After the National Socialist seizure of power readmitted as attorney and notary upon request; end of 1935 license as notary was revoked; worked as an attorney until at least 1936.
*Sources:* TK 33; *li; Verz.; DJ 36, S. 314; Liste 36; BArch, R 3001 PAK

**Ambos, Hans Dr.**
04/10/1897 Berlin - no information
*Home address:* Wichmannstr. 25, W 62
*Law firm address:* Dresdener Str. 124, SO 36
*Additional information:* Attorney at the LG I-III, at the AG Berlin-Mitte and notary. After the National Socialist seizure of power he was readmitted as attorney and notary upon request; end of 1935 license as notary was revoked, ceased working as an attorney before 1936; last lived in Berlin in a guesthouse; emigration to Brussels, Belgium, in May 1939; was transported to unoccupied France during the war and interned there.
*Sources:* Br.B. 32; TK 33; *li; DJ 36, S. 314; BArch, R 3001 PAK; VZ 39; BG

**Anders, Rudolf**
04/14/1889 Berlin - no information
*Home address:* Zähringer Str. 20-21, Wilmersdorf
*Law firm address:* Gleditschstr. 47, W 30
*Additional information:* He had participated in the First World War, 1914 as an orderly, 1915, after the second state examination in law, conscripted to the army; attorney (since 1919) at the KG (since 1922) and notary (since 1928); After the National Socialist seizure of power he was readmitted upon request, had to dissolve his law firm established with non-Jewish partner attorney Werda, moved the law firm to Charlottenburg; 1935 license as notary was revoked, worked as an attorney until general occupational ban in 1938; emigration.
*Sources:* Br.B. 32; TK 33; *li; DJ 36, S. 314; BArch, R 3001 PAK, PA; MRRAK; BG

**Apfel, Alfred Dr.**
03/12/1882 Düren/Eifel - 06/20/1940 Marseille, Frankreich
*Home address:* no information
*Law firm address:* Friedrichstr. 59/60, W 8 (Moca-Efti-Haus)

*Additional information:* 1900 he took his
school leaving examination; 1900-1903 he
completed his law studies; 1903 he took
his first state examination in law; 1906 he
completed his doctorate in Rostock; military
service, he attended a military academy, was
not promoted because of Jewish descent; he
was a war volunteer in 1914, he was awarded
the EK I; he resigned from the military service
in 1916 due to health reasons; then he was a
legal adviser in business; since 1919 he was
an attorney in Berlin, last at the LG I-III
and AG Berlin-Mitte, later also a notary, he
was a well-known criminal defence lawyer,
even in political processes, e.g. as one of the
representatives of Carl von Ossietzky; 1909–
1922 President of the Association of Jewish
Youth Clubs of Germany; until 1922 he was
a member of the board of directors in the CV,
then a member of the Zionist Association for
Germany. After the burning of the Reichstag
arrested on 02/28/1933, taken into so-called
"protective custody"; after release he flew to
France; on 08/23/1933 he was denaturalized.
He died in June 1940 in Marseilles at the age
of 58.
*Publications:* Behind the Scenes of German
Justice. Reminiscences of a German Barrister
1882-1933, London 1935.
*Sources:* Br.B. 32; TK 33; BArch, R 3001
PAK; BG; BHdE, Bd. 1, S. 17 (date of death:
06/19/1940); Walk; Lowenthal; Göpp., S. 266

**Apt, Bruno Dr.**
12/03/1880 Cosel - 12/19/1943 Theresienstadt
*Home address:* Mommsenstr. 22,
Charlottenburg
*Law firm address:* Schöneberger Ufer 34,
W 35
*Additional information:* Attorney at LG
I-III and notary. After the National Socialist
seizure of power he was readmitted as
attorney and notary upon request; in 1933 he
had to dissolve the partnership with Prof. Dr.
Max Apt (presumably his brother) and change
the law firm address; at the end of 1935 his
license as a notary was suspended; practiced
until general occupational ban in 1938;
was still working as a "consultant" from
his home. Transportation on 08/31/1942 to
Theresienstadt, died there in December 1943.
*Sources:* Br.B. 32; *li; DJ 36, S. 314;
MRRAK; Liste d. Kons., 15.3.39; Tel.B. 41;
BG; ThG; GB II

**Apt, Max Prof. Dr.**
06/16/1869 Groß-Strelitz - 12/11/1957 Berlin
*Home address:* Pücklerstr. 8, SO 36
*Law firm address:* Unter den Linden 39, NW 7
*Additional information:* Law studies in
Breslau, Leipzig, Berlin and Freiburg; obtained
doctorate in 1891 in Freiburg; assistant to the
Director of the National Bank of Germany
(later DANAT Bank); senior managing director
of the Elders Council of the Governing Council
of the Berlin Mercantile Community; in 1893
co-founder of the CV in Berlin; 1900-1937
board member of the Deutsch-Israelitischer
Gemeindebund (German Federation of
Jewish Communities) in Berlin; 1903-1920
in-house counsel to the Korporation der
Kaufmannschaft von Berlin (Association of
the Berlin Mercantile Community) ; 1906
co-founder, later trustee and honorary
professor of the Handelshochschule Berlin
(Berlin Commercial College); founder and
editor of trade journals, amongst others the
"Deutsche Wirtschaftszeitung," and editor
of the collection of texts entitled "Deutsche
Reichsgesetzgebung"; member of the German
Democratic Party (DDP) and of Bnai Brith;
Zionist official. After the National Socialist
seizure of power his license as attorney at the
LG I-III and as notary were revoked in May
1933. 1938 delegate of the Jewish Community
to Berlin at the Conference of Evian; 1939
emigration to Great Britain; return to Berlin
1954.
*Sources:* Br.B. 32; TK 33; JMBl. 19.5.33;
BArch, R 3001 PAK; BG; BHdE Bd. 1, S. 17
(date of death 12/16/1957); Walk; Göpp., S.
326; Lowenthal

**Arens, Fritz**
05/11/1893 Lubichow - no information
*Home address:* Kleiststr. 13, Charlottenburg
*Law firm address:* Wielandstr. 30,
Charlottenburg 4
*Additional information:* Attorney at LG I-III,
AG Charlottenburg and notary. After the
National Socialist seizure of power in 1933
he was still accredited as attorney and notary,
however, changed his law firm address. At the
end of 1935 his license as notary was revoked;
emigration via Great Britain to Buenos Aires,
Argentina, on 09/01/1936. A warrant was
issued against him for tax code violations.
*Sources:* Br.B. 32; TK 33; *li; DJ 36, S. 314;
BArch, R 3001 PAK; BG; Wolf, BFS

## Arndt, Adolf Dr.

03/12/1904 Königsberg - 02/13/1974 Kassel
*Home address:* Kurfürstendamm 186,
Charlottenburg
*Law firm address:* Lützowufer 19 b, W 35
*Additional information:* During the 1920s
he worked at the law firm address of the
well-known defense lawyer Prof. Alsberg.
He subsequently worked as a judge, among
other things he was a correspondent in
the proceedings against George Grosz
for blasphemy. Due to his insistent legal
advocacy, which he also espoused through
various legal publications, his political
activites attracted the attention of the
National Socialists. After the National
Socialist seizure of power this familiarity,
together with the fact that he was a "half-
Jew" (he had been baptised as a child),
became a personal threat. After the National
Socialist seizure of power he left his position
as judge. Surprisingly, also to him, in
August/September 1933 his application
for admission as a lawyer was granted. He
then formed a law partnership with the
attorney Fritz Schönbeck. He represented
various larger companies (Blum & Haas),
but also "degenerate" defamatory artists and
politically persecuted personalities such as
Wilhelm Leuschner, who was later murdered,
and the last chairman of the General German
Trade Union Confederation (ADGB),
Theodor Leipart. He was interested in fine
arts and acquired paintings by Xaver Fuhr,
Schmidt-Rottluff, amongst others. Through
his marriage to a woman who was regarded
as "Aryan," he was partially protected from
massive attacks, because of his "mixed race"
status he was allowed to work as an attorney
after the general occupational ban of 1938
(and not as a "consultant").
However, he could not practice unhindered,
e.g., he could no longer appear as a legal
representative in divorce proceedings of
Jewish and non-Jewish spouses. In the fall
of 1943 he was forced to work as an auditor
for the Askania factory, regarded as essential
for armament, a few months later, in July
1944, he was used by the Todt organization
as a forced laborer, amongst other at the
evacuation of the Gestapo headquarters in
Paris ("Aktion Hase"). Later he had to work
for a Saarland company. As a forced laborer,
he was forbidden to visit shelters during the
air raids of the Allieds. In January 1945,
after being weakened physically from various
serious illnesses, he reunited with his wife
and daughter, who had fled to Silesia from
Berlin, by means of falsified documents. He
returned to his office to prevent difficulties
for his superiors. A little later he made his
way to Silesia again to encourage his family
to flee westward. The family left with a
suitcase in February 1945 and found shelter
in Westphalia. He was still in danger of
being identified as a "Jew" and experienced
liberation in Westphalia. He was able to get
from there to Marburg, where his mother
lived, which was in the American zone. In
August 1945 he was admitted as an attorney
and notary in Marburg, for a while he was
also a senior public prosecutor. In November
1945 became undersecretary in the Hessian
Ministry of Justice.
As early as 1933 the Social Democratic
Reichstag delegate Otto Wels had left a
lasting impression on him. He championed
the social balance within society and became
a confidante of Kurt Schumacher and a
member of the SPD parliamentary group
in the German Bundestag. "Right" and
"democracy" were the leading ideas in his
political actions; he enjoyed a particularly
high reputation as a speaker. Under Willy
Brandt's aegis as governing mayor of Berlin,
he took over the office of Senator for Science
and Arts for one year during 1962/63. He
died in February 1974.
*Sources:* *li; JMBl. 2.9.33; LAB, Liste
Mschlg. 36; Tel.B. 41; Walk; Gosewinkel,
Dieter: Adolf Arndt. Die Wiederbegründung
des Rechtsstaats aus dem Geist der
Sozialdemokratie (1945-1961) [The rebirth
of the rule of law from the spirit of social
democracy (1945-1961)] , Bonn 1991;
Munzinger-Arch.; Ausk. d. Tochter, Dr. Y.
Arndt und des Sohnes Prof. Claus Arndt

## Arndt, Ernst Moritz

04/06/1901 Königsberg - 01/20/1980
*Home address:* Wilmersdorfer Str. 95,
Charlottenburg 4
*Law firm address:* Kaiserdamm 17,
Charlottenburg 5
*Additional information:* He was the brother
of Adolf Arndt. He was admitted to the
KG as an attorney; in April 1933 he was
subject to an occupational ban, but was soon

readmitted — which was peculiar, since he could not claim any exemptions. Because he was considered of "mixed race," he could work as an attorney until at least 1940 after the general occupational ban in 1938.
*Sources:* TK 33; *li; LAB, Liste Mschlg. 36; VZ 39; Tel.B. 41; Ausk. Nichte Dr. Y. Arndt; Ausk. Maria Haendcke-Hoppe-Arndt

**Arnheim, Charlotte Dr., geb. Peiser**
06/23/1904 Berlin - no information
*Home address:* no further information
*Law firm address:* Feuerbachstr. 7/9, Steglitz
*Additional information:* Attorney since 06/30/1932, after the National Socialist seizure of power she applied for readmission, she also stated in her argument that she was going through a divorce and could not expect any assistance from her husband, her readmission was denied and she was made subject to an occupational ban, "because she was not of Aryan descent."
*Sources:* JMBl. 33, S. 209; BArch, R 3001 PAK, PA

**Arnheim, Fritz Anselm Dr.**
05/06/1890 Berlin - internment 1942
*Home address:* Nürnberger Str. 66, Schöneberg
*Law firm address:* Kronenstr. 76, W 8
*Additional information:* Attorney at the LG I-III and notary. After the National Socialist seizure of power he was readmitted again as attorney and notary upon request; in 1933 he relocated his law firm; at the end of 1935 his license as a notary was revoked; he was admitted as an attorney up to the general occupational ban in 1938. No further information is available for the years until his transportation. His declaration of property was signed on 08/08/1942. He went to the collection point Artilleriestr. 31, was transported on 08/17/1942 to Theresienstadt and on 10/19/1944 was transported to Auschwitz.
*Sources:* Br.B. 32; TK 33; *li; DJ 36, S. 314; MRRAK; BArch, R 3001 PAK; BG; ThG; GB II

**Arnheim, Georg**
03/21/1872 - internment 1942
*Home address:* no further information available
*Law firm address:* Brunnenstr. 194, N 54

*Additional information:* Attorney at the LG I-III, AG Berlin-Mitte and notary. After the National Socialist seizure of power in 1933 his license as a notary was revoked, he was admitted as an attorney up to the general occupational ban in 1938. Transportation on 01/13/1942 to Riga.
Br.B. 32; TK 33; JMBl. 30.6.33, S. 202; *li; Liste 36; BArch, R 3001 PAK; MRRAK; VZ 39; GB II

**Arnheim, Hugo Dr., Judicial Councillor**
11/11/1862 Berlin - 02/26/1943 Theresienstadt
*Home address:* Waitzstr. 6, Charlottenburg
*Law firm address:* Landgrafenstr. 6, W 62
*Additional information:* Attorney at the KG and notary. After the National Socialist seizure of power readmitted as attorney and notary; at the end of 1935 his license as a notary was revoked; he was admitted as an attorney up to the general occupational ban in 1938. Transportation on 01/12/1943 to Theresienstadt, he died there after only a few weeks.
*Sources:* Br.B. 32; TK 33; *li; DJ 36, S. 314; BArch, R 3001 PAK; MRRAK; BG; g; ThG; GB II

**Arnheim, Julius Dr.**
12/26/1874 Alt-Valm - no information
*Home address:* Güntzelstr. 63, Wilmersdorf
*Law firm address:* Güntzelstr. 63, Wilmersdorf
*Additional information:* Attorney at the LG I-III and notary. After the National Socialist seizure of power readmitted as attorney upon request, his license as a notary was revoked in 1933. The partnership had to be dissolved in 1933, the law firm had to be relocated. Admitted as an attorney up to the general occupational ban of 1938. On 09/02/1940 he could emigrate to Mexico.
*Sources:* Br.B. 32; TK 33; JMBl. 30.6.33, S. 202; *li; MRRAK; BArch, R 3001 PAK; BG

**Arnheim, Rudolf Dr.**
02/26/1875 Mannheim - 07/01/1943 Theresienstadt
*Home address:* Pfalzburger Str. 85-86, W 15
*Law firm address:* Pfalzburger Str. 85-86, W 15
*Additional information:* Attorney at LG I-III, AG Charlottenburg and notary. After the National Socialist seizure of power in 1933

his license as a notary was revoked, upon request he was readmitted as an attorney up to the general occupational ban in 1938. He signed the declaration of property on 09/30/1942; collection point Artilleriestr. 31; on 10/03/1942 transported to Theresienstadt, where he perished in the summer of 1943.
*Sources:* Br.B. 32; TK 33; JMBl. 30.6.33, S. 202; *li; DJ 36, S. 314; BArch, R 3001 PAK; MRRAK; BG; ThG; GB II

**Arnold, Fritz W. Dr.**
02/03/1894 Charlottenburg - 12/21/1980 Lemgo
*Home address:* Konstanzer Str. 51, Wilmersdorf
*Law firm address:* Unter den Linden 71, NW 7
*Additional information:* He had been seriously injured as a participant in the First World War (leg amputation); attorney since 1926, admitted to LG I-III and AG Berlin-Mitte, at the same time notary. After the National Socialist seizure of power he was readmitted as an attorney and notary upon request, because he had been a "frontline fighter." At the end of 1935 his license as a notary was revoked; he practiced as an attorney up to the general occupational ban of 1938; thereafter he worked as a "consultant"; from 1939/40 he worked in the advisory council of the office of Pastor Grüber. At the end of September 1942 he managed to escape to Basel, Switzerland, with the help of "Unternehmen Sieben." 1946 he emigrated to New York, USA, where he studied American law. In the 1960s he returned to Germany, where he died in 1980.
*Sources:* Br.B. 32; TK 33; *li; DJ 36, S. 314; MRRAK; Liste d. Kons., 15.3.39; Tel.B. 41; BG; Göpp., S. 32; Ausk. Dorothee Fliess

**Aron, Ludwig Dr.**
07/13/1894 - no information
*Home address:* no further information
*Law firm address:* Friedrichstr. 59/60, W 8
*Additional information:* Attorney at LG I-III. After the National Socialist seizure of power general occupational ban on 06/16/1933.
*Sources:* Br.B. 32; TK 33; Liste d. nichtzugel. RA, 25.4.33; JMBl. 33, S. 253; BArch, R 3001 PAK, PA

**Arons, Albert Dr.**
08/12/1898 Berlin - 07/22/1948 Grenoble
*Home address:* Königsweg 24, Charlottenburg
*Law firm address:* Mohrenstr. 9, W 8
*Additional information:*
He had been seriously injured as a volunteer in the First World War and was awarded the EK. Was admitted as an attorney to LG I-III and AG Berlin-Mitte. After the National Socialist seizure of power he was readmitted as an attorney because of his "frontline" service.
In 1935 the family of four spent Christmas in Switzerland, there the parents informed their daughters that they would not be returning to Berlin. At the beginning of April the family arrived in Portugal; the preferred countries of emigration were "all filled up." (R. Arons). Previously, they had spent five days in Paris to make it appear that they were on vacation. The family had no connections in Portugal other than a business card that the grandmother had received from a woman who had emigrated to Portugal. This woman took the family in and helped them to build a new life.
He could no longer work as an attorney, because he did not have social contacts and his degrees were not recognized. Up to that point the career of a salesman was looked at with scorn, but now he had to turn to this line of activity to support his family. He tried to export sardines in oil, but failed. In 1948, he died from pulmonary emphysema during a vacation trip to Switzerland.
One daughter in Portugal graduated from high school and then studied philosophy and history. Up until the day he died the politically conservative father frequently found himself in conflict with the daughter, who was a political activist who adhered to more liberal views. In Berlin the family had a casual adherence to Jewish traditions, after the war broke out fundamental doubts about the existence of God grew in strength; the daughter became an atheist. She is quoted as saying: "Are you religious?" – "No, thank God!" The daughter came to identify with Portugal as her native land, for many years she spoke no German. She campaigned for political changes in Portugal, her son was temporarily a member of the Socialist government.

*Sources:* Br.B. 32; TK 33; *li; DJ 36, S. 106; BArch, R 3001 PAK, PA; BG; Ausk. R. Arons

**Aronsohn, Georg, Judicial Councillor**
10/03/1867 Bromberg –
01/17/1943-01/18/1943
Theresienstadt
*Home address:*
Regensburger Straße
*Law firm address:*
Kaiserallee 26, Wilmersdorf
*Additional information:* An attorney in
Bromberg, he opted for Germany in 1920
and moved with his family to Berlin. There
he was admitted as an attorney, most recently
at the LG I-III and the AG Charlottenburg
and he was appointed as a notary. After the
National Socialist seizure of power in 1933
he was readmitted as an attorney and notary
upon request, since he had been recognized
as an "elderly attorney." In 1934, he defended
his colleague Ludwig Bendix in a trial that
ended with an acquittal. At the end of 1935
his license as a notary was revoked. His law
firm was dissolved as part of the general
occupational ban of 11/30/1938, afterwards
he still worked as a "consultant." His
daughters managed to emigrate, his wife died
of cancer in July 1939. He was transported
on 10/03/1942 to Theresienstadt, where he
succumbed to a stroke after a few months.
The cause of the stroke was the knowledge
that his name was listed on a transportation
list "to the East." His second wife was taken
to Auschwitz after his death and murdered
with other relatives.
*Sources:* Br.B. 32; TK 33; *li; DJ 36, S.
314; MRRAK; ThG; GB II (here: date of
death given as 01/17/1943); Göpp., S. 238;
Proskauer, E.: Paths and detours (here: date of
death given as 01/18/1943)

**Aronsohn, Max, Judicial Councillor**
06/07/1854 Berlin - 01/04/1939
*Home address:* no further information
available
*Law firm address:* Potsdamer Str. 116 III, W 35
*Additional information:* Attorney at the KG;
after the National Socialist seizure of power
in 1933 he was readmitted upon request
(presumably as "elderly attorney"); he worked
as an attorney until the general occupational
ban of 1938. He died in 1939 at the age of 85.

*Sources:* Br.B. 32; TK 33, *li; DJ 36, S. 314;
BArch, R 3001 PAK; MRRAK; Tel.B. 38; BG

**Asch, Adolf Dr.**
02/27/1881 Posen (now known as Poznan) -
1972 London
*Home address:* Tauentzienstr. 11, W 50
*Law firm address:* Tauentzienstr. 11, W 50
*Additional information:* He had participated
in the First World War and was seriously
wounded. He returned as a war invalid with
50 per cent severe wounds. Admitted as an
attorney to the KG, at the same as a time
notary; after 1918 chairman of the Berlin
conciliation committee; in-house counsel
for Romanian law; board member of the
Verein für Bodenreform (Association for
Land Reform); board member of the Verein
der Kammergerichtsanwälte (Association of
Attorneys of the Court of Appeals in Berlin).
After the National Socialist seizure of power
he was made subject to an occupational ban
for six weeks as from April 1933, upon request
he was readmitted as attorney at the KG and
notary; since he had been recognized as a
"frontline fighter." At the end of 1935 his
license as a notary was revoked; he practiced
as an attorney until the general occupational
ban in 1938. Arrested on the Night of Broken
Glass of November 1938 and was interned in
the Sachsenhausen concentration camp; there
he contracted eye disease and sciatica; after his
release he worked as a "consultant" for a short
period. In January 1939 emigration to England;
lived in Manchester together with his wife
and his son, who had completed studies as a
chemist in Milan, until he joined the Air Force.
Worked as a packer from 1941-45. His wife
helped to support them with language teaching.
The daughter survived an internment camp in
France, later final relocation to London.
*Sources:* Br.B. 32; TK 33; *li; DJ 36, S. 314;
BArch, R 3001 PAK; MRRAK; LAB, Liste d.
Kons.; LBI; BG; Walk

**Asch, Albert Dr., Judicial Councillor**
1864 Posen - 1936 Berlin
*Home address:* no information
*Law firm address:* Nymphenburger Str. 7,
Schöneberg
*Additional information:* Attorney at the KG
and notary; was the father of Ernst and Walter;
after the National Socialist seizure of power
readmitted upon request, presumably as "elderly

attorney." At the end of 1935 his license as a notary was revoked and he was disbarred; died 1936 at the age of 72.
*Sources:* TK 33; *li; DJ 36, S. 314; BArch, R 3001 PAK; BG; BHdE Bd. 1, S. 22 (Ash, Ernest E.); Ausk. Ruth Arons, 6.12.1998

**Asch, Ernst Dr.**
03/15/1890 Posen (now known as Poznan) - September 1980 New York
*Home address:* Reichsstr. 37, Charlottenburg
*Law firm address:* Kurfürstendamm 185, W 15
*Additional information:* Son of attorney and notary Albert; brother of attorney Walter; 1908-11 study in Geneva, Munich, Berlin, Kiel and Breslau; 1914-1919 military judge, awarded the EK II; attorney since 1919, most recently at LG I-III, since 1923 also notary; international law specialist, legal advisor to domestic and foreign banks. After the National Socialist seizure of power in the summer of 1933 he was made subject to an occupational ban; 1938 brief detention; emigration to the Netherlands on 09/26/1938; in April 1940 he traveled further to Mexico; as from July 1940 in the USA; henceforth called himself Ernest Ash. As from 1940 investment consultant and stock market broker; also represented emigrants free of charge in reparation matters; died 1980 in New York.
*Sources:* Br.B. 32; TK 33; JMBl., S. 253; BG; BHdE Bd. 1, S. 22 (Ernest Ash); BArch, R 3001 PAK; SSDI; Ausk. Ruth Arons, 6.12.1998

**Asch, Walter Dr.**
04/08/1886 - 1972 (?) London
*Home address:* Berliner Str. 19, Charlottenburg
*Law firm address:* Friedrich-Karl-Ufer 2-4, NW 40
*Additional information:* Son of attorney and notary Albert; brother of attorney Ernst; worked temporarily as an attorney at AEG Berlin; attorney at the LG I-III. After the National Socialist seizure of power readmitted upon request, had to relocate his law firm in 1933; emigration to Great Britain in September 1938 (1936?); died in London in 1972.
*Sources:* Br.B. 32; TK 33; *li; BG; BHdE Bd. 1, S. 22 (Ash, Ernest E.); BArch, R 3001 PAK; Ausk. Ruth Arons, 6.12.1998

**Ascher, Bruno Dr.**
04/09/1887 Soldau/East Prussia - 08/26/1933 Berlin
*Home address:* Bellevuestr. 6a, W 9
*Law firm address:* Bellevuestr. 6a, W 9
*Additional information:* He had participated in the First World War, during which time he had contracted chronic stomach pain. Attorney at the LG I-III, the AG Berlin-Mitte and notary. After the National Socialist seizure of power, he was made subject to an occupational ban on 05/05/1933 that was rescinded after he had presented various clearance certificates and had provided proof of his frontline fighting activities. He died at the end of August 1933 at the age of 45.
*Sources:* Adr.B. 32; TK 33; Pr.J. 33, S. 390; BArch, R 3001 PAK, PA; Naatz-Album

**Ascher, Hermann**
01/12/1886 Berlin - 04/04/1942 Litzmannstadt/Lodz
*Home address:* Neue Königstr. 55-56, C 2
*Law firm address:* An der Spandauer Brücke 1b
*Additional information:* Attorney at the LG I-III and notary. After the National Socialist seizure of power his license as a notary was revoked; admitted as an attorney up to the general occupational ban in 1938. Transportation on 10/24/1942 to Litzmannstadt/Lodz; he died there six months later.
*Sources:* Br.B. 32; TK 33; JMBl. 30.6.33, S. 202; *li; Liste 36; MRRAK; BArch, R 3001 PAK; BG; GB II

**Aschheim, Carl Dr.**
01/17/1879 Berlin - transportation 1942
*Home address:* Landhausstr. 38, Wilmersdorf
*Law firm address:* Nürnberger Str. 53-55, W 50
*Additional information:* Attorney at the LG I-III and notary. After the National Socialist seizure of power in 1933 his license as a notary was revoked; he had to relocate his law firm; admitted as an attorney up to the general occupational ban in 1938. Date of declaration of property: 04/02/1942, transportation on 04/02/1942 to Warschau.
*Sources:* Br.B. 32; TK 33; JMBl. 33, S. 208; *li; BArch, R 3001 PAK; MRRAK; BG; GB II

**Aschkenasi, Ludwig**
03/07/1887 - no information
*Home address:* An der Apostelkirche 8, W 57

*Law firm address:* An der Apostelkirche 8,
W 57
*Additional information:* Attorney at the LG
I-III and notary; Gesellschafter der Jüdische
Verlag GmbH. After the National Socialist
seizure of power he was made subject to
an occupational ban in the spring of 1933;
emigration to Paris, France.
*Sources:* Br.B. 32; TK 33; Liste d. nichtzugel.
RA, 25.4.33; JMBl. 33, S. 253; BArch, R
3001 PAK; BG

**Auerbach, Dagobert Dr., JR**
07/27/1871 Posen (now known as Poznan) -
no information
*Home address:* Kaiser-Wilhelm-Platz 2-4,
Schöneberg
*Law firm address:* Kaiser-Wilhelm-Platz 2-4,
Schöneberg
*Additional information:* Attorney at the LG
I-III and notary, in partnership with Ernst
Pick; after the National Socialist seizure of
power in 1933 he was readmitted as attorney
and notary upon request; license as a notary
revoked at the end of 1935; admitted as an
attorney up to the general occupational ban in
1938; later emigration to Argentina.
*Sources:* Br.B. 32; TK 33; *li; DJ 36, S. 314;
MRRAK; BArch, R 3001 PAK; BG

**Auerbach, Ella, nee Levi**
01/15/1900 Frankfurt a. M. - 04/20/1999
New York
*Home address:* Matthäikirchplatz 5, W 35
*Law firm address:* Burgstr. 28, C 2
*Additional information:* After her first
state examination in law in 1922 Ella Levi
was sworn in as a clerk in Bad Homburg
during the same year. During her clerkship
she met Richard Auerbach, an attorney
from Berlin. They got married in 1925. Ella
could now continue her clerkship in Berlin.
After marriage she fluctuated as to whether
she should complete the traning, ultimately
decided to complete it. Two months before
the examination she was pregnant and took
leave. In 1926 their first daughter was born.
In February 1928 Ella took the second
state examination in law in Frankfurt; the
Frankfurter Zeitung reported this, because
she was the first female clerk at the Frankfurt
Higher Regional Court. On 03/18/1928 Ella
was the first woman to be admitted to the
Court of Appeals in Berlin, the Frankfurter

Zeitung published a report on this. In 1929
the second child, a son, was born. The
apartment of the family at Matthäikirchplatz
in Tiergarten was furnished in accordance
with current fashion trends of the time.
Until 1933 the couple worked together at
a law firm. After the National Socialist
seizure of power, Ella was made subject
to an occupational ban on 06/17/1933,
her husband, who was a former "frontline
fighter," was still allowed to work for a while,
until 1935 also as a notary.
After the Night of Broken Glass in November
1938, Richard was almost arrested and went
"underground." Now he was prepared to
heed his wife's urging to emigrate. In January
1939 the family emigrated to Great Britain,
because they had not been able to obtain
an emigration visa for the entire family.
Richard was interned in Great Britain at
the beginning of the war. After he had been
released again in July 1949, the whole family
was able to enter the USA in September 1940.
Ella had studied shorthand and typing. She
could find a job as a secretary and translator
in New York and could support the family.
In the meantime her husband retrained as
an auditor. In December 1940 she could
start work as a social worker at "Selfhelp for
German Emigrees," a self-help organization
started by Paul Tillich; later she was a board
member of this organization.
From 1950-53 Ella completed her education
as a social worker during evening courses at
Columbia University and thereafter took care
of the elderly. At the age of 66 she took four
semesters of comparative Jewish religious
history and later worked for a year at the
Federation of Jewish Philanthropies. She had
to give up this activity for health reasons and
worked for non-profit associations, amongst
others as president of the "sisterhood" of
the Habonim congegation and the women's
group of the Leo Baeck Institute. She died in
New York in 1999.
*Sources:* Br.B. 32; TK 33; Liste d. nichtzugel.
RA, 25.4.33; JMBl. 33, S. 209; BArch, R
3001 PAK, PA; BG; Jewish Immigr. U.S.A.,
Oral History, S. 5; BHdE Bd. 1, S. 24 (A.,
Richard Joseph); jurists; Ausk. Prof. Günther
und Frau Waltraud, 28.12.1998 u. 1999

**Auerbach, Felix**
01/30/1889 Gollantsch - transportation 1942

*Home address:* Helmstedter Str. 24, Wilmersdorf
*Law firm address:* Stresemannstr. 12, SW 11
*Additional information:* Attorney at LG I-III,
AG Berlin-Mitte and notary; after the National
Socialist seizure of power he was made subject
to an occupational ban in spring of 1933.
Transported on 07/11/1942, presumably to
Auschwitz.
*Sources:* Br.B. 32; TK 33; Liste d. nichtzugel.
RA, 25.4.33; JMBl. 33, S. 253; BArch, R 3001
PAK, PA; BG; GB II

**Auerbach, Friedlieb (Fritz) Dr.**
01/05/1888 - no information
*Home address:* no information
*Law firm address:* Dorotheenstr. 79, NW 7
*Additional information:* Had a law practice in
Berlin since 1918, most recently admitted to the
KG; after the National Socialist seizure of power
he was made subject to an occupational ban on
08/01/1933.
*Sources:* Br.B. 32; TK 33; Liste d. nichtzugel.
RA, 25.4.33; JMBl. 33, S. 282; BArch, R 3001
PAK, PA

**Auerbach, Gerhard**
02/19/1902 Berlin - no information
*Home address:* no information
*Law firm address:* Friedrichstr. 77, W 8
*Additional information:* Had a law practice
in Berlin since 1929, last admitted to the KG;
after the National Socialist seizure of power
he was made subject to an occupational ban
on 06/19/1933. He presumably emigrated to
Palestine.
*Sources:* Br.B. 32; TK 33; Liste d. nichtzugel.
RA, 25.4.33; JMBl. 33, S. 253; BArch, R 3001
PAK, PA

**Auerbach, Herbert Dr.**
07/27/1890 - no information
*Home address:* no information
*Law firm address:* Potsdamer Str. 138 a
*Additional information:* Attorney at the LG
I-III, AG Berlin-Mitte and notary; after the
National Socialist seizure of power he was made
subject to an occupational ban in the spring of
1933; emigrated 1936; a warrant was issued
against him for tax code violations.
*Sources:* Br.B. 32; TK 33; Liste d. nichtzugel.
RA; JMBl. 33, S. 253; BArch, R 3001 PAK;
Wolf, BFS

**Auerbach, Jakob (Isidor), Judicial Councillor**
05/30/188? - 06/20/1935

*Home address:* no information
*Law firm address:* Lützowufer 10
*Additional information:* Attorney at the LG I-III
and notary; after the National Socialist seizure of
power in 1933 he was readmitted upon request.
He died in 1935 at the age of 55 years.
*Sources:* Br.B. 32; TK 33; *li; LAB, Liste
15.10.33; BArch, R 3001 PAK; BG

**Auerbach, Jakob Dr.**
No information
*Home address:* Roonstr. 2, A 1
*Law firm address:* Roonstr. 2, A 1
*Additional information:* Attorney at the LG
I-III and notary. After the National Socialist
seizure of power in 1933 he was readmitted as
an attorney upon request, but license as a notary
was revoked; emigration to the Netherlands on
10/01/1937, disbarment on 12/27/1936.
*Sources:* Br.B. 32; TK 33; JMBl. 30.6.33,
S. 202; *li; BG; BArch, R 3001 PAK; Ausk.
Reich-Ranicki, 11.5.2000

**Auerbach, Kurt Berthold Dr.**
10/28/1893 – 03/24(28.?)/1941 Berlin
*Home address:* Mommsenstr. 22,
Charlottenburg
*Law firm address:* Lindenstr. 16/17, SW 68
*Additional information:* Attorney at the LG
I-III, AG Schöneberg and notary; after the
National Socialist seizure of power in 1933
he was readmitted upon request; end of 1935
license as notary was revoked; admitted as
attorney up to the general occupational ban in
1938. He died in 1941 at the age of 47 at the
Jewish Hospital.
*Sources:* Br.B. 32; TK 33; *li; DJ 36, S. 314;
MRRAK; BArch, R 3001 PAK; BG

**Auerbach, Leo**
No information
*Home address:* no information
*Law firm address:* Unter den Linden 56
*Additional information:* Attorney at the LG
I-III. After the National Socialist seizure of
power he was made subject to an occupational
ban in the spring of 1933; was in a relationship
with a "non-Jew" and later married; went to
France with a Mexican passport; became a
member of the Foreign Legion and managed
their library in North Africa; survived and lived
in Hesse after liberation.
*Sources:* Br.B. 32; TK 33; Liste d. nichtzugel.
RA; JMBl. 33, S. 220; BArch, R 3001 PAK;

Reich-Ranicki: Mein Leben, 1999, S. 137/38;
ergänz. Mitteil. 11.5.2000

**Auerbach, Leonhard Dr.**
10/23/1891 Berlin - 02/11/1961 Berlin
*Home address:* Lindauer Str. 8, Schöneberg
*Law firm address:* Kleiststr. 26, W 26
*Additional information:* Attorney at the LG
I-III and notary; after the National Socialist
seizure of power he was readmitted upon
request as attorney, but the joint law address
with a non-Jewish partner was dissolved;
1935 license as notary was revoked; 1938
general occupational ban as attorney.
Worked from 1939 to December 1940 in
the Grüber Office (for the support of "non-
Aryan" Christians; he belonged to the Reich
association of the same name); advisor on
imprisonment, concentration camps, eviction,
emigration affairs and legal questions,
afterwards as a "consultant"on a temporary
basis; was conscripted to do clean-up work,
from August to November 1943 at the
Wuhlheide labor camp; became seriously ill
and was operated upon by Grüber co-worker
Dr. Jaffé at home; then forced laborer in
an armament business and then an office
supply business. He had a so-called "mixed
race" marriage, his wife was regarded as
"Aryan."After 1945 once again attorney and
notary in Berlin (East), as of 1949 honorary
professor at the Free University of Berlin,
which he helped to establish.
*Sources:* Br.B. 32; TK 33; *li; DJ 36, S.
314; MRRAK; BArch, R 3001 PAK; Mitt.
bl. Reichsverband nichtarischer Christen
6.12.1934; BG; Göpp, S. 327f.

**Auerbach, Max Dr.**
08/11/1887 Berlin - no information
*Home address:* Lietzenburger Str. 13, W 15
*Law firm address:* Ritterstr. 54
*Additional information:* Attorney at the
KG and notary. After the National Socialist
seizure of power the question of his admission
as a lawyer and notary was disputed over
a period of several months. Finally he was
still admitted. At the end of 1935 his license
as a notary was revoked; before the general
occupational ban of 1938 he was removed
from the list of attorneys. He emigrated to
Great Britain.
*Sources:* Adr.B. 32; Pr.J. 33, S. 532 u. 840; DJ
36, S. 314; Liste 36; BArch, R 3001 PAK; BG

**Auerbach, Richard Joseph Dr.**
02/06/1892 Posen (now known as Poznan) -
09/01/1980 New York
*Home address:* Matthäikirchplatz 5, W 35
*Law firm address:* Burgstr. 28, C 2
*Additional information:* Studied in
Heidelberg, Berlin und Halle; 1914-18 soldier
in First World War, frontline duty; 1919
doctorate in Breslau; judge as from 1921, as
from 1923 attorney in Berlin; got to know
his later wife Ella in the mid-1920s; marriage
in 1925. Ella became his law partner in
1928. He was admitted as an attorney from
the beginning of 1933 at the LG I-III, at AG
Berlin-Mitte and also as a notary; 1921-
1938 board member of the Jewish student
association "Kartell Convent." After the
National Socialist seizure of power his wife
and other law partner, Dr. Max Raphael,
were disbarred. He went into partnership
with Wilhelm Goldberg. His wife continued
to help him with legal work. Disciplinary
proceedings were started against him, and
he was acquitted, despite violent anti-Semitic
agitation. His license as a notary was revoked
at the end of 1935; he worked as an attorney
up to the general occupational ban. He
barely escaped arrest after the pogrom in
November 1938 and had to go underground
for some time. His wife persuaded him to
emigrate. In January 1939 the family and
their two children went to Great Britain.
At the beginning of the war in 1939 he was
interned for four months on the Isle of Man.
After his release the family left the country
in September 1940 for New York, USA. For
a while his wife supported the family, while
he studied business with the objective of
becoming an auditor; they could not afford
renewed legal studies. 1945 examinations,
then worked until 1949 as an auditor,
thereafter self-employed; he also dealt with
reparations; official in Jewish organizations
and associations. The couple lived in New
York, where he died in 1980 at the age of 88.
*Sources:* Br.B. 32; TK 33; *li; LAB, 15.10.33;
DJ 36, S. 314; MRRAK; BArch, R 3001 PAK;
BG; BHdE Bd. 1, S. 24

**Aufrecht, Ernst**
No information
*Home address:* no information
*Law firm address:* Seydelstr. 31, SW 19
*Additional information:* Attorney at the LG

I-III, AG Berlin-Mitte and notary; after the National Socialist seizure of power in 1933 his license as a notary was revoked; worked as an attorney up to the general occupational ban in 1938.
*Sources:* Br.B. 32; TK 33; JMBl. 30.6.33, S. 202; *li; Liste 36; MRRAK; BArch, R 3001 PAK

# B

## Bab, Hans
10/19/1905 Schneidemühl - 02/12/1989 Chile
*Home address:* no information
*Law firm address:* Nürnberger Platz 3, W 50
*Additional information:* Attorney at the LG I-III and AG Berlin-Mitte. After the National Socialist seizure of power he was made subject to an occupational ban on 06/20/1933, despite numerous efforts to remain employed, he emigrated in a timely manner and most recently lived in Chile; he died there in 1989 at the age of 83.
*Sources:* TK 33; Liste d. nichtzugel. RA, 25.4.33; JMBl. 33, S. 253; BArch, R 3001 PAK, PA; Ausk. T. Krach

## Bach, Julian Dr.
01/30/1882 Posen (now known as Poznan) - 08/26/1942 Berlin
*Home address:* Auguststr. 14-15, Hospital N 4
*Law firm address:* Hauptstr. 156, Schöneberg
*Additional information:* Attorney at the LG I-III, AG Schöneberg and notary. After the National Socialist seizure of power in 1933 his license as a notary was revoked; he worked as an attorney up to the general occupational ban in 1938. He died on 08/26/1942 at the age of 60 in a hospital; more details are not available.
*Sources:* Br.B. 32; TK 33; JMBl. 33, S. 208; *li; LAB, Liste 15.10.33; MRRAK; BArch, R 3001 PAK

## Bachwitz, Willi
02/01/1884 Halle/Saale - no information
*Home address:* Kurfürstendamm 46 (15), W 15
*Law firm address:* Knesebeckstr. 59/60, W 15
*Additional information:* Attorney at the LG I-III and notary; after the National Socialist seizure of power in 1933 his license as a notary was revoked; law partnership with Georg Philipsborn was dissolved and law firm was relocated in 1933; he was a

member of the Reichsverband nichtarischer Christen (Reich Association of non-Aryan Christians); he was disbarred as an attorney on 04/01/1937. He emigrated to Beaufort West, South Africa.
*Sources:* Br.B. 32; TK 33; JMBl. 33, S. 208; *li; LAB, Liste 15.10.33; BArch, R 3001 PAK; Mitt.bl. Reichsverband nichtarischer Christen 6.12.1934; BG

## Bäcker, Benno Dr.
01/18/1893 - no information
*Home address:* no information
*Law firm address:* Rathenower Str. 5, NW 52
*Additional information:* Attorney since 1921, most recently at the LG I-III and at the AG Berlin-Mitte, notary since 1932. After the National Socialist seizure of power, he was made subject to an occupational ban on 05/23/1933.
*Sources:* Br.B. 32; TK 33; Liste d. nichtzugel. RA, 25.4.33; BArch, R 3001 PAK

## Badrian, Alfred Dr.
04/27/1878 Ober-Heiduk - 01/15/1942 Riga
*Home address:* Wielandstr. 34, Charlottenburg
*Law firm address:* Königstr. 48, C 2
*Additional information:* Attorney at the LG I-III, AG Charlottenburg and notary; after the National Socialist seizure of power in 1933 license as a notary was revoked; worked as an attorney up to the general occupational ban in 1938. On 01/13/1942 he was transported to Riga; was murdered there soon after.
*Sources:* Br.B. 32; TK 33; JMBl. 33, S. 234; *li; LAB, Liste 15.10.33; BArch, R 3001 PAK; MRRAK; BG; BdE; GB II

## Badrian, Erich
04/24/1898 Burg - no information
*Home address:* no information
*Law firm address:* Kaiser-Wilhelm-Str. 46
*Additional information:* Attorney at the KG. After the National Socialist seizure of power he was made subject to a general occupational ban in the spring of 1933. Emigration to Palestine on 05/16/1933.
*Sources:* Br.B. 32; TK 33; Liste d. nicht zugel. RA, 25.4.33; JMBl. 4.8.33, S. 253; BArch, R 3001 PAK; BG

## Badrian, Gerhard Dr.
10/13/1901 Kattowitz - transportation 1943
*Home address:* Württembergische Str. 33, W 15

*Law firm address:* Landsberger Allee 115/116, NO 18
*Additional information:* He was a dissident; attorney at the KG, most recently at the LG I. After the National Socialist seizure of power he was readmitted as an attorney up to the general occupational ban in 1938. Went underground as from September 1942. He was arrested and was transported to Auschwitz on 08/04/1943.
*Sources:* TK 33; *li; LAB, Liste 15.10.1933; BArch, R 3001 PAK; MRRAK; BG; GB II

**Badrian, Gustav, Judicial Councillor**
No information - 12/17/1935
*Home address:* no information
*Law firm address:* Dernburgstr. 49, Charlottenburg
*Additional information:* Attorney general at the LG I-III and notary. After the National Socialist seizure of power he was readmitted upon request (also as notary); died in December 1935.
*Sources:* Br.B. 32; TK 33; *li; DJ 36, S. 67; BArch, R 3001 PAK; BG

**Baer, Albert Dr.**
04/04/1888 - no information
*Home address:* no information
*Law firm address:* Friedrich-Ebert-Str. 2-3, W 9
*Additional information:* Attorney general at the LG I-III and notary. After the National Socialist seizure of power in the spring of 1933 he was made subject to an occupational ban.
*Sources:* Br.B. 32; TK 33; Liste d. nichtzugel. RA, 25.4.33; JMBl. 33, S. 253; BArch, R 3001 PAK

**Ball, Arthur Dr.**
03/07/1889 Philadelphia, USA - 02/15/1975 Colorado, USA
*Home address:* no information
*Law firm address:* Dorotheenstr. 31, NW 7
*Additional information:* He was baptized, as were his parents; attorney at the LG I-III and notary. After the National Socialist seizure of power he was briefly readmitted upon request. 1933 emigration to London, Great Britain. On 07/24/1934 he was disbarred in accordance with § 21 Paragraph 1 of the Attorney's Act (RAO). He later emigrated to the USA; an arrest warrant for tax evasion was issued against him. He died in Colorado just before his 87th birthday.

*Sources:* Br.B. 32; TK 33; *li; BArch, R 3001 PAK; Wolf, BFS

**Ball, Ernst Dr., Judicial Councillor**
No information
*Home address:* Potsdamer Str. 50, W 35
*Law firm address:* Viktoria-Luise-Platz 1, W 30
*Additional information:* Attorney at the LG I-III and notary. Ernst practiced at a law firm together with his brothers Fritz and Kurt Ball. After the National Socialist seizure of power in 1933 his license as a notary was revoked, in addition the Ball brothers were made subject to an occupational ban in June 1933. Ernst discontinued his membership in the Berlin Bar, the law firm was dissolved.
*Sources:* Jüd.Adr.B; Br.B. 32; TK 33; JMBl. 33, S. 234; Pr.J. 33, S. 502; BArch, R 3001 PAK; Ball-Kaduri

**Ball, Fritz Dr.**
07/19/1893 - November 1968
*Home address:* Eisenacher Str. 81, Schöneberg
*Law firm address:* Viktoria-Luise-Platz 1, W 30
*Additional information:* Since 1920 admitted as an attorney, also as a notary since 1930: after the National Socialist seizure of power he was arrested in March 1933 and detained and tortured in the savage concentration camp at the General Pape Str. barracks. He was released again shortly thereafter. The law firm, which he ran jointly with his brother Kurt and another relative, Ernst, had to be dissolved after Fritz and Kurt had been made subject to an occupational ban. He was transported to the Sachsenhausen concentration camp after Night of the Broken Glass in 1938. After his release he emigrated to the USA in 1939, where he changed his first name to Fred. He died 1968 in New York.
*Sources:* Br.B. 32; TK 33; JMBl. 30.6.33, S. 203; BArch, R 3001 PAK; Ball-Kaduri; BG; SSDI

**Ball, Kurt Dr.**
01/20/1891 Berlin - 05/29/1976 Tel Aviv
*Home address:* no information
*Law firm address:* Viktoria-Luise-Platz 1, W 30
*Additional information:* He worked at the Reich Ministry of Finance from 1920 -1926. In 1926 he established himself as an attorney specializing in tax matters (in a partnership with his brother Fritz and another relative, Ernst). He was admitted to the LG I-III,

at the same time he was a private lecturer at the Handelshochschule Berlin (Berlin Commercial College). At the beginning of 1933 he had still been elected as a member of the board of the RAK, from which he had to resign shortly thereafter because of political reasons. After the National Socialist seizure of power on 06/19/1933, the joint law firm had to be dissolved. Up to 1938 he worked as a tax consultant to Jewish emigrants, at the same time he was a member of the board from 1934-37 of the Zionist local branch in Berlin. During the wave of arrests after Night of the Broken Glass he was also arrested, he was interned at the Sachsenhausen concentration camp from 11/11/1938 to 12/16/1938. After his release he emigrated to Palestine; he extended his last name and henceforth he called himself Kurt-Jacob Ball-Kaduri. From 1943-1944, he began with the collection of witness statements on the Holocaust in Palestine. Upon his initiative this research center (Yad Vashem) was taken over by the state of Israel as a national memorial. Numerous publications (after 1945 under the name Kurt-Jakob Ball-Kaduri), amongst others: Das Leben der Juden in Deutschland im Jahre 1933 [The life of the Jews in Germany in 1933], Frankfurt/M. 1963
*Sources:* Br.B. 32, TK 33; Liste d. nichtzugel. RA, 25.4.33; JMBl. 28.7.33, S. 234; Verz.; Ball-Kaduri; Walk; Göpp., S: 267; BG

**Bamberger, Hans Dr.**
01/13/1892 Berlin - no information
*Home address:* no information
*Law firm address:* Motzstr. 77, W 30
*Additional information:* He was baptized (as was his father); attorney at LG I-III and notary. After the National Socialist seizure of power he was readmitted upon request, because he was recognized as a "frontline fighter" of the First World War. At the end of 1935 his license as a notary was revoked; in 1936 he received a subsistence allowance from the KG; he was admitted as an attorney up to the general occupational ban.
*Sources:* Br.B. 32; TK 33; *li; BG; LAB, Liste 15.10.33; DJ, 36, S. 314; MRRAK; BArch, R 3001 PAK, PA

**Bang, Ferdinand Dr.**
02/13/1889 Marburg - 05/12/1955 Berlin
*Home address:* Schillerstr. 15, Charlottenburg

*Law firm address:* Friedrichstr. 66, W 8
*Additional information:* Attorney at the LG I-III and notary. After the National Socialist seizure of power he was regarded as being of "mixed race." He was still admitted as both attorney and notary, however, he was listed as "Jewish." Later, due to the effects of war, he had to relocate his office several times. He was married to an "Aryan" woman, they had children. After liberation his request for compensation was denied, since he had hardly been subjected to restrictions, had always been able to exercise his profession; besides, his children had been members of the HJ and the BDM, he himself was a member of the NSV and Volkssturm ("People's storm"). In 1946 he was first appointed as a prosecutor and then as a judge. However, due to severe heart disease he was not able to carry out these tasks. In 1949 he was readmitted as an attorney. He died in 1955 in Berlin.
*Sources:* Br.B. 32; TK 33; *li; LAB, Liste 15.10.33; LAB, Liste Mschl.36; Tel.B. 41; LAB, RAK, PA; BG

**Barbasch, Ludwig Dr.**
08/28/1892 Berlin - 07/12/1967 Wiesbaden
*Home address:* no information
*Law firm address:* Königstr. 20/21, C 2
*Additional information:* 1918-19 Minister of State without portfolio in Mecklenburg during the revolutionary phase, he was sentenced to death after the suppression of the revolution, was later pardoned, active member of the KPD; from 1924-1933 criminal defense lawyer in Berlin, who specialized in politically charged cases (shared office with Hans Litten), admitted as an attorney at the AG Berlin-Mitte and at the LG I-III. After the National Socialist seizure of power arrested in March 1933, together with Hans Litten and Alfred Apfel; he was made subject to an occupational ban; until September 1933 imprisoned in Brandenburg, after liberation emigration via Switzerland and Italy to Palestine; 1956/57 return to Germany; since 1958 attorney in Wiesbaden, specialized in reparation affairs.
*Sources:* Adr.B. 32; TK 33; JMBl. 33, S. 220; GStA, Rep. 84 a, Nr. 20363; BG; Göpp., S. 328; Walk; Krach, S. 430

**Barczinski, Arthur Dr.**
02/27/1885 Allenstein - no information
*Home address:* no information

*Law firm address:* Uhlandstr. 167, W 15
*Additional information:* Attorney at the LG
I-III and notary; since 1921 he was no longer
a member of the Jewish synagogue. After the
National Socialist seizure of power he was
readmitted upon request; end of 1935 his license
as a notary was revoked; in 1933 he relocated
his law firm to Albrecht-Achilles-Str. 5.
*Sources:* Br.B. 32; TK 33; *li; DJ 36, S. 314;
Liste 36; LAB, Liste 15.10.33; BArch, R 3001
PAK; BG

**Baron, Fritz Dr.**
02/01/1905 - November 1980
*Home address:* no information
*Law firm address:* Eisenacher Str. 113, W 30
*Additional information:* Attorney at the LG
I-III and AG Berlin-Mitte. After the National
Socialist seizure of power occupational ban
in spring of 1933. Emigration to New York,
USA, called himself Fred henceforth; he died
in November 1980 in the USA.
*Sources:* TK 33; Liste d. nichtzugel. RA,
25.4.33; JMBl. 33, S. 209; BArch, R 3001
PAK; BG; SSDI

**Barth, Aron Dr.**
03/26/1890 Berlin - 1957 Tel Aviv
*Home address:* Auerbachstr. 15, Wilmersdorf
*Law firm address:* Auerbachstr. 15,
Wilmersdorf
*Additional information:* 1908-11 studied
in Berlin und Heidelberg; since 1916 an
attorney, most recently at the KG, later also a
notary; 1916-33 legal advisor to the DANAT-
Bank and the Hirsch Copper Corporation;
Zionist official, amongst others legal
counsel from 1921-38 at the World Customs
Organisation (WZO) Court, delegate to
the Zionist Congress and to the Congress
Court. After the National Socialist seizure
of power in the spring of 1933 he was made
subject to an occupational ban; emigration
to Haifa, Palestine, on 06/01/1934 (another
source suggests 1933). An arrest warrant
for tax evasion was issued against him. Up
to 1938 he was an attorney in Haifa, then
until 1957 vice president, later director of the
Anglo-Palestine Bank/Bank Leumi; official in
associations and institutions, amongst other
executive member of the Hebrew University of
Jerusalem and 1947-57 presiding judge of the
World Customs Organisation (WZO) Court;
died 1957 in Tel Aviv.

*Publications:* Orthodoxie und Zionismus
[Orthodoxy and zionism](1920) und div.
religiöse Schriften.
*Sources:* Adr.B. 32; TK 33; Liste d.
nichtzugel. RA, 25.4.33; JMBl. 23.6.33, S.
195; BArch, R 3001 PAK; BG; BHdE Bd. 1, S.
36; Walk; Lowenthal; Wolf, BFS

**Baruch, Bernhard**
07/04/1885 Munich - no information
*Home address:* Ansbacher Str. 54, Schöneberg
*Law firm address:* Pallasstr. 14, W 57
*Additional information:* Attorney at the KG
and notary. After the National Socialist seizure
of power in 1933 he was readmitted as attorney,
at first his license as a notary was revoked, then
re-appointed; had to relocate the law firm; at the
end of 1935 his license as a notary was revoked;
he was listed as an attorney until 1936 in the
Berlin business directory. Survived the National
Socialist regime; lived in Moltkestraße, Berlin-
Pankow after 1945.
*Sources:* Br.B. 32; Adr.B. 32 u. 36; *li; BArch,
R 3001 PAK; Aufbau (NY), 2.11.45; BG

**Basch, Walter**
11/29/1885 Berlin - no information
*Home address:* Schlüterstr. 45, W 15
*Law firm address:* Lützowstr. 83, W 35
*Additional information:* Attorney at the
KG and notary. After the National Socialist
seizure of power in 1933 his license as a
notary was revoked; worked as an attorney up
to the general occupational ban in 1938.
*Sources:* Br.B. 32; TK 33; *li; LAB, Liste
15.10.33; DJ 36, S. 314; MRRAK; BArch, R
3001 PAK; BG

**Baswitz, Felix**
No information - 1933
*Home address:* no information
*Law firm address:* Bülowstr. 17, W 57
*Additional information:* Attorney at the
KG and notary. After the National Socialist
seizure of power in 1933 his license as a
notary was revoked; continued to be admitted
to practice law; died in 1933.
*Sources:* Jüd.Adr.B; Br.B. 32; TK 33; JMBl.
33, S. 234; *li; Pr.J. 33, S. 839; BArch, R
3001 PAK

**Bauchwitz, Kurt Dr.**
07/12/1890 Halle/Saale - July 1974 Norfolk
(Massachusetts), USA

*Home address:* Bleibtreustr. 33, Charlottenburg
*Law firm address:* Kurfürstendamm 47, W 15
*Additional information:* Attorney at the LG I-III, at the AG Berlin-Mitte and notary; after the National Socialist seizure of power he was readmitted as an attorney and notary upon request; at the end of 1935 license as a notary was revoked; worked as an attorney until the general occupational ban of 1938; emigration to the USA in 1939; henceforth he changed his name to Roy C. Bates; died in 1974 at the age of 84.
*Sources:* Adr.B. 32; TK 33; *li; DJ 36, S. 314; MRRAK; BArch, R 3001 PAK; BG; SSDI

**Bauer, Franz**
11/29/1877 Berlin - transportation 1942
*Home address:* Solinger Str. 7, NW 87
*Law firm address:* Uhlandstr. 171/172, W 15
*Additional information:* He was Protestant; attorney at the LG I-III and notary. After the National Socialist seizure of power he was readmitted as an attorney and a notary; at the end of 1935 his license as a notary was revoked; he worked as an attorney up to the general occupational ban in 1938. He was transported to Auschwitz on 12/14/1942.
*Sources:* Br.B. 32; TK 33; *li; DJ 36, S. 314; MRRAK; BArch, R 3001 PAK; BG; GB II

**Baum, Max Dr.**
05/12/1884 Neugede - no information
*Home address:* no information
*Law firm address:* Motzstr. 54, W 30
*Additional information:* Baptized as a child, he took part in the First World War and was designated with the EK II. Kl. Attorney at the LG I-III. After the National Socialist seizure of power in 1933 he was readmitted, because he was regarded as a "frontline fighter." In 1937 he discontinued his membership in the Bar.
*Sources:* Br.B. 32; Adr.B. 32; TK 33; *li; BArch, R 3001 PAK; BG

**Baum, Siegfried**
03/09/1905 - no information
*Home address:* no information
*Law firm address:* Greifswalder Str. 9, NO 55
*Additional information:* Attorney at the LG I-III and AG Berlin-Mitte. After the National Socialist seizure of power he was made subject to an occupational ban in the spring of 1933. He survived the National Socialist regime and

later lived in Hessen.
*Sources:* Liste d. nichtzugel. RA, 25.4.33; JMBl. 33, S. 253; BArch, R 3001 PAK

**Baumer, Wilhelm von**
No information
*Home address:* no information
*Law firm address:* Auguste-Viktoria-Str. 4/II
*Additional information:* Attorney at the KG. He was disbarred in 1934 ("inactive 1934").
*Sources:* TK 33; *li; BArch, R 3001 PAK

**Becher, Carl (Karl) Dr.**
04/18/1888 - no information
*Home address:* Kaiserallee 206, W 15
*Law firm address:* Kaiserallee 206, W 15
*Additional information:* Attorney at the LG I-III and notary. After the National Socialist seizure of power in 1933 he was readmitted upon request; relocated his law firm in 1933; at the end of 1935 his license as a notary was revoked; he practiced law until the general occupational ban in 1938; emigration to Seattle, USA, via Great Britain on 03/23/1939.
*Sources:* Br.B. 32; TK 33; *li; LAB, Liste 15.10.33; DJ 36, S. 314; MRRAK; BArch, R 3001 PAK; BG

**Becher, Richard**
09/02/1875- no information
*Home address:* Fasanenstr. 73, W 15
*Law firm address:* Fasanenstr. 73, W 15
*Additional information:* Attorney at the LG I-III and notary. After the National Socialist seizure of power law firm was dissolved, license as a notary was revoked and relocation in 1933, readmitted as an attorney upon request - until 1937, then was disbarred. Emigration to Goldau, Switzerland, on 08/07/1937; he followed his wife, Elisabeth. An arrest warrant for tax evasion was issued against them.
*Sources:* Br.B. 32; TK 33; JMBl. 33, S. 282; *li; LAB, Liste 15.10.33; BArch, R 3001 PAK; BG; Wolf, BFS

**Beck, Kurt Dr.**
03/02/1890 Gdansk - no information
*Home address:* Hohenzollerndamm 8, Berlin W 15
*Law firm address:* Friedrichstr. 59/60, W 8
*Additional information:* He fought in the First World War. He had been undenominational since 1919; since 1920 admitted as an attorney

and since 1927 as a notary, practiced law in partnership with Alfred Apfel. After the National Socialist seizure of power he was made subject to an occupational ban, he was accused of "Communist activity." This probably occurred against the background of the fact that he could have claimed to be an exception from the occupational ban because he had been a "frontline fighter." Disbarment on 07/20/1933.
Sources: Br.B. 32; TK 33; JMBl. 33, S. 253; BArch, R 3001 PAK, PA; GStA, Rep. 84a, Nr. 20363

**Beck-Wardan, Kurt Dr.**
01/15/1892 Berlin - no information
*Home address:* Windscheidstr. 12, Charlottenburg
*Law firm address:* Königin-Luise-Str. 16, Charlottenburg
*Additional information:* He had participated in the First World War and subsequently suffered from his nerves. In 1924 he established himself as an attorney in Berlin, he was admitted as an attorney to LG I-III and to AG Charlottenburg. Since 1932 he used a double-barrelled name, his last name had been Beck before; his non-Jewish wife and their son who had been born in 1925 also adopted the name. He established a partnership together with the attorney Werner Salinger, was charged with several offenses, however, he retained his bar membership until 1933. After the National Socialist seizure of power he was disbarred on 06/06/1933 in accordance with § 3 d. of the Lawyers' RAG ("Communist activity"). This probably occurred against the background of the fact that he could have claimed to be an exception from the occupational ban against Jewish attorneys because he had been a "frontline fighter." He emigrated with his family to Istanbul. There he first worked as a clerk, after six months he established himself as an attorney together with a Turkish colleague. The German Consulate General obtained information about him from the State Department.
*Sources:* TK 33; LAB A Rep 343, AG Köpenick Vertretungsverbote, S. 19; JMBl. 33, S. 221; BArch, R 3001 PAK, PA; GStA, Rep. 84 a, Nr. 20363

**Beer, Fritz Dr.**
03/01/1895 - no information

*Home address:* no information
*Law firm address:* Schicklerstr. 13, O 27
*Additional information:* Attorney at the LG I-III and AG Berlin-Mitte. After the National Socialist seizure of power he was readmitted upon request; worked until the general occupational ban in 1938. Emigrated on 02/16/1938 to Panama, later went to the USA, where most recently he lived in New York under the name Fred and died in 1999 at the age of 104.
*Sources:* Br.B. 32; *li; LAB, Liste 36; Liste 15.10.33; MRRAK; BArch 3001, PAK; MRRAK; BG; SSDI

**Beer, Kurt**
06/18/1897 - June 1983
*Home address:* no information
*Law firm address:* Alexanderstr. 25, O 27
*Additional information:* Attorney since 1924, admitted to the LG I-III and to the AG Berlin-Mitte, notary since 1932. After the National Socialist seizure of power he was made subject to an occupational ban in June 1933. At first he emigrated to Palestine, later to the USA, where he eventually lived in Queens, NY; after 1945 he worked for URO.
*Sources:* Br.B. 32; TK 33; Liste d. nichtzugel. RA, 25.4.33; JMBl. 33, S. 221; BArch 3001, PAK; BG; SSDI; Ausk. Fontheim 6.4.2000

**Beermann, Hans Dr.**
06/08/1878 Berlin - 09/07/1940
*Home address:* Rüdesheimer Platz 11, Wilmersdorf
*Law firm address:* Bülowstr. 28, W 57
*Additional information:* Attorney at the LG I-III, AG Berlin-Mitte and notary. After the National Socialist seizure of power, he was first made subject to an occupational ban, which was revoked, thereupon readmitted as attorney upon request, but license as a notary was revoked; worked as an attorney up to the general occupational ban in 1938; died 1940 at the age of 72 and is buried at Weißensee.
*Sources:* Jüd.Adr.B.; Br.B. 32; TK 33; JMBl. 33, S. 220; *li; LAB, Liste 15.10.33; MRRAK; BArch R 3001, PAK; BG

**Beerwald, Joseph Dr.**
10/17/1895 Tilsit - no information
*Home address:* Livländische Str. 10, Wilmersdorf
*Law firm address:* Jägerstr. 63, W 8
*Additional information:* Attorney at the LG

I-III, at the AG Berlin-Mitte and notary. After the National Socialist seizure of power he was readmitted upon request; license as notary was revoked at the end of 1935; worked as an attorney up to the general occupational ban in 1938; emigrated to Great Britain.
*Sources:* Br.B. 32; TK 33; *li; LAB, Liste 15.10.33; DJ 36, S. 314; MRRAK; BArch, R 3001 PAK; BG

**Behr, Rudolf**
05/09/1894 - no information
*Home address:* no information
*Law firm address:* Eichhornstr. 1, W 9
*Additional information:* Attorney at the KG. After the National Socialist seizure of power in spring 1933 he was at first made subject to an occupational ban, however, later readmitted as attorney upon request; still listed as an attorney in 1938 in the business directory.
*Sources:* TK 33; Liste d. nichtzugel. RA, 25.4.33; *li; LAB, Liste 15.10.33; Br.B. 38; BArch, R 3001 PA

**Behrend, Hugo Dr.**
09/16/1876 - no information
*Home address:* Rubensstr. 25, Friedenau
*Law firm address:* Kantstr. 67, Charlottenburg
*Additional information:* Attorney at the AG Charlottenburg, at the LG I-III and notary. After the National Socialist seizure of power in the summer of 1933 he was made subject to an occupational ban. He was partially represented by attorney Dr. Benno Leyser.
*Sources:* TK 1933; JMBl. 33, S. 253; Pr.J. 33, S. 391; BArch, R 3001 PAK, PA

**Bein, Erwin Dr.**
05/07/1884 Berlin - no information
*Home address:* Landhausstr. 43
*Law firm address:* Kleiststr. 29, W 62
*Additional information:* Attorney at the LG I-III and notary. After the National Socialist seizure of power license as a notary was revoked in 1933, readmitted as an attorney upon request, relocated his law firm, worked until the general occupational ban in 1938; emigration to Great Brtain or USA on 02/26/1939.
*Sources:* Br.B. 32; TK 33; JMBl. 30.6.33, S. 202; *li; LAB, Liste 15.10.33; MRRAK; BArch, R 3001 PAK; BG

**Belkin, Hugo Dr.**
06/10/1878 Silesia - 12/29/1943
*Home address:* Sächsische Str. 44, Wilmersdorf
*Law firm address:* Kronenstr. 12/13, W 8
*Additional information:* Attorney at the LG I-III and notary. After the National Socialist seizure of power he was readmitted upon request; relocated his law firm in 1933; his license as an attorney was revoked in 1935; he worked as an attorney up to the general he was made subject to an occupational ban in 1938; his wife was Protestant. He died in 1943 at the age of 65, the more precise details of his death are unknown.
*Sources:* Br.B. 32; TK 33; *li; LAB, Liste 15.10.33; DJ 36, S. 314; MRRAK; BArch, R 3001 PAK; BG

**Benary, Otto**
11/24/1886 Berlin - no information
*Home address:* Derfflingerstr. 11
*Law firm address:* Nollendorfplatz 6, W 30
*Additional information:* Attorney at the LG I-III, AG Schöneberg and notary. After the National Socialist seizure of power he was made subject to an occupational ban in the spring of 1933. Emigration to Chile on 04/05/1939.
*Sources:* Adr.B. 32; TK 33; Liste d. nichtzugel. RA, 25.4.33; JMBl. 33, 195; BArch, R 3001 PAK; BG

**Benda, Heinrich Dr.**
01/29/1895 Berlin - no information
*Home address:* Lützowstr. 50
*Law firm address:* Dörnbergstr. 1, W 35
*Additional information:* War volunteer during the First World War, had lost an eye during the Battle of the Somme; he was Protestant. 1918 first state examination in law, 1922 second state examination in law; attorney since 1927, had also previously studied social and political science. After the National Socialist seizure of power he was made subject to an occupational ban. He naturally assumed that since he had been a "frontline fighter," he would be allowed to practice law; he submitted his military records, which were criticized by the judicial administration: "No request, but F." (which meant: no separate application, no declaration of loyalty, but "frontline fighter"). On 06/20/1933 he declared that "in line with the statutory provisions" he was "not an ethnic German." He would have been admitted to practice law, but now political reasons were being sought. The board of the KG requested

in August 1933 that he be made subject to an occupational ban. In the same letter to the Ministry of Justice, the president of the KG pointed out that he had been arrested together with the student Werner Levy on March 3, 1933, when both were posting leaflets with the words "Away with Hitler. Fight for the dictatorship of the proletariat! "The case was closed, however, the process was sufficient to disbar him, because he had been involved with "Communist affairs" (08/29/1933). He was made subject to an occupational ban.
*Sources:* Pr.J. 33, S. 466; BArch PAK, PA; BG

**Bendix, Erwin Dr.**
05/13/1885 Magdeburg - no information
*Home address:* Viktoria-Luise-Pl. 5, Schönebg.
*Law firm address:* Schlesische Str. 26, SO 36
*Additional information:* Attorney at the LG I-III and notary. After the National Socialist seizure of power he was readmitted upon request; at the end of 1935 his license as an attorney was revoked; he emigrated in October 1938 to London, Great Britain.
*Sources:* Br.B. 32; TK 33; *li; LAB, Liste 15.10.33; DJ 36, S. 314; MRRAK; BArch, R 3001 PAK; BG

**Bendix, Hans Dr.**
02/15/1903 Berlin - no information
*Home address:* Kurfürstendamm 73
*Law firm address:* Kurfürstendamm 184, W 15
*Additional information:* Attorney at the LG I-III and AG Charlottenburg. After the National Socialist seizure of power he was made subject to an occupational ban in the spring of 1933. His wife Esther was regarded as "Aryan."
*Sources:* Br.B. 32; TK 33; Liste d. nichtzugel. RA, 25.4.33; JMBl. 33, S. 234; BG

**Bendix, Ludwig Dr.**
06/28/1877 Dorstfeld (Westphalia) - 01/03/1954 Oakland (California), USA
*Home address:* no information
*Law firm address:* Zimmerstr. 84, SW 68
*Additional information:* He had been an attorney since 1907, later he also was admitted as a notary, at the same he also specialized in labor law. After the National Socialist seizure of power he was made subject to an occupational ban in May 1933

because of his involvement in "Communist affairs," although he had not been actively involved in this sense. He had, however, defended some important opponents of the National Socialists. The exemption as "elderly attorney" would have applied to him in accordance with § 2 of the Attorneys' Act (AG). As from 06/02/1933 he was taken into "protective custody" for four months; he was informed upon release that he needed to be "taught a lesson." After his release he tried to work as a legal adviser. A colleague reported him for working illegally as a legal adviser and for unfair competition. Although he won the trial, he felt morally defeated by the accompanying hate campaign. He was interned at the Dachau concentration camp from July 1935 to May 1937. Completely emaciated, he was released and ordered to emigrated to a country outside of Europe. In May 1937 he emigrated to Palestine. Because he could not tolerate the climate, he moved in 1947 to the USA to his son Richard (born 02/25/1916, lived in the USA since 1938), who was the Chair of Sociology in Berkeley, California. He died in California in 1954. Numerous publications, including in collaboration with Manfred Weiss: Zur Psychologie der Urteilstätigkeit des Berufsrichters und andere Schriften, mit einer biografischen Einleitung von Reinhard Bendix. [The psychology of the judicial process in professional judges and other writings, with a biographical introduction by Reinhard Bendix]
*Sources:* Br.B. 32; TK 33; JMBl. 33, S. 195; Naatz-Album; LBI Memoirs; Bendix, R.: Von Berlin nach Berkeley; Göpp., S. 268

**Benfey, Hans Dr.**
01/23/1888 Emmerstedt - no information
*Home address:* no information.
*Law firm address:* Pariser Platz 6 II, NW 7
*Additional information:* Attorney at the KG and notary. After the National Socialist seizure of power his licence as a notary was revoked, he was re-admitted as an attorney to the KG. He had been baptized a Catholic, he was regarded as "of mixed race, first degree," he was married to a non-Jewish wife and survived the National Socialist regime.
*Sources:* TK 33; JMBl. 33, S. 220; Liste 15.10.33; *li; LAB, Liste Mschlg. 36; Aufbau N.Y., 17.8.1945; BG

**Benjamin, Julian**
01/20/1896 Kulm - November 1969
*Home address:* Stübbenstr. 9, Schöneberg
*Law firm address:* Dorotheenstr. 30, NW 7
*Additional information:* He fought in the
First World War; attorney at the LG I-III and
notary; after the National Socialist seizure of
power he was acknowledged as a "frontline
fighter," thereafter he was re-admitted
upon request; at the end of 1935 his license
as a notary was revoked; up to the general
occupational ban in 1938 he worked as an
attorney. Later an entry "listed as away on
travel" was found. He could apparently
emigrate to the USA, where he finally lived in
California and died in 1969.
*Sources:* Br.B. 32; TK 33; *li; LAB, Liste
15.10.33; DJ 36, S. 314; MRRAK; BArch, R
3001 PAK; BG; SSDI (hier: *20.10.1896)

**Benjamin, Max Louis Dr.**
05/11/1885 Berlin - no information
*Home address:* Kaiserdamm 74,
Charlottenburg
*Law firm address:* Kaiserdamm 74,
Charlottenburg
*Additional information:* Attorney at the LG
I-III and notary. After the National Socialist
seizure of power he was readmitted, but had
to dissolve the law firm in 1933 and relocate;
at the end of 1935 his license as a notary was
revoked. Emigration to New York, USA.
*Sources:* Br.B. 32; TK 33; *li; LAB, Liste
15.10.33; DJ 36, S. 314; BArch, R 3001 PAK; BG

**Benjamin, Siegfried Dr.**
01/31/1885 Kulm - no information
*Home address:* Auf dem Grat 52, Zehlendorf
*Law firm address:* Alexanderstr. 5, C 25
*Additional information:* Attorney at the KG
and notary. Partnership with Martin Freund
and Hans Munter. After the National Socialist
seizure of power his license as a notary was
revoked. One partner left the law firm, and
the law firm had to relocate. Up to the general
occupational ban in 1938 he worked as an
attorney. Emigration to Tel Aviv, Palestine or
to Great Britain in March 1939.
*Sources:* TK 33; *li; Br.B. 32; JMBl. 33, 202;
LAB, Liste 15.10.33; MRRAK; BArch, R
3001 PAK; BG

**Ber, Hermann**
03/20/1876 Berlin - no information

*Home address:* Kurfürstendamm 205,
Charlottenburg
*Law firm address:* Jägerstr. 6, W 8
*Additional information:* Attorney at the LG
I-III and notary. After the National Socialist
seizure of power in 1933 his license as a notary
was revoked; he worked as an attorney until
the general occupational ban in 1938. His wife
Elise, whose maiden name has been Mierke,
was regarded as "Aryan." Emigration to
Amsterdam, the Netherlands on 04/15/1939.
*Sources:* Br.B. 32; TK 33; JMBl. 33, S. 234;
*li; LAB, Liste 15.10.33; MRRAK; BArch, R
3001 PAK; BG

**Beradt, Martin Dr.**
08/26/1881 Magdeburg -
11/26/1949 New York
*Home address:*
Joachimsthaler Str. 15, W 15
*Law firm address:*
Joachimsthaler Str. 25/26,
W 15
*Additional information:* In addition to his
legal activities, he published literary works
since 1909, amongst others "Go" (the story
of a troubled and anxious boy, who commits
suicide, appeared in 1909 in an edition of
30,000 copies), "Eheleute" and "Das Kind"
as well as works critical of the judicial system
(amongst others: [The judge], edited by
Martin Buber). At the beginning of the First
World War, he was found to be unfit for
military service because of an eye condition,
however, in 1915 he was put to work digging
trenches. When his suffering worsened, he was
dismissed by the military. His experiences were
narrated in an anti-war novel ("Erdarbeiter"
[Digger], in 1929 it was reissued under
the title "Schipper an der Front" [Shoveler
on the Front]). He expanded his law firm,
specialized in copyright law, was also admitted
as a notary; became legal counsel to the
Deutscher Automobilhändlerverband (German
Automobile Dealer Association), but also an
agent for Walther Rathenau and Heinrich
Mann. In "Weltbühne"[The World Stage] he
flagellated the disregard of personal rights and
the "normal German bourgeois way of life."
After the National Socialist seizure of power
he was readmitted as an attorney, however, his
license as an attorney was revoked; at the same
time his partnership with Dr. Ernst Rudolf
Katz and Dr. Georg Russ was dissolved and the

law firm was relocated. He later wrote in the narrative "Die Robe"[The Robe]: "When my license as an attorney was revoked in 1933, I received exact instructions where and with what deadline I had to deliver the volumes with documents, my register, the rubber stamp, the seal, the seal press ..." he had been admitted as an attorney to the KG up to the general occupational ban in 1938.

Shortly before the war started, on 07/17/1939, he was able to travel with his wife Charlotte, who was a journalist, to the USA (1940) via Great Britain. In his luggage he had the manuscript of this book entitled "Beide Seiten einer Straße" [Both sides of a road] (at first published under the title: "Straße der kleinen Ewigkeit" [The street of little eternity]), a description of Grenadierstraße in the Scheunen Quarter in Berlin; however, he could not find a publisher for it in New York. During the final years of his life Charlotte worked as a hairdresser to support them. In November 1949 he died half blind at the age of 68 in New York. Meanwhile, some of his works were republished.

*Sources:* Br.B. 32; TK 33; JMBl. 33, S. 234; *li; LAB, Liste 15.10.33; BArch, R 3001 PAK; MRRAK; BG; Hanno Kühnert: Von den Deutschen vergessen [Forgotten by the Germans]; in: Die Zeit, 11/30/1990. S. 76; With notes by Eike Geisel, in: Beide Seiten einer Straße.

**Berendt, Hugo**
05/07/1892 Rogasen - transported on 1943
*Home address:* Kurfürstendamm 177, W 15
*Law firm address:* Kaiser-Friedrich-Str. 61a, Charlottenburg
*Additional information:* Fought in the First World War; attorney at Charlottenburg, at the LG I-III and notary; after the National Socialist seizure of power he was readmitted as an attorney and notary, because he had been recognized as a "frontline fighter"; in 1935 his license as a notary was revoked and he was made subject to an occupational ban as an attorney in 1938. He was transported to Auschwitz on 09/10/1943.
*Sources:* Br.B. 32; TK 1933; *li; LAB, Liste 15.10.33; DJ 36, S. 314 (Behrendt); BArch, R 3001 PAK; MRRAK; BG; GB II

**Berent, Margarete Dr.**
07/09/1887 Berlin -
06/23/1965 New York
*Home address:* Spichernstr. 4, Wilmersdorf
*Law firm address:* Hallesches Ufer 14, SW 11
*Additional information:*
Daughter of a salesman, she already passed her exams to be a teacher at middle and high girls' schools at the age of 19. Only a year later, in 1910, she passed her school leaving examination in Berlin. Subsequently she studied law in Berlin and Erlangen. 1914 she completed her studies with a doctorate. Her dissertation entitled "Die Zugewinnstgemeinschaft der Ehegatten" [Community of accrued gains between spouses], which received the distinguished rating of magna cum laude. In 1915, this work was published as part of a prestigious academic series aimed at teachers at middle and high school girls' schools. (Over 40 years later, in 1958, it was used as material for the legal transformation of marital property and inheritance law in the Federal Republic of Germany.)

Despite an excellent dissertation, she could neither become a judge nor an attorney, since she needed to take the state examinations in law which she was not allowed to do as a woman. She worked as a legal aid worker in law offices and in legal aid centers for women. For a while she was employed by the city council. In the young Weimar Republic, in 1919, the Prussian Minister of Justice approved the admission of women to the state examinations in law. Shortly thereafter, on December 22, 1919, she passed her first state examination in law with the excellent "good" rating.

After a four-year clerkship and passing her second state examination in law she was appointed on March 7, 1925 as one of the first female attorneys in Prussia at the Berlin LG and at the Berlin AG. "In 1933 the law firm formed the basis of my existence. I had managed to expand it to such an extent I could maintain my own office and earn a decent income and travel abroad . . . I would like to mention that I enjoyed trust, respect and growing recognition . . . I spoke repeatedly on the radio, amongst others in Hamburg and in a series about family law for the Zentralinstitut für Erziehung und Unterricht (Central Institute for Education and Instruction . . ." (from the compensation documents)

She was committed to an obvious recognition of women in all professions, but above all in jurisprudence. She strived for the social and legal equality of women both in committees, as well as in her specific professional area, family law. At the same time, she was a member of the Assembly of Representatives of the Jewish Synagogue of Berlin, and amongst the leaders of the Prussian State Association of Synagogue Communities.

After the National Socialist seizure of power she was disbarred as an attorney on 06/19/1933, because she was Jewish; she was made subject to an occupational ban. From mid-1933 to November 1939 she worked for the Central Welfare Office for German Jews in Berlin and Cologne. From the summer of 1938 onwards, she sought to emigrate to the United States and was registered with the Consulate for an entry visa. However, because of the great number of applications she did not receive a response to her queue number. Finally, on November 30, 1939, after the beginning of the war, she fled via Switzerland to Italy and embarked on the S.S. Augustus to Chile, where she arrived at Valparaiso on December 28, 1939.

Up to July 1940 she lived in Chile and made a living as a language teacher. When she was able to obtain a US visa, she traveled to New York in August 1940. There an extensive network of aid and emigrant organizations existed.

She worked as a housekeeping aid and at the post office. 1942 she once again commenced with legal studies, mainly evening courses. She worked on the side, since she could only receive minimal financial support from relatives. From 1945 to 1950 she worked as a law clerk at a law firm. In 1948 she passed her Bachelor of Laws (LL.B.) examinations at the New York University Law School, 1949 the bar examination of the state of New York. In 1950, already 63 years old, she established herself as an attorney. She earned little money - too little. From 1953 until her death in 1965 she worked at the Legal Division of the City of New York. She did not return to Germany. Her brother and his family had been murdered in Auschwitz.

*Publications (selection):* Die Zugewinnstgemeinschaft der Ehegatten [The community of accrued gains between spouses], Breslau 1915, in the series Untersuchungen zur deutschen Staats- und Rechtsgeschichte [Studies in German governmental and legal history], [v.]123; Die Frau in den juristischen Berufen [Women in the legal profession]; in: Die Frau der Gegenwart [The contemporary woman], 1917, pp. 153-157; Die Frau als Richter [Women as judges]; in: "Juristische Wochenschrift" [Legal Weekly] 1920, p. 1012; Schutz von Frauen und Kindern im Entwurf zum Strafgesetzbuch [Protection of women and children in the draft to the criminal code]; in: Monatszeitschrift Deutscher Ärztinnen [German monthly for female doctors] 5th year, vol. 9; Das Jugendrecht im Entwurf des Einführungsgesetzes zum Straf- und Strafvollzugsgesetz [Juvenile law in the draft introductory act to the Criminal and Penal Code] in: Centralblatt für Jugendrecht und Jugendwohlfahrt [Central Gazette for juvenile law and youth welfare law], XXIth year, number 12.

*Sources:* Br.B. 32; Liste d. nichtzugel. RA, 25.4.33; JMBl. 33, S. 253; BArch, R 3001 PAK, PA; Entschädigungsbeh. Bln., Entsch. akte; BHdE Bd. 1, S. 53; Walk; Göpp., S. 268; Stiefel, Ernst/Mecklenburg, Frank: Deutsche Juristen im amerikanischen Exil (1933-1950) [German jurists in American exile [1933-1950)], Tübingen 1991, S. 76/77; Quack, Sibylle: Margarete Berent; in: Dick, Jutta/Sassenberg, Marina (Editor): Jüdische Frauen im 19. und 20. Jahrhundert. Lexikon zu Leben und Werk [Jewish women in the 19th and 20th centuries: a dictionary of their life and work], Hamburg 1993, S. 53-55; Häntzschel, Hiltrud: Eine neue Form der Bindung und Freiheit. Die Juristin Margarete Berent (1887-1965) [A new form of commitment and freedom. The jurist Margaret Berent], in: Häntzschel, Hiltrud/ Bußmann, Hadumod: Bedrohlich gescheit. Ein Jahrhundert Frauen und Wissenschaft [Dangerously intelligent. A century of women and scholarship in Bavaria] Munich 1997.

**Berg, Hermann Dr.**
No information
*Home address:* no information
*Law firm address:* Nikolsburger Platz 1

*Additional information:* Attorney at the LG I and notary; after the National Socialist seizure of power his licence as a notary was revoked in early 1933; a little later his law firm was dissolved.
*Sources:* TK 33; Adr.B. 33; JMBl. 33, S. 202; Pr.J. 33, S. 502; BArch, R 3001 PAK

**Berger, Erwin Dr.**
05/15/1901 - no information
*Home address:* no information
*Law firm address:* Kurfürstendamm 13, W 50
*Additional information:* Attorney at the LG I-III and at the AG Berlin-Mitte. After the National Socialist seizure of power he was made subject to an occupational ban in early 1933.
*Sources:* Br.B. 32; TK 33; Liste d. nichtzugel. RA, 25.4.33; JMBl. 33, S. 253; BArch, R 3001 PAK

**Berger, Fritz Dr.**
02/28/1902 Chemnitz - no information
*Home address:* Nassauische Str. 4, Wilmersdorf
*Law firm address:* Königstr. 33/36, C 2
*Additional information:* Attorney since 1932; admitted at the LG I-III and AG Berlin-Mitte. After the National Socialist seizure of power he was made subject to an occupational ban in early 1933; 1936-39 leader of the Palestine Office; 1939 delegate to the Zionist World Conference: emigration to Palestine. Tel Aviv; Studied archaeology, 1948-67 did archaeology research for the Israeli government, as well as working as a bookseller and archaeologist.
*Sources:* TK 33; Liste d. nichtzugel. RA, 25.4.33; JMBl. 33, S. 253; BArch, R 3001 PAK; Göpp., S. 269; BG

**Berger, Kurt**
07/21/1892 - 02/05/1936
*Home address:* no information
*Law firm address:* Rankestr. 34, W 50
*Additional information:* Attorney at the LG I-III and notary. After the National Socialist seizure of power he was readmitted. 1935 he was disbarred as an attorney as his license as a notary was revoked. He died in 1936 at the age of 44.
*Sources:* Br.B. 32; TK 33; *li; LAB, Liste 15.10.33; BArch, R 3001 PAK; BG

**Bergmann, Arthur Dr.**
12/16/1906 - 1979 Jerusalem

*Home address:* no information
*Law firm address:* Klosterstr. 65/67, C 2
*Additional information:* He was one of the six sons of the rabbi Bergmann. Attorney at the LG I-III and AG Berlin-Mitte. After the National Socialist seizure of power he was made subject to an occupational ban on 06/13/1933; he went to Saarland and in 1935 after reintegration into the German Reich he was accused of high treason and arrested. In 1936 he fled and emigrated to Palestine; he was an active participant in the development of the state of Israel, amongst others with the introduction of social security. He died at the age of 73 in Jerusalem.
*Sources:* TK 33; Liste d. nichtzugel. RA, 25.4.33; JMBl. 33, S. 253; BArch, R 3001 PAK, PA; Walk; Ausk. Werner Wolff, 22.9.1998

**Bergmann, Siegfried**
02/11/1878 Przeworsk - no information
*Home address:* Leibnizstr. 43, Charlottenburg
*Law firm address:* Neue Schönhauser Str. 1, N 54
*Additional information:* Attorney at the LG I-III, at the AG Berlin-Mitte and notary. In partnership with Dr. Erich Ilgner and Ernst Karfunkel. After the National Socialist seizure of power in 1933 he was made subject to a temporary ban on representation, which which was canceled and his license as a notary was revoked; upon request readmitted as a notary. Emigration.
*Sources:* Br.B. 32; JMBl. 33, S. 202; *li; LAB, Liste 15.10.33; BArch, R 3001 PAK; BG; Wolf, BFS

**Bergmann, Siegfried**
05/06/1887 Kobylin (Kr. Krotoschin) - no information
*Home address:* Wildensteiner Str. 7, Karlshorst
*Law firm address:* Friedrichstr. 246, SW 68
*Additional information:* Attorney since 1916, at first admitted to the OLG-Bezirk Breslau (Higher Regional Court District Breslau), since 1920 in Berlin. Was drafted in the First World War, but promptly dismissed as unfit for service, however, his three brothers served. After the National Socialist seizure of power in 1933 he was made subject to an occupational ban despite intense efforts on his part to be admitted longer. In his application he declared that he only employs "Aryan

personnel." Emigration on 11/04/1933 to Great Britain (according to BLHA Palästina). *Sources:* JMBl. 33, S. 209; BArch, R 3001 PAK, PA; BG: Akten OFP, BLHA, PrBr Rep. 36 A, OFP, Devisenstelle

**Bermann, Robert**
11/16/1900 Gleiwitz - no information
*Home address:* no information
*Law firm address:* Güntzelstr. 46, Wilmersdorf
*Additional information:* Legal advisor to the Stock Exchange in Berlin, later legal counsel to the Chamber of Industry and Commerce, discharged from this position on 03/31/1933 after the National Socialist seizure of power, because he was Jewish, for the same reason he was made suject to an occupational ban as an attorney with the KG on 07/01/1933; emigrated to London, Great Britain.
*Sources:* TK 33; Liste d. nichtzugel. RA, 25.4.33; JMBl. 33, S. 253; BArch, R 3001 PAK, PA; BG

**Berne, Jacob Dr.**
03/01/1879 Witkowo - no information
*Home address:* Admiral-von-Schröder-Str. 29, W 35
*Law firm address:* Herwarthstr. 4, NW 40
*Additional information:* Attorney at the LG I. After the National Socialist seizure of power in 1933 his license as a notary was revoked. He was also disbarred as an attorney in 1933 ("inactive"), although he was readmitted in the fall. Later emigrated to London, Great Britain.
*Sources:* TK 33; JMBl. 33, S. 202; *li; LAB, Liste 15.10.33; BArch, R 3001 PAK; BG

**Bernhard, Walter**
04/09/1877 Berlin - 09/05/1948 Berlin
*Home address:* no information.
*Law firm address:* Nollendorfplatz 1, W 30
*Additional information:* Attorney since 1907; since 1930 he was also a director of the Darmstadt and National Bank DANAT (which had experienced the most serious slump of all German banks during the global economic crisis); in addition he was also in-house counsel and liquidator of the banks Gebr. Arnhold and S. Bleichröder GmbH.

Another important client was the department store Hermann Tietz. By his own account, he had voted for the DVP during the last free elections; he was a Protestant.
After the National Socialist seizure of power he was readmitted as an attorney, he was recognized as a so-called "elder attorney." Before 1933, he had earned revenues between RM 134,000 (1931) and RM 85,000 (RM) (1932), they were reduced to RM 63,000 by the year 1938. In 1938 he was made subject to the general occupational ban as a Jewish attorney, but he could continue his work as a liquidator. No information about him is available up to his liberation from the National Socialist regime. He survived and was readmitted as an attorney in 1948, he died in the same year.
*Sources:* TK 33; Br.B. 32; *li; LAB, Liste 15.10.33; BArch, R 3001 PAK; MRRAK; LAB, RAK, PA

**Bernhardt, Martin Dr.**
05/11/1886 Kriewen - November 1979
*Home address:* Hagenstr. 31, Grunewald
*Law firm address:* Hindersinstr. 9, NW 40
*Additional information:* Attorney at the LG I. After the National Socialist seizure of power he was readmitted as an attorney; emigrated to the USA on 12/29/1937, he was disbarred as an attorney at the same time. He died at the age of 93. He last lived in New Jersey, USA.
*Sources:* Br.B. 32; TK 33; *li; LAB, Liste 15.10.33; BArch, R 3001 PAK; BG; SSDI

**Bernhardt, Walter**
04/12/1879 Berlin - 08/14/1961 Berlin
*Home address:* no information
*Law firm address:* Breite Str. 15, Steglitz
*Additional information:* Attorney at the LG I-III. After the National Socialist seizure of power in 1933 he was readmitted; in 1933 he had to relocate his law firm. His marriage was childless, therefore not a privileged "mixed race marraige" and later he became a "star bearer." He worked as a porter at the Stettin train station for a year, then a year later as an employee in various factories in the southeast of Berlin. "I was also forced by the Gestapo to give up my home and sell my belongings at giveaway prices." Readmitted as an attorney on 12/12/1946, he lived in Berlin-Steglitz until his death.
*Sources:* Br.B. 32; TK 33; *li; LAB, Liste 15.10.33; LAB, RAK, PA; BG

**Bernstein, Erich**
11/10/1905 Schwerin - 10/29/2003
*Home address:* no information
*Law firm address:* Mittelstr. 57/58, NW 7
*Additional information:* He was a civil
lawyer, he published the document entitled
"Irrtum und Geschäftsgrundlage" [Errors as
to the implicit basis of a contract]; attorney
at the LG I. After the National Socialist
seizure of power he was made subject to an
occupational ban on 06/26/1933, emigrated to
the USA; last lived in Fairfax, Virginia.
*Sources:* TK 33; Liste d. nichtzugel. RA,
25.4.33; JMBl. 33, S. 253; BArch, R 3001
PAK, PA; SSDI (Eric B.)

**Bernstein, Heimann, Judicial Councillor**
06/29/1852 Gnesen - 07/30/1940
*Home address:* Hanstedter Weg 15, Steglitz
*Law firm address:* Worpsweder Str. 9, Steglitz
*Additional information:* Attorney at the
LG I-III. After the National Socialist seizure
of power he was readmitted as an attorney,
presumably as "elder attorney:": his law
firm was relocated, he was disbarred on
11/01/1937.
*Sources:* Br.B. 32.; TK 33; *li; LAB, Liste
15.10.33; BArch, R 3001 PAK; BG

**Bernstein, Heinrich Siegfried**
05/04/1905 - no information
*Home address:* no information
*Law firm address:* Taubenstr. 50, W 8
*Additional information:* Attorney since 1931,
admitted at the LG I-III. After the National
Socialist seizure of power on 06/19/1933 he
was made subject to an occupational ban.
*Sources:* TK 33; Liste d. nichtzugel. RA, 25.4.33;
JMBl. 33, S. 253; BArch, R 3001 PAK, PA

**Bernstein, Otto**
05/07/1877 Leipzig - 02/09/1943
Theresienstadt
*Home address:* Mommsenstr. 65, W15 *Law
firm address:* Mommsenstr. 9, W 15
*Additional information:* Attorney at the KG.
He was Protestant: in addition to being an
attorney he was the editor of the journal "Bank-
Archiv" [Banking archive]. After the National
Socialist seizure of power he was readmitted as
an attorney until the general occupational ban in
1938; thereafter he retired. Date of declaration
of property : 10/23/1942; he was interned
at the collection point Große Hamburger

Str. 26, on 10/30/1942; he was transported to
Theresienstadt. He died there two months later.
*Sources:* TK 33; *li ; MRRAK; BG; ThG; GB
II; Göpp., S. 368

**Bernstein, Siegfried**
02/18/1885 - 07(10?)/15/1938
*Home address:* no information
*Law firm address:* Uhlandstr. 171, W 15
*Additional information:* Attorney at the LG I-III
and notary. After the National Socialist seizure
of power he was readmitted as an attorney; at the
end of 1935 his license as a notary was revoked;
he died in 1938 at the age of 53.
*Sources:* TK 33; *li; LAB, Liste 15.10.33; DJ
36, S. 314; BArch, R 3001 PAK

**Bernstein, Tobias Dr.**
No information
*Home address:* no information
*Law firm address:* Kurfürstendamm 50 III
*Additional information:* Attorney at the LG
I-III. After the National Socialist seizure of
power in 1933 he was disbarred as an attorney
("inactive"), in fall 1933 he was readmitted as
an attorney.
*Sources:* TK 33; *li; LAB, Liste 15.10.33; Pr.J.
33, S. 868; BArch, R 3001 PAK

**Bernstein, Werner Dr.**
03/17/1893 - no information
*Home address:* no information
*Law firm address:* Hinter der katholischen
Kirche 2, W 56
*Additional information:* Presumably the son
of Wilhelm, they worked together in a law firm.
Attorney at the LG I-III. After the National
Socialist seizure of power he was readmitted as
an attorney. He was still listed as an attorney
in 1936.
*Sources:* TK 33; *li; Liste 36; LAB, Liste
15.10.33; BArch, R 3001 PAK

**Bernstein, Wilhelm Dr., Judicial Councillor**
09/14/1856 Magdeburg - 11/12/1940
*Home address:* Kaiserallee 31, Wilmersdorf
*Law firm address:* Hinter der katholischen
Kirche 2, W 56
*Additional information:* Presumably the father
of Werner, joint law firm; attorney at the LG
I-III and notary. After the National Socialist
seizure of power in 1933 he was readmitted
as an attorney and a notary upon request; at
the end of 1935 his license as an attorney was

revoked; he was admitted as an attorney until the general occupational ban in 1938.
*Sources:* TK 33; *li; LAB, Liste 15.10.33; DJ 36, S. 314; BArch, R 3001 PAK; BG

**Besas, Georg Dr.**
09/10/1886 - 1933 Berlin
*Home address:* no information
*Law firm address:* Fasanenstr. 31, W 15
*Additional information:* Attorney at the LG I-III and notary. After the National Socialist seizure of power in 1933 his license as a notary was revoked; he committed suicide in 1933 at the age of 48 years.
*Sources:* TK 33; *li; BArch, R 3001 PAK; JMBl. 1933, S. 202; Pr.J. 33, S. 598; BG; g

**Beschütz, Julius Dr.**
08/27/1882 Salzwedel - 10/31/1943 Berlin
*Home address:* Nestorstr. 1, Wilmersdorf
*Law firm address:* Kronenstr. 66/67, W 8
*Additional information:* Attorney at the KG and notary; after the National Socialist seizure of power he was readmitted; at the end of 1935 his license as an attorney was revoked. Worked as an attorney until the general occupational ban in 1938. His wife Erna was regarded as "Aryan." He died in 1943 at the Jewish Hospital in Iranischen Straße.
*Sources:* *li; Liste 15.10.33; DJ 36, S. 314; BArch, R 3001 PAK; MRRAK; BG

**Besler, Manfred Dr.**
06/25/1894 Galicia - July 1981
*Home address:* Schillerstr. 124, Charlottenburg
*Law firm address:* Siegmundshof 13, NW 23
*Additional information:* He participated in the First World War; since 1924 practiced as an attorney in Berlin, admitted to the LG I-III. After the National Socialist seizure of power he was made subject to an occupational ban on 07/28/1933 (no recognition as "frontline fighter"). He emigrated to the USA; he last lived in Westchester, N.Y.
Br.B. 32; TK 33; Liste d. nichtzugel. RA, 25.4.33; JMBl. 33, S. 266; BArch, R 3001 PAK; SSDI (Fred B.)

**Besser, Alexander Dr.**
10/27/1899 - no information
*Home address:* no information
*Law firm address:* Kronenstr. 54, W 8
*Additional information:* Attorney at the LG

I-III and AG Berlin-Mitte. After the National Socialist seizure of power he was made subject to an occupational ban in early 1933. He survived the Nazi regime; after 1945 he lived in Hessen.
*Sources:* Br.B. 32; TK 33; Liste d. nichtzugel. RA, 25.4.33; JMBl. 33, S. 253; BArch, R 3001 PAK

**Beuthner, Ernst Dr.**
04/18/1878 Beuthen - transportation in 1941
*Home address:* Luitpoldstr. 37, Schöneberg
*Law firm address:* Behrenstr. 28, W 8
*Additional information:* Attorney at the LG I-III and notary. After the National Socialist seizure of power in 1933 he was made subject to a temporary representation ban and his license as a notary was revoked; supposedly he still worked as a consultant. Date of declaration of property: 10/12/1941; collection point Levetzowstr. 7-8; transportation on 10/18/1941 to Litzmannstadt/Lodz.
*Sources:* TK 33; JMBl. 33, S. 220; *li; MRRAK; BG; GB II

**Beutler, Dagobert**
08/29/1883 Czarnikau - transportation 1942
*Home address:* Sybelstr. 64, Charlottenburg
*Law firm address:* Oranienstr. 58 a, S 42
*Additional information:* Attorney at the LG I-III, at the AG Berlin-Mitte and notary, joint law firm partnership with his brother Jaques. After the National Socialist seizure of power he was readmitted upon request; at the end of 1935 his license as a notary was revoked; up to the general occupational ban in 1938 he worked as an attorney, then he still worked as a consultant. Date of declaration of property 10/2/1942; interned at the collection point Große Hamburger Str. 26; transportation on 10/03/1942 to Theresienstadt together with his brother Jaques; was transported from Theresienstadt to Auschwitz on 01/23/1943.
TK 33; *li; LAB, Liste 15.10.33; DJ 36, S. 314; MRRAK; Liste d. Kons., 15.3.39; BG; ThG; GB II

**Beutler, Jaques (also Jack)**
09/04/1879 Czarnikau - transportation 1942
*Home address:* Sybelstr. 64, Charlottenburg
*Law firm address:* Oranienstr. 58a, S 42
*Additional information:* Attorney at the KG and notary, he established a joint law firm partnership with his brother Dagobert. After the National Socialist seizure of power he was temporarily

disbarred and his license as a notary was revoked; was admitted as an attorney until the general occupational ban in 1938. Transportation on 10/03/1942 to Theresianstadt together with his brother Dagobert; transported on 10/23/1944 to Auschwitz.

*Sources:* TK 33; JMBl. 33, S. 202; *li; LAB, Liste 15.10.33; BArch, R 3001 PAK; MRRAK; BG; ThG; GB II

**Beutner, Joachim Dr.**
10/07/1897 Jüterbog - 08/08/1963 Berlin
*Home address:* Reichsstr. 105, Charlottenburg
*Law firm address:* Markgrafenstr. 46, W 8
*Additional information:*
He fought in the First World War, he was Protestant; attorney at the LG I-III and notary. After the National Socialist seizure of power he was regarded as "mixed race" (a grandparent was regarded as Jewish). Was allowed to continue work as an attorney and notary, because he was regarded as a "frontline fighter;" together with Wilhelm (presumably his brother) he established a law partnership; he could also continue his profession after the start of the war, however, because of his own origins and that of his wife he was not admitted to the corresponding professional association and was thus greatly disadvantaged. In 1943 the presiding judge of the KG stated that he had made the services of the employment office available to him, since he was not indispensible to the legal profession. In 1944 he was captured by the "Aktionsmitte" ("Action Center"), which was initiated by the Gestapo and carried out by the Todt Organization. To what extent he was involved in demolition work or similar was unclear, since he had suffered from tuberculosis since 1943. He survived the Nazi regime and applied for readmission as an attorney in January 1947. This request was initially denied, since he was to be called on to work as a judge or prosecutor. For reasons of illness, he stuck to his intention to work as an attorney again. In 1948/1949 he was readmitted as an attorney. He died in August 1963 at the age of 65 years in Berlin.
*Sources:* TK 33; Liste 15.10.33; *li; Liste Mschlg. 36; Tel.B. 41; LAB, RAK, PA

**Beutner, Wilhelm Dr.**
No information
*Home address:* no information
*Law firm address:* Markgrafenstr. 46, W 8
*Additional information:* Attorney at the KG and notary; he was Protestant. After the National Socialist seizure of power he was regarded as "mixed race" (a grandparent was regarded as Jewish). In 1933 he was readmitted as an attorney and notary; he established a law partnership with Joachim (presumably his brother); he was still listed as an attorney and notary in the 1943 business directory.
*Sources:* TK 33; *li; LAB, Liste 15.10.33; LAB, Liste Mschlg.36; BArch, R 3001 PAK; Tel.B. 41; Br.B. 43

**Bibro, Felix**
09/28/1903 no information
*Home address:* Schaperstr. 10, W 50
*Law firm address:* Klosterstr. 88/90, C 2
*Additional information:* Attorney at the LG I-III and AG Berlin-Mitte. After the National Socialist seizure of power in 1933 he was made subject to an occupational ban. He emigrated to Palestine.
*Sources:* TK 33; Liste d. nichtzugel. RA, 25.4.33; Pr.J. 33, S. 807; BArch, R 3001 PAK; BG

**Bieber, Friedrich Dr.**
07/25/1891 Lissa - transportation 1944
*Home address:* Woyrschstr. 45, W 35
*Law firm address:* Friedrichstr. 118/119, N 24
*Additional information:* He fought in the First World War; was a Protestant; attorney at the LG I-III and notary. After the National Socialist seizure of power he was readmitted as attorney and notary upon request, because he was recognized as a "frontline fighter"; he was prosecuted; after his conviction in 1935 he was disbarred. Date of declaration of property: 06/27/1933. Collection point Schulstr. 78; was transported on 07/12/1944 to Auschwitz.
*Sources:* TK 33; *li ; LAB, Liste 15.10.33; BArch, R 3001 PAK, PA; BG; GB II

**Bieber, Richard Dr., Judicial Councillor**
06/30/1858 Magdeburg - 09/19/1936
*Home address:* Kaiser-Wilhelm-Str. 53, C 2
*Law firm address:* Kaiser-Wilhelm-Str. 53, C 2
*Additional information:* Attorney at the LG I-III, at the AG Berlin-Mitte and notary.

After the National Socialist seizure of power in 1933 he was readmitted as attorney upon request. End of 1935 his license as a notary was revoked; he died in 1936 at the age of 78.
*Sources:* TK 33; *li; LAB, Liste 15.10.33; DJ 36, S. 314; BG

**Bieberfeld, Siegfried Dr.**
10/15/1881Lissa - 1944 Heidelberg
*Home address:* Mommsenstr. 14, Charlottenburg
*Law firm address:* Alexanderstr. 71, C 25
*Additional information:* Attorney at the LG I-III, AG Berlin-Mitte and notary. After the National Socialist seizure of power in 1933 his license as a notary was revoked, he was readmitted as an attorney upon request until the general occupational ban in 1938. He was a good chess player, as the son of a former chess partner recalled. He and his wife went "underground" during the war in Berlin, by living in a bombed out house. It is noted in files: "10/17/1942 reported to be unknown." Later they fled to Heidelberg and registered themselves as bombing victims under the last name of Biebinger. In this manner they could receive ration cards. He had to undergo an operation in 1944, upon which the surgeon noticed that he was Jewish. The doctor did not report him; however, he died following the operation. His wife managed to go abroad, the son of the family had already been sent away from Germany. He committed suicide in 1945.
*Sources:* Br.B. 32; TK 33; JMBl. 33, S. 202; *li; LAB, Liste 15.10.33; BArch, R 3001 PAK; Naatz-Album; MRRAK; BG; Ausk. Bers

**Bielschowsky, Ludwig Dr.**
02/06/1891 - no information
*Home address:* Kaiserallee 31, Wilmersdorf
*Law firm address:* Güntzelstr. 62, Wilmersdorf
*Additional information:* Attorney at the LG I-III and notary. After the National Socialist seizure of power in 1933 he was readmitted as an attorney; at the end of 1935 his license as a notary was revoked; in 1938 he was made subject to an occupational ban as an attorney.
*Sources:* TK 33; *li; Liste 36; LAB, Liste 15.10.33; MRRAK; BArch, R 3001 PAK

**Bielschowsky, Richard Dr.**
09/26/1895 - no information
*Home address:* no information

*Law firm address:* Meinekestr. 21, W 15
*Additional information:* Attorney at the LG I-III, at the AG Berlin-Mitte and notary. After the National Socialist seizure of power he was made subject to an occupational ban on 06/21/1933. His participation in the First World War was not regarded as deployment on the front, his request to be re-admitted as an attorney was declined.
*Sources:* Br.B. 32; TK 33; Liste d. nichtzugel. RA, 25.4.33; JMBL. 33, S. 253; BArch, R 3001 PAK, PA

**Biermann, Georg**
03/26/1890 Greifswald - 04/03/1945 Theresienstadt
*Home address:* Westfälische Str. 28, Wilmersdorf
*Law firm address:* no information
*Additional information:* Attorney at the LG I-III and AG Berlin-Mitte. After the National Socialist seizure of power he was made subject to a representation ban, subsequently an occupational ban. On 01/23/1943 he was transported from Berlin to Theresienstadt; he died there on 04/03/1945.
*Sources:* TK 33; JMBl. 7.7.33, S. 209; BArch, PAK; VZ 39; GB II

**Bileski, James**
02/25/1891 - no information
*Home address:* no information
*Law firm address:* Carmerstr. 15, Charlottenburg
*Additional information:* Attorney and notary; he was the youngest brother of Moritz; during the First World War he was a pilot for the Luftwaffe.
*Sources:* Jüd.Adr.B.; Br.B. 33; BArch, R 3001 PAK; Ausk. des Neffen J. Aival, 7./8.2001

**Bileski, Moritz Dr.**
04/01/1889 Frankenstein - 02/10/1946
*Home address:* Waitzstr. 12, Charlottenburg
*Law firm address:* Carmerstr. 15, Charlottenburg
*Additional information:*
He had fought in the First World War and was the recipient of the EK; he was a committed Zionist; he was an important member of the K.J.V. (Kartell jüdischer Verbindungen = Cartel of Jewish Connections). Already in the 1920s

he made his first attempt to settle in Palestine, however, conditions were difficult. He returned to Berlin in 1926 and established himself as an attorney at the KG, later also as a notary. After the National Socialist seizure of power, he applied for readmission with evidence that he had fought in the First World War. In July 1933 he emigrated - this time finally - with his family to Palestine and thereupon he was deleted from the list of attorneys. In Palestine he founded the Ahdut Ha'am Party together with Felix Rosenblüth (Rosen). He worked as an attorney until his death and published numerous artaicles. An obituary noted that he was "a jurist in accordance with his spiritual nature," who expected the fulfillment of justice from the law. This was a hindrance in political activities, he rebelled against power games that were primarily concerned with interests and reason of the state. He died in Tel Aviv at the age of 56.
*Sources:* TK 33; Liste d. nichtzugel. RA, 25.4.33; Pr.J. 33, S. 807; BArch, R 3001 PAK, PA; Ausk. d. Sohnes J. Aival

**Birnbaum, Marcus Dr.**
05/23/1890 Fulda - 03/06/1941 Amsterdam
*Home address:* Flotowstr. 7, NW 87
*Law firm address:* Leipziger Str. 113
*Additional information:* Member of the orthodox congregation Adass Jisroel, attorney at the LG I-III and notary. After the National Socialist seizure of power in 1933 he was made subject to an occupational ban. Emigration to Amsterdam, the Netherlands, on 02/01/1939, where he died two years later at the age of 50.
*Sources:* Br.B. 32; TK 33; JMBl. 33, S. 253; BArch, R 3001 PAK; BG

**Bischofswerder, Franz Dr.**
06/13/1888 Berlin - no information
*Home address:* Markgrafendamm 25, O 17
*Law firm address:* An der Spandauer Brücke 12, C 2
Attorney at the KG and notary. After the National Socialist seizure of power he was readmitted: at the end of 1935 his license as a notary was revoked; he worked as an attorney until the general he was made subject to an occupational ban in 1938; was used by the Jewish synagogue as an escort for the transport of Jewish refugees on 04/02/1939 to Richborough, Great Britain; he remained there and still emigrated to the USA in 1939; he

changed his name to Frank Bishop.
*Sources:* TK 33; *li; LAB, Liste 15.10.33; DJ 36, S. 314; MRRAK; BArch, R 3001 PAK; BG

**Bischofswerder, Isidor, Judicial Councillor**
02/07/1858 Wongrowitz - 01/27/1941 Berlin
*Home address:* Berkaer Str. 32-35, Altersheim der Jüd. Gemeinde (Retirement home of the Jewish Synagogue)
*Law firm address:* Keithstr. 21, W 62
*Additional information:* Presumably the father of Franz; attorney at the LG I-III and AG Charlottenburg. After the National Socialist seizure of power he was readmitted as attorney; worked as an attorney until the general occupational ban of 1938. Most recently lived in a retirement home of the Jewish Synagogue.
*Sources:* TK 33; *li; LAB, Liste 15.10.33; BArch, R 3001 PAK; MRRAK; BG

**Bittermann, Wilhelm**
No information- 04/19/1937
*Home address:* no information
*Law firm address:* Hardenbergstr. 19, Charlottenburg
*Additional information:* Attorney at the LG I-III, AG Berlin-Mitte and notary. After the National Socialist seizure of power in 1933 his license as a notary was revoked; he worked as an attorney until at least 1936.
*Sources:* TK 33; *li; LAB, Liste 15.10.33; Liste 36; BArch, R 3001 PAK

**Blach, Friedrich Samuel**
01/19/1884 Stralsund - August 1969
*Home address:* Mackensenstr. 5, Schöneberg
*Law firm address:* Pommersche Str. 7a, Wilmersdorf
*Additional information:* Attorney at the LG II. After the National Socialist seizure of power he was readmitted as an attorney upon request; 1937 emigration to New York, USA; he died in August 1969.
*Sources:* TK 33; *li; LAB, Liste 15.10.33; BArch,R 3001 PAK; BG; SSDI (Frederick B.)

**Blankenfeld, Fritz Dr.**
06/20/1889 Wangerin - no information
*Home address:* Salzburger Str. 7, Schöneberg
*Law firm address:* Linkstr. 19, W 9
*Additional information:* Attorney at the KG and notary. After the National Socialist seizure of power in 1933 he was readmitted

upon request; at the end of 1935 his license as a notary was revoked; he worked as an attorney until the general occupational ban in 1938; emigration on 09/01/1940 to Montevideo, Uruguay.
*Sources:* TK 33; *li; DJ 36, S. 314; MRRAK; BArch, R 3001 PAK; BG

**Blaschkauer, Rudolf, Judicial Councillor**
09/13/1862 Murowana - 12/11/1940
*Home address:* Wielandstr. 11, Charlottenburg
*Law firm address:* Wittelsbacher Str. 25, Wilmersdorf
*Additional information:* Attorney at the LG I-III and notary. After the National Socialist seizure of power in 1933 his license as a notary was revoked; he worked as an attorney until his disbarment on 09/24/1938.
*Sources:* TK 33; JMBl. 33, S. 208; *li; LAB, Liste 15.10.33; BG

**Blasse, Jakob**
07/14/1883 Koschmin - no information
*Home address:* Riehlstr. 7, Charlottenburg
*Law firm address:* Burgstr. 7, C 2
*Additional information:* Attorney at the LG I-III and notary; after the National Socialist seizure of power he was readmitted upon request; at the end of 1935 his license as a notary was revoked; he worked as an attorney up to the general occupational ban in 1938.
*Sources:* TK 33; *li; DJ 36, S. 314; BArch, R 3001 PAK; MRRAK; BG

**Blau, Bernhard**
12/14/1881 Stolp - no information
*Home address:* Eichenallee 9, Charlottenburg
*Law firm address:* Eichenallee 66, Charlottenburg
*Additional information:* Attorney at the KG and notary. After the National Socialist seizure of power in 1933 his license as a notary was revoked; he worked as an attorney up to the general occupational ban in 1938, then he still worked as a "consultant." He had a so-called "mixed race" marriage, his wife was regarded as "Aryan." He survived the National Socialist regime and after the liberation he lived in Charlottenburg.
*Sources:* TK 33; JMBl. 33, S. 202; *li; MRRAK; LAB, Liste d. Kons. 15.3.1939; BG

**Blau, Bruno Dr.**
09/10/1881 Marienwerder/Westpreußen - 08/21/1954 Freiburg i.Br.
*Home address:* Heinestr. 12 (Babelsberg)
*Law firm address:* Alexanderplatz 1, C 25
*Additional information:* Attorney at the LG I-III, AG Berlin-Mitte and notary. After the National Socialist seizure of power he was readmitted upon request; he shared his law office premises with his colleagues. In the summer of 1933 the minister of justice issued an order "that all such associations should be dissolved by the end of September. My colleague therefore rented another office and since all the offices were too big for me, I was also forced to look for another. In fact, since I could not find suitable offices in my old area, I had no choice but to move to another area" (Memoirs, page 26). When the former law office premises were closed, he had to pay a considerable amount of money and the termination of a contract with a telephone company had to be decided by the court, since he was not prepared to continue his obligations under the contract for several years. He referred to the predicament in the transfer of practice. After the court entered a verdict against him, he said that it had played a decisive role in the fact that "a Jewish judge was an assessor; and this was a former Senate president of the KG, who had been transferred to the much lower job of an appointee at the LG as a result of the aforementioned Law for the Restoration of the Professional Civil Service. The judge was the speaker for my case, and the decision largely depended on him. I had to find out for myself what I had learned from my previous practice, that the Jewish judges were taking a position which was directed against the Jewish party from an exaggerated objectivity. In other words, they wanted to avoid any appearance that they as Jews had incorrectly favored a Jewish person. Thus I lost the trial." (page 27f.).
At the end of 1935 his license as a notary was revoked. 1936 he relinquished his license to practice law, it was canceled on 02/24/1936. He emigrated to Prague; there he began to compile social statistics. In 1942 he was arrested and transferred to the Gestapo in Berlin. He had been suffering from stomach pain for a long time and had to stick to a diet; he became very ill in prison and could no longer walk by himself. He was therefore sent to the

Police Division of the Jewish Hospital. The chief physician diagnosed him with cancer. A radiologist treated him with high radiation doses, with the result that he was able to regain his mobility over the years. However, with a certain cancer diagnosis, he had apparently fallen into oblivion with the responsible Gestapo offices, even after the extremely unusual transfer in 1944 from the police station to the "free" station of the hospital, he was not transported. In this way he survived the Nazi era. After 1945, he emigrated to the United States, where he became prominent with various publications. He died in 1954 in Freiburg i.Br.

Numerous publications: Das Ausnahmerecht für die Juden in den europäischen Ländern 1933-1945 [The separate legal regime for Jews in European nations 1933-1945], New York 1952; Das Ausnahmerecht für die Juden in Deutschland 1933-1945 [The separate legal regime for Jews in Germany 1933-1945],1st, 2nd and 3rd ed. Düsseldorf 1954 and/or 1965; Die Kriminalität der deutschen Juden, o.J. [The crime rate of German Jews, without year]; The Jewish Population of Germany 1939-1945, without year; Zur Geschichte der Reichsvertretung [The history of the National Representative Agency of German Jews], manuscript, Frankfurt/M. 1937; Vierzehn Jahre Not und Schrecken, Memoiren [Fourteen years of need and and terror, memoirs], unpublished manuscript, USA, without year (ca. 1952).
*Sources:* TK 33; *li; Liste 15.10.33; LAB, Lis-te 36,; DJ 36, S. 314 u. 360; BArch, R 3001 PAK; BG; Grabstein

**Bley, Bruno Dr.**
09/27/1894 Berlin - no information
*Home address:* Wilhelmshöher Str. 29, Friedenau (1926)
*Law firm address:* Dorotheenstr. 77-78
*Additional information:* Since 1926 he was an attorney at the LG I-III. In the personnel file his religion is listed as "mosaic." After the National Socialist seizure of power on 05/23/1933 he was disbarred because of "non-Aryan"ancestry, on 06/07/1933 his admission was revoked. The file mentions: "The name of the lawyer Dr. Bruno Bley is listed in the list of Republican Association of Judges . . . "
*Sources:* Br.B. 32; TK 33; MvRRB; JMBl. 23.6.33, S. 195; BArch R 3001 PAK, PA

**Bleyberg, Max, Judicial Councillor**
No information
*Home address:* no information
*Law firm address:* Landsberger Allee 11/13
*Additional information:* Attorney at the LG I-III, AG Berlin-Mitte and notary. He was readmitted after the National Socialist seizure of power; at the end of 1935 his license as a notary was revoked; he was presumably disbarred on 01/15/1935 (other data state 1938).
*Sources:* TK 33; *li; LAB, Liste 15.10.33; DJ 36, S. 314; BArch, R 3001 PAK

**Bloch, Arthur Dr.**
1002/1883 Ratibor - no information
*Home address:* Pestalozzistr. 59, Charlottenburg
*Law firm address:* Kaiserallee 208, W 15
*Additional information:* Attorney at the KG and notary. After the National Socialist seizure of power in 1933 his license as a notary was revoked. He was disbarred as an attorney on 04/01/1937; he emigrated on 03/01/1937 to New York, USA.
*Sources:* TK 33; JMBl. 33, S. 208; *li; LAB, Liste 15.10.33; BArch, R 3001 PAK; BG

**Bloch, Paul**
No information
*Home address:* no information
*Law firm address:* Friedrichstr, 175, W 8
*Additional information:* Attorney and notary. After the National Socialist seizure of power he was readmitted as an attorney; at the end of 1935 his license as a notary was revoked; he worked as an attorney until the general occupational ban in 1938.
*Sources:* Adr.B. 32; *li: LAB, Liste 15.10.33; Liste 36; MRRAK; BArch, R 3001 PAK

**Block, Werner**
No information
*Home address:* No information
*Law firm address:* Kurfürstendamm 202, W 15
*Additional information:* Attorney at the KG. After the National Socialist seizure of power he was readmitted; he worked as an attorney until the general occupational ban in 1938.
*Sources:* TK 33; *li; LAB, Liste 15.10.33; Lis-te 36; MRRAK; BArch, R 3001 PAK

**Blum, Alfred Dr.**
No information
*Home address:* no information
*Law firm address:* Kurfürstendamm 32, W 15

*Additional information:* Attorney and notary; after the National Socialist seizure of power in 1933 his license as a notary was first revoked, thereupon he closed his law office.
*Sources:* JMBl. 33, S. 202; Pr.J. 33, S. 466; BArch, R 3001 PAK

**Blum, Arno Dr.**
10/12/1903 Berlin - June 1974 Jerusalem
*Home address:* no information
*Law firm address:* Kurfürstendamm 38/39
*Additional information:* Attorney since 1924, admitted to the LG I-III. After the National Socialist seizure of power in 1933 he was made subject to a general occupational ban. In the same year he emigrated to France; 1934 to Palestine. After 1945 every so often he was a legal adviser of the Israelische Mission (Israeli Mission) in Cologne, 1962-67 director general of the Israeli Court of Auditors.
*Sources:* Br.B. 32; TK 33; Liste d. nichtzugel. RA, 25.4.33; JMBl. 33, S. 253; BArch, R 3001 PAK; BG; Göpp., S. 270

**Blum, Hans Dr.**
07/02/1899 Berlin - no information
*Home address:* Grolmanstr. 41, Charlottenburg
*Law firm address:* Tauentzienstr. 8, W 50
*Additional information:* Attorney at the LG I-III and AG Berlin-Mitte. After the National Socialist seizure of power he was made subject to an occupational ban on 06/19/1933. He emigrated to Great Britain on 04/19/1939.
*Sources:* Adr.B. 32; TK 33; Liste d. nichtzugel. RA, 25.4.33; JMBl. 33, S. 253; BArch, R 3001 PAK, PA; BG

**Blumenfeld, Fritz Dr.**
08/16/1883 Neuruppin - transportation 1942
*Home address:* Kaiserplatz 2, Wilmersdorf
*Law firm address:* Potsdamer Str. 24/25, W 35
*Additional information:* Attorney at the LG I-III and notary. After the National Socialist seizure of power in 1933 his license as a notary was revoked, he was readmitted as an attorney until the general occupational ban in 1938. Emigration to Paris, France; on 11/04/1942 he was transported from Drancy to Auschwitz.
*Sources:* Br.B. 32; TK 33; JMBl. 33, S. 202; *li; MRRAK; BArch, R 3001 PAK; BG; GB II

**Blumenfeld, Paul**
05/22/1887 Forst/Lausitz - 08/09/1942 Berlin
*Home address:* Gontardstr. 3, C 25
*Law firm address:* Sophienstr. 5, N 54
*Additional information:* Attorney at the LG II and the AG Lichtenberg. After the National Socialist seizure of power in 1933 he was made subject to an occupational ban. He died in 1942 at the hospital in Auguststr. 14-15 at the age of 55.
*Sources:* TK 33; Liste d. nichtzugel. RA, 25.4.33; JMBl. 33, S. 202; BArch, R 3001 PAK; BG

**Blumenheim, Rudolf Dr.**
12/25/1900 Berlin - May 1978
*Home address:* no information
*Law firm address:* Friedrichstr. 203, SW 68
*Additional information:* Attorney at the LG I-III and AG Berlin-Mitte. After the National Socialist seizure of power he was made subject to an occupational ban on 06/19/1933. He emigrated to the USA, where he most recently lived in Palm Beach, Florida.
*Sources:* Adr.B. 32; TK 33; Liste d. nichtzugel. RA.; JMBl. 33, S. 253; BArch, R 3001 PAK, PA; SSDI (Bluemenheim)

**Blumenthal, Berthold Dr.**
02/26/1886 Berlin - 02/07/1941
*Home address:* no information
*Law firm address:* Nachodstr. 19, W 50
*Additional information:* Attorney at the LG I-III, AG Charlottenburg and notary. After the National Socialist seizure of power in 1933 his license as a notary was revoked; he was admitted as an attorney until the general occupational ban in 1938. He died in February 1941 shortly before his 55th birthday.
*Sources:* TK 33; JMBl. 33, S. 234; *li; Liste 36; MRRAK; BArch, R 3001 PAK; BG

**Blumenthal, Curt (Kurt) Dr.**
12/05/1883 - transportation 1943
*Home address:* Mommsenstr. 22, Charlottenburg
*Law firm address:* Schloßstr. 107, Steglitz
*Additional information:* Attorney at the LG I-III, AG Schöneberg and notary. After the National Socialist seizure of power in 1933 he was temporarily disbarred and his license as a notary was revoked; worked as an attorney until the general occupational ban in 1938, later forced labor. Date of declaration of

property: 01/17/1943, collection point Große Hamburger Str. 26; on 01/1943 transportation to Auschwitz.
*Sources:* TK 33; JMBl. 33, S. 202; *li; BArch, R 3001 PAK; MRRAK; BG; GB II

**Blumenthal, Erich Dr.**
10/31/1887 - no information
*Home address:* Brandenburgische Str. 42, Wilmersdorf
*Law firm address:* Wichmannstr. 28, W 62
*Additional information:* Attorney at the LG I-III and notary. After the National Socialist seizure of power in 1933 he was readmitted upon request; at the end of 1935 his license as an attorney was revoked; he worked as an attorney up to the general occupational ban in 1938; emigration to the USA.
*Sources:* Br.B. 32; TK 33; *li; DJ 36, S. 314; BArch, R 3001 PAK; MRRAK; BG

**Blumenthal, Erich Dr.**
08/24/1893 - no information
*Home address:* no information
*Law firm address:* Krausenstr. 12, (or Friedrichstr. 246, SW 68)
*Additional information:* Attorney at the LG I-III and notary. After the National Socialist seizure of power in 1933 he was made subject to an occupational ban; emigrated to Australia on 08/10/1939.
*Sources:* Br.B. 32; TK 33; JMBl. 33, S. 253; BArch, R 3001 PAK; BG

**Blumenthal, Julius Dr.**
03/17/1900 Gdansk – 12/03/1942 Sachsenhausen
*Home address:* no information
*Law firm address:* Oranienburger Str. 1
*Additional information:* Attorney at the LG I-III and AG Berlin-Mitte. After the National Socialist seizure of power he was made subject to an occupational ban on 05/26/1933; he was active in the Jewish community; as from 1939 he was a legal assistant of the Jüdisches Nachrichtenblatt (Jewish Bulletin) and leader of the legal division of the Jewish Synagogue. He was one of eight hostages who were shot in retaliation for employees of the Jewish community in Sachsenhausen who were listed to be transported, but escaped.
*Sources:* Br.B. 32; TK 33; LAB, Liste d. nichtzugel. RA. 25.4.33; JMBl.30.6.33, S. 203; BArch, R 3001 PAK; BG; GB II (3.12.1942);

Walk, nach Lowenthal, Bewährung, S.185; Göpp., S. 239 Sterbefallanzeige KZ Sachsenhausen

**Blumenthal, Otto Dr.**
01/18/1897 Berlin - 09/28/1988
*Home address:* Wilskistr. 66, Zehlendorf
*Law firm address:* Nürnberger Str. 66, W 50
*Additional information:* He fought in the First World War; he had many artistic and intellectual interests; together with Hans Richter he founded the Deutsche Liga für Unabhängigen Film (German League for Independent Film); attorney at the LG I-III and notary; brother-in-law of Udo Rukser, together they formed a law partnership. After the National Socialist seizure of power he was readmitted as an attorney and a notary, because he was recognized as a "frontline fighter." He was disbarred as an attorney on 10/01/1935. In November 1938 he was arrested and transported to the Dachau concentration camp. After his release in February 1939 he emigrated to Palestine, where he changed his name to B. Oded Bental; he took a job as a bank clerk, which he did not like. After 1945 he worked for URO in its Berlin office.
*Sources:* TK 33; *li; LAB, Liste 15.10.33; BArch, R 3001 PAK; BLHA, Rep. 36 A, OFP, Nr. A 427; Ausk. Hön-Museum, HEGAU; Ausk. Werner Wolff 3/2000

**Blumenthal, Siegfried Dr.**
08/31/1898 Berlin - 1974 Berlin
*Home address:* Karlsruher Str. 29, Wilmersdorf
*Law firm address:* Mommsenstr. 45, Charlottenburg
*Additional information:* Attorney at the LG I-III and AG Berlin-Mitte. After the National Socialist seizure of power in 1933 he was readmitted as an attorney. He worked as an attorney until the general occupational ban in 1938. After 11/09/1938 he was transported to the Sachsenhausen concentration camp; he was released with the condition that he had to emigrate to a non-European country; he emigrated to Palestine in March 1939; his mother and his sister were transported and murdered. In 1950 he returned to Berlin and worked in the judicial field.
*Sources:* TK 33; *li; LAB, Liste 15.10.33; MRRAK; BArch, R 3001 PAK; PA Sen.Just. Archiv 74/60; BG; Ausk. F. Flechtmann

**Boas, Fritz**
10/18/1889 - no information
*Home address:* no information
*Law firm address:* Potsdamer Str. 43, W 35
*Additional information:* He fought in the
First World War; attorney at the KG and
notary. After the National Socialist seizure
of power in 1933 he was readmitted as an
attorney, because he was recognized as a
"frontline fighter." In 1935 his license as
a notary was revoked; he worked as an
attorney until the general occupational ban
of 1938.
*Sources:* Br.B. 32; TK 33; *li; LAB, Liste
15.10.33; DJ 36, S. 314; MRRAK; BArch, R
3001 PAK, PA

**Boas, Hans Dr.**
04/18/1883 Berlin - transportation 1943
*Home address:* Kluckstr. 27, W 35
*Law firm address:* Viktoria-Luise-Platz 10
*Additional information:* Attorney at the LG
I-III and notary. After the National Socialist
seizure of power in 1933 he was readmitted
upon request; in 1935 his license as a notary
was revoked; he worked as an attorney until
the general occupational ban in 1938. On
03/03/1943 transportation to Auschwitz.
*Sources:* TK 33; *li; LAB, Liste 15.10.33; DJ
36, S. 314; MRRAK; BArch, R 3001 PAK;
BG; GB II

**Bobrecker, Alfred**
01/20/1868- 12/18/1934
*Home address:* Niersteiner Str. 6,
Wilmersdorf
*Law firm address:* Gontardstr. 4, C 25
*Additional information:* Attorney at the LG
1-III and notary. After the National Socialist
seizure of power his license as a notary was
revoked, he was readmitted as an attorney
upon request. His wife Martha was regarded
as "Aryan." He died in 1934 at the age of 66.
*Sources:* TK 33; JMBl. 33, S. 202; *li; BArch,
R 3001 PAK; BG

**Bochner, Ernst**
12/30/1872 Schönlanke - 10/04/1937
*Home address:* Tölzer Str. 29, Wilmersdorf
*Law firm address:* Bayreuther Str. 41, W 62
*Additional information:* Attorney at the
LG I-III. After the National Socialist seizure
of power in 1933 he was readmitted as an
attorney upon request. In 1936 he was still

working as an attorney; he died in 1937 at the
age of 74.
*Sources:* TK 33; *li; Liste 36; LAB, Liste
15.10.33; BArch, R 3001 PAK; BG

**Bodlaender, Rudolf Dr.**
01/19/1903 - no information
*Home address:* no information
*Law firm address:* Wera-Promenade 5,
Friedrichshagen
*Additional information:* After the National
Socialist seizure of power he was made subject
to an occupational ban in 1933.
*Sources:* Liste d. nichtzugel. RA, 25.4.33;
JMBl. 33, S. 253; BArch, R 3001 PAK

**Boehm, Erich**
05/18/1884 - no informationj
*Home address:* Altensteinstr. 59, Zehlendorf
*Law firm address:* Joachimsthaler Str. 11, W 15
*Additional information:* Attorney and
notary. After the National Socialist seizure
of power in 1933 his license as a notary was
revoked; he was readmitted as an attorney
upon request; his license as a notary was
revoked on 04/05/1934.
*Sources:* Pr.J. 33, S. 390; *li; LAB, Liste
15.10.33; BArch, R 3001 PAK

**Boehm, Julius Edgar**
08/17/1884 - no information
*Home address:* no information
*Law firm address:* Kurfürstendamm 197/98,
W 15
*Additional information:* Attorney at the LG
I-III and notary. After the National Socialist
seizure of power in 1933 he was readmitted
upon request. At the end of 1935 his license
as a notary was revoked; he worked as an
attorney until the general occupational ban.
*Sources:* TK 33; *li; LAB, Liste 15.10.33; DJ
36, S. 314; MRRAK; BArch, R 3001 PAK

**Boehm, Max, Judicial Councillor**
No information
*Home address:* Riehlstr. 3, Charlottenburg
(1931)
*Law firm address:* Belle-Alliance-Sr. 88, SW 61
*Additional information:* Attorney at the
KG and notary. After the National Socialist
seizure of power in early 1933 he was
temporarily banned from working; upon
request he was readmitted as an attorney and
notary; he was no longer listed in the 1936

personnel calendar of the Ministry of Justice.
*Sources:* Jüd.Adr.B.; *li, Liste d. nichtzugel.
RA, 25.4.33; LAB, Liste 15.10.33; BArch, R
3001 PAK

**Boenheim, Ernst Dr.**
No information
*Home address:* Geisbergstr. 34, W 30
*Law firm address:* Lützowplatz 27
*Additional information:* Attorney at the
KG; after the National Socialist seizure of
power of the board of the RAK he applied
as an attorney of the Rote Hilfe" (Red Aid)
to the PrMJ; afterwards there are no further
references in the bar association lists.
*Sources:* Jüd.Adr.B.; Br.B. 32; TK 33; Liste
d. nichtzugel. RA, 25.4.33 (Nachtrag); GStA,
Rep. 84a, Nr. 20363

**Boenheim, Kurt Dr.**
10/26/1886 Markgrabowa - no information
*Home address:* Flatowstr. 1
*Law firm address:* Charlottenstr. 59
*Additional information:* Attorney at the LG
I-III and notary. On 11/12/1926 he announced
his resignation from the Jewish Synagogue.
After the National Socialist seizure of power
he was made subject to an occupational ban
in July 1933; on 08/16/1933 he once again
became a member of the Jewish Synagogue.
*Sources:* Jüd.Adr.B.; Adr.B. 32; TK 33; JMBl.
15.7.33, S. 220/21; BArch, R 3001 PAK; BG

**Boerne, Ludwig Dr., Judicial Councillor**
No information
*Home address:* No information
*Law firm address:* Friedrichstr. 183, W 8
*Additional information:* Attorney at the
LG I-III and notary. After the National
Socialist seizure of power in 1933 he was
readmitted upon request. He was disbarred
on 10/07/1935.
*Sources:* TK 33; *li; LAB, Liste 15.10.33;
BArch, R 3001 PAK

**Böhm, Gustav, Dr. Judicial Councillor**
11/27/1885 Cottbus - ca. 1933
*Home address:* no information
*Law firm address:* Charlottenstr. 57, W 8 (?)
*Additional information:* Attorney at the LG
I Berlin since 08/03/1917. After the National
Socialist seizure of power he was disbarred on
06/09/1933 due to "non-Aryan" ancestry, on
06/16/1933 he was disbarred. He died in 1933

at the age of 48. More detailed circumstances
of his death are not known.
*Sources:* TK 33; JMBl. 7.7.33, S. 209; BArch,
R 3001 PAK

**Bokofzer, Erwin Dr.**
05/07/1889 - no information
*Home address:* no information
*Law firm address:* Nettelbeckstr. 7/8, W 62
*Additional information:* Attorney at the LG
I-III and AG Berlin-Mitte. After the National
Socialist seizure of power in 1933 he was
readmitted upon request; he worked as an
attorney up to the general occupational ban
in 1938.
*Sources:* TK 33; *li; LAB, Liste 36, Liste
15.10.33; MRRAK; BArch, R 3001 PAK

**Bonnem, Max Dr.**
06/26/1886 - 12/10/1937
*Home address:* Hektorstr. 9-10, Wilmersdorf
*Law firm address:* Lützow-Ufer 17, W 35
*Additional information:* Attorney at the LG
I-III and notary. After the National Socialist
seizure of power in April 1933 he was first
made subject to a representation ban, then
he was readmitted as an attorney. 1933 his
license as a notary was revoked, he died in
1937 at the age of 51.
*Sources:* TK 33; JMBl. 33, S. 202; *li; LAB,
Liste 15.10.33; BArch, R 3001 PAK; BG

**Bonnin, August Dr., Judicial Councillor**
No information
*Home address:* no information
*Law firm address:* Ritterstr. 66, SW 68
*Additional information:* Attorney at the LG
I-III and notary. After the National Socialist
seizure of power in 1933 his license as a
notary was revoked; he was still admitted as
an attorney in 1936.
*Sources:* TK 33; JMBl. 33, S. 202; *li; LAB,
Liste 36, Liste 15.10.33; BArch, R 3001 PAK

**Borg, Max**
01/07/1889 Gdansk - no information
*Home address:* no information
*Law firm address:* Behrenstr. 51/52, Mitte
*Additional information:* Attorney since
1932, admitted to the LG I-III. After the
National Socialist seizure of power he was
made subject to an occupational ban in
June 1933; he relocated his law office from
Kurfürstendamm 177 to Behrenstraße.

He was disbarred during the course of the merging of the three district courts, because he was no longer admitted to the newly formed LG. He supposedly emigrated to France.
*Sources:* TK 33; Pr.J. 33, S. 737; BArch, R 3001 PAK, PA; BG

**Boronow, Joseph (Josef)**
11/11/1880 Berlin - transportation 1943
*Home address:* Stülpnagelstr. 3, Charlottenburg
*Law firm address:* Großgörschenstr. 40, W 57
*Additional information:* Attorney and notary at the KG. After the National Socialist seizure of power in 1933 his license as a notary was revoked; he worked as an attorney up to the general occupational ban in 1938. After the occupational ban he was used for forced labor and was used as a worker. Date of declaration of property: 09/16/1943, collection point Große Hamburger Str. 26, transportion on 09/28/1943 to Auschwitz.
*Sources:* TK 33; JMBl. 33, S. 202; *li; Liste 36; LAB, Liste 15.10.33; MRRAK; BArch, R 3001 PAK; BG; GB II

**Brach, Max Dr.**
11/26/1887 Berlin - no information
*Home address:* Lützowstr. 3, W 35
*Law firm address:* Burgstr. 26
*Additional information:* Attorney at the LG I-III, at the AG Berlin-Mitte and notary. After the National Socialist seizure of power in early 1933 he emigrated to Amsterdam, the Netherlands on 06/01/1937, later to the USA.
*Sources:* Br.B. 32; TK 33; Liste d. nichtzugel. RA, 25.4.33; JMBl. 33, S. 209; BArch, R 3001 PAK; BG

**Bradt, Martin Dr.**
04/25/1877 Berlin - no information
*Home address:* Giesebrechtstr. 11, Charlottenburg
*Law firm address:* Steinplatz 1, Charlottenburg
*Additional information:* Attorney at the LG I-III, AG Berlin-Mitte and notary. After the National Socialist seizure of power in 1933 he was temporarily made subject to a ban on representation and his license as a notary was revoked; he was admitted as an attorney until the general occupational ban in 1938. Emigration to Glasgow, Great Britain.

*Sources:* TK 33; JMBl. 33, S. 208; *li; LAB, Liste 15.10.33; MRRAK; BArch, R 3001 PAK; BG

**Brandt, Arthur**
06/21/1893 Züllichau - 01/24/1989 Lugano
*Home address:* Tauentzienstr. 12a, W 50
*Law firm address:* Tauentzienstr. 12a, W 50
*Additional information:* One of the most prominent defenders of the Weimar Republic, he became well known because of his representation in the sensational "Cheka"political trial (1925); he had connections with "Rote Hilfe Deutschland" (Red Aid Germany); he worked in a law partnership with Hans Fraustedter. After the National Socialist seizure of power he was regarded as politically unpopular in the view of the National Socialists; the RAK had reported him. Emigration in March 1933 to London, Great Britain; a warrant was issued against him for tax code violations. 1938 he continued to the USA. Attorney at the Supreme Court in Massachusetts. 1953 he returned to Berlin, worked as an attorney until 1970, he later moved to Lugano, where he died in 1989.
Numerous publications, amongst others "Denkschrift der Verteidigung" [The brief of the defense], New edition, 1979
*Sources:* TK 33; JMBl. 33, S. 253; BArch, R 3001 PAK; GStA, Rep. 84 a, Nr. 20363; Göpp., S. 330; Ausk. T. Krach; Wolf, BFS; Schneider, Schwarz, Schwarz

**Brandt, Heinrich, Judicial Councillor**
02/14/1872 Warsaw - no information
*Home address:* Goethestr. 11, Lichterfelde
*Law firm address:* Goethestr. 11, Lichterfelde
*Additional information:* Attorney at AG Lichterfelde. After the National Socialist seizure of power he was readmitted as an attorney. He was disbarred in the late fall of 1933. He survived the National Socialist regime and after 1945 lived in Berlin-Wilmersdorf.
*Sources:* TK 33; *li; Pr.J. 9.11.33, S. 633; BArch, R 3001 PAK; BG

**Brandus, Werner Dr.**
02/18/1899 Magdeburg - no information
*Home address:* no information
*Law firm address:* Charlottenstr.55, W 8
*Additional information:* Attorney at the LG

I-III and AG Berlin-Mitte. After the National Socialist seizure of power he was disbarred as an attorney on 03/19/1933.
*Sources:* Adr.B. 32; TK 33; Liste d. nichtzugel. RA, 25.4.33; JMBl. 33, S. 253; BArch, R 3001 PAK

**Brasch, Paul (Isidor)**
03/21/1884 Posen (now known as Poznan) - transportation 1942
*Home address:* Bamberger Str. 36, W 30
*Law firm address:* Kantstr. 8, Charlottenburg
*Additional information:* Attorney at the KG and notary. After the National Socialist seizure of power he was readmitted; at the end of 1935 his license as a notary was revoked; he worked as an attorney until the general occupational ban of 1938; emigration to Brussels, Belgium in 1939; after the start of the war he was interned as a former officer; on 08/31/1942 he was transported from Drancy to Auschwitz.
*Sources:* TK 33; *li; LAB, Liste 15.10.33; DJ 36, S. 314; MRRAK; BArch, R 3001 PAK; BG; g; GB II

**Brass, Alfons Dr.**
05/17/1888 - no information
*Home address:* no information
*Law firm address:* Alte Jakobstr. 124
*Additional information:* Attorney at the KG and notary. After the National Socialist seizure of power he was made subject to an occupational ban on 06/20/1933.
*Sources:* Br.B. 32; TK 33; LAB, Liste d. nichtzugel. RA, 25.4.33; JMBl. 4.8.33, S. 253; BArch, R 3001 PAK

**Brauer, Hans Dr.**
11/17/1899 - no information
*Home address:* Rosenthaler Str. 43, N 54
*Law firm address:* Rosenthaler Str. 43, N 54
*Additional information:* Attorney at the KG. After the National Socialist seizure of power he was made subject to a general occupational ban in April 1933; later he was readmitted as an attorney; still listed as an attorney in the business directory until 1935.
*Sources:* TK 33; Liste d. nichtzugel. RA; *li; LAB, Liste 15.10.33; BArch, R 3001 PAK; Br.B. 35

**Braun, Emilie, nee Melchior**
12/03/1897 Hamburg - no information
*Home address:* no information

*Law firm address:* Motzstr. 88, W 30
*Additional information:* Since 10/22/1932 she was admitted as a female attorney to the LG I-III. After the National Socialist seizure of power she was made subject to an occupational ban on 06/24/1933; emigration to France.
*Sources:* TK 33; Liste d. nichtzugel. RA, 25.4.33; JMBl. 33, S. 220; BArch, R 3001 PAK, PA; BLHA, PrBr Rep. 36 A, OFP Dev. St.

**Braun, Kurt Dr.**
09/13/1897 Berlin - September 1985
*Home address:* Küstriner Str. 5, Charlottenburg
*Law firm address:* Nollendorfplatz 6, W 30
*Additional information:* Since 1916 he studied in Berlin; 1917-18 at the war navy; 1922 doctorate in Breslau; from 1923 he was a district court judge in Berlin-Lichterfelde; since 1924 an attorney, most recently he was admitted to the LG I-III, AG Berlin-Mitte, later also a notary, specialized in business law. After the National Socialist seizure of power in April 1933 he was made subject to an occupational ban, upon request he was readmitted; he worked as an attorney up to the general occupational ban in 1938. Emigration to London, Great Britain, on 05/10/1939; to the USA in 1940; 1940-42 economic policy research at the University of New Hampshire, Durham; 1942-51 Brookings Institution, Washington, D.C.; 1944-45 also adviser to the U.S.-War Ministry, at the same time he was a guest professor at the Howard University, Washington, D.C.; 1960-67 head of the West European Division at the Statistical Office of the U.S. Department of Labor; lived in Alexandria, Virginia in 1975, died 1985.
*Sources:* TK 33; *li; LAB, Liste d. nichtzugel. RA, 25.4.33, Liste 15.10.33 DJ 36, S. 314; MRRAK; BArch, R 3001 PAK; BG; BHdE Bd. 1, S. 87 (Geb.dat.: 13.9.1899); SSDI

**Brée, Hans**
04/30/1890 Stolp - no information
*Home address:* no information
*Law firm address:* Schadowstr. 4/5, NW 7
*Additional information:* He was a "frontline fighter" and was baptized a Protestant; but he left the church in 1933 because he vetoed their attitude toward National Socialism. Attorney at the LG I-III. After the National Socialist seizure of power he was readmitted as an attorney. He was regarded as "mixed race"

(his father was Jewish). He still worked as an attorney in 1943. Due to his good contacts to Jewish families, who also were amongst his clients, he was persistently persecuted by the Gestapo, the Customs Investigation Office and the Vermögensverwertungsstelle (Asset Reclamation Office) and finally was used as a forced laborer by the Todt organization. After 1945 he was readmitted as an attorney and a notary. 1965 he was disbarred, because he had moved away from Berlin.
*Sources:* *li; LAB, Liste 15.10.33; Liste Mschlg. 36; Tel.B. 41; Br.B. 43; LAB, RAK PA

**Breit, Georg**
05/22/1873 Nimptsch - 12/31/1941 Litzmannstadt/Lodz
*Home address:* Mommsenstr. 66, Charlottenburg
*Law firm address:* Friedrichstr. 166, W 8
*Additional information:* Attorney at the KG and notary. After the National Socialist seizure of power in 1933 he was readmitted upon request; at the end of 1935 his license as a notary was revoked; he worked as an attorney up to the general occupational ban in 1938. Date of declaration of property: 10/23/1941; collection point Levetzowstr. 7-8; transportation on 11/01/1941 to Litzmannstadt/Lodz, he died there two months later.
*Sources:* *li; LAB, Liste 15.10.33; BArch, R 3001, PAK; MRRAK; BG; GB II

**Breslau, Alexander Dr.**
04/26/1900 Berlin - 04/17/1969 Montreux, Switzerland
*Home address:* Kurfürstendamm 155 b, Wilmersdorf
*Law firm address:* Grolmanstr. 27, Charlottenburg
*Additional information:* He left the Jewish Synagogue in 1931, attorney at the KG. After the National Socialist seizure of power he was made subject to an occupational ban in early 1933. He emigrated to France and there married Henriette Schmidthals from Berlin. When the Nazis invaded France, the couple fled to the USA via Portugal. He soon obtained a position as commentator at the radio in Washington (Schmidthals).
*Sources:* BArch, R 3001 PAK; BG; Ausk. Dr. Walter Schmidthals, 2.12.1998

**Breslauer, Walter Dr.**
07/03/1890 Berlin - 1981 London
*Home address:* no information
*Law firm address:* Mohrenstr. 51
*Additional information:* 1908-11 legal studies in Berlin and Freiburg; co-founder of the Jüdischer Liberale Jugendverein (Jewish Liberal Youth Association); 1912 first state examination in law; 1914 doctorate in Göttingen; 1918 second state examination in law; since 1919 he was an attorney, most recently admitted to the KG, as from 1928 also a notary; 1931-36 also an administration director of the Jewish Synagogue in Berlin; 1925-32 member, 1931-32 chair of the Association Meeting of the Prussian State Association of Jewish Congregations. After the National Socialist seizure of power he was made subject to an occupational ban in 1933; 1936 emigration to Great Britain via Switzerland, 1936-37 he studied at the London School of Economics; 1937-72 he was an attorney in London; 1940 he was interned on the Isle of Man; 1940-41 he studied at the Polytechnic in London, and graduated as an accountant; 1941-46 he was an accountant; 1945 he was the co-founder of the Council of Jews from Germany, he was engaged in reparation and in many Jewish organizations; he died in 1981 in London.
*Publications:* The Private International Law of Succession in England, America and Germany, 1937
*Sources:* Br.B. 32; TK 33; LAB, Liste d. nichtzugel. RA, 25.4.33; JMBl. 33, S. 209; BArch, R 3001 PAK; BHdE Bd. 1, S. 92, ; Göpp., S. 271; Lowenthal

**Brinkenhoff, Kurt (Curt) Dr.**
12/22/1892 Berlin - transportation 1943
*Home address:* No information
*Law firm address:* Waitzstr. 23, Charlottenburg
*Additional information:* Attorney at the LG I-III, AG Charlottenburg and notary. After the National Socialist seizure of power in 1933 he was temporarily made subject to a representation ban; upon request he was readmitted. At the end of 1935 his license as a notary was revoked; he worked as an attorney up to the general occupational ban in 1938. In 1943 he was transported to Auschwitz.
*Sources:* Br.B. 32; TK 33; *li; LAB, Liste d.

nichtzugel. RA, 25.4.33; Liste 15.10.33; DJ 36, S. 314; MRRAK; BArch, R 3001 PAK; Naatz-Album; BG; GB II

**Brock, Hugo Dr.**
04/10/1882 Gnesen - 08/18/1942 Riga
*Home address:* Bayernallee 7, Charlottenburg
*Law firm address:* Kleiststr. 15, W 62
*Additional information:* Attorney at the KG and notary. After the National Socialist seizure of power in 1933 he was temporarily made subject to a representation ban and his license as a notary was revoked; he worked as an attorney up to the general occupational ban in 1938. Transportation on 08/15/1942 to Riga, he was murdered there on the day of his arrival on 08/18/1942.
*Sources:* TK 33; JMBl. 33, S. 202; *li; LAB, Liste 15.10.33; MRRAK; BArch, R 3001 PAK; BG; BdE; GB II

**Brock, Isidor Dr., Judicial Councillor**
08/17/1853(1858?) Gnesen - 09/20/1940 Berlin
*Home address:* Flotowstr. 8, NW 87, Tiergarten
*Law firm address:* Chausseestr. 123, N 4
*Additional information:* Presumably the father of Hugo; attorney at the LG I-III and notary. After the National Socialist seizure of power he was temporarily made subject to a ban on representation and his license as a notary was revoked; he worked as an attorney until the general occupational ban in 1938. He died in 1940 at the age of 87.
*Sources:* TK 33; JMBl. 33, S. 208; *li; LAB, Liste 15.10.33; MRRAK; BArch, R 3001 PAK; BG

**Brock, Walter Dr.**
12/14/1901 - no information
*Home address:* no information.
*Law firm address:* Tauentzienstr. 7 b, W 50
*Additional information:* Attorney at the LG I-III and AG Berlin-Mitte. After the National Socialist seizure of power he was made subject to an occupational ban on 06/19/1933.
*Sources:* Adr.B. 32; TK 33; Liste d. nichtzugel. RA, 25.4.33; JMBl. 33, S. 253; BArch, R 3001 PAK, PA

**Broder, Ernst W. Siegbert**
03/27/1888 - 1970 Lugano
*Home address:* no information

*Law firm address:* Kronenstr. 16, W 8
*Additional information:* Attorney at the LG I-III, AG Berlin-Mitte and notary. After the National Socialist seizure of power he was made subject to an occupational ban on 06/20/1933. He emigrated to Shanghai, China, he later presumably went to Switzerland, where he died in 1970 at the age of 82.
*Sources:* Br.B. 32; TK 33; LAB, Liste d. nichtzugel. RA, 25.4.33; JMBl. 33, S. 253; BArch, R 3001 PAK, PA; BG

**Brodnitz, Julius Dr., Judicial Councillor**
08/19/1865 Posen - 03/16/1936 Berlin
*Home address:* Schillstr. 9, W 62
*Law firm address:* Prinzregentenstr. 94, Wilmersdorf
*Additional information:* Attorney at the LG I-III and notary; 1920-1936 chairman of the CV and active member of the Jewish Reform Community in Berlin. After the National Socialist seizure of power in 1933 his license as a notary was revoked; he was readmitted as an attorney; co-founder of the Reichsvertretung der Juden.
*Sources:* TK 33; JMBl. 33, S. 202; *li; Liste 36; LAB, Liste 15.10.33; BArch, R 3001 PAK; BG; Krach, S. 431; Ladwig-Winters, Freiheit, S. 290

**Broecker, Rudolf von, Dr.**
08/12/1879 Berlin - 03/10/1950 Berlin
*Home address:* Potsdamer Str. 48, Lichterfelde
*Law firm address:* Karlstr. 107, Lichterfelde
*Additional information:* He had fought in the First World War, he was Protestant. Attorney at the LG I-III, AG Schöneberg and notary; 1922-1932 member of the "Stahlhelm" (Steel Helmet) and later also a member of the NSDAP (The National Socialist German Workers' Party). After the National Socialist seizure of power he was regarded as "mixed race," in 1933 he was readmitted as an attorney and notary. Despite his origins he sought to support National Socialist politics, he was also a "Blockwart" (block leader), as was established in a letter to

the vice-president of the KG in 1947. For this reason his application for re-admittance as a lawyer after 1945 was rejected; after 1949 he was readmitted, after he had only been classified as a nominal Nazi.
*Sources:* TK 33; *li; LAB: Liste Mschlg. 36; Tel.B. 41; BG; LAB, RAK, PA

**Broh, James Dr., Judicial Councillor**
11/09/1867 Perleberg - no information
*Home address:* Mansfelder Str. 34, Wilmersdorf
*Law firm address:* Memhardtstr. 20, C 25
*Additional information:* Attorney at the LG I-III, AG Berlin-Mitte and notary; member of the USPD, then KAPD, 1930 member of the KPD; he defended Max Hoelz in 1921; he later defended the person accused of murdering Horst Wessel; the "Rote Hilfe" (Red Aid) paid him about RM 3,200. After the National Socialist seizure of power in 1933 he was imprisoned for a short time; in May 1933 he was still reported by the board of the RAK to the PrMJ, an occupational ban followed. He emigrated to France with his wife in April 1933. During his exile he was active in journalism.
*Sources:* Br.B. 32; Jüd.Adr.B.; TK 33; GStA, Rep. 84 a, Nr. 20363 (Hanns B.); JMBl. 30.6.33; BArch, R 3001 PAK; BG; BHdE; Schneider, Schwarz, Schwarz, S. 99

**Bromberg, Hugo Dr.**
01/26/1890 Cottbus - no information
*Home address:* Borstellstr. 18, Südende, Steglitz
*Law firm address:* Passauer Str. 4, W 50
*Additional information:* Attorney and notary. After the National Socialist seizure of power in 1933 he was readmitted; at the end of 1935 his license as an attorney was revoked; he worked until 1938 as an attorney. His wife was regarded as "non-Jewish."
*Sources:* *li; LAB, Liste 15.10.33; DJ 36, S. 314; Liste 36; MRRAK; BArch, R 3001 PAK; BG

**Bruck, Georg, Judicial Councillor**
05/18/1869 Frankenstein - 11/07/1940
*Home address:* Dragonerstr. 32, N 54, Mitte
*Law firm address:* Chausseestr. 17 II, N 4
*Additional information:* Attorney at the LG I-III and AG Charlottenburg. After the National Socialist seizure of power he was readmitted as an attorney; he was listed in the

business directory for the last time in 1935. He died in 1940 at the age of 71.
*Sources:* Br.B. 32 u. 35; TK 33; *li; BArch, R 3001 PAK; BG

**Bruck, Martin Dr.**
04/12/1878 Neiße - transportation 1942
*Home address:* Roscherstr. 4, Charlottenburg
*Law firm address:* Königstr. 34/36, C 2
*Additional information:* Attorney at the LG I-III, AG Berlin-Mitte and notary. After the National Socialist seizure of power his license as an attorney was revoked in 1933; worked as an attorney up to the general occupational ban in 1938. Transported from 06/24/1942 to 06/26/1942 from Berlin to Minsk.
*Sources:* TK 33; JMBl. 33, S. 208; *li; LAB, Liste 15.10.33, Liste 36; MRRAK; BArch, R 3001 PAK; VZ 39; GB II

**Brückmann, Harry**
No information
*Home address:* no information
*Law firm address:* Oranienstr. 145/146, S 42
*Additional information:* Attorney at the LG I-III and notary. After the National Socialist seizure of power in 1933 his license as a notary was revoked; he worked as an attorney until 04/20/1937, then he was disbarred.
*Sources:* TK 33; JMBl. 33, S. 202; *li; LAB, Liste 36, Liste 15.10.33; BArch, R 3001 PAK

**Brumm, Fritz Dr.**
02/06/1885 Neustadt a.d.W. - 12/31/1944
*Home address:* Flensburger Str. 25, NW 87
*Law firm address:* Alt-Moabit 109, NW 40
*Additional information:* Attorney at the LG I-III and AG Berlin-Mitte. After the National Socialist seizure of power in 1933 he was readmitted; in 1937 he was disbarred as an attorney. According to the BG he was "declared dead" on 12/31/1944.
*Sources:* TK 33; *li; LAB, Liste 15.10.33; BArch, R 3001 PAK; BG

**Brün, Paul Dr.**
04/28/1889 Berlin - 1970 Haifa, Israel
*Home address:* Cecilienallee 10, Dahlem
*Law firm address:* Kurfürstendamm 195, W 15
*Additional information:* Attorney at the LG I-III, AG Charlottenburg

and notary. After the National Socialist seizure of power he was made subject to a ban on representation in early 1933, then he was readmitted; at the end of 1935 his license as a notary was revoked; he worked as an attorney until the general occupational ban in 1938. After 11/09/1938 he was transported to the Sachsenhausen concentration camp; in January 1939 he was released with the condition that he had to emigrate. Emigration to Great Britain; in April 1946 to Palestine.
*Sources:* TK 33; *li; LAB, Liste d. nichtzugel. RA, 25.4.33, Liste 15.10.33; DJ 36, S. 314; Naatz-Album; MRRAK; BArch, R 3001 PAK; BG

### Brünn, Max Friedrich Dr.
10/17/1896 Berlin - No information
*Home address:* Bamberger Str. 28 (until 5/37)
*Law firm address:* Bamberger Str. 59, W 50
*Additional information:* Attorney at the KG and notary. After the National Socialist seizure of power he was readmitted upon request; at the end of 1935 his license as a notary was revoked; he was disbarred as an attorney on 07/15/1939. Emigration to London, Great Britain.
*Sources:* *li; LAB, Liste 15.10.33; DJ 36, S. 314; BArch, R 3001 PAK; BG

### Bry, Herbert
11/26/1887 Thorn - no information
*Home address:* Leibnizstr. 60, Charlottenburg
*Law firm address:* Kantstr. 4, Charlottenburg
*Additional information:* Attorney at the LG I-III and notary. After the National Socialist seizure of power in 1933 he was readmitted; he was disbarred on 11/07/1934; emigration to Tel Aviv, Palestine.
*Sources:* TK 33; *li; LAB, Liste 15.10.33; BArch, R 3001 PAK; BG

### Buchholz, Heinrich Dr.
10/26/1902 Berlin - July 1987
*Home address:* Wielandstr. 27/28, W 15
*Law firm address:* Wilhelmstr. 130, SW 68
*Additional information:* He was first admitted as an attorney on 12/16/1932. After the National Socialist seizure of power he was made subject to an occupational ban on 06/25/1933. Emigration to the USA; he died there in 1987 at the age of 84.
*Sources:* Jüd.Adr.B.; JMBl. 30. 6.33, S. 203; Liste d. nichtzugel. RA, 25.4.33; BArch, R 3001 PAK, PA; SSDI

### Buckwitz, Hans Dr.
10/17/1900 - no information
*Home address:* no information
*Law firm address:* Kurfürstendamm 22, W 15
*Additional information:* Attorney at the LG I-III and AG Berlin-Mitte. After the National Socialist seizure of power he was made subject to an occupational ban on 06/17/1933.
*Sources:* Adr.B. 32; TK 33; Liste d. nichtzugel. RA; JMBl. 33, S. 253; BArch, R 3001 PAK, PA

### Bud, Franz
01/31/1900 - no information
*Home address:* no information
*Law firm address:* Schönhauser Allee 6/7, N 54
*Additional information:* Attorney at the KG; former student at the French Gymnasium, married to a jurist. After the National Socialist seizure of power he was made subject to an occupational ban in early 1933. Emigration to the USA via Paris; in Paris he founded a tie factory; later he worked in the USA as an optician.
*Sources:* TK 33; Liste d. nichtzugel. RA, 25.4.33; BArch, R 3001 PAK; Ausk. E. Proskauer

### Buka, Hans Dr.
07/14/1886 - approximately 1937
*Home address:* no information
*Law firm address:* Kantstr. 162, Charlottenburg
*Additional information:* Attorney at the KG and notary. After the National Socialist seizure of power he was readmitted; at the end of 1935 his license as a notary was revoked; he still worked as an attorney until at least 1936; however, he went bankrupt, according to the son of a colleague, and took his own life.
*Sources:* *li; LAB, Liste 15.10.33, Liste 36; BArch, R 3001 PAK; Ausk. Fontheim, 6.4.2000

### Bukofzer, Karl
09/28/1885 Schwetz - transportation in 1942
*Home address:* Fehrbelliner Str. 79, NW 54
*Law firm address:* Burgstr. 30 II, C 2
*Additional information:* Attorney at the LG I-III, AG Berlin-Mitte and notary. After the National Socialist seizure of power he was readmitted; at the end of 1935 his license as a notary was revoked; he worked as an attorney until the general occupational ban in 1938; transportation on 09/05/1942 to Riga.

*Sources:* TK 33; *li; DJ 36, S. 314; MRRAK; BArch, R 3001 PAK; BG; BdE; GB II

**Burak, Arthur**
01/19/1902 - no information
*Home address:* no information
*Law firm address:* Hermannplatz 9, S 59
*Additional information:* Attorney at the LG I-III and AG Neukölln. After the National Socialist seizure of power he was made subject to an occupational ban in spring of 1933.
*Sources:* TK 33; Liste d. nichtzugel. RA, 25.4.33; JMBl. 33, S. 253; BArch, R 3001 PAK

**Bürgner, Hans Dr.**
12/17/18832 Berlin - no information
*Home address:* Ruhlaer Str. 7, Schmargendorf
*Law firm address:* Kurfürstendamm 24, W 15
*Additional information:* Attorney at the LG I-III, AG Berlin-Mitte and notary. After the National Socialist seizure of power in the spring of 1933 he was temporarily disbarred, then readmitted; At the end of 1935 his license as an attorney was revoked; emigration to London, Great Britain, later he changed his name to Burgner.
*Sources:* TK 33; *li; LAB, Liste 15.10.33; DJ 36, S. 314; MRRAK; BArch, R 3001 PAK; BG; Ausk. Werner Wolff, 22.9.1998

**Buschke, Albrecht Dr.**
10/02/1904 Berlin - no information
*Home address:* no information
*Law firm address:* Lützowstr. 60 a, W 35
*Additional information:* Attorney at the KG. After the National Socialist seizure of power he was made subject to an occupational ban on 06/17/1933, despite more intensive efforts to continue working.
*Sources:* Liste d. nichtzugel. RA, 25.4.33; JMBl. 33, S. 209; BArch, R 3001 PAK, PA

**Busse, Ernst, Judicial Councillor**
03/13/1867 Lobsens -no information
*Home address:* Georg-Wilhelm-Str. 12, Wilmersdorf
*Law firm address:* Grunewaldstr. 42, Schöneberg
*Additional information:* He was a Protestant, attorney at the KG and notary. After the National Socialist seizure of power his license as a notary was revoked, he was readmitted as an attorney up to the general occupational ban in 1938. Date of the declaration of property:

06/21/1943; collection point Große Hamburger Str. 26, transportation on 06/30/1943 on Theresienstadt. He survived, returned to Berlin and lived in Zehlendorf after the war.
*Sources:* TK 33; JMBl. 33, S. 202; *li; MRRAK; BArch, R 3001 PAK; BG; Liste der Theresienstadt-Überlebenden

**Byk, Rudolf Dr.**
11/16/1887 Berlin - 03/11/1937
*Home address:* In der Halde 14, Zehlendorf
*Law firm address:* Mohrenstr. 9, W 8
*Additional information:* Attorney at the LG I-III and notary. After the National Socialist seizure of power in 1933 his license as a notary was revoked; he worked as an attorney until at least 1936. He died in 1937 at the age of 50.
*Sources:* TK 33; JMBl. 33, S. 202; *li; LAB, Liste 15.10.33; Liste 36; BArch, R 3001 PAK; BG

# C

**Calé, Richard Dr.**
05/17/1883 - no information
*Home address:* no information
*Law firm address:* Maaßenstr. 27, W 62
*Additional information:* Attorney at the KG and notary. After the National Socialist seizure of power in 1933 his license as a notary was revoked; he was disbarred in 1938 before the general occupational ban. Emigration to the USA.
*Sources:* TK 33; JMBl. 33, S. 202; *li; LAB, Liste 15.10.33; Liste 36; Br.B. 38; DJ 38, S. 1705; BArch, R 3001 PAK; NY Publ. Lib. (Am. Com.), NY Publ. Lib. file Grüneberg

**Callmann, Curt Dr.**
12/22/1883 Briesen - 10/16/1944 Auschwitz
*Home address:* Martin-Luther-Str. 25, Schöneberg
*Law firm address:* Potsdamer Str. 56, W 35
*Additional information:* Attorney at the LG I-III, AG Schöneberg and notary. After the National Socialist seizure of power in 1933 he was readmitted. His license as a notary was revoked in 1935; he worked as an attorney up to the general occupational ban in 1938. Date of declaration of property: 12/07/1942, collection point Gerlachstr. 20, transportation on 12/15/1942 to Theresienstadt; from there he was transported to Auschwitz on 10/16/1944.

where he was murdered shortly after his arrival.
*Sources:* TK 33; *li; LAB, Liste 15.10.33; DJ 36, S. 314; MRRAK; BG; ThG; GB II

### Calmon, Curt Dr.
08/23/1884 - no information
*Home address:* no information
*Law firm address:* Unter den Linden 16, W 8
*Additional information:* Attorney at the LG I. After the National Socialist seizure of power he was readmitted; he was still working as an attorney on 12/04/1936; he was then disbarred.
*Sources:* TK 33; *li; LAB, Liste 15.10.33; Liste 36

### Carlebach, Alfred Dr.
01/28/1887 Frankfurt a. M. - no information
*Home address:* no information
*Law firm address:* Viktoriastr. 4 a, W 35
*Additional information:* Attorney at the LG I-III and notary; he left the Jewish congregation on 09/09/1931; from 1929-1933 he worked at a law firm in partnership with Erich Koch-Weser. After the National Socialist seizure of power in 1933 he was readmitted; at the end of 1935 his license as a notary was revoked; on 05/04/1936 he was also disbarred as an attorney; emigration to Great Britain.
*Sources:* Adr.B. 32; TK 33; *li; LAB, Liste 15.10.33; DJ 36, S. 314; BG

### Caro, Erich Dr.
08/20/1891 Berlin - no information
*Home address:* Machandelweg 1, Charlottenburg
*Law firm address:* Wilhelmstr. 44, W 8
*Additional information:* Attorney at the KG and notary. After the National Socialist seizure of power he was readmitted; at the end of 1935 his license as an attorney was revoked, he worked as an attorney until the general occupational ban in 1938, then he was admitted as a "consultant." He emigrated in early 1939 via Porto Allegre, Brazil (presumably together with a relative Ernst, a further dependant, Herbert, already lived there); shortly thereafter he relocated to the USA; arrival in New York on 04/15/1939.
*Sources:* TK 33; *li; LAB, Liste 15.10.33; DJ 36, S. 314; MRRAK; BArch, R 3001 PAK; Liste d. Kons., 15.3.39; BG

### Caro, Ernst
11/26/1873 Berlin - no information
*Home address:* Joachimsthaler Str. 11, W 15,
*Law firm address:* Joachimstaler Str. 11, W 15
*Additional information:* Attorney at the KG and notary; in 1921 he left the Jewish congregation. After the National Socialist seizure of power in 1933 his license as a notary was revoked; up to the general occupational ban in 1938 he worked as an attorney. Emigration to Porto Allegre, 1939 (presumably together with a relative, Erich, a further dependent, Herbert, already lived there).
*Sources:* TK 33; JMBl. 33, S. 202; *li; LAB, Liste 15.10.33; MRRAK; BArch, R 3001 PAK; BG

### Caro, Herbert Moritz Dr.
10/16/1906 Berlin - no information
*Home address:* no information
*Law firm address:* Jägerstr. 59/60, W 8
*Additional information:* Attorney at the LG I-III and AG Tempelhof. After the National Socialist seizure of power in early 1933 he was made subject to an occupational ban. Emigration to France in April 1933; returned to Germany in 1934, emigration to Porto Allegre, Brazil, in April 1935 (presumably he followed Ernst and Erich); in 1967 he still lived in Brazil.
*Sources:* TK 33; Liste d. nichtzugel. RA, 25.4.33; JMBl. 33, S. 234; BArch, R 3001 PAK; BG

### Casper, Paul
07/25/1903 - no information
*Home address:* Lützowufer 10, W 35
*Law firm address:* Lützowufer 10, W 35
*Additional information:* Attorney at the KG; after the National Socialist seizure of power in early 1933 he was made subject to an occupational ban, emigration before 07/25/1938 to Portugal.
*Sources:* JMBl. 33, S. 203; BArch, R 3001 PAK; BG

### Casper, Paul Dr.
04/08/1891 Berlin - no information
*Home address:* Xantener Str. 2, W 15
*Law firm address:* Mittelstr. 25, NW 7
*Additional information:* Attorney at the LG I-III and notary. After the National Socialist seizure of power in early 1933 he was readmitted upon request; at the end of 1935 his license as a notary was revoked; he worked

as an attorney until the general occupational ban in 1938. In the wake of 11/09/1938 he was arrested, until the middle of 1939 he was interned at the Sachsenhausen concentration camp; after his release he emigrated to London, Great Britain.
*Sources:* Jüd.Adr.B.; TK 33; Adr.B. 33; Liste d. nichtzugel. RA, 25.4.33; *li; LAB, Liste 15.10.33; DJ 36, S. 314; MRRAK; BArch, R 3001 PAK; BG

**Cassel, Alfred**
6.10.1881 Berlin - Deportation 1943
*Home address:* Sächsische Str. 5, W 15
*Law firm address:* Am Karlsbad 1 a, W 35
*Additional information:* Attorney at the LG I-III and notary. After the National Socialist seizure of power in 1933 his license as a notary was revoked, he was readmitted as an attorney up to the general occupational ban in 1938. Transportation on 03/12/1943 to Auschwitz.
*Sources:* TK 33; JMBl. 33, S. 208; *li; LAB, Liste 15.10.33; MRRAK; BArch, R 3001 PAK; BG; GB II

**Cassirer (Casirer), Alfred Dr.**
09/14/1882 Kattowitz - no information
*Home address:* Droysenstr. 7, Charlottenburg
*Law firm address:* Kurfürstendamm 225, W 15
*Additional information:* Attorney at the LG I-III, AG Charlottenburg and notary. After the National Socialist seizure of power in 1933 his license as a notary was revoked; he worked as an attorney up to the general occupational ban in 1938.
*Sources:* TK 33; JMBl. 33, S. 202; *li; Liste 36; LAB, Liste 15.10.33; MRRAK; BArch, R 3001 PAK; BG

**Castro, Carlos de Dr.**
12/18/1895 - no information
*Home address:* no information
*Law firm address:* Leipziger Str. 112, W 8
*Additional information:* Attorney at the LG I-IIII, AG Berlin-Mitte and notary. After the National Socialist seizure of power in 1933 he was readmitted; at the end of 1935 his license as a notary was revoked; he worked as an attorney up to the general occupational ban in 1938.
*Sources:* TK 33; *li; LAB, Liste 15.10.33; DJ 36, S. 314; DJ 38, S. 1811; MRRAK; BArch, R 3001 PAK; Liste 36

**Catleen, Hermann**
02/15/1882 Hohensalza - 1942 (?) London
*Home address:* Wittenbergplatz 1, W 62
*Law firm address:* Jägerstr. 11, W 8
*Additional information:* Attorney at the LG I-IIII and notary. After the National Socialist seizure of power he was readmitted; at the end of 1935 his license as a notary was revoked; he worked as an attorney up to the general occupational ban in 1938; he practiced during his last years from his private home; emigration to London, Great Britain, on 11/03/1938; he presumably died there in 1942.
*Sources:* TK 33; *li; LAB, Liste 15.10.33; DJ 36, S. 314; MRRAK; BArch, R 3001 PAK; BG

**Charles, Hugo Dr.**
03/23/1879 Rothenburg a.d.O. –
No information
*Home address:* Meinekestr. 25, W 15
*Law firm address:* Meinekestr. 25, W 15
*Additional information:* Attorney at the LG I-III and notary. After the National Socialist seizure of power in 1933 his license as an attorney was revoked; he worked as an attorney until the general occupational ban in 1938; emigration, presumably to Australia.
*Sources:* TK 33; JMBl. 33, S. 202; *li; LAB, Liste 15.10.33; MRRAK; BArch, R 3001 PAK; BG

**Cheim, Sally**
11/22/1889 Berlin - no information
*Home address:* Fredericiastr. 15, Charlottenburg
*Law firm address:* An der Spandauer Brücke 2, C 2
*Additional information:* Attorney at the LG I-III and notary. After the National Socialist seizure of power he was readmitted; at the end of 1935 his license as a notary was revoked; he worked as an attorney up to the general occupational ban in 1938; then he still worked as a "consultant." Emigration to the USA on 08/21/1939.
*Sources:* TK 33; *li; LAB, Liste 15.10.33; DJ 36, S. 314; MRRAK; Liste der Kons.; BG

**Chodziesner, Dorothea, geb. Galliner**
10/29/1904 - 11/06/1943 Concepcion, Chile
*Home address:* Feuerbachstr. 13, Finkenkrug
*Law firm address:* Sybelstr. 19, Charlottenburg
*Additional information:* Dorothea's father

was the liberal Rabbi Julius Galliner, her uncle, Moritz Galliner, was also an attorney, her father-in-law, Ludwig, also was an attorney. After the National Socialist seizure of power she was made subject to an occupational ban on 06/09/1933. Her husband emigrated in 1939 to Great Britain, where he was interned after the beginning of the war as a "hostile foreigner" and transported to Australia. 1939/40 Dorothea escaped with her four-year-old son, first to Great Britain and and from there further to Chile. On 11/06/1943 she died there at the age of 39. After the internment was lifted, her husband joined the army and then settled permanently in Australia. In 1945 his 10-year-old son, who had lived in Chile until then, went to live with him. Her father-in-law died in Theresienstadt. Her sister-in-law, the well-known lyricist Gertrud Kolmar, was murdered in Auschwitz.
*Sources:* Liste d. nichtzugel. RA., 25.4.33; JMBl. 33, S. 221; BArch, R 3001 PAK, PA; Ausk. d. Sohnes, 26.10.99

**Chodziesner, Fritz**
01/19/1906 Berlin - 07/29/1990 Berlin
*Home address:* no information
*Law firm address:* Kurfürstendamm 14/15, W 50
*Additional information:* Since 1931 he was an attorney in Berlin. After the National Socialist seizure of power in early 1933, he was made subject to an occupational ban. He still worked at the law firm of his father Max for a certain period of time and then worked for various Jewish organizations, among others the Aid Organization for Jews in Germany as an emigration adviser. Emigration to Montevideo, Uruguay, later relocation to Buenos Aires; he returned to Berlin in 1945 and was readmitted as an attorney.
*Sources:* Liste, d. nichtzugel. RA, 25.4.33; BArch, R 3001 PAK; LAB, RAK PA; Ausk. E. Proskauer

**Chodziesner, Ludwig, Judicial Councillor**
08/28/1861Obersitzko - 02/13/1943 Theresienstadt
*Home address:* Speyerer Str. 10, Schöneberg
*Law firm address:* Manteuffelstr. 9/13, Finkenkrug, Falkensee
*Additional information:* Attorney since 1891, at first a partner of Dr. Max Wronker, later a sole practitioner. He was known as a defense

lawyer, notably in the trial against Count Philip to Eulenburg, an influential politician and confidant of the Emperor. He was also involved in the sensational process against the family of Count Kwilecki, later in the Adlon trial and in the divorce proceedings of the Count von der Schulenburg. The Chodziesner family had produced several jurists, two brothers, a nephew, and the daughter-in-law were also attorneys. There was also a close connection to the Benjamin family; the Schoenflies cousin was the mother of Walter and Georg Benjamin. Ludwig's daughter, Gertrud Kolmar (the German mame of the city of Chodzies), had been recognized as a lyricist with the support of her father. He was readmitted as an attorney after the National Socialist seizure of power, he was recognized as "elder attorney." On 07/1936 he was disbarred after working as an attorney for 45 years. Six years later he was asked to prepare himself for transportation to Theresienstadt. George Benjamin's wife, Hilde, helped him to pack his belongings. She was also an attorney and was made subject to an occupational ban after 1933 because of Communist activities [later she became the Minister of Justice of the DDR (German Democratic Republic)]. He signed a declaration of property on 09/07/1942. He went to the collection point Große Hamburger Str. 26 and was transported on 09/09/1942 to Theresienstadt, where he died only six months later. His daughter Gertrud Kolmar was murdered in Auschwitz.
*Sources:* TK 33; *li; DJ 36, S. 314; BG; ThG; GB II; Marbacher Magazin, 63/1993, Johanna Woltmann: Gertrud Kolmar 1894-1943; dies.: Gertrud Kolmar - Leben und Werk, Göttingen 1995

**Chodziesner, Max, Judicial Councillor**
11/21/1869 Woldenberg - 1950 Montevideo
*Home address:* Berliner Str. 159, Wilmersdorf
*Law firm address:* Kurfürstendamm 14/15, W 50
*Additional information:* Attorney at the LG I-III, AG Schöneberg and notary. After the National Socialist seizure of power in 1933 his license as a notary was revoked. he was readmitted as an attorney, since he was recognized as an "elder attorney;" he worked as an attorney until at least 1936; emigration to Uruguay, Montevideo, with his son Fritz;

he died there in 1950. Max was the brother of Ludwig.
*Sources:* TK 33; JMBl. 33, S. 208; *li; TK 36; Br.B. 36; BG

**Chodziesner, Siegfried Dr.**
07/18/1872 - no information
*Home address:* Kastanienallee 23, Charlottenburg
*Law firm address:* Kastanienallee 23, Charlottenburg
*Additional information:* 1894-97 studied in Berlin, he established himself as an attorney there, last admitted to the LG I-III, AG Charlottenburg and also as notary; he met the sexologist Magnus Hirschfeld in 1903 and defended him in 1904 together with the attorney Wronker against the accusation that he had offended the surveyed students with his survey on sexual orientation; he was a member of the Scientific Humanitarian Committee (WHK), which was committed to the abolition of paragraph 175 and the emancipation of homosexuals; from 1918/19 until the end of 1923 board member of the Magnus Hirschfeld-Stiftung, which funded the Institute of Sexual Sciences. After the National Socialist seizure of power in 1933 his license as a notary was revoked; in late fall 1933 he was disbarred. 1938 emigration with his wife Minnie to Florence, later to Montevideo, Uruguay.
*Sources:* Br.B. 33; Adr.B. 37; TK 33; JMBl. 33, S. 208; Pr.J. 33, S. 633; BArch, R 3001 PAK; Johanna Woltmann: Gertrud Kolmar – Leben und Werk, Göttingen 1995; BG; Ausk. Ralf Dose, Magnus-Hirschfeld-Gesellschaft

**Chone, Paul Dr.**
11/27/1884 - no information
*Home address:* Nymphenburger Str. 1, Schöneberg
*Law firm address:* Lutherstr. 47, W 62
*Additional information:* Attorney at the LG I-III, AG Berlin-Mitte and notary. After the National Socialist seizure of power in 1933 he was readmitted as an attorney; at the end of 1935 his license as a notary was revoked; he worked as an attorney until the general occupational ban in 1938; emigration to Palestine on 03/06/1939.
*Sources:* TK 33; *li; LAB, Liste 15.10.33; DJ 36, S. 314; MRRAK; BArch, R 3001 PAK; BG

**Cohen, Ernst Dr.**
10/31/1880 Mönchengladbach - no information
*Home address:* Konstanzer Str. 30, Wilmersdorf
*Law firm address:* Jägerstr. 11, W 8
Attorney at the LG I-III and notary. After the National Socialist seizure of power in 1933 he was readmitted; his license as a notary was revoked in 1935. Emigration to the Netherlands.
*Sources:* TK 33; *li; LAB, Liste 15.10.33; DJ 36, S. 314; BArch, R 3001 PAK; BG

**Cohen, Willy Max**
02/25/1905 - no information
*Home address:* no information.
*Law firm address:* Friedrichstr. 62, W 8
*Additional information:* In April 1932 he was admitted as an attorney at the LG I-III and AG Berlin-Mitte. After the National Socialist seizure of power he was made subject to an occupational ban in early 1933.
*Sources:* TK 33 (Wilhelm); Liste d. nichtzugel. RA, 25.4.33; JMBl. 33, S. 253; BArch, R 3001 PAK, PA

**Cohn, Alexander, Judicial Councillor**
04/26/1865 Kamin - 09/06/1942 Theresienstadt
*Home address:* Berkaer Str. 32-35, Altersheim der Jüdischen Gemeinde
*Law firm address:* Meinekestr. 23, W 15
*Additional information:* Attorney at the LG I-III and notary. After the National Socialist seizure of power in 1933 his license as an attorney was revoked; he worked as an attorney up to the general occupational ban in 1938. He last lived at the retirement home of the Jewish Synagogue; on 08/17/1942 he was transported from Berlin to Theresienstadt; he died there on 09/06/1942, a few days after arrival.
*Sources:* TK 33; JMBl. 33, S. 202; *li; LAB, Liste 15.10.33; BArch, R 3001 PAK; Naatz-Album; MRRAK; BG; GII

**Cohn, Arne Georg**
01/03/1886 - no information
*Home address:* Kaiserallee 22, W 15
*Law firm address:* Potsdamer Str. 118 a, W 35
*Additional information:* Attorney at the LG

I-III and notary. After the National Socialist seizure of power he was made subject to an occupational ban in early 1933. Emigration to Copenhagen, Denmark.
*Sources:* Br.B. 32; TK 33; Liste d. nichtzugel. RA, 25.4.33; JMBl. 7.7.33, S. 209; BG

**Cohn, Arthur**
12/07/1881 Berlin - no information
*Home address:* Herderstr. 2, Charlottenburg
*Law firm address:* Potsdamer Str. 103, W 35
*Additional information:* Attorney at the KG and notary. After the National Socialist seizure of power in 1933 his license as an attorney was revoked; emigration to Lucerne, Switzerland, presumably in April 1937.
*Sources:* TK 33; JMBl. 33, S. 202; *li; LAB, Liste 15.10.33; BArch, R 3001 PAK; BG

**Cohn, Benno Dr.**
09/30/1894 Lobsens - 11/24/1975 Tel Aviv
*Home address:* no information.
*Law firm address:* Kaiser-Wilhelm-Str. 36, C 25
*Additional information:* Since 1925 he was an attorney, admitted to the LG I-III and AG Berlin-Mitte. After the National Socialist seizure of power he was temporarily made subject to a ban on representation; after 1933 he did not work as an attorney, since his income had declined too much. Emigration to Palestine in 1938; after the founding of the state of Israel he was a member of the Knesset, from 1951-59 he was the president of the Israeli Civil Servant Disciplinary Court; he continued to be active as a politician; he was a witness in the Eichman trial.
*Sources:* Br.B. 32; TK 33; *li; LAB, Liste 15.10.33; BArch, R 3001 PAK; MRRAK; Göpp., S. 272; BG; Trial of A. Eichmann, Vol. VI, p. 233, 267, 1976, 2228

**Cohn, Edgar**
04/05/1905 - no information
*Home address:* no information
*Law firm address:* Alexanderstr. 15, C 25
*Additional information:* Attorney at the LG I-III and AG Berlin-Mitte. After the National Socialist seizure of power he was made subject to an occupational ban on 05/31/1933, intercession supporting his request to be readmitted, amongst others from two National Socialists, did not change anything. He emigrated and was naturalized.
*Sources:* TK 33; Liste d. nichtzugel. RA, 25.4.33; JMBl. 33, S. 220; BArch, R 3001 PAK, PA; BG

**Cohn, Erich**
11/17/1899 - 1967 Zürich
*Home address:* Kurfürstendamm 163
*Law firm address:* Kurfürstendamm 225, W 15
*Additional information:* Attorney at the LG I-III and AG Berlin-Mitte. After the National Socialist seizure of power he was readmitted; on 07/10/1934 he was disbarred. Emigration to London, Great Britain, on 10/26/1936; later to the USA. He died l967 in Zurich.
*Sources:* TK 33; JMBl. 33, S. 202; *li; LAB, Liste 15.10.33; BArch, R 3001 PAK; BG

**Cohn, Erich Dr.**
08/09/1887 - no information
*Home address:* no information
*Law firm address:* Lennéstr. 4, W 9
*Additional information:* Attorney since 1913, last at the LG I-III and AG Charlottenburg, notary since 1924. After the National Socialist seizure of power his license as an attorney was revoked in June 1933. He was disbarred on 08/03/1934.
*Sources:* TK 33; JMBl. 33, S. 202; *li; BArch, R 3001 PAK

**Cohn, Ernst Dr.**
12/10/1885 Berlin - 11/25/1941 Kowno
*Home address:* Kaiserdamm 86, Charlottenburg
*Law firm address:* Turmstr. 20, NW 21
*Additional information:* Attorney at the LG I-III, AG Berlin-Mitte and notary. After the National Socialist seizure of power in 1933 his license as a notary was revoked; he worked as an attorney up to the general occupational ban in 1938. Finally he worked as an unskilled laborer at Winterschall AG, Spritzgußwerk Fusor Berlin-Rudow, Kanalstr. 103-115; date of declaration of property: 11/13/1941; collection point Levetzowstr. 7-8; transportation on 11/17/1941 to Kowno, was murdered there.
*Sources:* TK 33; JMBl. 33, S. 202; *li; LAB, Liste 15.10.33; BArch, R 3001 PAK; Liste 36; MMRAK; BG; GB II

**Cohn, Eugen**
No information
*Law firm address:* Kleiststr. 16, W 62

*Additional information:* Attorney at the LG I-III and AG Berlin-Charlottenburg; after the National Socialist seizure of power in early 1933 he was made subject to an occupational ban.
*Sources:* Adr.B. 33; JMBl. 33, S. 221; BArch, R 3001 PAK

**Cohn, Fritz Simon**
09/23/1875 Berlin - 09/02 1943 Theresienstadt
*Home address:* Rosenheimer Str. 29 a, Schöneberg
*Law firm address:* Zimmerstr. 60 I, SW 68
*Additional information:* He was a dissident (since 1913). Attorney at the LG I-III and notary. After the National Socialist seizure of power in 1933 his license as a notary was revoked; he worked as an attorney until the general occupational ban in 1938. His wife was regarded as "Aryan." He stayed at the Jewish Hospital; date of declaration of property: 06/18/1943; transportation on 06/16/1943 to Theresienstadt, he died there after three months.
*Sources:* TK 33; Pr.J. 33, S. 466; *li; MRRAK; BG; ThG; GB II

**Cohn, Georg**
06/15/1884 Lobsens - 03/29/1944 Theresienstadt
*Home address:* Solinger Str. 11, Tiergarten
*Law firm address:* Bendlerstr. 17, W 35
*Additional information:* Attorney at the KG and notary; one of the important attorneys of the Red Cross in the 1920s. After the National Socialist seizure of power readmitted as an attorney; he was disbarred in 1934. Last an unpaid employee of the Reichsvertretung; date of declaration of property: 08/27/1942; collection point Große Hamburger Str. 26; transportation on 09/02/1942 to Theresienstadt, there he died at the end of March 1944.
*Sources:* TK 33; *li; LAB, Liste 15.10.33; BArch, R 3001 PAK; BG; ThG; GB II; Schneider, Schwarz, Schwarz

**Cohn, Georg**
01/04/1893 Rostock - no information
*Home address:* Zähringerstr. 2, Wilmersdorf
*Law firm address:* Potsdamer Str. 118, W 35
*Additional information:* Attorney at the KG and notary. After the National Socialist seizure of power in 1933 he was readmitted;

at the end of 1935 his license as a notary was revoked; he worked as an attorney up to the general occupational ban in 1938. Emigration to Grimsby, Great Britain. After 1945 he became a specialist in reparations.
*Sources:* TK 33; *li; DJ 36, S. 314; BArch, R 3001 PAK; MRRAK; BG; Ausk. E. Prokauer

**Cohn, Gerhard**
12/16/1885 Glogau - no information
*Home address:* Hansemannstr. 6, W 35
*Law firm address:* Potsdamer Str. 138, W 9
*Additional information:* Attorney at the LG I-III and notary; in 1932 he was still a board member of the RAK; after the National Socialist seizure of power in 1933 he was forced to resign as a board member of the RAK; he was readmitted as an attorney and notary; at the end of 1935 his license as a notary was revoked; he worked as an attorney until the general occupational ban of 1938; emigration to Helsingborg, Sweden.
*Sources:* TK 33; *li; LAB, Liste 15.10.33; DJ 36, S. 314; Liste 36; Verz.; BArch, R 3001 PAK; MRRAK; BG

**Cohn, Hans**
03/31/1892 Thorn - no information
*Home address:* Potsdamer Str. 99, W 35
*Law firm address:* Potsdamer Str. 99, W 35
*Additional information:* Attorney at the LG I-III, AG Schöneberg and notary. After the National Socialist seizure of power he was made subject to an occupational ban in June 1933.
*Sources:* Br.B. 32; TK 33; JMBl. 21.8.33, S. 266; BArch, R 3001 PAK; Naatz-Album; BG

**Cohn, Harry Dr.**
02/12/1896 - 03/17/1981 Argentina
*Home address:* no information
*Law firm address:* Schinkelplatz 1/2, W 56
*Additional information:* Son of the attorney, notary, and judicial councillor Sally Cohn. The family could be traced to living in Prussia since the beginning of the 19th century. Because of a physical handicap (restriction of the right upper arm),

Cohn could not participate in the First World War, despite reporting as a volunteer, since he was classified as unfit for fighting with a weapon. He instead reported, as soon as possible, to the Vaterländischer Hilfsdienst (Patriotic Assistance Service) (06/11/1917-11/30/1918). After the end of the war he completed his studies, obtained his doctorate (in Greifswald) and passed the second state examination in law with the grade "good." He established himself as an attorney at the end of 1924 in Berlin, he was admitted to the district courts I, II and III. In 1924 he was also a member of the supervisory board of Union Treuhand Aktiengesellschaft. He was later appointed as a notary.

After the National Socialist seizure of power he was made subject to an occupational ban on 06/09/1933. His application for re-admission with reference to his patriotic mission was rejected. He immigrated to Argentina in 1933, where he passed another legal examination. His sons had been born in 1927 and 1929. He also supported his mother Martha (Knesebeckstrasse 90, Charlottenburg 2) and his sister. Although he managed to establish himself professionally in Argentina, he never felt at home there culturally and socially.
*Sources:* Br.B. 32; TK 33; Liste d. nichtzugel. RA, 25.4.33; JMBl. 33, S. 266; BArch, R 3001 PAK, PA; Ausk. Dan Grunfeld, LA, 2005

**Cohn, Heinz Dr.**
06/06/1901 Potsdam - Januar 1975
*Home address:* Landshuter Str. 14, W 30
*Law firm address:* Dircksenstr. 26/27, C 25
Attorney at the KG. After the National Socialist seizure of power occupational ban on 05/26/1933. In a number of letters, he insists that he is dependent on his profession, since he has to support his wife, child, parents and parents-in-law. However, his application for re-admission was rejected. He worked as a foreign exchange consultant. Emigration in January of 1939; he last lived under the name of Henry in New York.
*Sources:* Br.B. 32; TK 33; Liste d. nichtzugel. RA, 25.4.33; BArch, R 3001 PAK, PA; BG; SSDI

**Cohn, Henry Dr.**
[01/06/1895 Berlin - transportation 1942
*Home address:* Neue Kantstr. 4, Charlottenburg
*Law firm address:* Königstr. 50, C 2
Attorney at the LG I-III and notary. After the National Socialist seizure of power in 1933 he was readmitted; at the end of 1935 his license as a notary was revoked; he worked as an attorney up to the general occupational ban in 1938; then he still worked as a "consultant." Transportation on 06/25/1942 to Theresienstadt.
*Sources:* TK 33; *li; LAB, Liste 15.10.33; DJ 36, S. 314; Naatz-Album; MRRAK; BG; ThG; GB II

**Cohn, Julius**
04/20/1886 - 08/28/194220.4.1886 - 28.8.1942
*Home address:* Brunnenstr. 25, N 54
*Law firm address:* Brunnenstr. 25, N 54
Attorney at the LG I-III and notary. After the National Socialist seizure of power in 1933 his license as a notary was revoked; he worked as an attorney up to the general occupational ban in 1938. He died in 1942 at the age of 56. He was buried at Weißensee.
*Sources:* TK 33; JMBl. 33, S. 202; *li; LAB, Liste 15.10.33; Liste 36; BArch, R 3001 PAK; MRRAK; BG

**Cohn, Louis, Judicial CouncillorR**
01/17/1882 Gostaczyn - no information
*Home address:* Landshuter Str. 16, W 30
*Law firm address:* Landshuter Str. 28, W 30
Attorney at the KG. After the National Socialist seizure of power in April 1933 he was made subject to a ban on representation; then he was readmitted; he was disbarred in September 1935. Emigration on 05/27/1939, originally intended itinerary via Cuba to the USA; since no mooring permit was issued for the ship in Cuba, compulsory return transport to England; presumably later emigrated to Palestine.
*Sources:* TK 33; *li; LAB, Liste 15.10.33; BArch, R 3001 PAK; BLHA, OFP, Dev.st; BG

**Cohn, Oskar Dr.**
10/15/1869 Guttentag - 11/02/1934 Geneva
*Home address:* Levetzowstr. 16 a, NW 87

*Law firm address:* Neue Friedrichstr. 69, C 2
Attorney since 1897. Last admitted to the
LG I-III and also as a notary; 1912-1920
member of the Reichstag (SPD/USPD),
1921-24 member of the Landtag of Prussia
(SPD); board member of the League for
Human Rights; he committed himself to the
rights of the Eastern Jews, in the sense of
national minority protection; active in Jewish
organizations; he was the law partner of
Rudolf Sachs; he was defense counsel in the
famous Bullerjahn trial. After the National
Socialist seizure of power by the National
Socialists he was directly threatened; the RAK
listed him "because of communist activity."
He fled in early 1933 to Paris, France, later to
Switzerland, where he died in 1934. He was
disbarred in the summer of 1933.
*Sources:* TK 33; JMBl. 21.8.33, S. 266; GStA,
Rep. 84 a; Nr. 20363; BArch, R 3001 PAK;
BG; LBI, NY, Sachs, R. S. 12/14; Krach, S.
431; Schneider, Schwarz, Schwarz; Ludger
Held: Oskar Cohn, 2002

**Cohn, Otto Dr.**
06/12/1892 Berlin - 10/29/1942 Riga
*Home address:* no information
*Law firm address:* Köpenicker Str. 115, SO 16
*Additional information:* Attorney at the
LG I-III, AG Berlin-Mitte and notary. After
the National Socialist seizure of power he
was made subject to an occupational ban
on 06/09/1933; later he worked in Jewish
cultural affairs representation. Transportation
on 10/26/1942 to Riga, he was murdered
shortly after arrival on 10/29/1942.
TK 33; Liste d. nichtzugel. RA,
25.4.33;JMBL. 33, S. 253; BArch, R 3001
PAK, PA; BG; BdE; GB II

**Cohn, Rudolf Dr.**
04/05/1890 - no information
*Home address:* Pannierstr. 13, Neukölln
*Law firm address:* Mohrenstr. 11/12, W 8
*Additional information:* Attorney at the LG
I-III and notary. After the National Socialist
seizure of power in 1933 he was readmitted;
at the end of 1935 his license as an attorney
was revoked; up to the general occupational
ban in 1938 he worked as an attorney;
emigration to Malmö, Sweden.
*Sources:* TK 33; *li; LAB, Liste 15.10.33; DJ
36, S. 314; MRRAK; BArch, R 3001 PAK;
BG

**Cohn, Siegbert Dr.**
08/19/1891 Berlin - 03/18/1933
*Home address:* Mommsenstr. 67,
Charlottenburg
*Law firm address:* Ritterstr. 54
*Additional information:* Attorney at the LG
I-III and notary. He died in March 1933 at
the age of 41.
*Sources:* Br.B. 32; JMBl. 13.4.33, S. 16;
BArch, R 3001 PAK; BG

**Cohn-Bendit, Erich**
11/26/1902 Berlin - 08/14/1959 Frankfurt a. M.
*Home address:* no information
*Law firm address:* Taubenstr. 50
*Additional information:* Attorney at the LG
I-III and AG Schöneberg; he added his mother's
maiden name to his name as part of his listing
in the list of attorneys, to distinguish himself
from the more than 20 other attorneys with
the last name Cohn; politically to the left,
he worked as a lawyer for the "Rote Hilfe"
(Red Aid); amongst others he represented the
attorney Hans Litten, who had been expelled
for political reasons because of allegedly
negligent negotiations and party political
propaganda from a trial because of the attacks
of SA (Sturmabteilung - armed and uniformed
branch of the NSDAP) gangs on a garden plot
(Felseneck trial).
After the National Socialist seizure of power
he was made subject to an occupational ban
in April 1933. His name was on a persecution
list "because of Communist activity." The
list also included amongst others Alfred
Apfel, Ludwig Bendix and Hilde Benjamin.
Occupational ban in early 1933; he emigrated
in 1933 with his partner and future wife
Herta to Paris, France; he could only find
temporary work; his wife supported the
family; he moved in the circles of political
exiles, he was friends with amongst others
Hannah Arendt and Walter Benjamin; at
the beginning of the war he was imprisoned
as a "hostile foreigner;" he fled from the
internment camp, since he feared extradition
to the Germans; he scraped by in the
unoccupied part of France, where he found
refuge with his family in Montauban and
Moissac. After the occupation of South-West
France by the Wehrmacht arrest threatened.
The couple was warned, went underground
and lived under a foreign name until the
liberation of the country.

After the war, the family moved to Cailly-sur-Eure in Normandy, where the couple ran an orphanage for Jewish children until 1948; subsequently they lived in Paris again. He returned to Germany alone in 1952, without his wife and children, he established himself as an attorney in Frankfurt with great success, he dealt mainly with compensation and reparation issues and he won several proceedings in the face of established case law that went against him; he died in 1959. He was the father of Gabriel (born in 1936) and Daniel (born in 1945).

*Sources:* Adr.B. 32; TK 33; Liste d. nichtzugel. RA, 25.4.33; GStA, Rep. 84a, Nr. 20363; JMBl. 7.7.33, S. 209; Schneider, Schwarz, Schwarz; Elisabeth Young-Bruehl: Hannah Arendt; Ausk. T. Krach; Stamer, Sabine: Cohn-Bendit. Die Biografie, Hamburg/Wien 2001

**Cohn-Biedermann, Leo Dr., Judicial Councillor**
10/18/1870 Konitz - no information
*Home address:* Wielandstr., W 15
*Law firm address:* Rosenthaler Str. 43, C 54
*Additional information:* Attorney at the LG I-III, AG Berlin-Mitte and notary. After the National Socialist seizure of power in 1933 his license as a notary was revoked; he was disbarred as an attorney on 07/31/1936; emigration to Palestine.
*Sources:* TK 33; JMBl. 33, S. 202; *li; LAB, Liste 15.10.33; BArch, R 3001 PAK; BG

**Cohn-Lempert, Georg Dr.**
2.5.1882 - 15.4.1968 Berlin
*Home address:* Motzstr. 90, Wilmersdorf
*Law firm address:* Motzstr. 90 (vor der Neunummerierung Nr. 42)
*Additional information:* He fought in the First World War. He was admitted as an attorney at the LG I-III and at AG Tempelhof. In the Attorneys' Chambers at the Großbeerenstraße Court there was a blackboard on which his name was printed and one could always see in which room he was currently present (a memory of his daughter). After the National Socialist seizure of power in 1933 his license as a notary was revoked, he was re-admitted as an attorney upon request, since he had been a "frontline

fighter." In the same year he agreed to a separation of property with his wife, who was regarded as "non-Jewish." In this way she was financially independent and she could purchase a lot in the Sudeten mountains and have a small house built on it.

The couple had two children, they lived in a so-called "privileged mixed-race marriage." The revoking of his license as a notary definitely left a financial mark, but in 1934 the missing revenue of the notaryship could be compensated for by the takeover of the representation of German FIAT within a certain framework. He could still work as an attorney until the general occupational ban in 1938. Subsequently he sought to be admitted as a "consultant;" this, however, was rejected. He left the Jewish Synagogue on 12/12/1940, in the hope of facilitating life for his daughters. Although this was no longer permitted, he was still baptized by a priest known to him. At the same time the family was much closer to the Jewish faith from a religious orientation than the Christian one and at least the father always followed different dietary laws, even if he did not insist on a basic kosher household. Moreover, he had not adhered to the rules of faith when he chose his wife. For his daughters, however, the question of religion had a subordinate value; they were always astonished when looking at the drawings on the match boxes, "Who were the Jews who were depicted there, for we did not know anyone who looked like that?" They were subjected to "customary" exclusion, according to the National Socialist racial laws, so the older daughter had to leave school at the age of 16 in 1934 and could not take a high school diploma.

He was forced to work for the Kranol company, which manufactured water bottles. In 1943, after the family had been bombed, they escaped to their house in Krummhübel in the Sudeten Mountains. The well-known writer Else Ury, who wrote the "Nesthäkchen" books, also lived there. He only joined his family later. His status as a Jew was not known in the Sudeten Mountains; he and his wife experienced the end of National Socialism there. The daughters immediately returned to Berlin, He and his wife could not get to Berlin until 1959. Here he settled down as a lawyer again. Until his death, he lamented the fact that no

one was particularly interested in the fate of "those who returned" and that former Nazis, such as Hans Globke, very soon were once again appointed as top government officials. As a positive sign during the time of persecution, his daughter still has evidence that the Reich Bar Association (Reichs-Rechtsanwaltkammer) supported the family with a monthly amount of 100 RM (from 1943 to 1945) (presumably his wife had sought this support). He died in 1968 shortly before his 87th birthday.
*Sources:* TK 33; JMBl. 33, S. 202; *li; LAB, Liste 15.10.33; Liste 36; MRRAK; BArch, R 3001 PAK; BG; LAB, RAK PA; Ausk. d. Tochter I. Cohn-Lempert

**Cohn-Linde, Bruno Dr.**
03/13/1893 Linde - March 1986 Santa Barbara, USA
*Home address:* Pariser Str. 4, W 15
*Law firm address:* Kurfürstendamm 23, W 15
Attorney at the LG I-III, AG Berlin-Mitte and notary. After the National Socialist seizure of power he was readmitted; his license as a notary was revoked in 1935. Emigration to the USA via Denmark on 10/31/1936; at first he lived under the name Bruno Linde in Santa Barbara, California, where he died in 1986.
*Sources:* TK 33; *li; BG; LAB, Liste 15.10.33; DJ 36, S. 314; BArch, R 3001 PAK; SSDI

**Cohnberg, Bruno Dr., Judicial Councillor**
04/11/1872 0 10/22/1934
*Home address:* no information
*Law firm address:* Kurfürstendamm 220, W 15
Attorney at the LG I-III, AG Charlottenburg and notary. After the National Socialist seizure of power in 1933 his license as a notary was revoked, he was re-admitted as an attorney. He died in 1934.
*Sources:* *li; Br.B. 32; TK 33; JMBl. 33, S. 220; LAB, Liste 15.10.33; BArch, R 3001 PAK; Naatz-Album

**Cohnberg, Franz-Theodor**
04/01/1905 - no information
*Home address:* no information
*Law firm address:* Emser Str. 1, Wilmersdorf
He had only been admitted to the KG on 03/09/1933. He was made subject to an occupational ban on 06/23/1933.
*Sources:* Liste d. nichtzugel. RA, 25.4.33; JMBl. 33, S. 253; BArch, R 3001 PAK, PA

**Cohnitz, Ernst, Judicial Councillor**
No information
*Home address:* no information
*Law firm address:* Bellevuestr. 5
Attorney at the LG I-III and notary. After the National Socialist seizure of power he was disbarred in 1933.
*Sources:* Adr.B. 32; TK 33; Pr.J. 33, S. 443; BArch, R 3001 PAK

**Conrad, Max**
No information
*Home address:* no information
*Law firm address:* Kurländer Allee 29, Charlottenburg
After the National Socialist seizure of power he was readmitted as an attorney.
*Sources:* *li; BArch, R 3001 PAK

**Coper, Alexander Dr.**
10/17/1891 - 02/06/1958 Berlin
*Home address:* Rüdesheimer Platz 10, Wilmersdorf;
*Law firm address:* Taubenstr. 14, W 8
He fought in the First World War and was disabled (his leg had been amputated); attorney at the LG I-III and notary; after the National Socialist seizure of power in 1933 he was re-admitted; in 1935 his license as a notary was revoked. After the general occupational ban as an attorney in 1938 he still worked as a "consultant." Instead of the compulsory name "Israel" he selected the name "Berl." From Nov. 1943 to March 1944 he was imprisoned for an indisputable allegation, the alleged falsification of food ration cards. He was released, but shortly afterwards, on June 21, 1944, his wife Magdalena died in a bomb attack on Berlin. While he had been protected by the status of his "privileged mixed-race marriage," because his wife was considered "Aryan" and the couple had children, that protection lapsed after the death of his wife. On 09/15/1944 he was arrested, on 10/27/1944 he was transported to Theresienstadt; his experiences there have been recorded in poems. The children were used for forced labor. He survived and lived in

Wilmersdorf after the liberation.
Sources: TK 33; *li; LAB, Liste 15.10.33;
DJ 36, S. 314; Naatz-Album; MRRAK; BG;
Ausk. d. Sohnes, Prof. H. Coper

**Cornel, Theodor Dr., Judicial Councillor**
No information
Home address: no information
Law firm address: Bayreuther Str. 41
Attorney at the LG I and notary; after the
National Socialist seizure of power he was
disbarred in 1933.
Sources: Br.B. 33; TK 33; Pr.J. 33, S. 442/ 443

**Corny, Dagobert Dr.**
09/09/1885 Berlin - no information
Home address: Behrenstr. 50 (1931)
Law firm address: Möckernstr. 131, SW 11
Attorney at the LG I-III and AG Schöneberg,
worked for the "Rote Hilfe" (Red Aid). After
the National Socialist seizure of power he was
made subject to an occupational ban.
Sources: Adr.B. 32; Jüd.Adr.B; TK 33; LAB,
Liste d. nichtzugel. RA, 25.4.33 (Nachtrag);
JMBl. 33, S. 209; BArch, R 3001 PAK; BG;
Schneider, Schwarz, Schwarz

**Corwegh, Fritz Geh.
Judicial Councillor**
01/04/1873 Breslau - 1951
Lugano
Home address:
Landhausstr. 41,
Wilmersdorf
Law firm address:
Landhausstr. 41 III, Wilmersdorf
Additional information: Fought in the First
World War, was awarded the EK. Attorney
at the LG I-III. After the National Socialist
seizure of power he was readmitted, since
he was recognized as a "frontline fighter";
he was disbarred on 10/11/1935; emigration
to Lugano, Switzerland, in May 1939. He
was supported by his brother-in-law, who
had been dismissed as an official and took a
position in Peking working for IG Farben. He
died in 1951 in Lugano.
Sources: *li; LAB, Liste 15.10.33; BArch, R
3001 PAK; BG; Ausk. d. Enkels Dr. E. Haas

**Cossmann, Richard Dr.**
08/12/1858 - 06/16/1933
Home address: no information
Law firm address: Neue Königstr. 21

Additional information: Attorney at the LG
I. He died during the first half of the year in
1933; he was buried at Weißensee.
Sources: Br.B. 32; TK 33; JMBl. 33, S. 266;
BArch, R 3001 PAK; BG (Cohsmann)

**Cronheim, Fritz**
11/06/1898 Berlin - 11/25/1941 Kowno
Home address: Passauer Str. 14, W 50
Law firm address: Lützowstr. 60 a, W 62
Additional information: Attorney since 1925,
admitted to the LG I-III and AG Berlin-Mitte.
After the National Socialist seizure of power
he was made subject to an occupational ban
on 06/10/1933. Transportation on 11/17/1941
to Kowno, where he was murdered a few days
after his arrival.
Sources: Adr.B. 32; TK 33; Liste d.
nichtzugel. RA., 25.4.33; JMBl. 33, S. 253;
BArch, R 3001 PAK, PA; BG; BdE; GB II

**Czapski, Georg Dr.**
06/01/1895 - no information
Home address: Schlüterstr. 12, Charlottenburg
Law firm address: Friedrichstr. 187/188, W 8
Additional information: Attorney at the LG
I-III, AG Berlin-Mitte and notary. After the
National Socialist seizure of power in 1933
he was readmitted; at the end of 1935 his
license as a notary was revoked. Emigration
presumably to the Netherlands before 1938;
in 1940 he lived in Stockholm, in 1976 he was
living in The Hague, the Netherlands.
Sources: TK 33; *li; LAB, Liste 15.10.33; DJ
36, S. 314; MRRAK; BArch, R 3001 PAK; BG

# D

**Daffis, Walther**
02/16/1901 Berlin-Charlottenburg - July 1978
Home address: no information
Law firm address: Kronenstr. 12/13, W 8
Additional information: He was Protestant.
Attorney since 1929, admitted to the LG I-III
and AG Charlottenburg. After the National
Socialist seizure of power he was made subject
to an occupational ban on 06/09/1933. His
wife Eleonore was regarded as "Aryan."
Emigration in 1933 at first to South Africa;
later he lived in Palm Beach, Florida, USA.
Sources: Adr.B. 32; TK 33; Liste d. nichtzugel.
RA.; JMBl. 33, S. 234; BArch, R 3001 PAK,
PA; BLHA, OFP, Dev.st.; BG; SSDI

**Dahl, Erich Dr.**
05/23/1898 Bielefeld - no information
*Home address:* Bamberger Str. 23,
Schöneberg
*Law firm address:* Potsdamer Str. 13
*Additional information:* Attorney at the
KG, allegedly also worked in the financial
sector. After the National Socialist seizure
of power in 1933 he was made subject to an
occupational ban. Emigration to Worthing,
Sussex, Great Britain on 02/01/1939.
*Sources:* Br.B. 32; TK 33; JMBl. 33, S. 203;
BArch, R 3001 PAK; BG

**Dahlheim, Kurt Dr.**
03/20/1883 Berlin - no information
*Home address:* Branitzer Platz 6,
Charlottenburg
*Law firm address:* Ebereschenallee 23,
Charlottenburg
*Additional information:* "Frontline fighter"
in the First World War; baptized as a
Protestant. Attorney and notary at the LG
I-III. After the National Socialist seizure of
power he was readmitted. He was regarded
as "mixed race" (two grandparents were
regarded as Jewish). He was able to work
until at least 1943, further fate unknown.
*Sources:* TK 33; *li; LAB, Liste 15.10.33;
Liste Mschlg.36; BArch, R 3001 PAK; Tel.B.
41; Br.B. 43

**Dalberg, Rudolf Dr.**
02/19/1885 Brilon - no information
*Home address:* Friedrich-Wilhelm-Str. 14,
W 8
*Law firm address:* Markgrafenstr. 38, W 56
*Additional information:* Attorney at the KG.
After the National Socialist seizure of power
he was made subject to an occupational ban
after April 1933; readmitted upon request
until the general occupational ban in 1938.
Emigration to London, Great Britain on
12/09/1938; he lived there until 1950.
*Sources:* TK 33; *li; Liste d. nichtzugel. RA,
25.4.33; LAB, Liste 15.10.33; MRRAK;
BArch, R 3001 PAK; BG

**Dalen, Fritz Dr.**
12/10/1880 Bromberg - 03/01/1942 Berlin
*Home address:* Joachim-Friedrich-Str. 7,
Halensee
*Law firm address:* Ulmenstr. 1,
Lichterfelde-Ost

*Additional information:* Attorney at the
LG I-III and notary. After the National
Socialist seizure of power he was readmitted.
In 1935 his license as an attorney was
revoked; he was disbarred as an attorney on
01/28/1936. He committed suicide in March
1942, presumably in light of the threat of
transportation.
*Sources:* TK 33; *li; LAB, Liste 15.10.33; DJ
36, S. 314; BArch, R 3001 PAK; BG; GB II

**Dalsheim, Friedrich Dr.**
10/25/1895 - no information
*Home address:* no information
*Law firm address:* Königin-Augusta-Str. 51
*Additional information:* Attorney at the KG.
After the National Socialist seizure of power
he was readmitted; still worked as an attorney
in 1936.
*Sources:* TK 33 u. 36; *li; BArch, R 3001
PAK; Liste 36

**Daniel, Arthur**
04/06/1866 - 12/04/1933
*Home address:* Rahnsdorf, Seestr. 30
*Law firm address:* Wallstr. 76/79, SW 19
*Additional information:* Attorney at the LG
I-III and notary. After the National Socialist
seizure of power his license as a notary was
revoked in 1933; he died in December 1933 at
the age of 67; he was buried at Weißensee.
*Sources:* TK 33; JMBl. 33, S. 202; *li; BArch,
R 3001 PAK; BG

**Daniel, Fritz Dr.**
12/19/1900 - June 1979
*Home address:* no information
Kanzlei: Bülowstr. 1, W 57
*Additional information:* He was Protestant.
Attorney at the LG I-III and AG Schöneberg.
After the National Socialist seizure of power
he was made subject to an occupational ban
on 06/09/1933. Emigration to the USA, he last
lived under the name Fred in San Francisco.
*Sources:* Adr.B. 32; TK 33; Liste d.
nichtzugel. RA, 25.4.33; JMBl. 33, S. 253;
BArch, R 3001 PAK; SSDI (Fred D.)

**Dannenbaum, Fritz Dr.**
02/25/1879 Berlin - 07/04/1940 Richmond,
England
*Home address:* Rauchstr. 5, W 35
*Law office address:* Roonstr. 5, NW 40
*Additional information:* Attorney at the LG

I-III. After the National Socialist seizure of power he was made subject to an occupational ban in early 1933. Emigration on 08/22/1938 to Richmond, Great Britain; he died there in 1940.
*Sources:* Br.B. 32; TK 33; Liste d. nichtzugel. RA, 25.4.33; JMBl. 33, S. 253; BArch, R 3001 PAK; BG

**Dannenberg, Ernst Dr.**
01/07/1892 Stettin - no information
*Home address:* Emser Str. 22, Wilmersdorf
*Law office address:* Nürnberger Str. 66, W 50
*Additional information:* Attorney at the LG 1-III and notary. After the National Socialist seizure of power he was made subject to an occupational ban at the beginning of April 1933, from the end of April he was again authorized to represent in trials, then readmitted; at the end of 1935 his license as a notary was revoked; worked as an attorney until the general occupational ban in 1938; emigration to London, Great Britain, on 08/08/1939.
*Sources:* TK 33; *li; Liste d nichtzugel. RA, (Nachtrag), 25.4.33; DJ 36, S. 314; Liste 36; LAB, Liste 15.10.33; MRRAK; BArch, R 3001 PAK; BG

**Danziger, Ernst**
06/07/1904 - no information
*Home address:* no information
*Law office address:* Kaiser-Wilhelm-Str. 36, C 25
*Additional information:* Attorney since 1931; admitted at the LG I-III and AG Berlin-Mitte. After the National Socialist seizure of power he was made subject to an occupational ban on 05/23/1933; emigration in September 1933 to Palestine.
*Sources:* TK 33; Liste d. nichtzugel. RA, 25.4.33; JMBl. 33, S. 209; BArch, R 3001 PAK; BG

**Danziger, Georg Jacques Dr.**
05/19/1883 Posen (now known as Poznan) - 01/03/1960 New York
*Home address:* Margaretenstr. 13, W 9
*Law office address:* Margaretenstr. 8, W 35
*Additional information:* Attorney at the LG I-III and notary, specialist in the field of patent and trademark law. After the National Socialist seizure of power his license as a notary was revoked in 1933; he worked as an attorney up to the general occupational

ban in 1938; afterwards he worked at the Meinhardt Law office as an attorney. Emigration to Great Britain on 03/28/1939, he was completely destitute; later he went to the USA, where he worked as a corporate consultant; from 1955 he called himself George. His sister and his brother died in the concentration camps. After the war he became an honorary member of the German Association for the Protection of Intellectual Property and Copyright.
*Sources:* TK 33 (Jacques); JMBl. 33, S. 208; *li; LAB, Liste 15.10.33; BArch, R 3001 PAK; BG; Göpp., S. 274

**Danziger, Gerhard Dr.**
07/19/1884 Halberstadt - no information
*Home address:* Waldmannstr. 21, Lankwitz
*Law office address:* Waldmannstr. 21, Lankwitz
*Additional information:* Attorney at the KG. After the National Socialist seizure of power he was readmitted until the general occupational ban in 1938. Emigration to Santon, Great Britain; was interned as a "hostile foreigner" on the Isle of Man.
*Sources:* TK 33; *li; LAB, 15.10.33; BArch, R 3001 PAK; MRRAK; BG

**Danziger, Kurt**
10/28/1876 Thorn - no information
*Home address:* Wielandstr. 35, Charlottenburg
*Law office address:* Motzstr. 38, Wilmersdorf
*Additional information:* Attorney at the LG I-III, AG Berlin-Mitte and notary. After the National Socialist seizure of power in 1933 his license as a notary was revoked; he worked as an attorney until the general occupational ban in 1938. Emigration to the USA via Spain on 06/06/1941.
*Sources:* TK 33; JMBl. 33, S. 202; *li; LAB, 15.10.33; BArch, R 3001 PAK; MRRAK; BG

**David, Leo**
No information
*Home address:* Prager Str. 6, Wilmersdorf
*Law office address:* Krausenstr. 12, W 8
*Additional information:* Attorney at the LG I; after the National Socialist seizure of power he was made subject to an occupational ban in early 1933. Emigration to Palestine; return to Hessen, Germany.
*Sources:* Adr.B. 33; JMBl. 33, S. 253; BArch, R 3001 PAK; BG

### Davidsohn, Franz Sally Dr.

07/08/1874 Hohensalza - transportation 1942
*Home address:* Wilhelmsaue 136,
Wilmersdorf
*Law office address:* no information
*Additional information:* Attorney at the LG
I-III, AG Berlin-Mitte and notary. After the
National Socialist seizure of power in 1933
his license as a notary was revoked, then he
was disbarred as an attorney. Collection point
Große Hamburger Str. 26; transportation on
08/11/1943 to Theresienstadt; on 05/16/1944
to Auschwitz.
*Sources:* Br.B. 32; TK 33; JMBl. 33, S. 202
(Sally); Pr.J. 33, S. 466 (Sally); BArch, R 3001
PAK; BG; GB II

### Davidsohn, Leo Dr., Judicial Councillor

02/15/1878 - 07/10/1937
*Home address:* Uhlandstr. 171-172
*Law office address:* Steinplatz 1,
Charlottenburg
*Additional information:* Attorney at the LG
I-III, AG Berlin-Mitte and notary; in 1932 he
was still a member of the board of the RAK.
After the National Socialist seizure of power
his license as a notary was revoked in 1933.
In 1936 he still worked as an attorney, last in
his priviate residence. He died in 1937 at the
age of 69.
*Sources:* TK 33; JMBl. 33, S. 220; *li; Liste
36; BG

### Deuren, Arnold van Dr.

1875 - 1942
*Home address:* Monbijouplatz 10, C 2
*Law office address:* Monbijouplatz 10, C 2
*Additional information:* Attorney at the
LG I-III, AG Berlin-Mitte and notary. After
the National Socialist seizure of power in
1933 his license as a notary was revoked, he
was readmitted as an attorney. Emigration
to the Netherlands in 1935; he committed
suicide there in 1942 after occupation by the
German troops.
*Sources:* TK 33; JMBl. 33, S. 220; *li; LAB,
Liste 15.10.33; BArch, R 3001 PAK; BG; GB II

### Deutsch, Leo

12/13/1873 Breslau - no information
*Home address:* Dragonerstr. 32, C 2, Mitte
*Law office address:* Lothringer Str. 42, N 54
*Additional information:* Attorney at the LG
I-III, AG Berlin-Mitte and notary. After the

National Socialist seizure of power in 1933 he
was readmitted; at the end of 1935 his license
as an attorney was revoked; up to the general
occupational ban in 1918 he was working as
an attorney; presumably he emigrated.
*Sources:* TK 33; *li; Liste 36; LAB, Liste
15.10.33; DJ 36, S. 314; MRRAK; BArch, R
3001 PAK; BG

### Dickmann, Wilhelm Dr.

10/13/1900 Hermsdorf - 10/28/1987
Alexandria, Virginia, USA
*Home address:* Babelsberger Str. 49,
Wilmersdorf
*Law office address:* Landgrafenstr. 1, W 62
*Additional information:* He fought in the
First World War as a 17-year-old. His mother
was Protestant, he himself had also been
baptized. He initially worked as an attorney
at the Weil Law Office, later he worked as a
solo practitioner, he was admitted to the LG
I-III and AG Berlin-Mitte. After the National
Socialist seizure of power he was readmitted
because of his status as a "frontline fighter."
He worked up to the general occupational ban
in 1938; on 12/02/1938 he could emigrate
to the USA. There he worked at various jobs
("night checker" at a restaurant, he worked
11.5 hours per day, he wrote short stories
and articles). He called himself William.
He received one of the rare scholarships of
the American Committee for the Guidance
of Professional Personnel and in 1943
he completed the examinations for legal
studies at the University of Pennsylvania in
Philadelphia. He became a naturalized U.S.
citizen and started working for the U.S. Civil
Service in 1943. He was an officer in the U.S.
Army; he worked as a member of the staff in
the Legal Department of the American High
Commissioner General Clay. In this function
he was the author of the Control Council
(Kontrollratsgesetz) Act No. 46 (02/25/1945)
on the dissolution of Prussia. His parents and
sister were killed. In the post-1945 period, he
intensively endeavored to alleviate the plight
of the German population. He lived close to
Washington in Virginia with his wife Ilka,
nee Deutsch, daughter of the former Prague
rabbi and a medical doctor herself. He felt
accepted: "My wife and I will be buried in the
same cemetery as Kennedy," was his desire.
His wife died in 1983, Dickman died four
years later.

*Sources:* TK 33; *li; LAB; Liste 15.10.33; MRRAK; BArch, R 3001 PAK, PA; MRRAK; NY Publ.Lib. (Am.Com.) Dickmann; BG; Göpp., S. 275; various autobiographical writings (private print); Ausk. Lomski; Ausk. Anne Halle

**Dittmann, Fritz**
07/20/1885 Berlin - no information
*Home address:* Bamberger Str. 32, W 30, Schöneberg
*Law office address:* Behrenstr. 26 a, W 8
*Additional information:* Attorney at the LG I-III, AG Schöneberg and notary. After the National Socialist seizure of power in 1933 he was readmitted upon request. He was regarded as "mixed race first class." He was a Protestant; he still worked as an attorney and notary until at least 1942/43. He survived the National Socialist regime and lived in Charlottenburg after 1945.
*Sources:* TK 33; *li; LAB; Liste 15.10.33; BArch, R 3001 PAK; LAB, Liste Mschl. 36; Tel.B. 41; Br.B. 43; BG

**Domke, Martin Dr.**
09/11/1892 Berlin - 1980
*Home address:* Bendlerstr. 30, W 35
*Law firm address:* no information
*Additional information:* Attorney at the LG I-III and notary, he was a friend of Walter Benjamin. After the National Socialist seizure of power he was made subjct to an occupational ban in 1933; emigration to Paris, France on 01/01/1934; he went to the USA on 01/01/1934, he was a professor there since 1950; 1958 chair of the Commission for Arbitration of International Commercial Law Cases; in 1967 he received the Federal Republic of Germany's Great Cross of Merit; he died in 1980.
*Sources:* TK 33; JMBl. 33, S. 253; BArch, R 3001 PAK; BG; Göpp., S. 275; Internet: www.wbenjamin.org/giessen_convolute.html, Nachdruck eines FAZ-Artikels

**Donig, Arthur Dr.**
11/13/1881 Frankfurt a. M. - 07/26/1958
*Home address:* Fasanenstr. 20, Charlottenburg
*Law firm address:* Friedrichstr. 64, W 8
*Additional information:* Attorney at the KG and notary. After the National Socialist seizure of power in 1933 he was readmitted upon request; at the end of 1935 his license as a

notary was revoked; he worked as an attorney until the general occupational ban in 1938; emigration to Buenos Aires, Argentina in 1939; in 1950 he was living under the name Arturo in Buenos Aires; he worked as an auctioneer.
*Sources:* *li; LAB; Liste 15.10.33; DJ 36, S. 314; MRRAK; BArch, R 3001 PAK; BG

**Donig, Martin Dr.**
01/25/1902 - October 1965
*Home address:* Nassauische Str. 61, Wilmersdorf
*Law firm address:* Ritterstr. 80, SW 68
*Additional information:* Attorney at the KG. After the National Socialist seizure of power he was made subject to an occupational ban in early 1933. Emigration to San Francisco, USA on 05/31/1938; he died in 1965 in the USA.
*Sources:* Br.B. 32; TK 33; JMBl. 33, S. 203; BArch, R 3001 PAK, BG; Göpp., S. 275; SSDI

**Dorn, Wilhelm Dr.**
07/18/1890 Oekel-Hermsdorf - no information
*Home address:* Wichmannstr. 3
*Law firm address:* Mohrenstr. 52, W 8
Attorney at the LG I-III and notary. After the National Socialist seizure of power in 1933 he was readmitted; at the end of 1935 his license as a notary was revoked; emigration in March 1937 to Italy; he returned in 1945 and established himself in Lower Saxony.
*Sources:* TK 33; *li; LAB; Liste 15.10.33; DJ 36, S. 314; BArch, R 3001 PAK; BG

**Dresdner, Erwin Dr.**
11/07/1888 Beuthen - no information
*Home address:* Wilmersdorfer Str. 77, Charlottenburg
*Law firm address:* Zimmerstr. 92/93, SW 68
*Additional information:* Attorney at the KG and notary. After the National Socialist seizure of power in 1933 he was readmitted; at the end of 1935 his license as a notary was revoked; he worked as an attorney until the general occupational ban in 1938.
*Sources:* TK 33; *li; LAB; Liste 15.10.33; DJ 36, S. 314; Liste 36; BArch, R 3001 PAK; MRRAK; BG

**Dresdner, Harry**
08/12/1885 Dubbeln - no information
*Home address:* Brandenburgische Str. 41, W 15
*Law firm address:* Keithstr. 14 a, W 62

*Additional information:* Attorney at the LG I-III. After the National Socialist seizure of power he was readmitted until the general occupational ban in 1938. Emigration to Wellington, New Zealand.
*Sources:* TK 33; *li; LAB; Liste 15.10.33; MRRAK; BArch, R 3001 PAK; BG

**Dresel, Alfred**
01/03/1891 Berlin - no information
*Home address:* Amselstr. 15, Dahlem
*Law firm address:* Amselstr. 15, Dahlem
*Additional information:* Attorney at the KG. After the National Socialist seizure of power he was made subject to an occupational ban in early 1933; emigration to London, Great Britain on 12/27/1938; board member of the Council of Jews from Germany; in 1977 he was living in Oxshott, Great Britain.
*Sources:* TK 33; Liste d. nichtzugel. RA, 25.4.33; JMBl. 33, S. 203; BG; BArch, R 3001 PAK; Göpp., S. 276

**Drucker, Erich Dr.**
No information
*Home address:* no information
*Law firm address:* Berliner Allee 242, Weißensee
*Additional information:* Attorney at the LG I-III and AG Weißensee. After the National Socialist seizure of power he was made subject to an occupational ban in early 1933.
*Sources:* TK 33; Liste d. nichtzugel. RA, 25.4.33; JMBl. 33, S. 221

**Drucker, Paul Dr.**
09/04/1895 Berlin - 08/01/1959 presumably Mexico
*Home address:* Thomasiusstr. 15, NW 40
*Law firm address:* Potsdamer Str. 92, W 57
*Additional information:* Attorney at the LG I-III and AG Berlin-Mitte. After the National Socialist seizure of power in 1933 he was readmitted; at the end of 1935 his license as an attorney was revoked; he worked as an attorney up to the general occupational ban in 1938; emigration to Mexico on 02/14/1939.
*Sources:* TK 33; *li; LAB, Liste 15.10.33; DJ 36, S. 314; Naatz-Album; MRRAK; BG

# E

**Ebers, Georg Dr.**
No information - 04/28/1935
*Home address:* no information
*Law firm address:* Französische Str. 47, W 8
*Additional information:* Attorney and notary at the LG I-III. After the National Socialist seizure of power in 1933 he was readmitted; he died in 1935.
*Sources:* Br.B. 32; TK 33; *li; LAB, Liste 15.10.33

**Ebstein, Curt Dr.**
02/05/1899 Berlin - 1984 USA
*Home address:* no information
*Law firm address:* Behrenstr. 27, W 8
*Additional information:* Attorney at the LG I-III and AG Mitte. After the National Socialist seizure of power he was readmitted until the general occupational ban in 1938; emigration to the USA on 05/25/1941; he died there in 1984.
*Sources:* TK 33; *li; LAB, Liste 15.10.33; MRRAK; BG; SSDI

**Eckstein, Curt Dr.**
04/30/1890 Dewangen-Reichenbach - transportation 1944
*Home address:* An der Spandauer Brücke 12, C 2
*Law firm address:* Mittelstr. 18, NW 7
*Additional information:* Attorney at the KG and notary. After the National Socialist seizure of power in 1933 he was readmitted; at the end of 1935 his license as a notary was revoked; he worked as an attorney until the general occupational ban in 1938; he was captured in 1939 in Borgsdorf, Niederbarnim, during the population census.
*Sources:* Br.B. 32; *li; LAB, Liste 15.10.33; DJ 36, S. 314; MRRAK; BG; GB II

**Eckstein, Ernst**
05/22/1886 Göttingen (Hannover?) - transportation 1942
*Home address:* Kurfürstendamm 224, W 15
*Law firm address:* Kurfürstendamm 224, W 15
*Additional information:* Attorney at the KG. After the National Socialist seizure of power he was made subject to an occupational ban in spring 1933; emigration to France.

Transportation on 09/16/1942 from Drancy to Auschwitz.
*Sources:* Br.B. 32; TK 33; Liste d. nichtzugel. RA, 25.4.33; BG; GB II

**Eckstein, Ludwig**
09/16/1901 Hannover - no information
*Home address:* no information
*Law firm address:* Hardenbergstr. 27, Charlottenburg
*Additional information:* Attorney at the KG. After the National Socialist seizure of power he was made subject to an occupational ban on 07/13/1933; emigration; after the end of the war he returned to Berlin; he was readmitted as an attorney.
*Sources:* TK 33; Liste d. nichtzugel. RA, 25.4.33; JMBl. 33, S. 282; BArch, R 3001 PAK, PA; Ausk. Werner Wolff, 22.9.1998

**Edel, Robert Dr.**
02/04/1904 Charlottenburg - no information
*Home address:* Berliner Str. 2, Charlottenburg
*Law firm address:* no information
*Additional information:* Since February 1932 he was admitted as an attorney at the LG I-III and AG Charlottenburg. After the National Socialist seizure of power he was made subject to an occupational ban on 06/09/1933.
*Sources:* TK 33; JMBl. 26.7.33, S. 234; BArch, R 3001 PAK, PA

**Edelstein, Friedrich (Fritz) Gustav Dr.**
02/21/1895 Berlin - 1956 USA
*Home address:* Ilmenauer Str. 10, Wilmersdorf
*Law firm address:* Motzstr. 38, Wilmersdorf
*Additional information:* Attorney at the LG I-III and notary; he was Protestant. After the National Socialist seizure of power in 1933 he was readmitted; at the end of 1935 his license as a notary was revoked; he worked as an attorney until the general occupational ban in 1938; he belonged to the Reich Association of Non-Aryan Christians. Emigration to the USA on 03/18/1941.
*Sources:* TK 33; *li; DJ 36, S. 314; BArch, R 3001 PAK; Mitt.bl. Reichsverband nichtarischer Christen, 6.12.1934; MRRAK; Naatz-Album; BG

**Eger, Herbert**
11/19/1882 Berlin - 05/25/1963
*Home address:* no information
*Law firm address:* Schloßstr. 1, Pankow
*Additional information:* Attorney at the LG I-III, AG Pankow and notary. After the National Socialist seizure of power in 1933 his license as a notary was revoked; he was admitted as an attorney until the general occupational ban in 1938; 1938 he was transported to Sachsenhausen concentration camp. His wife Marie was regarded as "Aryan." Emigration to Great Britain on 06/13/1939.
*Sources:* TK 33; Pr.J. 33, S. 532; *li; LAB, Liste 15.10.33; MRRAK; BArch, R 3001 PAK; BG; Ausk. des Sohnes

**Ehrenfried, Gustav Dr.**
04/07/1872 - 02/02/1939
*Home address:* Schwäbische Str. 29, W 30
*Law firm address:* Augsburger Str. 57, W 50
*Additional information:* Attorney at the LG I-III and notary. After the National Socialist seizure of power in 1933 his license as a notary was revoked; he worked as an attorney until the general occupational ban in 1938. He died in early 1939, he was buried at Weißensee.
*Sources:* TK 33; JMBl. 33, S. 220; *li; LAB; Liste 15.10.33; MRRAK; BArch, R 3001 PAK; BG

**Ehrlich, Friedrich Dr.**
09/08/1889 Iserlohn - transportation 1942
*Home address:* Wartburgstr. 24, Schöneberg
*Law firm address:* Rosenthaler Str. 44, C 54
*Additional information:* Attorney at the LG I-III, AG Berlin-Mitte and notary. After the National Socialist seizure of power he was made subject to an occupational ban in early 1933. He was used for forced labor, last as a worker; date of declaration of property: 11/23/1942, collection point Große Hamburger Str. 26; transportation on 11/29/1942 to Auschwitz
*Sources:* Br.B. 32; TK 33 (Fritz); Liste d. nichtzugel. RA, 25.4.33; JMBl. 33, S. 253; BArch, R 3001 PAK; BG; GB II

**Ehrlich, Hugo Dr.**
06/10/1881 Alt Beru - 11/24/1940 Berlin
*Home address:* Giesebrechtstr. 15, Charlottenburg

*Law firm address:* Lennéstr. 7, W 9
*Additional information:* Attorney at the LG I-III and notary. After the National Socialist seizure of power in 1933 his license as a notary was revoked; worked as an attorney until the general occupational ban in 1938; he last practiced as an attorney in his apartment; he died in 1940 at the age of 59; he was buried at Weißensee.
*Sources:* Br.B. 32; JMBl. 33, S. 202; *li; LAB, Liste 15.10.33; Liste 36; MRRAK; BArch, R 3001 PAK; BG

**Ehrlich, Kurt**
02/16/1886 Magdeburg - no information
*Home address:* Fasanenstr. 68, W 15
*Law firm address:* Fasanenstr. 68, W 15
*Additional information:* Attorney at the LG I-III and notary. After the National Socialist seizure of power in 1933 he was readmitted; at the end of 1935 his license as a notary was revoked; he worked as an attorney until the general occupational ban in 1938.
*Sources:* TK 33; *li; LAB, Liste 15.10.33; DJ 36, S. 314; Liste 36; MRRAK; BArch, R 3001 PAK; BG

**Ehrmann, Ernst**
06/01/1904 Berlin - no information
*Home address:* no information
*Law firm address:* Jägerstr. 13
*Additional information:* Attorney at the LG I-III. After the National Socialist seizure of power he was made ubject to an occupational ban in early 1933.
*Sources:* Adr.B. 32; TK 33; Liste d. nichtzugel. RA, 25.4.33; JMBl. 33, S. 234; BArch, R 3001 PAK

**Eichelbaum, Eva**
09/08/1901 - no information
*Home address:* no information
*Law firm address:* Neue Ansbacher Str. 17, W 50
*Additional information:* Attorney since 1929, admitted at the LG 1-III and AG Berlin-Mitte. After the National Socialist seizure of power she was made subject to an occupational ban on 06/09/1933. Her application to continue working as an attorney was rejected.
*Sources:* TK 33; Liste d. nichtzugel. RA, 25.4.33; JMBl. 33, S. 234; BArch, R 3001 PAK, PA

**Eichelbaum, Kurt Dr.**
05/25/1890 - July 1967 New York
*Home address:* Badensche Str./Ecke Babelsberger Str.
*Law firm address:* Taubenstr. 8/9, W 8
*Additional information:* Soldier during First World War; attorney (since 1919), last at the LG I-III, and notary (since 1927). After the National Socialist seizure of power he was made subject to an occupational ban on 05/29/1933; his war service was not recognized as "frontline fighting." He had worked for several prominent Swiss companies. In June 1933 he left Berlin with his wife and son; in Switzerland, however, the family only received a temporary residency permit, from there they went to Italy; they could still take their extensive library with them. In early 1939 they were able to obtain a visa for Cuba, after many intensive efforts. Fortunately the family was allowed to go ashore. After one and a half years of waiting, the family managed to enter the USA, but there they remained "alien enemies" for a long time," then they received U.S. citizenship. The family managed to struggle along by taking various temporary jobs; the son soon became the main breadwinner. Kurt was finally happy to get a job at the department store Macy's. While he and his wife had a precarious social status, the son became a sergeant in the U.S. Army and came with the U.S troops to Berlin. Kurt lived in the neighborhood Queens in New York until his death; he died in 1967 at the age of 77.
*Sources:* Adr.B. 32; TK 33; Liste d. nichtzugel. RA.; JMBl. 33, S. 209; BArch, R 3001 PA; SSDI; Engelmann, Bernt: Die unfreiwilligen Reisen des Putti Eichelbaum [The involuntary trips of Putti Eichelbaum], Göttingen 1996

**Eisenberg, Fritz Dr.**
02/25/1889 Berlin - transportation 1943
*Home address:* Wittelsbacher Str. 13
*Law firm address:* Charlottenstr. 58, W 8
*Additional information:* Attorney at the KG (since 1919) and notary (since 1929). After the National Socialist seizure of power in early 1933 he was made subject to an occupational ban as an attorney and notary. Transportation to Auschwitz on 03/01/1943.

*Sources:* Br.B. 32; TK 33; Liste d. nichtzugel. RA, 25.4.33; Pr.J. 33, S. 466; BArch, R 3001 PAK; BG; GB II

**Eisenmann, Adolf Dr.**
10/22/1887 Frankfurt a. M. - no information
*Home address:* no information
*Law firm address:* Ansbacher Str. 35, W 50
*Additional information:* Soldier in the First World War, was awarded with the EK I/II; attorney (since 1921) at the LG I-III and AG Berlin-Mitte, and notary (since 1927). After the National Socialist seizure of power in 1933 he was readmitted; on 11/14/1935 his license as a notary was revoked as part of the general dismissal of Jewish notaries; he was disbarred as an attorney on 11/30/1938 in light of the general occupational ban.
*Sources:* TK 33; *li, LAB, Liste 15.3.33; DJ 36, S. 314; MRRAK; BArch, R 3001 PAK

**Eisenstaedt, Alfred Dr.**
01/21/1874 Berlin - no information
*Home address:* Hallesche Str. 18, SW 11
*Law firm address:* Kronenstr. 76, W 8
*Additional information:* Attorney at the LG I-III and notary. After the National Socialist seizure of power in 1933 his license as a notary was revoked; he was working as an attorney until the general occupational ban in 1938.
*Sources:* TK 33; JMBl. 33, S. 202; *li; Liste 36; MRRAK; BArch, R 3001 PAK; BG

**Eisenstaedt, Nathan, Judicial Councillor**
08/26/1866 Stuhm - 11/02/1941Berlin
*Home address:* Pariser Str. 24, W 15
*Law firm address:* Tauentzienstr. 14, W 50
*Additional information:* Attorney at the KG and notary. After the National Socialist seizure of power in 1933 his license as a notary was revoked; he worked as an attorney until the general occupational ban in 1933; he died in November 1931 at the age of 75 in Berlin.
*Sources:* TK 33; JMBl. 33, S. 202; *li; Liste 36; LAB, Liste 15.10.33; BArch, R 3001 PAK; MRRAK; BG

**Eisenstaedt, Siegfried Dr.**
04/09/1884 Berlin - 10/29/1942 Riga
*Home address:* no information
*Law firm address:* Friedrichstr. 91-92, NW 7
*Additional information:* Attorney at the LG I-III. After the National Socialist seizure of power in 1933 he was temporarily made subject to a ban on representation, he was readmitted until the general occupational ban in 1938. Transportation on 10/26/1942 on Riga, there he was murdered shortly after arrival.
*Sources:* Br.B. 32; TK 33; Liste d. nichtzugel. RA, 25.4.33; Liste 36; MRRAK; BArch, R 3001 PAK; BG; BdE; GB II

**Eisner, Anita**
07/25/1900 Berlin - 04/12/1950 Berlin
*Home address:* no information
*Law firm address:* Lützowstr. 69, W 35
*Additional information:* Attorney since 1927, admitted to the LG I-III. She had financed her studies with difficulty, because her father succumbed to a heart attack in 1914 when he was arrested by the British as a civilian prisoner on a trip to Antwerp. After the National Socialist seizure of power she was made subject to an occupational ban on 05/26/1933; then authorized representative in the house and property administration of numerous Jewish emigrants. She was in constant contact with the National Socialist authorities within the framework of this activity: "I remember, for example .... that in a single week I had five summons before the customs investigation and the Gestapo, summons where one never knew at that time whether one was going to emerge free or be deterred without any reason ... Not only did I have to witness that all of my relatives, including my nearly 80-year-old mother and my only sister, furthermore all my remaining friends in Germany had been evacuated and completely exterminated by the Nazis ... I also had to witness how dozens of my clients and relatives entrusted to me by friends and clients had to make their way into nothingness. From March 1943 until the seizure of Berlin, for more than two years, I had to live illegally, I did not receive any food ration cards and mostly not know what I was living on and where I would spend the next night." During this period, Anita wrote to a friend in Alsace with the help of an intermediary; the letters show how difficult it was for her to endure the persecution. She could not enter air raid shelters; she happened to be in Dresden when the devastating bombings took place, she fled into the forest. She tried to make ends meet with philosophical writings; she survived and

was admitted to the practice of law in 1947, whereby she turned down requests that she allow herself to be taken into consideration as a candidate for the judiciary. She died in 1950 at the age of 49.
*Sources:* TK 33; JMBl. 33, S. 209; BArch, R 3001, PAK, PA; Aufbau (NY), 28.09.45 (Geb. dat.: 25.07.09); LAB, RAK, PA; BG; Ausk. F. Flechtmann, André Hugel

### Eisner, Ernst Dr.
03/12/1895 - no information
*Home address:* Landshuter Str. 28, W 30
*Law firm address:* Landshuter Str. 28, W 30
*Additional information:* Attorney at the LG I-III and notary. After the National Socialist seizure of power in 1933 he was readmitted; at the end of 1935 his license as a notary was revoked; he worked as an attorney up to the general occupational ban in 1938, thereafter he was still admitted as a "consultant." Emigration to London, Great Britain.
*Sources:* TK 33; *li; LAB, Liste 15.10.33; DJ 36, S. 314; MRRAK; BArch, R 3001 PAK; Liste der Kons. v. 23.2.1939; BG

### Eisner, Hermann Dr.
10/16/1897 Gleiwitz - 10/29/1977 Berlin
*Home address:* Sybelstr. 69 (?), Charlottenburg
*Law firm address:* Friedrichstr. 85 II, W 8
*Additional information:* Attorney since 1926, admitted at the LG I-III and AG Berlin-Mitte; he was also on the management board of the Engelhardt Group. He was the husband of the beloved actress Camilla Spira (known as the hostess in the operetta "Im Weißen Rössl"). After the National Socialist seizure of power he was readmitted. At the end of 1935 his license as a notary was revoked; he worked as an attorney until the general occupational ban in 1938. He had to give up his board seat as early as 1934. During an interview Camilla Spira noted: "He was so German ... I tried to make it clear to him that this was not a labor camp, but death was awaiting him." After finally being persuaded by his wife, he emigrated to the Netherlands; there the persecutors caught up with him and in 1943 he went to the Westerbork concentration camp. He survived and returned to Berlin. In 1947 he was readmitted as an attorney; he was still active as a notary until 1973; most recently he had relocated his law firm to his apartment in Dahlem.

*Sources:* TK 33; *li; LAB, Liste 15.10.33; DJ 36, S. 314; MRRAK; BArch, R 3001, PAK; BG; LAB, RAK PA; Ausk. d. Tochter Susanne T.

### Eisner, Wilhelm Dr.
08/12/1900 - no information
*Home address:* no information.
*Law firm address:* Prager Platz 3, Wilmersdorf
*Additional information:* Admitted as an attorney since 12/21/1932. After the National Socialist seizure of power he was made subject to an occupational ban on 06/10/1933; he then moved from Berlin to Gleiwitz.
*Sources:* Liste d. nichtzugel. RA, 25.4.33; JMBl. 33, S. 253; BArch, R 3001 PAK, PA

### Elb, Joseph Paul Dr.
04/24/1899 Fürth - 03/07/1942
*Home address:* no information
*Law firm address:* Schiffbauerdamm 29 a
*Additional information:* Attorney at the LG I-III. After the National Socialist seizure of power he was readmitted; he was still listed as an attorney in the 1938 business directory; he died in March 1942 at the age of 42; the circumstances of his death are not known.
*Sources:* TK 33; *li; Liste 36; LAB, Liste 15.10.33; Br.B. 38; BArch, R 3001 PAK

### Elden, Walter Dr.
08/10/1905 Berlin - no information
*Home address:* no information
*Law firm address:* Lindenstr. 43, SW 19
*Additional information:* Attorney at the LG I-III and AG Berlin-Mitte, first admitted at the end of 1932. After the National Socialist seizure of power he was made subject to an occupational ban on 06/09/1933.
*Sources:* TK 33; Liste d. nichtzugel. RA, 25.4.33; JMBl. 33, S. 234; LAB, Liste 15.10.33; BArch, R 3001 PAK, PA

### Elias, Ludwig Dr.
09/19/1891 Berlin - no information
*Home address:* no information
*Law firm address:* Markgrafenstr. 78, SW 68
*Additional information:* Attorney at the LG I-III. After the National Socialist seizure of power he was made subject to an occupational ban in early 1933.
*Sources:* Adr.B. 32; TK 33; Liste d. nichtzugel. RA, 25.4.33; JMBl. 33, S. 234; BArch, R 3001 PAK, PA

**Elkeles, Heinrich Dr.**
04/15/1887 Posen (now known as Poznan) -
transportation 1943
*Home address:* Passauer Str. 2, Schöneberg,
W 50
*Law firm address:* Kaiser-Wilhelm-Str. 59, C 2
*Additional information:* Attorney at the LG
I-III, AG Mitte and notary. After the National
Socialist seizure of power in 1933 he was
readmitted; at the end of 1935 his license
as a notary was revoked; until the general
occupational ban in 1938 he worked as an
attorney; since 1939 he was a board member
of the Reich Association of Jewish Provincial
Community Organizations, a director of
Jüdische Landarbeit GmbH, a division of
the Reich Association. Transportation on
06/16/1943 to Theresienstadt, from there he
was transported on 10/28/1944 to Auschwitz
and murdered there.
*Sources:* TK 33; *li; LAB, Liste 15.10.33;
MRRAK; BArch, R 3001 PAK, PA; BG; ThG;
GB II; Göpp., S. 241

**Elkeles, Ludwig Dr.**
03/10/1902 Posnan - no information
*Home address:* no information
*Law firm address:* Jägerstr. 19, W 8
*Additional information:* Attorney at the LG
I-III. After the National Socialist seizure of
power he was made subject to an occupational
ban on 06/10/1933. His mother sought the
readmission of her son by writing a letter to
Reich President Hindenburg; her other son,
a doctor, had been affected by the exclusion
policy and had become unemployed. The
answer was succint: "Your son Ludwig will not
be readmitted as an attorney." He emigrated in
1934 to Gdansk or Warsaw.
*Sources:* TK 33; Liste d. nichtzugel. RA,
25.4.33; JMBl. 33, S. 220; BArch, R 3001
PAK, PA; BG

**Elkisch, Walter Dr.**
07/01/1889 Berlin - March 1972
*Home address:* no information
*Law firm address:* Sächsische Str. 2, W 15
*Additional information:* Attorney at the
LG I-III and AG Charlottenburg. After the
National Socialist seizure of power he was
readmitted; he worked as an attorney until at
least 1936; emigration to the USA, last lived
in New York.
*Sources:* TK 33; *li; LAB, Liste 15.10.33;
Liste 36; SSDI

**Elsaß, Arthur Dr.**
03/26/1896 Landsberg - no information
*Home address:* Martin-Luther-Str. 9, W 30
*Law firm address:* Martin-Luther-Str. 9, W 30
*Additional information:* Attorney at the
KG and notary. After the National Socialist
seizure of power in 1933 he was re-admitted;
at the end of 1935 his license as a notary was
revoked; he worked as an attorney until the
general occupational ban in 1938, thereafter
he worked as a "consultant," on 05/20/1942
he was still living in Berlin.
TK 33; *li; LAB; Liste 15.10.33; DJ 36, S.
314; MRRAK; Liste d. Kons., 15.4.39; BG

**Elsbach, Alwin (Albin), Judicial Councillor**
05/29/1863 Walldorf - 02/11/1944 Auschwitz
*Home address:* Stülerstr. 7 (vorher Hitzigstr.)
*Law firm address:* Hitzigstr. 8, W 35
*Additional information:* Attorney at the LG
I-III and notary. After the National Socialist
seizure of power in 1933 his license as a
notary was revoked; he was disbarred on
02/01/1938. Emigration to the Netherlands;
there he was arrested and at the beginning of
1944 he was transported from Westerbork to
Auschwitz.
*Sources:* TK 33; JMBl. 33, S. 202; *li; LAB,
Liste 15.10.33; BArch, R 3001 PAK; BG
(Albin E.); GB II (Albin E.)

**Emanuel, Albert Dr.**
04/17/1892 Hannover - no information
*Home address:* Konstanzer Str. 51
*Law firm address:* Neue Friedrichstr.
78, C 2
*Additional information:* Attorney at the LG
I-III, AG Berlin-Mitte and notary. After the
National Socialist seizure of power in 1933
he was readmitted; at the end of 1935 his
license as a notary was revoked; he worked
as an attorney until the general occupational
ban in 1938, thereafter he was still admitted
as a "consultant." Emigration presumably on
01/15/1939.
*Sources:* TK 33; *li; LAB, Liste 15.10.33; DJ 36,
S. 314; MRRAK; Liste d. Kons., 15.4.39; BG

**Emanuel, Otto, Judicial Councillor**
11/07/1859 Rodenberg - 01/03/1940
*Home address:* Hauptstr. 119 bei Schneider,
Schöneberg
*Law firm address:* Hauptstr. 119 I,
Schöneberg

*Additional information:* Attorney at the LG I-III. After the National Socialist seizure of power he was readmitted as an attorney until the general occupational ban in 1938.
*Sources:* TK 33; *li; Liste 36; LAB, Liste 15.10.33; MRRAK; BArch, R 3001 PAK; BG

**Engel, Carl, Judicial Councillor**
06/02/1870 Schönlanke - 01.12.1943 Theresienstadt
*Home address:* Niebuhrstr. 67, Charlottenburg
*Law firm address:* Hardenbergstr. 13, Charlottenburg
*Additional information:* Attorney at the LG I-III and notary. After the National Socialist seizure of power in 1933 he was readmitted; at the end of 1935 his license as a notary was revoked; he worked as an attorney until the general occupational ban in 1938. Transportation on 08/11/1942 to Theresienstadt, he died there on 01/12/1943.
*Sources:* TK 33; *li; LAB, Liste 15.10.33; DJ 36, S. 314; MRRAK; BG; ThG; GB II

**Engelbert, Sally Fritz Dr.**
04/04/1886 Gudensberg - 03/22/1958 Berlin
*Home address:* Ilmenauer Str. 9, Wilmersdorf
*Law firm address:* Unter den Linden 66, NW 7
*Additional information:*
He had fought in the First World War and had been awarded the EK I/II; since 1919 he was an attorney, last at the LG I-III and AG Berlin-Mitte; in a law partnership with Johannes Werthauer; notary since 1924. He was, amongst others, the executor of Louis Ullstein's will.
On 04/01/1933 Roland Freisler appeared at the law firm and ordered its closure. He was readmitted as attorney and notary; comrades of his former regiment had interceded on his behalf. At first he relocated his law firm to Königstraße. With the occupational ban against Jewish officials his license as a notary was revoked in January 1936; he was disbarred as an attorney in 1938; he worked until 1941 as a "consultant." His wife Emilie was regarded as "non-Jewish," the marriage was regarded as "privileged," the couple had two children. On 12/11/1942 he was arrested by the Gestapo. He was at the Wuhlheide labor camp until 05/02/1943.

He survived and was readmitted as an attorney on 07/04/1945, on 03/14/1947 as a notary. In 1947 he also became city councillor for Greater Berlin and in 1951 a member of the Judges Election Committee. Despite massive political pressure, he was still legal advisor to the Police Presidents, both in the East and the West. He died in Berlin in 1958.
*Sources:* *li; LAB, Liste 15.10.33; BArch, R 3001 PAK; MRRAK; Liste d. Kons.; 15.3.39; LAB, RAK PA; BG; Ausk. Lieselotte Kuhlmann (Tochter), 29.1.1999; 14.4.2000

**Erlanger, Henry**
09/19/1872 Frankfurt a. M. - 10/06/1942 Theresienstadt
*Home address:* Corneliustr. 22, Lankwitz
*Law firm address:* Fasanenstr. 67, W 15
*Additional information:* Attorney at the KG. After the National Socialist seizure of power he was readmitted; he worked as an attorney until the general occupational ban in 1938. In 1942 he was living at the retirement home on Gerlachstr. 18-21. On 09/14/1942 he was transported to Theresienstadt and died there after only a few days.
*Sources:* Br.B. 32; TK 33; *li; MRRAK; BArch, R 3001 PAK; BG; ThG; GB II

**Eulau, Friedrich Dr.**
07/07/1888 Frankfurt a. M. - no information
*Home address:* no information
*Law firm address:* no information
*Additional information:* Worked as an attorney in Berlin since 1919, last at the LG I-III and at the AG Wedding; he was Jewish. After the National Socialist seizure of power he was made subject to an occupational ban in early 1933.
*Sources:* TK 33 (Fritz); JMBl.28.4. u. 12.5.33; BArch, R 3001 PAK, PA

**Exiner, Martin**
12/21/1885 Militsch - no information
*Home address:* no information
*Law firm address:* Königin-Augusta-Str. 23, W 35
*Additional information:* Attorney at the LG I-III and notary. After the National Socialist seizure of power in 1933 he was readmitted; his license as a notary was revoked in 1933; he worked as an attorney until the general occupational ban in 1938.
*Sources:* TK 33; *li; LAB, Liste 15.10.33; DJ 36, S. 314; Liste 36; MRRAK; BArch, R 3001 PAK

**Eyck, Erich Dr. phil.**
12/07/1878 Berlin - 06/23/1964 London
*Home address:* Lützowstr. 60, W 35
*Law firm address:* Magdeburger Str. 5, W 35
*Additional information:* Since 1898 he
studied law, political science and history
in Freiburg and Berlin; he obtained his
doctorate in 1904; as from 1906 he
established himself as an attorney, last at
the KG and notary; 1915-20 city councillor
in Charlottenburg, 1920-30 city councillor
in Berlin; he also worked as a journalist
(Berliner Tageblatt, Vossische Zeitung); he
was a member of the DDP and/or State Party,
of the Democratic Club, of the governing
board of the CV. After the National Socialist
seizure of power in 1933 his license as a
notary was revoked, he was readmitted as
an attorney because of his status as "elder
attorney." In 1937 emigration to Great
Britian via Lonon, in London he pursued
history studies, delivered guest lectures in
Oxford and London and was again active as
a journalist; in 1953 he received the Große
Bundesverdienstkreuz (Great Federal Cross
of Merit); he published historical studies, but
because of his decidedly liberal history, the
recognition of the German professional world
had long been denied him; he died in 1964 in
London.
*Publications:* Bismarck, 3 vols. 1941, 1943,
1944 (Zurich); Geschichte der Weimarer
Republik [History of the Weimar Republic], 2
vols. 1954, 1956, amongst others.
*Sources:* JMBl. 33, S. 202; *li; BG: LAB,
OFP-Akten; BHdE1933, Bd.1; LAB, Liste
15.10.33; BArch, R 3001 PAK; Krach, S.432;
Göpp., S. 278

# F

**Fabian, Erich Dr.**
08/23/1883 Berlin - no information
*Home address:* Am Karpfenpfuhl 14-16,
Zehlendorf
*Law firm address:* Eisenzahnstr. 66, Halensee
*Additional information:* Attorney
since 1909, last at the LG I-III and AG
Charlottenburg, notary since 1923; he had
fought in the First World War, was awarded
the EK II; in 1926 he was the vice president
of Bnai Brith Loge, later he resigned. After
the National Socialist seizure of power he

was readmitted, because he was recognized
as a "frontline fighter" (highlighted green
in personnel files) and "elderly attorney"
(highlighted blue in personnel files). In
regard to his admission as a notary, a red
"N" was recorded in the personnel file; in
1935 his license as a notary was revoked.
An application for further admission as a
"Jewish notary" was personally rejected by
State Secretary Roland Freisler. He was active
as an attorney until the general occupational
ban in 1938. Emigration to Great Britain on
07/14/1939.
*Sources:* TK 33; *li; LAB, Liste 15.10.33; DJ
36, S. 314; MRRAK; BArch, R 3001 PAK,
PA; BG

**Fabian, Franz Dr.**
04/12/1888 Berlin - no information
*Home address:* no information
*Law firm address:* Kochstr. 22-26, SW 68
*Additional information:* Attorney at
the LG I-III. After the National Socialist
seizure of power he was made subject to an
occupational ban in early 1933. Emigration
to Santiago Los Leones, Chile.
*Sources:* Adr.B. 32; TK 33; Liste d.
nichtzugel. RA; JMBl. 33, S. 209; BArch, R
3001 PAK; BG

**Fabian, Fritz Dr.**
12/20/1874 Tuchel - 04/02/1942
Litzmannstadt/Lodz
*Home address:* Sybelstr. 66, Charlottenburg
*Law firm address:* Unter den Linden 42, NW 7
*Additional information:* Attorney at the
LG I-III, AG Berlin-Mitte and notary. After
the National Socialist seizure of power his
license as a notary was revoked in 1933; he
was readmitted as an attorney; he worked as
an attorney until the general occupational
ban in 1938. Date of declaration of property:
10/15/1941; collection point Levetzowstr.
7-8; transportation from 10/27/1941 to
10/29/1941 to Litzmannstadt/Lodz, he died
there at the beginning of April 1942.
*Sources:* TK 33; JMBl. 33, S. 220; *li; LAB,
Liste 15.10.33; MRRAK; BArch, R 3001
PAK; BG; GB II

**Fabian, Heinz Kurt Dr.**
12/07/1877 - no information
*Home address:* no information
*Law firm address:* Klopstockstr. 37, NW 87

*Additional information:* After the National Socialist seizure of power he was made subject to an occupational ban; he was disbarred.
*Sources:* BArch, R 3001 PAK; Liste d. nichtzugel. RA, 25.4.33 (Nachtrag)

**Fabian, Martin**
16.12.1894 Strelno - no information
*Home address:* Sybelstr. 42 at Neumann, Charlottenburg
*Law firm address:* Kleiststr. 19, Schöneberg
*Additional information:* Attorney at the LG I-III. After the National Socialist seizure of power he was re-admitted; he worked as an attorney until 07/15/1937, then he was disbarred.
*Sources:* TK 33; *li; LAB, Liste 15.10.33; Liste 36; BArch, R 3001 PAK; BG

**Fabian, Walter**
10/03/1886 Tuchel - 08/20/1951
*Home address:* no information
*Law firm address:* Kurfürstendamm 184
*Additional information:* Attorney at the LG I-III and notary. After the National Socialist seizure of power in April 1933 he was made subject to an occupational ban in July 1933. He was a member of the Reich Association of Non-Aryan Christians. His wife was regarded as "non-Aryan." He survived the National Socialist regime and lived in Steglitz afterwards.
*Sources:* Br.B. 32; TK 33; Liste nichtzugel. RA, 25. 4. 33; JMBl. 33, S. 209; BArch, R 3001 PAK, (PA vorh.); Mitt.bl. Reichsverband nicht-arischer Christen, 6.12.1934; BG

**Faerber, Erich Dr.**
09/06/1891 Berlin - no information
*Home address:* no information
*Law firm address:* Nürnberger Platz 6, W 50
*Additional information:* Attorney at the LG I-III, AG Berlin-Mitte and notary. After the National Socialist seizure of power in 1933 he was readmitted; at the end of 1935 his license as a notary was revoked; he worked as an attorney until the general occupational ban in 1938.
*Sources:* TK 33; *li; LAB, Liste 15.10.33; DJ 36, S. 314; Liste 36; MRRAK; BArch, R 3001 PAK

**Falk, Hans Dr.**
07/16/1888 Breslau - transportation 1941
*Home address:* Niebuhrstr. 64, Charlottenburg
*Law firm address:* Jägerstr. 40, W 56
*Additional information:* Attorney at the LG I-III, AG Berlin-Mitte and notary. After the National Socialist seizure of power he was readmitted in 1933; at the end of 1935 his license as a notary was revoked; he worked as an attorney until the general occupational ban in 1938. He was later used for forced labor and employed as a laborer; he had to move several times. Date of declaration of property: 01/15/1941; collection point Levetzowstr. 7-8, transportation on 10/24/1941 to Litzmannstadt/Lodz.
*Sources:* Br.B. 32; TK 33; *li; LAB, Liste 15.10.33; DJ 36, S. 314; MRRAK; BArch, R 3001 PAK; Naatz-Album; BG; GB II

**Falkenberg, Josef**
10/31/1881 Berlin - 12/15/1962
*Home address:* Salzburger Str. 17, Schöneberg
*Law firm address:* Seydelstr. 26, SW 19
*Additional information:* Attorney since 1911, last at the LG I-III; notary since 1924; he had voted for the SPD during the last free elections according to his own data. After the National Socialist seizure of power in 1933 his license as a notary was revoked; he worked as an attorney until the general occupational ban in 1938; then he was admitted as a "consultant." His income losses were highest in the years 1938/39 (total income between RM 1,800.- and 2,958. - RM), he could otherwise record an income of up to RM 5,328. - RM. His wife Maria was regarded as "non-Jewish." He survived the National Socialist regime and was readmitted as an attorney in 1950 and as a notary in 1954. He died on 12/15/1962 in Berlin.
*Publications:* Aufsätze zur Gewerbefreiheit
*Sources:* TKK 33; JMBl. 33, S. 202; *li; LAB, Liste 15.10.33; MRRAK; Naatz-Album; BG; LAB, RAK, PA

**Falkenheim, Albert Dr.**
07/24/1891 Königsberg - no information
*Home address:* no information
*Law firm address:* Mohrenstr. 54/55, W 8
*Additional information:* Attorney at the LG I-III
and notary. After the National Socialist seizure
of power in 1933 he was readmitted; his license
as a notary was revoked at the end of 1935; he
still worked as an attorney until 04/06/1938.
*Sources:* TK 33; *li; LAB, Liste 15.10.33; DJ
36, S. 314; Liste 36; BArch, R 3001 PAK

**Falkenstein, Eberhard Dr.**
05/31/1881 Berlin - no information
*Home address:* Herwarthstr. 1, Lichterfelde
*Law firm address:* Unter den Linden 56, NW 7
*Additional information:* Attorney at the LG
I-III and notary; he was a Protestant. After the
National Socialist seizure of power in 1933
his license as a notary was revoked; he was
regarded as "mixed race" (one grandparent
was Jewish); he could still practice as an
attorney until at least 1942/43.
*Sources:* TK 33; *li; Pr.J. 33, S. 565; BArch, R
3001 PAK; LAB, Liste Mschlg. 36; Tel.B. 41;
Br.B. 43; BG

**Faß, Fritz Dr.**
02/20/1890 Neuwied - no information
*Home address:* no information
*Law firm address:* Friedrichstr. 203, SW 68
*Additional information:* He had fought in the
First World War; attorney at the LG I-III and
AG Schöneberg. After the National Socialist
seizure of power he was not recognized as a
"frontline fighter," he was made subject to an
occupational ban on 06/08/1933, since he was
regarded as a Jew, even though he was "mixed
race." He presumably emigrated to Italy: there
is a reference in his personal file in the RJM
that the Reich Bar Association still claimed an
outstanding contribution of RM 60.
*Sources:* Br.B. 32; TK 33; Liste d. nichtzugel.
RA, 25.4.33; JMBl. 33, S. 209; LAB, Liste
15.10.33; BArch, R 3001 PAK, PA; BG

**Feblowicz, Max**
06/08/1881 - 06/12/1935 Berlin
*Home address:* Hardenbergstr. 14,
Charlottenburg
*Law firm address:* Bismarckstr. 12,
Charlottenburg
Attorney at the LG I-III, AG Charlottenburg
and notary. After the National Socialist seizure

of power in 1933 his license as a notary was
revoked, he was readmitted as a lawyer, he
died in 1935 at the age of 54.
*Sources:* TK 33; JMBl. 33, S. 220; *li; LAB,
Liste 15.10.33; BArch, R 3001 PAK; BG

**Feblowicz, Samuel**
07/14/1901 Obornik - no information
*Home address:* no information
*Law firm address:* Joachimsthaler Str. 38,
Charlottenburg
*Additional information:* Attorney since
1927, admitted at the LG I-III and AG
Charlottenburg; he also exercised mandates
for the Red Cross. After the National Socialist
seizure of power he was made subject to an
occupational ban on 06/09/1933. Some of the
clients continued their approval and praised his
efforts against corruption. Despite all efforts,
the occupational ban was upheld. He emigrated
in July 1933 to France.
*Sources:* TK 33; Liste d. nichtzugel. RA,
25.4.33 (Supplement); JMBl. 33, S. 221;
BArch, R 3001 PAK, PA; BG; Schneider,
Schwarz, Schwarz

**Feder, Ernst Dr.**
03/18/1881 - 03/29/1964 Berlin
*Home address:* Welterpfad 76, Tempelhof
*Law firm address:* Marburger Str. 17, W 50
*Additional information:* Attorney at the
KG and notary; member of the Republican
Association of Judges, also active as a
journalist. After the National Socialist seizure
of power in 1933 his license as a notary was
revoked; emigration via Switzerland to Paris,
France, 1933. Admission not officially deleted
until 1935; emigration to Brazil in July 1941;
return to Berlin (West) 1957.
*Sources:* TK 33; MVRRB; Pr.J. 33, S. 390; *li;
LAB, Liste 15.10.33; BArch, R 3001 PAK; BG

**Feidelberg, Karl Dr.**
07/03/1894 Altena - no information
*Home address:* Orberstr. 28-29, Grunewald
*Law firm address:* Orberstr. 28-29,
Grunewald
*Additional information:* Attorney at the LG
I-III, AG Berlin-Mitte and notary. After the
National Socialist seizure of power he was
readmitted until his emigration to Tel Aviv,
Palestine, on 10/20/1934.
*Sources:* TK 33; *li; LAB, Liste 15.10.33;
BArch, R 3001 PAK

**Feiertag, Kurt Dr.**
11/22/1884 - transportation1943
*Home address:* Witzlebenstr. 18,
Charlottenburg
*Law firm address:* Krausenstr. 70, W 8
*Additional information:* Attorney at the
LG I-III, AG Berlin-Mitte and notary. After
the National Socialist seizure of power in
1933 his license as a notary was revoked;
he practiced as an attorney until the general
occupational ban in 1938. Transportation on
03/03/1943 to Auschwitz.
*Sources:* TK 33; Pr.J. 33, S. 390; *li; LAB,
Liste 15.10.33; Liste 36; BArch, R 3001 PAK;
MRRAK; BG; GB II

**Feig, Ernst**
06/09/1880 Gleiwitz - 04/26/1942
Sachsenhausen
*Home address:* Tellstr. 11, Neukölln
*Law firm address:* Schlesische Str. 39
*Additional information:* Attorney at the
LG I-III. After the National Socialist seizure
of power in 1933 he was disbarred. He was
murdered in April 1942 in Sachsenhausen.
*Sources:* Adr.B. 32; TK 33; BArch, R 3001
PAK; BG; GB II

**Feig, Otto, Judicial Councillor**
02/18/1864 Tarnowitz - no information
*Home address:* Vorbergstr. 8, Schöneberg
*Law firm address:* Beuthstr. 10 II, SW 19
*Additional information:* Attorney at the LG
I-III, AG Berlin-Mitte and notary. After the
National Socialist seizure of power he was
readmitted. He worked as an attorney until
08/18/1938, then he was disbarred. His wife
was regarded as "non-Jewish." He survived
and lived in Pankow after 1945.
TK 33; JMBl. 33, S. 202; *li; Liste 36; LAB,
Liste 15.10.33; BArch, R 3001 PAK; BG

**Feige, Richard Dr.**
06/14/1880 Liegnitz - no information
*Home address:* Brandenburgische Str. 42,
Wilmersdorf
*Law firm address:* Potsdamer Str. 134 a, W 9
*Additional information:* Attorney at the
KG and notary. He was Protestant. After
the National Socialist seizure of power in
1933 his license as a notary was revoked;
he worked as an attorney until the general
occupational ban in 1938. Emigration to the
USA on 06/18/1941.

*Sources:* TK 33; JMBl. 33, S. 202; *li; LAB,
Liste 15.10.33; MRRAK; BArch, R 3001
PAK; BG

**Feige, Walter Dr.**
12/20/1883 Berlin - no information
*Home address:* Konstanzer Str. 2, W 15
*Law firm address:* Potsdamer Str. 134 a
*Additional information:* Attorney at the LG
I-III, AG Berlin-Mitte and notary. After the
National Socialist seizure of power he was
made subject to an occupational ban in early
1933. Emigration to the USA in 1941.
*Sources:* Br.B. 32; TK 33; Liste d. nichtzugel.
RA, 25.4.33; JMBl. 33, S. 202; BArch, R
3001 PAK; BG (mit abw. Geb.jahr: 1885)

**Feilchenfeld, Daniel, Judicial Councillor**
06/27/1868 Kulm - no information
*Home address:* Friedrich-Wilhelm-Str. 20, W 35
*Law firm address:* Friedrich-Wilhelm-Str. 20,
W 35
*Additional information:* Attorney at the
LG I-III and notary. After the National
Socialist seizure of power in 1933 his license
as a notary was revoked; he practiced as an
attorney until the general occupational ban of
1938; emigration to the Dominican Republic.
*Sources:* TK 33; JMBl. 33, S. 202; *li; LAB,
Liste 15.10.33; MRRAK; BArch, R 3001
PAK; BG

**Feilchenfeld, David**
08/28/1877 Thorn – 1952 (?) Berlin
*Home address:* Schönhauser Allee 90, N 113
*Law firm address:* Monbijouplatz 4, N 24
*Additional information:* Attorney and
notary. After the National Socialist seizure of
power in 1933 he was readmitted; he worked
as an attorney until the general occupational
ban in 1938, then he was active as a
"consultant." His wife was regarded as "non-
Jewish." He still worked until 1944 in Berlin.
He survived the Nazi regime; in 1946 he
was arrested by the Soviet military police; he
was released and could once again establish
himself as an attorney. He died (presumably)
in 1952 in Berlin-Grunewald.
*Sources:* TK 33; * li; LAB, Liste 15.10.33; DJ
36, S. 314; MRRAK; Liste. d. Kons., 15.4.39;
BG; LAB, RAK, PA

**Feilchenfeld, Max**
05/01/1874 Thorn - no information

*Home address:* Kommandantenstr. 1, SW 19
*Law firm address:* Kommandantenstr. 1, SW 19
*Additional information:* Attorney at the LG
I-III and notary. After the National Socialist
seizure of power in 1933 his license as a
notary was revoked; he worked as an attorney
until the general occupational ban of 1938.
Emigration to Manila, Philippines.
*Sources:* TK 33; JMBl. 33, S. 202; *li; LAB,
Liste 15.10.33; MRRAK; BArch, R 3001
PAK; BG

**Feinberg, Dagobert Dr.**
04/10/1905 Luisenhof/Memel – No
information
*Home address:* no information
*Law firm address:* Tauentzienstr. 18a, W 50
*Additional information:* Attorney at the LG
I-III and AG Berlin-Charlottenburg, in a law
firm partnership with Dr. Herbert Fiegel.
After the National Socialist seizure of power
he was made subject to an occupational ban
in early 1933. Emigration to Palestine.
*Sources:* Adr.B. 32; Liste d. nichtzugel. RA
(dort als „Feigenberg"); JMBl. 33, S. 221;
BArch, R 3001 PAK; Ausk. E. Proskauer

**Feld, Arthur Dr.**
12/11/1884 Friedeberg - no information
*Home address:* Kurfürstendamm 210,
Charlottenburg
*Law firm address:* Potsdamer Str. 33
*Additional information:* Attorney at the
LG I-III and notary. After the National
Socialist seizure of power in 1933 his license
as a notary was revoked in June of 1933, in
September he was disbarred as an attorney.
*Sources:* Br.B. 32; TK 33; JMBl. 33, S. 202;
Pr.J. 33, S. 391; BArch, R 3001 PAK; BG

**Feld, Erwin Dr.**
11/22/1890 Berlin - no information
*Home address:* Paulsborner Str. 10, Halensee
*Law firm address:* Potsdamer Str. 83, W 57
*Additional information:* Attorney at the LG
I-III, AG Berlin-Mitte and notary. After the
National Socialist seizure of power in 1933 he
was readmitted; at the end of 1935 his license
as a notary was revoked; he worked as an
attorney until the general occupational ban in
1938. Emigration to Shanghai, China.
*Sources:* TK 33; *li; DJ 36, S. 314; MRRAK;
BArch, R 3001 PAK; BG

**Ferester, Max**
12/11/1890 Berlin - February 1971
*Home address:* Neue Ansbacher Str. 18, W 50
*Law firm address:* Neue Ansbacher Str. 18,
W 50
*Additional information:* Attorney at the KG,
at the same time a city councillor. After the
National Socialist seizure of power in 1933
he was readmitted; he worked as an attorney
until the general occupational ban in 1938.
Emigration to Havana, Cuba; later he went to
the USA, where he died in 1971 at the age of 80.
*Sources:* TK 33; *li; LAB, Liste 15.10.33;
MRRAK; BArch, R 3001 PAK; BG; SSDI

**Fernbach, Fritz Dr.**
12/16/1888 Sprottau - no information
*Home address:* no information
*Law firm address:* Dorotheenstr. 34, NW 7
*Additional information:* He fought in the First
World War; attorney since 1921, admitted
at the LG I. After the National Socialist
seizure of power his war service during
the First World War was not recognized as
"frontline fighting;" he was made subject to an
occupational ban on 09/25/1933.
*Sources:* Adr.B. 32; Liste d. nichtzugel. RA,
25.4.33; JMBl. 33, 17.6.33, S. 184; BArch, R
3001 PAK, PA

**Fiegel, Herbert Dr. Dr.**
07/14/1898 Berlin - no information
*Home address:* Tauentzienstr. 18 a, W 50
*Law firm address:* Tauentzienstr. 18 a, W 50
*Additional information:* Attorney at the LG
I-III and AG Mitte, in a law partnership with
Dr. Dagobert Feinberg. After the National
Socialist seizure of power he was readmitted;
he was disbarred on 04/06/1934 "upon
request;" emigration to Palestine; later he was
active with the URO. Br.B. 32; TK 33; *li;
*Sources:* LAB, Liste 15.10.33; BArch, R 3001
PAK; BG; Ausk. E. Proskauer

**Fink, Arthur Dr.**
03/30/1882 Bromberg - 01/16/1934
Darmstadt
*Home address:* Nikolassee, Zehlendorf
*Law firm address:* Uhlandstr. 29,
Charlottenburg
*Additional information:* Attorney at the
LG I-III, AG Schöneberg and notary, in
a partnership with Betti Fink. After the
National Socialist seizure of power in 1933

his license as a notary was revoked; he was readmitted as an attorney. He committed suicide in 1934 in Darmstadt at the age of 52.
*Sources:* Br.B. 32; TK 33; JMBl. 33, S. 202; *li; LAB, Liste 15.10.33; BArch, R 3001 PAK; BG; GB II

**Fink, Betti**
08/13/1891 Pleschen - no information
*Home address:* Uhlandstr. 29, Charlottenburg
*Law firm address:* Uhlandstr. 29, Charlottenburg
*Additional information:* Attorney at the KG; joint law partnership with Arthur Fink. After the National Socialist seizure of power he was made subject to an occupational ban in early 1933. Betti emigrated on 05/24/1935 to Ramat Gan, Palestine.
*Sources:* TK 33; Liste d. nichtzugel. RA, 25.4.33; JMBl. 33, S. 203; BArch, R 3001 PAK; BG

**Finkelstein, Hermann Dr.**
02/17/1905 Berlin-Charlottenburg - no information
*Home address:* no information.
*Law firm address:* Droysenstr. 6, Charlottenburg
*Additional information:* Attorney at the LG I-III and AG Charlottenburg. After the National Socialist seizure of power he was made subject to an occupational ban on 07/13/1933.
*Sources:* TK 33; Liste d. nichtzugel. RA, 25.4.33; JMBl. 21.8.33, S. 266; BArch, R 3001 PAK, PA

**Fischer, Alfred**
No information - transportation
*Home address:* Pfalzburger Str. 60, Wilmersdorf
*Law firm address:* Tauentzienstr. 8, W 50
*Additional information:* Attorney at the KG and notary. After the National Socialist seizure of power he was readmitted in 1933; at the end of 1935 his license as a notary was revoked; he was disbarred in 1936. Emigration to Prague, Czechoslovakia in 1934; he was arrested there and transported to Litzmannstadt/Lodz.
*Sources:* Br.B. 32; TK 33; *li; LAB, Liste 15.10.33; DJ 36, S. 314; BArch, R 3001 PAK; BG; g

**Fischer, Fritz Dr.**
07/01/1888 Kattowitz - no information

*Home address:* no information
*Law firm address:* Kurfürstendamm 38/39, W 15
*Additional information:* Attorney at the LG I-III, AG Schöneberg and notary; he was made subject to an occupational ban in early 1933.
*Sources:* TK 33; Liste d. nichtzugel. RA, 25.4.33 (Nachtrag); JMBl. 33, S. 221 (Friedrich); BArch, R 3001 PAK

**Fischer, Han(n)s Dr.**
02/16/1894 Berlin - no information
*Home address:* Hohenzollerdamm 96, Grunewald
*Law firm address:* Potsdamer Str. 129/130, W 9
*Additional information:* Attorney at the LG I-III and notary. After the National Socialist seizure of power he was readmitted in 1933; at the end of 1935 his license as a notary was revoked; he practiced as an attorney until the general occupational ban in 1938.
*Sources:* TK 33; *li; LAB, Liste 15.10.33; DJ 36, S. 314; MRRAK; BArch, R 3001 PAK; Naatz-Album; BG

**Fischer, James Dr.**
08/22/1870 - 08/30/1938
*Home address:* Kaiserplatz 1, Wilmersdorf
*Law firm address:* Rheinstr. 21, Friedenau
*Additional information:* Attorney at the LG I-III, AG Berlin-Mitte and notary; he had his name changed from Cohn to Fischer. After the National Socialist seizure of power in 1933 his license as a notary was revoked; he was admitted as an attorney until 1938; he died in 1938 a week after his 68th birthday, he was buried at Weißensee.
*Sources:* TK 33; JMBl. 33, S. 266; *li; LAB, Liste 15.10.33; BArch, R 3001 PAK; BG

**Fischer, Oskar Dr.**
09/20/1882 Berlin - after 1945, Berlin
*Home address:* Bismarckstr. 66, Charlottenburg
*Law firm address:* Seydelstr. 26, C 19
*Additional information:* Attorney and notary. After the National Socialist seizure of power in 1933 he was readmitted; at the end of 1935 his license as a notary was revoked; he worked as an attorney up to the general occupational ban in 1938. Emigration to London on 07/15/1939. After the end of the war he visited Berlin every year; he died at the

Tempelhof Airport from a heart attack.
*Sources:* TK 33; *li; LAB, Liste 15.10.33; DJ
36, S. 314; MRRAK; BArch, R 3001 PAK;
BG; Ausk. Frau Brigitte Rothert, 27.1.1999

**Flatau, Ernst Dr.**
10/31/1885 Berlin - no information
*Home address:* Konstanzer Str. 1,
Wilmersdorf
*Law firm address:* Kurfürstendamm 24, W 15
*Additional information:* Attorney at the KG
and notary; management board and owner of
a property management in Schöneberg. After
the National Socialist seizure of power in 1933
his license as a notary was revoked, he was
readmitted as an attorney until the general
occupational ban in 1938. Emigration to the
province of Belluno in Italy on 03/08/1939;
since ca. 1947 he lived in New York; in 1967
he was a member of the board of the American
Association of Former European Jurists.
*Sources:* TK 33; JMBl. 33, S. 220; *li; LAB,
Liste 15.10.33; MRRAK; BArch, R 3001
PAK; American Association of Former
European Jurists, LBI Arch. 6546; BG

**Flater, Alfred**
06/10/1882 Neustettin - transportation in 1942
*Home address:* Hallesches Ufer 58, SW 11,
Kreuzberg
*Law firm address:* Friedrichstr. 203, SW 68
*Additional information:* Attorney at the LG I-III,
AG Tempelhof and a notary. After the National
Socialist seizure of power in 1933 his license as
a notary was revoked, he was readmitted as an
attorney until the general occupational ban in
1938; he was granted a maintenance subsidy from
the Reich Bar Association. Date of declaration
of property: 12/22/1941, transportation on
01/19/1942 to Riga.
*Sources:* TK 33; JMBl. 33, S. 202; *li; LAB,
Liste 15.10.33; MRRAK; BArch, R 3001
PAK; BG; BdE; GB II

**Flato, Fritz Dr.**
01/04/1895 Berlin - 1945
New York
*Home address:*
Kommandantenstr. 63-64,
SW 19
*Law firm address:*
Kommandantenstr. 63-64,
SW 19
*Additional information:* Attorney since 1925,

admitted at the LG I-III and AG Tempelhof,
later also a notary, he was active in the
Scientific Humanitarian Committee (since
at least 1929), as board member at times,
until its dissolution in 1933; he advocated
for the abolishment of § 175 (which made
homosexual acts between men punishable).
After the National Socialist seizure of power
he was readmitted. He was a close friend
of Kurt Hiller since childhood, in 1933 he
endeavored to have him released from the
Oranienburg concentration camp; in 1934 he
was disbarred; at the end of 1935 he emigrated
to the USA. A warrant was issued against him
for tax code violations. His mother followed
him in 1937, the family estate was confiscated
in 1938. He called himself Fred after 1943 and
still lived in New York after 1945. According
to the memory of Kurt Hiller, he is said to
have committed suicide "living in the most
bitter misery."
*Sources:* TK 33; *li; BG; Wolf, BFS; Hiller,
Kurt: Leben gegen die Zeit; Reinbek 1969 u.
1973, S. 285 (Bd.1) u. 105 (Bd.2); Ausk. E.
Proskauer; Ausk. Jens Dobler

**Fleischmann, Hugo Dr.**
01/09/1876 Fürth - no information
*Home address:* Keithstr. 20, W 62
*Law firm address:* Wilhelmstr. 89 a, W 8
*Additional information:* Attorney at the LG
I-III. After the National Socialist seizure of
power he was made subject to an occupational
ban in early 1933. Emigration to Veracruz,
Mexico, on 05/28/1939.
*Sources:* Adr.B. 32; TK 33; Liste d.
nichtzugel. RA, 25.4.33; JMBl. 7.7.33, S. 209;
BArch, R 3001 PAK; BG

**Fliess, Julius Dr.**
10/18/1876 Bernau -
03/02/1955 Berlin
*Home address:* Bleibtreustr.
27, Charlottenburg
*Law firm address:*
Potsdamer Str. 103, W 35
*Additional information:*
He fought during the First World War and
was seriously wounded; he was awarded
various medals for his combat mission. He
was an attorney at the KG and a notary, in
1932 he was also a board member of the
RAK. After the National Socialist seizure of
power he was re-admitted upon request; in

1935 his license as a notary was revoked; in 1938 he was disbarred; up to 1942 he was still active as a "consultant." On 09/30/1942 he was able to flee with his family to Basel, Switzerland (within the framework of "Unternehmen Sieben," which was initiated by Von Canaris and Von Dohnanyi). In 1947 he returned from Switzerland to Berlin. In 1948 he was readmitted as an attorney, later also as notary; he died in 1955 in Berlin. *Sources:* TK 33; *li; LAB, Liste 15.10.33; DJ 36, S. 314; Liste 36; MRRAK; Liste d. Kons., 15.4.39; BG; LAB, RAK PA; Ausk. Dorothee Fliess; Meyer, Winfried: Unternehmen Sieben – Eine Rettungsaktion

### Foerder, Herbert Dr.

03/25/1901 Berlin - 06/10/1970 Tel Aviv
*Home address:* no information
*Law firm address:* Charlottenstr. 53, W 8
*Additional information:* Attorney at the LG I-III and AG Berlin-Mitte. After the National Socialist seizure of power he was made subject to an occupational ban in early 1933. In 1933 he emigrated to Palestine; there he became a co-founder and until 1957 director of the Middle Classes Housing Association; henceforth he called himself Yeshayahu; 1949-57 member of the Knesset, since 1957 chairman of the board of the Leumi Bank (National Bank).
*Sources:* Br.B. 32; TK 33; Liste d. nichtzugel. RA, 25.4.33; JMBl. 33, S. 253; BArch, R 3001 PAK; BG; Göpp., S.279

### Fontheim, Georg Martin Dr.

08/30/1881 Berlin - transportation 1943
*Home address:* Kaiserdamm 67, C 9 (today: Heerstr. 15/15 a)
*Law firm address:* Joachimsthaler Str. 3, Charlottenburg 2
*Additional information:* Attorney at the LG I-III and notary, brother of Kurt, his clients included members of the Hohenzollern family. After the National Socialist seizure of power his license as a notary was revoked in 1933; he worked as an attorney until his occupational ban in 1938. Afterwards several clients continued to seek advice; billing was done via an "Aryan" attorney, who was a friend of his, which was a risk for him. In February 1941,

the family of four was ordered to vacate their apartment within eight days to make it available to "German citizens." The family then moved in with relatives. He was transported to Auschwitz on January 12, 1943, together with his wife Charlotte and his daughter Eva. His son Ernst was the only one of the family who survived. *Sources:* TK 33; JMBl. 33, S. 202; *li; LAB, Liste 15.10.33; MRRAK; BArch, R 3001 PAK; BG; GB II; Ausk. des Sohnes, 6. u. 15.6.2000

### Fontheim, Kurt Dr.

11/10/1882 Berlin - 1976 Baden-Baden
*Home address:* Uhlandstr. 25, W 50
*Law firm address:* Kurfürstendamm 13, W 50
*Additional information:* Attorney at the KG, brother of Georg Martin. After the National Socialist seizure of power he was readmitted; he was disbarred in October 1936. 1936 emigration first to Switzerland, from there to the unoccupied zone in the south of France in 1941, then further to Portugal and finally to the USA. In the 1960s he returned to Europe; however, he did not settle anywhere. It was only in his old age that he lived permanently in Baden-Baden, where he died at the age of 93. *Sources:* TK 33; *li; LAB, Liste 15.10.33; DJ 36, S. 276; BArch, R 3001 PAK; BG; Ausk. des Neffen, 6. u. 15.6.2000

### Fraenkel, Alfred Dr.

09/05/1882 Laurahütte - no information
*Home address:* Prager Str. 7, W 50
*Law firm address:* Marburger Str. 11, W 50
*Additional information:* He was a dissident. Attorney at the LG I-III and notary. After the National Socialist seizure of power in 1933 his license as a notary was revoked; he was admitted as an attorney until 07/14/1938; emigration to Lucerne, Switzerland. *Sources:* TK 33; JMBl. 33, S. 202; *li; LAB, Liste 15.10.33; BArch, R 3001 PAK; BG

### Fraenkel, Ernst Dr.

12/26/1898 Cologne - 03/28/1975 Berlin
*Home address:* Eschwegering 23, Tempelhof
*Law firm address:* Alte Jakobstr. 155, SW 68
*Additional information:* After an accelerated school leaving examination, he fought in the First World War after he had barely turned 18, he was seriously injured; he studied law at Frankfurt a. M. and Heidelberg; he was a dissident, member of the SPD; later he became

advisor to the Metal Workers' Union, he was in a law partnership with Franz L. Neumann, the law firm was located at the Metal Workers' building. After the National Socialist seizure of power he was made subject to an occupational ban in April 1933, which however, was repealed, since he had been recognized as a "frontline fighter," until the general occupational ban in 1938 he was admitted at the KG. He defended numerous political prisoners from 1933-38, he also worked in the political underground, which meant an additional threat to him. His wife Hannah, nee Pickel (born on 03/13/1904), was regarded as "Aryan."

He was the author of the only critical study on National Socialism that originated in Germany itself, later published under the title "Der Doppelstaat" ("The Dual State"). 1938 emigration to the USA via Great Britain; he received one of the rare scholarships of the American Committee for the Guidance of Professional Personnel; he studied law and completed his studies in 1941. After a short period of working as a lawyer he was active as a managing director in various refugee organizations; he took over a research project until, after he had acquired American citizenship, he was able to take a position at a state institution [Foreign Economic Administration (FEA)]. After the end of World War II, he remained in the U.S. government service and went to South Korea as a legal adviser to help build democracy. When the war broke out, the couple was evacuated. Under pressure from Otto Suhr, he returned to Berlin in 1951, worked at the Deutsche Hochschule für Politik (German Academy for Politics), at the same time at the Free University of Berlin, he taught political science there, he took part in the merger of the two institutions; he became a full professor at the Otto Suhr Institute until his retirement in 1967. He was awarded the Große Bundesverdienstkreuz (Great Federal Cross of Merit) and the Ernst Reuter plaque. He died in 1975 in Berlin.
*Publications:* among others Gesammelte Schriften, Bd. 1-4 [Collected writings, vols. 1-4], 1999-2004
*Sources:* TK 33; *li; Liste d. nichtzugel. RA, 25.4.33; MRRAK; BArch, R 3001 PAK, PA; NY Publ. Lib.; FU-Archiv; BG; Göpp. S. 335/36; OSI, Fraenkel-Projekt; SLW noch unveröffentlichte Biografie Ernst Fraenkels

[still unpublished biography of Ernst Fraenkel]

### Fraenkel, Ernst
09/26/1902 Berlin - no information
*Home address:* Niebuhrstr. 71, Charlottenburg
*Law firm address:* Lützowufer 30, W 62
*Additional information:* Attorney since 1928, last at the KG. After the National Socialist seizure of power he was made subject to an occupational ban on 07/13/1933. He emigrated on 06/09/1933 to France, lived in Paris.
*Publications:* Dein Recht als Ausländer [Your right as a foreigner], Paris 1936
*Sources:* TK 33; JMBl. 33, S. 266; Liste d. nichtzugel. RA, 25.4.33 (Nachtragsliste); BArch, R 3001 PAK, PA; BG

### Fraenkel, Herbert Dr.
05/27/1872 - 01/21/1939
*Home address:* Wielandstr. 38, Charlottenburg
*Law firm address:* Lützowufer 30, W 62
*Additional information:* Attorney at the LG I-III, AG Berlin-Mitte and notary. After the National Socialist seizure of power his license as a notary was revoked in 1933, he was readmitted as an attorney, he practiced until the general occupational ban in 1938; he committed suicide in 1939 at the age of 76; he was buried at Weißensee.
*Sources:* TK 33; JMBl. 33, S. 202; *li; LAB, Liste 15.10.33; Liste 36; MRRAK; BArch, R 3001 PAK; BG; g

### Fraenkel, Max Dr.
10/01/1887 Frankfurt a. M. - no information
*Home address:* no information
*Law firm address:* no information.
*Additional information:* After the National Socialist seizure of power he was made subject to an occupational ban on 07/13/1933; emigration 1933 to Paris, France. A warrant was issued against him for tax code violations. BArch, R 3001 PAK, PA; Wolf, BFS

### Fraenkel, Siegfried Dr.
12/16/1887 - no information
*Home address:* no information
*Law firm address:* Bülowstr. 13, W 57
*Additional information:* Attorney at the LG I-III. After the National Socialist seizure of power he was made subject to an occupational ban on 05/20/1933.

*Sources:* TK 33; Liste d. nichtzugel. RA, 25.4.33; JMBl. 33, S. 195; BArch, R 3001 PAK, PA

**Fraenkel, Walter Dr.**
No information
*Home address:* no information
*Law firm address:* Behrenstr. 50, W 8
*Additional information:* Attorney at the LG I-III, at the AG Berlin-Mitte and notary. After the National Socialist seizure of power his license as a notary was revoked in 1933; he was still active as an attorney until 08/19/1936.
*Sources:* Br.B. 32; TK 33; JMBl. 33, S. 202; *li; Liste 36; LAB, Liste 15.10.33; BArch, R 3001 PAK

**Fränkel, Eduard Dr.**
05/06/1874 Berlin - no information
*Home address:* Kaiserdamm 6, Charlottenburg
*Law firm address:* Französische Str. 17, W 8
*Additional information:* Attorney at the LG I-III, at the AG Berlin-Mitte and notary. After the National Socialist seizure of power, he was readmitted in 1933; his license as a notary was revoked in 1935; he worked as an attorney until the general occupational ban in 1938. Emigration to Rio de Janeiro, Brazil, on 10/29/1940.
*Sources:* TK 33; *li; LAB, Liste 15.10.33; DJ 36, S. 314; MRRAK; BArch, R 3001 PAK; BG

**Fränkel, Heinz Julian Dr.**
08/18/1901 - no information
*Home address:* no information
*Law firm address:* Behrenstr. 14, W 8
*Additional information:* After the National Socialist seizure of power he was made subject to an occupational ban in early 1933. Emigration to New York, USA via Paris; after 1945 he returned to Germany.
*Sources:* Adr.B. 32; TK 33; Liste der nicht-zugel. RA, 25.4.1933; BArch, R 3001 PAK; Ausk. E. Proskauer

**Fränkel, Heinz Dr.**
06/18/1900 Berlin - no information
*Home address:* no information
*Law firm address:* Jägerstr. 10
Admitted as an attorney since 1927. After the National Socialist seizure of power he was made subject to an occupational ban on 05/29/1933.
*Sources:* TK 33; BArch, R 3001 PAK, PA

**Fränkel, Max Dr.**
11/19/1888 Ostrowo - no information
*Home address:* Regensburger Str. 27, W 50
*Law firm address:* Hohenzollernstr. 2, W 10
*Additional information:* After the National Socialist seizure of power he was made subject to an occupational ban on 05/23/1933. Emigration to New York, USA.
*Sources:* Liste d. nichtzugel. RA, 25.4.33; JMBl. 33, S. 266; BArch, R 3001 PAK, PA; BG

**Fränkel, Rudolf Dr.**
02/20/1890 Berlin - before 1945
*Home address:* no information
*Law firm address:* Friedrich-Karl-Ufer 2/4, NW 40
*Additional information:* He was a Protestant; attorney at the LG I-III. After the National Socialist seizure of power he was made subject to an occupational ban on 05/29/1933. His wife was regarded as "Aryan." He was purported to have died before 1945 in a prison.
*Sources:* Adr.B. 32; TK 33; Liste d. nicht-zugel. RA, 25.4.33; JMBl. 33, S. 209; BArch, R 3001 PAK, PA; BG

**Fränkel, Siegfried Dr.**
08/28/1888 Oppeln - December 1975 New York
*Home address:* Aschaffenburger Str. 18, Schöneberg
*Law firm address:* Schönhauser Allee 6
*Additional information:* Attorney at the LG I-III, AG Berlin-Mitte and notary. After the National Socialist seizure of power he was made subject to an occupational ban on 05/26/1933. He had intensively tried to avert the occupational ban, however, without success. Presumably he emigrated (in the files "from 06/15/1939"); died in 1975 in New York at the age of 87.
Br.B. 32; TK 33; Liste d. nichtzugel. RA, 25.4.33; JMBl. 33, S. 253; BArch, R 3001 PAK, PA; BG; SSDI

**Fraenkl, Viktor, Judicial Councillor**
No information
*Home address:* No information
*Law firm address:* Habsburger Str. 2, W 30
*Additional information:* Attorney at the LG I-III; after the National Socialist seizure of power he was disbarred in 1933, on the file card of the RMJ it is noted: "inactive 1933."
*Sources:* JMBl. 33, 19.5.33; BArch, R 3001 PAK

**Fragstein und Niemsdorff, Edgar von**
03/06/1883 - no information
*Home address:* no information
*Law firm address:* Augsburger Str. 35
*Additional information:* Attorney at the
LG I-III, AG Charlottenburg and notary; he
was a Catholic. After the National Socialist
seizure of power his license as a notary was
revoked in 1933; he was regarded as "mixed
race first degree"; he represented numerous
clients who were equally affected; after 1938
he was allowed to continue practicing; he
survived the National Socialist regime and
was readmitted as an attorney after 1945.
*Sources:* Adr.B. 32; TK 33; JMBl. 33, S.
220; LAB, Liste Mschlg. 36; Liste der zugel.
Anwälte nach 45

**Franck, Hugo Dr.**
06/30/1872 Einbeck - 1967 Vancouver
*Home address:* Fasanenstr. 22, W 15
*Law firm address:* Fasanenstr. 22, W 15
*Additional information:* He was a soldier
during the First World War; attorney at
LG I-III and AG Berlin-Mitte; his home
and law firm were in a middle-class house,
near the Kurfürstendamm and close to the
Fasanenstraße Synagogue. After the National
Socialist seizure of power he was re-admitted
as an attorney, because he had been a
"frontline fighter." He still practiced in 1936.
Emigration to San Francisco, 1938; later to
Vancouver in British Columbia, Canada,
where he died in 1967.
*Sources:* *li; LAB, Liste 15.10.33; BArch, R
3001 PAK; Liste 36; BLHA, OFP-Akten; BG;
SSDI; AoR, Kanada

**Frank, Karl (Carl) Dr.**
05/19/1874 - 11/01/1935
*Home address:* no information
*Law firm address:* Taubenstr. 23 a, W 8
*Additional information:* Attorney at the LG
I-III, AG Berlin-Mitte and notary. After the
National Socialist seizure of power his license
as a notary was revoked in 1933; he was
readmitted as an attorney; he died in 1935 at
the age of 61, he was buried at Weißensee.
*Sources:* Br.B.32; TK 33; JMBl. 33, S. 202;
*li; LAB, Liste 15.10.33; BG

**Frank, William Dr.**
01/01/1903 Berlin - April 1977
*Home address:* no information

*Law firm address:* Leipziger Str. 119, W 8
Attorney at the KG. After the National
Socialist seizure of power he was made
subject to an occupational ban in early 1933.
Emigration to the USA in 1936 via Cuba;
since 1937 he lived in the USA; he died in
1977, he last lived in New York.
*Sources:* TK 33; Liste d. nichtzugel. RA,
25.4.33; JMBl. 33, S. 209 (Willie); BArch, R
3001 PAK; BG; SSDI

**Frankenstein, Ernst Dr.**
05/31/1881 Dortmund - 10/28/1959 London
*Home address:* no information
*Law firm address:* Behrenstr. 23, W 8
*Additional information:* Attorney at the LG
I-III and notary, specialized in international
private law. After the National Socialist
seizure of power in 1933 his license as a
notary was revoked; he was disbarred in
1934; by then he had emigrated to France;
in 1936 he emigrated to Great Britain. A
warrant was issued against him for tax code
violations. In 1959 he died at the age of 78 in
London.
*Sources:* Br.B. 32; TK 33; JMBl. 33, S. 208;
*li; Philo-Lexikon, S. 604; NY Publ. Lib.
(Am. Com.) Weigert, Julius B.; Wolf, BFS

**Frankfurter, Gerhard Dr.**
03/17/1902 Berlin - no information
*Home address:* no information
*Law firm address:* Nikolsburger Platz 2
*Additional information:* Attorney at the LG
I-III, AG Berlin-Mitte and notary. After the
National Socialist seizure of power he was
made subject to an occupational ban in early
1933. He emigrated in 1933 to Great Britain.
*Sources:* Adr.B. 32; TK 33; Liste d.
nichtzugel. RA, 25.4.33; JMBl. 33, S. 209;
BArch, R 3001 PAK; BG

**Frankfurter, Hans**
09/21/1901 Berlin - no information
*Home address:* no information
*Law firm address:* Lützowufer 30, W 62
*Additional information:* Attorney at the LG
I-III. After the National Socialist seizure of
power he was made subject to an occupational
ban in early 1933; he was regarded as "mixed
race first degree," in 1943 he "was arrested
at work."
*Sources:* Liste d. nichtzugel. RA, 25.4.33;
JMBl. 33, S. 220; BArch, R 3001 PAK; BG

**Frankfurter, Richard Otto Dr.**
12/12/1873 Bielitz - 02/02/1953 Montevideo
*Home address:* Nassauische Str. 49,
Wilmersdorf
*Law firm address:* Nikolsburger Platz 2,
Wilmersdorf
*Additional information:* Attorney at the LG
I-III and notary; well-known film attorney, in
addition to being an author of the world stage.
After the National Socialist seizure of power
in 1933 his license as a notary was revoked, he
was re-admitted as an attorney, on 09/11/1934
he was disbarred. Emigration via Switzerland
to Montevideo, Uruguay, on 09/01/1934.
*Sources:* TK 33; JMBl. 33, S. 202; *li; LAB,
Liste 15.10.33; BArch, R 3001 PAK; BG;
Göpp., S. 280; Ausk. F. Flechtmann

**Franz, Günter Curt**
04/22/1898 Berlin-Charlottenburg -
04/20/1962 Berlin
*Home address:* no information
*Law firm address:* Speyerer Str. 15/16, W 30
*Additional information:* Since 1927 attorney at
the LG I-III. After the National Socialist seizure
of power he was readmitted. He was regarded
as "mixed race first degree," his wife Oda was
regarded as "non-Jewish." He was still listed
as an attorney in the business directory in
1942/43. He was forced to work for the Todt
Organization. In 1946 he was readmitted as
an attorney, after 1945 he lived in Schöneberg
again.
*Sources:* TK 33; *li; LAB, Liste 15.10.33,
Liste Mschlg. 36; Br.B.43; BArch, R 3001
PAK; BG; LAB, RAK, PA

**Fraustaedter, Hans**
06/16/1897 Berlin - no information
*Home address:* no information
*Law firm address:* Tauentzienstr. 12 a, W 50
*Additional information:* Attorney at the KG.
After the National Socialist seizure of power
he was made subject to an occupational ban
on 06/02/1933.
*Sources:* Br.B. 32; TK 33; Liste d. nichtzugel.
RA, 25.4.33; JMBl. 33, S. 203; BArch, R
3001 PAK, PA

**Frentzel, Gerhard Dr.**
03/15/1896 Berlin - no information
*Home address:* Nassauische Str. 57,
Wilmersdorf
*Law firm address:* Nassauische Str. 57,
Wilmersdorf

*Additional information:* Attorney at the
LG I-III; since 1925 he worked for the
Deutsche Industrie und Handelstag (The
Association of German Chambers of Industry
and Commerce); he voted for the DVP
during the last free elections according to
his own data. After the National Socialist
seizure of power he was readmitted as an
attorney; he was regarded as "mixed race
first degree;" member of the NSV and of the
NS-Reichskriegerbundes (Kyffhäuserbund)
[National Socialist Reich Warrior Society
(Kyffhäuser League)]; had to vacate his
workplace "within a few hours in November
1938;" he worked as an attorney and tax
consultant until at least 1942/43; he was
forced to work for the Todt Organization, but
was declared unfit for duty. He survived the
Nazi regime and lived in Wilmersdorf again
after 1945; in 1947 he was readmitted as an
attorney.
*Sources:* TK 33; *li; Liste 15.10.33; LAB,
Liste Mschlg. 36; BArch, R 3001 PAK; BG;
LAB, RAK PA

**Freudenheim, Martin Dr.**
11/23/1887 Berlin - no information
*Home address:* Kaiser-Wilhelm-Str. 43, Mitte
*Law firm address:* Steinplatz 1,
Charlottenburg
*Additional information:* Attorney at the LG
I-III, AG Berlin-Mitte and notary. After the
National Socialist seizure of power in 1933 he
was readmitted; at the end of 1935 his license
as a notary was revoked; he worked as an
attorney until the general occupational ban in
1938; he survived the Nazi regime and lived
in Friedrichshain after 1945.
*Sources:* TK 33; *li; LAB, Liste 15.10.33; DJ
36, S. 314; MRRAK; BArch, R 3001 PAK;
BG

**Freudenstein, Hugo**
10/18/1883 Alfeld - no information
*Home address:* Hessenallee 11,
Charlottenburg
*Law firm address:* Friedrichstr. 56/57
*Additional information:* Attorney at the
KG and notary. After the National Socialist
seizure of power he waas made subject to an
occupational ban in the summer of 1933. He
emigrated to Amsterdam, the Netherlands, on
03/24/1938.
*Sources:* Br.B. 32; TK 33; JMBl. 4.8.33, S.
253; BArch, R 3001 PAK; BG

**Freudenstein, Kurt Dr.**
01/02/1891 Berlin - no information
*Home address:* Geisbergstr. 33 bei Graetz,
Schöneberg
*Law firm address:* Französische Str. 52, W 8
*Additional information:* Attorney at the LG
I-III and notary. After the National Socialist
seizure of power he was made subject to an
occupational ban as an attorney and notary
on 05/29/1933; later he was an employee of
the RV.
*Sources:* Br.B. 32; TK 33; Liste d. nichtzugel.
RA, 25.4.33; JMBl. 33, S. 209; BArch, R
3001 PAK, PA; BG

**Freund, Georg Dr., Judicial Councillor**
11/02/1857 Breslau - 1938
*Home address:* Bayerische Str. 5, W 15
*Law firm address:* Kurfürstendamm 35, W 15
*Additional information:* Attorney at the LG
I-III and notary; he was a Protestant. After
the National Socialist seizure of power he was
readmitted; at the end of 1935 his license as a
notary was revoked; until 08/02/1938 he was
still working as an attorney, he died in 1938.
*Sources:* TK 33; *li; LAB, Liste 15.10.33; DJ
36, S. 314; Liste 36; BArch, R 3001 PAK; BG

**Freund, Hans**
12/16/1901 Kattowitz - no information
*Home address:* no information
*Law firm address:* Potsdamer Str. 125, W 9
*Additional information:* Attorney at the KG.
After the National Socialist seizure of power
he was made subject to an occupational ban
on 06/10/1933.
*Sources:* Br.B. 32; Liste d. nichtzugel. RA,
25.4.33; JMBl. 33, S. 209; BArch, R 3001
PAK, PA; BG

**Freund, Heinrich Dr.**
09/14/1885 Lodz - 01/03/1948 Palo Alto, USA
*Home address:* Neue Kantstr. 12,
Charlottenburg
*Law firm address:* Meinekestr. 7, W 15
*Additional information:* Fought in the First
World War; attorney at the LG I-III and
notary; he worked closely with Udo Rukser
and founded the journal "Ostrecht" with
him. The journal, later called "Zeitschrift für
Ostrecht," focused on the problems of political
reorganization. Particular attention was paid to
legal issues related to the Soviet Union. He had
a personal relationship to the subject through
his marriage. His wife Vera was a Russian who

had grown up in St. Petersburg. The publication
of the magazine was discontinued, after
the departure of the Jewish editor had been
demanded after 1933. He was baptized, his wife
was considered "Aryan" after the takeover of
the National Socialists. He was re-admitted as
an attorney and notary upon request, because
he had been recognized as a "frontline fighter."
At the end of 1935 his license as a notary was
revoked; after the general occupational ban in
1938 he worked as a "consultant." Emigration
in April 1939 to England; there he was interned
as an "alien enemy," at the beginning of 1941
he was transported to Australia, there he was
in a camp for four years. After his release he
worked as a salesman and a journalist; he was
ill and destitute. He was not able to be reunited
with his wife and his son, who had had to stay
in Great Britain, until 1946/1947. In 1947 he
received a contract for a research project at
Stanford University, California. He died two
months after his arrival in the USA. His sister
and mother were murdered by the regime.
*Sources:* Br.B. 32; TK 33; *li; LAB, Liste
15.10.33; DJ 36, S. 314; BArch, R 3001
PAK; MRRAK; Osteuropa-Recht [Eastern
European law], Special edition 1/1960, pp.
2-5 (Obituary Rukser); corrections Henry
Finlay (son) 03/05 and 09/16/1999

**Freund, Hermann Dr.**
01/06/1880 Landshut - 10/09/1933
*Home address:* Heinrichstr. 9 a, Zehlendorf
*Law firm address:* Berliner Str. 49/50,
Neukölln
*Additional information:* Attorney at the LG
I-III, at the AG Neukölln and notary. After
the National Socialist seizure of power he had
to dissolve his law firm in 1933; emigration to
France, there he died in October 1933 from
sepsis.
*Sources:* Br.B. 32; TK 33; Pr.J. 33, S. 443;
BArch, R 3001 PAK; BG

**Freund, Martin**
03/22/1886 Breslau - no information
*Home address:* no information
*Law firm address:* Alexanderstr. 5, C 25
*Additional information:* Attorney at the LG
I-III and notary. After the National Socialist
seizure of power in 1933 he was readmitted;
at the end of 1935 his license as a notary was
revoked; he practiced as an attorney until
the general occupational ban; presumably he
emigrated (memo: "as of 11/05/19").

*Sources:* TK 33; *li; DJ 36, S. 314; Liste 36; MRRAK; BArch, R 3001 PAK; BG

### Freund, Rudolf Dr.

07/19/1877 - no information
*Home address:* Miquelstr. 81, Dahlem
*Law firm address:* Jägerstr. 6, W 8
Attorney at the LG I and AG Mitte; after the National Socialist seizure of power in 1933 he was disbarred. Afterwards he worked as an auditor from his home address. Emigration to Cuba on 10/21/1941, later to the USA.
*Sources:* Jüd.Adr.B.; Adr.B. 33; Pr.J. 33, S. 391; BArch, R 3001 PAK; BG

### Freund, Wilhelm Dr.

07/27/1881 Potsdam - 12/20/1942
*Home address:* Elsässer Str. 11, Mitte
*Law firm address:* Behrenstr. 35, W 56
*Additional information:* Attorney at the LG I. After the National Socialist seizure of power he was readmitted as an attorney; he was most recently listed in the 1937 business directory. His wife was regarded as "non-Jewish." He died in 1942, he was buried at Weißensee.
*Sources:* TK 33; *li; LAB, Liste 15.10.33, Liste 36; Br.B. 37; BArch, R 3001 PAK; BG

### Freundlich, Ernst Dr.

12/27/1896 Posen (now known as Poznan) - no information
*Home address:* Berkaer Str. 30, Grunewald
*Law firm address:* Invalidenstr. 111, N 4
*Additional information:* Attorney at the LG I-III, AG Berlin-Mitte and notary. After the National Socialist seizure of power he was readmitted; his license as a notary was revoked in 1935; he practiced as an attorney until the general occupational ban in 1938, in a joint law partnership with Herbert (presumably his brother).
*Sources:* *li; LAB, Liste 15.10.33; DJ 36, S. 314; Liste 36; MRRAK; BArch, R 3001 PAK; BG

### Freundlich, Herbert Dr.

08/23/1893 Posen (now known as Poznan) - no information
*Home address:* Invalidenstr. 111, N 4
*Law firm address:* Invalidenstr. 111, N 4
*Additional information:* Attorney at the KG and notary. After the National Socialist seizure of power he was readmitted; his license as a notary was revoked at the end of 1935; he practiced as an attorney until the general occupational ban in 1938 in a joint law partnership with Ernst (presumably his brother), thereafter he was admitted as a "consultant."
*Sources:* *li; LAB, Liste 15.10.33, DJ 36, S. 314; Liste 36; MRRAK; BArch, R 3001 PAK; Liste der Kons.v.23.2.1939; BG

### Freundlich, Ludwig Dr.

09/19/1878 Neustettin - no information
*Home address:* Helmstedter Str. 26, Wilmersdorf
*Law firm address:* Krausenstr. 70, W 8
*Additional information:* Attorney at the LG I-III, AG Schöneberg and notary. After the National Socialist seizure of power his license as a notary was revoked in 1933; he still practiced as an attorney until 1937. Emigration to London, Great Britain.
*Sources:* TK 33; JMBl. 33, S. 208; *li; LAB, Liste 15.10.33, Liste 36; BArch, R 3001 PAK; BG

### Freundlich, Salo Dr.

10/07/1897 - no information
*Home address:* Trabener Str. 14, Grunewald
*Law firm address:* Linkstr. 29, W 9
*Additional information:* Attorney at the LG I-III and AG Charlottenburg. After the National Socialist seizure of power he was made subject to an occupational ban in early 1933. Emigration to London, Great Britain, in April/May 1939.
*Sources:* Adr.B. 32; TK 33; Liste d. nichtzugel. RA, 25.4.33; JMBl. 33, S. 234; LAB, Liste 15.10.33; BArch, R 3001 PAK; BG

### Frey, Erich Max Dr. jur. Dr. phil.

10/16/1882 Breslau - 03/30/1964 Santiago de Chile
*Home address:* Bellevuestr. 21/22, W 9
*Law firm address:* Bellevuestr. 5, W 9
*Additional information:* Attorney since 1911. He was one of Berlin's best known defense attorneys. He was involved in the trial against the members of the "Ringverein Immertreu," against the student Krantz in the eye-catching "Steglitzer student murder trial," as well as in the trial of the killing of Horst Wessels he was the defense attorney. Because of his prominence, he was severely

endangered after the National Socialist seizure of power. The RAK also named him as one of the attorneys who had participated in Communist activities. Emigration in 1933 via Paris to South America, where he died in 1964 in Santiago de Chile.
*Publications:* Ich beantrage Freispruch (Memoiren) [I request acquittal (memoirs)], 1959
*Sources:* Adr.B. 32; BArch, R 3001 PAK; Walk, S. 102; Krach, S.433; Göpp., S. 280; AoR, Ausst.

**Freyhan, Max Dr.**
07/28/1881 Breslau - no information
*Home address:* Altonaer Str. 25, NW 87
*Law firm address:* Altonaer Str. 25, NW 87
*Additional information:* Attorney at the LG I-III and notary. After the National Socialist seizure of power in 1933 his license as a notary was revoked; he worked as an attorney until the general occupational ban in 1938; he emigrated to London, Great Britain.
*Sources:* TK 33; JMBl. 33, S. 220; *li; LAB, Liste 15.10.33; MRRAK; BArch, R 3001 PAK; BG

**Freymann, Kurt Dr.**
05/09/1887 Danzig - no information
*Home address:* Rothenburgstr. 11, Steglitz
*Law firm address:* Dorotheenstr. 80
*Additional information:* Attorney at the LG I-III and notary. After the National Socialist seizure of power he was disbarred on 09/16/1933 in the course of the merging of the district courts. He emigrated in 1933 to Italy. A warrant was issued against him for tax code violations.
*Sources:* Br.B. 32; TK 33; Pr.J. 33, S. 443; BArch, R 3001 PAK, PA; Wolf, BFS

**Friedeberg, Hans Dr.**
01/18/1890-01/18/1890 Posen (now known as Poznan) - 05/11/1953
*Home address:* Grunewaldstr. 44, Schöneberg
*Law firm address:* Eisenacher Str. 83, W 30
*Additional information:* Attorney since 1921, most recently at the LG I-III and AG Schöneberg, and notary; up to 1933 he had an average income of between RM 18,000 and RM 22,000. After the National Socialist

seizure of power he was made subject to an occupational ban in April 1933, then he was readmitted; at the end of 1935 his license as a notary was revoked; he worked as an attorney until the general occupational ban in 1938, thereafter he was admitted as a "consultant." Up to 1939 his income lowered by RM 2,100; up to 1944 it rose again to RM 12,000. His wife was regarded as "non-Jewish." He had been arrested during the "November action" in 1938 and imprisoned in Sachsenhausen. He survived the National Socialist regime and was readmitted in 1948 as an attorney and as a notary. Later he lived on Konstanzer Str. 3.
*Sources:* TK 33; Liste d. nichtzugel. RA, 25.4.33; *li; LAB, Liste 15.10.33; DJ 36, S. 314; MRRAK; BG; LAB, RAK, PA

**Friedeberg, Max Dr.**
04/23/1875 Magdeburg - no information
*Home address:* Potsdamer Str. 18, Lichterfelde
*Law firm address:* Ehrenbergstr. 11/14, O 17
*Additional information:* Attorney at the LG I and notary. After the National Socialist seizure of power in 1933 his license as a notary was revoked; on 11/21/1935 he was "disbarred upon request." He emigrated via the Netherlands to New York, USA on 12/23/1938.
*Sources:* TK 33; JMBl. 33, S. 220; *li; LAB, Liste 15.10.33; BG

**Friedenthal, Felix Dr.**
03/25/1874 Breslau - no information
*Home address:* Birkbuschstr. 38, Steglitz
*Law firm address:* Großgörschenstr. 40, W 57
*Additional information:* Attorney at the KG and notary. After the National Socialist seizure of power in 1933 his license as a notary was revoked; he was readmitted as attorney until the general occupational ban in 1938, he emigrated to Great Britain in 1939.
*Sources:* TK 33; JMBl. 33, S. 208; *li; LAB, Liste 15.10.33; MRRAK; BArch, R 3001 PAK; BG

**Friedlaender, Bruno Dr., Judicial Councillor**
10/04/1889 Berlin - 03/19/1942
*Home address:* Gleimstr. 16, Prenzlauer Berg
*Law firm address:* Potsdamer Str. 22 b, W 9
*Additional information:* Attorney at the LG I-III and notary. After the National Socialist seizure of power in 1933 his license as a

notary was revoked; he worked as an attorney until the general occupational ban in 1938. He was Protestant, his wife was regarded as "non-Jewish." He committed suicide in March 1942 at the age of 52.
*Sources:* TK 33; JMBl. 33, S. 208; *li; Liste 15.10.33; Liste 36; MRRAK; BArch, R 3001 PAK; BG

**Friedlaender, Eugen Dr.**
09/15/1878 Berlin - 06/16/1952 New York
*Home address:* Beymestr. 1, Grunewald
*Law firm address:* Margaretenstr. 8
*Additional information:* Attorney at the LG I-III and notary; soldier during the First World War. He specialized in commercial law, he was nevertheless considered one of the representatives of the civil action incidental to criminal proceedings in the Helfferich trial. Helfferich had accused Finance Minister Mathias Erzberger of various offenses and spread propaganda against him in one of his publications. In this trial Erzberger wanted to act against the power of the press. Helfferich was defended among others by Max Alsberg; he was sentenced, but received a comparatively mild sentence. The agitation against Erzberger, which had always been antisemitic, had an effect: on the way out of the court Erzberger was attacked by a young man with a revolver. His defender Eugen walked in and tried to snatch the gun from the man, but he could still fire two shots, Erzberger was injured, but not fatally thanks to the support of his lawyer. One year later, Erzberger was the victim of another assassination attempt of the political right.
He went abroad in March/April 1933 at the beginning of the exclusionary measures and did not return to Germany. Nevertheless, he filed a request to be readmitted, which was granted because he was recognized as a "frontline fighter." His two children traveled independently to the Netherlands to Italy, because they had heard that the borders were to be closed. From there the family went to Switzerland. 1934 he is noted as "inactive" in the documents on his legal activity. In 1937 he and his wife followed his son to the USA, where he lived in New York until his death in 1952.

*Sources:* Br.B. 32; TK 33; BArch, R 3001 PAK; LAB, B Rep. 025-02, Nr. 1133/55, Rep. 58, Akte 69, Bd. 1-16, Film 334-336; BLHA, OFP-Akten; Ausk. Tom Freudenheim, Ausk. des Sohnes H. Friedlaender

**Friedlaender, Ewald Kurt Dr.**
01/24/1880 Berlin - October 1944 Auschwitz
*Home address:* Bleibtreustr. 15-16, Charlottenburg
*Law firm address:* Wilhelmstr. 44, W 8
*Additional information:* Attorney at the LG I-III and notary. After the National Socialist seizure of power in 1933 his license as a notary was revoked; he worked as an attorney until the general occupational ban in 1938. He emigrated to the Netherlands; he was arrested there and transported on 02/26/1944 from Westerbork to Theresienstadt; on 10/09/1944 he was transported to Auschwitz and was murdered there.
*Sources:* TK 33; JMBl. 33, S. 208; *li; Liste 15.10.33; MRRAK; BArch, R 3001 PAK; BG; GB II

**Friedlaender, James Dr.**
02/25/1877 Berlin - 07/23/1943 Sobibor
*Home address:* no information
*Law firm address:* Tile-Wardenberg-Str. 13, NW 87
*Additional information:* Attorney at the LG I-III and notary. After the National Socialist seizure of power in 1933 his license as a notary was revoked; he worked as an attorney until the general occupational ban in 1938. On 07/20/1943 he was transported from Westerbork to Sobibor and he was murdered there after his arrival.
*Sources:* Br.B. 32; TK 33; JMBl. 33, S. 208; *li; Liste 15.10.33; MRRAK; BArch, R 3001 PAK; Naatz-Album; GB II

**Friedlaender, Karl Dr.**
04/09/1882 Pleß - no information
*Home address:* no information
*Law firm address:* Händelstr. 3
*Additional information:* Attorney at the LG I-III and notary. After the National Socialist seizure of power in 1933 his license as a notary was revoked, he was also temporarily made subject to a ban as an attorney, upon

request he was readmitted, he still worked as
an attorney up to 09/20/1936.
*Sources:* TK 33; JMBl. 33, S. 208; *li; LAB,
Liste 15.10.33; BArch, R 3001 PAK

**Friedlaender, Kurt Dr.**
08/17/1894 Berlin - no information
*Home address:* Mommsenstr. 70,
Charlottenburg
*Law firm address:* Jägerstr. 8, W 8
*Additional information:* Admitted as an
attorney at the LG Berlin and AG Schöneberg;
after the National Socialist seizure of
power he was disbarred. He emigrated on
08/27/1939 to London, Great Britain.
*Sources:* Adr.B. 33; Pr.J. 33, S. 502; BArch, R
3001 PAK; BG

**Friedlaender, Leo, Judicial Councillor**
No information - 1934
*Home address:* no information
*Law firm address:* Meraner Platz 2,
Schöneberg
*Additional information:* Attorney at the LG
I-III and notary. After the National Socialist
seizure of power he was readmitted.
*Sources:* TK 33 (Leopold); *li; BArch, R 3001
PAK

**Friedländer, Eduard Dr.**
02/16/1894 Berlin - no information
*Home address:* Köpenicker Str. 95, SO 16
*Law firm address:* Markgrafenstr. 78
*Additional information:* Attorney at the
KG and notary. After the National Socialist
seizure of power he was made subject to a
ban on representation in early 1933, first he
was disbarred, then he was readmitted; at
the end of 1935 his license as a notary was
revoked; he worked as an attorney until
1937; he emigrated to Sao Paulo, Brazil, on
02/15/1937.
*Sources:* Adr.B. 32; Liste d. nichtzugel. RA,
25.4.33; JMBl. 33, S. 203; DJ 36, S. 314; Liste
36; BArch, R 3001 PAK; BG

**Friedländer, Ernst**
06/02/1888 Potsdam - 07/05/1944 Berlin
*Home address:* Mehlitzstr. 3, Wilmersdorf
*Law firm address:* Hohenzollerndamm 198,
Wilmersdorf
*Additional information:* Attorney at the LG
I-III, AG Berlin-Mitte and notary. After the
National Socialist seizure of power he was

readmitted in 1933; at the end of 1935 his
license as a notary was revoked; he worked
as an attorney until the general occupational
ban in 1938. His wife Gerda was regarded as
non-Jewish. He died in 1944 at the age of 56
and was buried at Weißensee.
*Sources:* TK 33; *li; Liste 15.10.33; DJ 36, S.
314; MRRAK; BArch, R 3001 PAK; BG

**Friedländer, Hans**
12.09.1901 Berlin - no information
*Home address:* no information
*Law firm address:* Kaiser-Wilhelm-Str. 3, C 2
*Additional information:* Attorney at the LG
I-III and AG Berlin-Mitte. After the National
Socialist seizure of power he was made subject
to an occupational ban on 07/13/1933.
*Sources:* Br.B. 32; TK 33; Liste d. nichtzugel.
RA, 25.4.33; JMBl. 21.8.33, S. 266; BArch,
R 3001 PAK

**Friedländer, Heinrich Dr.**
07/13/1885 Brieg - 10/27/1959 Frankfurt a. M.
*Home address:* no information
*Law firm address:* Herwarthstr. 4, NW 40
*Additional information:* Attorney at the LG
I-III and notary; he specialized in trade and
anti-trust law. After the National Socialist
seizure of power he was re-admitted; at
the end of 1935 his license as a notary was
revoked; he worked as an attorney until
the general occupational ban in 1938.
He emigrated in November 1938 to the
USA; lectureship in Havana, Cuba, later
he returned to the USA. He returned to
Germany, from 1950 he was an attorney in
Frankfurt/M; he died there in 1959.
*Sources:* TK 33; *li; DJ 36, S. 314; Liste 36;
Liste 15.10.33; BArch, R 3001 PAK; Philo-
Lexikon, S. 604; MRRAK; Göpp. S. 336

**Friedmann, Gustav**
12/24/1897 Hamburg - 03/31/1936
*Home address:* no information
*Law firm address:* Kleiststr. 35, W 62
*Additional information:* Attorney since
1929, admitted to the LG I-III and AG Berlin-
Mitte. After the National Socialist seizure of
power he was made subject to an occupational
ban on 06/08/1933; he died in March 1936;
he was buried at Weißensee.
*Sources:* Br.B. 32; TK 33; Liste d. nichtzugel.
RA, 25.4.33; JMBl. 33, S. 220; Liste
15.10.33; BArch, R 3001 PAK, PA; BG

**Friedmann, Hans Dr.**
03/12/1882 Glogau - no information
*Home address:* Kurfürstendamm 59-60,
Charlottenburg
*Law firm address:* Behrenstr. 63, W 8
*Additional information:* Attorney at the LG
I-III. After the National Socialist seizure of
power he was readmitted. He emigrated to
Rio de Janeiro, Brazil, on 07/24/1937.
*Sources:* TK 33; *li; Liste 15.10.33; BArch, R
3001 PAK; BG

**Friedmann-Friters, Alfred Dr.**
04/13/1880 Berlin - no information
*Home address:* Burggrafenstraße
*Law firm address:* Taubenstr. 8/9, W 8
*Additional information:* Attorney at the
KG and notary. After the National Socialist
seizure of power his license as a notary was
revoked; he was disbarred in 1936; already in
1934 he emigrated to Switzerland. A warrant
was issued against him for tax code violations.
*Sources:* TK 33; JMBl. 33, S. 253; *li; Liste
15.10.33; BArch, R 3001 PAK; BG; Wolf, BFS

**Frost, Ismar Dr.**
12/09/1889 Oppeln - no information
*Home address:* Chausseestr. 130, N 4
*Law firm address:* Chausseestr. 130, N 4
*Additional information:* Attorney at the LG
I-III, AG Charlottenburg and notary. After
the National Socialist seizure of power he was
made subject to an occupational ban in early
1933; at the end of 1935 his license as a notary
was revoked; in 1936 he was still working as
a lawyer. He emigrated via Czechoslovakia to
Zurich, Switzerland.
*Sources:* Br.B. 32; TK 33; Liste d. nichtzugel.
RA, 25.4.33; *li; Liste 15.10.33; DJ 36, S.
314; Liste 36; BArch, R 3001 PAK; BG

**Fuchs, Franz Eugen Dr.**
02/11/1899 Berlin - transportation 1942
*Home address:* Kurfürstenstr. 115, W 6
*Law firm address:* Potsdamer Str. 38
*Additional information:* Attorney at the LG
I-III and notary; he was a board member of
the RAK until at least 1932; member of the
executive board of the CV. After the National
Socialist seizure of power he was made
subject to an occupational ban in April 1933;
he once again had right of representation at
trials as from the end of April; later he was
readmitted; at the end of 1935 his license

as a notary was revoked; he worked as an
attorney until the general occupational ban in
1938, thereafter he worked as a "consultant";
as from 1939 in the Reichsvereinigung der
Juden in Deutschland (Reich's Federation of
the Jews in Germany). He was imprisoned
at the Alexanderplatz police prision since
approximately 06/12/1942; transported from
06/24/1942 to 06/26/1942 to Minsk.
*Sources:* Br.B. 32; TK 1933; Nachtragsliste
25.4.33; DJ 36, S, 314; Liste der Kons.;
MRRAK; BG; GB II; Göpp., S. 244

**Fuchs, Herbert Dr.**
05/26/1886 Tarnowitz - transportation 1943
*Home address:* Meinekestr. 4, W 15
*Law firm address:* Meinekestr. 4, W 15
*Additional information:* Attorney at the
LG I-III, AG Berlin-Mitte and notary,
he was a Protestant. After the National
Socialist seizure of power he was made
subject to an occupational ban in April
1933, his license as a notary was revoked;
he was readmitted as an attorney until the
general occupational ban in 1938, then until
the beginning of June 1942 as a legal aid
worker and later with the dissolution of law
firms of "consultants," in accordance with
the declaration of property of 06/22/1942
"officially approved Jewish aid worker in the
consultant practice H. Friedeberg;" at the
same time he was a "collector" of outstanding
claims of transported colleagues in favor of
the Reich Bar Association. Date of declaration
of property: 06/22/1943; collection point
Große Hamburger Str. 26; transportation on
06/20/1943 to Theresienstadt; from there he
was transported on 10/09/1944 to Auschwitz.
*Sources:* TK 33; Liste d. nichtzugel. RA,
25.4.33; JMBl. 33, S. 234; *li; Liste 15.10.33;
Liste 36; MRRAK; BArch, R 3001 PAK; BG;
ThG; GB II

**Fuchs, Martin Dr.**
04/15/1889 - no information
*Home address:* no information
*Law firm address:* Potsdamer Str. 117, W 35
*Additional information:* Attorney at the KG
and notary. After the National Socialist seizure
of power he was readmitted; at the end of 1935
his license as a notary was revoked; he was
disbarred as an attorney on 09/20/1937.
*Sources:* TK 33; *li; DJ 36, S. 314; BArch, R
3001 PAK

**Fürth, Hugo Dr.**
02/27/1888 Glogau - 03/18/1956 Sydney
*Home address:* Fredericiastr. 28,
Charlottenburg
*Law firm address:* Friedrichstr. 66 III, W 8
*Additional information:* Attorney at the
LG I-III, AG Berlin-Mitte and notary. After
the National Socialist seizure of power in
1933 his license as a notary was revoked; he
was listed as an attorney until the general
occupational ban in 1938; in 1937 he
emigrated to Sydney, Australia; there he ran a
paper and cardboard factory.
*Sources:* TK 33; JMBl. 33, S. 208; *li; Liste
36; MRRAK; BArch, R 3001 PAK; BG; Ausk.
Henry Finlay

**Fürth, Walter Dr.**
08/08/1894 Wurzing - No information
*Home address:* Koenigsallee 65, Grunewald
*Law firm address:* Potsdamer Str. 121, W 35
*Additional information:* Soldier during First
World War; he was a Catholic; attorney at
the LG I-III and AG Tempelhof. After the
National Socialist seizure of power he was
readmitted; he was regarded as "mixed race."
He was active as an attorney until the general
occupational ban in 1938. He emigrated to
London, Great Britain, 1939; he was in the
service of the British military government
after 1945.
*Sources:* TK 33; *li; BG; Liste 36; Liste
Mschlg. 36; MRRAK; BArch, R 3001 PAK

**Fuß, Max**
03/31/1879 Schrimm - transportation 1943
*Home address:* Uhlandstr. 39, W15
*Law firm address:* Uhlandstr. 39, W 15
*Additional information:* Attorney at the LG
I-III and notary. After the National Socialist
seizure of power in 1933 his license as a
notary was revoked; he worked as an attorney
until the general occupational ban in 1938.
Transportation on 03/12/1943 to Auschwitz.
*Sources:* JMBl. 33, S. 208; *li; MRRAK;
BArch, R 3001 PAK; BG; GB II

**Futter, Matthias Dr.**
12/20/1891 Dubrauke - September 1977
*Home address:* Helfferichstr. 44-46, Dahlem
*Law firm address:* Parkstr. 46, Dahlem
*Additional information:* Attorney at the LG
I-III and notary. After the National Socialist
seizure of power he was made subject to an
occupational ban in early 1933. He emigrated
in 1938 via Italy or via Switzerland to New
York, USA; he changed his name to Matthew;
he died in 1977 at the age of 85.
*Sources:* Br.B. 32; TK 33; Liste d. nichtzugel.
RA; JMBl. 33, S. 209; BArch, R 3001 PAK;
BG; SSDI

# G

**Gabriel, Georg Dr.**
10/04/1894 Exin - no information
*Home address:* no information
*Law firm address:* An der Spandauer Brücke 2
*Additional information:* Attorney and
notary, after the National Socialist seizure of
power he was readmitted upon request. He
emigrated in December 1933 to Palestine.
*Sources:* *li; BArch, R 3001 PAK; BG

**Galewski, Erwin Dr.**
01/02/1899 Pleschen - no information
*Home address:* Kurfürstendamm 167, W 15
*Law firm address:* Kurfürstendamm 167
*Additional information:* Since 1931 admitted
to the LG I-III; after the National Socialist
seizure of power he was made subject to an
occupational ban in July 1933.
*Sources:* Liste d. nichtzugel. RA, 25.4.33; JMBl.
21.8.33; S. 266; BArch, R 3001 PAK, PA

**Galliner, Moritz Dr.**
04/23/1884 Zinten -
12/28/1942 Berlin
*Home address:* Speyerer Str.
10, Schöneberg
*Law firm address:*
Lutherstr. 20/21, W 62
*Additional information:*
He was a religious Jew. He belonged to
the Representative Assembly of the Jewish
Reform Synagogue of Berlin. He denied
Zionism; for him, Judaism was a religion;
otherwise he adhered to German culture.
Politically, he supported the SPD. Attorney
and notary, as an attorney he practiced
in all areas, he also appeared in political
trials. After the National Socialist seizure of
power his license as a notary was revoked;
he was readmitted as an attorney until the
general occupational ban in 1938; thereafter
he worked as a "consultant." In 1941 he
was forced to work as a laborer at Siemens

in Siemensstadt. An attempt at emigration failed. He and his wife had received a visa for Cuba, but it was forged. Their son was sent to distant relatives to England, their daughter to North America. On the day before transportation he and his wife committed suicide. The couple was buried at Weißensee.
*Sources:* *li; JMBl. 33, S. 220; BArch, R 3001 PAK; MRRAK; BLHA: OFP-Akte; BG; GB II; Ausk. P. Galliner (Sohn), A. Neuman (Tochter); AoR Ausst.

### Gans, Ernst Dr.
07/08/1892 Hörde - 9.9.1992
*Home address:* Rognitzstr. 12, Charlottenburg
*Law firm address:* Landgrafenstr. 1, W 62
*Additional information:* He wrote his lawyers' trainee examination in 1914 and was immediately summoned to the military. He served in the army until the end of the First World War and was awarded the EK I/II. He obtained his doctorate in 1920 in Erlangen and passed his second state examination in law. While studying, he was active in a dueling fraternity (Licaria in the Cartel Convent), which was also a fraternity against antisemitic student groups. He went to Berlin as an assessor, here he entered the renowned practice of Dr. Bruno Weil, an additional partner at that time was Wilhelm Dickmann. Later he was also appointed as a notary. After the National Socialist seizure of power his license as a notary was revoked, he was readmitted as an attorney, because he had been recognized as a "frontline fighter." His license as a notary was revoked in 1935. His revenues continued to decline, but in 1937-38 they no longer covered his expenses. The couple was allowed to leave Germany, however, before they left they were plundered: RM 103,000 for Reich flight tax and RM 43,181 for Jewish property tax. In order to take along their own furniture, paintings, as well as personal jewelry, RM 60,750 had to be paid without replacement "for exporting purposes." Because of the limited possibility for the transfer of foreign exchange the couple suffered a further loss in the amount of RM 37,600. The couple received an affidavit for the US, where they arrived on October 10, 1938. There they could rely on the support of their acquaintances, but limited language skills were an obstacle to professional activity. They managed to keep their heads above water with unskilled

labor (amongst others the sticking of labels on marmalade bottles). Only in 1940 did he find a permanent position as a sales representative. After the USA entered the war, he was no longer allowed to visit companies that were working on war orders. Only after six months and thorough examination was this restriction lifted. He managed to establish a secure position at the National Greeting Card Company. The couple settled down near Detroit, where they were active in various social clubs. At the age of 70, in 1962, he once again turned to legal activity, a close relationship with the German Consulate General developed. As from 1964, he was admitted in Berlin as an attorney under the exemption of the residence obligation and took over various reparation proceedings. He died in 1992; he last lived in Southfield, Michigan.
*Sources:* *li; BArch, R 3001, PAK; DJ 36, S. 314; BG; Jewish Immigrants . . . in the U.S.A., Oral History, S. 35; SSDI

### Gaßmann, Karl Dr.
05/29/1876 Gleiwitz - no information
*Home address:* Giesebrechtstr. 19, Charlottenburg
*Law firm address:* Wielandstr. 30, Charlottenburg
*Additional information:* After the National Socialist seizure of power his license as a notary was revoked in 1933; he worked as an attorney until the general occupational ban in 1938. He emigrated on 09/03/1941 via Spain to Uruguay.
*Sources:* JMBl. 33; S. 208; *li; Liste 36; BArch, R 3001 PAK; MRRAK; BG

### Gaßmann, Walter Dr.
11/16/1891 Gleiwitz - 04/18/1939
*Home address:* no information
*Law firm address:* Kurfürstenstr. 78
*Additional information:* After the National Socialist seizure of power he was made subject to an occupational ban in early 1933; in April 1939 he died at the age of 48.
*Sources:* Adr.B. 32; Liste d. nichtzugel. RA, 24.4.33.; JMBl. 33; S. 253; BArch, R 3001 PAK; BG

### Gerhard, Stephan, Judicial Councillor
No information - 02/09/1936
*Home address:* no information
*Law firm address:* Lennéstr. 6, W 9
*Additional information:* After the National

Socialist seizure of power he was readmitted as an attorney and a notary; his license as a notary was revoked in 1935; according to the handwritten entry in the list drawn up and supplemented in 1933, he died in February 1936.
*Sources:* *li; LAB, Liste 15.10.33; DJ 36, S. 314, S. 360; BArch, R 3001 PAK

**Germer, Paul Dr.**
07/29/1882 Schloppe - no information
*Home address:* Potsdamer Str. 138, W 35
*Law firm address:* Potsdamer Str. 56 I, W 35
*Additional information:* After the National Socialist seizure of power he was readmitted as an attorney and notary (until 1935); his wife was regarded as "non-Jewish"; he worked as an attorney until the general occupational ban in 1938.
*Sources:* *li; Liste 15.10.33; Liste 36; DJ 36, 314; BArch, R 3001 PAK; BG

**Gerschel, Justinus Dr.**
06/16/1881 - 1934
*Home address:* no information
*Law firm address:* Von-der-Heydt-Str. 16, W 35
*Additional information:* Attorney and notary; after the National Socialist seizure of power in 1933 he was readmitted; he died in 1934 at the age of 53.
*Sources:* *li; LAB, Liste 15.10.33; BArch, R 3001 PAK

**Gerson, Georg Dr.**
05/24/1887 Frankfurt/Oder - no information
*Home address:* Nassauische Str. 62, Wilmersdorf
*Law firm address:* Friedrichstr. 59/60
*Additional information:* Attorney since 1913 and notary; he was chairman of the Jewish School Association. After the National Socialist seizure of power his license as a notary was first revoked, then he was disbarred as an attorney in the course of the merging of the district courts. In 1933 he emigrated to Palestine; an arrest warrant for tax evasion was issued against him.
*Sources:* Adr.B. 32; JMBl. 33, S. 208; BArch, R 3001 PAK, PA; Naatz-Album; Wolf, BFS

**Gerson, Heinrich**
04/02/1904 Hamm - no information
*Home address:* Bleibtreustr. 32, W 15
*Law firm address:* Klopstockstr. 7
*Additional information:* After the National Socialist seizure of power he was made subject to an occupational ban on 05/26/1933.
*Sources:* Adr.B. 32; Liste d. nichtzugel. RA, 25.4.33; JMBl. 33; S. 203; BArch, R 3001 PAK, PA

**Glaser, Fritz Dr.**
10/09/1890 Krotoschin - 04/13/1974
*Home address:* Wartburgstr. 16, Schöneberg
*Law firm address:* Charlottenstr. 71, W 8
*Additional information:* Attorney and notary; after the National Socialist seizure of power he was readmitted; his license as a notary was revoked in 1935; he worked as an attorney until the general occupational ban on 1938. Emigration in 1939 to Great Britain, he changed his name to Fred; he was presumably a brother of Ludwig and Martin; he died in 1974 at the age of 83.
*Sources:* Adr.B. 32; *li; DJ 36, S. 314; Liste 36; LAB, Liste 15.10.33; BArch, R 3001, PAK; MMRAK; BG; Ausk. B. Dombek, 2000

**Glaser, Kurt**
04/18/1885 Brieg - no information
*Home address:* Stormstr. 7, Charlottenburg
*Law firm address:* Kurstr. 34/35, SW 19
*Additional information:* Attorney and notary; after the National Socialist seizure of power he was readmitted; his license as a notary was revoked in 1935; he worked as an attorney until the general occupational ban in 1938. He emigrated to Tel Aviv, Palestine, on 11/12/1939.
*Sources:* *li; LAB, Liste 15.10.33; DJ 36, S. 314; BArch, R 3001 PAK; MRRAK; BG

**Glaser, Ludwig**
03/08/1889 Krotoschin - no information
*Home address:* no information
*Law firm address:* Friedrichstr. 207, SW 68
*Additional information:* Attorney at the KG; after the National Socialist seizure of power he was made subject to an occupational ban as an attorney in early 1933. Ludwig was presumably a brother of Fritz and Martin. He emigrated to the Netherlands in July 1933.
*Sources:* Br.B. 32; Liste d. nichtzugel. RA, 25.4.33; BArch, R 3001 PAK, PA; BG

**Glaser, Martin**
06/21/1883 Krotoschin - no information
*Home address:* no information
*Law firm address:* Mauerstr. 91
*Additional information:* Attorney and notary;
after the National Socialist seizure of power
in 1933 his license as a notary was revoked;
thereupon he requested in September 1933
to be disbarred as an attorney. Martin was
presumably a brother of Fritz and Ludwig. He
emigrated to the Netherlands, 1933.
*Sources:* JMBl. 33, S. 208; Pr.J. 33, S. 443;
BArch, R 3001 PAK, PA; BG

**Glaser, Paul Dr.**
03/25/1903 Berlin-Wilmersdorf - no
information
*Home address:* no information
*Law firm address:* Burggrafenstr. 11, W 62
*Additional information:* After the National
Socialist seizure of power he was made subject
to an occupational ban in April 1933.
*Sources:* TK 33; Liste d. nichtzugel. RA,
25.4.33; JMBl. 33, S. 253; BArch, R 3001
PAK

**Glaß, Paul Dr.**
10/08/1885 Schneidemühl - 12/24/1939 Berlin
*Home address:* Ansbacher Str. 9, Schöneberg
*Law firm address:* Bergstr. 145, Neukölln
*Additional information:* Attorney and
notary; in 1927 he ceased to be a practicing
Jew. After the National Socialist seizure of
power in 1933 he was readmitted; his license
as a notary was revoked in 1933; he worked
as an attorney until the general occupational
ban in 1938. In the documents of the file of
the Berlin Remembrance Book his death is
listed as 12/24/1939; he spent his final days at
the Jewish Hospital in Iranischen Straße.
*Sources:* *li; LAB, Liste 15.10.33; DJ 36, S.
314; BArch, R 3001 PAK; BG

**Glass, Salo Dr., Judicial Councillor**
01/20/1880 Raschkow - no information
*Home address:* Barbarossastraße 50,
Schöneberg
*Law firm address:* Große Frankfurter Str. 141,
O 17
*Additional information:* Attorney and
notary; after the National Socialist seizure
of power in 1933 his license as a notary was
revoked; he was readmitted as an attorney.
He emigrated in 1933; he was disbarred as an

attorney in 1934. An arrest warrant for tax
evasion was issued against him.
*Sources:* *li; LAB, Liste 15.10.33; BArch, R
3001 PAK; Wolf, BFS

**Glogauer, Julius Dr.**
09/06/1885 Hannover - no information
*Home address:* no information
*Law firm address:* Olivaer Platz 11
*Additional information:* He was an attorney at
the KG (since 1912) and notary (since 1924); he
was disbarred due to various offenses at the end
of February/beginning of March 1933.
*Sources:* TK 33; JMBl. 33, 10. u.17.3.33;
BArch, R 3001 PAK, PA

**Glogauer, Richard Dr.**
03/08/1892 Berlin - no information
*Home address:* no information
*Law firm address:* Fasanenstr. 67
*Additional information:* He dissolved his law
firm during the first six months of 1933.
*Sources:* TK 33; Br.B.32; BArch, R 3001
PAK; JMBl. 33, S. 253; BG

**Glückmann, Adolf**
01/14/1904 - no information
*Home address:* no information
*Law firm address:* Rosenthaler Str. 52, N 54
After the National Socialist seizure of power
he was made subject to an occupational ban
in early 1933.
*Sources:* Liste d. nichtzugel. RA, 25.4.33;
JMBl. 33, S. 234; BArch, R 3001 PAK

**Glücksmann, Alfred Dr.**
09/24/1875 - no information
*Home address:* Paulinenstr. 2, Lichterfelde
*Law firm address:* Neue Wilhelmstr. 1, NW 7
*Additional information:* Attorney at the KG;
after the National Socialist seizure of power
he was disbarred in 1933. In January 1939
he emigrated to Tel Aviv, Palestine. Later he
returned to Berlin.
TK 33; JMBl. 33, S. 266; BG

**Glücksmann, Heinrich Dr.**
10/13/1886 Königshütte - no information
*Home address:* Motzstr. 91, W 30
*Law firm address:* Schellingstr. 6, W 9
*Additional information:* Attorney and
notary; after the National Socialist seizure
of power in 1933 his license as a notary was
revoked; he was readmitted as an attorney

until 11/02/1935. Emigration to Palestine.
*Sources:* *li; LAB, Liste 15.10.33; JMBl. 33,
S. 208; BArch, R 3001 PAK; BG

**Glücksmann, Herbert Dr.**
03/06/1904 Bielitz - no information
*Home address:* no information
*Law firm address:* Köpenicker Str. 41, SO 16
*Additional information:* After the
National Socialist seizure of power he was
made subject to an occupational ban on
06/12/1933.
*Sources:* Liste d. nichtzugel. RA, 25.4.33;
BArch, R 3001 PAK, PA

**Glücksmann, Leo**
12/29/1875 Kobylin - transportation 1943
*Home address:* Kommandantenstr. 34,
Kreuzberg
*Law firm address:* Kommandantenstr. 34,
Kreuzberg
*Additional information:* Attorney and
notary; after the National Socialist seizure
of power he was readmitted; his license as a
notary was revoked in 1935. Transportation
on 09/10/1943 to Theresienstadt. Ffrom
there he was transported to Auschwitz on
05/18/1944.
*Sources:* *li; LAB, Liste 15.10.33; DJ 36, S.
314; Liste 36; BArch, R 3001 PAK; MRRAK;
BG; ThG; GB II

**Glücksmann, Siegfried**
No information
*Home address:* no information
*Law firm address:* no information
*Additional information:* Attorney and
notary; after the National Socialist seizure of
power he was made subject to an occupational
ban until July 1933.
*Sources:* TK 33; JMBl. 33, S. 209; BArch, R
3001 PAK

**Godin, Reinhard, Baron von**
No information
*Home address:* Maienstr. 5, Zehlendorf
*Law firm address:* Wilhelmstr. 69 a
*Additional information:* Attorney and notary;
after the National Socialist seizure of power
in 1933 he still had not been listed as "non-
Jewish," later he was regarded as "mixed
race," because he had a Jewish grandparent.
He was Catholic and married. He was allowed
to work again after the general occupational

ban in 1938. He survived and was immediately
readmitted after 1945.
*Sources:* Adr.B. 32; LAB, Liste Mschlg. 36;
Tel.B. 41; Verz. zugel. Anw. 45

**Goetzel, Walther Dr.**
02/18/1888 Berlin
- 10/26/1965
*Home address:* no
information
*Law firm address:*
Charlottenstr. 56, W 8
*Additional information:*
Attorney since 1914, notary since 1924;
expert on tenancy law. He was a member of
the French Reformed Church Berlin. After the
National Socialist seizure of power in 1933
his license as a notary was revoked; he was
readmitted as an attorney. His wife Erna was
regarded as non-Jewish; he himself as "mixed
race first degree." He survived and in 1947 he
was readmitted as an attorney and a notary.
*Sources:* *li; JMBl. 33, S. 220; LAB, Liste
15.10.33, Liste Mschl. 36; BArch, R 3001
PAK; BG; LAB, RAK, PA

**Goldbaum, Wenzel Dr.**
09/19/1881 Lodz - 05/15/1960 Lima, Peru
*Home address:* no information
*Law firm address:* Wilhelmstr. 52
*Additional information:* Studied in Munich,
Berlin and Marburg; obtained a doctorate in
1906; attorney (since 1909) and notary, he
specialized in copyright and theater law, in law
partnership with Gerhard Jacoby; until 1933
he was the first secretary and legal advisor of
the Association of German Playwrights and
Stage Composers.
After the National Socialist seizure of power the
law firm was dissolved. He emigrated in early
1933 to Paris, France. An arrest warrant for
tax evasion was issued against him. In 1936 he
moved to Ecuador and there, together with his
sons, he founded a life insurance company; he
published a journal for copyright law (six issues);
since 1939 he worked for the Swiss journal
"Le droit d'ateur" as the South American
correspondent. In 1946 he was the representative
for Ecuador at the Copyright Convention in
Washington; later he moved to Peru and he died
in Lima in 1960 at the age of 78.
*Sources:* Adr.B. 32; BArch, R 3001 PAK; Pr.J.
33, S. 701; Philo-Lexikon, S. 604; BG; BHdE
Bd. I, S. 229; Wolf, BFS; Göpp., S. 282

**Goldberg, Bruno Dr.**
11/08/1892 Berlin - November 1977
New York
*Home address:* Akazienstr. 28, Schöneberg
*Law firm address:* Kaiser-Allee 203, W 15
*Additional information:* Attorney and notary; after the National Socialist seizure of power he was readmitted; he was disbarred on 12/14/1934. He emigrated in 1934 to Paris, France, later to the Netherlands, then to New York in the USA. A warrant was issued against him for tax code violations. He died 1977 in New York.
*Sources:* *li; LAB, Liste 15.10.33; BArch, R 3001 PAK; BG; Wolf, BFS

**Goldberg, Georg**
12/23/1883 Berlin - transportation 1944
*Home address:* Uhlandstr. 184, Charlottenburg
*Law firm address:* Friedrichstr. 136, N 24
*Additional information:* Attorney and notary; after the National Socialist seizure of power he was readmitted; he relocated his law firm; at the end of 1935 his license as a notary was revoked; until the general occupational ban in 1938 he worked as an attorney. His wife was regarded as "Aryan," he himself ceased to be a practicing Jew. Presumably his wife died in 1943; after working as a laborer, he was subsequently arrested on 07/09/1944 and went to the collection point Schulstr. 78, N 65. On 07/13/1944 he was transported to Theresienstadt; from there he was transported on 10/28/1944 to Auschwitz.
*Sources:* TK 33; Liste d. nichtzugel. RA, 25.4.33; *li; Liste 36; DJ 36, S.314; BArch, R 3001 PAK; MRRAK; BG; ThG; GB II

**Goldberg, Georg**
01/24/1902 - November 1982
*Home address:* no information
*Law firm address:* Alexanderstr. 38
*Additional information:* Attorney at the KG; after the National Socialist seizure of power occupational ban in April 1933. He emigrated to the USA, he changed his name to George; he died at the age of 80.
*Sources:* TK 33; Br.B. 32; Liste d. nichtzugel. RA, 25.4.33; JMBl. 33, S.203; BArch, R 3001 PAK; SSDI

**Goldberg, Wilhelm Wolf**
08/13/1875 Guben - no information
*Home address:* Kantstr. 4, Charlottenburg

*Law firm address:* Kantstr. 4, Charlottenburg
*Additional information:* Attorney and notary; after the National Socialist seizure of power in 1933 his license as a notary was revoked, he was readmitted as an attorney; in 1936 he was still working as an attorney, in 1937 he survived an honorable court hearing with a reprimand, although the National Socialist press had been violently agitated against him. Emigration to London, Great Britain, in November 1938.
*Sources:* JMBl. 33, S. 208; *li; Liste 36; LAB, Liste 15.10.33; BArch, R 3001 PAK; BG

**Goldberger, Manfred**
06/02/1881 Berlin
- 01/20/1943
*Home address:* Rosenheimer Str. 27, W 30
*Law firm address:* Kufsteiner Str. 2, Schöneberg
*Additional information:* Attorney and notary; he was a Protestant; after the National Socialist seizure of power in 1933 he was readmitted; until the general occupational ban in 1938 he worked as an attorney, afterwards as an asset manager. Date of declaration of property: 03/17/1942, transportation on 03/28/1942 to Piaski; he died on 01/20/1943.
*Sources:* Adr.B. 32; *li; DJ 36, S. 314; LAB, Liste 15.10.33; Liste 36; BArch, R 3001 PAK; Naatz-Album; BG; GB II

**Goldmann, Eduard, Judicial Councillor**
10/20/1854 - 01/01/1939
*Home address:* Rüsternallee 23, Charlottenburg
*Law firm address:* Potsdamer Str. 118, W 35
*Additional information:* He was a major civil rights activist, attorney and notary; after the National Socialist seizure of power he was re-admitted; in 1935 his license as a notary was revoked; he died in 1939 at the age of 84; he was buried at Weißensee.
*Sources:* *li; LAB, Liste 15.10.33; DJ 36, S. 314; Liste 36; BArch, R 3001 PAK; Philo-Lexikon, S: 603; BG

**Goldschmidt, Alexander, Judicial Councillor**
05/19/1878 - 01/21/1937
*Home address:* Adalbertstr. 41, Kreuzberg
*Law firm address:* Eislebener Str. 6, W 50

*Additional information:* Attorney and notary; after the National Socialist seizure of power in 1933 his license as a notary was revoked, he was readmitted as a notary; he worked as an attorney until his death in 1937; he was buried at Weißensee.
*Sources:* *li; JMBl. 33, S. 202; LAB, Liste 15.10.33; Liste 36; BArch, R 3001 PAK; BG

**Goldschmidt, Bernhard,** transportation 1941
*Home address:* Schaperstr. 31, W 50
*Law firm address:* Friedrichstr. 49, SW 68
*Additional information:* Attorney at the KG; after the National Socialist seizure of power he was made subject to an occupational ban in early 1933; subsequently he presumably worked as a bookkeeper. Transportation with the First Transport on 10/18/1941 to Lodz/Litzmannstadt.
*Sources:* TK 33; JMBl. 33, S. 282; BArch, R 3001 PAK; BG; GB II

**Goldschmidt, Ernst**
12/21/1895 Peine - no information
*Home address:* Auguste-Victoria-Str. 62, Schmargendorf
*Law firm address:* Hardenbergstr. 27, Charlottenburg
*Additional information:* Attorney and notary; after the National Socialist seizure of power in 1933 he was readmitted; he had to relocate his law office; his license as a notary was revoked in 1935; until August 1938 he was still admitted as an attorney, presumably emigrated on 09/1/1938.
*Sources:* Br.B. 32; TK 33; *li; LAB, Liste 15.10.33; DJ 36, S. 314; Liste 36; MRRAK; BG

**Goldschmidt, Ernst Dr.**
01/20/1885 Koblenz - 12/21/1949
*Home address:* Hohenzollerndamm 102, Dahlem
*Law firm address:* Landshuter Str. 27, W 30
*Additional information:* Attorney and notary; after the National Socialist seizure of power he was readmittted; his license as a notary was revoked in 1935; he worked as an attorney until the general occupational ban in 1938; at the same time he was active at the private Goldsmith School, located at Roseneck, which had been established by his wife, Dr. Leonore Goldschmidt. The Goldschmidt School became a refuge for many Jewish students who had to leave their original schools. It had over 500 students, of whom more than 75 lived at the school. The school tried to prepare its students for a life in Great Britain, whilst it e.g. could confer a certificate of the University of Cambridge. The students were in a difficult position, often completely unprepared, since they had been confronted with anti-Semitic attacks and exclusion measures in their original schools. Often, they were relegated by these schools; mostly they decided to change schools themselves after having been terrorized by their teachers or classmates. The Goldschmidt school was also a port of call for the teachers who had been dismissed from civil servant status or for young teachers, who were no longer allowed to be employed as Jews in state schools. The school felt committed to tolerance and humanity. The school fee amounted to RM 360 per year and was therefore within the framework of the various private schools that accepted Jews (there were about 4% non-Jewish students at the Goldschmidt school). The school was closed in November 1939. Previously many children had been taken to safety in Great Britain with numerous children's transports. Ernst was to be arrested in the wake of the Night of the Broken Glass throughout the Reich on November 9, 1938, but was able to flee to Denmark with the night train. From there he traveled to Great Britain where he stayed for four months. In March 1939 he returned to Berlin, in accordance with a guarantee that his wife had reached, trusting that he would not be arrested. His wife needed him, because the school was experiencing legal and administrative difficulties. In fact, he remained unharmed. The couple emigrated to Great Britain in July 1939, where his wife again opened a school in Folkstone. He supported his wife with this endeavor. With the intensified attacks on the English coast, the school had to be integrated with another in Newport, Monmouthshire, thus losing its independence. Shortly before the transfer, he was interned for about a year on the Isle of Man as an "enemy alien." After his release, he was recognized as a refugee from Nazi oppression. He struggled to make a living as a company representative in Stoke-on-Trent. In 1947 he and his wife moved to London, where the small company could be expanded. In 1949 he became ill with cancer, he died in the same year just before his 65th birthday.

*Sources:* Br.B. 32; TK 33; *li; LAB, Liste 15.10.33; DJ 36, S. 314; Liste 36; MRRAK; BG; BArch, R 3001, PAK; Meyhöfer, Rita: Gäste in Berlin? Jüdisches Schülerleben in der Weimarer Republik und im Nationalsozialismus [Guests in Berlin? Jewish student life in the Weimar Republic and under National Socialism]. Hamburg 1996; Information of the son Rudi G.

### Goldschmidt, Fritz

07/07/1892 - 10/31/1970
*Home address:* Luitpoldstr. 32, Schöneberg
*Law firm address:* Luitpoldstr. 32, Schöneb.
*Additional information:* Attorney at the KG and notary; after the National Socialist seizure of power he was made subject to an occupational ban in early 1933. After emigration to Palestine, he returned to Germany, where he died in 1970; he was buried in Berlin at the Jewish Cemetery on Heerstraße.
*Sources:* Br.B. 32; JMBl. 33, S. 209; BArch, R 3001, PAK; BG; Ausk. E. Proskauer; Jüd. Friedh. Heerstr.

### Goldschmidt, Hans Dr.

06/08/1904 Krefeld - 02/28/1990
*Home address:* no information
*Law firm address:* Lützowufer 17, W 10
*Additional information:* Attorney at the KG; after the National Socialist seizure of power he was made subject to an occupational ban on 06/17/1933, despite intensive efforts on his part to avoid this. He migrated to the USA, where he most recently lived in New York.
*Sources:* Br.B. 32; Liste d. nichtzugel. RA, 25.4.33; JMBl. 33, S. 203; BArch, R 3001 PAK, PA; BG; SSDI

### Goldschmidt, Heinz

09/17/1903 Berlin - no information
*Home address:* no information
*Law firm address:* Warschauer Str. 15, O 34
*Additional information:* After the National Socialist seizure of power he was made subject to an occupational ban on 05/29/1933.
*Sources:* Adr.B. 32; Liste d. nichtzugel. RA, 25.4.33; JMBl., S. 209; BArch, R 3001 PAK, PA

### Goldschmidt, Hermann Dr.

09 (04.?)/24/1896 Praust - Auschwitz
*Home address:* no information
*Law firm address:* Hohenzollerndamm 198, Wilmersdorf

*Additional information:* After the National Socialist seizure of power he was readmitted; he worked as an attorney up to the general occupational ban in 1938. He died at Auschwitz.
*Sources:* *li; LAB, Liste 15.10.33; BArch, R 3001, PAK; MRRAK; BG; GB II

### Goldschmidt, Ivan

10/22/1878 Berlin - transportation 1944
*Home address:* Kurfürstenstr. 127, W 62
*Law firm address:* Lennéstr. 10, W 9
*Additional information:* Attorney and notary; after the National Socialist seizure of power in 1933 he was readmitted; in 1935 his license as a notary was revoked; he was admitted as an attorney until the general occupational ban. Transportation on 01/20/1944 from Berlin to Auschwitz.
*Sources:* *li; LAB, Liste 15.10.33; DJ 36, S. 314; BArch, R 3001 PAK; MRRAK; BG (Iwan G.); GB II

### Goldschmidt, Karl Dr.

08/14/1890 Frankfurt am Main - August 1975 New York
*Home address:* Knesebeckstraße 32, Charlottenburg and/or Wachtelallee 18, Dahlem
*Law firm address:* Dorotheenstr. 80
*Additional information:* Attorney in Berlin since 1921; at the same time he was a legal advisor (Jakob Michael Group, Emil Koester Firm); after the National Socialist seizure of power on 08/08/1933 he was made subject to an occupational ban; 1935 he emigrated to The Hague, the Netherlands, later to New York, USA. An arrest warrant for tax evasion was issued against hime. He died 1975 in New York.
*Sources:* TK 33; Pr.J. 33, S. 868; BArch, R 3001 PAK, PA; Wolf, BFS

### Goldschmidt, Kurt

08/21/1889 Berlin - no information
*Home address:* Köpenicker Str. 6, SO 36
*Law firm address:* Köpenicker Str. 6, SO 36
*Additional information:* After the National Socialist seizure of power he was made subject to an occupational ban on 05/26/1933; although he had fought as a soldier in the First World War, he had not been recognized as a "frontline fighter." His wife was a physician, her admission was also revoked. This meant that the family of four had no income.

*Sources:* Br.B. 32; Liste d. nichtzugel. RA, 25.4.33; JMBl. 33, S. 203; BArch, R 3001 PAK, PA

**Goldschmidt, Leonhard**
03/12/1901 Hannover - no information
*Home address:* no information
*Law firm address:* no information
*Additional information:* Attorney at the KG since 1930; after the National Socialist seizure of power he was made subject to an occupational ban on 07/13/1933.
*Sources:* BArch, R 3001 PAK, PA

**Goldschmidt, Siegfried Dr.**
07/08/1880 Filehne - no information
*Home address:* Kurfürstenstr. 89, W 35
*Law firm address:* Königin-Augusta-Str. 20, W 35
*Additional information:* He fought in the First World War, he had been awarded the EK II. Attorney and notary; after the National Socialist seizure of power in 1933 his license as a notary was revoked, he was readmitted as an attorney until the general occupational ban in 1938. He emigrated via Sweden to Milan, Italy on 03/14/1939.
*Sources:* JMBl. 33, S. 220; *li; LAB, Liste 15.10.33; BArch, R 3001 PAK; BG

**Goldschmidt, Wilhelm Dr.**
11/05/1903 Berlin - no information
*Home address:* no information
*Law firm address:* Levetzowstr. 12, NW 87
*Additional information:* Attorney at the KG; after the National Socialist seizure of power he was made subject to an occupational ban on 06/09/1933.
*Sources:* Liste d. nichtzugel. RA, 25.4.33; JMBl. 33, S. 203; BArch, R 3001 PAK, PA

**Goldstandt, Herbert Dr.**
04/03/1901 Hohensalza - no information
*Home address:* no information
*Law firm address:* Kronenstr. 16, W 8
*Additional information:* Attorney at the KG; he was Protestant; after the National Socialist seizure of power he was made subject to an occupational ban on 06/30/1933; he emigrated to Switzerland.
*Sources:* Liste d. nichtzugel. RA, 25.4.33; BArch, R 3001 PAK, PA

**Goldstein, Hans W.M. Dr.**
01/27/1892 Aschersleben - no information

*Home address:* Werftstr. 8, NW 40
*Law firm address:* Unter den Linden 16, W 8
*Additional information:* Attorney and notary; after the National Socialist seizure of power he was made subject to an occupational ban in early 1933, his license as a notary was revoked; he was readmitted as an attorney until the general occupational ban in 1938. His wife Dora was regarded as "Aryan." He emigrated to London, Great Britain, on 01/02/1939, he changed his name to John Jürgen Granville.
*Sources:* TK 33; Liste d. nichtzugel. RA, 25.43.33; *li; LAB, Liste 15.10.33; DJ 36, S. 314; Liste 36; BArch, R 3001 PAK, PA; MRRAK; BG

**Goldstein, Hans**
10/26/1885 Herford - 05/28/1933
*Home address:* no information
*Law firm address:* Wilhelmstr. 55, W
*Additional information:* Attorney and notary; he fought in the First World War. After the National Socialist seizure of power he was made subject to an occupational ban. He was not recognized as a "frontline fighter," various letters of recommendation, which had to be submitted in the application for readmission in April 1933, praise his "patriotic attitude." He died at the end of May 1933 at the age of 48.
*Sources:* JMBl. 7.7.33; BArch, R 3001 PAK, PA

**Goldstein, Ismar**
09/28/1880 Lipine - transportation 1942
*Home address:* Konstanzer Str. 3, W 15
*Law firm address:* Gleditschstr. 46, W 30
*Additional information:* Attorney at the KG; after the National Socialist seizure of power in 1933 his license as a notary was revoked; he worked as an attorney until the general occupational ban in 1938, thereafter he still worked as a "consultant." He was arrested in 1942, transportation on 10/19/1942 to Riga.
*Sources:* JMBl. 33, S. 220; *li; LAB, Liste 15.10.33; BArch, R 3001 PAK; BG; BdE; GB II

**Goldstein, Rudolf Dr. jur. et rer. pol.**
01/01/1885 Stargard - 01/12/1974 Berlin
*Home address:* Mommsenstr. 42, Charlottenburg
*Law firm address:* Friedrichstr. 192, W 8
*Additional information:* He was a Protestant; he fought in the First World War, he was

awarded the EK II. Attorney since 1913 and notary since 1924; after the National Socialist seizure of power he was readmitted in 1933 as an "elderly attorney" and as a "frontline fighter;" he was regarded as "mixed race first degree," he belonged to the Reich Association of Non-Aryan Christians; he was also still allowed to practice after 1938, without becoming a "consultant." Apparently his wife was regarded as "non-Jewish," since she was allowed to own property. He wrote: "... to escape seizure by the Todt Organization, I took a position in June 1944 at Phrix GmbH ... in Silesia. From there I was seized to dig trenches in Silesia from August 1944 to January 1945." He survived and was readmitted as an attorney in 1949.
*Sources:* *li; LAB, Liste 15.10.33; BArch, R 3001, PAK; Mitt.bl. Reichsverband nichtarischer Christen, 6.12.1934; LAB, RAK, PA; BG

### Goldstrom, Siegfried Dr.
06/18/1882 Bütow - 11/08/1948 London
*Home address:* Pariser Str. 20, W 15
*Law firm address:* Kurfürstendamm 24, W 15
*Additional information:* Attorney and notary; after the National Socialist seizure of power in 1933 his license as a notary was revoked; he was readmitted as an attorney; he still worked as an attorney until the general occupational ban in 1938. He emigrated to London, Great Britain in August 1939; he died there in 1948.
*Sources:* JMBl. 33, S. 208; *li; LAB, Liste 15.10.33; Liste 36; BArch, R 3001 PAK; BG

### Goldstücker, Max
12/06/1878 Breslau - transportation 1941
*Home address:* Sigmaringer Str. 30, Wilmersdorf/ Barbarossastr. 84 (40?)
*Law firm address:* Friedrich-Wilhelm-Str.18
*Additional information:* Attorney and notary; after the National Socialist seizure of power he was made subject to an occupational ban in 1933. No further information until declaration of property on 10/31/1941; collection point Levetzowstr. 7-8; transportation on 10/18/1941 to Litzmannstadt/Lodz.
*Sources:* Br.B. 32; TK 33; Liste d. nichtzugel. RA, 25.4.33; JMBl. 21.8.33, S. 266; BArch, R 3001, PAK; BG; GB II

### Golinski, Siegfried Dr.
04/11/1884 Jarotschin - no information

*Home address:* Augsburger Str. 33, Charlottenburg
*Law firm address:* Zimmerstr. 22, SW 68
*Additional information:* Attorney and notary; after the National Socialist seizure of power in 1933 his license as a notary was revoked, he was readmitted as an attorney, he was still working as an attorney until ca. 1936.
*Sources:* JMBl. 33, S. 220; *li; LAB, Liste 15.10.33; Liste 36; BArch, R 3001 PAK; BG

### Golm, Ernst Dr.
12/21/1885 Berlin - no information
*Home address:* no information
*Law firm address:* Olivaer Platz 7, W 15
*Additional information:* Attorney and notary; after the National Socialist seizure of power his license as a notary was revoked in 1933; he was readmitted as an attorney; until December 1937 he was still working as an attorney.
*Sources:* *li; LAB, Liste 15.10.33; Liste 36; BArch, R 3001 PAK

### Goltzen, Arthur, Judicial Councillor
10/03/1870 Berlin - no information
*Home address:* Martin-Luther-Str. 12, W 62
*Law firm address:* Markt 1, Spandau
He had fought in the First World War; attorney and notary; after the National Socialist seizure of power he was readmitted; since he had been recognized as a "frontline fighter." He was a Protestant. He was regarded as "mixed race first class." He was still working as an attorney in 1936.
*Sources:* *li; LAB, Liste 15.10.33, Liste Mschlg. 36; BArch, R 3001 PAK; BG

### Goßmann, Georg, Judicial Councillor
No information
*Home address:* no information
*Law firm address:* Martin-Luther-Str. 89, W 30
*Additional information:* Attorney and notary; after the National Socialist seizure of power he was readmitted; his license as a notary was revoked in 1935; he was still working as an attorney until 1937.
*Sources:* *li; LAB, Liste 15.10.33; DJ 36, S. 314; Liste 36; BArch, R 3001 PAK

### Gotthelf, Alfred Dr., Judicial Councillor
09/05/1861 Berlin - 12/01/1942 Theresienstadt
*Home address:* Barbarossastr. 52, W 30

*Law firm address:* Maaßenstr. 35, W 30
*Additional information:* Attorney and
notary; after the National Socialist seizure
of power he was readmitted; his license as a
notary was revoked in 1935; he worked as
an attorney until the general occupational
ban in 1938; he last relocated his law office
to his home. No further information until
his declaration of property on 08/07/1942;
collection point Große Hamburger Str.
26, transportation on 08/13/1942 to
Theresienstadt.
*Sources:* *li; LAB, Liste 15.10.33; DJ 36, S.
314; Liste 36; BArch, R 3001 PAK; MRRAK;
BG; ThG; GB II

**Gottlieb, Fritz**
05/01/1903 Breslau - no information
*Home address:* no information
*Law firm address:* Wichmannstr. 5
*Additional information:* After the National
Socialist seizure of power he was made subject
to an occupational ban on 07/14/1933.
*Sources:* Br.B. 32; Liste d. nichtzugel. RA,
25.4.33; JMBl. 21.8.33; BArch, R 3001 PAK

**Gottlieb, Joseph Dr.**
07/13/1901 Lysiec - no
information
*Home address:*
Kurfürstendamm 13, W 50
*Law firm address:*
Oranienburger Str. 13/14,
N 24
*Additional information:* After the National
Socialist seizure of power he was made
subject to an occupational ban in early 1933.
Emigration to Tel Aviv, Palestine.
*Sources:* Br.B. 32; Liste d. nichtzugel. RA,
25.4.33; JMBl. 33, S. 195; BArch, R 3001
PAK; Naatz-Album; BG

**Gottschalk, Alfred Dr.**
03/16/1899 Sassin - no information
*Home address:* no information
*Law firm address:* Uhlandstr. 161, W 15
*Additional information:* Attorney and
notary; after the National Socialist seizure of
power he was readmitted in 1933; his license
as a notary was revoked in 1935; he worked
as an attorney until the general occupational
ban in 1938. Emigration to Shanghai, China.
*Sources:* *li; LAB, Liste 15.10.33; DJ 36, S.
314; BArch, R 3001 PAK; BG

**Gottschalk, Leopold, Judicial Councillor**
06/19/1862 Königsfeld - no information
*Home address:* Martin-Luther-Str. 10,
Schöneberg
*Law firm address:* Potsdamer Platz 1, W 9
*Additional information:* Attorney and
notary; after the National Socialist seizure
of power his license as a notary was revoked
in 1933, he was readmitted as attorney; he
worked as an attorney up to the general
occupational ban in 1938. Emigration to
Bolivia on 05/31/1939.
*Sources:* TK 33; *li; LAB, Liste 15.10.33;
BArch, R 3001 PAK; BG

**Gottschalk, Martin**
02/06/1881 Berlin-Charlottenburg
- 09/20/1939
*Home address:* Wielandstr. 29 bei Wolff,
Charlottenburg
*Law firm address:* Helmstedter Str. 11 I,
Wilmersdorf
*Additional information:* Attorney at the KG;
after the National Socialist seizure of power
he was readmitted; he worked as an attorney
until the general occupational ban in 1938.
He died in 1939 at the age of 58, he was
buried at Weißensee.
*Sources:* *li; LAB, Liste 15.10.33; BArch, R
3001 PAK

**Grabower, Robert**
08/31/1905 Berlin - no information
*Home address:* Bamberger Str. 14, Wilmersdorf
*Law firm address:* Hohenstaufenstr. 24, W 30
*Additional information:* First admitted
1932/33; after the National Socialist
seizure of power he was made subject to an
occupational ban in early 1933. Emigration to
London, Great Britain.
*Sources:* Liste d. nichtzugel. RA, 25.4.33;
JMBl. 33, S. 209; BArch, R 3001 PAK; BG

**Graetz, Ernst Dr.**
02/28/1895 - no information
*Home address:* no information
*Law firm address:* Taubenstr. 35, W 8
*Additional information:* Attorney and
notary; after the National Socialist seizure of
power his license as a notary was revoked on
09/11/1933.
*Sources:* Adr.B. 32; TK 33; Liste d.
nichtzugel. RA 25.4.33; Pr.J. 33, S. 565;
BArch, R 3001 PAK, PA

**Graetzer, Franz Dr.**
09/23/1884 Berlin - no information
*Home address:* Berliner Str. 146,
Charlottenburg
*Law firm address:* Berliner Str. 146,
Charlottenburg
*Additional information:* Attorney and
notary; after the National Socialist seizure
of power in 1933 he was readmitted as
attorney and notary; his license as a notary
was revoked in 1935; he worked as an
attorney until the general occupational ban
in 1938. He emigrated to New York, USA
(presumably) before March 1939.
*Sources:* *li; LAB, Liste 15.10.33; DJ 36, S.
314; Liste 36; BArch, R 3001 PAK; BG

**Graetzer, Walter Dr.**
06/23/1882 Magdeburg - no information
*Home address:* Oranienburger Str. 23, N 24
*Law firm address:* Monbijouplatz 11, N 24
*Additional information:* After the National
Socialist seizure of power he was readmitted
as an attorney and worked until 08/22/1938.
Emigration on 06/30/1939 to Shanghai, China.
*Sources:* *li; LAB, Liste 15.10.33; Liste 36;
BArch, R 3001 PAK; BG

**Graff, Wilhelm**
01/05/1901 Berlin-Charlottenburg - May
1978
*Home address:* no information
*Law firm address:* Kurfürstendamm 224, W 15
*Additional information:* After the National
Socialist seizure of power he was made subject
to an occupational ban on 07/13/1933. After
emigration, he changed his name to William;
he last lived in Hawaii, USA; he died at the
age of 77.
*Sources:* Br.B. 32; Liste d. nichtzugel. RA,
25.4.33; JMBl. 33, S. 282; BArch, R 3001
PAK, PA; SSDI

**Grau, Julius**
04/13/1884 Berlin - transportation 1941
*Home address:* Flotowstr. 10, NW 87,
Tiergarten
*Law firm address:* Behrenstr. 30, W 8
*Additional information:* Attorney at the
KG and notary; after the National Socialist
seizure of power in 1933 he was readmitted;
his license as a notary was revoked in 1935;
he still worked as an attorney until the general
occupational ban in 1938, thereafter he was

admitted as a "consultant." Transportation
with the First Transport on 10/18/1941 to
Litzmannstadt/Lodz.
*Sources:* *li; LAB, Liste 15.10.33; DJ 36, S.
314; Liste 36; BArch, R 3001 PAK; MRRAK;
Liste der Kons. v. 23.2.1939; BG; GB II

**Grau, Richard, Dr.**
07/29/1899 Berlin - October 1970
*Home address:* no information
*Law firm address:* Flensburger Str. 3, NW 87
*Additional information:* Attorney at the KG;
after the National Socialist seizure of power he
was re-admitted until the general occupational
ban in 1938. He emigrated to the USA; he began
studies at a law school in California; he applied
for a scholarship with American Committee;
however, his application was rejected; he last
lived under the name Richard Graw in Berkeley,
California; he died in 1970 at the age of 71.
*Sources:* *li; LAB, Liste 15.10.33; BArch, R
3001 PAK; NY Publ. Lib. (Am. Com.) Grau;
SSDI

**Grau, Walter Dr.**
05/25/1893 Berlin - 09/27(28?)/1942
*Home address:* Gustloffstr. 51,
Charlottenburg
*Law firm address:* Flensburger Str. 3, NW 87
*Additional information:* Attorney and
notary; after the National Socialist seizure
of power he was readmitted; his license as a
notary was revoked in 1935; he was admitted
as an attorney until the general occupational
ban in 1939, then he still worked as a
"consultant." He was a Protestant; at the
end of September 1942 he committed suicide
at the age of 51, presumably in view of the
imminent transportation.
*Sources:* *li; LAB, Liste 15.10.33; DJ 36, S.
314; MRRAK; Liste d. Kons. 15.4.39; BArch,
R 3001 PAK; BG; GB II

**Graul, Georg**
01/26/1887 Berlin - 11/26/1958 Berlin
*Home address:* Beerenstr. 58, Zehlendorf
*Law firm address:* Französische Str. 21, W 8
*Additional information:* He was Protestant;
attorney (since 1925) and notary (1930);
he had previously worked in industry. His
revenues were between RM 5,000 and 8,000
p.a. He was a Freemason and had fought
in the First World War. In 1932 he joined
the "Stahlhelm" (Steel helmet), his political

orientation was German-nationalist. After the National Socialist seizure of power in 1933 he was readmitted, he had been recognized as a "frontline fighter." Because he was regarded as "mixed race" he was exempted from the general occupational ban in 1938. His only son died in September 1939 during the occupation of Poland. This circumstance temporarily protected him from further persecution, but he was constantly threatened. However, he managed to, as he himself noted, "again and again put off a determination of my ancestry." He was allowed to continue practicing and employed Fritz Rosenthal, who had gone underground, at his office. On 10/23/1944 he was arrested by the Gestapo within the framework of "Aktion Mitte [a Nazi paramilitary organization comprised of four laborers that worked on building projects in the employ of the Todt Organization]" as "mixed race first degree" and "on 11/06/1944 he was brought to the special work camp Zerbst Airport." In January he received a short vacation. He was able to obtain a temporary exemption because of a "medical report" and went underground until the end of the war. He survived and lived in Zehlendorf after liberation. He immediate received his readmittance as attorney and notary.
*Sources:* *li; LAB, Liste 15.10.33; Liste Mschl. 36; BG; LAB, RAK PA

**Gronemann, Sammy**
03/21/1875 Strasburg, West Prussia - 03/06/1953 Tel Aviv
*Home address:* Monbijouplatz 10
*Law firm address:* Tauentzienstr. 13
*Additional information:* Attorney since 1906 in Berlin, later also notary, had also studied at the Berlin Rabbinical Seminary. Since 1901 he was a delegate at Zionist congresses, at the same time an official in Zionist federations; in 1920 he published the successful novel "Tohuwabohu [Hullabaloo]," which had as its content the situation of the Berlin Jews in its various facets; additional publications: "Hawdoloh" and "Zapfenstreich [Tattoo]" (1923), "Schalet, Beiträge zur Philosophie des Wenn schon [Schalet (casserole dish of Ashkenazi Jewish cuisine for the lunch meal on Shabbat), contributions to the philosophy

if already]" (1927); for many years he was legal counsel of the Association of German Authors. After the National Socialist seizure of power in 1933 he was disbarred. He emigrated to France in 1933, from there to Tel Aviv, Palestine in 1936; He was active in Irgun Olei Merkas Europa (Association of Immigrants from Central Europe); in 1946 he published his autobiography "Erinnerungen eines Jecken [Memoirs of a German-speaking Jewish emigrant of the 1930s in Palestine]." His writings have been reissued in recent years.
*Sources:* Br.B. 32; BArch, R 3001 PAK; Pr.J. 33, S. 443 u. 868; BG; BHdE Bd. 2,1, S. 417; Göpp., S. 284; Walk, S. 126; autobiographical writings: Erinnerungen [Memoirs] (erschienen 2002/2004)

**Groß, Jakob**
07/18/1886 Graudenz - no information
*Home address:* no information
*Law firm address:* Anhalter Str. 4, SW 11
*Additional information:* Attorney and notary; after the National Socialist seizure of power in 1933 he was readmitted as an attorney and notary; his license as a notary was revoked in 1935; he was disbarred on 03/15/1937. He emigrated to Haifa, Palestine.
*Sources:* *li; LAB, Liste 15.10.33; DJ 36, S. 314; Liste 36; BArch, R 3001 PAK

**Grossmann, Edgar Dr.**
03/29/1887 Strasburg, West Prussia - November 1974
*Home address:* Meinekestr. 9
*Law firm address:* Rathenower Str. 3, NW 40
*Additional information:* Attorney and notary; after the National Socialist seizure of power he was made subject to an occupational ban in early 1933. He emigrated to Great Britain in August 1939; he later became an American citizen and changed his name to Edgar
*Sources:* TK 33; Br.B. 32; Liste d. nichtzugel. RA, 25.4.33; JMBl. 33, S. 220/1; BArch, R 3001 PAK; BG; SSDI

**Grossmann, Hans Sigismund Dr.**
08/26/1902 Berlin - 11/13/1974 New York
*Home address:* Budapester Str. 47, at Wallfisch, W 30
*Law firm address:* Kaiser-Wilhelm-Str. 46, C 2

*Additional information:* After the National Socialist seizure of power he was made subject to an occupational ban in July 1933. He emigrated to Teheran; during the Second World War he was in a British internment camp in Himalaya from 1941-1945, subsequently he had to remain in India until 1947; he went to New York, USA, in 1947, in 1952 he became an American citizen; there he worked as an attorney specializing in reparation affairs.
*Sources:* Adr.B. 33; TK 33; JMBl. 28.7.33; BG; Ausk. der Tochter Atina Grossmann

**Grün, Alfred Dr.**
11/20/1882 Stettin - before 1953
*Home address:* Wielandstr. 18, Charlottenburg
*Law firm address:* Wielandstr. 18, Charlottenburg
*Additional information:* Attorney and notary; after the National Socialist seizure of power in 1933 he was re-admitted; his license as a notary was revoked in 1935; he worked as an attorney until the general occupational ban in 1938. His wife Else was regarded as "Aryan." He survived and lived in Charlottenburg after liberation.
*Sources:* *li; LAB, Liste 15.10.33; DJ 36, S. 314; Liste 36; BArch, R 3001 PAK, PA; Verz. zugel. Anw. 45; BG

**Grün, Benno**
02/02/1879 - 01/06/1938
*Home address:* Boothstr. 27, Lichterfelde
*Law firm address:* Belle-Alliance-Str. 106, SW 61
*Additional information:* Attorney at the KG and notary; after the National Socialist seizure of power in 1933 he was readmitted as an attorney and notary; his license as a notary was revoked in 1935; he worked as an attorney until his death in 1938; he died in 1938 at the age of 58.
*Sources:* *li; LAB, Liste 15.10.33; DJ 36, S. 314; Liste 36; BArch, R 3001 PAK; Mitt. der Reichs-Rechtsanwaltskammer 1938; BG

**Gruenbaum, Hans Dr.**
03/16/1903 Berlin - 01/08/1992 Israel
*Home address:* Dahlmannstr. 28, Charlottenburg
*Law firm address:* Kurfürstendamm 202, W 15
*Additional information:* Since 1930 he was admitted as an attorney at the KG, he worked in partnership with Dr. Hannes. After the National Socialist seizure of power he was made subject to an occupational ban on 06/09/1933. His father, Judicial Councillor Martin Simon Gruenbaum, was also an attorney in Berlin.
Hans was a Zionist and emigrated together with his brother Ernst to Palestine; his bride followed him there from Berlin. They cultivated a small farm in the middle of the desert with difficulty, surrounded by Arab neighbors, growing vegetables and fruit, keeping chickens and goats. For a long time they were dependent on support from Germany, however, that ceased when the situation for Jews in Germany became worse. The couple had two children.
His parents died in Theresienstadt, his mother-in-law in Litzmannstadt/Lodz. In 1954 he went to Munich for the URO, later to London. In 1970 he returned to Israel, where he became director of the URO. His daughter Naomi Blumenthal later became a member of the Knesset for Likud.
*Sources:* BArch, R 3001 PAK, PA ; BG; Korr. I. Sholeq; Bericht Gertrud Gruenbaum, geb. Dobriner

**Gruenbaum, Martin Simon, Judicial Councillor**
06/13/1864 Riesenburg - 10/26/1942 Theresienstadt
*Home address:* Dahlmannstr. 26, Charlottenburg
*Law firm address:* An der Spandauer Brücke 9
*Additional information:* Attorney and notary; after the National Socialist seizure of power in 1933 his license as a notary was revoked; later he was also disbarred and his law firm was dissolved. His son Hans was made subject to an occupational ban and decided to go to Palestine together with his brother Ernst. For Simon this was no way out, he visited his sons in their new home in 1936

and 1939, but always returned to Germany. He believed that older Jews would be left alone. However, the situation worsened, when food was rationed, their housekeeper of many years helped energetically. Until their transport she took care of the couple. On 09/08/1942 Simon signed a declaration of property; he went to the collection point Große Hamburger Str. 26. On 09/10/1942 he was transported to Theresienstadt and died a few weeks later; his wife also died in Theresienstadt.
*Sources:* Br.B. 32; TK 33; JMBl. 33, S. 208; Pr.J. 33, S. 532; BArch, R 3001, PA (G., Hans); BG; ThG; GB II; Ausk. Ilana Soreq

**Grünberg, Adolf, Judicial Councillor**
01/20/1869 Strzalkowo - no information
*Home address:* Bismarckstr. 97-98, Charlottenburg
*Law firm address:* Rankestr. 3, W 50
*Additional information:* Attorney and notary; after the National Socialist seizure of power he was readmitted in 1933; his license as a notary was revoked in 1935; he worked as an attorney until the general occupational ban in 1938. He emigrated to Montevideo, Uruguay, on 09/12/1940.
*Sources:* *li; LAB, Liste 15.10.33; DJ 36, S. 314; BArch, R 3001 PAK; Liste 36; MRRAK; BG

**Grünberg, Alfred Dr.**
12/07/1903 Hindenburg - no information
*Home address:* no information
*Law firm address:* Viktoriastr. 28, W 10
*Additional information:* After the National Socialist seizure of power he was made subject to an occupational ban in early 1933.
*Sources:* Liste d. nichtzugel. RA, 25.4.33; Pr.J. 33, S. 565; BArch, R 3001 PAK

**Grünberg, Hans Dr.**
08/25/1892 Magdeburg - no information
*Home address:* no information
*Law firm address:* Kurfürstendamm 177, W 15
*Additional information:* He had fought in the First World War; attorney (since 1924) and notary (since 1930); after the National Socialist seizure of power in 1933 he was, however, not recognized as a "frontline fighter." The admission was withdrawn in the course of the merging of the Berlin district courts.
*Sources:* Adr.B. 32; Liste d. nichtzugel. RA, 25.4.33; BArch, R 3001 PAK, PA

**Grünberg, Leopold Dr., Judicial Councillor**
03/30/1864 Bötzow - transportation 1942
*Home address:* Trautenaustr. 16, Wilmersdorf
*Law firm address:* Dircksenstr. 26/27, C 25
*Additional information:* Attorney and notary; after the National Socialist seizure of power in 1933 his license as a notary was revoked; he was readmitted as an attorney until the general occupational ban in 1938. Transportation on 08/12/1942 to Theresienstadt, from there he was transported on 09/26/1942 to Treblinka.
*Sources:* *li; LAB, Liste 15.10.33; JMBl. 33, S. 208; BArch, R 3001 PAK; BG; GB II

**Grüneberg, Curt Dr.**
12/24/1895 Berlin - no information
*Home address:* no information
*Law firm address:* Meinekestr. 8, W 15
*Additional information:* Attorney and notary, at the same time legal counsel of Allgemeine Fleischer-Zeitung AG. in Berlin. After the National Socialist seizure of power he was readmitted; in 1935 his license as a notary was revoked; he was still working as an attorney in 1936. He emigrated to the USA; in 1939 he applied for a scholarship from American Committee, which was presumably rejected.
*Sources:* *li; DJ 36, S. 314; Liste 36; BArch, R 3001 PAK; NY Publ. (Lib. Am. Com.), Grüneberg

**Grüneberg, Kurt Dr.**
12/28/1887 Cologne-Ehrenfeld - February 1985 New York
*Home address:* Altonaer Str. 2, NW 87
*Law firm address:* Siegmundshof 1, NW 87
*Additional information:* Attorney, on 01/23/1933 RA, on 01/23/1933 he was also appointed as notary; after the National Socialist seizure of power in 1933 he was readmitted; his license as a notary was revoked in 1935; on 05/02/1938 he was disbarred as an attorney. He emigrated to New York, USA, where he died in 1985 with the name of Kurt Grune.
*Sources:* *li; LAB, Liste 15.10.33; DJ 36, S. 314; BArch, R 3001 PAK; SSDI; BG

**Grünstein, Charlotte**
03/23/1905 Berlin - no information
*Home address:* no information
*Law firm address:* Prager Platz 6, Wilmersdorf

*Additional information:* Was admitted in May 1932 as an attorney; after the National Socialist seizure of power he was made subject to an occupational ban on 06/12/1933.
*Sources:* Liste d. nichtzugel. RA, 25.4.33; JMBl. 21.8.33, S. 266; BArch, R 3001 PAK, PA

**Gumpel, Harry**
01/06/1888 Berlin - 11/25/1941 Kowno
*Home address:* Xantener Str. 15 a
*Law firm address:* Kurfürstendamm 225, W 15
*Additional information:* Attorney and notary; after the National Socialist seizure of power in 1933 he was readmitted; his license as a notary was revoked in 1935; he was still working as an attorney until the general occupational ban in 1938. Transportation on 11/17/1941 to Kowno, where he was murdered.
*Sources:* *li; LAB, Liste 15.10.33; DJ 36, S. 314; Liste 36; BArch, R 3001 PAK; MRRAK; BG; BdE; GB II

**Gumpert, Franz Dr.**
06/29/1907 Berlin-Charlottenburg - no information
*Home address:* Kleiststr. 42, at Neuländer, W 62
*Law firm address:* no information
*Additional information:* He had only been admitted to the Bar on 03/17/1933. He was disbarred in the spring of 1933. He emigrated in 1933 to British India.
*Sources:* Liste d. nichtzugel. RA, 25.4.33; BArch, R 3001 PAK, PA; BG

**Gumpert, Hans Dr.**
07/10/1890 Berlin - 1962
*Home address:* Mommsenstr. 56, Charlottenburg
*Law firm address:* Mommsenstr. 56, Charlottenburg
*Additional information:* Attorney and notary; he practiced law from his apartment of 285 m² in Charlottenburg, where his parents had lived before him. His wife Kitty, who died in 1998 at the age of 91, was regarded as "Aryan," the marriage was regarded as privileged, since they had a child (born in ca. 1938). After the National Socialist seizure of power in 1933 he was readmitted. His license as a notary was revoked in 1935. After the general occupational ban for Jewish attorneys in 1938

he worked as a "consultant." Faced with the threat, the couple hid in Staaken for some time, then returned to the apartment. Ms. Gumpert knew her way around Berlin and knew where she could find food for the family; the neighborhood was aware of the troubled situation. He survived and practiced after the liberation, in his apartment as before, once again as attorney and notary until his death in 1962.
*Sources:* *li; LAB, Liste 15.10.33; DJ 36, . 314; MRRAK; BG; Ausk. E. Proskauer; Ausk. Müller

**Gundermann, Alfons**
09/16/1904 - no information
*Home address:* no information
*Law firm address:* Oranienstr. 10/11, SO 36
*Additional information:* After the National Socialist seizure of power he was made subject to an occupational ban on 06/13/1933.
*Sources:* Liste d. nichtzugel. RA, 25.4.33; BArch, R 3001 PAK, PA

**Gutfeld, Walter Dr.**
02/13/1897 Berlin - no information
*Home address:* no information
*Law firm address:* Viktoria-Luise-Platz 1, W 30
*Additional information:* Attorney at the KG; after the National Socialist seizure of power he was made subject to an occupational ban on 08/24/1933.
*Sources:* Liste d. nichtzugel. RA, 25.4.33 (Nachtrag); BArch, R 3001 PAK

**Gutmann, Konrad Dr.**
07/25/1880 Berlin - December 1951
*Home address:* Stübbenstr. 1, Schöneberg
*Law firm address:* Bayerischer Platz 110, Schönberg
*Additional information:* Attorney and notary; after the National Socialist seizure of power in 1933 he was readmitted; his license as a notary was revoked in 1935; he was disbarred and made subject to an occupational ban in 1938; he emigrated to New York, USA, on 09/28/1938.
*Sources:* *li; LAB, Liste 15.10.33; BArch, R 3001 PAK; Liste 36; BG

**Guttmann, Alexander Dr.**
12/19/1894 Mannheim - no information
*Home address:* Kurfürstendamm 22, W 15
*Law firm address:* Kurfürstendamm 22, W 15

*Additional information:* Attorney at the KG and notary; after the National Socialist seizure of power in 1933 he was readmitted; his license as a notary was revoked in 1935. He became entangled in legal proceedings due to so-called "racial defilement" (Rassenschande) which refers to sexual relations between "non-Aryans" and "Aryans." He was disbarred within the framework of the general occupational ban in 1938. He emigrated to Great Britain; after 1945 he returned to Germany as an employee of the URO.
*Sources:* *li; LAB, Liste 15.10.33; DJ 36, S. 314; BArch, R 3001 PAK; MRRAK; BG; Ausk. Wolff, Werner, 22.9.1999

**Guttmann, Hans**
04/17/1904 Breslau - no information
*Home address:* no information
*Law firm address:* Alexanderstr. 71, C 25
*Additional information:* After the National Socialist seizure of power he was made subject to an occupational ban on 06/23/1933. His personal file contains a note that he did not submit an unconditional declaration of loyalty as requested; he had stated in his application for readmittance that he recognized the "provisions of the Reich law as binding" (04/10/1933).
*Sources:* Liste d. nichtzugel. RA, 25.4.33; JMBl. 33, S. 209; BArch, R 3001 PAK, PA

**Guttmann, Julius, Judicial Councillor**
02/05/1855 - 01/01/1936 Berlin
*Home address:* Kurfürstendamm 200, Wilmersdorf
*Law firm address:* Klosterstr. 43, C 2
*Additional information:* Attorney and notary; after the National Socialist seizure of power in 1933 he was readmitted. His license as a notary was revoked in 1935. He died in 1936 in Berlin at the age of 81, he was buried at Weißensee.
*Sources:* *li; LAB, Liste 15.10.33; DJ 36, S. 210; BArch, R 3001 PAK; BG

**Guttmann, Leonhard, Judicial Councillor**
05/02/1869 Brieg - 09/23/1942 Theresienstadt
*Home address:* Wallstr. 21-22, C 2
*Law firm address:* Wallstr. 21-22, C 2
*Additional information:* Attorney and notary; after the National Socialist seizure of power in 1933 his license as a notary was revoked, he was readmitted as attorney, he

worked until the general occupational ban in 1938. On 08/31/1942 he was transported to Theresienstadt, where he died a few weeks later.
*Sources:* *li; LAB, Liste 15.10.33; JMBl. 33, S. 208; Liste 36; BArch, R 3001 PAK; BG; ThG; GB II

**Guttmann, Oskar**
06/19/1885 Hildesheim - transportation 1943
*Home address:* Speyerer Str. 10, W 30
*Law firm address:* Motzstr. 62, W 30
*Additional information:* Attorney at the KG and notary; after the National Socialist seizure of power in 1933 he was readmitted; his license as a notary was revoked in 1935; he worked as an attorney until the general occupational ban in 1938. Later collecting guardian at the RV, District Office Berlin, Oranienburger Str. 31. Date of declaration of property: 05/09/1943; transportation on 05/19/1943 to Theresienstadt, from there he was transported on 10/19/1944 to Auschwitz.
*Sources:* *li; LAB, Liste 15.10.33; DJ 36, S. 314; Liste 36; BArch, R 3001 PAK; MRRAK; GB II; Göpp., S. 245

**Guttmann, Wilhelm Dr.**
09/25/1903 Gleiwitz - no information
*Home address:* no information
*Law firm address:* Berliner Str. 146, Charlottenburg
*Additional information:* Attorney at the KG; after the National Socialist seizure of power he was made subject to an occupational ban in June 1933.
*Sources:* Liste d. nichtzugel. RA, 25.4.33; JMBl. 33, S. 203; BArch, R 3001 PAK

**Guttsmann, Max Dr., Judicial Councillor**
06/23/1858 Rybnik - 12/27/1941
*Home address:* Droysenstr. 7, Charlottenburg
*Law firm address:* Friedrichstr. 206
*Additional information:* Attorney and notary; after the National Socialist seizure of power he was made subject to an occupational ban in 1933. He died in 1941 at the age of 83, he was buried at Weißensee.
*Sources:* TK 33; JMBl. 33, 2.6.33; BArch, R 3001 PAK; BG

# H

**Haase, Berthold Dr.**
04/30/1874 - 01/22/1938 Meranoo
*Home address:* no information
*Law firm address:* Innsbrucker Str. 5
Attorney at the KG and notary; he intensively
dealt with the "Eastern Jewish question" in
the 1920s (CV Zeitung, 1923); as a jurist he
specialized in international law. After the
National Socialist seizure of power in 1933
his license as a notary was revoked; in 1935,
after the "Nuremberg laws" were released,
he dissolved his practice and applied to be
disbarred. "Thus, during my 62nd year,
my career came to an end, during which I
dedicated myself with seriousness and joy to the
care of the law, and in which I had used my best
powers for the preservation and strengthening
of German culture" (LBI). A little later his
daughter emigrated to Palestine with his
granddaughter. He died in 1938 at the age of 65
in Meranoo.
*Sources:* *li; LAB, Liste 15.10.33; BArch,
R 3001 PAK; LBI NY, Memoirs: Mein Leben.
Was in ihm geschah und wie ich es erlebte
[Memoirs: My life. What happened during it
and how I experienced it] 1935, unpublished
manuscript; BG

**Haase, Ernst-Friedrich Dr.**
10/27/1904 Rybnik - no information
*Home address:* no information
*Law firm address:* Bayreuther Str. 41, W 62
*Additional information:* After the National
Socialist seizure of power he was readmitted;
he worked until April 1936 as an attorney. In
1936 he emigrated to Chile, he presumably
returned to Germany.
*Sources:* *li; LAB, Liste 15.10.33; Liste 36;
BArch, R 3001 PAK; BG

**Haberland, Kurt Dr.**
10/17/1896 Berlin - 06/05/1942 Mauthausen
*Home address:* Nördlinger Str. 3, Schöneberg
*Law firm address:* Charlottenstr. 60, W 8
*Additional information:* Attorney at the KG;
after the National Socialist seizure of power
he was readmitted; he worked as an attorney
until the general occupational ban in 1938.
Transportation; died 1942 in Mauthausen.
In the 1950s litigation concerning the valuable
estate of Kurt Haberland took place on several
judicial levels. The litigation was undertaken

between his former fiancée, whom he had not
been able to marry because of the racist laws
and the family members of the deceased. Finally,
his fiancée was awarded the legacy because she
was recognized as his potential spouse.
*Sources:* *li; LAB, Liste 15.10.33; Liste 36;
BArch, R 3001 PAK; MRRAK; BG; GB II;
Ausk. Sabine Meyer, Lüne-burg; Kopie des
Urteils v. 26.6.1956

**Hadra, Arthur, Judicial Councillor**
No information - 1938
*Home address:* no information
*Law firm address:* Genthiner Str. 22, W 35
*Additional information:* Attorney and notary;
after the National Socialist seizure of power
in 1933 his license as a notary was revoked;
he was readmitted as an attorney; presumably
he was working as an attorney until his death
in 1938.
*Sources:* TK 33; JMBl. 33, S. 208; *li; LAB,
Liste 15.10.33; Liste 36; BArch, R 3001 PAK

**Hadra, Herbert**
02/14/1903 Groß-Strehlitz - April 1979
*Home address:* No information
*Law firm address:* Schönhauser Allee 126, N 58
*Additional information:* After the National
Socialist seizure of power he was made subject
to an occupational ban on 06/10/1933. He
emigrated to the USA, where he last lived in
Queens, New York.
*Sources:* TK 33; Liste d. nichtzugel.RA.
25.4.33; JMBl. 33, S. 234; BArch, R 3001
PAK; SSDI

**Haendel, Richard Dr.**
09/11/1883 Landsberg/Warthe - no
information
*Home address:* no information
*Law firm address:* Alexanderplatz 1, C 25
*Additional information:* Attorney and notary;
after the National Socialist seizure of power in
1933 his license as a notary was revoked, He
was readmitted as an attorney upon request;
however, he was disbarred during the same
year.
*Sources:* TK 33; JMBl. 33, S. 208; Pr.J.33, S.
868; *li; BArch, R 3001 PAK

**Hagelberg, Ernst Dr.**
07/12/1876 Berlin - transportation 1942
*Home address:* Kaiserdamm 72,
Charlottenburg

*Law firm address:* Joachimsthaler Str. 43/44, Charlottenburg 2
*Additional information:* Attorney and notary, specializing in land register and notary law; after the National Socialist seizure of power his license as a notary was revoked, he was readmitted as an attorney; he worked up to the general occupational ban in 1938. Transportation on 10/19/1942 to Riga.
*Sources:* TK 33; JMBl. 33, S. 208; LAB, Liste 15.10.33; *li; Liste 36; BArch, R 3001 PAK; MRRAK; BG; BdE; GB II

**Hahn, Franz, Judicial Councillor**
12/15/1869 Liegnitz - no information
*Home address:* Grolmanstr. 36, Charlottenburg
*Law firm address:* Grolmanstr. 36, Charlottenburg
*Additional information:* Attorney and notary; after the National Socialist seizure of power in 1933 his license as a notary was revoked, he was readmitted as an attorney; he worked as an attorney until the general occupational ban in 1938. He emigrated to South Africa on 05/17/1939.
*Sources:* TK 33; JMBl. 33, S. 208; *li; LAB, Liste 15.10.33; BArch, R 3001 PAK; MRRAK; BG

**Halpert, Dodo Hans Dr.**
08/22/1863 Quednau - 1938 Berlin
*Home address:* Güntzelstr. 61, Wilmersdorf
*Law firm address:* Neue Bayreutherstr. 7, W 30
*Additional information:* Attorney and notary, he was also active in the "Rote Hilfe" (Red Aid) setting; after the National Socialist seizure of power in 1933 he was "dismissed as a notary upon request," he was readmitted as an attorney; he worked until the general occupational ban in 1938; ca. the beginning of 1938 he committed suicide.
*Sources:* JMBl. 33, S. 252; *li; LAB, Liste 15.10.33; Liste 36; BArch, R 3001 PAK; BG; Schneider, Schwarz, Schwarz; Ausk. Y. Arndt, Korr. Claus Arndt

**Hamburger, Adolf Dr.**
09/18/1887 Schwagrau - 10/17/1962 New York
*Home address:* Uhlandstr. 27, Charlottenburg
*Law firm address:* Uhlandstr. 27, Charlottenburg
*Additional information:* After his legal studies he completed pharmaceutical studies; he became a specialist in the field of pharmacy law with this combination of specialist knowledge and also worked as legal counsel of the German Association of Pharmacists and corporate counsel of the "Credit Union of German Pharmacists;" he supported the SPD. After the National Socialist seizure of power he was made subject to an occupational ban as attorney and notary in early 1933; he emigrated to New York, USA, in 1934; he renewed legal studies of six semesters at St. John's University; as from 1939 he established himself as an attorney in New York; he was in great demand as a German-American attorney; he was a legal employee of the German-speaking "New Yorker Volkszeitung [New York News]" and also later a consultant of the German General Consulate in New York; after 1949 he was admitted at the LG Wiesbaden, especially in reparation affairs. He died in October 1962 from heart failure.
*Sources:* Br.B. 32; Liste d. nichtzugel. RA, 25.4.33; JMBl. 33, S. 282; BG; Pharmazeutische Zeitung 107 (1962), S. 1560 (Nachruf); Leimkugel, Frank: Wege jüdischer Apotheker, 2. Aufl. 1991, S. 30, 107f., 135

**Hamburger, Alfred Dr.**
02/10/1900 Berlin - November 1984
*Home address:* no information
*Law firm address:* Stresemannstr. 11
*Additional information:* Attorney at the KG; after the National Socialist seizure of power he was made subject to an occupational ban on 06/26/1933, he was previously admitted to the KG; he emigrated to the USA; there he applied for a scholarship in 1940; he last lived in New York; he died in 1984 at the age of 84.
*Sources:* Br.B. 32; Liste d. nichtzugel. RA, 25.4.33; JMBl. 33, S. 209; BArch, R 3001 PAK; NY Publ. Lib. (Am.Com.) Hamburger; SSDI (Fred H.)

**Hamburger, Fritz Dr.**
02/07/1883 Kattowitz - no information
*Home address:* Viktoria-Luise-Platz 10, Schöneberg
*Law firm address:* Landshuter Str. 2, Schöneberg
*Additional information:* After the National Socialist seizure of power he was made subject to an occupational ban in early 1933. He emigrated to Copenhagen, Denmark, on 02/15/1934.
*Sources:* Br.B. 32; Liste d. nichtzugel. RA,

25.4.33; JMBl. 21.8.33, S. 267; BArch, R
3001 PAK; BG

**Hamburger, Georg Dr.**
04/10/1891 Berlin -
08/03/1944 Theresienstadt
*Home address:*
Eisenzahnstr. 6, Halensee
*Law firm address:*
Kronenstr. 64/65, W 8
*Additional information:*
He was baptized at the age of five; 1908 he
completed his school leaving examination;
1912 he took his first state examination in law;
he fought in the First World War (1915-18),
which interrupted his clerkship; 1919 he took
his second state examination in law. Attorney
(since 1919) and notary (since 1927); he still
was a member of the board of the RAK in
1932. After the National Socialist seizure of
power he was regarded as a Jew; after 1933
he was readmitted as an attorney, because he
fell under the exception made for "frontline
fighters." Amongst others, he represented
relatives of the members of the Wertheim
department store family. In 1935 his license
as a notary was revoked. After the general
occupational ban for attorneys in 1938 he
was readmitted as a "consultant." He was a
board member of the Reich Association of
Non-Aryan Christians and later a member
of the Paulus Bund; he was a member of the
Confessing Church, after the beginning of
the war he also helped the congregation's
representatives; he corresponded with the
theologian Helmut Gollwitzer; he concerned
himself with theological writings, read the
Bible in Hebrew and Greek, he exchanged
views within the Dogmatic Working Group;
he helped to smuggle out of the country Karl
Barth's "Church Dogmatics," v. II/2, with
a reinterpretation of individual chapters
of the letter from the Romans. The threat
to his person grew. Attempts to flee were
unsuccessful. On 09/29/1941 he told Gollwitzer
of his bitterness: ". . . [since] I don't have
relatives or people close to me to share this with
me, I am really left completely alone here . . ."
In 1942, in view of the intensified
"evacuations," the number of suicides
increased. He sought Gollwitzer's advice, as
to whether one could escape transportation
"to the East" by means of suicide and he
deemed exceptions justified. Gollwitzer tried

to support him theologically and generally
rejected this step. In October 1942 he escaped
the first transportation. On June 21, 1943,
he signed his declaration of property, which
included all of his remaining property.
Subsequently he went to the collection point
Große Hamburger Str. 26 in Berlin-Mitte.
He was transported to Theresienstadt on
06/30/1943. Arthur Goldschmidt had already
set up a Protestant church there. He held Bible
studies here, he was not allowed to preach,
since he was not ordained. Malnutrition
had so weakened him that he had to cancel
a session. Arthur Kaufmann gave him
Communion: "The surrender of this already
almost complete man was shattering and
without complaint, like a prayer, he whispered
that God had forsaken him." At the beginning
of August 1944 he died of tuberculosis.
*Sources:* *li; LAB, Liste 15.10.33; DJ 36,
S. 314; Liste d. Kons., 15.4.39; BLHA,
OFP-Akte; Naatz-Album; BG; ThG; GB II;
Biogramm zu Georg Hamburger [Biography
on Georg Hamburger] by Hartmut Ludwig,
in: "Ihr Ende schaut an..." Evangelische
Märtyrer des 20. Jahrhunderts [Protestant
martyrs of the 20th century] edited by Harald
Schultze/Andreas Kurschat, Leipzig 2006

**Hamburger, Karl Wilhelm, Judicial
Councillor**
05/14/1866 Görlitz - 01/07/1941
*Home address:* Nymphenburger Str. 1,
Schöneberg
*Law firm address:* Stresemannstr. 11, SW 11
*Additional information:* Attorney and
notary; after the National Socialist seizure
of power in 1933 his license as a notary was
revoked; he was still working as an attorney
until 1936; he died in 1941 at the age of 74.
*Sources:* *li; JMBl. 33, S. 208; LAB, Liste
15.10.33; Liste 36; BArch, R 3001 PAK; BG

**Hamburger, Leopold Dr.**
02/01/1900 Berlin - no information
*Home address:* no information
*Law firm address:* Blücherplatz 2, SW 61
*Additional information:* After the National
Socialist seizure of power he was made subject
to an occupational ban in early 1933. He
emigrated in 1936 to Palestine.
*Sources:* Br.B. 32; Liste d. nichtzugel. RA,
25.4.33; JMBl. 21.8.33, S. 267; BArch, R
3001 PAK; BG

**Hamburger, Sally**
06/27/1882 Königshütte - transportation 1942
*Home address:* Stolzenfelsstr. 2, Karlshorst
*Law firm address:* Müllerstr. 177, N 65
*Additional information:* Attorney and
notary; after the National Socialist seizure of
power in 1933 he was readmitted; license as
a notary was revoked in 1935; he still worked
as an attorney until the general occupational
ban in 1938. Transportation on 03/28/1942
to Piaski.
*Sources:* *li; LAB, Liste 15.10.33; DJ 36, S.
314; Liste 36; MRRAK; BArch, R 3001 PAK;
BG; GB II

**Hamburger, Werner**
03/20/1901 Küstrin - no information
*Home address:* no information
*Law firm address:* Kurfürstendamm 216, W 15
*Additional information:* After the National
Socialist seizure of power he was made subject
to an occupational ban on 05/20/1933.
*Sources:* Liste d. nichtzugel. RA, 25.4.33
(Nachtrag); JMBl. 33, S. 209; BArch, R 3001
PAK, PA

**Hammer, Hans Hermann Dr.**
11/02/1895 Berlin - transportation 1942
*Home address:* no information
*Law firm address:* Mauerstr. 80, W 8
*Additional information:* After the National
Socialist seizure of power he was made subject
to an occupational ban on 05/31/1933. He
emigrated to France. There his pursuers
caught up with him; on 09/07/1942 he was
transported from Drancy to Auschwitz.
*Sources:* Liste d. nichtzugl. RA., 25.4.33;
JMBl. 33, S. 209; BArch, R 3001 PAK, PA;
BG; GB II

**Hammerschlag, Heinz Erich Dr.**
07/09/1902 - no information
*Home address:* Fasanenstr. 41 (1931)
*Law firm address:* Kronenstr. 3, W 8
*Additional information:* After the National
Socialist seizure of power he was made subject
to an occupational ban in June 1933.
*Sources:* Br.B. 32; Liste d. nichtzugel. RA,
25.4.33; JMBl. 33, S. 209; BArch, R 3001 PAK

**Hammerschmidt, Fritz**
11/21/1894 Cottbus - transportation 1944
*Home address:* Babelsberger Str. 52/
Prinzregentenstr. 92, Wilmersdorf

*Law firm address:* Kantstr. 19, Charlottenburg
*Additional information:* Attorney at the KG;
he ran a law firm together with his brother
Walter. After the National Socialist seizure
of power in 1933 he was made subject to
an occupational ban, subsequently he was
readmitted and worked as an attorney until
the general occupational ban in 1938. Later he
worked as a forced laborer; date of declaration
of property: 02/29/1944; collection point
Schulstr. 78; transportation on 03/09/1944 to
Auschwitz. His wife, who had been transported
at the same time, survived Auschwitz, went to
the Ravensbrück concentration camp and was
liberated by the allied troops.
*Sources:* Adr.B. 32; Br.B. 32; Liste d.
nichtzugel. RA, 25.4.33; *li; LAB, Liste
15.10.33; Liste 36; MRRAK; BArch, R 3001
PAK; BG; GB II; Hammerschmidt, Wolfgang:
Spurensuche. Zur Geschichte der jüdischen
Familie Hammerschmidt, Cottbus, Gießen
1996

**Hammerschmidt, Walter**
05/14/1900 Cottbus - December 1938
*Home address:* no information
*Law firm address:* Kantstr. 19,
Charlottenburg
*Additional information:* Walter practiced
law together with his brother Fritz at the
same law firm. After the National Socialist
seizure of power he was made subject to an
occupational ban in early 1933. For the years
up to 1938 no information is available. After
the Night of Broken Glass in November 1938
he was arrested and sent to Sachsenhausen
concentration camp. Immediately after his
release, he died of sepsis in December 1938.
When Prof. Sauerbruch wanted to carry out
a post mortem examination on the corpse, it
was seized by the Gestapo.
Adr.B. 32; Liste d. nichtzugel. RA 25.4.33;
*Sources:* JMBl. 33, S. 253; BArch, R 3001
PAK; Göpp., S. 246; Hammerschmidt,
Wolfgang: Spurensuche. Zur Geschichte der
jüdi-schen Familie Hammerschmidt, Cottbus,
Gießen 1996

**Hammerstein, Julius Dr.**
12/10/1879 Mohrungen - transportation 1943
*Home address:* Romberger Str. 17, NO 18
*Law firm address:* Frankfurter Str. 142, O 17
*Additional information:* Attorney and
notary; after the National Socialist seizure

of power his license as a notary was revoked in 1933; he worked as an attorney until the general occupational ban in 1938. Transportation on 03/06/1943 to Auschwitz.
*Sources:* JMBl. 33, S. 220; *li; LAB, Liste 15.10.33; Liste 36; BArch, R 3001 PAK; MRRAK; BG; GB II

**Hanff, Paul**
11/30/1891 Berlin - 11/25/1941 Kowno
*Home address:* no information
*Law firm address:* Kurfürstendamm 197/98, W 15
*Additional information:* Attorney and notary; after the National Socialist seizure of power in 1933 he was readmitted; his license as a notary was revoked in 1935; he still worked as an attorney until the general occupational ban in 1938. He was transported to Kowno on 11/17/1941 and was murdered there shortly thereafter.
*Sources:* Adr.B. 32; Br.B. 32; *li; LAB, Liste 15.10.33; DJ 36, S. 314; Liste 36; MRRAK; BArch, R 3001 PAK; BG; BdE; GB II

**Hannes, Martin Dr.**
10/13/1881 Görlitz - no information
*Home address:* Kurfürstendamm 202, W 15
*Law firm address:* Kurfürstendamm 202, W 15
*Additional information:* Attorney and notary; after the National Socialist seizure of power in 1933 he was readmitted; his license as a notary was revoked in 1935; he worked as an attorney until the general occupational ban in 1938. He emigrated to Sydney, Australia, on 07/01/1939.
*li; LAB, Liste 15.10.33; DJ 36, S. 314; Liste 36; MRRAK; BArch, R 3001 PAK; BG

**Hartstein, Willy Dr.**
01/17/1901 Berlin - no information
*Home address:* no information
*Law firm address:* Klosterstr. 43, C 2
*Additional information:* After the National Socialist seizure of power he was made subject to an occupational ban in early 1933. He emigrated to Palestine on 02/01/1939, later returned to Berlin.
*Sources:* Br.B. 32; Liste der nichtzugel. RA, 25.4.33; JMBl. 33, S. 209; BArch, R 3001 PAK; BG

**Hartwich, Waldemar, Judicial Councillor**
12/16/1854 Letschin - 10/05/1941 Berlin

*Home address:* Königsallee 16 a bei Unger, Grunewald
*Law firm address:* Nachodstr. 26, W 50
*Additional information:* After the National Socialist seizure of power he was readmitted, he still worked as an attorney until 03/28/1938. He died in 1941 at the retirement home of the Jewish Synagogue on Iranische Str.
*Sources:* Br.B. 32; *li; LAB, Liste 15.10.33; Liste 36; BArch, R 3001 PAK; BG

**Harz, Moses Dr.**
09/08/1905 Hadworna (East Galicia) - no information
*Home address:* no information
*Law firm address:* Helmstedter Str. 26, Wilmersdorf
*Additional information:* After the National Socialist seizure of power he was made subject to an occupational ban on 06/12/1933.
*Sources:* Liste d. nichtzugel. RA, 25.4.33; JMBl. 33, S. 209; BArch, R 3001 PAK, PA

**Hauptmann, Kurt Dr.**
09/21/1892 Berlin - no information
*Home address:* no information
*Law firm address:* Nollendorfstr. 11/12, W 30
After the National Socialist seizure of power he was made subject to an occupational ban in early 1933.
*Sources:* Adr.B. 32; Jüd.Adr.B.; Liste d. nichtzugel. RA, 25.4.33; JMBl. 33, S. 253; BArch, R 3001 PAK

**Hausen, Willy Dr.**
09/11/1888 Zeitz - no information
*Home address:* Kaiserallee 212, W 15
*Law firm address:* Kaiserallee 214/215, W 15
*Additional information:* Attorney at the KG and notary; after the National Socialist seizure of power he was made subject to an occupational ban in April 1933; his license as a notary was revoked and he was disbarred on 06/09/1933.
*Sources:* Jüd.Adr.B.; Br.B. 32; Liste d. nichtzugel. RA, 25.4.33; BArch, R 3001 PAK

**Haußmann, Fritz Dr.**
11/10/1885 Ratibor - no information
*Home address:* no information
*Law firm address:* Lietzenburger Str. 30
*Additional information:* He fought in the First World War; attorney and notary, he specialized in trade and antitrust law. After the National Socialist seizure of power in 1933 he was

readmitted; in 1935 his license as a notary was revoked, he worked as an attorney until the general occupational ban in 1938.
Sources: *li; LAB, Liste 15.10.33; TK 36; Liste 36; Philo-Lexikon, S. 604; MRRAK; BArch, R 3001 PAK

**Hayn, Julius, Judicial Councillor**
08/24/1870 Kempen - no information
Home address: Kohlisstr. 94, Mahlsdorf-Lichtenberg
Law firm address: Friedrichstr. 192, W 8
Additional information: Attorney and notary; after the National Socialist seizure of power in 1933 his license as a notary was revoked, he worked as an attorney until the general occupational ban in 1938. His wife was regarded as non-Jewish.
Sources: JMBl. 33, S. 208; *li; LAB, Liste 15.10.33; Liste 36; MRRAK; BArch, R 3001 PAK; BG

**Hayn, Louis (Ludwig)**
05/08/1885 Leobschütz - no information
Home address: Falterweg 13, Grunewald
Law firm address: Charlottenstr. 59, W 8
Additional information: Attorney and notary; after the National Socialist seizure of power he was made subject to an occupational ban in early 1933. He emigrated to Merano, Italy, then to Palma de Mallorca in Spain, later he lived in Barcelona.
Sources: Adr.B. 32; Liste d. nichtzugel. RA 25.4.33; JMBl. 33, S. 203; BArch, R 3001 PAK; BG

**Heidenfeld, Joachim Dr.**
02/09/1879 Oppeln - after 1950
Home address: Limonenstr. 25, Lichterfelde and/or Eisenacher Str. 35, Schöneberg
Law firm address: Elßholzstr. 23, W 57
Additional information: Attorney and notary, after the National Socialist seizure of power in 1933 he was readmitted; his license as a notary was revoked in 1935; he was still working as an attorney in 1936. He emigrated to Johannesburg, South Africa.
Sources: Adr.B. 32; LAB, Liste 15.10.33; DJ 36, S. 314; Liste 36; BArch, R 3001 PAK; BG: LAB,OFP-Akten; Ausk. Martin Glass

**Heilborn, Gustav, Judicial Councillor**
No information - 1938
Home address: no information

Law firm address: Albrechtstr. 6, Steglitz
Additional information: Attorney and notary; after the National Socialist seizure of power in 1933 his license as a notary was revoked, he worked as an attorney until 12/24/1937; he died in 1938.
Sources: JMBl. 33, S. 208; *li; LAB, Liste 15.10.33; Liste 36; MRRAK

**Heilborn, Theodor Dr.**
09/08/1883 Kosel - July 1969
Home address: Kottbusser Damm 2, SW 29
Law firm address: Kottbusser Damm 2, SW 29
Additional information: Attorney and notary; after the National Socialist seizure of power his license as a notary was revoked; he presumably worked as an attorney until the general occupational ban in 1938. He emigrated to the USA in May 1940, he died there at the age of 85.
Sources: JMBl. 33, S. 208; *li; LAB, Liste 15.10.33; MRRAK (vermutlich fälschlich: Heilbronn); BArch, R 3001 PAK; SSDI; BG; Ausk. Vera Fassberg

**Heilbronn, Arthur, Judicial Councillor**
09/27/1865 Königsberg - 03/05/1943 Theresienstadt
Home address: Bamberger Str. 37, W 30/ Berchtesgadener Str. 14, Schöneberg
Law firm address: Lindenstr. 81, SW 68
Additional information: Attorney and notary; after the National Socialist seizure of power his license as a notary was revoked in 1933, he worked as an attorney until the general occupational ban in 1938. Thereafter estate curator and executor; date of declaration of property: 08/06/1942; collection point Große Hamburger Str. 26; transportation on 09/02/1942 to Theresienstadt, there he died six months later.
Sources: JMBl. 33, S. 208; *li; LAB, Liste 15.10.33; Liste 36; MRRAK; BArch, R 3001 PAK; BG; ThG; GB II

**Heilbut(h), Ilse Dr.**
04/26/1904 Berlin - no information
Home address: no information
Law firm address: Wassertorstr. 1, S 42
Additional information: After the National Socialist seizure of power he was made subject to an occupational ban on 06/10/1933.
Sources: Liste d. nichtzugel. RA, 25.4.33; JMBl. 33, S. 234; BArch, R 3001 PAK, PA

Heiman(n)sohn, Rudolf
06/07/1904 Berlin - December 1977
*Home address:* no information
*Law firm address:* Frankfurter Allee 87, O 112
*Additional information:* After the National
Socialist seizure of power he was made subject
to an occupational ban on 06/12/1933. He
emigrated to the USA, lived in Queens in New
York, he changed his last name to Heimanson;
he died at the age of 73.
*Sources:* Liste d. nichtzugel. RA, 25.4.33; JMBl.
33, S. 234; BArch, R 3001 PAK, PA; SSDI

Heims, Eduard Dr.
11/28/1884 Berlin - September 1964 California
*Home address:* Mohrenstr. 54/55, W 8
*Law firm address:* Markgrafenstr. 36, W 56
*Additional information:* He was known
as Heymann until 1917. Both parents were
already Protestant. He studied law in Tübingen,
Halle and Berlin; he completed his doctoral
thesis at the Friedrich-Wilhelms-Universität
in Berlin, which was particularly demanding,
with the grade summa cum laude; he worked
scientifically and theoretically in the field of
criminal law, church law and international
law. 1912-14 he was an (assistant) judge in
Berlin; 1914-19 he was a senior civil servant in
the Foreign Trade Department of the German
Foreign Office; 1919-23 he was a staff member
of Walter Simons (amongst others 1920/21
Foreign Secretary) and in the Reich Finance
Administration, as well as legal counsel of the
Reich Association of German Industry; 1923-25
he was admitted as a lawyer at the KG, then
at the LG I-III; 1926-36 at the same time he
was a director general of the Gesellschaft für
Hypothekenberatung (Company for Mortgage
Advice) with headquarters in Berlin and
Baltimore/USA.
After the National Socialist seizure of power he
was made subject to an occupational ban in the
early summer of 1933; 1937 he emigrated to Los
Angeles, USA; he established himself as a farmer
in California, where he died in 1964.
*Sources:* JMBl. 7.7.33; S. 209; Liste nicht
zugel. RA, 25.4.33; BArch, R 3001 PAK, PA;
BG; BHdE Bd. 1, S. 280; SSDI

Heine, Kurt Dr.
02/04/1889 Waren - no information
*Home address:* no information
*Law firm address:* Niebuhrstr. 5,
Charlottenburg

*Additional information:* After the National
Socialist seizure of power he was made subject
to an occupational ban on 06/13/1933.
*Sources:* Liste d. nichtzugel. RA, 25.4.33;
JMBl. 33, S. 209; BArch, R 3001 PAK

Heinitz, Anton Dr.
12/24/1885 Berlin - no information
*Home address:* Salzbrunner Str. 42,
Grunewald
*Law firm address:* Charlottenstr. 55, W 8
*Additional information:* Brother of Günther;
attorney and notary; after the National
Socialist seizure of power he was readmitted;
his license as a notary was revoked in 1935;
he worked as an attorney until the general
occupational ban in 1938. He emigrated
to London, Great Britain, on 09/28/1938.
His mother committed suicide in 1940; his
brother Günther was murdered in Auschwitz
in 1943.
*Sources:* Adr.B. 32; *li; LAB, Liste 15.10.33;
DJ 36, S. 314; Liste 36; MRRAK; BArch, R
3001 PAK; BG; Göpp., S. 247

Heinitz, Günther
01/21/1892 Berlin - transportation 1943
*Home address:* Münchener Str. 37, W 30/
Französische Str. 13-14
*Law firm address:* Charlottenstr. 55, W 8
*Additional information:* Attorney at the KG;
he worked at the the law firm of his father,
Ernst, which he continued with his brother
Anton after his father's death. After the
National Socialist seizure of power in 1933
he was made subject to an occupational ban.
From 1939 he worked at "Büro Grüber," a
Protestant relief organization for "non-Aryan
Christians" (filing department); he was last
subjected to forced labor at Weser-Flugzeugbau
GmbH (from 03/01/1941); on 02/02/1943 he
was transported to Auschwitz. His mother
committed suicide in February 1940.
*Sources:* Adr.B. 32; TK 33; Liste d.
nichtzugel. RA, 25.4.33; BArch, R 3001 PAK;
BG; GB II; Göpp., S. 247

Hennig, Martin Dr.
02/23/1898 Neumark - no information
*Home address:* Steinplatz 2, Charlottenburg
*Law firm address:* Joachimsthaler Str. 11, W 15
*Additional information:* Attorney and
notary; after the National Socialist seizure of
power he was readmitted in 1933; his license

as a notary was revoked in 1935; he was still working as an attorney in October 1936. He emigrated to Palestine in 1936.
Sources: *li; LAB, 15.10.33; DJ 36, S. 314; Liste 36; BArch, R 3001 PAK; BG

**Henoch, Robert Dr.**
02/09/1884 - no information
Home address: Stromstr. 3, Charlottenburg
Law firm address: Schadowstr. 4/5, NW 7
Additional information: In October 1933 he was readmitted as attorney and notary; the time when his license as a notary was revoked (at the latest at the end of 1935) is not known; he worked as an attorney until at least October 1936; he emigrated to New York, USA in May 1939.
Sources: *li; LAB, 15.10.33; Liste 36; BArch, R 3001 PAK; BG: LAB, OFP-Akten, Nr. 349/44

**Henschel, Ernst**
10/14/1878 Breslau - no information
Home address: Claudiusstr. 13, NW 87
Law firm address: Müllerstr. 177, N 65
Additional information: Attorney and notary; after the National Socialist seizure of power in 1933 his license as a notary was revoked; he was disbarred on 04/29/1938. He emigrated to London, Great Britain in September 1938.
Sources: JMBl. 33, S. 208; *li; LAB, 15.10.33; BArch, R 3001 PAK; BG

**Henschel, Franz Dr.**
06/01/1888 Berlin - no information
Home address: Johannisberger Str. 5, Wilmersdorf
Law firm address: Taubenstr. 13, W 8
Additional information: He was a dissident; attorney at the KG and notary; after the National Socialist seizure of power in 1933 he was readmitted; his license as a notary was revoked in 1935; he was still working as an attorney until the general occupational ban in 1938; he survived and was readmitted as an attorney after 1945.
Sources: *li; DJ 36, S. 314; Liste 36; MRRAK; BArch, R 3001, PAK; LAB, 15.10.33; LAB, RAK, PA Werthauer; Verz. zugel. Anw.45; BG

**Henschel, Georg**
03/19/1887 Berlin - no information

Home address: Oranienburger Str. 60-63, N 24
Law firm address: An der Spandauer Brücke 9, C 2
Additional information: Attorney at the KG and notary; after the National Socialist seizure of power his license as a notary was revoked on 07/03/1933; he was disbarred as an attorney on 11/10/1936; he presumably emigrated to Denmark.
Sources: Br.B. 32; *li; LAB, 15.10.33; BArch, R 3001 PAK; BG

**Henschel, Martin, Judicial Councillor**
No information - 1933
Home address: no information
Law firm address: Friedrichstr. 72, W 8
Additional information: Attorney and notary; after the National Socialist seizure of power in 1933 he was readmitted; he died a little later.
Sources: TK 33; *li; LAB, 15.10.33; Pr.J. 33, S. 679; BArch, R 3001 PAK

**Henschel, Moritz**
02/17/1879 Breslau - ca. 1947 Jerusalem
Home address: Lietzenburger Str. 8, W 15
Law firm address: Lietzenburger Str. 30, W 15
Additional information: He fought in the First World War and was awarded the EK II. Attorney at the KG and notary; until 1933 he was a member of the board of the Berlin Bar Association; after the National Socialist seizure of power in 1933 he was readmitted; his license as a notary was revoked in 1935; he worked as an attorney until the general occupational ban in 1938. Transportation on 06/16/1943 to Theresienstadt. There he was the head of the division for leisure activities. He survived the camp and went to Jerusalem after liberation, where he died in 1947.
Sources: TK 33; *li; Liste 36; MRRAK; BArch, R 3001 PAK; BG; Aufbau, N.Y., 12.10.1945; Ausk. Beate Meyer

**Henschel, Richard Dr.**
09/06/1889 Berlin - no information
Home address: no information
Law firm address: Friedrichstr. 72, W 8
Additional information: Attorney and notary; after the National Socialist seizure of power he was made subject to an occupational ban on 07/14/1933. He made a request to be readmitted, however, his service during the First World War was not recognized as

"front line fighting." He emigrated to Lisbon, Portugal, on 04/01/1936.
*Sources:* Adr.B. 32; Liste d. nichtzugel. RA. 25.4.33; Pr.J. 33, S. 502; BArch, R 3001 PAK; BG

**Hepner, Heinrich Dr.**
10/31/1885 Görlitz - 07/10/1958 Chile
*Home address:* no information
*Law firm address:* Potsdamer Str. 118 c, W 35
*Additional information:* Attorney at the KG and notary; since 1912 he was admitted as attorney, at first at the law firm of Dr. Eugen Fuchs; later he was in the First World War service as a liaison officer between the Red Cross and the troops; 1921 marriage to Käthe Halberstam, birth of three children. After the National Socialist seizure of power in 1933 his license as a notary was revoked; he was readmitted as an attorney, he worked until the general occupational ban in 1938. He was arrested and transported to Sachsenhausen in connection with the Night of Broken Glass of November 1938, he was released on 12/22/1938 after being able to present a visa to Cuba that his wife had obtained. The family traveled to Cuba via the Netherlands and Great Britain, but could not go ashore, because the government had changed and the visa was declared invalid. The family managed to travel to Chile via Panama and Peru and found a home there. He died here at the age of 72.
*Sources:* JMBl. 33, S. 208; *li; Liste 36; LAB, Liste 15.10.33; MRRAK; BArch, R 3001 PAK; BG; Ausk. Lore Hepner, 2006

**Hepner, Julius Dr.**
05/29/1886 Beuthen - no information
*Home address:* Von-der-Heydt-Str. 2, W 10
*Law firm address:* Kaiser-Wilhelm-Str. 53, C 2
*Additional information:* Attorney and notary; in 1932 he was still a board member of the Bar Association. After the National Socialist seizure of power he was readmitted; his license as a notary was revoked in 1935; he worked as an attorney until the general occupational ban in 1938. He emigrated to Stockholm, Sweden. His wife Marie was regarded as "Aryan."
*Sources:* TK 33; *li; LAB, 15.10.33; TK 36; Liste 36; BArch, R 3001 PAK; BG

**Herrmann, Max**
03/09/1883 Breslau - no information
*Home address:* Nürnberger Str. 14/15, W 50
*Law firm address:* Alexanderstr. 32
*Additional information:* In 1910 he passed his second state examination in law; he was an attorney and notary; after the National Socialist seizure of power in 1933 his license as a notary was revoked in 1933, subsequently he was disbarred on 09/10/1934, already in October 1933 he was no longer listed in the directory of Berlin attorneys. He emigrated to France on 10/01/1933.
*Sources:* Jüd.Adr.B.; TK 33; JMBl. 33, S. 208; BArch, R 3001 PAK

**Herrmann, Siegfried**
05/06/1877 Wehlau - transportation 1942
*Home address:* no information
*Law firm address:* Alexanderstr. 55, O 27
*Additional information:* Attorney and notary; after the National Socialist seizure of power in 1933 he was readmitted; in 1935 his license as a notary was revoked; he worked as an attorney until the general occupational ban in 1938. Transportation on 01/13/1942 from Berlin to Riga.
*Sources:* TK 33; *li; LAB, 15.10.33; DJ 36, S. 314; Liste 36; MRRAK; BArch, R 3001 PAK; GB II; BArch R 1509 RSA

**Herrnberg, Felix Dr.**
07/01/1889 Allenstein - 03/27/1942 Litzmannstadt/Lodz
*Home address:* Eisenacher Str. 106, Schöneberg
*Law firm address:* Ansbacher Str. 17, W 50
*Additional information:* He was the brother-in-law of the former Berlin police chief, Bernhard Weiss, who had been particularly hostile to the Nazi press. After the National Socialist seizure of power in April 1933 he was made subject to an occupational ban; he was readmitted, because he had fought as a "frontline fighter" during the First World War. In 1935 his license as a notary was revoked; in 1936 he was disbarred. On 10/24/1941 he was transported to Litzmannstadt/Lodz, where he died a few months later.
*Sources:* Br.B.32; Liste d. nichtzugel. RA, 25.4.33; JMBl. 33, S. 209; Liste 36; DJ 36, S. 314; BArch, R 3001 PAK, PA; BG; GB II

**Herrnstadt, Ernst Dr.**
10/16/1906 Gleiwitz - no information
*Home address:* no information
*Law firm address:* Leipziger Str. 123 a, W 8
*Additional information:* Attorney at the
KG (since 1931); after the National Socialist
seizure of power he was made subject to an
occupational ban on 06/02/1933.
*Sources:* Liste d. nichtzugel. RA, 25.4.33;
BArch, R 3001 PAK, PA

**Hertzberg, Georg Dr.**
11/17/1872 Neuruppin - 10/29/1942
Theresienstadt
*Home address:* Frobenstr. 27, W 35,
Schöneberg
*Law firm address:* Markt 4/5, Spandau
*Additional information:* Attorney and
notary; after the National Socialist seizure of
power in 1933 he was readmitted; in 1935 his
license as a notary was revoked; he worked
as an attorney until the general occupational
ban in 1938. Transportation on 08/27/1942
to Theresienstadt. There he died after a few
months.
*Sources:* *li; LAB, 15.10.33; DJ 36, S. 315;
MRRAK; BArch, R 3001 PAK; BG; ThG;
GB II

**Herz, Franz Dr.**
03/12/1878 Jessnitz - 03/05/1943
*Home address:* Karlsruher Str. 28 bei
Bernstein, Wilmersdorf-Halensee
*Law firm address:* Köpenicker Str. 195, SO 36
*Additional information:* Attorney and notary;
after the National Socialist seizure of power
in 1933 his license as a notary was revoked;
he was readmitted as an attorney and worked
until 1937; he died in 1943 a week before his
75th birthday, he was buried at Weißensee.
*Sources:* TK 33; *li; LAB, 15.10.33; TK 36;
Liste 36; BArch, R 3001 PAK; BG

**Herzberg, Hans Dr.**
06/22/1893 Essen - 1969 Sao Paulo, Brazil
*Home address:* Württembergallee 26-27,
Charlottenburg
*Law firm address:* Nollendorfplatz 6, W 30
*Additional information:* Attorney and
notary. After the National Socialist seizure of
power he was readmitted; in 1935 his license
as a notary was withdrawn; he worked as an
attorney until the general occupational ban in
1938. He emigrated to Brazil in 1939.

*Sources:* *li; LAB, 15.10.33; DJ 36, S. 315;
MRRAK; BArch, R 3001 PAK; BG; BHdE
Bd. 1, S. 290 (Rolf Herzberg)

**Herzfeld, Arthur Dr.**
08/15/1877 Dortmund - transportation 1943
*Home address:* Martin-Luther-Str. 25, W 30,
Schöneberg
*Law firm address:* Seydelstr. 31, SW 19
*Additional information:* Attorney and
notary; after the National Socialist seizure
of power in 1933 his license as a notary was
revoked; he worked as an attorney until the
general occupational ban in 1938; later he
worked as an executor. Date of declaration
of property: 02/28/1943; transportation to
Auschwitz on 03/03/1943.
*Sources:* Adr.B. 32; JMBl. 33, S. 253; *li;
LAB, 15.10.33; Liste 36; MRRAK; BArch, R
3001 PAK; BG; GB II

**Herzfeld, Joseph Dr.**
12/18/1953 Neuss - 07/27/1939 Ritten/South
Tyrol
*Home address:* no information
*Law firm address:* Französische Str. 13/14
*Additional information:* He had completed
a commercial apprenticeship; from 1874 he
worked at an insurance bank in New York,
from 1878-80 he studied at the Columbia Law
School; from 1881 to 1885 he worked as an
attorney in New York. 1885-87 he did his legal
studies in Berlin; an attorney since 1892; later
also a notary. He traveled to Cuba, Mexico
and Canada. Because of his education he had
a thorough knowledge of Anglo-Saxon law.
1887 he was a member of the SPD, from 1898-
1906 and 1912-1918 he was a member of the
Reichstag for the SPD. He especially concerned
himself with the affairs of agricultural workers.
Herzfeld was among the opponents of the 1914
war within the SPD, he was co-founder of the
USPD in 1917, he changed to the KPD in 1920,
and was the Reichstag delegate from 1920-24,
co-founder and attorney of the "Rote Hilfe"
(Red Aid), member of the board of trustees
of the children's homes of the Red Aid (which
took care of children when their parents were
imprisoned); defense counsel for the KPD,
among others during the Tescheka trial; was
also active internationally for the Red Aid.
After the National Socialist seizure of power
he was at risk as a politically active jurist. The
RAK reported in May 1933 to the Prussian

Ministry of Justice that since March 6, 1925 he had been a permanent defender on behalf of the Red Aid, "at the same time it was emphasized that he was non-Aryan." He was made subject to an occupational ban in 1933. He emigrated to Zurich, Switzerland in 1933; he took over the representation of German emigrants before Swiss courts at the age of more than 80; then he moved to South Tyrol. There he died in 1939 at the age of 86.
*Sources:* GHStA, Rep. 84a, Nr. 20363; JMBl. 33, S. 209; BArch, R 3001 PAK; Göpp., S. 287; Schneider, Schwarz, Schwarz, S. 160/61

**Herzfeld, Robert Dr.**
09/22/1888 Berlin - no information
*Home address:* no information
*Law firm address:* Potsdamer Str. 129/130
*Additional information:* During the 1920s he was a lawyer for "Rote Hilfe" (Red Aid), like Joseph Herzfeld, with whom he temporarily shared an office. After the National Socialist seizure of power he was made subject to an occupational ban on 08/07/1933. In his case a "communist activity" (§ 3) was given as a justification, in addition to being "non-Aryan" (§ 1 Subsection 1 of the Law of 04/07/1933).
*Sources:* Liste d. nichtzugel. RA, 25.4.33; JMBl. 21.8.33, S. 267; BArch, R 3001 PAK, PA; Schneider, Schwarz, Schwarz, S. 162

**Herzog, Hans Dr.**
06/13/1891 Berlin - no information
*Home address:* no information
*Law firm address:* Mohrenstr. 54/55, W 8
*Additional information:* Attorney and notary; after the National Socialist seizure of power he was readmitted; on 02/17/1935 he was disbarred.
*Sources:* *li; LAB, 15.10.33; BArch, R 3001 PAK; DJ 36, S. 315

**Herzog, Martin**
04/07/1895 Posen (now called Poznan) - no information
*Home address:* no information
*Law firm address:* Flemmingstr. 3, Steglitz
*Additional information:* Attorney since 1931; after the National Socialist seizure of power he was made subject to an occupational ban on 06/27/1933; in August 1933 he emigrated to Palestine.
*Sources:* Liste d. nichtzugel. RA, 25.4.33; JMBl. 33, S. 209; BArch, R 3001 PAK, PA; BG

**Heydemann, Walter Dr.**
06/03/1896 Berlin - no information
*Home address:* Meinekestr. 20, Charlottenburg
*Law firm address:* Meinekestr. 20, W 15
*Additional information:* He and his brothers were members of a Jewish student union, which during the 1920s was involved in brawls with Nazi groups. Attorney and notary; in 1933 he was readmitted; his license as a notary was revoked in 1935; he worked as an attorney until the general occupational ban in 1938. He emigrated to New York, USA, on 12/24/1938.
*Sources:* Adr.B. 32; *li; LAB, 15.10.33; DJ 36, S. 315; Liste 36; BArch, R 3001 PAK; MRRAK; BG; Ausk. E. Proskauer

**Heymann, Adolf, Judicial Councillor**
05/12/1861 Selchow - transportation 1942
*Home address:* Blankenfeldestr. 4, C2, Mitte
*Law firm address:* Blumenstr. 49, O 27
*Additional information:* Attorney and notary; after the National Socialist seizure of power in 1933 his license as a notary was revoked; he worked as an attorney until the general occupational ban in 1938. Transportation on 07/30/1942 to Theresienstadt.
*Sources:* JMBl. 33, S. 208; *li; LAB, 15.10.33; MRRAK; BArch, R 3001, PAK; Naatz-Album ("Andreas H."); BG; ThG; GB II

**Heymann, Ernst Dr., Judicial Councillor**
01/18/1888 Cologne - no information
*Home address:* Fasanenstr. 58, W 15
*Law firm address:* Badstr. 61, N 20
*Additional information:* Attorney and notary; after the National Socialist seizure of power in 1933 he was readmitted; his license as a notary was revoked in 1935, he worked as an attorney until the general occupational ban in 1938. He emigrated to New York, USA, on 04/28/1939.
*Sources:* *li; LAB, 15.10.33; DJ 36, S. 315; BArch, R 3001 PAK; MRRAK; BG

**Heymann, Hans Dr.**
05/20/1882 Dortmund - no information

*Home address:* Bayreuther Str. 38, W 62
*Law firm address:* Friedrich-Ebert-Str. 15, W 9
*Additional information:* Attorney at the
KG and notary; after the National Socialist
seizure of power he was readmitted; he
worked as an attorney until the general
occupational ban in 1938, thereafter he was
still working as a "consultant." He emigrated
to Sydney, Australia.
*Sources:* *li; LAB, Liste 15.10.33; BArch,
R 3001 PAK; MRRAK; Liste der Kons. v.
23.2.1939; BG

**Heymann, Hugo Dr., Judicial Councillor**
No information
*Home address:* no information
*Law firm address:* Brückenstr. 6 b, SO 16
*Additional information:* Attorney and notary;
after the National Socialist seizure of power
in 1933 his license as a notary was revoked; he
was readmitted to work as an attorney until
the general occupational ban in 1938.
*Sources:* JMBl. 33, S. 208; *li; LAB, Liste
15.10.33; Liste 36; BArch, R 3001 PAK;
MRRAK

**Hilb, Karl Dr.**
12/23/1894 Mannheim - no information
*Law firm address:* Kronenstr. 66; W 8
*Additional information:* He fought in the
First World War from 1915-1918 and was
awarded the EK II. and the Baden Silver
Medal of Merit on a ribbon; he had been
admitted to the Bar in Mannheim in 1924,
had then settled in Haifa in 1926 and studied
"Palestinian and other Near-Eastern law,
namely Turkish, Syrian and Arabic law and
French and English colonial law," in 1927
he passed the appropriate examinations,
until 1930 he practiced as an attorney in
Palestine. In 1930 he returned to Germany and
established himself as an attorney in Berlin.
After the National Socialist seizure of power,
he applied for readmission to the Bar on
04/10/1933, pointing out his status as a
"frontline fighter." The proof of EK II. was,
however, not sufficient. He was very self-
assured, pointing out that such an honor was
only awarded in connection with "frontline
fighting."
In November 1933 the board of the RAK
reported to the KG judge that he was in
Haifa, Palestine. The vice president of the

KG, Goetsch, initiated the disbarment, which
occurred on 12/09/1933.
*Sources:* Adr.B. 33; Pr.J. 33, S. 839; BArch, R
3001 PAK, PA

**Hilb, Robert Dr.**
02/20/1891 Berlin - no information
*Home address:* no information
*Law firm address:* Kurfürstenstr. 88, W 62
*Additional information:* He was Protestant;
attorney (since 1921) and notary (since
February 1933); after the National Socialist
seizure of power he was made subject to an
occupational ban on 05/31/1933.
*Sources:* Adr.B. 32; Liste d. nichtzugel. RA.;
JMBl. 33, S. 253; BArch, R 3001 PAK, PA

**Hiller, Gerhard**
03/05/1906 Berlin - 08/08/1991
*Home address:* no information
*Law firm address:* Nollendorfplatz 6, W 30
*Additional information:* He had attended
the Konigstädtische Gymnasium in Berlin
and began his legal studies in 1924. They
were difficult to finance after the death of his
mother (the father had already died in 1915).
On March 24, 1932, he was admitted to the
bar, and in December of the same year he got
married. After the National Socialist seizure
of power he requested to be readmitted,
however, since he could not claim any of the
grounds for exemption, he was made subject
to an occupational ban on 07/06/1933. He
emigrated to the USA, he changed his first
name to Gary, last lived in Forest Hills, New
York, died at the age of 85.
*Sources:* Adr.B. 33; JMBl. 33, S. 234; BArch,
R 3001 PAK, PA; SSDI

**Hiller, Walter Dr.**
09/04/1889 Berlin - transportation 1941
*Home address:* no information
*Law firm address:* Regensburger Str. 2, W 50
*Additional information:* Attorney and
notary; after the National Socialist seizure
of power he was first disbarred, then
readmitted; his license as a notary was
suspended at the latest at the end of 1935, he
still worked as an attorney until 04/05/1938.
He was transported on 11/01/1941 to Lodz/
Litzmannstadt.
*Sources:* Adr.B. 32; TK 36; Liste 36; BArch,
R 3001 PAK; BG; GB II

**Hintze, Walter Dr.**
11/24/1904 Stettin - no information
*Home address:* Prinzregentenstr. 84,
Wilmersdorf
*Law firm address:* Lutherstr. 33, W 62
*Additional information:* After the National
Socialist seizure of power he was regarded
as "mixed race," because he had a Jewish
grandparent. He was Protestant. In 1933 he
was readmitted; in 1940 he was still working
as an attorney.
*Sources:* *li; LAB, Liste 15.10.33; Liste
Mschlg. 36; Tel.B. 41; BG

**Hirsch, Hermann**
06/27/1885 Messingwerk - 1935 Jerusalem
*Home address:* Winklerstr. 28, Grunewald
*Law firm address:* Winklerstr. 28, Grunewald
*Additional information:* After the National
Socialist seizure of power he was readmitted
in 1933. He emigrated to Jerusalem, Palestine,
on 12/15/1934; he died there in 1935 at the
age of 50.
*Sources:* TK 33; *li; BArch, R 3001 PAK; BG

**Hirsch, Hugo, Judicial Councillor**
01/26/1899 Grünberg/Silesia - no information
*Home address:* Kurfürstendamm 14/15, W 50
*Law firm address:* Kurfürstendamm 14/15,
W 50
*Additional information:* Attorney and
notary; after the National Socialist seizure of
power in 1933 he was readmitted; his license
as a notary was revoked in 1935; he still
worked as an attorney until the end of the
general occupational ban in 1936.
*Sources:* Jüd.Adr.B.; *li; LAB, Liste 15.10.33;
DJ 36, S. 315; Liste 36; MRRAK; BArch, R
3001 PAK

**Hirsch, Martin Dr.**
12/15/1890 Berlin - no information
*Home address:* Hoffmann-von-Fallersleben-
Platz, Wilmersdorf
*Law firm address:* Eichhornstr. 1, W 9
*Additional information:* He was the in-house
counsel to the Ignaz Petschek Group; in 1933
he was readmitted as attorney and notary;
his license as a notary was revoked at the
latest at the end of 1935; he emigrated to
San Francisco, USA in 1938.
*Sources:* Adr.B. 32; *li; LAB, Liste 15.10.33;
DJ 36, S. 315; BArch, R 3001 PAK; BG

**Hirsch, Martin Dr.**
10/31/1897 Rogasen - no information
*Home address:* no information
*Law firm address:* Friedrichstr. 49 a, SW 68
*Additional information:* Attorney since
1925; after the National Socialist seizure of
power he was made subject to an occupational
ban on 06/23/1933.
*Sources:* Adr.B. 32; Liste d. nichtzugel. RA,
25.4.33; JMBl. 33, S. 253; BArch, R 3001
PAK, PA

**Hirsch, Paul Dr., Judicial Councillor**
No information
*Home address:* Knesebeckstr. 61, W 15
*Law firm address:* Knesebeckstr. 61, W 15
*Additional information:* Attorney at the KG
and notary; after the National Socialist seizure
of power in 1933 his license as a notary was
revoked; he was readmitted as an attorney
until the general occupational ban in 1938.
*Sources:* TK 33; Jüd.Adr.B; JMBl. 33, S. 208;
*li; LAB, Liste 15.10.33; Liste 36; MRRAK;
BArch, R 3001 PAK

**Hirsch, Salli Dr.**
06/27/1885 Heinrichswalde, East Prussia -
11/21/1950 Jerusalem
*Home address:* no information
*Law firm address:* Kurfürstendamm 234, W 50
*Additional information:* 1914-18 he fought
in the First World War, he was awarded the
EK II; attorney and notary; he was a board
member of the Jewish Synagogue in Berlin and
an official in Jewish and Zionist associations,
amongst others a delegate at Zionist congresses;
he repeatedly made trips to Palestine. After the
National Socialist seizure of power in 1933 he
was readmitted; in 1935 his license as a notary
was revoked; upon request he was disbarred
on 11/04/1935. He emigrated to Palestine in
November 1935; until 1949 he worked at a
law firm in Jerusalem; he was furthermore
active in numerous functions in institutions and
associations; he also wrote contributions for
the "Haaretz" newspaper; he died in 1950 in
Jerusalem.
*Sources:* *li; LAB, Liste 15.10.33; BArch, R
3001 PAK; BG; BHdE Bd.1, S. 300 f.

**Hirsch, Walter Dr.**
04/07/1896 Schwetz - transportation 1941
*Home address:* Tauentzienstr. 7, W 50
*Law firm address:* Tauentzienstr. 7, W 50

*Additional information:* Attorney and notary; after the National Socialist seizure of power he was readmitted; in 1935 his license as a notary was revoked; he worked as an attorney until the general occupational ban in 1938, thereafter he was admitted as a "consultant." Date of declaration of property: 10/21/1941; he went to the collection point Levetzowstr. 7-8; transportation on 10/24/1941 to Litzmannstadt/Lodz.
*Sources:* *li; LAB, Liste 15.10.33; DJ 36, S. 315; MRRAK; Liste d. Kons., 15.4.39; BArch, R 3001 PAK; BG; GB II

**Hirschberg, Erich Dr.**
01/05/1883 Roggenau - 05/18/1961
*Home address:* Lietzensee-Ufer 9, Charlottenburg
*Law firm address:* Lietzensee-Ufer 9, Charlottenburg
*Additional information:* He was Protestant; during his studies he was a member of a (dueling) fraternity; attorney (since 1911) and notary (since 1924); he presumably was the brother of Oscar; up to 1933 he had an average income of RM 30,000 p.a. After the National Socialist seizure of power in 1933 his license as a notary was revoked; his revenue decreased to RM 6,000 p.a. In 1938 his license as a notary was revoked within the framework of the general occupational ban. He emigrated to Shanghai, China; he returned to Berlin in 1947; in 1954 he was readmitted as attorney and notary.
*Sources:* JMBl. 33, S. 208; *li; LAB, Liste 15.10.33; BArch, R 3001 PAK; MRRAK; BG; LAB, RAK, PA

**Hirschberg, Ernst Dr.**
09/14/1894 Berlin - transportation 1943
*Home address:* Fasanenstr. 42, W 15
*Law firm address:* Prenzlauer Str. 18, C 25
*Additional information:* Attorney and notary; after the National Socialist seizure of power in 1933 he was readmitted; in 1935 his license as a notary was revoked; he still worked as an attorney until the general occupational ban in 1938. He was later forced to work as a laborer and was used at Tornado, Müllerstr. 30, N 65. Transportation on 01/12/1943 to Theresienstadt; from there he was transported on 09/28/1944 to Auschwitz.

*Sources:* *li; LAB, Liste 15.10.33; DJ 36, S. 315; Liste 36; BArch, R 3001 PAK; MRRAK; BG; GB II

**Hirschberg, Franz Dr.**
05/02/1893 Berlin - transportation 1943
*Home address:* Ludwigkirchstr. 9, W 15
*Law firm address:* Badstr. 60, N 20
*Additional information:* Attorney and notary; after the National Socialist seizure of power he was disbarred and his license as a notary was revoked. The official notification of his death in 1933 seems to be incorrect, since he emigrated to France. There the pursuers caught up with him. Transportation on 03/04/1943 from Drancy to Majdanek.
*Sources:* JMBl. 33, S. 282; Liste d. nichtzugel. RA, 25.4.33; BArch, R 3001 PAK; BG; GB II

**Hirschberg, Hans Dr.**
No information
*Home address:* No information
*Law firm address:* Nollendorfstr. 15, Schöneberg (1932)
*Additional information:* Attorney and notary; after the National Socialist seizure of power he was made subject to an occupational ban in 1933.
*Sources:* Br.B. 32; JMBl. 33, S. 253; BArch, R 3001 PAK

**Hirschberg, Oscar Dr.**
10/19/1889 Roggenau - no information
*Home address:* Solinger Str. 7, NW 87
*Law firm address:* no information
*Additional information:* After the National Socialist seizure of power he was made subject to an occupational ban on 06/06/1933. He emigrated to Shanghai, China on 07/21/1939.
*Sources:* Liste d. nichtzugel. RA, 25.4.33; JMBl. 33, S. 234; BArch, R 3001 PAK, PA; BG

**Hirschberg, Paul Dr., Judicial Councillor**
01/02/1869 Posen - 10/05/1942 Theresienstadt
*Home address:* Waitzstr. 6, Charlottenburg
*Law firm address:* Stresemannstr. 105, SW 11
*Additional information:* After the National Socialist seizure of power he was readmitted; he worked as an attorney until the general occupational ban in 1938. Transportation on 07/17/1942 to Theresienstadt; he died there a few weeks later.
*Sources:* *li; LAB, Liste 15.10.33; Liste 36; BArch, R 3001 PAK; MRRAK; BG; ThG; GB II

**Hirschel, Max Dr., Judicial Councillor**
04/09/1861 - 02/18/1935
*Home address:* no information
*Law firm address:* Bendlerstr. 17, W 35
*Additional information:* After the National
Socialist seizure of power in 1933 he was
readmitted as an attorney; in 1935 he died at
the age of 74, he was buried at Weißensee.
*Sources:* TK 33; *li; LAB, Liste 15.10.33;
BArch, R 3001 PAK; BG

**Hirschfeld, Erwin Dr.**
05/01/1887 Dortmund - no information
*Home address:* Jenaer Str. 5, Wilmersdorf
*Law firm address:* Jenaer Str. 17, Wilmersdorf
*Additional information:* Attorney (since 1919)
and notary (since 1929); after the National
Socialist seizure of power he was made subject
to an occupational ban on 06/12/1933. He
emigrated to France.
*Sources:* Br.B. 32; JMBl. 33, S. 220/1; Liste d.
nichtzugel. RA, 25.4.33; BArch, R 3001 PAK,
PA; Wolf, BFS

**Hirschfeld, Georg Dr.**
11/27/1879 Berlin - no information
*Home address:* Kaiser-Wilhelm-Str. 59, C 2
(1931)
*Law firm address:* Kaiser-Wilhelm-Str. 59, C 2
*Additional information:* Attorney and
notary, in a law partnership with Ludwig
Hirschfeld (no relation specified); after
the National Socialist seizure of power his
license as a notary was revoked in 1933;
he still worked as an attorney until the
general occupational ban in 1938; he lived in
Germany at the time of the 1939 census.
*Sources:* Adr.B. 32; JMBl. 33, S. 208; *li;
LAB, Liste 15.10.33; Liste 36; BArch, R 3001
PAK; MRRAK; VZ 39

**Hirschfeld, Leo Dr.**
04/19/1887 Berlin - 04/11/1933
*Home address:* Alexanderstr. 24
*Law firm address:* Friedrichstr. 4
*Additional information:* Attorney and
notary; he died in April 1933 shortly before
his 46th birthday.
*Sources:* TK 33; JMBl. 28.4.33; BArch, R
3001 PAK, PA; BG

**Hirschfeld, Ludwig**
01/15/1893 Berlin - no information
*Home address:* no information

*Law firm address:* Kaiser-Wilhelm- Str. 59, C 2
*Additional information:* Attorney and
notary; in a law partnership with Georg
Hirschfeld (no relation specified); after the
National Socialist seizure of power in 1933
he was readmitted; in 1935 his license as a
notary was revoked; he still worked as an
attorney until 04/01/1937.
*Sources:* *li; DJ 36, S. 315; Liste 36; BArch, R
3001 PAK; BG

**Hirschfeld, Maurice**
12/31/1899 Berlin - no information
*Home address:* no information
*Law firm address:* Potsdamer Str. 35, Spandau
*Additional information:* After the National
Socialist seizure of power he was made subject
to an occupational ban in the spring of 1933.
He emigrated to Palestine on 12/27/1938.
*Sources:* Br.B. 32; Liste d. nichtzugel. RA,
04/25/1933; JMBl. 08/21/1933; p. 267;
BArch, R 3001 PAK; BG

**Hirschfeldt, Hermann, Judicial Councillor**
10/26/1862 Bovin - 08/03/1942
Theresienstadt
*Home address:* Iranische Str. 3, N 65/
Bamberger Str. 31, Schöneberg
*Law firm address:* Kaiser-Wilhelm-Str. 19, C 2
*Additional information:* After the National
Socialist seizure of power he was readmitted;
he worked as an attorney until the general
occupational ban in 1938. Transportation on
07/06/1942 to Theresienstadt; he died there
nearly a month later at the age of 79.
*Sources:* TK 33; *li; LAB, Liste 10/15/1933;
BArch, R 3001 PAK; BG; ThG; GB II
(Hirschfeld)

**Hirschland, Karl Dr.**
07/12/1881 Essen - 12/29/1946 USA
*Home address:* Maaßenstr. 13, W 62
*Law firm address:* Lützowufer 17
*Additional information:* Attorney (since
1914) at the LG I-III; after the National
Socialist seizure of power he was disbarred
during the course of the merging of the
district courts in January of 1934. He
emigrated in 1933 to France; 1936 to the
USA. An arrest warrant for tax evasion was
issued against him. He died at the end of 1946
in the USA.
*Sources:* Br.B. 32; BArch, R 3001 PAK, PA;
Wolf, BFS

**Hirschowitz, Aron Dr.**
03/22/1885 Insterburg - no information
*Home address:* Kurfürstendamm 173, W 15
*Law firm address:* Linkstr. 30, W 9
*Additional information:* Attorney and
notary; after the National Socialist seizure
of power in 1933 his license as a notary was
revoked, he worked as an attorney until
the general occupational ban in 1938. He
emigrated, however, information about
the destination varies: Shanghai, China on
12/09/1938, or Honduras on 11/12/1940.
*Sources:* Br.B. 32; Pr.J. 33, p. 466; *li; LAB,
Liste 10/15/1933; BArch, R 3001 PAK; BG

**Hirsch-Rheinshagen, Richard Dr.**
No information
*Home address:* no information
*Law firm address:* Lietzenburger Str. 7, W 15
*Additional information:* Attorney at the
KG and notary; after the National Socialist
seizure of power he was made subject to an
occupational ban as attorney and notary in
early 1933.
*Sources:* Br.B. 32; Liste d. nichtzugel. RA,
04/25/1933; JMBl. 08/04/1933

**Hirsch-Wagner, Walter**
03/11/1888 Göttingen - no information
*Home address:* no information
*Law firm address:* Friedrichstr. 160
*Additional information:* He fought in the
First World War; attorney at the LG I-III
(1919) and notary (1929); after the National
Socialist seizure of power he was made subject
to an occupational ban in 1933; he lived in
Salerno, Italy, in 1934; from there he still
tried in vain to be readmitted, because of his
status as a "frontline fighter." He possibly
remained in Italy.
*Sources:* JMBl. 06/30/1933; Liste nichtzugel.
RA, 04/25/1933; BArch, R 3001 PAK, PA

**Hirschwald, Franz Dr.**
02/16/1882 Berlin - no information
*Home address:* Uhlandstr. 165-166, W 15
*Law firm address:* Behrenstr. 49, W 8
*Additional information:* He was a Protestant;
"frontline" duty as a soldier during the First
World War; after the National Socialist
seizure of power in 1933 he was readmitted.
He was regarded as "mixed race," because he
had two Jewish grandparents; in 1941 he was
still practicing as an attorney and a notary.

He survived and after 1945 he was again
admitted as an attorney in West Berlin.
*Sources:* TK 33; *li; LAB, Liste 10/15/1933,
Liste Mschlg. 36; Tel.B. 41; Verz. zugel. Anw.
45; BG

**Hoch, Rudolf Dr.**
11/21/1891 Gdansk - no information
*Home address:* Lietzenburger Str. 33, W 15
*Law firm address:* Hardenbergstr. 19,
Charlottenburg
*Additional information:* Attorney at the
KG and notary; after the National Socialist
seizure of power in 1933 he was readmitted;
in 1935 his license as a notary was revoked;
he worked as an attorney until the general
occupational ban in 1938. He emigrated to
London, Great Britain, on 04/15/1939.
*Sources:* *li; LAB, Liste 10/15/1933; DJ 36, p.
315; BArch, R 3001 PAK; MRRAK; BG

**Hoeniger, Franz Dr.**
03/30/1875 Hohensalza - Berlin
*Home address:* Am Karlsbad 27, Tiergarten
*Law firm address:* Am Karlsbad 27,
Tiergarten
*Additional information:* He was a dissident.
Attorney at the KG and notary; after the
National Socialist seizure of power in 1933
his license as a notary was revoked; his wife
Henriette was regarded as "Aryan." He worked
as an attorney until the general occupational
ban in 1938. He committed suicide, the date
and the circumstances are not known.
*Sources:* JMBl. 33, p. 208; *li; LAB, Liste
10/15/1933; Liste 36; BArch, R 3001 PAK;
MRRAK; BG; GB II (CD-ROM)

**Hoffmann, Bruno**
11/22/1883 Lyck - no information
*Home address:* Hohenzollerndamm 47 a,
Grunewald
*Law firm address:* Hohenzollerndamm 47 a,
Grunewald
*Additional information:* Attorney and notary;
after the National Socialist seizure of power
in 1933 he was readmitted; his license as a
notary was revoked in 1935; he still worked
as an attorney until the general occupational
ban in 1938. He lived in a "privileged mixed-
race marriage," i.e. his wife was regarded as
"Aryan" and the couple had children of their
own. He survived and after the liberation he
lived in the Berlin Zehlendorf district.

*Sources:* *li; LAB, Liste 10/15/1933; DJ 36, p. 315; Liste 36; BArch, R 3001 PAK; MRRAK; Verz. zugel. Anw. 45; BG

**Hoffnung, Rudolf Dr.**
01/02/1889 Luckenwalde - no information
*Home address:* Französische Str. 49, W 8
*Law firm address:* Unter den Linden 56
*Additional information:* He fought in the First World War; attorney since 1924; after the National Socialist seizure of power he was made subject to an occupational ban on 06/06/1933. His request to be readmitted was rejected, because his service during the First World War was not regarded as "frontline duty." Emigration to Palestine.
*Sources:* Adr.B. 32; JMBl. 33, p. 209; Liste d. nichtzugel. RA, 04/25/1933; BArch, R 3001 PAK, PA; BG

**Hoffstaedt, Wilhelm, Judicial Councillor**
No information
*Home address:* No information
*Law firm address:* Innsbrucker Str. 5, Schöneberg
*Additional information:* Attorney and notary; after the National Socialist seizure of power in 1933 his license as a notary was revoked; he worked as an attorney until the general occupational ban in 1938.
*Sources:* TK 33; JMBl. 33, p. 208; *li; LAB, Liste 10/15/1933; Liste 36; MRRAK

**Hohenstein, Werner**
05/26/1892 Stettin - no information
*Home address:* Grolmanstr. 32-33, Charlottenburg
*Law firm address:* Grolmanstr. 32-33, Charlottenburg
*Additional information:* He moved to Berlin with his family as a child and passed his school leaving examination in 1911. From 1911 to 1914 he studied law in Freiburg, Munich and Berlin. In March 1915 he passed the legal traineeship examination at the KG. He subsequently was a soldier, he was seriously wounded. After the legal traineeship he passed his assessor examination in 1922 and temporarily worked in the judicial service, but later switched over to business and worked as legal counsel at a bank in Gdansk. In 1925 he returned to Berlin and established himself as an attorney; in 1932 he was appointed as a notary.

After the National Socialist seizure of power he was readmitted in 1933 as a "frontline fighter." Later he wrote: "I had a purely commercial practice. My clientele came from the textile trade of large-scale manufacture, the oil and metal trade. My income in 1929, the first year after I established myself, was about 6,000 Reichsmark and it steadily increased until I emigrated, although my license as a notary, which had been granted in 1932, was revoked again in 1935 because of the Nuremberg Laws." In 1937 he married Dorothea, who was 13 years younger than him and worked as a medical doctor. A little later her admission to practice was revoked, just like her husband in 1938. In November 1938, he was arrested and interned at the Sachsenhausen concentration camp as part of the Pogrom throughout the Reich. At the beginning of December he was free again. The couple had already previously received an immigration certificate for Palestine. When applying for a passport, their assets had to be disclosed to the Directorate-General. Afterwards the couple was informed: ". . . from this, the 3 instalments of the Jewish property tax of ca. RM 3,200 each, which still have to be paid." He had applied for admission as a "consultant," which was granted to him after the general occupational ban. The Palestine Office worked on the request for emigration to Palestine, the passage with Palestine & Orient Lloyd and the trip on March 22, 1939 from Trieste on the steamer Galilea were booked. The couple received their passports just in time, but the entry visa was only valid until 12/31/1938 and had to be extended. The Palestine Trust Office of the Jews in Germany, Potsdamer Straße 72, 2 Hof, demanded a (reduced) flagship fee of RM 10,500. After payment of the sum, he received a "C certificate" for emigration to Palestine. A total of at least RM 20,000 had already been paid to official agencies. Until the day of departure, he had to report daily to his relevant police district, Grolmannstrasse, corner of Kurfürstendamm. On 03/19/1939 the couple left Berlin to travel to Trieste, where they were to board the ship which was to take them to Haifa. Shortly before his departure, he asked the head of the police station at Division II for a "homeland certificate." In addition to the passport, this home ticket was to document the connection to Germany and make a return possible. However, the regular renewal of the "homeland certificate" became obsolete with the start of the war and the closure of the consulate in Palestine.

Life in the new country was difficult. "Since I had attended a classical high school, I lacked the necessary language skills in Hebrew and English. In order to keep me afloat, I tried to start a peddler coffee trade. This did not bring in any money and had to be stopped at the outbreak of the war, because at that time the compulsory management of food was immediately introduced, households were connected to certain stores by means of food ration cards and thereby intermediate trade was excluded." Another venture in trade failed. His wife could not practice her profession as a medical doctor and could not contribute money for living expenses. The couple sold any possessions they could; furniture, books, a grammophone, crystal and porcelain. In December 1945 he was able to find a job with the American Porcelain Tooth Company Ltd. "Until then I had been without an income."

In the 1950s he filed an application for reparation. In May 1960 an amount of DM 8,000 was awarded to him. At the same time the couple applied to emigrate back to Germany. It will forever remain uncertain as to whether the two ever saw Germany again. They presumably died in Tel Aviv in the 1980s. Apparently they did not have any children. Their documents were found by J. Schlör in an antique shop in Tel Aviv.
*Sources:* *li; LAB, Liste 10/15/1933; DJ 36, p. 315; MRRAK; Liste d. Kons. 38; BG; Schlör, J.: Von Berlin nach Tel Aviv [From Berlin to Tel Aviv], Menora 1994, pages 231-261

**Holdheim, Gerhard Dr.**
11/26/1892 - no information
*Home address:* no information
*Law firm address:* Waitzstr. 6, Charlottenburg
*Additional information:* After the National Socialist seizure of power he was made subject to an occupational ban in 1933.
*Sources:* Br.B. 32; Liste d. nichtzugel. RA, 04/25/1933; JMBl. 33, p. 209; BArch, R 3001 PAK

**Holdheim, Kurt Julius Dr.**
08/09/1888 Berlin - 01/29/1949 Berlin

*Home address:* Schlüterstr. 45, W 15
*Law firm address:* Tauentzienstr. 7 b, W 50
*Additional information:* When he was a student he belonged to a dueling fraternity; he fought as a soldier during the First World War; attorney (since 1919) and notary (since 1925) at a law firm together with Arthur Hornthal, specialized in rental and housing law. After the National Socialist seizure of power he was readmitted, because he was recognized as a "frontline fighter;" in 1935 his license as a notary was revoked; 1938 occupational ban as attorney; he was admitted as a "consultant." He emigration to Haifa, Palestine, on 11/19/1939; in 1947 he returned to Berlin and was readmitted as an attorney and a notary; he died 1949 in Berlin.
*Sources:* *li; LAB, Liste 10/15/1933; DJ 36, p. 315; MRRAK; Liste d. Kons. v. 04/15/1939; BArch, R 3001 PAK; LAB, RAK, PA; BG

**Hollaender, Adolf Dr.**
No information
*Home address:* no information
*Law firm address:* Kurfürstenstr. 51, W 35
*Additional information:* Attorney and notary; after the National Socialist seizure of power he was made subject to an occupational ban in early 1933.
*Sources:* Br.B. 32; Liste d. nichtzugel. RA, 04/25/1933; BArch, R 3001 PAK; Naatz-Album

**Hollander, Gottfried Dr.**
04/23/1876 Wreschen - transportation 1943
*Home address:* Oranienburger Str. 3, later no. 4, C 2
*Law firm address:* An der Spandauer Brücke 8, C 2
*Additional information:* Attorney and notary; after the National Socialist seizure of power in 1933 he was readmitted; his license as a notary was revoked in 1935; he worked as an attorney until the general occupational ban in 1938. Transportation on 03/01/1943 to Auschwitz.
*Sources:* Adr.B. 32; *li; LAB, Liste 10/15/1933; BArch, R 3001 PAK; Naatz-Album; BG; GB II

**Holländer, Karl Dr., Judicial Councillor**
08/02/1868 Berlin - no information
*Home address:* Claudiusstr. 4 and Mahler-str.
12, Dahlem (1933)
*Law firm address:* Friedrichstr. 65 a, W 8
*Additional information:* Attorney and
notary: He left the Jewish Synagogue
in October 1931; upon request he was
readmitted as an "elder attorney." He offered
to refrain from his own admission in favor of
his son Ulrich. This was denied. He emigrated
in 1933 to Amsterdam, the Netherlands. In
the legal files it is noted: "inactive 1934."
An arrest warrant for tax evasion was issued
against him.
*Sources:* JMBl. 33, p. 208; *li; LAB, Liste
10/15/1933; BArch, R 3001 PAK; BG; Wolf, BFS

**Holländer, Ludwig Dr.**
08/05/1877 Berlin - 02/09/Berlin
*Home address:* Hohenzollerndamm 196,
Wilmersdorf
*Law firm address:* Hohenzollerndamm 196,
Wilmersdorf
*Additional information:* Legal counsel and
later director of the CV Berlin; founder of the
Philo Verlag; board member of the DDP Berlin;
after the National Socialist seizure of power
in 1933 his license as a notary was revoked, he
was admitted as an attorney until his death in
February 1936, he was buried at Weißensee.
*Sources:* JMBl. 33, p. 208; *li; LAB, Liste
10/15/1933; BArch, R 3001 PAK; BG; Krach,
p. 433

**Holländer, Ulrich Gert Dr.**
02/24/1904 Berlin - no information
*Home address:* no information
*Law firm address:* Friedrichstr. 65 a, W 8
(previously Taubenstr. 44)
*Additional information:* Attorney at the
KG; the son of the attorney and notary Dr.
Karl Holländer; after the National Socialist
seizure of power he was made subject to an
occupational ban on 05/26/1933. His father
offered the Ministry of Justice to refrain from
his own admission in favor of his son Ulrich.
This was denied.
*Sources:* Br.B. 32; Liste d. nichtzugel. RA,
04/25/1933; JMBl. 33, p. 203; BArch, R 3001
PAK, PA

**Holz, Hans Dr.**
03/27/1902 - October 1970

*Home address:* no information
*Law firm address:* Uhlandstr. 194 a,
Charlottenburg (1932), later: Dorotheenstr.
64, NW 7
*Additional information:* Attorney (since
1930) and notary; after the National Socialist
seizure of power he was made subject to an
occupational ban on 06/06/1933. Emigration
to the USA, last lived in Forest Hills, New
York. He died at the age of 68.
*Sources:* Adr.B. 32; Liste d. nichtzugel. RA,
04/25/1933; JMBl. 33, p. 209; BArch, R 3001
PAK, PA; SSDI

**Holz, Ignaz, Judicial Councillor**
12/24/1853 Posen - no information
*Home address:* Fasanenstr. 28,
Charlottenburg
*Law firm address:* Kurfürstenstr. 105, W 62
*Additional information:* Attorney and
notary; after the National Socialist seizure of
power he was readmitted in 1933; his license
as a notary was revoked in 1935; he was still
working as an attorney until 08/22/1938.
*li; LAB, Liste 10/15/1933; DJ 36, p. 315;
Liste 36; BArch, R 3001 PAK; BG

**Holz, Leonhard Dr.**
07/11/1882 Berlin - 1945 Flossenbürg
*Home address:* no information
*Law firm address:* Ludwigkirchplatz 12
*Additional information:* Attorney since
1910, later also a notary; soldier in the First
World War, was wounded and was awarded
the EK; member of the SPD; 1920-21 he was
city councillor; as an attorney he specialized
in rental law. After the National Socialist
seizure of power he was thrown down the
steps by a Storm Trooper commando at the
Berlin District Court on 04/30/1933 and
was mistreated. In the middle of May 1933
he fled with his second wife to Paris. After
postgraduate study he worked as an attorney
again. His first wife and their daughter also
followed him to Paris; the daughter went to
Colombia with her husband. After the death
of his second wife, he and his first wife
Herta were interned in France in 1940;
on 03/27/1944 he was transported from
Drancy to Auschwitz. Herta was murdered
in Auschwitz. At the end of January 1945
he was transported from Auschwitz to
Mauthausen; on 03/03/1945 further to the
Flossenbürg concentration camp.

*Sources:* Br.B. 32; BArch, R 3001 PAK; BG; Verfolgte Berl. Stadtverordnete u. Magistratsmitgl.; GB II

**Horn, Georg**
04/09/1880 - 12/27/1936
*Home address:* Neue Königstr. 88, Prenzlauer Berg
*Law firm address:* Neue Königstr. 40, NO 43
*Additional information:* Attorney and notary; after the National Socialist seizure of power his license as a notary was revoked in 1933; he was readmitted as an attorney; he died in 1936 at the age of 56, he is buried at Weißensee.
*Sources:* *li; BArch, R 3001 PAK; JMBl. 33, p. 220; BG

**Hornthal, Arthur**
No information - 1935
*Home address:* no information
*Law firm address:* Tauentzienstr. 7 b, W 50
*Additional information:* Attorney and notary, in a law partnership with Kurt Holdheim; after the National Socialist seizure of power in 1933 his license as a notary was revoked; he was readmitted as an attorney, he worked until 1934; he died in 1935.
*Sources:* Br.B. 32; JMBl. 33, p. 208; *li; LAB, Liste 10/15/1933; BArch, R 3001 PAK

**Horowitz, Simon Dr.**
01/16/1884 Thorn - no information
*Home address:* Droysenstr. 15, Charlottenburg
*Law firm address:* An der Spandauer Brücke 12, C 2
*Additional information:* Attorney and notary; after the National Socialist seizure of power in 1933 his license as a notary was revoked; he was readmitted as an attorney; he worked until the general occupational ban in 1938. He emigrated to Tel Aviv, Palestine on 04/15/1939
*Sources:* JMBl. 33, p. 208; *li; LAB, Liste 10/15/1933; Liste 36; BG

**Horrwitz, Hugo, Judicial Councillor**
No information
*Home address:* no information
*Law firm address:* Brückenallee 8, NW 87
*Additional information:* Attorney and notary; joint law firm with Walter; after the National Socialist seizure of power in 1933 he was readmitted; in 1935 his license as a notary was revoked; he worked as an attorney until the general occupational ban in 1938.
*Sources:* *li; LAB, Liste 10/15/1933; DJ 36, p. 315; Liste 36; MRRAK; BArch, R 3001 PAK

**Horrwitz, Walter Dr.**
03/20/1900 Berlin - no information
*Home address:* no information
*Law firm address:* Brückenallee 8, NW 87
*Additional information:* In 1933 Hugo and Walter merged their law firms. Before Walter's law office was in Charlottenstr. 48. In April 1933 he was made subject to an occupational ban, upon request he was readmitted; he worked as an attorney until at least 1936. Br.B. 32; Liste d. nichtzugel. RA, 04/25/1933
*Sources:* *li; LAB, Liste 10/15/1933; Liste 36; BArch, R 3001 PAK

**Horwitz, Alfred**
10/31/1876 Berlin - 02/18/1940
*Home address:* Lützowufer 10, Tiergarten
*Law firm address:* Aschaffenburger Str. 19
*Additional information:* He was a dissident; attorney and notary; after the National Socialist seizure of power in 1933 his license as a notary was revoked; his wife Katharina was regarded as non-Jewish. He was readmitted as an attorney until the general occupational ban in 1938. He died in 1940 at the age of 63.
*Sources:* JMBl. 33, p. 208, *li; LAB, Liste 10/15/1933; Liste 36; BArch, R 3001 PAK; MRRAK; BG

**Horwitz, Arthur**
11/05/1882 Berlin - no information
*Home address:* Prinzregentenstr. 23, Wilmersdorf
*Law firm address:* Prinzregentenstr. 23, Wilmersdorf
*Additional information:* Attorney at the KG and notary; after the National Socialist seizure of power in 1933 his license as a notary was revoked; he was readmitted as an attorney; he worked until the general occupational ban in 1938. He emigrated to Montevideo, Paraguay, on 01/10/1939.
*Sources:* JMBl. 33, p. 266; *li; LAB, Liste 10/15/1933; BArch, R 3001 PAK; MRRAK; BG

**Horwitz, Heinrich Dr.**
06/20/1899 - no information
*Home address:* no information
*Law firm address:* Kurfürstenstr. 119, W 62
*Additional information:* After the National Socialist seizure of power he was made subject to an occupational ban on 06/10/1933; in 1933 he moved to Stuttgart.
*Sources:* Adr.B. 32; Liste d. nichtzugel. RA, 04/25/1933; JMBl. 33, p. 253; BArch, R 3001 PAK, PA

**Hurtig, Franz**
07/25/1900 Hannover - transportation 1943
*Home address:* Niebuhrstr. 74, Charlottenburg
*Law firm address:* Alexanderstr. 44, C 25
*Additional information:* After the National Socialist seizure of power he was made subject to an occupational ban on 06/07/1933, despite his request for readmittance, his voluntary war service was not recognized as "frontline fighting." Transportation on 02/19/1943 to Auschwitz.
*Sources:* Adr.B. 32; Liste d. nichtzugel. RA 04/25/1933; JMBl. 33, p. 253; BArch, R 3001 PAK, PA; BG; GB II

**Hurwitz, Walter**
12/18/1892 Berlin-Tegel - 1942 transportation
*Home address:* Kurfürstendamm 201, W 15
*Law firm address:* Kurfürstendamm 201, W 15
*Additional information:* After the National Socialist seizure of power he was readmitted, in 1936 he was still working as an attorney. He emigrated to France; transportation on 08/10/1942 to Auschwitz.
*Sources:* *li; LAB, Liste 10/15/1933; Liste 36; BArch, R 3001 PAK; BG; GB II

# I

**Igel, Karl**
05/25/1900 Kattowitz - no information
*Home address:* no information
*Law firm address:* Greifswalder Str. 226, NO 55
*Additional information:* After the National Socialist seizure of power he was made subject to an occupational ban on 06/09/1933. He emigrated in the summer of 1933 to Palestine.
*Sources:* Liste d. nichtzugel. RA, 04/25/1933; JMBl. 33, p. 234; BArch, R 3001 PAK; BG

**Ilgner, Erich Dr.**
01/01/1895 Berlin - no information
*Home address:* Meisenbusch 58, Zehlendorf-Machnow
*Law firm address:* Neue Schönhauser Str.1, N 54
*Additional information:* Attorney at the KG, joint law firm partnership with Siegfried Bergmann and Ernst Karfunkel. After the National Socialist seizure of power he was made subject to an occupational ban in 1933. He emigrated to France or Belgium in 1933.
*Sources:* Br.B. 32; Liste d. nichtzugel. RA, 04/25/1933; JMBl. 33, p. 203; BArch, R 3001 PAK; BG

**Illch, Max**
08/20/1872 Frankfurt a. M. - no information
*Home address:* Tannenbergallee 3, Charlottenburg
*Law firm address:* Charlottenstr. 56, W 8
*Additional information:* In 1932 he was still a board member of the RAK; after the National Socialist seizure of power in 1933 his license as a notary was revoked; he was readmitted as an attorney. He emigrated to Rome, Italy, on 02/26/1936.
*Sources:* TK 33; *li; LAB, Liste 10/15/1933; JMBl. 33, p. 220; Liste 36; BG

**Imberg, Franz, Judicial Councillor**
12/27/1865 Berlin - 02/03/1942 Berlin
*Home address:* Potsdamer Str. 113 (1941)
*Law firm address:* Potsdamer Str. 113
*Additional information:* Attorney and notary; after the National Socialist seizure of power in 1933 he was readmitted in 1933; his license as a notary was revoked in 1935. He committed suicide on 02/03/1942.
*Sources:* *li; LAB, Liste 10/15/1933; DJ 36, p. 315; Liste 36; BArch, R 3001 PAK; MRRAK; Vz 39; GB II

**Imberg, Leo**
01/10/1879 Berlin - 09/14/1942 Theresienstadt
*Home address:* Richard-Wagner-Str. 5, Charlottenburg
*Law firm address:* Sesenheimer Str. 29, Charlottenburg
*Additional information:* Attorney and notary; after the National Socialist seizure of power in 1933 his licence as a notary was revoked; he still worked as an attorney until

07/29/1936. Transportation on 08/28/1942, he died there a few days later.
*Sources:* JMBl. 33,p. 208; *li; LAB, Liste 10/15/1933; Liste 36; BG; ThG; GB II

**Immerwahr, Kurt Dr.**
03/03/1888 Berlin - 04/07/1942
*Home address:* Bleibtreustr. 27, W 15
*Law firm address:* no information
*Additional information:* After the National Socialist seizure of power occupational ban in early 1933; he died in 1942 at the age of 54.
*Sources:* Jüd. Adr.B.; Liste d. nichtzugel. RA, 04/25/1933; JMBl. 33, p. 209; BArch, R 3001 PAK; BG

**Indig, Alexander Dr., Judicial Councillor**
No information - 1934
*Home address:* no information
*Law firm address:* Charlottenstr. 60, W 8
*Additional information:* Attorney and notary; after the National Socialist seizure of power in 1933 his license as a notary was revoked; "inactive 1934;" he died in the same year.
*Sources:* *li; LAB, Liste 10/15/1933; JMBl. 33, p. 208; BArch, R 3001 PAK

**Isaac, Martin Dr.**
No information
*Home address:* Schaperstr. 35, W 50
*Law firm address:* Schaperstr. 35, W 50
*Additional information:* Attorney and notary; after the National Socialist seizure of power in 1933 his license as a notary was revoked; he worked as an attorney until the general occupational ban in 1938. He emigrated to Jerusalem, Palestine.
*Sources:* *li; LAB, Liste 10/15/1933; JMBl. 33, p. 208; BArch, R 3001 PAK; MRRAK; BG

**Isaacsohn, Abraham, Judicial Councillor**
10/30/1866 Brietzig - 09/25/1942 Theresienstadt
*Home address:* Mommsenstr. 6, Charlottenburg
*Law firm address:* Mommsenstr. 6, Charlottenburg
*Additional information:* Attorney and notary; after the National Socialist seizure of power in 1933 his license as a notary was revoked, he was readmitted as an attorney, he still worked until the general occupatoinal

ban in 1938. Date of declaration of property: 08/10/1942; transportation on 08/17/1942 to Theresienstadt; he died there soon after.
*Sources:* JMBl. 33, p. 208; *li; LAB, Liste 10/15/1933; Liste 36; BArch, R 3001 PAK; Naatz-Album; BG; ThG; GB II

**Isaacsohn, Martin Dr.**
12/14/1882 Rastenburg - no information
*Home address:* Kaiserstr. 22-24, C 25
*Law firm address:* Kaiserstr. 22-24, C 25
*Additional information:* Attorney (since 1910) and notary (since 1924); after the National Socialist seizure of power he applied to be readmitted; however, his license as a notary was revoked on 06/28/1933, despite all statements of good repute (Leumundsbekundungen); on 10/02/1933 he was disbarred. He emigrated to France on 10/01/1933.
*Sources:* Jüd.Adr.B.; JMBl. 33, p. 208; Pr.J. 33, p. 502; BArch R 3001 PAK, PA; BG

**Isay, Hermann Prof. Dr.**
09/07/1873 Berlin - 03/21/1938 Berlin
*Home address:* no information
*Law firm address:* Maienstr. 2, W 62
*Additional information:* Attorney (since 1901) at the KG and notary; 1919 private lecturer; since 1935 visiting lecturer at the TH Berlin. After the National Socialist seizure of power in 1933 his license as a notary was revoked; in 1934 he was dismissed as a visiting lecturer; in 1936 he was still working as an attorney. He died in 1938 after a serious illness.
*Publications:* Internationales Wettbewerbsrecht [International Competition Law], vol. I, Europa [Europe], together with attorney Mettetal, Paris, 1937
*Sources:* Br.B. 32; JMBl. 33, p. 208; *li; LAB, Liste 10/15/1933; Liste 36; Göpp., p. 224

**Isay, Rudolf Dr.**
01/01/1886 Trier - 04/14/1956 Bonn
*Home address:* Maienstr. 2, W 62
*Law firm address:* Maienstr. 2, W 62
*Additional information:* He was a Protestant. Legal studies in Heidelberg, Berlin and Bonn; 1908 doctorate; he established himself as an attorney in Berlin, later also a notary; he became prominent with publications on mining law. After the National Socialist seizure of power in 1933 his license as a

notary was revoked; he was readmitted as an attorney; he was a member of the Reich Association of Non-Aryan Christians; emigration to Brazil on 10/24/1935; he moved to the jungle (Rolandia) and there became a coffee farmer; in 1951 he returned to Germany and was a visiting lecturer at Universität Bonn.
Sources: *li; LAB, Liste 10/15/1933; JMBl. 33, p. 208; BArch, R 3001 PAK; Mitt. bl. Reichsverband nichtarischer Christen, 12/06/1934; BG; BHdE Vol. 2,1, p. 552; Göpp. p. 341; Isay, Rudolf: Aus meinem Leben [From my life], Weinheim 1960

### Israel, Fritz Dr.
11/10/1902 - no information
Home address: Rosenheimer Str. 17, Schöneberg
Law firm address: Friedrichstr. 208, SW 68
Additional information: Attorney since 1932; after the National Socialist seizure of power he was made subject to an occupational ban on 05/31/1933.
Sources: Liste d. nichtzugel. RA, 04/25/1933; JMBl. 33, p. 209; BArch, R 3001 PAK

### Israel, Georg R. Albrecht
07/13/1897 Berlin - 01/02/1986 Chertsey, England
Home address: Neidenburger Allee 7, Charlottenburg
Law firm address: Reichskanzlerplatz 2, Charlottenburg
Additional information: He had studied law in Berlin, he also took the second state examination in law there and was admitted as an attorney in February 1925. Numerous publications in: "Grundeigentum", in "Reichs-Verwaltungsblatt" and in "Preußisches Verwaltungsblatt."
After the National Socialist seizure of power in early 1933 he was made subject to an occupational ban. He was a dissident, his wife Erna was of non-Jewish origin. Other than the occupational ban he was also hit by a publication ban, an article that had already been accepted was no longer published in May 1933, because he was regarded as a Jew. After the occupational ban he still remained general representative for a former client. According to his daughter, he was imprisoned from November 1943, first at the Große Hamburger Straße collecting station, then at the Alexanderplatz police prison, then -

from May 1944 to 04/21/1945, just before the end of the war - at the collecting station in Schulstrasse at the premises of the Jewish Hospital. His son died at the Großbeeren forced labor camp from epidemic typhus. His daughter was rescued by means of a children transport rescue mission to Great Britain. After the liberation he worked in his profession again. From 1950, at the latest, he practiced as an attorney and notary in Berlin-Charlottenburg. He died in 1986 at the age of 88 during a family visit to Great Britain.
Sources: Br.B. 32; Liste d. nichtzugel. RA, 04/25/1933; JMBl. 08/21/1933, p. 267; BArch, R 3001 PAK; BG; information daughter Ruth B. 12/2001

### Israel, Hugo Dr.
12/06/1885 Kassel - no information
Home address: Corneliusstr. 4 a, W 10
Law firm address: Französische Str. 35-37
Additional information: Former legal counsel of the Dresdner Bank; after the National Socialist seizure of power he was made subject to an occupational ban in early 1933. He emigrated to Amsterdam, the Netherlands, 1933.
Sources: Br.B. 32; Liste d. nichtzugel. RA 04/25/1933; JMBl. 33, p. 209; BArch, R 3001 PAK; BG

### Israel, Paul
06/29/1876 Königsberg - no information
Home address: Hohenstaufenstr. 60 I, Schöneberg
Law firm address: Wollankstr. 1, Pankow
Additional information: Attorney and notary; after the National Socialist seizure of power he was made subject to an occupational ban in early 1933; in 1939 he was still living in Berlin.
Sources: Br.B. 32; Liste d. nichtzugel. RA, 04/25/1933 (addendum list); BArch, R 3001 PAK; VZ 39

### Israelski, Leopold
07/28/1873 - 05/19/1936
Home address: Kaiserdamm 23, Charlottenburg
Law firm address: Alexanderplatz 5
Additional information: Attorney and notary; after the National Socialist seizure of power in 1933 his license as a notary was revoked; he was readmitted as an attorney.

Worked until his death in 1936, he was buried at Weißensee.
*Sources:* *li; LAB, Liste 10/15/1933; JMBl. 33, p. 220; Liste 36; BG

**Israelski, Werner Julius**
05/12/1903 Dirschau - 06/09/1994
*Home address:* Bayernallee 36, Charlottenburg
*Law firm address:* Klosterstr. 80/2, C 2
*Additional information:* After the National Socialist seizure of power he was made subject to an occupational ban in early 1933. He emigrated to New York, USA, after 06/29/1938; he last lived under the name Werner Illing in Los Angeles, California.
*Sources:* Adr.B. 32; Liste d. nichtzugel. RA, 04/25/1933; JMBl. 33, p. 253; BArch, R 3001 PAK; BG; SSDI

**Issing, Julius Dr., Judicial Councillor**
No information
*Home address:* no information
*Law firm address:* Fasanenstr. 44, W 15
*Additional information:* Attorney and notary; after the National Socialist seizure of power in 1933 his license as a notary was revoked; he was readmitted as an attorney; he was disbarred on 07/19/1934.
*Sources:* JMBl. 33, p. 208; *li; LAB, Liste 10/15/1933; BArch, R 3001 PAK

**Ittmann, Julius**
No information
*Home address:* no information
*Law firm address:* Alexanderstr. 22, C 25
*Additional information:* Attorney and notary; after the National Socialist seizure of power in 1933 his license as a notary was revoked, he was readmitted as an attorney, he still worked until 06/11/1936.
*Sources:* JMBl. 33, p. 208; *li; LAB, Liste 10/15/1933; Liste 36; BArch, R 3001 PAK

**Ivers, Hellmut Dr.**
05/30/1903 Berlin - no information
*Home address:* Düsseldorfer Str. 5, W 5
*Law firm address:* Bayreuther Str. 11, W 30
*Additional information:* Attorney since 1932; after the National Socialist seizure of power he was made subject to an occupational ban until 06/12/1933.
*Sources:* Liste d. nichtzugel. RA, 04/25/1933; JMBl. 33, p. 234; BArch, R 3001 PAK, PA

# J

**Jackier, Alfred Dr.**
10/09/1893 - no information
*Home address:* no information
*Law firm address:* Wielandstr. 30, Charlottenburg
*Additional information:* Attorney and notary; after the National Socialist seizure of power he was made subject to an occupational ban in April 1933; he was readmitted; both his licenses to practice law and to work as a notary were revoked on 04/25/1934. He emigrated to Palestine, returned to Berlin after 1945.
*Sources:* *li; Br.B. 32; LAB, Liste 10/15/1933; BArch, R 3001 PAK, PA; information E. Proskauer

**Jacob, Erwin**
06/04/1901 Berlin - February 1983
*Home address:* no information
*Law firm address:* Chausseestr. 31, N 4
*Additional information:* After the National Socialist seizure of power he was made subject to an occupational ban in the summer of 1933; he was nevertheless still legally active. He emigrated to Cuba; he applied for a scholarship with American Committee; he acquired American citizenship.
*Sources:* Liste d. nichtzugel. RA, 04/25/1933; JMBl. 07/15/1933; p. 221; BArch, R 3001 PAK; NY Publ. Lib.(Am. Com.) Jacob, E.; SSDI

**Jacob, Siegfried Kurt Dr.**
02/12/1884 Tremessen - 06/20/1954 Berlin
*Home address:* Niebuhrstr. 64, Charlottenburg
*Law firm address:* Köpenicker Str. 114, SO 16
*Additional information:* Attorney (since 1912) and notary (since 1919); soldier in the First World War. After the National Socialist seizure of power in 1933 he was readmitted, because he was recognized as a "frontline fighter;" in 1935 his license as a notary was revoked; in 1938 he was made subject to a general occupational ban for Jewish attorneys. All of his furniture and also his practice equipment were confiscated without compensation by the Gestapo. He sent his wife and son to England; he himself was arrested and went to a concentration camp. He succeeded, however, in being sent to a prison where he remained until the end of the war. In 1947 he was readmitted as an attorney and a notary. He practiced until his death in

1954 in 52 Müllerstr. As a consequence of the imprisonment, he was often so weak that he could only receive his clients in bed (he also lived in the office). On his office door there was the sign "Closed because of overcrowding."
*Sources:* *li; LAB, Liste 10/15/1933; MRRAK; BG; information E. Proskauer

**Jacob, Walter Eugen Dr.**
10/29/1887 Breslau - 02/02/1935
*Home address:* no information
*Law firm address:* Hallesches Ufer 6, SW 11
*Additional information:* Attorney and notary; after the National Socialist seizure of power he was readmitted as an attorney, his status as a Jew was only ascertained later; he worked as an attorney until his death in February 1935.
*Sources:* Br.B. 32; TK 33; LAB, Liste 10/15/1933

**Jacobi, Ludwig Dr.**
06/09/1895 Nörenberg - transportation 1944
*Home address:* Lindenallee 25/Knesebeckstr. 28/Droysenstr. 18, Charlottenburg
*Law firm address:* Wilmersdorfer Str. 64, Charlottenburg
*Additional information:* After the National Socialist seizure of power he was readmitted; he worked as an attorney until the general occupational ban in 1938. Last leader of the Palestine Office. Transportation on 02/02/1942 to Theresienstadt; on 09/29/1944 transported to Auschwitz.
*Sources:* TK 33; *li; LAB, Liste 10/15/1933; Liste 36; BArch, R 3001 PAK; MRRAK; BG; GB II; Göpp., p. 248

**Jacobi, Max Dr.**
05/12/1878 Insterburg - 08/13/1943 Theresienstadt
*Home address:* Rieppelstr. 2, Spandau-Siemensstadt
*Law firm address:* Nonnendammallee 101, Siemensstadt
*Additional information:* Attorney at the Court of Appeals in Berlin; after the National Socialist seizure of power he was readmitted; he was disbarred in 1935. Date of declaration of property: 01/18/1943, collection station Gerlachstr. 18-21; transportation on 01/28/1943 to Theresienstadt, he died there six months later.
*Sources:* *li; LAB, Liste 10/15/1933; BArch, R 3001 PAK; BG; ThG; GB II

**Jacobowitz, Heinz Dr.**
07/12/1906 - no information
*Home address:* Hufelandstr. 45, NO 55
*Law firm address:* Königin-Augusta-Str. 7, W 9
*Additional information:* Attorney since 1932, after the National Socialist seizure of power he was made subject to an occupational ban on 05/31/1933.
*Sources:* TK 33; Liste d. nichtzugel. RA, 04/25/1933; BArch, R 3001 PAK, PA

**Jacobowitz, Ludwig**
12/05/1890 Tost - no information
*Home address:* no information
*Law firm address:* Alexanderplatz 1, C 25
*Additional information:* Attorney and notary; after the National Socialist seizure of power he was readmitted; in 1935 his license as a notary was revoked; he was disbarred before November 1938. He emigrated to the Netherlands.
*Sources:* TK 33; *li; LAB, Liste 10/15/1933; BArch, R 3001 PAK; BG

**Jacobowitz, Samuel Dr.**
01/28/1885 Woinicz/Galicia - no information
*Home address:* no information
*Law firm address:* Oranienburger Str. 59, N 24
*Additional information:* After the National Socialist seizure of power he was readmitted; he was still working as an attorney in 1938.
*Sources:* TK 33; *li; Liste 36; BArch, R 3001 PAK

**Jacobs, Hans Dr.**
10/15/1902 Berlin-Neukölln - no information
*Home address:* Bergstr. 145, Neukölln
*Law firm address:* Bergstr. 145, Neukölln
*Additional information:* Attorney since 04/01/1932; after the National Socialist seizure of power he lived in Spain in early 1933, but nevertheless requested readmittance, this was however rejected, since he was "non-Aryan." He was disbarred on 09/05/1933. He went from Spain to Switzerland; he was living in Switzerland in 1934.
*Sources:* BArch, R 3001 PAK, PA (P. 16, 08/23/1933); Pr.J. 33, p. 443; BG

**Jacobs, Heinrich Dr.**
04/14/1902 Deutsch-Wilmersdorf - August 1981
*Home address:* no information

*Law firm address:* Potsdamer Str. 138, W 9
*Additional information:* He passed both state examinations in law with the grade of "good," he was admitted as an attorney to the KG in 1928, he shared an office with Dr. Harri Wolff. After the National Socialist seizure of power he applied to be readmitted in April 1933. The application was rejected because he was of "non-Aryan descent" and could not claim any of the grounds for exemption, which meant an occupational ban. He emigrated to the USA, he last lived in New York, he changed his first name to John; he died in 1981 at the age of 79.
*Sources:* Liste d. nichtzugel. RA, 04/25/1933 (Nachtrag); JMBl. 33, p. 203; BArch, R 3001 PAK; SSDI

**Jacobsohn, Carl (Karl), Judicial Councillor**
07/23(29?)/1866 Nakel - 03/31(04/01?)/1938
*Home address:* Berliner Allee 5, Weißensee and Bolivarallee 5, Charlottenburg
*Law firm address:* Bergstr. 145, Neukölln
*Additional information:* Attorney at the KG and notary; after the National Socialist seizure of power he was readmitted; in 1935 his license as a notary was revoked; he died in 1938 at the age of 71.
*Sources:* *li; LAB, Liste 10/15/1933; DJ 36, p. 315; Liste 36; BArch, R 3001 PAK; BG

**Jacobsohn, Ernst Dr.**
No information
*Home address:* no information
*Law firm address:* Linkstr. 39, W 9
*Additional information:* Attorney and notary; after the National Socialist seizure of power he was readmitted; on 11/01/1935 his admission was "deleted upon request," after the notaryship was revoked for Jewish officials.
*Sources:* *li; LAB, Liste 10/15/1933; BArch, R 3001 PAK

**Jacobsohn, Friedrich (Fritz) Dr.**
05/20/1888 Berlin - 07/28/1936 Berlin
*Home address:* Spichernstr. 7, W 15
*Law firm address:* Kalkreuthstr. 4, W
*Additional information:* After the National Socialist seizure of power in 1933 he was readmitted as an attorney. He died in 1936 at the age of 48 from the long-term effects of a war injury.
*Sources:* Br.B. 32; *li; LAB, Liste 10/15/1933; Liste 36; BArch, R 3001 PAK; BG

**Jacobsohn, Hans Dr.**
02/12/1905 Goldap - 03/31/1972
*Home address:* no information
*Law firm address:* Warmbrunner Str. 33, Grunewald
*Additional information:* Attorney at the KG; Protestant; at first he was an attorney at a law firm with Erich and Paul Simon, as well as Erich Cohn, Königstr. After the National Socialist seizure of power in 1933 he was made subject to a temporary representation ban, then he was readmitted. He was exempted from the general occupational ban in 1938, because he was regarded as "mixed race," he still worked until at least 1941, amongst others for the NITAG; he escaped persecution because his documents with the authorities were destroyed by a bomb; after 1945 he first went to Hamburg, later as a board member of the NITAG (Napthaindustrie und Tankanlagen AG) to Kassel; he died in 1972.
*Sources:* TK 33; Liste d. nichtzugel. RA, 04/25/1933; *li; Liste Mschl. 36; Tel.B. 41; BArch, R 3001 PAK; VZ 39; information of his son-in-law

**Jacobsohn, Julian Dr.**
03/10/1902 - December 1966
*Home address:* no information
*Law firm address:* Große Frankfurter Str. 115, No. 18
*Additional information:* Attorney since 1931 with the LG I-III and with AG Pankow; after the National Socialist seizure of power he made a request to be readmitted in early 1933, but could not cite any reasons for an exemption; as a result he was made subject to an occupational ban. He emigrated to the USA, there he last lived in New York.
*Sources:* Liste d. nichtzugel. RA, 04/25/1933; JMBl. 33, p. 253; BArch, R 3001 PAK, PA; BG; SSDI

**Jacobsohn, Julian Dr., Judicial Councillor**
06/11/1866 Posen - no information
*Home address:* Taubertstr. 5, Grunewald
*Law firm address:* Wielandstr. 25, W 15
*Additional information:* Attorney and notary; after the National Socialist seizure of power his license as a notary was revoked in 1933, he was readmitted as an attorney; he worked as an attorney until the general occupational ban in 1938.

*Sources:* JMBl. 33, p. 208; *li; LAB, Liste 10/15/1933; Liste 36; BArch, R 3001 PAK; MRRAK

 **Jacobsohn, Kurt Dr.**
09/02/1897 Deutsch-Eylau - transportation 1944
*Home address:* Große Hamburger Str. 26, N 4; Gieselerstr. 12, Wilmersdorf, C 2; Monbijouplatz 4
*Law firm address:* Kurfürstendamm 37, W 15
*Additional information:* Attorney and notary; after the National Socialist seizure of power he was readmitted; in 1935 his license as a notary was revoked; occupational ban as attorney in 1938, he still worked as a "consultant," as from 1942 he was a steward at the collection point Große Hamburger Str. 26 and was used with the collecting service. Bruno Blau describes him as a "spy" for the Gestapo. He had probably tried in this way to escape transportation. He was nevertheless arrested on February 20, 1944 and deported to Theresienstadt on February 23, 1944. From there he was transported to Auschwitz on 05/15/1944.
*Sources:* *li; Br.B.32; LAB, Liste 10/15/1933; DJ 36, p. 315; MRRAK; Liste d. Kons. 04/15/1939; Tel.B. 41; Naatz-Album; BG; GB II; Blau, B., Vierzehn Jahre Not und Schrecken [Fourteen years of distress and fright], p. 70

**Jacobsohn, Robert Dr.**
02/25/1900 Berlin - no information
*Home address:* Friedrichstr. 226-227, SW 68
*Law firm address:* Lindenstr. 16/17
*Additional information:* After the National Socialist seizure of power he was made subject to an occupational ban in early 1933. He emigrated to Rio de Janeiro, Brazil, on 08/20/1936; after 1945 he returned to Berlin, lived in Wilmersdorf.
*Sources:* Br.B. 32; Liste d. nichtzugel. RA, 04/25/1933; JMBl. 33, p. 209; BArch, R 3001, PAK; BG

**Jacobsohn, Sally Dr.**
11/09/1876 Schönlanke - no information
*Home address:* Giesebrechtstr. 16, Charlottenburg
*Law firm address:* Giesebrechtstr. 16, Charlottenburg

*Additional information:* After the National Socialist seizure of power readmitted; he was still working as an attorney until the general occupational ban in 1938. He emigrated to Havana, Cuba, then Houston, USA.
*Sources:* Liste 36; LAB, Liste 10/15/1933; BArch, R 3001 PAK; MRRAK; BG

**Jacobson, Günther Dr.**
10/08/1896 - no information
*Home address:* no information
*Law firm address:* Friedrichstr. 131, N 24
*Additional information:* Attorney at the KG; after the National Socialist seizure of power in 1933 readmitted.
*Sources:* li; LAB, Liste 10/15/1933; BArch, R 3001 PAK

**Jacobson, Julius Dr., Judicial Councillor**
No information
*Home address:* no information
*Law firm address:* Invalidenstr. 134, N 4
*Additional information:* After the National Socialist seizure of power he was readmitted, died in 1934.
*Sources:* *li; LAB, Liste 10/15/1933; BArch, R 3001 PAK

**Jacoby, Albrecht Georg Dr.**
05/25/1898 Berlin - 01/01/1953
*Home address:* Meinekestr. 26, Charlottenburg
*Law firm address:* Meinekestr. 26, Charlottenburg
*Additional information:* Attorney and notary; after the National Socialist seizure of power he was made subject to an occupational ban in early 1933. He emigrated via Switzerland to London, Great Britain, on 10/08/1938.
*Sources:* Br.B. 32; Liste d. nichtzugel. RA., 04/25/1933; JMBl. 33, p. 209; BArch, R 3001 PAK; BG

**Jacoby, Alfred Dr.**
05/24/1885 - no information
*Home address:* no information
*Law firm address:* Behrenstr. 37, W 8
*Additional information:* After the National Socialist seizure of power readmitted; he was still working as an attorney in 1936.
*Sources:* TK 33; *li; Liste d. nichtzugel. RA, 04/25/1933 (Addendum, here Jakobi); LAB, Liste 10/15/1933; Liste 36; BArch, R 3001 PAK

**Jacoby, Ernst Dr.**
12/13/1878 Berlin - transportation 1942
*Home address:* Bayerische Str. 6/Salzburger
Str. 17 (June 1942), Schöneberg
*Law firm address:* Motzstr. 53, W 30
*Additional information:* Attorney and
notary; after the National Socialist seizure of
power in 1933 he was readmitted; in 1935 his
license as a notary was revoked; he worked
as an attorney until the occupational ban in
1938, thereafter as a "consultant."
Date of declaration of property: 03/27/1942;
transportation on 03/28/1942 to Piaski.
*Sources:* *li; LAB, Liste 10/15/1933; DJ 36, p.
315; Liste 36; Liste d. Kons.; BG; GB II

**Jacoby, Gerhard Dr. jur. et rer. pol.**
07/30/1891 Berlin - 08/19/1960 New York
*Home address:* Bregenzer Str. 19, W 15
*Law firm address:* Rankestr. 30, W 50
*Additional information:* 1912 he completed
his state examination in law; 1913 he received
a doctorate in law; 1914-18 he fought in First
World War, he was awarded the EK II; 1921 he
received a doctorate in political science from
Würzburg; as from 1921 he was an attorney in
Berlin, admitted to the KG, later also a notary;
established a law partnership with Wenzel
Goldbaum; specialized in copyright and theater
law; worked amongst others for the S. Fischer
Verlag, the UFA and many stage performers
and authors; co-founder and legal counsel of
GEMA. After the National Socialist seizure
of power in 1933 he was readmitted; during
the same year he emigrated to Jerusalem,
Palestine via France; there he worked as a legal
and financial adviser; in 1937 he went to the
USA with a tourism visa, after an interim stay
in Canada, with a regular entry visa; 1939-
60 he was with the World Jewish Congress;
1949-60 he was a representative of the WJC
with Unesco; 1951-52 he was also WJC
representative in Germany; participated in the
founding of the Central Council of Jews in
Germany; died in 1960 in New York.
*Sources:* *li; LAB, Liste 10/15/1933; DJ 36, p.
315; BG; BHdE vol. I, p. 326; Göpp., p. 289

**Jacoby, Gustav Dr.**
03/10/1904 New York - August 1985
*Home address:* no information
*Law firm address:* Bregenzerstr. 4, W 15
*Additional information:* 1905 was the return
of the family to Germany; as from 1922
he completed his legal studies in Freiburg

i.Br., Berlin and Leipzig; 1927 he received his
doctorate. After the National Socialist seizure of
power he was made subject to an occupational
ban as an attorney in early 1933; he emigrated
to the USA in June 1933; 1933-35 he renewed
his legal studies at New York University and
Columbia University; at the same time he
worked as an expert in German law; he became
a U.S. citizen; as from 1936 he was admitted
as an attorney in New York; he was active in
Jewish and other institutions and associations.
*Sources:* Liste d. nichtzugel. RA, 04/25/1933;
BArch, R 3001 PAK; BG; BHdE vol. I, p. 326;
Jewish Immigrants . . . in the U.S.A., Oral
History, pages 51-52; SSDI

**Jacoby, Hellmut**
07/05/1903 - no information
*Home address:* no information
*Law firm address:* Wartburgstr. 19,
Schöneberg
*Additional information:* Attorney with the
LG II. After the National Socialist seizure of
power he was made subject to an occupational
ban in early 1933.
Liste d. nichtzugel. RA, 04/25/1933; JMBl. 33,
p. 209; BArch, R 3001 PAK

**Jacoby, Max Dr.**
11/19/1874 Braunsberg - 01/07/1942 Berlin
*Home address:* Aschaffenburger Str. 20, W 30
*Law firm address:* Potsdamer Str. 84 a, W 57
*Additional information:* Attorney and notary;
after the National Socialist seizure of power
in 1933 his license as a notary was revoked;
he was readmitted as an attorney, he was
still working as an attorney until the general
occupational ban in 1938. He died in 1942 at
the Jewish Hospital.
*Sources:* JMBl. 33, p. 208; *li; LAB, Liste
10/15/1933; Liste 36; BArch, R 3001 PAK;
MRRAK; VZ 39; BG: LAB, OFP files

**Jacoby, Moritz S.**
06/11/1883 Berlin - 08/18/1942 Riga
*Home address:* Landhausstr. 25 a,
Wilmersdorf
*Law firm address:* Landsberger Str. 83, C 25
*Additional information:* Attorney and notary;
after the National Socialist seizure of power
in 1933 readmitted; in 1935 his license as a
notary was revoked; he worked as an attorney
until at least 1936; on 08/15/1942 he was
transported to Riga, there he was murdered
shortly after arrival.

*Sources:* *li; LAB, Liste 10/15/1933; DJ 36, p. 315; Liste 36; BArch, R 3001 PAK; BdE; GB II; information Dr. Hermann Simon

### Jacusiel, Alfred Dr.
02/09/1901 Berlin - no information
*Home address:* Spandauer Str. 9, C 2
*Law firm address:* Mohrenstr. 51, W 8
*Additional information:* Attorney at the KG, he also published; after the National Socialist seizure of power he was made subject to an occupational ban in early 1933. Alfred was the son of Kurt.
*Sources:* Br.B. 32; Liste d.nichtzugel. RA, 04/25/1933; JMBl. 33, p. 203; BArch, R 3001 PAK, PA

### Jacusiel, Hans Dr.
06/27/1903 - no information
*Home address:* no information
*Law firm address:* Fasanenstr. 30, W 15
*Additional information:* Attorney since 1928; after the National Socialist seizure of power he was made subject to an occupational ban on 05/31/1933. Hans was the son of Kurt.
*Sources:* Br.B. 32; Liste d. nichtzugel. RA, 04/25/1933; JMBl. 33, p. 220; BArch, R 3001 PAK

### Jacusiel, Kurt, Judicial Councillor
06/24/1868 Schwetz - no information
*Home address:* Mohrenstr. 51, W 8
*Law firm address:* Mohrenstr. 51, W 8
*Additional information:* Joint law partnership with his half brother Max, he was the father of Alfred and Hans; after the National Socialist seizure of power in 1933 his license as a notary was revoked. He was readmitted as an attorney until the general occupational ban in 1939. He emigrated to Santiago de Chile, Chile.
*Sources:* JMBl. 33, p. 208; li; LAB, Liste 10/15/1933; BArch, R 3001 PAK; MRRAK; BG

### Jacusiel, Max Dr.
06/04/1882 Berlin - no information
*Home address:* Sven-Hedin-Str. 20, Zehlendorf
*Law firm address:* Mohrenstr. 51, W 8
*Additional information:* Joint law partnership with his half brother Kurt; after the National Socialist seizure of power in 1933 his license as a notary was revoked, he was readmitted as an attorney. He

emigrated to Amsterdam, the Netherlands, on 01/15/1936.
*Sources:* JMBl. 33, p. 208; *li; LAB, Liste 10/15/1933; BArch, R 3001 PAK; BG

### Jaffa, Sally Dr.
07/15/1879 Insterburg - no information
*Home address:* Seebergsteig 19, Wilmersdorf, Grunewald
*Law firm address:* Dircksenstr. 26/27, C 25
*Additional information:* Attorney and notary; after the National Socialist seizure of power his license as a notary was revoked in 1935; he worked as an attorney until the general occupational ban in 1938. He emigrated to London, Great Britain.
*Sources:* *li; LAB, Liste 10/15/1933; DJ 36, p. 315; Liste 36; BArch, R 3001 PAK; MRRAK; BG

### Jaffé, Elisabeth
09/18/1901 - no information
*Home address:* no information
*Law firm address:* Maaßenstr. 25, W 30
*Additional information:* Attorney at the KG (since 1928); after the National Socialist seizure of power he was made subject to an occupational ban on 06/02/1933.
*Sources:* Br.B. 32; Liste d. nichtzugel. RA, 04/25/1933; BArch, R 3001 PAK, PA

### Jaffé, Leo Dr.
08/13/1889 Zduny - no information
*Home address:* no information
*Law firm address:* Am Karlsbad 21
*Additional information:* Attorney (since 1924) and notary (1930). After the National Socialist seizure of power he emigrated in August 1933 to Haifa, Palestine; in Israel he worked as a representative for life insurance; he returned to Germany in June 1956; he was readmitted as an attorney on 08/22/1956 and as a notary on 08/31/1956; he moved to Munich in 1959 and established himself as an attorney there.
*Sources:* Br.B. 32; TK 33, BArch, R 3001, PAK; LAB, RAK, PA

### Jaffe, Max Dr.
07/15/1883 Wreschen - no information
*Home address:* Bayerischer Platz 6, W 30
*Law firm address:* Bayerischer Platz 6, W 30

*Additional information:* Attorney and notary; after the National Socialist seizure of power in 1933 he was readmitted; his license as a notary was revoked at the latest in 1935; he was disbarred as an attorney on 03/31/1936. He emigrated to Tel Aviv, Palestine.
*Sources:* TK 33; *li; LAB, Liste 10/15/1933; BArch, R 3001 PAK; BG

**Jaffé, Walter Dr.**
04/25/1876 Berlin - no information
*Home address:* Prager Str. 7, Wilmersdorf
*Law firm address:* Zimmerstr. 87, SW 68
*Additional information:* Attorney and notary; after the National Socialist seizure of power in 1933 he was readmitted; his license as a notary was revoked at the latest in 1935; he was a member of the Reich Association of Non-Aryan Christians. He emigrated to Paris, France, on 08/31/1938.
*Sources:* *li; LAB, Liste 10/15/1933; BArch, R 3001 PAK; Mitt.bl. Reichsverband nichtarischer Christen, 12/06/1934; BG

**Jalowicz, Hermann Dr.**
06/12/1877 Berlin -
03/18/1941 Berlin
*Home address:* Prenzlauer Str. 9, Mitte
*Law firm address:* Prenzlauer Str. 19 a, C 25
*Additional information:* He came from a poor, religious, law-abiding family. He financed his legal studies by being a working student. During the First World War he was a soldier at the military court in the conquered eastern territories. Already during his studies he was actively involved in Zionist activities, he was a member of the Bar-Kochba gymnastics club and edited its monthly association body, the "Jüdische Turnzeitung" (Jewish Gymnastics Newspaper). After the First World War he opened his own law firm (later with a notary); his wife presided over the office. He was an attorney with a strong sense of justice. On the other hand, he was not interested in business aspects.
After the National Socialist seizure of power he was readmitted upon his request, since he was recognized as a "frontline fighter." His license as a notary was revoked; in 1935 he visited the second Maccabiah Games, his friends supported travel costs. Since his wife had been ill for several years, emigration was not a possibility. After her death in June 1938 he gave up his law firm and apartment, the furniture had to be sold dirt cheap. The Palestinian Authority's promise of a certificate of emigration to Palestine was not kept. His financial predicament was dire. As a former notary, who at that time had official status, he received only a small pension. In 1938 he no longer sought permission to be a "consultant," since the expected revenues would not have covered the costs of the firm. He died in 1941 at the age of 63; "his life energy was sapped" (grandson Hermann Simon).
*Sources:* *li; LAB, Liste 10/15/1933; DJ 36, p. 315; Liste 36; BArch, R 3001 PAK; MRRAK; BG; information H. Simon, CJ

**Jandorf, Julius Dr.**
05/24/1882 Hengstfeld - no information
*Home address:* no information
*Law firm address:* Mauerstr. 53, W 8
*Additional information:* Attorney and notary; after the National Socialist seizure of power in 1933 his license as a notary was revoked; he was readmitted as an attorney up to his disbarment on 12/10/1935.
*Sources:* *li; LAB, Liste 10/15/1933; JMBl. 33, p. 208; Liste 36; BArch, R 3001 PAK

**Jankuhn, Alfred**
03/07/1906 Berlin - no information
*Home address:* Ilmenauer Str. 2, Wilmersdorf
*Law firm address:* Mittelstr. 25, NW 7
*Additional information:* After the National Socialist seizure of power in 1933 he was readmitted; this was an unusual process, since he could not have been an "elder attorney" or "frontline fighter," the only reason for exemption in 1933 could have been that his father had died during the First World War. Checking the files is not possible, since they have been lost. He was a Protestant, he was regarded as "mixed-race first degree" and could still practice in 1941, he survived and lived in Wilmersdorf after the liberation.
*Sources:* *li; Liste Mschlg. 36; BArch, R 3001 PAK; Tel.B. 41; Verz. zugel. Anw. 45; BG

**Jarecki, Jacob, Judicial Councillor**
08/17/1862 Wreschen - 10/15/1942 Theresienstadt
*Home address:* Gerlachstr. 18-21, C 2 (Retirement home of the Jewish Synagogue)

*Law firm address:* Prinzregentenstr. 6, Wilmersdorf
*Additional information:* Attorney and notary; after the National Socialist seizure of power in 1933 his license as a notary was revoked; he worked as an attorney until the general occupational ban in 1938. Transportation on 09/14/1942 to Theresienstadt; he died there a month later.
*Sources:* JMBl. 33, p. 208; *li; LAB, Liste 10/15/1933; Liste 36; BArch, R 3001 PAK; BG; ThG; GB II

**Jarecki, Samuel**
No information - 06/01/1938
*Home address:* no information
*Law firm address:* Potsdamer Str. 118 c, W 35
*Additional information:* Attorney and notary; after the National Socialist seizure of power in 1933 his license as a notary was revoked; he was still working as an attorney in 1936; he died in 1938.
*Sources:* JMBl. 33, p. 208; *li; LAB, Liste 10/15/1933; Liste 36

**Jessel, Herbert Dr.**
05/20/1892 Breslau - no information
*Home address:* Westfälische Str. 17
*Law firm address:* Unter den Linden 8, W 8
*Additional information:* Attorney at the KG; after the National Socialist seizure of power he was readmitted; he worked as an attorney until the general occupational ban in 1938. He emigrated to Surrey, Great Britain, on 08/22/1939.
*Sources:* *li; LAB, Liste 10/15/1933; Liste 36; MRRAK; BG

**Joachim, Günther**
03/08/1880 Berlin - 03/29/1933 Berlin
*Home address:* no information
*Law firm address:* Königstr. 53/54; C 2
*Additional information:* Attorney since 1928; SPD member.
He was transported by the SA (Sturmabteilung = Storm Troopers) in March 1933 and was imprisoned and killed in the SA-barracks Jüdenstraße and ULAP. His death was only listed in September 1933 (JMBl.). He was buried at Weißensee.
*Sources:* Br.B. 32; TK 33; JMBl. 2.9.33, p. 281; BArch, R 3001 PAK; BG; Friedh.W.Sterbereg.; Krach, p. 434; Schilde et al., p. 63, 215; Sandvoss 1994, p. 34

**Joachim, Walter**
09/16/1891 Berlin - 10/29/1942 Riga
*Home address:* Kantstr. 33, Charlottenburg
*Law firm address:* Goethepark 26, Charlottenburg
*Additional information:* After the National Socialist seizure of power he was made subject to an occupational ban in early 1933. Date of declaration of property: 10/21/1942; transportation on 10/26/1942 to Riga; he was murdered there shortly after arrival.
*Sources:* Br.B. 32; JMBl. 33, p. 221; Liste d. nichtzugel. RA, 04/25/1933; BArch, R 3001 PAK; BG; BdE; GB II

**Joachimczyk, Willy Dr.**
07/06/1883 Posen - 07/01/1942 Auschwitz
*Home address:* Tirpitzufer 64, W 35
*Law firm address:* Kanzlei: Friedrichstr. 187/188, W 8
*Additional information:* Attorney and notary; after the National Socialist seizure of power in 1933 he was readmitted; in 1935 his license as a notary was revoked; he still worked as an attorney until the general occupational ban in 1938. He was transported to Auschwitz under unknown circumstances and was murdered there on 07/01/1942.
*Sources:* *li; LAB, Liste 10/15/1933; DJ 36, p. 315; Liste 36; MRRAK; BG; GB II; information Weißleder

**Joel, Günther Dr.**
No information
*Home address:* no information
*Law firm address:* Französische Str. 35/39, W 56
*Additional information:* After the National Socialist seizure of power in 1933 he was readmitted as an attorney, he was regarded as "mixed race," he was still working in 1936; he survived and was readmitted as an attorney and notary after 1945.
*Sources:* *li; LAB, 10/15/1933; Liste Mschlg. 36; TK 36; BArch, R 3001 PAK; Verz. zugel. Anw. 45

**Jolenberg, Hans**
10/01/1891 Berlin - no information
*Home address:* no information
*Law firm address:* Dorotheenstr. 19, NW 7
*Additional information:* Attorney since 1918; after the National Socialist seizure of

power he was made subject to an occupational ban at the beginning of June 1933.
*Sources:* Br.B. 32; Liste d. nichtzugel. RA, 04/25/1933 (hier: Jelenberg); JMBl. 07/07/1933; p. 209; BArch, R 3001 PAK, PA

### Jonas, Albert Dr.
03/03/1898 Berlin - March 1985
*Home address:* no information
*Law firm address:* Französische Str. 28, W 56
*Additional information:* Attorney at the KG (since 1924); after the National Socialist seizure of power he was made subject to an occupational ban on 05/20/1933. He emigrated to the USA, last lived in New York.
*Sources:* Br.B. 32; Liste d. nichtzugel. RA, 04/25/1933; BArch, R 3001 PAK, PA; SSDI

### Jonas, Fritz
05/24/1891 Berlin - no information
*Home address:* no information
*Law firm address:* Französische Str. 15, W 8
*Additional information:* Attorney and notary; he was also active in providing legal protection to the "Rote Hilfe" (Red Aid). After the National Socialist seizure of power the executive board of the RAK mentioned to the Prussian Ministry of Justice that "[he], according to the notification of SS Section III," received fees from the "Rote Hilfe," at the same time it was emphasized that he was "non-Aryan." A little later he was made subject to an occupational ban. He emigrated to Shanghai, China; in 1952 he was living in Brazil.
*Sources:* GHStA, Rep. 84a, Nr. 20363; Liste d. nichtzugel. RA, 04/25/1933 (Addendum); JMBl. 33, p. 209; BArch, R 3001 PAK; BG; Schneider, Schwarz, Schwarz, p. 171

### Jonas, Ludwig Dr.
11/24/1875 Sagan - transportation 1942
*Home address:* Rosenheimer Str. 22, Schöneberg
*Law firm address:* Rosenheimer Str. 22, Schöneberg
*Additional information:* Attorney and notary; after the National Socialist seizure of power in 1933 he was readmitted; his license as a notary was revoked in 1935; he still worked as an attorney until the general occupational ban in 1938. Date of declaration of property: 08/09/1942; collecting station Große Hamburger Str. 26; transportation on

08/19/1942 to Theresienstadt; on 05/16/1944 he was transported to Auschwitz.
*Sources:* *li; LAB, Liste 10/15/1933; Liste 36; BArch, R 3001 PAK; BG; GB II

### Jonas, Max Dr.
06/19/1903 Fränkisch-Crumbach - no information
*Home address:* Lindenallee 28, Charlottenburg
*Law firm address:* Schöneberger Ufer 42, W 35
*Additional information:* After the National Socialist seizure of power he was made subject to an occupational ban in early 1933. He emigrated to Great Britain in November 1933.
*Sources:* Br.B. 32; Liste d. nichtzugel. RA, 04/25/1933; JMBl. 33, p. 220; BArch, R 3001 PAK; BG

### Joseph, Benno
09/02/1873 Nakel - no information
*Home address:* Kronprinzenstr. 8, Weißensee
*Law firm address:* Badstr. 26, N 20
*Additional information:* Attorney and notary; after the National Socialist seizure of power in 1933 his license as a notary was revoked; he still worked as an attorney until the general occupational ban in 1938.
JMBl. 33, p. 208; *li; LAB, Liste 10/15/1933; Liste 36; BArch, R 3001 PAK

### Joseph, Eugen Dr.
05/08/1882 Berlin - transportation 1942
*Home address:* Neue Ansbacher Str. 7 a; Gustloffstr. 55, Charlottenburg
*Law firm address:* Potsdamer Str. 37, W 35
*Additional information:* Attorney and notary; after the National Socialist seizure of power he was readmitted; his license as a notary was revoked in 1935; he still worked as an attorney until the general occupational ban in 1938. Date of declaration of property: 11/24/1942; collecting station Große Hamburger Str. 26; transportation on 11/29/1942 to Auschwitz.
*Sources:* *li; LAB, Liste 10/15/1933; DJ 36, p. 315; Liste 36; BArch, R 3001 PAK; MRRAK; BG; GB II

### Joseph, Otto Hermann
01/31/1897 Berlin - no information
*Home address:* Paulsborner Str. 92, W 15
*Law firm address:* Jägerstr. 18, Mitte

*Additional information:* Attorney at the KG and notary; after the National Socialist seizure of power he dissolved his law firm. The other sources are contradictory: presumably he emigrated in 1934 to Paris, France. An arrest warrant for tax evasion was issued against him.
*Sources:* Br.B. 32; Pr.J. 33, p. 773; BArch, R 3001 PAK; BG; Wolf, BFS

**Josephsen, Albert**
09/21/1878 Neutomischel - no information
*Home address:* Aschaffenburger Str. 5 bei Müller, Wilmersdorf
*Law firm address:* Unter den Linden 60, NW 7
*Additional information:* Attorney and notary; after the National Socialist seizure of power in 1933 his license as a notary was revoked, he was readmitted as an attorney; he worked until the general occupational ban in 1938; he was a member of the Reich Association of Non-Aryan Christians.
*Sources:* JMBl. 33, p. 208; *li; Liste 36; MRRAK; BG; LAB, Liste 10/15/1933; BArch, R 3001 PAK; Mitt.bl. Reichsverband nichtarischer Christen, 12/06/1934

**Josephsen, Georg**
01/08/1876 Neutomischel - no information
*Home address:* no information
*Law firm address:* Hardenbergstr. 9 a, Charlottenburg
*Additional information:* Attorney at the KG; after the National Socialist seizure of power he was made subject to an occupational ban in early 1933.
*Sources:* JMBl. 33, p. 253; Liste d. nichtzugel. RA, 04/25/1933; BArch, R 3001 PAK; BG

**Josephsen, Richard**
06/15/1880 - no information
*Home address:* no information
*Law firm address:* Hardenbergstr. 9 a, Charlottenburg
*Additional information:* Attorney and notary: after the National Socialist seizure of power in 1933 his license as a notary was revoked, he was readmitted as an attorney, he was disbarred on 10/12/1935.
*Sources:* JMBl. 33, p. 208; *li; LAB, Liste 10/15/1933; BArch, R 3001 PAK

**Juda, Alfred Dr.**
06/16/1904 Berlin - no information
*Home address:* no information

*Law firm address:* Neue Königstr. 10, NO 43
*Additional information:* Attorney since 1931; after the National Socialist seizure of power he was made subject to an occupational ban on 05/31/1933. He emigrated on 08/20/1939 to London, Great Britain.
*Sources:* Liste d. nichtzugel. RA, 04/25/1933; JMBl. 33, p. 209; BArch, R 3001 PAK; BG

**Juda, Josef Dr.**
07/04/1901 - no information
*Home address:* no information
*Law firm address:* Behrenstr. 23, W 8
*Additional information:* Attorney since 1930, after the National Socialist seizure of power he was made subject to an occupational ban on 06/12/1933.
*Sources:* Liste d. nichtzugel. RA, 04/25/1933; JMBl. 33, p. 253; BArch, R 3001 PAK, PA

**Judesis, Arthur**
04/26/1889 Königsberg - 11/10/1938 Berlin
*Home address:* no information
*Law firm address:* Taubenstr. 21, W 8
*Additional information:* Attorney and notary; after the National Socialist seizure of power in 1933 he was readmitted; in 1935 his license as a notary was revoked, he worked as an attorney until 11/19/1937.
He was killed in the context of the Night of Broken Glass on 11/10/1938 at the age of 49 years.
*Sources:* *li; LAB, Liste 10/15/1933; DJ 36, p. 315; Liste 36; BArch, R 3001 PAK; Naatz-Album; BG; GB II

**Juliusberger, Erich Dr.**
04/24/1886 Breslau - transportation 1943
*Home address:* Königin-Augusta-Str. 48
*Law firm address:* Potsdamer Str. 134; Potsdamer Str. 123 a, W 35; Nürnberger Str. 66, Schöneberg
*Additional information:* He had passed his first state examination in law in Breslau in 1908, his second state examination in law in 1913, from 1914 until his release in 1919 military service, especially on the West Front, he received multiple awards, amongst others the EK II. Kl. Attorney (since 1914) and notary (since 1924). After the National Socialist seizure of power

in 1933 his license as a notary was revoked; he was readmitted as an attorney, he last practiced from his private home; he was used as a forced laborer and employed as a worker. Date of declaration of property: 01/11/1943; collecting station Große Hamburger Str. 26; transportation on 01/29/1943 to Auschwitz. Erich was presumably the brother of Fritz.
*Sources:* TK 33; Pr.J. 33, p. 390; *li; TK 36, p. 53; Tel.B. 38; LAB, Liste 10/15/1933; Liste 36; BArch, R 3001 PAK, PA; MRRAK; BG; GB II

### Juliusberger, Fritz Dr.
03/06/1884 Breslau - 01/30/1943 Auschwitz
*Home address:* Knesebeckstr. 22, Charlottenburg
*Law firm address:* Unter den Linden 14, W 8
*Additional information:* He had broken away from the Jewish religion. After the National Socialist seizure of power in 1933 his license as a notary was revoked; he was readmitted as an attorney until the general occupational ban in 1938; his wife Klara was regarded as non-Jewish. He was transported to Auschwitz under unknown circumstances and was murdered on 01/30/1943.
*Sources:* TK 33; BR. B. 32; JMBl. 33, p. 208; *li; Liste 36; BArch, R 3001 PAK; MRRAK; BG; GB II

### Just, Arthur Dr.
02/21/1895 Berlin - no information
*Home address:* Kurfürstendamm 216, W 15
*Law firm address:* Kurfürstendamm 216, W 15
*Additional information:* After the National Socialist seizure of power he was readmitted and worked as an attorney until the general occupational ban in 1938.
*Sources:* *li; LAB, Liste 10/15/1933; Liste 36; BArch, R 3001 PAK; MRRAK; BG

# K

### Kahlenberg, Hermann Dr.
01/05/1876 Bremen - no information
*Home address:* Fasanenstr. 48, Wilmersdorf
*Law firm address:* Lützow-Ufer 5 a, W 35
*Additional information:* After the National Socialist seizure of power in 1933 he was readmitted; on 04/24/1934 he was disbarred. He emigrated to Amsterdam, the Netherlands, on 06/30/1938, later to London, Great Britain.
*Sources:* *li; LAB, Liste 10/15/1933; BArch, R 3001 PAK; BG: LAB, OFP files

### Kahn, Bernhard Dr.
01/13/1887 - no information
*Home address:* no information
*Law firm address:* Hohenzollernstr. 25, W 35
*Additional information:* After the National Socialist seizure of power he was readmitted; he still worked as an attorney until the general occupational ban in 1938; he presumably emigrated to Shanghai.
*Sources:* *li; LAB, 10/15/1933; Liste 36; BArch, R 3001 PAK; MRRAK

### Kahn, Heinrich Dr.
04/27/1902 - no information
*Home address:* no information
*Law firm address:* Barbarossastr. 21, W 30
*Additional information:* In 1931 he was also active in providing legal protection to the Red Aid. After the National Socialist seizure of power he was made subject to an occupational ban in early 1933.
Liste d. nichtzugel. RA, 04/25/1933 (Addendum); JMBl. 33, p. 203; BArch, R 3001 PAK; Schneider, Schwarz, Schwarz, p. 173

### Kahn, Rudolf Dr.
10/15/1896 Germersheim - no information
*Home address:* no information
*Law firm address:* Friedrich-Ebert-Str. 15, W 9
*Additional information:* After the National Socialist seizure of power in 1933 he was readmitted; on 11/20/1936 he was disbarred, he presumably emigrated to Shanghai.
*Sources:* TK 33; *li; Liste 36; BG; LAB, Liste 10/15/1933; BArch, R 3001 PAK; Information E. Proskauer

### Kahn, Wilhelm Dr.
04/28/1903 - no information
*Home address:* no information
*Law firm address:* Schmidtstr. 24/25, SO 16
*Additional information:* After the National Socialist seizure of power he was made subject to an occupational ban in early 1933.
*Sources:* Liste d. nichtzugel. RA, 04/25/1933; JMBl. 33, p. 253; BArch, R 3001 PAK

### Kaiser, Hermann Georg Dr.
01/13/1904 Mardorf - 10/14/1992
*Home address:* no information
*Law firm address:* Friedrichstr. 166
*Additional information:* 1922-25 he completed his legal studies in Marburg, Gießen and Frankfurt a. M.; 1925 he passed

his first state examination in law; 1927 he received his doctorate; 1929 he passed his second state examination in law; as from December 1929 he wa an attorney in Berlin, admitted to the KG. After the National Socialist seizure of power he was made subject to an occupational ban in 1933; in May 1938 he was suspected by the Gestapo in Rostock as an informer, thereupon he emigrated to Great Britain via Belgium; as from February 1940 he went to the USA; at first he was an owner of a supply company for the oil industry, as from 1949 he owned a petroleum and gas company; he was active in numerous institutions and associations, he last lived in Tulsa, Oklahoma.
*Sources:* Br.B. 32; BArch, R 3001 PAK; Pr.J. 33, p. 502; BG; BHdE vol. 1, p. 344; SSDI

**Kalisch, Hans Dr.**
09/29/1877 Berlin - no information
*Home address:* no information
*Law firm address:* Motzstr. 58, W 30
Attorney and notary; after the National Socialist seizure of power in 1933 his license as a notary was revoked, he was readmitted as an attorney - he worked until the general occupational ban in 1938. His wife was regarded as non-Jewish.
*Sources:* JMBl. 33, p. 220; *li; Liste 36; BArch, R 3001 PAK

**Kalischer, Ernst**
03/19/1881 Berlin - no information
*Home address:* Potsdamer Str. 121, W 35
*Law firm address:* Potsdamer Str. 129/130, W 9
*Additional information:* Attorney and notary; after the National Socialist seizure of power in 1933 his license as a notary was revoked; he was readmitted as an attorney, disbarment on 09/17/1936; he emigrated to Rio de Janeiro, Brazil, on 09/08/1936.
*Sources:* JMBl. 33, p. 208; *li; LAB, Liste 10/15/1933; Liste 36; BArch, R 3001 PAK; BG

**Kalischer I, Fritz Dr.**
12/14/1881 Berlin -
08/06/1964 Tessin
*Home address:* Meineckestr. 4, Charlottenburg
*Law firm address:* Potsdamer Str. 138, W 9
*Additional information:*
Attorney at the KG (since 1912); He was

Protestant, he fought in the First World War from 1915 to the end of the war; he shared a law office with Dr. Hans Kaufmann. After the National Socialist seizure of power in 1933 he was readmitted; he was able to claim that he was both a "frontline fighter" as well as an "elder attorney." In 1936 he was taken into "protective custody" and he was accused of a foreign exchange offense. In the meantime, his offices were closed, even the appointed representative, attorney Alfred Maaß, was only admitted entry after an application with the Ministry of the Interior. The Chief Prosecutor at the District Court rejected the opening of court proceedings against him, because there was no sufficient evidence. At this time, he had been in protective custody for six months and was under the command of the Gestapo. He continued working after his release until the general occupational ban in 1938. In order to avoid his legal first name "Israel," he now called himself Feleg Kalischer. He was still admitted as a "consultant." Since he lived in a "mixed race marriage" and had two children with his wife and the marriage was regarded as "privileged," he was still protected for a period of time.
In 1942, the couple decided to leave Berlin and moved to a vacation home of the family in Bad Schwarzbach in the Jizera Mountains in Silesia. From there, Ms. Kalischer had to go to Berlin several times to extend her food ration cards. The family was not deregistered in Berlin to avoid further inquiries. In Bad Schwarzbach it was thought that Fritz was staying in Berlin. In this way he managed to go underground. The daughter of school age was informed about the situation and knew that she had to stay silent. In the case of danger, a hiding place for Fritz was installed in the chimney of the house. The housekeeper and maid of the youngest child, Aunt Minna, remained faithful to the family. She had to witness how her former employer, for whom she had been working for twenty years and whom she loved, was suddenly picked up with an unknown destination because she was Jewish. Also supported by some neighbors who had been informed of the situation, the family survived the time of distress. However, with the advance of the Soviet troops, security had not yet been fully achieved. Thus an attack took place, since

the rumor was spread that something could be gotten "from the Jews." However, after the end of the war, Fritz was able, in other cases, to defend himself by referring to his Jewish star. In 1946 he moved back to Berlin and immediately established himself as an attorney. His former secretary took up her old job. He relocated his office from Grolmannstraße to Mommsenstr. 22.
*Sources:* Br.B. 32; TK 33; *li; LAB, Liste 10/15/1933; Liste 36; BArch, R 3001 PAK, PA; MRRAK; Verz. zugel. Anw. 45; information of the daughter

### Kalischer, Fritz
10/15/1884 Berlin - no information
*Home address:* no information
*Law firm address:* Friedrichstr. 93, NW 7
*Additional information:* Attorney at the KG (since 1915); after the National Socialist seizure of power he applied to be readmitted as an attorney in April 1933. In the "Declaration of Loyalty" addressed to the Prussian Minister of Justice, he wrote: "I must declare, Your Excellency, with reference to the decree of 5 April 1933 . . . that I recognize the situation created by the facts." According to the editor, this explanation was insufficient. As a result, he was made subject to an occupational ban. He emigrated to Northfields, Great Britain, on 07/02/1938.
*Sources:* Br.B. 32; TK 33; Liste d. nichtzugel. RA, 04/25/1933; JMBl. 33, p. 203; BArch, R 3001 PAK, PA; BG

### Kallmann, Arthur Dr.
04/16/1873 Stargard - 03/14/1943 Theresienstadt
*Home address:* Geisbergstr. 41, W 30
*Law firm address:* Geisbergstr. 41, W 30
*Additional information:* Since ca. 1903 he was an established attorney at the District Courts I-III, later also a notary; he published the "Deutscher Juristen-Kalender" [German legal calendar] (1914 and 1930). He really wanted to become a judge, however, he would have had to be baptized according to the informal rules of the Prussian administration of justice. He rejected this, although he was not religious at all, his son reports. After the National Socialist seizure of power in 1933 he was

readmitted as an "elder" attorney, however, his license as a notary was revoked. He practiced until the general occupational ban in 1938. Date of declaration of property: 08/11/1942; collecting station Gerlachstr. 18-21; transportation on 10/03/1942 to Theresienstadt, where he died on 03/14/1943. His wife was transported to Auschwitz in October 1944 and was murdered there. His daughter, Eva, born on 03/20/1921 in Berlin, was transported to Riga on 10/26/1942 and was murdered there on 10/29/1942. The son of the family, Helmut (born 1922), was sent to Great Britain unaccompanied in 1938. After the war broke out he was interned in Great Britain as an "alien enemy," eventually transported to Canada and further interned there. He was released in 1943 and made ends meet with various jobs. In 1946, he began studying musicology in Toronto and later became a professor and specialist in Canadian music.
*Sources:* JMBl. 33, p. 208; *li; LAB, Liste 10/15/1933; Liste 36; BArch, R 3001 PAK; MRRAK; BG; ThG; GB II; information of Helmut Kallmann (son) 1999, 2006; Ausst. AoR, Kanada

### Kallmann, Curt
05/09/1885 Berlin - no information
*Home address:* Bendlerstr. 8
*Law firm address:* Bellevuestr. 14, W 9
*Additional information:* Attorney and notary; after the National Socialist seizure of power he was readmitted; in 1935 his license as a notary was revoked; he still worked as an attorney until the general occupational ban in 1938. He emigrated to Sweden.
*Sources:* *li; LAB, Liste 10/15/1933; DJ 36, p. 315; Liste 36; BArch, R 3001 PAK; MRRAK; BG

### Kallmann, Siegmund Dr.
03/11/1887 Reetz - no information
*Home address:* Tempelhofer Ufer 1 c, SW 61
*Law firm address:* Tempelhofer Ufer 1 c, SW 61
*Additional information:* Attorney and notary; after the National Socialist seizure of power his license as a notary was revoked, he gave up his activity, in 1934 he emigrated to Switzerland. An arrest warrant for tax evasion was issued against him.
*Sources:* Br.B. 32; TK 33; Pr.J. 33, p. 466; Wolf, BFS

**Kamm, Dagobert**
06/18/1890 - no information
*Home address:* no information
*Law firm address:* Große Frankfurter
Str. 121, NO 18
*Additional information:* Attorney and
notary; after the National Socialist seizure of
power he was readmitted; in 1935 his license
as a notary was revoked; he was still working
as an attorney until 11/07/1937.
*Sources:* *li; LAB, Liste 10/15/1933; DJ 36, p.
315; Liste 36; BArch, R 3001 PAK

**Kamnitzer, Eugen**
06/23/1881 Gilgenburg - no information
*Home address:* Düsseldorfer Str. 51, W 15
*Law firm address:* Königstr. 49, C 2
*Additional information:* Attorney and
notary; after the National Socialist seizure
of power in 1933 his license as a notary was
revoked; he worked as an attorney until the
general occupational ban. He emigrated to
Rio de Janeiro, Brazil, on 02/17/1939.
*Sources:* JMBl. 33, p. 208; *li; LAB, Liste
10/15/1933; BArch, R 3001 PAK; MRRAK; BG

**Kann, Richard Dr.**
11/05/1874 Hannover - 12/06/1942 Berlin
*Home address:* Neue Ansbacher Str. 6, W 50,
Tiergarten
*Law firm address:* Schöneberger Ufer 46, W 35
*Additional information:* Well-known civil
attorney;; attorney at the KG and notary;
before 1933, he was a member of the
executive board of the Berlin Bar Association
and of the legal provincial examination
commission. After the National Socialist
seizure of power in 1933 his license as a
notary was revoked, he worked as an attorney
until the general occupational ban in 1938;
after that he was admitted as a "consultant."
In 1942, he and his wife, Susanne,
committed suicide in the face of the imminent
deportation. He was buried at Weißensee.
*Publications:* among others "Zeitschrift für
Deutschen Zivilprozess" [Journal of German
Civil Procedure]
*Sources:* JMBl. 33, p. 208; *li; LAB, Liste
10/15/1933; Liste 36; Philo-Lexikon, p. 604;
Liste d. Kons. 04/15/1939;
MRRAK; BG; GB II; Göpp., p. 233

**Kantorowicz, Fritz**
11/19/1885 1885 Posen - no information

*Home address:* no information
*Law firm address:* Joachimsthaler Str. 16, W 15
*Additional information:* Attorney and
notary; after the National Socialist seizure
of power in 1933 his license as a notary was
revoked; he worked as an attorney until the
general occupational ban in 1938. He went
underground and survived.
*Sources:* JMBl. 33, p. 208; *li; LAB, Liste
10/15/1933; Liste 36; BArch, R 3001 PAK; BG

**Kantorowicz, Ludwig Dr.**
05/05/1900 Samter - no information
*Home address:* no information
*Law firm address:* Kaiserstr. 25 a, C 25
*Additional information:* Attorney since 1927;
after the National Socialist seizure of power
he was made subject to an occupational ban
on 06/10/1933. He emigrated to Great Britain.
*Sources:* Br.B. 32; JMBl. 33, p. 253; Liste d.
nichtzugel. RA, 04/25/1933; BArch, R 3001
PAK, PA; BG

**Kantorowicz, Max Dr.**
09/06/1876 Posen - no information
*Home address:* no information
*Law firm address:* Neue Königstr. 19 c, NO 43
*Additional information:* Attorney and
notary; presumably legal counsel of the
"Komische Oper" (Comic Opera); after the
National Socialist seizure of power in 1933
his license as a notary was revoked; he still
worked as an attorney until the general
occupational ban in 1938. He emigrated to
Bolivia on 06/03/1939.
*Sources:* JMBl. 33, p. 208; *li: LAB, Liste
10/15/1933; Liste 36; MRRAK; BG

**Kareski, Paul Dr.**
02/09/1884 Posen - 10/29/1942 Riga
*Home address:* Landsberger Str. 66/67, C 25,
Mitte
*Law firm address:* Landsberger Str. 66/67,
C 25
*Additional information:* Attorney and
notary; after the National Socialist seizure
of power in 1933 his license as a notary
was revoked; he was readmitted as an
attorney; he was still working in 1936; he
was last an honorary inspector at the Jewish
Culture Association. Date of declaration of
property: 10/20/1942, deportation to Riga on
10/26/1942. He was murdered shortly after
arrival.

*Sources:* JMBl. 33, p. 208; *li; LAB, Liste 10/15/1933; Liste 36; BArch, R 3001 PAK; BG; BdE; GB II

**Karfunkel, Ernst**
11/28/1880 Berlin - no information
*Home address:* no information
*Law firm address:* Neue Schönhauser Str. 1, N 54
*Additional information:* Attorney and notary; after the National Socialist seizure of power in 1933 his license as a notary was revoked, he worked as an attorney until the general occupational ban in 1938. Emigration.
*Sources:* JMBl. 33, p. 220; *li; LAB, Liste 10/15/1933; Liste 36; BArch, R 3001 PAK; MRRAK; BG

**Karger, Alfred Joseph Dr.**
05/26/1891 Magdeburg - no information
*Home address:* Wielandstr. 15, Charlottenburg/ Krottnauerstr. 22, Zehlendorf
*Law firm address:* Fasanenstr. 77, Charlottenburg
*Additional information:* Attorney and notary; after the National Socialist seizure of power in 1933 he was made subject to an occupational ban. He emigrated to Ecuador on 10/16/1941; highly likely that he returned to Germany.
*Sources:* Adr.B. 32; TK 33; JMBl. 33, p. 253; BArch, R 3001 PAK; BG: BAK, Kartei schulpfl. Kinder; BAK, Emigrations- u. Sterbedatei; LAB, OFP files; BAP, 15.09 RSA

**Karger, Fritz Dr.**
05/13/1903 Berlin - no information
*Home address:* Von-der-Heydt-Str. 4, W 35
*Law firm address:* Hallesches Ufer 16, SW 11
*Additional information:* Attorney at the LG I-III and AG Berlin-Mitte. After the National Socialist seizure of power in 1933 he was made subject to an occupational ban. 1936 he emigrated to Basel, Switzerland.
*Sources:* Adr.B. 32; TK 33; JMBl. 33, p. 220; BArch, R 3001 PAK; BG; BHdE vol. I, p. 349 (Heinz Karger)

**Karpen, Alfred Dr.**
06/28/1890 Berlin - no information
*Home address:* Motzstr. 81, Wilmersdorf
*Law firm address:* Motzstr. 51, Wilmersdorf
*Additional information:* Attorney at the KG and notary; after the National Socialist seizure of power he was readmitted; he was in closer contact to Dagobert Pincus; his license as a notary was revoked in 1935; he was made subject to an occupational ban as attorney in 1936, then he was still working as a "consultant," he survived by going underground, after 1945 he was readmitted; he practiced until the end of his 87th year, 1977, in Xantener Str. 16, then he canceled his membership in the Bar Association.
*Sources:* *li; LAB, Liste 10/15/1933; DJ 36, p. 315; Liste 36; MRRAK; Liste d. Kons. V. 04/15/1939; Verz. zugel. Anw.45; LAB, RAK, PA; BG

**Karsen, Arthur Dr.**
08/30/1881 - no information
*Home address:* Kaiserstr. 30-32, Spandau
*Law firm address:* Markt 1, Spandau
*Additional information:* Attorney and notary; after the National Socialist seizure of power in 1933 his license as a notary was revoked, he was readmitted as an attorney; he worked until the general occupational ban in 1938; he was a member of the Reich Association of non-Aryan Christians. He emigrated to Great Britain in April/May 1939.
*Sources:* JMBl. 33, p. 208; *li; LAB, Liste 10/15/1933; MRRAK; Mitt.bl. Reichsverband nichtarischer Christen, 12/06/1934; BG

**Kaskel, Joseph**
03/13/1892 Posen - 09/05/1989 USA
*Home address:* Habelschwerter Allee 26, Zehlendorf-Dahlem
*Law firm address:* Friedrichstr. 79 a, W 8
*Additional information:* Attorney at the KG (since 1922) and notary (since 1927); he was a Protestant; he fought during the First World War. After the National Socialist seizure of power in 1933 he was readmitted, because he had been recognized as a "frontline fighter;" his license as a notary was revoked on 01/28/1936; he was made subject to an occupational ban as attorney in 1938. He emigrated to the USA; after the end of the war he reestablished a law office, which supervised bilateral mandates; freed from the residence obligation, he was once again admitted as an attorney in Berlin; in 1967 he was a member of the board of the American Association of Former European Jurists, N.Y.; he changed his name to Kaskell, he last lived in New York, he died at the age of 97.

*Sources:* *li, LAB, Liste 10/15/1933; DJ 36, p. 315; BArch, R 3001 PAK; MRRAK; LBI, NY; BG; LAB, RAK PA; American Association of Former European Jurists, LBI Ar 6546

### Kassel, Heinrich
02/26/1882 - 03/01/1937
*Home address:* no information
*Law firm address:* Pariser Platz 6, NW 7
*Additional information:* Attorney at the KG and notary; after the National Socialist seizure of power in 1933 his license as a notary was revoked; he worked as an attorney until his death in 1937.
*Sources:* JMBl. 33, p. 208; *li; LAB, Liste 10/15/1933; Liste 36; BArch, R 3001 PAK

### Katschak, Alfred Dr.
11/21/1892 - 02/25/1938
*Home address:* no information
*Law firm address:* Behrenstr. 14/16, W 8
After the National Socialist seizure of power he was readmitted; his status as a "Jewish" attorney had only been determined in the course of 1933. He died in February 1938 at the age of 46.
*Sources:* LAB, Liste 10/15/1933; BArch, R 3001 PAK

### Katschke, Hans
04/10/1902 - no information
*Home address:* Aschaffenburger Str.23, Wilmersdorf (1931)
*Law firm address:* Charlottenstr. 71, W 8
*Additional information:* After the National Socialist seizure of power he was made subject to an occupational ban in in early 1933. He emigrated to South America, presumably to Montevideo.
*Sources:* Br.B. 32; Jüd.Adr.B., JMBl. 33, p. 253; BArch, R 3001 PAK; information E. Proskauer

### Katschke, Walter
08/20/1893 Berlin - no information
*Home address:* Giesebrechtstr. 18, Charlottenburg
*Law firm address:* Landshuter Str. 18, W 30
*Additional information:* Attorney and notary; after the National Socialist seizure of power in 1933 he was readmitted; his license as a notary was revoked in 1935; he worked as an attorney until the general

occupational ban in 1938. He emigrated to London, Great Britain, on 12/31/1938, later presumably to Palestine/Israel.
*Sources:* *li; LAB, Liste 10/15/1933; DJ 36, p. 315; BArch, R 3001 PAK; MRRAK; BG; information E. Proskauer

### Katz, Arthur Dr.
09/06/1902 - no information
*Home address:* no information
*Law firm address:* Neue Promenade 3, C 2
*Additional information:* Attorney at the KG; he was made subject to an occupational ban in early 1933. He emigrated to Palestine.
*Sources:* Liste d. nichtzugel. RA, 04/25/1933; BArch, R 3001 PAK; BG

### Katz, Erich Dr.
04/28/1893 Marienburg - no information
*Home address:* no information
*Law firm address:* Kronenstr. 64, W 8
*Additional information:* Attorney and notary; after the National Socialist seizure of power he was readmitted upon his own request; however, he was disbarred in the same year; later he was presumably working as a sales representative.
*Sources:* *li; LAB, Liste 10/15/1933; Pr.J. 33, p. 633; BArch, R 3001 PAK; Naatz-Album; BG

### Katz, Ernst Rudolf Dr.
07/10/1894 - no information
*Home address:* no information
*Law firm address:* Joachimsthaler Str. 25/26, W 15
*Additional information:* After the National Socialist seizure of power in 1933 he was readmitted; he worked as an attorney until 05/01/1938.
*Sources:* *li; LAB, Liste 10/15/1933; Liste 36; BArch, R 3001 PAK

### Katz, Gerhard Dr.
03/31/1906 Berlin - May 1975
*Home address:* no information
*Law firm address:* Eisenzahnstr. 65, Halensee
*Additional information:* After the National Socialist seizure of power he was made subject to an occupational ban on 06/10/1933, he emigrated on 11/04/1938 to Boston, USA, he changed his first name to Gerald.
*Sources:* Liste d. nichtzugel. RA, 04/25/1933; JMBl. 33, p. 221; BArch, R 3001 PAK; SSDI; BG

### Katz, Hanna Dr.

10/23/1895 Berlin -
07/28/1982 New York
*Home address:* Waitzstr. 7,
Charlottenburg
*Law firm address:*
Schadowstr. 1 b, NW 7
*Additional information:*
Hanna was the first woman at the law faculty
of the Friedrich-Wilhelms-Universität in Berlin
to write a doctoral thesis, entitled "Gaps
in the employment contract." In 1930 she
established herself as an attorney. She was
allowed to continue to work as an attorney
after the National Socialist seizure of power
in 1933, because she was a member of the
Trademark Committee of the International
Law Association, where she held the office of
secretary. This office was linked to attorney
admission. In order to prevent an English
representative from succeeding, she was
granted the license as an attorney in 1933,
although she did not meet the requirements
of the Attorney Act of 04/07/1933. The Reich
Association of German National Attorneys,
the Chamber of Industry and Commerce
of Berlin and the Federal Foreign Office
advocated this.
After the occupational ban in 1938 she was
the only woman working as a "consultant."
In addition to being an attorney, she was an
English interpreter. Before she was able to
flee from Germany, they plundered various
state offices, later her valuables deposited in
Germany were seized by her (Jewish) chief
representative. Hanna emigrated to New
York, USA, on 06/06/1941, where she again
studied law and completed the Bachelor of
Law; a little later she also passed the bar
examination. Meanwhile she could become
an American citizen. In 1946, she became
an attorney again, the main focus of her
work was trademark law, law against unfair
competition and antitrust law.
In 1954, under the emancipation of the
residence obligation in Berlin, she was
readmitted as an attorney. She was a
member of the Association of the Bar of the
City of New York and the American Bar
Association. In addition, she was active in
various committees of Jewish organizations.
In 1967, she was a member of the board of the
American Association of Former European
Jurists. She died in 1982 at the age of 86.

*Sources:* LAB, A Rep. 343, AG Köpenick,
Vertr.V.; *li; LAB, Liste 10/15/1933; Liste 36;
Liste d. Kons. 03/15/1939; BArch, R 3001
PAK, PA; LAB, B Rep 025-05 nr. 1852/55
(WGA); BG; LBI NY; American Association
of Former European Jurists, LBI Ar 6546,
Otto and Frances Walter Foundation, NY;
Juristinnen; Ausst. AoR, NY

### Katz, Herbert

05/6(7)/1902 Schneidemühl - 05/17/1943
Auschwitz
*Home address:* Müllerstr. 154, N 65,
Wedding
*Law firm address:* Müllerstr. 154, N 65,
Wedding
*Additional information:* After the National
Socialist seizure of power he was made subject
to an occupational ban on 06/12/1933. He
was transported on 04/19/1943 to Auschwitz
and was murdered there on 05/17/1943.
*Sources:* Liste d. nichtzugel. RA, 04/25/1933
JMBl. 33, p. 253; BArch, R 3001 PAK, PA;
VZ 39; BG; GB II

### Katz, Leo, Judicial Councillor

11/26/1870 Zabrze - before August 1951
*Home address:* no information
*Law firm address:* Tiergartenstr. 2, W 35
Attorney and notary; after the National
Socialist seizure of power in 1933 his license
as a notary was revoked, he was still working
as an attorney in 1936. He emigrated on
09/25/1941 to Montevideo, Uruguay.
*Sources:* JMBl. 33, p. 208; *li; LAB, Liste
10/15/1933; Liste 36; BG

### Katz, Siegfried

08/12/1887 Rastenburg - 10/29/1942 Riga
*Home address:* Sächsische Str. 75, W 15,
Wilmersdorf
*Law firm address:* Seydelstr. 3, SW 19
*Additional information:* Attorney and
notary; after the National Socialist seizure of
power in 1933 he was readmitted; his license
as a notary was revoked in 1935; he was
still working as an attorney until the general
occupational ban in 1938; he last practiced
from his private home. Transportation on
10/26/1942 to Riga; he was murdered there
shortly after arrival.
*Sources:* *li; LAB, Liste 10/15/1933; DJ 36, p.
315; Liste 36; BArch, R 3001 PAK; MRRAK;
BG; BdE; GB II

**Katz, Walter Dr.**
01/05/1893 Falkenberg - 02/20/1943
Auschwitz
*Home address:* Kantstr. 129, Charlottenburg
*Law firm address:* Brückenstr. 1, SO 16, later
Alexanderstr. 42, C 2
*Additional information:* Attorney and
notary: after the National Socialist seizure
of power he was readmitted; in 1935 his
license as a notary was revoked; he worked
as an attorney until the general occupational
ban in 1938, later he was still working as a
"consultant." His wife Gertrud was regarded
as "Aryan." He was sent to a concentration
camp on 01/13/1943" (Gestapo, 12/16/1943).
He was murdered in Auschwitz.
*Sources:* *li; LAB, Liste 10/15/1933; DJ 36, p.
315; MRRAK; Liste d. Kons. v. 04/15/1939;
BArch, R 3001 PAK; BG; GB II

**Katz, Willy Dr.**
12/29/1892 - no information
*Home address:* no information
*Law firm address:* Friedrichstr. 204
After the National Socialist seizure of power
he was made subject to an occupational ban
in early 1933.
*Sources:* Br.B. 32; Liste d. nichtzugel. RA,
04/25/1933; JMBl. 33, p. 195; BArch, R
3001 PAK

**Katzenstein, Martin Dr.**
03/08/1886 Eschwege - 1948 Chile
*Home address:* Lentzeallee 5 a, Dahlem
*Law firm address:* Potsdamer Str. 124, W 9
*Additional information:* Attorney and
notary; he was temporarily a law partner
of Prof. Max Alsberg; after the National
Socialist seizure of power in 1933 he was
readmitted, but relocated the law firm a few
houses further to Potsdamer Str. 118 c, a
house in which there were already four other
law firms established. In 1935 his license as
a notary was revoked; he was still working
as an attorney until the general occupational
ban in 1938. He emigrated on 07/27/1939 to
Santiago de Chile, where he died in 1948.
*Sources:* Adr.B. 32; *li; LAB, Liste
10/15/1933; DJ 36, p. 315; Liste 36; BArch, R
3001 PAK; MRRAK; BG; information Irene
Schmied, NY, 2001

**Katzenstein, Max Dr.**
03/06/1890 Frankfurt a. Main - no
information

*Home address:* Sybelstr. 62, Charlottenburg
*Law firm address:* Bleibtreustr. 32, W 15
*Additional information:* After the National
Socialist seizure of power he was made
subject to an occupational ban in early 1933.
He emigrated to Jerusalem, Palestine, on
08/22/1934.
*Sources:* Liste d. nichtzugel. RA, 04/25/1933
JMBl. 33, p. 234; BArch, R 3001 PAK; BG

**Katzenstein, Werner Dr.**
03/04/1893 Berlin - no information
*Home address:* no information
*Law firm address:* Apostel-Paulus-Str. 18,
Schöneberg
*Additional information:* Attorney at the
KG and notary; after the National Socialist
seizure of power he was readmitted. He
emigrated in 1934. An arrest warrant for tax
evasion was issued against him.
*li; LAB, Liste 10/15/1933; BArch, R 3001
PAK; Wolf, BFS

**Kauffmann, Werner Dr.**
11/07/1901 Berlin
- 03/18/1970
*Home address:* no
information
*Law firm address:* Alt-
Moabit 110, NW 40
*Additional information:*
After the National Socialist seizure of
power, he was regarded as "mixed race,"
in accordance with the so-called race laws,
his father was Jewish. He himself was a
Protestant. He was at first a member of the
DNVP (Deutschnationale Volkspartei =
German National People's Party), in 1933
he changed to the SPD (Sozialdemokratische
Partei Deutschlands = Social Democratic
Party of Germany). However, this
membership does not seem to have become
known any further. The decisive factor
for his career as an attorney was his "race
affiliation." Thus his career as a judge came
to an end in 1933: "On the basis of the
law for the adjustment of the civil service
at that time [he] was placed on leave and
discharged at the end of July 1933 [as a court
judge from the judicial service] . . . After
long efforts and multiple refusals by the
Berlin Bar Association, the president of the
Court of Appeals in Berlin and the National
Socialist Association of German Legal
Professionals, [he] finally succeeded, through

the intercession of Dr. Nadler, the head of the department in the then Prussian Ministry of Justice . . . to gain admission as an attorney in Berlin by means of a transitional hardship regulation"(resume 1946).

He was allowed to pursue his profession until the end of the Nazi regime. He was made subject to various disadvantages. Thus he was, for example, not a member of the National Socialist Association of German Professionals, which led to constant unpleasant disputes and explanations among the clients. Added to this the exclusion of defenses with the People's Court, of representations with the Labor Court, of guardianships and trusteeships, counsel for the defense appointed by the court and mostly also of legal aid." He could escape his mandatory obligation for the Todt Organization by the fortunate circumstance that his files at the Charlottenstraße Employment Office burned at the right time, as he writes in his resume. In 1945, he was immediately readmitted as an attorney and notary, albeit temporarily. He left the legal profession in 1952, when he was named senate director in the judicial administration.

*Sources:* JMBl. 08/04/1933; Liste Mschlg. 36; Tel.B. 41; LAB, RAK, PA; Verz. zugel. Anw. 45; Information Landesverw. Amt

**Kaufmann, Bruno Paul**
10/28/1881 Berlin - no information
*Home address:* Auerbachstr. 4, Grunewald
*Law firm address:* Jägerstr. 12, W 8
*Additional information:* Attorney and notary; after the National Socialist seizure of power in 1933 he was readmitted; his license as a notary was revoked in 1935; he worked as an attorney until the general occupational ban in 1938; thereafter he was still admitted as a "consultant." He emigrated to Great Britain (or to the USA) on 01/31/1939.
*Sources:* *li; LAB, Liste 10/15/1933; DJ 36, p. 315; BArch, R 3001 PAK; MRRAK; Liste der Kons. v. 02/23/1939; BG

**Kaufmann, Hans**
05/14/1901 Berlin - no information
*Home address:* Laubenheimer Str. 20, Wilmersdorf
*Law firm address:* Markobrunnerstr. 1, Wilmersdorf

*Additional information:* Attorney since 1929; after the National Socialist seizure of power he was first made subject to a ban on representation on 05/31/1933, then an occupational ban in early summer 1933, he was disbarred in July 1933.
*Sources:* Jüd.Adr.B.; TK 33; LAB, A Rep. 343, AG Köpenick, Vertr.V.; JMBl. 33, p. 253; BArch R 3001 PAK, PA

**Kaufmann, Hans Dr.**
02/02/1885 - ca. 1944
*Home address:* Lützowstr. 97, W 35
*Law firm address:* Potsdamer Str. 138, W 9
*Additional information:* He fought as an officer during the First World War at the Western Front, amongst others before Verdun, last in the rank of a lieutenant. He was seriously wounded (in the jaw and shoulder, was later severely impaired when talking and eating), he was awarded the EK II.Kl. Attorney (since 1912) and notary (since 1919); since 1918 he was a member of the Deutschen Staatspartei (DDP) (German State Party), since 1925 he was a member of the "Reichsbanner." After the National Socialist seizure of power he was readmitted. In 1935, he refused to give up his notaryship during the course of the general "removal of Jewish notaries," but ultimately had to submit. A short time later he was accused of "foreign exchange profiteering" and on 05/28/1936 he was taken in protective custody, evidently he had helped with the transfer of money abroad. His judicial activity and his awareness of the severity of his deed had particularly been taken into account in his sentencing. He was sentenced to eight years in prison. Shortly before his release from the Luckau prison he died of a disease. He had been disbarred on 09/04/1936 in conjunction with his imprisonment.
*Sources:* Jüd.Adr.B.; Br.B. 32; *li; LAB, Liste 10/15/1933; Liste 36; BArch, R 3001 PAK, PA; Blau, Vierzehn Jahre . . . , p. 35; BG

**Kaufmann, Lothar Dr.**
04/18/1901 - no information
*Home address:* Starnberger Str. 6, Schöneberg
*Law firm address:* Mittelstr. 18, NW 7
*Additional information:* Attorney since 1929; after the National Socialist seizure of power he was made subject to an occupational ban on 06/12/1933. He emigrated to London, Great Britain.

*Sources:* Liste d. nichtzugel. RA, 04/25/1933; JMBl. 33, p. 220; BArch, R 3001 PAK, PA; BG

### Kaufmann, Max Dr.

08/04/1885 - no information
*Home address:* no information
*Law firm address:* Kurfürstendamm 46, W 15
*Additional information:* Attorney and notary; after the National Socialist seizure of power in 1933 he was readmittted; he was regarded as "mixed race." He emigrated to Brazil.
*Sources:* *li; LAB, Liste 10/15/1933; Liste Mschlg. 36; BArch, R 3001 PAK; BG

### Kayser, Franz Dr.

07/02/1897 Berlin-Weißensee - June 1983
*Home address:* Reichstr. 2, Charlottenburg
*Law firm address:* Kaiserdamm 82, Charlottenburg 9
*Additional information:* In October 1933 he was admitted further as an attorney; he was made subject to an occupational ban in 1938 at the latest; he emigrated to New York, USA on 09/01/1938, there he changed his first name to Francis, he last lived in New York.
*Sources:* TK 33; *li; LAB, Liste 10/15/1933; BArch, R 3001 PAK; MRRAK; BG; SSDI

### Keidanski, Alfred

08/19/1904 Berlin-Charlottenburg - August 1976
*Home address:* no address
*Law firm address:* Niebuhrstr. 56, Charlottenburg
*Additional information:* After the National Socialist seizure of power he was made subject to an occupational ban on 06/12/1933. He emigrated to the USA, he changed his name to Keidanz, he last lived in New York.
*Sources:* Liste d. nichtzugel. RA, 04/25/1933; JMBl. 33, p. 209; BArch, R 3001 PAK, PA; SSDI

### Kempner, Friedrich Dr.

07/20/1892 Berlin - July 1981
*Home address:* Matthäikirchplatz 13, W 35
*Law firm address:* Markgrafenstr. 46, W 8
*Additional information:* Attorney and notary; after the National Socialist seizure of power he was readmitted; in 1935 his license as a notary was revoked; he worked as an attorney until the general occupational ban in 1938. He emigrated to the USA, where he last

lived in New York; he changed his first name to Frederick.
*Sources:* *li; LAB, Liste 10/15/1933; BArch, R 3001 PAK; BG; SSDI

### Kempner, Ludwig

07/10/1876 Berlin - 12/17/1942
*Home address:* Kaiserdamm 27, Charlottenburg
*Law firm address:* Neue Königstr. 6, NO 43
*Additional information:* After the National Socialist seizure of power he was readmitted, he worked as an attorney until the general occupational ban in 1938; he died in 1942 at the age of 66, he was buried at Weißensee.
*Sources:* *li; LAB, Liste 10/15/1933; Liste 36; MRRAK; BG

### Kienitz, Gustav

12/01/1859 Landsberg/Warthe - no information
*Home address:* Goethepark 11 (1939)
*Law firm address:* Schloßstr. 18, Pankow
*Additional information:* After the National Socialist seizure of power in 1933 he was readmitted, he was a Protestant; he was regarded as "mixed race," he could therefore also work as an attorney after the general occupational ban in 1938; he still lived in Berlin in 1941.
*Sources:* *li; LAB, Liste 10/15/1933; Liste Mschl. 36; Tel.B. 41

### Kiewe, Hans Dr.

12/27/1890 - 09/02/1963 Santiago de Chile
*Home address:* no information
*Law firm address:* Kochstr. 19, SW 68
*Additional information:* Attorney and notary; after the National Socialist seizure of power he was made subject to an occupational ban in early 1933. He emigrated to Chile; there he died in 1963 at the age of 72.
*Sources:* Br.B. 32; Liste d. nichtzugel. RA, 04/25/1933; JMBl. 33, p. 234; BArch, R 3001 PAK; Dok. Jüd. Museum Berlin 93/3/44

### Kirchheimer, Hilde, nee Rosenfeld, later Neumann

04/13/1905 Berlin - 09/11/1959 Berlin
*Home address:* no information
*Law firm address:* Joachimstaler Str. 41, Charlottenburg
*Additional information:* Daughter of the attorney and left-wing SPD politician

Kurt Rosenfeld; she was a dissident; "Realgymnasium" (secondary school) in Berlin; legal studies in Freiburg i. Br., Berlin and Bonn; member of Marxist student groups, as from 1925 sge was a member of the SPD in Berlin; she had a clerkship in Berlin and Erfurt; she married the attorney Otto Kirchheimer, and in 1930 they had a daughter; 1932 she became an attorney at the KG, also took on mandates in the legal protection order of the "Rote Hilfe" (Red Aid). After the National Socialist seizure of power she was threatened by several factors: her own political activity, the fact that she was the daughter of a politically active father, in addition she was of Jewish descent. In April 1933 she fled to France; in Germany the occupational ban went into effect on 07/13/1933; from 1933-1939 she was an official of the MOPR/International Red Aid; she assisted with the defence committee for those accused of the Reichtstag fire and in the International Jurist Association; in 1935, she went to the Soviet Union for one year to study law; in 1936 she joined the KPD (Kommunistische Partei Deutschlands = Communist Party of Germany); she returned to France, where she was interned in early 1940 for a month in Rieucros (at Pamiers); 1941 she emigrated to the USA via Mexico. In the same year she and Otto Kirchheimer were divorced, he had already lived in the USA for a long time; she married the doctor Rudolf Neumann (1899-1962), among others he worked in 1936 as leader of the medical corps of the International Brigade in Spain. She worked for political and cultural exile associations [amongst others "Bewegung Freies Deutschland" (The Movement for a Free Germany); Heinrich Heine Club] and for exile publications ["Demokratische Post" (Democratic Post)]. In early 1947 she returned with her husband to East Berlin; they joined the SED (Socialist Unity Party of Germany); from 1947 they took over various tasks in the establishment of the judicial system in the SBZ (Sowjetische Bezatsungszone = Soviet Occupational Zone), then in the DDR (Deutsche Demokratische Republik = German Democratic Republic), among others 1949-1950 she was president of the LG Berlin (East) and in 1950-1953 Chief Magistrate for Justice in Berlin; at the same time she was Deputy Head of the Justice Division of the Governing Board of the SED (Sozialistische Einheitspartei Deutschlands = Socialist Unity

Party of Germany), she taught at the Karl Marx Party School at the Central Committee of the SED; she had a close collaboration with Hilde Benjamin; 1953-1959 she was editor-in-chief of the journal "Neue Justiz;" 1958-1959 she was an honorary secretary of the Association of Democratic Jurists of Germany; in 1958 she was awarded the Patriotic Order of Merit in bronze, a year later the Order's Banner of Work; she died 1959 in Berlin.
*Sources:* Liste d. nichtzugel. RA, 04/25/1933; JMBl. 33, p. 282; BArch, R 3001, PAK, PA; BHdE, Bd. 1; Benjamin, Hilde, amongst others (Publisher): Zur Geschichte der Rechtspflege der DDR 1945-1949 [On the history of judicature of the DDR 1945-1949], Berlin 1976; Brentzel, Marianne: Die Machtfrau [The power woman]. Hilde Benjamin 1902-1989. Berlin 1997, p. 389; Wer war wer in der DDR? [Who was who in the GDR (German Democratic Republic)?], Berlin 2000; Schneider, Schwarz, Schwarz, see 224/25; Juristinnen, 2006, pages 280/81; information Frank Schale, 2005/06

**Kirchheimer, Otto Dr.**
11/11/1905 Heilbronn - 11/22/1965 Silversprings
*Home address:* no information
*Law firm address:* Zikadenweg 78, Eichkamp
*Additional information:* He studied law, philosophy and sociology; doctorate with Carl Schmitt; he was a member of the left-wing SPD, he published in the journal "Gesellschaft" published by Rudolf Hilferding. He was in close association with Franz L. Neumann and Ernst Fraenkel, with whom he completed his legal traineeship during his clerkship. He married Hilde Rosenfeld, nee Kirchheimer, in 1930 their daughter was born; he was an attorney since 1932; aside from being an attorney, he was active as a teacher at trade union schools. After the National Socialist seizure of power he was made subject to an occupational ban on 07/13/1933. He emigrated with his wife to Paris, later alone to the USA; there he worked at the Institute for Social Research in New York; from 1943 to 1955 he was a scholarly adviser to the State Department; in 1955 he accepted a professorship for Political Science at the New School of Social Research, 1962 he was appointed Professor for Public Law and Government at Columbia University, New York. Through numerous guest professorships he assisted with development

work for the discipline of political science in Germany. After his death in the USA, he was, in accordance with his wishes, buried in his birthplace of Heilbronn.
*Publications:* Politische Justiz [Political justice], 1. Aufl. [1st edition] Neuwied 1965; Von der Weimarer Republik zum Faschismus: Die Auflösung der demokratischen Rechtsordnung; Politik und Verfassung [From the Weimar Republic to fascism: the dissolution of the democratic legal order; politics and constitution]. Frankfurt a.M., 1964
*Sources:* Liste d. nichtzugel. RA, 04/25/1933; JMBl. 08/21/1933; BArch, R 3001 PAK, PA; Bleek, Wilhelm: Geschichte der Politikwissenschaft in Deutschland [History of Political Science in Germany], Munich 2001; Schale, Frank: Zwischen Engagement und Skepsis. Eine Studie zu den Schriften von Otto Kirchheimer [Between Commitment and Skepticism. A study of the writings of Otto Kirchheimer], Baden-Baden 2006

**Kirsch, Leonhard Dr.**
12/01/1896 Obornik - no information
*Home address:* no information
*Law firm address:* Unter den Linden 61, NW 7
*Additional information:* He passed the first state examination in law in 1919 in Celle, the second in 1923. After the National Socialist seizure of power he was disbarred as an attorney on 12/18/1933.
*Sources:* Jüd.Adr.B.; Pr.J. 33, p. 868; BArch R 3001, PAK, PA

**Kirschbaum, Moritz Dr., Judicial Councillor**
01/31/1864 Dortmund - 09/29/1942 Theresienstadt
*Home address:* Jenaer Str. 5, Wilmersdorf
*Law firm address:* Schwerinstr. 27, Zehlendorf
*Additional information:* After the National Socialist seizure of power he was readmitted; he was still working as an attorney in 1936. Transportation on 09/11/1942 to Theresienstadt; he died there only a few days later.
*Sources:* *li; LAB, Liste 10/15/1933; Liste 36; BG; ThG; GB II

**Kirschberg, Paul Dr.**
04/30/1883 - 06/22/1934
*Home address:* no information

*Law firm address:* Potsdamer Str. 37, W 35
*Additional information:* Attorney at the KG and notary; after the National Socialist seizure of power in 1933 his license as a notary was revoked, he was readmitted as an attorney; he died in 1934 at the age of 51 and was buried at Weißensee.
*Sources:* JMBl. 33, p. 208; *li; LAB, Liste 10/15/1933; BArch, R 3001 PAK; BG

**Kirschner, Heinrich Heimann, Judicial Councillor**
04/14/1865 Posen - 10/19/1942 Theresienstadt
*Home address:* Bayreuther Str. 13, W 30
*Law firm address:* Neue Kantstr. 32, Charlottenburg
*Additional information:* Attorney and notary; after the National Socialist seizure of power in 1933 his license as a notary was revoked; he was still working as an attorney until the general occupational ban in 1938. Transportation on 10/03/1942 to Theresienstadt, he died there two weeks later.
*Sources:* JMBl. 33, p. 208; *li; LAB, Liste 10/15/1933; Liste 36; MRRAK; ,BG; ThG; GB II

**Klausner, Edith Dr., nee Speer**
06/16/1879 Berlin - 05/28/1941
*Home address:* Augsburger Str. 71, W 50
*Law firm address:* Augsburger Str. 71, W 50
*Additional information:* In her family the daughters were given the same educational opportunities as the sons. Her older three sisters had confidently chosen their professions, they had become a medical doctor, a novelist and a sculptor. She accepted her first job in 1904 as a social worker at a so-called employment agency for the poor. Jobs were provided in the industrial sector, but also in nursing and the business sector. After the outbreak of the First World War, she set up her own workshops, where women were trained in a very short time to work for qualified positions in industry. After the war, she gave up her position in 1920 and studied political science and law; in 1922 she received her doctorate from the University of Tübingen with a dissertation entitled "Arbeitsnachweis

und Arbeitsvertrag [The employment agency and the employment contract]." In 1929 she became the first judge at the AG. At the end of 1931 she established herself as an attorney at the LG I-III and at the AG Berlin-Mitte. During this period she had an annual salary of about RM 20,000, p.a. and supported her sister Judith Speer, the sculptress and her husband, as well as a nephew. After the National Socialist seizure of power she was made subject to an occupational ban in early 1933. Her sister Judith had died early, she gave up her large apartment and moved in with her brother-in-law Paul Speer in a smaller apartment in Kleiststrasse; together they traveled to Italy. In 1934 they got married; her husband was regarded as non-Jewish. She received a pension from her previous place of employment, with which she supported her husband and his son. Her sisters emigrated to the USA, one died soon thereafter and left Edith her money, the other sister also helped her. In 1939, according to the census records, she was said to have worked at the Ministry of Justice. She died in May 1941 after a heart attack, she was buried at Weißensee.
*Sources:* Adr.B. 33; TK 33; Liste d. nichtzugel. RA, 04/25/1933; JMBl. 33, p. 267; BG; Juristinnen, pages 413-1415

**Klee, Alfred Dr.**
01/21/1875 Berlin - 1943 Westerbork
*Home address:* Tauentzienstr. 13, Charlottenburg
*Law firm address:* Tauentzienstr. 13, Charlottenburg
*Additional information:* Legal studies in Heidelberg, Berlin, Munich and Bonn; in 1901 he took his first state examination in law; in 1902 he received his doctorate in Heidelberg; since 1902 he was an attorney in Berlin, later also a notary; he was a close friend of Sammy Gronemann; he was active as an official in the Jewish Synagogue of Berlin and in Zionist organizations; as an attorney he committed himself to the legal persecution of anti-Semites. After the National Socialist seizure of power his license as a notary was revoked, he worked as an attorney until the general occupational ban in 1938; he served temporarily on the Presidential Committee

of the Reichsvertretung (Reich's Deputation); his house was searched by the Gestapo, thereupon he escaped to Rotterdam, the Netherlands on 11/15/1938; in the summer of 1943 he was arrested together with family members and transported to the Westerbork transportation camp; there he died under unknown circumstances. His wife was transported to Bergen-Belsen. She received a visa to Palestine, her request to take her grandchildren with her was denied. She stayed with them and died of starvation in the camp. She was buried in one of the mass graves.
*Sources:* Pr.J. 33, p. 390; *li; LAB, Liste 10/15/1933; Liste 36; MRRAK; DJ 1938, p. 2019; BG; GB II; BHdE vol. 1, p. 368; Göpp., p. 250

**Klein, Caesar, Judicial Councillor**
No information - 10/01/1935
*Home address:* no information
*Law firm address:* Grünstr. 4, Köpenick
*Additional information:* Attorney and notary; after the National Socialist seizure of power in 1933 he was readmitted; he died in 1935.
*Sources:* *li; LAB, Liste 10/15/1933

**Kleyff, Bruno**
04/02/1888 - April 1967
*Home address:* No information
*Law firm address:* Potsdamer Str. 129/130, W 9
*Additional information:* Attorney and notary; after the National Socialist seizure of power in 1933 he was readmitted; license as notary was revoked in 1935, he still worked as an attorney until the general occupational ban in 1938. He emigrated to the USA, he changed his last name to Clive, he last lived in Queens, New York.
*Sources:* *li; LAB, Liste 10/15/1933; Liste 36; BArch, R 3001 PAK; SSDI

**Knoche, Fritz Dr.**
01/19/1886 Berlin - 09/07/1942 Auschwitz
*Home address:* Motzstr. 81, Wilmersdorf
*Law firm address:* Motzstr. 51, Wilmersdorf
*Additional information:* Attorney at the KG and notary; after the National Socialist seizure of power in 1933 his license as a notary was revoked; he was readmitted as an attorney; he was still working as an attorney in 1936. He emigrated to Amsterdam, the Netherlands; 1942 he was transported from Auschwitz to Westerbork, he was murdered there.

*Sources:* JMBl. 33, p. 220; *li; LAB, Liste 10/15/1933; Liste 36; BArch, R 3001 PAK; BG; GB II

### Knopf, Albert, Judicial Councillor
06/18/1863 - 11/26/1936
*Home address:* Güntzelstr., Wilmersdorf
*Law firm address:* Mittelstr. 57/58, NW 7
*Additional information:* Attorney and notary; after the National Socialist seizure of power in 1933 his license as a notary was revoked, he was readmitted as an attorney; he still worked as an attorney until his death; he died in 1936 at the age of 83 and was buried at Weißensee.
*Sources:* JMBl. 33, p. 208; *li; LAB, Liste 10/15/1933; Liste 36; BG: Friedh.W. Sterbereg.

### Knopf, Harry Dr.
01/14/1887 Berlin - no information
*Home address:* Uhlandstr. 28, W 15
*Law firm address:* Kurfürstendamm 185, W 15
*Additional information:* Attorney and notary; in a joint law partnership with Hans Liebrecht and Ernst Asch; after the National Socialist seizure of power in 1933 his license as a notary was revoked; he was admitted as an attorney until the occupational ban in 1938. He emigrated to Palestine.
*Sources:* Jüd.Adr.B.; Br.B. 32; *li; LAB, Liste 10/15/1933; Liste 36; BArch, R 3001 PAK; BG

### Kober, Leopold
01/30/1876 Schildberg - no information
*Home address:* Traunsteiner Str. 61, W 30
*Law firm address:* Oranienstr. 47a, S 42
Attorney and notary; after the National Socialist seizure of power in 1933 he was readmitted; license as a notary was revoked in 1935; he was admitted as an attorney until the general occupational ban in 1938. He emigrated to Amsterdam, the Netherlands, from there presumably to the USA.
*Sources:* *li; LAB, Liste 10/15/1933; DJ 36, p. 315; Liste 36; MRRAK; BG

### Kobylinski, Martin Dr.
01/01/1886 Berlin - no information
*Home address:* Speyerer Str. 19, W 30, Schöneberg
*Law firm address:* Kronenstr. 76, W 8
*Additional information:* Attorney and notary; after the National Socialist seizure of power in 1933 his license as a notary was

revoked; he was still working as an attorney until the general occupational ban in 1938. He emigrated to Chicago, USA in 1939.
*Sources:* JMBl. 33, p. 208; *li; LAB, Liste 10/15/1933; Liste 36; BArch, R 3001 PAK; MRRAK; BG

### Koch, Ernst (später: Ernesto) Dr.
09/30/1892 Berlin - no information
*Home address:* Sachsenplatz 12, Charlottenburg
*Law firm address:* Charlottenstr. 56, W 8
*Additional information:* Legal studies in Freiburg, Heidelberg and Berlin; 1914-18 he was a participant in the First World War; attorney as from 1921, last admitted to the LG I-IIII, later also a notary; joint law partnership with Fritz Koch; since 1923 he was married to the psychoanalyst Lucy Adelheid, nee Schwalbe. After the National Socialist seizure of power he was readmitted; at the end of 1935 his license as a notary was revoked; he was admitted as an attorney until 10/01/1936; 1936, he emigrated to Sao Paulo, Brazil; 1936-37 he was a partner in a small lamp factory; as from 1937 he was an employee in a law office; he was active in the Jewish Synagogue Sao Paulo, 1956-67 he was a board member and president, then an honorary president; he worked as an attorney in reparation affairs; he lived in Sao Paulo in 1975.
*Sources:* TK 33; *li; LAB, Liste 10/15/1933; DJ 36, p. 315; Liste 36; BArch, R 3001 PAK; BG; BHdE Bd. 1, S. 376

### Koch, Fritz Dr.
02/11/1887 Berlin - no information
*Home address:* Dahlmannstr. 23, Charlottenburg
*Law office address:* Charlottenstr. 56, W 8
*Additional information:* Attorney at the KG and notary; he had a joint partnership with Ernst Koch; after the National Socialist seizure of power in 1933 he was readmitted; his license as a notary was revoked in 1935; he was still listed as an attorney until 10/01/1936.
*Sources:* *li; LAB, Liste 10/15/1933; BArch, R 3001 PAK

### Koch, Richard Dr.
07/22/1873 Berlin - no information
*Home address:* Sybelstr. 65, Charlottenburg
*Law firm address:* Alexanderstr. 58, O 27
*Additional information:* Attorney (since 1900) and notary (since 1912); he was

Protestant; in the 1920s he was a member of the DVP (Deutsche Volkspartei = German People's Party), later of the DNVP (Deutschnationale Volkspartei = German National People's Party). It only turned out in 1935 that he was regarded as "mixed race first degree," he retained his admission and was still practicing in 1941; in his personal file there are notes that he was retired from the summer of 1944 onwards. A final note dates to February 1945; he appears to have survived and to have gone to Munich.
*Sources:* TK 33: BArch, R 3001 PAK, PA; Tel.B.41

### Koch, Richard M.

07/29/1895 Berlin - no information
*Home address:* Bayreuther Str. 38, W 62
*Law firm office:* Leipziger Str. 54/56, SW 19
*Additional information:* He was in the army from 1914 until his release in 1919; he had fought in Galicia and Flanders and had been captured by the British. After his release he completed his legal training, he established himself as an attorney (1925), later also a notary (1927); he had changed his original name Cohn to Koch, which was later mentioned in various letters. After the National Socialist seizure of power he was made subject to an occupational ban, which was lifted again, however, after he had been recognized as a "frontline fighter." In 1935 his license as a notary was revoked, he still worked as an attorney until the general occupational ban in 1938, previously he received a formal reprimand from the Bar Association, because he had been convicted of charging extortionate rent. [He had rented an apartment to a client.] After the occupational ban he was still allowed to work as a "consultant" in 1939.
*Sources:* TK 33; *li; LAB, Liste 10/15/1933; DJ 36, p. 315; Liste 36 ; BArch, R 3001 PAK, PA; MRRAK (Richard M. K.)

### Kocheim, Edmund Dr.

11/04/1884 Posen - 01/17/1950
*Home address:* Kurfürstendamm 66, W 15
*Law firm address:* Potsdamer Str. 29, W 35
*Additional information:* Attorney (since 1912) and notary (since 1920); after the National Socialist seizure of power he was readmitted; in 1935 his license as a notary was revoked, he worked as an attorney until

the general occupational ban in 1938. His wife Herta was regarded as non-Jewish. The couple emigrated to Shanghai, China, where they lived from April 1940 to July 1947. He returned to Berlin. He was readmitted as an attorney and notary. His law office was located at W 15, Bayerische Str. 31. He died in 1950 at the age of 75.
*Sources:* *li; LAB, Liste 10/15/1933; DJ 36, p. 315; BArch, R 3001 PAK; MRRAK; LAB, RAK, PA; BG

### Kochmann, Ludwig

06/08/1886 Ostrowo - no information
*Home address:* Motzstr. 40, Schöneberg
*Law firm address:* Potsdamer Str. 79, W 57
*Additional information:* Attorney and notary; after the National Socialist seizure of power in 1933 he was readmitted; his license as a notary was revoked in 1935; he worked as an attorney until the general occupational ban in 1938.
*Sources:* *li; LAB, Liste 10/15/1933; DJ 36, p. 315; Liste 36; BArch, R 3001 PAK; MRRAK; BG

### Kochmann, Walther Dr.

03/06/1888 Dresden - 09/03/1936
*Home address:* no information
*Law firm address:* Friedrichstr. 85, W 8
*Additional information:* Attorney and notary, the law firm was very busy, moreover. He was legal counsel of an industry association; after the National Socialist seizure of power in 1933 he was readmitted; his license as a notary was revoked in 1935 due to loss of mandates. The development drove him to suicide at the age of 48. His widow and daughter were able to save themselves, supported by resistance circles.
*Sources:* *li; LAB, Liste 10/15/1933; DJ 36, p. 315; Liste 36; BArch, R 3001 PAK; BG; information Dahns, 2003

### Koch-Weser, Erich

02/26/1875 Bremerhaven - 10/19/1944
Fazenda Janita, Brazil
*Home address:* no information
*Law firm address:* Viktoriastr. 4 a, W 35
*Additional information:* After high school graduation he studied in Oldenburg; 1893 to 1897 he studied in Munich (economics, law); he was Protestant; 1901 to 1909 he was mayor in Delmenhorst, until 1913 he was

a town clerk in Bremerhaven, until 1919 he was mayor in Kassel; he was a member of the Oldenburg state parliament (1901 to 1909), in the Bremen township (1909 to 1913) and in the Prussian House of Lords (1913 until 1918); 1918 he was a founding member of the DDP (Deutsche Demokratische Partei = German Democratic Party), 1924 to 1930 its chairman. His political goal was to develop Germany as a divided unitary state, with the preservation of Prussia and a greater autonomy of the provinces. 1919 he was a DDP member of the Weimar National Assembly, then until 1930 delegate of the Reichstag; 1919 to 1921 he was Reich Minister of the Interior; June 1928 to May 1929 he was Reich Minister of Justice; he had to step down for reasons of proportional representation, a center man took his place. The press, comprising various political backgrounds, regretted his decision. Admitted as an attorney to the KG, later also as a notary; he had a joint law partnership with Alfred Carlebach and his son Reimer. He was a member of the Executive Committee of the Association of German Jurists until 1933. After the seizure of power by the National Socialists he was already very exposed because of his political past. Only later it became known that he was regarded as "mixed race," since his mother came from a Jewish family. In April 1933 he was made subject to an occupational ban. The revocation of admission as an attorney and notary, which was reported in the "Justiz- und Ministerialblatt," seems to have been repealed, because in 1936 he still practiced.

He emigrated to Brazil; he bought a coffee plantation and founded the municipality of Rolandia in the state of Parana with other refugees from Germany; he died in 1944 at the age of 67. His grandson Caio was born in Brazil in the same year.

*Sources:* Liste d. nichtzugel. RA, 04/25/1933; TK 33; JMBl. 33, p. 234; JMBl. 33, p. 282; *li; LAB, Liste Mschlg. 36; TK 36; BArch, R 3001, PAK, PA; Ausstell. AoR, 2000; Auerbach Hellmuth, short biography in: Benz/Graml: Biographisches Lexikon zur Weimarer Republik [Biographical dictionary on the Weimar Republic] 1988, pages 186/187

**Koch-Weser, Reimer**
07/03/1906 Delmenhorst - no information
*Home address:* no information
*Law firm address:* Viktoriastr. 4 a, W 35

*Additional information:* Attorney since the 1920s, son and partner of Erich. After the National Socialist seizure of power he was further admitted, obviously his partially Jewish origins only became known later, for in October 1933 he was still listed without identification in the Berlin directory of attorneys (* li), but this was soon corrected. On 10/10/1934 he was disbarred. He had gone to the USA. He later probably lived with his family and father in Brazil, his son Caio was born there.
*Sources:* TK 33; *li; Korr. Liste arischer Anw., 10/15/1933; BArch, R 3001 PAK, PA

**Koepke, Willi Dr.**
No information
*Home address:* no information
*Law firm address:* Unter den Linden 71, W 8
*Additional information:* Fought in the First World War, he was Protestant. He was only admitted after 1933; presumably his "non-Aryan" origins were at first not known; in 1936 he was regarded as "mixed race," he was active with this status as an attorney even into the war. He survived the war and was immediately readmitted as an attorney and notary.
*Sources:* TK 36; Liste Mschlg. 36; Tel.B. 41; BArch, R 3001 PAK; Verz. zugel. Anw. 45

**Köhler, Alfred Dr.**
01/26/1876 Berlin
- 10/27/1970
*Home address:* Kantstr. 4, Charlottenburg
*Law firm address:* Kantstr. 4, Charlottenburg
*Additional information:* Attorney and notary; after the National Socialist seizure of power in 1933 he was readmitted; in 1935 his license as a notary was revoked; he still worked as an attorney until the general occupational ban in 1938. He was always in danger: "I was occasionally arrested on the street in a Jewish raid and imprisoned in the Alexanderplatz Police Prison." In 1942 he was released from the collecting station Große Hamburger Strasse. Apparently, he had been arrested for transportation. His sisters, who had been arrested at the same time, were murdered in the concentration camp. He survived and lived in Wilmersdorf after the liberation. He was readmitted as an attorney in 1945; he died in 1974 at the age of 94.

*Sources:* *li; LAB, Liste 10/15/1933; DJ 36, kP. 315; Liste 36; MRRAK; BG; LAB, RAK, PA

**Kohn, Alfred**
10/09/1894 Karlsbad - no information
*Home address:* no information
*Law firm address:* Blücherstr. 4
*Additional information:* Attorney and notary; after the National Socialist seizure of power he was readmitted; in 1935 his license as a notary was revoked. In 1937 he was disbarred as an attorney.
*Sources:* *li; DJ 36, p. 315; Liste 36; BArch, R 3001 PAK

**Kollenscher, Max Dr.**
09/27/1875 Posen - beginning 1937
*Home address:* Altonaer Str. 21, NW 87
*Law firm address:* Kurfürstendamm 61, W 15
*Additional information:* Attorney and notary; board member of the Jewish Synagogue in Berlin. He emigrated to Jerusalem, Palestine, on 07/15/1933; he was only disbarred in 1935; an arrest warrant for tax evasion was issued against him.
*Sources:* JMBl. 33, p. 208; *li; LAB, Liste lk10/15/1933; BG; Wolf, BFS; Göpp., p. 224f. (with partially different information)

**Kolsen, Hermann, Judicial Councillor**
12/13/1859 Schwerin - 08/26/1942
*Home address:* Barbarossastr. 50, W 30; Prinzregentenstr. 78, Wilmersdorf
*Law firm address:* Prinzregentenstr. 78, Wilmersdorf
*Additional information:* Attorney and notary; he was a Protestant; after the National Socialist seizure of power in 1933 he was readmitted; in 1935 his license as a notary was revoked; he was still working as an attorney in 1936; in 1942 at the age of 83 he committed suicide; presumably in the face of imminent deportation.
*Sources:* *li; LAB, Liste 10/15/1933; Liste 36; BG; GB II

**Königsberger, Alfons Dr.**
11/08/1878 - 11/07/1933
*Home address:* Motzstr. 31, Schöneberg
*Law firm address:* Potsdamer Str. 119
*Additional information:* Attorney and notary: after the National Socialist seizure of power he was made subject to an occupational ban in early 1933; he died during the same

year, one day before his 55th birthday; he was buried at Weißensee.
*Sources:* Br.B. 32; TK 33; Liste d. nichtzugel. RA, 04/25/1933; BG

**Königsberger, Hans Dr.**
02/18/1895 - 01/10/1934
*Home address:* Kunz-Buntschuh-Str. 7, Wilmersdorf-Grunewald
*Law firm address:* Meinekestr. 11, W 15
*Additional information:* Attorney at the KG and notary; after the National Socialist seizure of power in 1933 he was readmitted; he died in 1934 at the age of 38; he was buried at Weißensee.
*Sources:* *li; LAB, Liste 10/15/1933; BArch, R 3001 PAK; BG

**Königsberger, Ludwig Dr.**
12/17/1898 Berlin - 06/11/1976
*Home address:* no information
*Law firm address:* Augsburger Str. 46, W 50
*Additional information:* He received a medal of honor for his service during the First World War. After the National Socialist seizure of power he was made subject to an occupational ban in early 1933. He emigrated to Great Britain. After 1945 he was readmitted in Berlin as an attorney and specialized in reparation affairs; he represented, among others, a case concerning the recognition of uninterrupted period of service for all pensioners.
*Sources:* Br.B. 32; Liste d. nichtzugel. RA, 04/25/1933; BArch, R 3001 PAK; information from the son, 10/01

**Königsberger, Semmy**
07/24/1900 Pleschen - transportation 1942
*Home address:* no information
*Law firm address:* Lothringer Str. 54, N 54
*Additional information:* After the National Socialist seizure of power he was made subject to an occupational ban on 06/12/1933. Transportation on 03/28/1942 to Piaski.
*Sources:* Liste d. nichtzugel. RA, 04/25/1933; JMBl. 33, p. 253; BArch, R 3001 PAK, PA; BG; GB II

**Koplowitz, Leo Dr.**
03/24/1994 Gogolin - no information
*Home address:* Dorotheenstr. 64, NW 7
*Law firm address:* Dorotheenstr. 64, NW 7
*Additional information:* Attorney and notary; after the National Socialist seizure

of power in 1933 his license as a notary was revoked, he was readmitted as an attorney until the general occupational ban in 1938. He emigrated to London, Great Britain before 11/28/1938.
*Sources:* JMBl. 33, p. 234; *li; LAB, Liste 10/15/1933; Liste 36; BArch, R 3001 PAK; MRRAK; BG (Koplowotz)

### Korach, Carl Dr.
10/11/1887 Berlin - June 1982
*Home address:* Kurfürstendamm 93, Wilmersdorf
*Law firm address:* Leipziger Str. 114, W 8
*Additional information:* Attorney and notary; in October 1933 he was readmitted; after the National Socialist seizure of power in 1933 he was readmitted; in 1935 his license as a notary was revoked; he worked as an attorney until the general occupational ban. He emigrated to the USA, where he lived in Queens, New York and died at the age of 94.
*Sources:* *li; LAB, Liste 10/15/1933; DJ 36, p. 315; Liste 36; BArch, R 3001 PAK; MRRAK; BG; SSDI

### Korn, Alfred Dr., Judicial Councillor
No information
*Home address:* no information
*Law firm address:* Kaiser-Wilhelm-Str. 89, Lankwitz
*Additional information:* Attorney and notary; after the National Socialist seizure of power in 1933 he was readmitted; on 10/17/1934 his licenses as an attorney and notary were revoked.
*Sources:* *li; LAB, Liste 10/15/1933

### Korn, Kurt
08/03/1899 - November 1982
*Home address:* no information
*Law firm address:* Oranienburger Str. 60/63, N 24
*Additional information:* After the National Socialist seizure of power he was made subject to an occupational ban on 06/10/1933. He emigrated to the USA, last lived in Queens, New York.
*Sources:* Br.B. 32; Liste d. nichtzugel. RA, 04/25/1933; JMBl. 33, p. 220; BArch, R 3001 PAK, PA; SSDI

### Kornicker, Gerhard
10/20/1903 Breslau - no information
*Home address:* no information
*Law firm address:* Leipziger Str. 30, W 8

*Additional information:* He was, as he said of himself, "nationalist-minded," nevertheless, after the National Socialist seizure of power he was made subject to an occupational ban on 05/26/1933.
*Sources:* Br.B. 32; Liste d. nichtzugel. RA, 05/24/1933; JMBl. 33, p. 203; BArch, R 3001 PAK, PA

### Kosterlitz, Arthur Dr.
08/09/1885 Strehlitz - no information
*Home address:* Passauer Str. 14, Schöneberg
*Law firm address:* Kurfürstendamm 224, W 15
*Additional information:* Attorney and notary; after the National Socialist seizure of power in 1933 he was readmitted; in 1935 his license as a notary was revoked; he worked as an attorney until the general occupational ban in 1938. He emigrated to London, Great Britain, on 12/01/1938.
*Sources:* *li; LAB, Liste 10/15/1933; DJ 36, p. 315; Liste 36; BArch, R 3001 PAK; MRRAK; BG

### Kosterlitz, Martin
02/27/1891 Pleß - March 1968
*Home address:* no information
*Law firm address:* Budapester Str. 26, W 62
*Additional information:* Attorney and notary; after the National Socialist seizure of power he was readmitted; in 1935 his license as a notary was revoked; he worked as an attorney until 09/23/1937. He emigrated to the USA, he last lived in Oakland, California.
*Sources:* *li; LAB, Liste 10/15/1933; Liste 36; BArch, R 3001 PAK; BG; SSDI

### Kozower, Philipp
01/29/1894 Berlin - transportation 1943
*Home address:* Oranienburger Str. 9-10, C 2, Mitte
*Law firm address:* Poststr. 12, C 2
*Additional information:* Attorney and notary; after the National Socialist seizure of power in 1933 he was readmitted; his license as a notary was revoked in 1935; he worked as an attorney until the general occupational ban in 1938. Board member of the RV as well as of the JKV, for which he also worked as a department head. On 01/28/1943 he was transported to Theresienstadt, from there he was transported on 10/12/1944 to Auschwitz.

*Sources:* *li; LAB, Liste 10/15/1933; DJ 36, p. 315; Liste 36; BArch, R 3001 PAK; MRRAK; BG; GB II; Göpp., p. 251; Naatz-Album

**Krämer, Ludwig Dr.**
08/30/1898 Giessen - 05/05/1989
*Home address:* no information
*Law firm address:* Joachimsthaler Str. 43/44, Charlottenburg
*Additional information:* Attorney at the KG; after the National Socialist seizure of power he was made subject to an occupational ban in early 1933. He emigrated to the USA, changed his name to Lewis Kramer, he last lived in New York.
*Sources:* Br.B. 32; Liste d. nichtzugel. RA, 04/25/1933; JMBl. 08/21/1933, p. 266; BArch, R 3001 PAK; SSDI

**Kraus, Martin**
10/10/1885 Berlin - October 1968 New York
*Home address:* Prinzenstr. 42, SW 19
*Law firm address:* Prinzenstr. 42, SW 19
*Additional information:* Attorney and notary; after the National Socialist seizure of power in 1933 his license as a notary was revoked; he was readmitted as an attorney, but still worked until the general occupational ban in 1938. He emigrated to New York, USA, where he died in 1968.
*Sources:* JMBl. 33, p. 208; *li; LAB, Liste 10/15/1933; Liste 36; BArch, R 3001 PAK; BG; SSDI; Information Cohn-Lempert

**Kremm, Fritz Dr.**
01/29/1893 Friesack - transportation 1943
*Home address:* Münchener Str. 45, W 30, Schöneberg
*Law firm address:* Potsdamer Str. 114, W 35
*Additional information:* After the National Socialist seizure of power in 1933 he was readmitted; he still worked as an attorney until the general occupational ban in 1938. He was later used in Berlin for forced labor, last used by the Willi A. Sasse Company. Date of declaration of property: 03/05/1943; collecting station Große Hamburger Str. 26; transportation on 03/17/1943 to Theresienstadt, from there he was transported on 09/28/1944 to Auschwitz.
*Sources:* *li; LAB, Liste 10/15/1933; Liste 36; BArch, R 3001 PAK; MRRAK; BG; GB II

**Krohn, Hugo Dr.**
01/13/1881 Pyritz - no information

*Home address:* Wittelsbacher Str. 18 or 15, Wilmersdorf
*Law firm address:* Wittelsbacher Str. 15
*Additional information:* Attorney and notary; after the National Socialist seizure of power in 1933 his license as a notary was revoked, he still worked as an attorney until 1938. He emigrated to London, Great Britain, on 05/27/1939.
*Sources:* JMBl. 33, p. 208; *li; LAB, Liste 10/15/1933; Liste 36; BArch, R 3001 PAK; MRRAK; BG

**Kroll, Siegfried**
10/13/1902 - no information
*Home address:* no information
*Law firm address:* Würzburger Str. 6, W 50
*Additional information:* Attorney since 1931; after the National Socialist seizure of power he was made subject to an occupational ban on 06/12/1933.
*Sources:* Liste d. nichtzugel. RA, 04/25/1933; JMBl. 08/21/1933, p. 267; BArch, R 3001 PAK, PA

**Kroner, Ludwig**
06/14/1906 - no information
*Home address:* no information
*Law firm address:* Schellingstr. 6, W 9
*Additional information:* After the National Socialist seizure of power, he made intensive efforts to avert the impending occupational ban, in vain: he was made subject to an occupational ban on 06/13/1933. He emigrated to Palestine in October 1933.
*Sources:* TK 33; Liste d. nichtzugel. RA, 04/25/1933; JMBl. 33, p. 253; BArch, R 3001 PAK, PA; BG

**Kronheim, Siegbert**
05/04/1886 Samotschin - 01/26/1943 Theresienstadt
*Home address:* Trautenaustr. 16, Wilmersdorf; Schillerstr. 14, Charlottenburg
*Law firm address:* Anhalter Str. 4, SW 11
*Additional information:* Attorney and notary; after the National Socialist seizure of power in 1933 he was readmitted; his license as a notary was revoked in 1935; he still worked as an attorney until the general occupational ban in 1938. Date of declaration of property: 09/17/1942; collecting station Große Hamburger Str. 26; transportation on 09/21/1942 to Theresienstadt; he died there four months later.

Sources: *li; LAB, Liste 10/15/1933; DJ 36, p. 315; Liste 36; MRRAK; BG; ThG; GB II

**Krotoschiner, Kurt Dr.**
03/21/1897 Berlin - no information
*Home address:* Sächsische Str. 71, W 15 (1932)
*Law firm address:* Kurfürstendamm 211, W 15
*Additional information:* Attorney at the KG; after the National Socialist seizure of power he was disbarred on 06/23/1933.
Sources: Br.B. 32; Jüd.Adr.B.; JMBl. 07/07/1933; BArch, R 3001 PAK

**Krüger, Hans**
01/07/1903 - no information
*Home address:* no information
*Law firm address:* Motzstr. 37, Wilmersdorf
*Additional information:* After the National Socialist seizure of power he was made subject to an occupational ban in early 1933. He emigrated to the Netherlands on 08/17/1933.
Sources: Liste d. nichtzugel. RA, 04/25/1933; JMBl. 33, p. 253; BArch, R 3001 PAK

**Kuhn, Werner Julius**
06/02/1899 Berlin - no information
*Home address:* Kurfürstendamm 175-176, Wilmersdorf
*Law firm address:* Kleiststr. 34, W 62
*Additional information:* After the National Socialist seizure of power in 1933 he was readmitted; he was still working as an attorney until the general occupational ban in 1938. He emigrated to Sydney, Australia.
Sources: *li; Liste 36; MRRAK; BG

**Kümmel, Hugo**
12/16/1904 Dortmund - no information
*Home address:* no information
*Law firm address:* Bülowstr. 44, W 57
*Additional information:* After the National Socialist seizure of power he was made subject to an occupational ban in July 1933.
Sources: Liste d. nichtzugel. RA, 04/25/1933; JMBl. 33, p. 253; BArch, R 3001 PAK

**Kuntz, Siegfried**
10/03/1871 - 01/24/1937
*Home address:* Bülowstr. 85, Schöneberg
*Law firm address:* Bülowstr. 85, W 57
*Additional information:* Attorney and notary; after the National Socialist seizure of power in 1933 he was readmitted; his license as a notary was revoked in 1935; he worked as an attorney until his death in

1937; he died at the age of 65; he was buried at Weißensee.
Sources: *li; LAB, Liste 10/15/1933; DJ 36, p. 315; Liste 36; BG

**Kunz, Bruno, Dr.**
05/02/1881 Xions - no information
*Home address:* Meinekestr. 3, Charlottenburg
*Law firm address:* Kurfürstendamm 216, W 15
*Additional information:* Attorney and notary; after the National Socialist seizure of power in 1933 his license as a notary was revoked; he was still admitted as an attorney until the general occupational ban in 1938. He emigrated on 12/10/1940.
Sources: *li; LAB, Liste 10/15/1933; JMBl. 33, p. 208; Liste 36; MRRAK; BG

**Kunz, Georg**
03/04/1898 Görlitz - transportation in 1943
*Home address:* Lützowstr. 60 a, W 35
*Law office address:* Genthiner Str. 16, W 35
*Additional information:* Attorney since 1927; after the National Socialist seizure of power he was made subject to an occupational ban on 06/10/1933. Transportation on 10/14/1943 to Auschwitz.
Sources: Br.B. 32.; Liste d. nichtzugel. RA, 04/25/1933; JMBl. 33, p. 253; BArch, R 3001 PAK, PA 65347; BG; GB II

**Kurnik, Karl Dr.**
05/15/1888 Stettin - no information
*Home address:* Paulsborner Str. 75, Wilmersdorf
*Law office address:* Königstr. 220/221, C 2
*Additional information:* Attorney and notary; after the National Socialist seizure of power in 1933 he was readmitted; his license as a notary was revoked in 1935. He emigrated to Zurich, Switzerland before 05/16/1938; 1940 to Havana, Cuba.
Sources: *li; LAB, Liste 10/15/1933; DJ 36, p. 315; Liste 36; BArch, R 3001 PAK; MRRAK; BG: LAB, OFP files; Naatz-Album

**Kurtzig, Arnold Dr.**
12/07/1898 Grünberg - October 1973
*Home address:* Charlottenbrunner Str. 46, Wilmersdorf
*Law office address:* An der Spandauer Brücke 14, C2

*Additional information:* Also defense counsel in the environment of the "Rote Hilfe" (Red Aid); brother of Paul, with whom he worked in a joint partnership; after the National Socialist seizure of power he was made subject to an occupational ban in 1933. His admission at all three regional courts was revoked in June 1933. He emigrated to France on 02/27/1933, later he evidently went to the USA, he last lived in Arlington, Virginia; he died in 1973 at the age of 74.
*Sources:* Liste d. nichtzugel. RA, 04/25/1933 (addendum); JMBl. 33, p. 221; BArch R 3001 PAK; BG; Schneider, Schwarz, Schwarz, p. 186; SSDI

**Kurtzig, Paul**
10/25/1899 Grünberg - no information
*Home address:* no information
*Law office address:* An der Spandauer Brücke 14, C 2
*Additional information:* As an attorney he was active in 1926 in the legal protection order of the "Rote Hilfe" (Red Aid); brother and law partner of Arnold; after the National Socialist seizure of power he was made subject to an occupational ban in 1933, he was disbarred on 07/20/1933.
*Sources:* Liste d. nichtzugel. RA, 04/25/1933 (addendum); JMBl. 08/21/1933; BArch, R 3001 PAK; Schneider, Schwarz, Schwarz, p. 186/87

**Kurzweg, Alfred**
12/07/1882 Chemnitz - 02/14/1943 Theresienstadt
*Home address:* Prinzregentenstr. 3, Wilmersdorf
*Law firm address:* Münzstr. 24, C 25
*Additional information:* Attorney and notary; after the National Socialist seizure of power in 1933 he was readmitted; his license as a notary was revoked in 1935; he was still working as an attorney until the general occupational ban in 1938, thereafter as a "consultant." Date of declaration of property: 08/17/1942. Transportation on 10/03/1942 to Theresienstadt, he died there in February 1943.
*Sources:* *li; LAB, Liste 10/15/1933; Liste 36; Liste d. Kons. v. 04/15/1939; BG; ThG; GB II

**Kuttner, Erich Dr.**
12/16/1892 Forst
- 12/15/1955
*Home address:* Kleiststr. 23, W 62
*Law firm address:* Friedrichstr. 44, SW 68
*Additional information:* He volunteered as a soldier in the First World War; attorney at the KG (since 1921) and notary (since 1928); after the National Socialist seizure of power in 1933 he was readmittted; because he was recognized as a "frontline fighter;" in 1935 his license as an attorney was revoked; he worked as an attorney until the general occupational ban in 1938. He emigrated to Argentina. He was married and had a daughter. He returned and was readmitted as an attorney in Berlin in 1952.
*Sources:* *li; LAB, Liste 10/15/1933; DJ 36, jP. 315; Liste 36; BArch, R 3001 PAK, PA 65464; MRRAK; BG: BAP, 15.09 RSA; LAB, RAK, PA

**Kuttner, Hermann**
07/22/1886 Berlin - no information
*Home address:* Potsdamer Str. 39 a
*Law firm address:* Potsdamer Str. 39/39 a
*Additional information:* Attorney (since 1913) and notary; after the National Socialist seizure of power his license as a notary was revoked on 06/30/1933; he was readmitted as an attorney, he worked until the general occupational ban in 1938. He emigrated on 08/26/1939.
*Sources:* Br.B. 32; JMBl. 33, p. 208; Liste 36; BArch, R 3001 PAK, PA; BG; Naatz-Album

**Kuznitzky, Heinz Georg Dr.**
05/25/1889 Halle a.d. Saale - no information
*Home address:* Laubenheimer Str. 1, Wilmersdorf
*Law firm address:* Unter den Linden 54/55
*Additional information:* Attorney and notary; after the National Socialist seizure of power he emigrated on 05/01/1933.
*Sources:* Br.B. 32; JMBl. 33, 05/26/1933; BArch, R 3001 PAK; BG

# L

**Labischin, Kurt Dr.**
08/24/1900 Posen - no information
*Home address:* no information
*Law firm address:* Zimmerstr. 92-93, SW 68
*Additional information:* After the National Socialist seizure of power he was made subject to an occupational ban in early 1933; he presumably survived the NS regime.
*Sources:* Br.B. 32; Liste d. nichtzugel. RA, 04/25/1933; JMBl. 08/21/1933, p. 267; BArch, R 3001 PAK

**Lachmann, Heinz Ulrich Dr.**
08/23/1898 Bremen - no information
*Home address:* Salzbrunner Str. 27
*Law firm address:* Viktoriastr. 10, W 10
*Additional information:* Attorney and notary in a joint law partnership with Kurt Lachmann; after the National Socialist seizure of power he was readmitted in 1933; his license as a notary was revoked in November 1935; he worked as an attorney until the general occupational ban in 1938. He emigrated to Great Britain.
*Sources:* *li; LAB, Liste 10/15/1933; DJ 36, p. 315; Liste 36; BArch, R 3001 PAK; MRRAK; BG

**Lachmann, Jean**
10/09/1879 - 02/20/1936
*Home address:* Eisenzahnstr. 66
*Law firm address:* Königstr. 20/21, C 2
*Additional information:* Attorney and notary; after the National Socialist seizure of power in 1933 he was readmitted; his license as a notary was revoked in 1935; he died in 1936, he was buried at Weißensee.
*Sources:* *li; LAB, Liste 10/15/1933; BG: Friedh.W.Sterbereg.

**Lachmann, Kurt Dr.**
01/01/1886 (1888?) Berlin - presumably 1938
*Home address:* Konstanzer Str. 5, W 15
*Law firm address:* Viktoriastr. 10, W 10
*Additional information:* Attorney and notary in a joint law partnership with Heinz Lachmann; he resigned from the Jewish Synagogue in 1927; after the National Socialist seizure of power in 1933 his license as a notary was revoked; he was still working as an attorney in 1936; he presumably died in 1938.

*Sources:* Jüd.Adr.B.; JMBl. 33, p. 208; *li; LAB, Liste 10/15/1933; Liste 36; BG

**Lachmann, Leo, Judicial Councillor**
09/05/1865 - 06/14/1936
*Home address:* no information
*Law firm address:* Alexanderstr. 42, O 27
*Additional information:* Attorney and notary; after the National Socialist seizure of power in 1933 his license as an attorney was revoked; he died in 1936 at the age of 70; he was buried at Weißensee.
*Sources:* JMBl. 33, p. 208; *li; LAB, Liste 10/15/1933; Liste 36; BG

**Lachmann, Max**
No information
*Home address:* no information
*Law firm address:* Kaiser-Allee 104, Friedenau
*Additional information:* Attorney at the KG and notary; after the National Socialist seizure of power in 1933 he was readmitted; his license as a notary was revoked in 1935; he was still working as an attorney until the general occupational ban in 1938.
*Sources:* Br.B. 32; *li; LAB, Liste 10/15/1933; DJ 36, p. 315; Liste 36; MRRAK

**Lachotzki, Werner Dr.**
11/22/1904 Beeskow - no information
*Home address:* Neue Kantstr. 28 (1939)
*Law firm address:* Uhlandstr. 194 a, Charlottenburg
*Additional information:* After the National Socialist seizure of power he was made subject to an occupational ban in early 1933; he was still living in Berlin in 1939; he certainly survived the National Socialist regime and worked again as a jurist later.
*Sources:* Liste d. nichtzugel. RA, 04/25/1933; JMBl. 33, p. 220; BArch, R 3001 PAK; VZ 39

**Lachs, Reinhold Dr.**
10/20/1894 Berlin - no information
*Home address:* no information
*Law firm address:* Händelstr. 18, NW 87
*Additional information:* 1912-16 he completed his legal studies in Berlin and Freiburg i. Br.; fought in the First World War in 1915-16; 1918 he received his doctorate in Heidelberg; 1921-22 he was an assistant judge in Berlin; from 1922-25 he worked as an attorney in the German Clearing office

for Prewar Debts; from 1925 he worked as an attorney in Berlin, last at the LG I-III. After the National Socialist seizure of power he was made subject to an occupational ban in early 1933. He emigrated to Great Britain in July 1933; 1934-37 he renewed his legal studies; 1937 he was admitted to the London Bar Association; 1939-45 he was assistant to Counsel in Chambers; 1940 he was interned for a short time; 1945-47 he was a legal advisor of the German Division in the Foreign Office; 1947 he was the legal advisor of the Control Commission for Germany; 1947-50 he was an attorney; as from 1950 he was a managing director, as from 1956 he was a legal advisor with the Jewish Trust Corp. for Germany; 1969 he retired; in 1977 he lived in London, Great Britain.
*Sources:* Br.B. 32; TK 33; Liste d. nichtzugel. RA, 04/25/1933; JMBl. 33, p. 253, BArch, R 3001 PAK; BG; BHdE 1980, Bd. 1, p. 408

**Ladewig, Fritz, Judicial Councillor**
05/28/1870 Criwitz - no information
*Home address:* Bundesratufer 1, Tiergarten
Law office: Müllerstr. 177, N 65
*Additional information:* Attorney and notary; after the National Socialist seizure of power in April 1933 he was made subject to an occupational ban; his license as a notary was revoked; he was readmitted as an attorney; he was a member of the Reich Association of non-Aryan Christians; he was disbarred upon request on 08/30/1935. Emigration.
*Sources:* Liste d. nichtzugel. RA, 04/25/1933; *li; LAB, Liste 10/15/1933; BG; Mitt. bl. Reichsverband nichtarischer Christen, 12/06/1934

**Ladewig, Hans Carl**
09/06/1886 Berlin - no information
*Home address:* Kronenstr. 4/5, W 8
*Law firm address:* Kronenstr. 4/5, W 8
*Additional information:* Attorney and notary; law partnership with Max Lichtwitz and Ernst Loewe; after the National Socialist seizure of power in 1933 he was readmitted; 1935 his license as a notary was revoked; he was disbarred on 09/11/1937. He emigrated to Italy.
*Sources:* *li; LAB, Liste 10/15/1933; DJ 36, p. 315; Liste 36; Naatz-Album; BG

**Lagro, Max Dr.**
09/06/1874 Nakel - transportation 1942
*Home address:* Konstanzer Str. 59, Wilmersdorf/Knesebeckstr. 68-69, Joachimsthaler Str. 7-8 ?, Charlottenburg
*Law firm address:* Knesebeckstr. 68/69, Charlottenburg
*Additional information:* Attorney and notary; after the National Socialist seizure of power his license as a notary was revoked in 1933; he worked as an attorney until the general occupational ban in 1938. Last conscripted as forced laborer at Iris Type GmbH, SO 36, Kottbusser Ufer 41; date of declaration of property: 08/23/1942; transportation on 09/05/1942 to Riga.
*Sources:* *li; LAB, Liste 10/15/1933; Liste 36; BG; BdE; GB II

**Lamm, Fritz Dr.**
12/21/1876 Görlitz - 12/03/1942 Sachsenhausen
*Home address:* Blumes Hof 15, W 15, Tiergarten
*Law firm address:* Rosenheimer Str. 23, W 30
*Additional information:* Attorney and notary; since 1908 he also worked for the Jewish Synagogue in Berlin; 1924 he was a legal advisor and then deputy chairman of the Welfare and Youth Office of the Synagoguge; lecturer in welfare courses. After the National Socialist seizure of power in 1933, his license as a notary was revoked, he was still working as an atttorney until the general occupational ban in 1938. He was shot dead as a hostage for escaped members of the Jewish Synagogue in Sachsenhausen.
*Sources:* JMBl. 33, p. 208; *li; LAB, Liste 10/15/1933; Liste 36; BG; GB II; Göpp., p. 252

**Lamm, Richard Dr.**
08/12/1889 Berlin - no information
*Home address:* Achenbachstr. 13, W 50
*Law firm address:* Achenbachstr. 13, W 50
*Additional information:* Attorney, at the same time involved in the women's clothing factory Gebr. Lamm oHG; after the National Socialist seizure of power he was readmitted; in 1934 his admission was deleted upon request. He emigrated to Paris, France, on 09/01/1938.
*Sources:* *li; LAB, Liste 10/15/1933; BArch, R 3001 PAK; BG

**Landau, Adolf, Judicial Councillor**
05/15/1862 Bingen - 08/06/1943
Theresienstadt
*Home address:* Walter-Fischer-Str. 2,
Wilmersdorf
*Law firm address:* Grolmanstr. 32/33,
Charlottenburg
*Additional information:* After the National
Socialist seizure of power he was readmitted,
he was still working until the general
occupational ban in 1938. Transportation on
03/17/1943 to Theresienstadt, he died there a
few months later.
*Sources:* TK 33; *li; LAB, Liste 10/15/1933;
Liste 36; BG; ThG; GB II

**Landau, Felix Dr., Judicial
Councillor**
No information
- 04/13/1935
*Home address:* no
information
*Law firm address:* Unter
den Linden 39, NW 7
*Additional information:* Attorney and
notary; after the National Socialist seizure
of power he was readmitted in 1933. He died
in 1935.
*Sources:* TK 33; *li; LAB, Liste 10/15/1933;
Naatz-Album

**Landau, Ludwig Dr.**
08/24/1882 Berlin - 09/19/1951 London
*Home address:* no information
*Law firm address:* Kleiststr. 15, W 62
*Additional information:* After the
National Socialist seizure of power he was
readmitted; he was still working as an
attorney until the general occupation in
1938. He emigrated to Great Britain, he
died there in 1951.
*Sources:* TK 33; *li; LAB, Liste 10/15/1933;
Liste 36; BArch, R 3001 PAK; MRRAK; BG

**Landsberg, Ernst Dr.**
01/13/1883 Berlin - no information
*Home address:* Uhlandstr. 169/170, W 15
*Law firm address:* Uhlandstr. 169/170, W 15
*Additional information:* Attorney and
notary; after the National Socialist seizure of
power his license as a notary was revoked; he
still worked as an attorney until the general
occupational ban in 1938. He emigrated to
Mercedes, Uruguay; 1948 to Cape Town,
South Africa.

*Sources:* JMBl. 33, p. 220; *li; LAB, Liste
10/15/1933; Liste 36; BArch, R 3001 PAK;
MRRAK; BG

**Landsberg, Franz**
07/17/1880 Berlin - no information
*Home address:* Gerkrathstr. 8,
Zehlendorf-Nikolassee
*Law firm address:* Hinter der katholischen
Kirche 2, W 8
*Additional information:* Attorney and notary;
after the National Socialist seizure of power
his license as a notary was revoked in 1933,
he worked as an attorney until the general
occupational ban in 1938. He emigrated to
London, Great Britain on 06/07/1939.
*Sources:* JMBl. 33, p. 208; *li; LAB, Liste
10/15/1933; Liste 36; MRRAK; BArch, R
3001 PAK; BG

**Landsberg, Hans Dr.**
06/24/1882 Berlin - no information
*Home address:* Kufsteiner Str. 5, Schöneberg
*Law firm address:* Berchtesgadener Str. 27,
Schöneberg
*Additional information:* Attorney and
notary; after the National Socialist seizure of
power his license as an attorney was revoked,
he worked as an attorney until the general
occupational ban in 1938. His wife, Gertrud,
nee Pakebusch, was regarded as non-Jewish.
*Sources:* JMBl. 33, p. 220; *li; LAB, Liste
10/15/1933; Liste 36; BArch, R 3001 PAK;
MRRAK; BG

**Landsberg, Hans Julius**
05/04/1890 Berlin - October 1973
*Home address:* Uhlandstr. 169, W 15,
Charlottenburg
*Law firm address:* Meinekestr. 22,
Charlottenburg
*Additional information:* Attorney at the KG
(since 1922) and notary (since 01/09/1933 );
after the National Socialist seizure of power in
1933 he was made subject to an occupational
ban. He recalled: "As a result of the National
Socialist Jewish legislation, as a Jew I was
disbarred as an attorney and my license as a
notary was revoked . . ." 1939 he emigrated to
Chile; he returned and was readmitted as an
attorney in Berlin in 1967.
*Sources:* Br.B. 32; Liste d. nichtzugel. RA,
04/25/1933; JMBl. 33, p. 203; BArch, R 3001
PAK; BG: BAP 15.09 RSA; LAB, OFP files;
LAB, RAK, PA

**Landsberg, Otto Dr.**
12/04/1869 Rybnik, Oberschlesien -
12/09/1957 Baarn, the Netherlands
*Home address:* Südwestkorso 21, Friedenau
*Law firm address:* Dorotheenstr. 29
*Additional information:* After his high
school examination he completed his legal
studies in Berlin 1887-1890; he became a
member of the SPD; 1895 he established
himself as an attorney in Magdeburg; 1903-
1909 he was city councillor in Magdeburg;
1912 he occupied a Reichstag seat; in the SPD
Reichstag faction he was an exponent of the
right wing; he represented a national policy
in 1914 at the beginning of the First World
War and campaigned for the granting of war
credits; in the November Revolution 1918/19
he was one of three SPD representatives in the
Council of People's Deputies; 1919 he was a
member of the Weimar National Assembly;
in February 1919 he became the Reich
Minister of Justice and later a member of the
delegation at the negotiations of the Treaty
of Versailles; he resigned from his ministry in
protest against the terms of the peace treaty;
from 1920-23 he was an envoy in Brussels,
Belgium; in 1924 he returned to Berlin and
established himself as an attorney, later he
also established himself as a notary; from
1924-33 he was once again a member of the
Reichstag; he was one of the legal experts
of the SPD fraction; in 1925 he was a legal
advisor to Reich President Ebert regarding the
Munich libel suit brought by him due to the
so-called "stab in the back" allegations that
had been brought against him. He did not
practice his faith but was politically opposed
to anti-Semitism.
After the National Socialist seizure of
power in early 1933 he was made subject
to an occupational ban; in August 1933 he
emigrated via Czechoslovakia, Switzerland
and Belgium to the Netherlands: in 1938
he was denaturalized from the German
Reich; after the German occupation of
the Netherlands from 1940-45 he lived
underground, hidden by friends; after the end
of the war he lived in the Netherlands, where
he died in 1957.
*Sources:* Br.B. 32; JMBl. 33, 06/02/1933;
Liste d. nichtzugel. RA, 04/25/1933; BArch,
R 3001 PAK; BG; BHdE vol. 1, p. 415; Benz/
Graml: Biographisches Lexikon [Biographical
lexicon], 1988

**Landsberg, Willy Dr.**
07/21/1884 Berlin - no information
*Home address:* no information
*Law firm address:* Chausseestr. 16, N 4
*Additional information:* Attorney and
notary; his grandfather already had been
baptized, he was a Protestant. After the
National Socialist seizure of power in
1933 he was regarded as "mixed race,"
his license as a notary was revoked
in accordance with § 3 of the law of
04/07/1933], thereupon he relinquished his
law firm in October 1933.
*Sources:* Br.B. 32; JMBl. 33, p. 208; Pr.J. 33,
p. 532; BArch R 3001 PAK, PA

**Landsberger, Arthur, Judicial Councillor**
No information
*Home address:* Köpenicker Str. 108, SO 16
*Law firm address:* Kantstr. 29,
Charlottenburg
*Additional information:* Attorney, Judicial
Council and notary (not to be confused with
the author of the same name, who was also an
attorney); after the National Socialist seizure
of power in 1933 his license as a notary was
revoked; he worked as an attorney until the
general occupational ban in 1938.
*Sources:* Adr.B. 31; Jüd.Adr.B.; JMBl. 33,
p. 208; *li; LAB, Liste 10/15/1933; Liste 36;
MRRAK

**Landsberger, Egon Dr.**
02/18/1896 Berlin - 01/30/1941 Dachau
*Home address:* Stierstr. 5, Schöneberg
*Law firm address:* Markgrafenstr. 43, W 56
*Additional information:* After the National
Socialist seizure of power he was readmitted,
he was still working as an attorney until the
general occupational ban in 1938; his wife,
Jenny, nee Weichert was regarded as non-
Jewish; on 07/03/1940 he was transported
to the Sachsenhausen concentration camp
under unknown circumstances, from there
he was taken on 09/05/1940 to the Dachau
concentration camp; at the end of January
1941 he was murdered in Dachau.
*Sources:* *li; LAB, Liste 10/15/1933; Liste 36;
BArch, R 3001 PAK; MRRAK; BG; GB II

**Landsberger, Friedrich Dr.**
05/24/1889 Rosenberg - no information
*Home address:* Hohenzollerndamm 47 a,
Wilmersdorf

*Law firm address:* Kurfürstendamm 206/2207, W 15
*Additional information:* After the National Socialist seizure of power he was readmitted; he was still working as an attorney until the general occupational ban in 1938. Emigration on 12/14/1939.
*Sources:* *li; LAB, Liste 10/15/1933; Liste 36; BArch, R 3001 PAK; MRRAK; BG

**Landsberger, Hans Herbert Dr.**
06/19/1905 Berlin - 07/14/1981 Ridgefield, USA
*Home address:* no information.
*Law firm address:* Invalidenstr. 111, NW 4
*Additional information:* Attorney at the KG; after the National Socialist seizure of power he was made subject to an occupational ban in early 1933. He emigrated to Paris, France; interned in 1939, fled to Spain in 1942; emigrated to New York, USA in 1943.
*Sources:* Liste d. nichtzugel. RA, 04/25/1933; JMBl. 33, p. 203; BArch, R 3001 PAK; BG; SSDI

**Landsberger, Kurt Dr.**
02/20/1890 Berlin - 10/27/1978
*Home address:* no information
*Law firm address:* Friedrich-Ebert-Str. 1, W 9
*Additional information:* He fought in the First World War; he was a dissident, his wife was of non-Jewish origins; he was admitted as an attorney since 1921; in 1927 he became a notary; he was in a law partnership with Leopold Landsberger. After the National Socialist seizure of power in 1933 he was readmitted, because he was recognized as a "frontline fighter," in 1935 his license as a notary was revoked; he worked as an attorney until the general occupational ban in 1935, then he still worked as a "consultant." After the Pogrom in 1938 he was transported to the Sachsenhausen concentration camp in 1938, he was freed again. His work as a consultant improved his economic situation. He managed to survive, protected by the "mixed marriage." After the end of the war he was readmitted as an attorney on 07/08/1945. He was a member of the management board of the Board Association and remained a member of the advisory board until 02/13/1963, he was at the same time the chairman of the Court of Honor until 05/06/1952 and from 05/07/1952 until 02/19/1958 an associate of the Honorary Court Senate. He lived and in 1949 was

still practicing as an attorney and notary in Charlottenburg, Schlüterstr.
*Sources:* *li; LAB, Liste 10/15/1933; DJ 36, p. 315; Liste 36; MRRAK; Liste d. Kons., 04/15/1939; BG; LAB, RAK, PA; information B. Dombek

**Landsberger, Leopold Dr.**
02/26/1887 - no information
*Home address:* no information
*Law firm address:* Friedrich-Ebert-Str. 1, W 9
*Additional information:* Attorney and notary; in a law partnership with Kurt Landsberger. After the National Socialist seizure of power in 1933 he was readmitted; his license as a notary was revoked in 1935; in 1936 he was still working as an attorney; he presumably emigrated to the Netherlands.
*Sources:* *li; LAB, Liste 10/15/1933; DJ 36, p. 315; Liste 36; BArch, R 3001 PAK

**Landsberger, Richard (Robert) Dr.**
04/10/1873 Berlin - 11/15/1941 Berlin
*Home address:* no information
*Law firm address:* Tempelhofer Ufer 23/24, SW
*Additional information:* Attorney and notary; after the National Socialist seizure of power in 1933 his license as a notary was revoked; he worked as an attorney until the general occupational ban in 1938; he died in 1941 at the Jewish Hospital at the age of 68.
*Sources:* JMBl. 33, p. 208; *li; LAB, Liste 10/15/1933; Liste 36; MRRAK; BG

**Landshoff, Fritz Dr.**
01/01/1885 - 03/19/1938
*Home address:* Kottbusser Damm 9, SW 29
*Law firm address:* Dresdener Str. 3, SO 36
*Additional information:* Attorney and notary; after the National Socialist seizure of power in 1933 his license as a notary was revoked, he was still practicing as an attorney until 1936, he last practiced from his private home; he died in 1938 at the age of 53, he was buried at Weißensee.
*Sources:* JMBl. 33, p. 208; *li; LAB, Liste 10/15/1933; Liste 36; BArch, R 3001 PAK; BG: Fried.W. Sterbereg.

**Landshut, Arnold**
05/30/1900 Neumark - no information
*Home address:* no information
*Law firm address:* Frankfurter Allee 18, O 34
*Additional information:* Attorney since 1925; after the National Socialist seizure of

power he was made subject to an occupational ban until 06/07/1933; he emigrated to Palestine in October 1933.
*Sources:* Br.B. 32; JMBl. 33, p. 234; Liste d. nichtzugel. RA, 04/25/1933; BArch, R 3001 PAK, PA; BG

**Lange, Kurt**
No information - April 1933
*Home address:* Neue Ansbacher Str. 12, W 50
*Law firm address:* Berliner Str. 9, Wilmersdorf
*Additional information:* The attorney and notary took his own life in view of the events in April 1933. He went into the Wannsee near the Swedish Pavilion.
*Sources:* Jüd.Adr.B.; Br.B. 32; Wochenblatt für den Synagogenbezirk Erfurt [Weekly magazine for the synagogue district of Erfurt], 04/21/1933; JMBl. 04/28/1933

**Langenbach, Otto Dr.**
No information
*Home address:* no information
*Law firm address:* Potsdamer Str. 129/130, W 9
*Additional information:* Attorney at the KG and notary; after the National Socialist seizure of power in 1933 his license as a notary was revoked, he was still working as an attorney in 1936.
*Sources:* JMBl. 33, p. 208; *li; LAB, Liste 10/15/1933; Liste 36

**Laserstein, Botho Dr.**
07/31/1901 Chemnitz - 03/09/1955
*Home address:* no information.
*Law firm address:* Kurfürstendamm 14/15, W 50
*Additional information:* Attorney since 1928 in a law firm with Max Chodziesner; in addition to his law practice he published political essays [among others in "Weltbühne" (World stage)] and film reviews. After the National Socialist seizure of power , the board of the RAK reported to the Prussian Ministry of Justice that he had published "several articles in the communist newspapers 'Berlin in the morning' and 'Welt am Abend' (World in the evening)," emphasizing at the same time that he was "non-Aryan." He was made subject to an occupational ban in June 1933. He emigrated to France in 1933; from 1936 to 1940 he was a translator with the French Postal Ministry; from 1940-1951 he was a

high school teacher of English and German at Catholic boarding schools, last in Dijon. In 1943 his wife and daughter were transported from France and murdered. His parents and brother were also victims of the Holocaust. He returned to Germany in 1951 and took over a position as prosecutor in Düsseldorf on 08/01/1951 "on a trial basis and at any time revocable;" in publications he argued against rearmament and the repeatedly discussed reintroduction of the death penalty; in his writings he also advocated for the rights of homosexuals, who were still threatened with criminal prosecution by the continued application of Paragraph 175 in its tighter version of 1935; because of his commitment, which included criticism of the judicial bureaucracy, he was transferred mid-1953 as a magistrate to Essen for disciplinary reasons. At the same time, his senior bosses began covert investigations, including baseless allegations, to find grounds for his dismissal from the civil service. Finally, he was dismissed from public service at the beginning of 1955, because "for constitutional reasons he would not be able to adapt himself to the profession of judge or public prosecutor in the future and even to embody a professional ethos, which would (be) expected from representatives of this class. (File note of the Ministry of Justice, North Rhine-Westphalia, 11/19/1954). He was thus faced with economic ruin (also because a settlement process pending since 1951 in Berlin did not progress). After the termination, he tried for the first time to take his own life. He tried in vain for inclusion as a brother in the Benedictine Abbey of Maria Laach. On March 9, 1955 he committed suicide.
*Publications:* numerous political essays and film reviews
*Sources:* GHStA, Rep. 84a, Nr. 20363; JMBl. 33, p. 282; BArch, R 3001, PAK; Information E. Proskauer; Hoven, Herbert (editor): Der unaufhaltsame Selbstmord des Botho Laserstein [The unstoppable suicide of Botho Laserstein], Frankfurt/M.1990; Göpp., pages 345/6

**Latte, Felix**
04/19/1886 Berlin - no information
*Home address:* Barbarossastr. 44, W 30
*Law firm address:* Stresemannstr. 103
*Additional information:* Attorney at the KG and notary; after the National Socialist

seizure of power in 1933 he was readmitted; in 1935 his license as a notary was revoked; he worked as an attorney until the general occupational ban in 1938. He emigrated to Shanghai, China, on 05/08/1939.
*Sources:* *li; LAB, Liste 10/15/1933; DJ 36, p. 315; Liste 36; MRRAK; BG

**Latte, Max, Judicial Councillor**
06/13/1857 - 11/10/1934
*Home address:* Martin-Luther-Str. 88, W 30
*Law firm address:* Martin-Luther-Str. 88, W 30
*Additional information:* Attorney and notary; in October 1933 he was readmitted; he died in 1934 at the age of 77.
*Sources:* *li; LAB, Liste10/15/1933; BG: Friedh.W.Sterbereg.

**Lazar, Walter**
09/04/1880 Königsberg - transportation 1943
*Home address:* Grolmanstr. 32, Charlottenburg
*Law firm address:* Neue Kantstr. 1, Charlottenburg
*Additional information:* Attorney and notary; after the National Socialist seizure of power in 1933 he was readmitted; his license as a notary was revoked in 1935, he was still working as an attorney until the general occupational ban in 1938. Date of declaration of property; 01/07/1943; collecting station Große Hamburger Str. 26; transportation on 01/12/1943 to Auschwitz.
*Sources:* *li; LAB, Liste 10/15/1933; DJ 36, p. 315; Liste 36; MRRAK; BArch, R 3001 PAK; BG; GB II

**Lazarus, Hans Dr.**
12/19/1887 Berlin - no information
*Home address:* no information.
*Law firm address:* Potsdamer Str. 122/123, W 35
*Additional information:* Attorney (since 1918) and notary (since 1929); after the National Socialist seizure of power he was made subject to an occupational ban on 06/09/1933.
*Sources:* Br.B. 32; Liste d. nichtzugel. RA, 04/25/1933; JMBl. 33, p. 209; BArch, R 3001 PAK, PA

**Lebin, Ernst Dr., Judicial Councillor**
No information
*Home address:* no information
*Law firm address:* Friedrichstr. 44, SW 68

*Additional information:* Attorney and notary; after the National Socialist seizure of power in 1933 his license as a notary was revoked; he still worked as an attorney until the general occupational ban in 1938. According to the nephew of his law partner Dr. Erich Kuttner Lebin was arrested in 1938; he was released again, but he died soon after from the consequences of the detention.
*Sources:* TK 33; JMBl. 33, p. 208; *li; LAB, Liste 10/15/1933; Liste 36; information Gorski

**Ledermann, Franz**
10/16/1889 Hirschberg - no information
*Home address:* Genthiner Str. 5, Schöneberg
*Law firm address:* Genthiner Str. 5 a, Schöneberg
*Additional information:* Attorney and notary; after the National Socialist seizure of power he was made subject to an occupational ban in early 1933; he emigrated to Amsterdam, the Netherlands on 10/01/1933.
*Sources:* Br.B.32; JMBl. 33, p. 221; Liste d. nichtzugel. RA, 04/25/1933; BArch, R 3001 PAK; BG: LAB, OFP files

**Leffmann, Ernst Dr.**
04/23/1899 Cologne - 03/22/1972 Arnheim
*Home address:* no information
*Law firm address:* Fasanenstr. 67, W 15
*Additional information:* He had passed one of the state examinations with the rarely awarded grade "very good;" he was an attorney since 1926. After the National Socialist seizure of power he was made subject to an occupational ban on 07/13/1933. At that time, however, he was already no longer in the country, he had left Germany on March 20, 1933. Previously, on 03/08/1933, he had given a lecture at the trade union confederation. SA men who had stormed this event abused him. He was delivered home the next morning, badly injured. His ear canal had been smashed with a rifle butt and he also had blood poisoning. He escaped from Germany. In August 1933 he established himself with his wife and two children in Arnheim and he founded a chemical factory. From December 1942 to October 1943, he and his wife and daughter went underground, but they were discovered

and deported via the Westerbork transit camp to Bergen-Belsen. The son went underground at a different location.

In April 1945, the family was transported with thousands of other prisoners in the direction of Theresienstadt. Due to the advancing front the train travelled aimlessly through Germany for 14 days and came to a halt on April 20, 1945 in the Langennaundorfer Forest at Tröbitz in the current district of Elbe-Elster, because a destroyed railway bridge prevented the onward journey. On April 23, 1945, the Red Army freed more than 2,500 seriously ill people from the cattle carriages.

He returned to his legal profession after the liberation. In 1953 he received "final approval" as an attorney at the KG in Berlin; freed from a residence requirement, he remained living in Arnheim. In 1960 he took on a teaching assignment for banking law at the University of Cologne. He also worked on the 9th edition (1969) of "Kommentars zum Gesetz gegen den unlauteren Wettbewerb" ["Commentary on the law against unfair competition"] by Alfred Rosenthal. He died in 1972 in Arnheim.
*Sources:* Br.B. 32; Liste d. nichtzugel. RA, 04/25/1933; JMBl. 08/21/1933, p. 267; BArch, R 3001 PAK, PA; information E.J. Numann, 11/02/1999

**Lehmann, Alfred Dr.**
01/07/1898 Berlin - no information
*Home address:* Freisinger Str. 15, W 30
*Law firm address:* Nassauische Str. 36, Wilmersdorf
*Additional information:* Attorney at the KG and notary; after the National Socialist seizure of power in 1933 he was readmitted; his license as a notary was revoked in 1935; he was still working as an attorney until the general occupational ban in 1938; there is a high certainty that he survived the National Socialist regime and later worked as an attorney again.
*Sources:* *li; LAB, Liste 10/15/1933; DJ 36, p. 315; Liste 36; MRRAK; BG

**Lehmann, Georg Dr.**
No information - April 1933
*Home address:* Innsbrucker Str. 29, Schöneberg
*Law firm address:* Am Karlsbad 29

*Additional information:* Attorney and notary; in view of the circumstances in April 1933, he committed suicide by taking pills.
*Sources:* Jüd.Adr.B.; Br.B. 32; Wochenblatt für den Synagogenbezirk Erfurt [Weekly magazine for the synagogue district of Erfurt], 04/21/1933; JMBl. 05/26/1933

**Lehmann, Manfred Dr.**
09/23/1897 - no information
*Home address:* Weberstr. 51, no. 15
*Law firm address:* Bayerische Str. 33, W 30
*Additional information:* After the National Socialist seizure of power he was readmitted; he was disbarred on 10/04/1937. He emigrated to Palestine.
*Sources:* Br.B. 32; *li; LAB, Liste 10/15/1933; Liste 36; BArch, R 3001 PAK; BG

**Leidert, Heinrich Dr.**
08/26/1879 Deutsch-Nettkow - no information
*Home address:* Am Karlsbad 2, W 35
*Law firm address:* Am Karlsbad 2, W 35
*Additional information:* Attorney and notary; after the National Socialist seizure of power in 1933 his license as a notary was revoked; he worked as an attorney until the general occupational ban in 1938. His wife Elisabeth, nee Knüppel, was regarded as non-Jewish; he emigrated to Shanghai, China, on 08/21/1939; in 1947 he returned to Steglitz, Berlin.
*Sources:* JMBl. 33, p. 208; *li; LAB, Liste 10/15/1933; Liste 36; MRRAK; BG

**Leiser, Hermann**
08/26/188-026.8.1880 Thorn - 05/25/1937 Berlin
*Home address:* no information
*Law firm address:* Schönhauser Allee 87
*Additional information:* Attorney and notary; after the National Socialist seizure of power in 1933 his license as a notary was revoked; he was readmitted as an attorney; he died in 1937 at the age of 57, according to his son, the film producer Erwin Leiser, he died from grief. He was buried at the Jewish cemetery Weißensee. His wife fled to England, his son Erwin followed her via Sweden.
*Sources:* Br.B. 32; JMBl. 33, p. 208; *li; Liste 36; BArch, R 3001 PAK; BG; information Renée Gundelach

**Lelewer, Hermann Dr.**
08/09/1891 Posen - 07/20/1946 Tel Aviv
*Home address:* no information
*Law firm address:* Tauentzienstr. 13, W 50
*Additional information:* Studied in Berlin,
Freiburg i.Br. and Heidelberg; 1913 he received
his doctorate in Berlin; in 1913 he traveled
through Palestine; from 1914-18 he fought
during the First World War; from 1919 he was
an attorney at the KG, later also a notary; he
was legal counsel of the Association of German
Writers; a member of the Representative
Assembly of the Jewish Synagogue Berlin;
official in Zionist organizations and Jewish
sport associations, amongst others he was
responsible for the 1st World Maccabiah
1932 in Palestine. After the National Socialist
seizure of power he was made subject to an
occupational ban in early 1933. He emigrated
to Great Britain in March 1933, to Palestine
in 1934; he was director of Jibaneh, an
organization for land acquisition in Palestine;
he was an active official of the Jewish sports
movement; he died in 1946 in Tel Aviv.
*Sources:* Br.B. 32; TK 33; Liste d. nichtzugel.
RA, 04/25/1933; JMBl. 08/04/1933, p. 253;
BArch, R 3001 PAK; BG; BHdE vol. 1, p.
429/30

**Lemchen, Heinrich**
11/23/1879 Czarnikau - no information
*Home address:* Adalbertstr. 7, SO 36
*Law firm address:* Adalbertstr. 7, SO 36
*Additional information:* Attorney and
notary; after the National Socialist seizure of
power in 1933 he was readmitted; in 1935 his
license as a notary was revoked. He emigrated
to Porto Alegre, Brazil, on 12/30/1936; he
was only disbarred as an attorney in 1938.
*Sources:* *li; LAB, Liste 10/15/1933; DJ 36, p.
315; Liste 36; BG: LAB, OFP files

**Lenk, Arthur**
04/30/1883 Berlin - no information
*Home address:* Kleine Präsidentenstr. 3
*Law firm address:* Kleine Präsidentenstr. 3
*Additional information:* Attorney and notary;
after the National Socialist seizure of power
in 1933 his license as a notary was revoked; he
was readmitted as an attorney; he participated
in a court of honor proceeding in May 1936;
as a consequence he was disbarred.
*Sources:* KJMBl. 33, p. 220; *li; Liste 36; BG:
LAB, OFP files; LAB, Rep. 68; Acc. 3017 No.
23; BArch, R 3001 PAK

**Lenzen, Felix Dr., Judicial Councillor**
01/10/1866 Trebnitz - no information
*Home address:* Helmstedter Str. 12,
Wilmersdorf
*Law firm address:* Leipziger Str. 105, W 8
*Additional information:* Attorney and
notary; after the National Socialist seizure
of power in 1933 his license as a notary was
revoked; he worked as an attorney until the
general occupational ban in 1938; he was a
member of the Reich Association of non-
Aryan Christians.
*Sources:* JMBl. 33, p. 220; *li; LAB, Liste
10/15/1933; Liste 36; MRRAK; BG; Mitt.
bl. Reichsverband nicht-arischer Christen,
12/06/1934

**Lenzen, Georg**
11/16/1875 Schwiebus - no information
*Home address:* Schönhauser Allee 8, N 54
*Law firm address:* Knesebeckstr. 72/73,
Charlottenburg
*Additional information:* Attorney and
notary; after the National Socialist seizure
of power his license as a notary was
revoked, he worked as an attorney until the
general occupational ban in 1938; he could
still have emigrated before the beginning of
the war; he lived in Brazil with his daughter
from his first marriage.
*Sources:* JMBl. 33, p. 208; *li; LAB, Liste
10/15/1933; Liste 36; MRRAK; BG: LAB,
OFP files; information F. Dudzus, 03/00

**Leopold, Botho Dr.**
06/21/1900 Hannover - no information
*Home address:* no information
*Law firm address:* Heilbronner Str. 13, W 30
*Additional information:* Attorney since
1932; after the National Socialist seizure of
power he was made subject to an occupational
ban on 05/27/1933. He emigrated to the
Netherlands.
*Sources:* Liste d. nichtzugel. RA, 04/25/1933;
JMBl. 33, p. 203; BArch, R 3001 PAK; BG

**Less, Siegfried Dr.**
06/25/1893 - no information
*Home address:* no information
*Law firm address:* Schönhauser Allee 136, N 58
*Additional information:* After the National
Socialist seizure of power he was made subject
to an occupational ban in early 1933.
*Sources:* Liste d. nichtzugel. RA, 04/25/1933;
JMBl. 33, p. 209; BArch, R 3001 PAK

**Lesser, Alfred Dr.**
01/26/1885 Berlin - no information
*Home address:* Stromstr. 4, Charlottenburg
*Law firm address:* Kurfürstendamm 224,
W 15
*Additional information:* Attorney and
notary; after the National Socialist seizure
of power in 1933 his license as a notary
was withdrawn; he worked as an attorney
until the general occupational ban in 1938.
His wife, Rosa, who was born in 1899,
was regarded as "Aryan;" in 1938 he was
imprisoned in Sachsenhausen; after the
liberation he emigrated to Melbourne,
Australia, on 04/30/1939.
*Sources:* JMBl. 33, p. 208; *li; LAB, Liste
10/15/1933; Liste 36; BArch, R 3001 PAK;
MRRAK; BG

**Lesser, Friedrich Karl**
07/19/1871 Berlin - no information
*Home address:* Grunewaldstr. 46,
Schöneberg
*Law firm address:* Habsburger Str. 12, W 30
*Additional information:* Attorney at the
KG and notary; cavalry captain; after the
National Socialist seizure of power in 1933
his license as a notary was revoked, he was
readmitted as an attorney; he was Protestant,
his wife was regarded as non-Jewish, he
himself was regarded as "mixed race," he was a
member of the Reich Association of Non-Aryan
Christians; he was still practicing law in 1941.
*Sources:* *li; LAB, Liste 10/15/1933, Liste
Mschlg. 36; Tel.B. 41; BG: BAP, 15.09
RSA; Mitt.bl. Reichsverband nichtarischer
Christen, 12/06/1934

**Lesser, Ludwig**
10/20/1882 Königsberg - no information
*Home address:* Landhausstr. 13,
Wilmersdorf
*Law firm address:* Tiergartenstr. 2, W 35
*Additional information:* Attorney and
notary; after the National Socialist seizure of
power in April 1933 he was readmitted upon
request; in 1935 his license as a notary was
revoked, he worked as an attorney until the
general occupational ban. His wife Elsbeth
was regarded as non-Jewish. He emigrated to
the USA on 10/12/1939.
*Sources:* Liste d. nichtzugel. RA, 04/25/1933;
*li; LAB, Liste 10/15/1933; DJ 36, p. 315;
Liste 36; BArch, R 3001 PAK; MRRAK; BG

**Lesser, Martin Dr.**
03/09/1884 - 01/25/1935
*Home address:* no information
*Law firm address:* Charlottenstr. 55, W 8
*Additional information:* Attorney and
notary; after the National Socialist seizure
of power in 1933 his license as a notary was
revoked; he was readmitted as an attorney. He
died in 1935 at the age of 50.
*Sources:* JMBl. 33, p. 208; *li; BG; Walk, p. 223

**Leszynsky, Eduard Dr.**
1877 Hameln - 1952 Kfar Jedidjah, Israel
*Home address:* Lynarstr. 3, Grunewald
*Law firm address:* Bayreuther Str. 36, W 62
*Additional information:* He turned to
Zionism at an early age; he was co-founder
of Hasmonea; attorney at the LG I-III and
notary; after the National Socialist seizure
of power in 1933 his license as a notary was
revoked, he was disbarred on 06/18/1935.
In 1935 he emigrated with his family to
Palestine; there he was involved in the
development of Jaarot Hakarmel.
*Sources:* Br.B. 32; Adr.B. 33; TK 33; JMBl.
33, p. 208; *li (Leszynski); LAB, Liste
10/15/1933; Walk; BHdE vol. 2.2, p. 713
(Rudolf Leszynski); information Maria
Haendcke-Hoppe-Arndt

**Levi, Alfred Dr.**
11/27/1877 Nordhausen - no information
*Home address:* Zähringerstr. 26, Wilmersdorf
*Law firm address:* Hubertusallee 14,
Grune-wald
*Additional information:* After the National
Socialist seizure of power he was readmitted;
he still worked as an attorney until
09/16/1938. He had broken away from the
Jewish faith, his wife Charlotte was non-
Jewish; he survived and after the liberation he
lived at his original address.
*Sources:* TK 33; *li; LAB, Liste 10/15/1933;
Liste 36; BG

**Levin-Goldschmidt, Robert Dr.,
Judicial Councillor**
05/03/1863 Berlin - 03/09/1936 Berlin
*Home address:* no information
*Law firm address:* Französische Str.
557/58, W 8
*Additional information:* Attorney at the LG
I-III and notary. After the National Socialist
seizure of power in 1933 his license as a

notary was revoked, he was readmitted as an attorney. He died in 1936 at the age of 73 in Berlin.

*Sources:* TK 33; JMBl. 33, p. 220; *li; LAB, Liste 10/15/1933; Liste 36; BG; BHdE vol. 1, p. 240 (Hubert B. Grant)

**Levinsohn, Heinrich**
06/07/1894 Berlin - 1945 Palestine
*Home address:* no information
*Law firm address:* Dorotheenstr. 77/78, NW 7
*Additional information:* Alongside his law practice, he was active in the fight against anti-Semitism. Attorney and notary; after the National Socialist seizure of power in 1933 he was readmitted. He was disbarred on 10/01/1935. He emigrated to Palestine; there he worked for the Organization of Immigrants from Central Europe (Irgun Olej Merkas Europe).
*Sources:* TK 33; *li; LAB, Liste 10/15/1933; BArch, R 3001 PAK; Walk, p. 226

**Levot, Hans Dr.**
04/03/1896 Cologne - no information
*Home address:* Kaiserkorso 152, Tempelhof
*Law firm address:* Kaiserkorso 152, Tempelhof
*Additional information:* He was Catholic; he fought in the First World War; after the National Socialist seizure of power in 1933 he was readmitted, since he had been recognized as a "frontline fighter." He was regarded as "mixed race," his wife as non-Jewish; he still practiced law in 1941. He survived and after 1945 he was readmitted as an attorney and notary.
*Sources:* TK 33; *li; LAB, Liste 10/15/1933; Liste Mschlg. 36; Tel.B. 41; Verz. zugel. Anw. 45; BG

**Levy, Arthur Dr.**
No information
*Home address:* Rosenthaler Str. 34/35, N 54
*Law firm address:* Rosenthaler Str. 34/35, N 54
*Additional information:* After the National Socialist seizure of power he was readmitted; he was still working as an attorney until the general occupational ban in 1938.
*Sources:* *li; LAB, Liste 10/15/1933; Liste 36; MRRAK

**Levy, Arthur Dr.**
No information

*Home address:* no information
*Law firm address:* Friedrichstr. 208, SW 68
*Additional information:* Attorney and notary; after the National Socialist seizure of power in 1933 he was readmitted; his license as a notary was revoked at the latest in 1935; he still worked as an attorney until the general occupational ban in 1938.
*Sources:* *li; LAB, Liste 10/15/1933; Liste 36; MRRAK

**Levy, Ernst Dr.**
12/23/1881 - 03/26/1934
*Home address:* Westfälische Str. 17, Wilmersdorf
*Law firm address:* Kurfürstendamm 216, W 15
*Additional information:* Attorney and notary; after the National Socialist seizure of power in 1933 he was readmitted; according to the handwritten entry in the edited list of 10/15/1933 in the archives of the state, he died on 03/26/1934 at the age of 53.
*Sources:* *li; LAB, Liste 10/15/1933

**Levy, Felix Dr.**
10/10/1886 Königsberg - 01/10/1955 Düsseldorf
*Home address:* Reichstr. 84, Charlottenburg
*Law firm address:* Ritterstr. 11, S 42
*Additional information:*
Attorney and notary; after the National Socialist seizure of power in 1933 he was readmitted; in 1935 his license as a notary was revoked; he continued to work as an attorney. In 1936 he made sure that his two children could live with his sister in South Tyrol. At the time of the Night of the Broken Glass in 1938, he visited his family there. He was warned by telephone not to return to Germany. The children were sent to England. He did not receive a visa until the end of 1939 and went to Ecuador. He established himself in Quito, where he spent the war years. After the war he returned to Europe, first to London. In cooperation with the British Control Commission he found a job in Germany. In Düsseldorf he still worked for a year and a half at a county law court until his retirement.
*Sources:* *li; LAB, Liste 10/15/1933; DJ 36, p. 315; Liste 36; BArch, R 3001 PAK; BG; information attorney Erdmann; information son L. B. Levy, 12/07/1998; 01/08/1999

**Levy, Fred Dr.**
09/27/1898 - April 1981
*Home address:* Kaiserallee 17, W 15
*Law firm address:* Joachimsthaler Str. 3, Charlottenburg
*Additional information:* He had lost his left arm as a soldier during the First World War. Attorney and notary; after the National Socialist seizure of power he was readmitted, because he was recognized as a "frontline fighter;" his license as a notary was revoked in 1935; after an occupational ban in 1938 he worked as an attorney, he worked as a "consultant" until 1941, in 1941 he emigrated to the USA, there he applied for a scholarship. The application was rejected because he was too old and also seriously disabled. He had difficulties earning a living, since he was only able to do certain jobs because of his serious injury. He last lived in New York, he died at the age of 82.
*Sources:* *li; LAB, Liste 10/15/1933; Liste 36; Liste d. Kons. v. 04/15/1939; Naatz-Album; NY Publ. Lib. (Am. Com.) Levy, Fred; BG; SSDI

**Levy, Friedrich Franz**
10/20/1888 Berlin - no information
*Home address:* no information
*Law firm address:* Friedrichstr. 208, SW 68
*Additional information:* Attorney (since 1919) and notary (since 1929); after the National Socialist seizure of power he was made subject to an occupational ban in early 1933. He emigrated in December 1933 to Palestine.
*Sources:* Br.B. 32; Liste d. nichtzugel. RA, 04/25/1933; BArch, R 3001 PAK, PA; BG

**Levy, Georg Dr.**
08/26/1879 - 03/05/1938
*Home address:* Engeldamm 8, Mitte
*Law firm address:* Köpenicker Str. 103, SO 16
*Additional information:* Attorney and notary; after the National Socialist seizure of power in 1933 his license as a notary was revoked; he still worked as an attorney in 1936, he worked in a law firm together with Hans; he died in 1938 at the age of 58 and was buried at Weißensee.
*Sources:* JMBl. 33, p. 208; *li; LAB, Liste 10/15/1933; Liste 36; BG: Friedh.W.Sterbereg.

**Levy, Hans**
04/15/1885 Berlin - 11/30/1941 Riga
*Home address:* Engeldamm 8, SO 16, Mitte
*Law firm address:* Köpenicker Str. 103, SO 16
*Additional information:* Attorney and notary; after the National Socialist seizure of power he was readmitted; in 1935 his license as a notary was revoked; he worked as an attorney until the general occupational ban in 1938, at the George L. Kanzlei law firm. He was used for forced labor, last as a driver; date of declaration of property: 11/24/1941; collecting station Levetzowstr. 7-8; transportation on 11/27/1941 to Riga; he was murdered there shortly after arrival on 11/30/1941.
*Sources:* *li; LAB, Liste 10/15/1933; DJ 36, p. 315; Liste 36; BArch, R 3001 PAK; MRRAK; BG; BdE; GB II

**Levy, Hans J.**
12/18/1902 - no information
*Home address:* no information
*Law firm address:* Landsberger Allee 125, NO 18
*Additional information:* Attorney since 1929; after the National Socialist seizure of power he was made subject to an occupational ban on 06/07/1933. He emigrated to Sydney, Australia via France.
*Sources:* Br.B. 32; Liste d. nichtzugel. RA, 04/25/1933; JMBl. 33, p. 221; BArch, R 3001 PAK; BG

**Levy, Hugo, Judicial Councillor**
No information
*Home address:* Seydelstr. 13, C 19
*Law firm address:* Seydelstr. 13, C 19
*Additional information:* Attorney and notary; after the National Socialist seizure of power in 1933 his license as a notary was revoked. He emigrated to Palestine 1935/36.
*Sources:* JMBl. 33, p. 220; *li; LAB, Liste 10/15/1933; Liste 36; BG

**Levy, Jack (Jakob)**
05/06/1889 - no information
*Home address:* Landhausstr. 2, Wilmersdorf
*Law firm address:* Tauentzienstr. 6
*Additional information:* He had fought in the First World War, amongst others as a balloon observer at the big battle in Flanders. Attorney (since 1920) and notary (since 1930); after the seizure of power by the

National Socialists in 1933 he was on leave for health reasons, he traveled to Palestine, returned in 1934. His license as a notary was revoked; until 1935 no decision had been made about his admission as an attorney. He emigrated in 1939.
*Sources:* Br.B. 32; TK 33; BArch, R 3001 PAK, PA; BG

**Levy, Kurt Dr.**
07/24/1898 Guben - transportation 1943
*Home address:* Trautenaustr. 20, Motzstr. 74, Wilmersdorf
*Law firm address:* Motzstr. 35, W 30
*Additional information:* Attorney at the KG and notary; after the National Socialist seizure of power in 1933 he was readmitted; 1935 his license as a notary was revoked; he worked as an attorney until the general occupational ban in 1938, then he still worked as a "consultant;" he was an employee of the Reich Association of Jews in Germany. Transportation on 06/16/1943 to Theresienstadt; from there he was transported on 10/28/1944 to Auschwitz.
*Sources:* *li; LAB, Liste 10/15/1933; DJ 36, p. 315; Liste 36; MRRAK; Liste d. Kons. of 03/15/1939; BArch, R 3001 PAK; BG; GB II

**Levy, Martin**
02/11/1878 Berlin - transportation 1943
*Home addresss:* Habsburger Str. 11, Schöneberg
*Law firm address:* Schwäbische Str. 29, W 30; Later: Potsdamer Str. 31 a
*Additional information:* Attorney and notary; after the National Socialist seizure of power in 1933 his license as a notary was revoked, he worked as an attorney until the general occupational ban in 1938. His wife, Olga, nee Schwahn, was of non-Jewish origins. He was last used as a worker for forced labor; date of declaration of property: 03/01/1943; transportation on 03/04/1943 to Auschwitz.
*Sources:* Br.B. 32; * li; LAB, Liste 10/15/1933; DJ 36, p. 315; Liste 36; MRRAK; BG; GB II

**Levy, Rudolf Dr.**
10/15/1893 - no information
*Home address:* no information
*Law firm address:* Badensche Str. 13, Wilmersdorf
*Additional information:* After the National Socialist seizure of power he was made subject to an occupational ban in early 1933.

*Sources:* Liste d. nichtzugel. RA, 04/25/1933; JMBl. 33, p. 221; BArch, R 3001 PAK

**Levy, Siegbert Dr.**
02/02/1891 - no information
*Home address:* no information
*Law firm address:* Kantstr. 8, Charlottenburg
*Additional information:* Attorney and notary; after the National Socialist seizure of power he was made subject to an occupational ban in early 1933. He emigrated to Sao Paulo, Brazil in April 1939.
*Sources:* Br.B. 32; Liste. d. nichtzugel. RA, 04/25/1933; JMBl. 33, p. 234; BArch, R 3001 PAK; BG

**Lewek, Leo Dr.**
11/12/1889 - 04/24/1936
*Home address:* no information
*Law firm address:* Meraner Str. 11, Schöneberg
*Additional information:* Attorney and notary; after the National Socialist seizure of power in 1933 he was readmitted; in 1935 his license as a notary was revoked; he worked as an attorney until his death in 1936; he died at the age of 46.
*Sources:* *li; LAB, Liste 10/15/1933; Liste 36; BArch, R 3001 PAK

**Lewin, Alfred Dr.**
05/18/1902 - 01/30/1993
*Home address:* no information
*Law firm address:* Mohrenstr. 48, W 8
*Additional information:* Attorney at the KG; after the National Socialist seizure of power he was made subject to an occupational ban in early 1933. He emigrated via Czechoslovakia in September 1933, later to the USA; he last lived in Los Angeles, California.
*Sources:* Br.B. 32; Liste d. nichtzugel. RA, 04/25/1933; JMBl. 33, p. 209; BArch, R 3001 PAK; BG; SSDI

**Lewin, Heinrich Dr.**
01/12/1887 - no information
*Home address:* no information
*Law firm address:* Frankfurter Allee 85, O 112
*Additional information:* After the National Socialist seizure of power he was made subject to an occupational ban as an attorney and notary in early 1933.

*Sources:* Br.B. 32; Liste d. nichtzugel. RA, 04/25/1933; BArch, R 3001 PAK; Naatz-Album

**Lewin, Martin Dr.**
09/29/1884 Berlin - no information
*Home address:* Meinekestr. 5, W 15
Law firm addresss: Friedrichstr. 77, W 8
*Additional information:* Attorney and notary; after the National Socialist seizure of power his license as a notary was revoked in 1933; he still worked as an attorney until the general occupational ban in 1938. He emigrated to Panama on 12/12/1940.
*Sources:* JMBl. 33, p. 208; *li; LAB, Liste 10/15/1933; Liste 36; BArch, R 3001 PAK; MRRAK; BG

**Lewin-Bauer, Arthur Dr.**
02/18/1885 Berlin - no information
*Home address:* Bayerische Str. 9, Schöneberg
*Law firm address:* Königstr. 48, C 2
*Additional information:* Attorney at the KG and notary; after the National Socialist seizure of power in 1933 he was readmitted; in 1935 his license as a notary was revoked; he worked as an attorney until the general occupational ban in 1938. He emigrated overseas.
*Sources:* *li; LAB, Liste 10/15/1933; DJ 36, p. 315; Liste 36; BArch, R 3001 PAK; MRRAK; BG

**Lewinneck, Siegfried**
12/22/1883 - 02/22/1937
*Home address:* no information
*Law firm address:* Neue Schönhauer Str. 10, N 54
*Additional information:* Attorney and notary; after the National Socialist seizure of power in 1933 he was readmitted; his license as a notary was revoked in 1935; he died in 1937 at the age of 54; he was buried at Weißensee.
*Sources:* *li; LAB, Liste 10/15/1933; DJ 36, p. 315; Liste 36; BArch, R 3001 PAK; BG

**Lewinnek, Ernst Dr.**
04/07/1898 Schwedt - no information
*Home address:* no information
*Law firm address:* Gertraudenstr. 23, C 19
*Additional information:* Attorney since 1924; after the National Socialist seizure of power he was made subject to an occupational ban on 06/10/1933. He emigrated in June 1940 to Shanghai, China.

*Sources:* Br.B. 32; Liste d. nichtzugel. RA, 04/25/1933; JMBl. 33, p. 253; BArch, R 3001 PAK; BG

**Lewinski, Moritz**
10/06/1881 - no information
*Home address:* no information
*Law firm address:* Neue Königstr. 43, NO 43
*Additional information:* Attorney and notary; after the National Socialist seizure of power in 1933 his license as a notary was revoked; he worked as an attorney until the general occupational ban in 1938; he survived, after 1945 he lived in Spandau.
*Sources:* JMBl. 33, p. 208; *li; LAB, Liste 10/15/1933; Liste 36; BArch, R 3001 PAK; MRRAK; BG

**Lewinsky, Hans Benjamin Dr.**
10/12/1907 Berlin - no information
*Home address:* Heilbronner Str. 13, Schöneberg
*Law firm address:* Stresemannstr. 12, SW 11
*Additional information:* After the National Socialist seizure of power he was made subject to an occupational ban in early 1933. He emigrated to the USA on 12/23/1938.
*Sources:* Liste d. nichtzugel. RA, 04/25/1933; JMBl. 33, 06/16/1933; BArch, R 3001 PAK; BG

**Lewinsohn, Alfred**
08/28/1885 - no information
*Home address:* no information
*Law firm address:* Breite Str. 40, Pankow
*Additional information:* Attorney and notary; after the National Socialist seizure of power in 1933 his license as a notary was revoked; he was removed from the list of attorneys on 08/14/1936; he already emigrated to Palestine in November 1935.
*Sources:* JMBl. 33, p. 208; *li; LAB, Liste 10/15/1933; Liste 36; BArch, R 3001 PAK; BG

**Lewinsohn, Georg Dr.**
01/16/1880 Berlin - transportation 1943
*Home address:* Potsdamer Str. 16, Tiergarten
*Law firm address:* Eichhornstr. 8, W 9
*Additional information:* Attorney and notary; after the National Socialist seizure of power his license as a notary was revoked on 07/03/1933; he was disbarred as an attorney on 10/17/1935. Date of declaration of property: 03/05/1943; transportation on 03/06/1943 to Auschwitz.

*Sources:* JMBl. 33, p. 220; *li; LAB, Liste 10/15/1933; BArch, R 3001 PAK; BG; GB II

**Lewinsohn, Josef Dr.**
05/03/1882 Elbing - transportation 1942
*Home address:* Rückertstr. 8, N 54, Mitte
*Law firm address:* Lennéstr. 10, W 9
*Additional information:* Attorney and notary; after the National Socialist seizure of power in 1933 his license as a notary was revoked; he worked as an attorney until the general occupational ban in 1938. Transportation on 01/25/1942 to Riga.
*Sources:* JMBl. 33, p. 220; *li; LAB, Liste 10/15/1933; Liste 36; MRRAK; BG; GB II

**Lewinsohn, Max Dr., Judicial Councillor**
11/15/1871 Berlin - 02/12/1943 Auschwitz
*Home address:* Mommsenstr. 66, Charlottenburg
*Law firm address:* Landsberger Str. 66/67, C 25
*Additional information:* Attorney and notary; after the National Socialist seizure of power in 1933 his license as a notary was revoked; he was disbarred as an attorney on 01/01/1937. He emigrated to the Netherlands; he was transported on 02/09/1943 from Westerbork to Auschwitz. There he was murdered on the day after arrival.
*Sources:* *li; LAB, Liste 10/15/1933; Liste 36; BG; GB II

**Lewy, Fritz Dr.**
08/23/1898 Insterburg - no information
*Home address:* Turiner Str. 48, N 65, Wedding
*Law firm address:* Neue Königstr. 19 c, NO 43
*Additional information:* After the National Socialist seizure of power in 1933 he was readmitted, he still worked as an attorney until the general occupational ban in 1933. He had broken away from the Jewish faith. His wife Charlotte was regarded as non-Jewish, the marriage was regarded as "privileged" according to the NS criteria, since the couple had children. He was used for forced labor as from 1943. He survived and after 1945 he was readmitted.
*Sources:* TK 33; *li; LAB, Liste 10/15/1933; Liste 36; BArch, R 3001 PAK; MRRAK; LAB, RAK, PA Werthauer; Entschädigungsbehörde Berlin, files 3531 (E. Bukofzer); BG

**Lewy, Georg**
02/02/1880 - 06/19/1939
*Home address:* Olivaer Platz 4, Wilmersdorf
*Law firm address:* Kurfürstendamm 38/39, W 15
*Additional information:* Attorney and notary; after the National Socialist seizure of power in 1933 he was readmitted; his license as a notary was revoked in 1935; he was still working as an attorney until the general occupational ban in 1938; he died in June 1939, he was buried at Weißensee.
*Sources:* *li; LAB, Liste 10/15/1933; DJ 36, p. 315; Liste 36; BArch, R 3001 PAK; MRRAK; BG

**Leyser, Benno Dr.**
05/31/1879 Berlin-Charlottenburg - transportation 1943
*Home address:* Berliner Str. 111, Charlottenburg
*Law firm address:* Berliner Str. 127, Charlottenburg
*Additional information:* Attorney and notary; after the National Socialist seizure of power in 1933 his license as a notary was revoked, he was still working as an attorney until the general occupational ban in 1938. Date of declaration of property: 12/28/1942, collecting station Große Hamburger Str. 26, transportation on 01/12/1943 to Auschwitz.
*Sources:* JMBl. 33, p. 208; *li; LAB, Liste 10/15/1933; Liste 36; BG; GB II

**Leyser, Fritz**
11/10/1883 Königsberg - no information
*Home address:* Meierottostr. 10, Wilmersdorf
*Law firm address:* no information
*Additional information:* Attorney and notary; after the National Socialist seizure of power in 1933 his license as a notary was revoked. On 06/11/1934 he was disbarred. He emigrated to Spain.
*Sources:* JMBl. 33, p. 208; BArch, R 3001 PAK; BG

**Licht, Ernst Dr.**
09/24/1900 Berlin - Sachsenhausen
*Home address:* no information
*Law firm address:* Martin-Luther-Str.90, W 30
*Additional information:* He had volunteered for military service, but immediately after he was drafted, he suffered from life-threatening

typhus. He was subsequently released. He established himself as an attorney in Berlin; after the National Socialist seizure of power, his participation in the First World War was not recognized as frontline fighting; he was made subject to an occupational ban on 05/31/1933. He did not want to emigrate; when he decided to flee in 1940, it was too late. He and his wife were arrested when crossing the border to the Netherlands and imprisoned in Gelsenkirchen. From there he was transported to Sachsenhausen, where he died on 08/15/1940; his wife died in Ravensbrück.
*Sources:* Liste d. nichtzugel. RA, 04/25/1933; JMBl. 33, p. 209; BArch, R 3001 PAK, PA; BG; GB II; information of the son of L. Königsberger, 10/2001

**Lichtwitz, Max**
05/07/1902 Berlin - 12/16/1942 Auschwitz
*Home address:* Kantstr. 30, Charlottenburg
*Law firm address:* Kronenstr. 4/5, W 8
*Additional information:* Law partnership with Hans Carl Ladewig and Ernst Loewe; after the National Socialist seizuure of power he was made subject to an occupational ban in April 1933; subsequently he was readmitted, presumably until 1939 (on a letterhead dated 07/28/1939 the occupation is deleted); he was last an employee of the Jewish Cultural Administration (JKV). Date of declaration of property: 12/05/1942, collecting station Große Hamburger Str. 26; transportation on 12/09/1942 to Auschwitz; he was murdered there six days after arrival.
*Sources:* Br.B. 32; Liste d. nichtzugel. RA, 04/25/1933; *li; LAB, Liste 10/15/1933; Liste 36; BArch, R 3001 PAK; MRRAK; NY Publ. Lib. (Am.Com.) Jacob, Erwin (he was named an advocate); BG; GB II; Naatz-Album

**Liebeck, Siegfried Dr.**
01/12/1885 - no information
*Home address:* no information
*Law firm address:* Königin-Augusta-Str. 7, W 9
*Additional information:* Attorney and notary; after the National Socialist seizure of power in 1933 he was readmitted; in 1935 his license as a notary was revoked; he was still working as a notary in 1936.
*Sources:* *li; LAB, Liste 10/15/1933; DJ 36, p. 315; Liste 36

**Liebenthal, Robert Dr., Judicial Councillor**
11/24/1854 Memel - 09/06/1942
*Home address:* no information
*Law firm address:* Martin-Luther-Str. 25
*Additional information:* Attorney at the KG and notary; after the National Socialist seizure of power he was made subject to an occupational ban in early 1933.
*Sources:* Br.B. 32; Liste d. nichtzugel. RA, 04/25/1933; BG

**Liebenthal, Werner Dr.**
01/20/1888 Berlin - no information
*Home address:* no information
*Law firm address:* Martin-Luther-Str. 25, Schöneberg
*Additional information:* Attorney (since 1920) and notary (since 1926); after the National Socialist seizure of power he was made subject to an occupational ban on 07/06/1933.
*Sources:* JMBl. 33, p. 221; BArch, R 3001 PAK, PA

**Liebenwalde, Heinrich**
03/16/1890 Berlin - 10/29/1942 Riga
*Home address:* no information
*Law firm address:* Münzstr. 19, C 25
*Additional information:* Attorney (since 1918) and notary (since 1928); after the National Socialist seizure of power he was made subject to an occupational ban on 05/27/1933. He was deported to Riga on 10/26/1942 and was murdered there shortly after his arrival.
*Sources:* Liste d. nichtzugel. RA, 04/25/1933; JMBl. 33, p. 209; BArch, R 3001 PAK; BG; BdE; GB II

**Lieber, Fritz Dr.**
11/07/1905 Kossow/Galicia - no information
*Home address:* no information
*Law firm address:* Wallnertheaterstr. 23, O 27
*Additional information:* He was admitted as an attorney on 03/03/1933; he was immediately made subject to a professional ban on 06/12/1933.
*Sources:* Jüd.Adr.B.; Liste nichtzugel. RA, 04/25/1933; JMBl. 07/28/1933, p. 234; BArch, R 3001 PAK, PA

**Liebert, Kurt (Curt) Dr.**
12/09/1882 - 06/16/1942
*Home address:* no information
*Law firm address:* Ritterstr. 42/43, SW 68
*Additional information:* Attorney and
notary; after the National Socialist seizure of
power in 1933 he was readmitted; his license
as a notary was revoked in 1935; he was
still working as an attorney until the general
occupational ban in 1938. He died in 1942 at
the age of 59.
*Sources:* *li; LAB, Liste 10/15/1933; DJ 36,
p. 315; Liste 36; BArch, R 3001 PAK;
MRRAK; BG

**Liebes, Curt Dr.**
03/21/1892 Posen - 12/24/1951
*Home address:* Prager Platz 6, Wilmersdorf
*Law firm address:* Prager Platz 6,
Wilmersdorf
*Additional information:* Attorney at the
KG and notary; after the National Socialist
seizure of power in 1933 he was readmitted;
emigration.
*Sources:* *li; LAB, Liste 10/15/1933; BArch, R
3001 PAK; BG

**Liebling, Karl Dr.**
09/22/1873 Leipzig - no
information
*Home address:* An der
Spandauer Brücke 7, C 2
*Law firm address:* An der
Spandauer Brücke 4-5, C 2
*Additional information:*
Attorney and notary; after the National
Socialist seizure of power in 1933 his license
as a notary was revoked, he was still working
as an attorney until the general occupational
ban in 1938. He emigrated to London, Great
Britain, on 03/14/1939.
*Sources:* JMBl. 33, p. 208; *li; LAB, Liste
10/15/1933; Liste 36; MRRAK; Naatz-
Album; BG

**Liebrecht, Hans Dr.**
01/12/1899 - no information
*Home address:* no information
*Law firm address:* Kurfürstendamm 185, W 15
*Additional information:* After the National
Socialist seizure of power in 1933 he was
readmitted; he worked as an attorney until
the general occupational ban in 1938.
Emigration.

*Sources:* Br.B. 32; *li; LAB, Liste 10/15/1933;
Liste 36; BArch, R 3001 PAK; BG: LAB,
OFP files

**Liedtke, Ernst**
07/25/1875 Christburg -
12/17/1933 Berlin
*Home address:* Blumeshof
13, W 35
*Law firm addresss:*
Blumeshof 13, W 35
*Additional information:*
He had studied in Königsberg; he married in
1910; he was baptized in 1914; he had three
daughters. Participation in First World War
(secret service activity). After completion of
legal education legal counsel among others
at Bosbau & Knauer, thereafter he was an
attorney at the KG. After the National Socialist
seizure of power in 1933 his license as a notary
was revoked, he was readmitted as an attorney;
however, he lapsed rapidly. According to his
wife, he died "heartbroken" in December 1933
because he could not overcome the situation.
His funeral was attended by many.
*Sources:* TK 33; JMBl. 33, p. 220; *li;
information of the grandchild, A. Liedtke, as
well as S. May

**Liemann, Willy**
09/14/1892 - no information
*Home address:* no information
*Law firm address:* Westarpstr. 1, W 30
*Additional information:* After the National
Socialist seizure of power in 1933 he was
readmitted, in 1936 he was still working as an
attorney.
*Sources:* Br.B. 32; *li; LAB, Liste 10/15/1933;
Liste 36; BArch, R 3001 PAK

**Liepmann, Kurt Dr.**
07/21/1887 Oschersleben - before 05/15/1942
*Home address:* Xantener Str. 15 a, W 15,
Wilmersdorf
*Law firm address:* Königstr. 22/24, C 2, (last
in his private home)
*Additional information:* After the National
Socialist seizure of power he was readmitted,
he was still working as an attorney until
at least 1936. He emigrated to Belgium in
1939; 1942 in France in Camp de la Plage
internment camp in Argelés sur Mer, located
on the border with Spain, he was arrested; he
died there.

*Sources:* *li; LAB, Liste 10/15/1933; Liste 36; BArch, R 3001 PAK; BG: LAB OFP files

**Lindemann, Hugo**
01/30/1874 - 01/16/1936
*Home address:* no information
*Law firm address:* Potsdamer Str. 118, W 35
*Additional information:* Attorney and notary; after the National Socialist seizure of power in 1933 his license as a notary was revoked, he was readmitted as an attorney.
*Sources:* JMBl. 33, p. 220; *li; LAB, Liste 10/15/1933; BG

**Lindenstrauß, Erich**
08/30/1899 - before 1969
*Home address:* no information.
*Law firm address:* Motzstr. 14, W 30
*Additional information:* Attorney and notary; brother of Leo and Walter; attorney since 1926; after the National Socialist seizure of power he was made subject to an occupational ban on 06/10/1933, although he was supposed to have been a soldier in the First World War. In 1933 he emigrated as the first of his family to Palestine and overtook an activity in the Havaara Office, to ensure the most extensive possible transfer of property to Palestine. Later, the office was relocated to Egypt, Erich returned to Palestine in 1939 and established himself in Jerusalem. In the meantime, his four brothers and sister also lived in the country. He went into administration, he worked in the civil service after the founding of the State of Israel.
*Sources:* Br.B. 32; Liste d. nichtzugel. RA, 04/25/1933; JMBl. 33, p. 253; BArch, R 3001 PAK, PA; information of the niece Alisa Rosen, conference 6/99

**Lindenstrauß, Leo Dr.**
04/08/1897 - before 1967
*Home address:* no information
*Law firm address:* Monbijouplatz 12, N 24
*Additional information:* Soldier during the First World War; attorney and notary, he had specialized in family law; brother of Erich and Walter; after the National Socialist seizure of power in 1933 he was readmitted; in 1935 his license as a notary was revoked, he was still admitted as an attorney for a short time, in January 1936 he emigrated to Palestine, like his brothers Eric and Walter. Although a convinced Zionist, he would

never have left Germany if he had not been urged to do so. To adjust to life in the still little-developed Palestine was particularly hard for him and his family, because one of the three children was disabled. He tried to make a living with various activities, amongst others he worked for a travel and insurance agency that also partially organized the transport of oranges. After the outbreak of war, demand for both travel and oranges declined. He did not possess the necessary financial resources for further legal training; he took a job in the administration, he worked for the Israeli government after the state of Israel was founded.
*Sources:* *li; LAB, Liste 10/15/1933; DJ 36, p. 315; Liste 36; BArch, R 3001 PAK; BG; information of the daughter Alisa Rosen, conference 6/1999

**Lindenstrauß, Walter**
03/12/1904 - 1977 Haifa
*Home address:* no information
*Law firm address:* Große Hamburger Str. 20, N 24
*Additional information:* Attorney since 1930; the youngest of the Lindenstrauß brothers; he was made subject to an occupational ban on 07/13/1933. Emigration in March 1939 to Palestine. He managed to settle successfully in Palestine. After the founding of the State of Israel, he became director of the Industrial Bank in Haifa; at times he took over the office of city councillor, later he was a honorary citizen. He died in 1977, meanwhile a street in Haifa has been named after him.
*Sources:* Br.B. 32; Liste d. nichtzugel. RA, 04/25/1933; JMBl. 08/21/1933, p. 267; BArch, R 3001 PAK, PA; information of Micha L., son 06/06

**Linz, Walter Dr.**
01/14/1898 - no information
*Home address:* no information
*Law office address:* Lützowstr. 83, W 35
*Additional information:* After the National Socialist seizure of power in 1933 he was readmitted, he was still working as an attorney until the general occupational ban in 1938.
*Sources:* *li; LAB, Liste 10/15/1933; Liste 36; BArch, R 3001 PAK; MRRAK

**Lion, Max Dr.**
06/08/1883 Dortmund - 12/02/1951
New York
*Home address:* Kurfürstendamm 188, W 15
*Law firm address:* Kurfürstendamm 188/189,
W 15
*Additional information:* He studied law,
philosophy and music in Geneva, Lucerne,
Munich and Berlin; 1901 he received his
doctorate Dr. jur.; attorney (since 1911, last
at the LG I-III and AG Berlin-Mitte) and
notary (since 1924) in Berlin; 1920-33 he was
a lecturer in tax and finance law at the Berlin
Commercial College; 1927-33 he was an
editor of the quarterly journal "Steuer- und
Finanzrecht [Tax and Financial Law]." After
the National Socialist seizure of power in
1933 his license as a notary and his teacher
license were revoked, he was readmitted as an
attorney. 1935 he emigrated to Amsterdam,
the Netherlands; 1937 he went to New York,
USA; he died 1951 in New York.
*Sources:* TK 33; JMBl. 33, p. 220; *li; LAB,
Liste 10/15/1933; BArch, R 3001 PAK; Philo-
Lexikon, p. 604; BG; BHdE vol. 2,2, p. 734;
Göpp., p. 299; Walk, p. 238

**Lion, Paul Dr.**
02/08/1895 Bonn - 07/03/1942 Auschwitz
*Home address:* no information
*Law firm address:* Friedrichstr. 175, W 8
*Additional information:* Attorney since
1925; after the National Socialist seizure
of power he was made subject to an
occupational ban on 06/13/1933. He was
Protestant; later he moved back to his
birthplace Bonn; on 06/22/1942 he was
transported to Auschwitz and was murdered
there.
*Sources:* Br.B. 32; Liste d. nichtzugel. RA,
04/25/1933; JMBl. 33, p. 253; BArch, R 3001
PAK, PA; GB II

**Lipmann-Wulf, Fritz, Judicial Councillor**
02/04/1871 Berlin - June 1941 Berlin
*Home address:* Keithstr. 12 and/or 25,
Tiergarten
*Law firm address:* Kronstr. 8/9, W 8
*Additional information:* Attorney at the LG
I-III, AG Berlin-Mitte and notary; he was
Protestant; after the National Socialist seizure
of power in 1933 his license was revoked;
he was still working as an attorney until
the general occupational ban in 1938. He
committed suicide in June 1941 in Berlin.

*Sources:* TK 33; JMBl. 33, p. 208; *li; LAB,
Liste 10/15/1933; Liste 36; MRRAK; BG;
g; GB II; BHdE, vol. 2,2, p. 734 (Peter
Lipman-Wulf)

**Lippmann, Carl (Karl) Dr.**
06/03/1892 Berlin - no information
*Home address:* Kurfürstendamm 196
Law firm adddress: Kurfürstendamm 233, W 50
*Additional information:* Attorney and
notary; after the National Socialist seizure of
power in 1933 he was readmitted; in 1935 his
license as a notary was revoked; he was still
working as an attorney until the end of 1935.
He emigrated in 1935. A warrant was issued
against him for tax code violations.
*Sources:* *li; LAB, Liste 10/15/1933; DJ 36,
p. 315; Liste 36; BArch, R 3001 PAK; BG;
Wolf, BFS

**Lipschitz, Alfred (Aron)**
10/02/1884 Flatow - no information
*Home address:* Wielandstr. 38,
Charlottenburg
*Law firm address:* Behrenstr. 30, W 8
*Additional information:* Attorney and
notary; after the National Socialist seizure
of power in 1933 his license as a notary
was revoked; he was still admitted as an
attorney until the general occupational ban
in 1938. He emigrated to Amsterdam, the
Netherlands, on 05/27/1939.
*Sources:* JMBl. 33, p. 208; *li; Liste 36;
BArch, R 3001 PAK; MRRAK; BG

**Lipschitz, Hans Dr.**
01/22/1893 - no information
*Home address:* no information
*Law firm address:* Mommsenstr. 31,
Charlottenburg 4
*Additional information:* Attorney at the KG;
after the National Socialist seizure of power
he was readmitted; he was still working as an
attorney in 1936.
*Sources:* *li; LAB, Liste 10/15/1933; Liste 36;
BArch, R 3001 PAK

**Lissauer, Fritz Dr.**
10/20/1874 Berlin - 03/07/1937 Berlin
*Home address:* no information
*Law firm address:* Berliner Str. 4, Wilmersdorf
*Additional information:* He was not only an
attorney but also a composer of songs and
operas. After the National Socialist seizure
of power in 1933 his license as a notary was

revoked; he was probably a member of the Jewish Synagogue in Berlin; he worked as an attorney until his death in March 1937.
*Sources:* JMBl. 33, p. 208; *li; LAB, Liste 10/15/1933; Liste 36; Walk, p. 240; SLW, Freiheit und Bindung [Freedom and bonding], p. 299

**Lißner, Jakob, Judicial Councillor**
12/01/1869 Wronke - transportation 1943
*Home address:* Pfalzburger Str. 24, W 15, Wilmersdorf
*Law firm address:* Neue Königstr. 70
*Additional information:* Attorney and notary; after the National Socialist seizure of power in 1933 his license as a notary was revoked; he still worked as an attorney until the general occupational ban in 1938. Transportation on 03/17/1943 to Theresienstadt; from there he was transported on 05/18/1944 to Auschwitz.
*Sources:* JMBl. 33, p. 208; *li; LAB, Liste 10/15/1933; Liste 36; MRRAK; BG; GB II (Jacob L.)

**Littauer, Alfred**
03/17/1890 Berlin - transportation 1942
*Home address:* no information
*Law firm address:* Greifswalder Str. 46
*Additional information:* Attorney and notary; after the National Socialist seizure of power he was made subject to an occupational ban as attorney and notary in early 1933. He emigrated to France. On 08/10/1942 he was transported from Drancy to Auschwitz.
*Sources:* Br.B. 32; JMBl. 33, p. 266; Pr.J. 33, p. 391; BArch, R 3001 PAK; BG; GB II

**Litten, Hans Joachim Dr.**
06/19/1903 Halle a.d. Saale - 02/04/1938 Dachau
*Home address:* no information
*Law firm address:* Königstr. 20/21
*Additional information:*
He was an attorney in Berlin since 1928: he became known for his defense of communist workers who had been involved in fights with National Socialists (amongst others the Felseneck trial). In the Eden Palace trial in 1931 he heard Adolf Hitler as a witness; his clever questioning strategy made Hitler extremely miserable. This resulted in a deep hostility of Hitler against him.

Hans, son of a Christian mother and a Jewish father and also a Protestant, saw himself as a champion of justice. Rather a loner and esthete, he was regarded for his tireless commitment to workers, communists, in some cases even in the legal protection order of the "Rote Hilfe" (Red Aid), as a representative of the "left advocacy." After the Reichstag fire in 1933 he was arrested and taken to several concentration camps. During his detention, he was made subject to an occupational ban by the judicial authorities. His mother tried in vain, even at the highest levels, for his release. He was brutally tortured during detention. Nevertheless, he worked —until his death—on a translation of the "Heliand," an Old Saxon epic that came into being ca. 830. The epic represents the life story of Christ in alliteration verse. In 1938 Litten commited suicide at the age of 34 in the Dachau concentration camp.
*Sources:* Liste nichtzugel. RA, 04/25/1933; JMBl. 33, p. 203; BArch, R 3001 PAK; BG; g; GB II; Aufbau (NY), 08/01/1947; BHdE vol. 2,2, p. 737 (Fritz Julius Litten); Litten, Irmgard: Eine Mutter kämpft [A mother is fighting]. Rudolstadt 1947; Krach, p. 434; Schneider, Schwarz, Schwarz, pages197-202; Ausst. AoR, 2004; information attorney Abesser

**Littmann, Ernst**
04/14/1904 - no information
*Home address:* Berliner Str. 143, Charlottenburg
*Law firm address:* Belle-Alliance-Str. 106, SW 61
*Additional information:* Attorney and notary; after the National Socialist seizure of power in 1993 his license as a notary was revoked; he was disbarred as an attorney on 08/06/1935. He emigrated to Copenhagen, Denmark.
*Sources:* JMBl. 33, S. 266; *li; LAB, Liste 10/15/1933; BArch, R 3001 PAK; BG

**Littmann, Herbert**
05/02/1903 Berlin - no information
*Home address:* no information
*Law firm address:* Helmstedter Str. 5, Wilmersdorf
*Additional information:* After the National Socialist seizure of power he was made subject to an occupational ban on 06/10/1933. He emigrated to Palestine in October 1935.

*Sources:* Liste d. nichtzugel. RA, 04/25/1933; JMBl. 07/07/1933, p. 209; BArch, R 3001 PAK, PA; BG

**Löb, Abraham Dr.**
04/20/1884 - 11/03/1937
*Home address:* Güntzelstr. 3, Wilmersdorf
*Law firm address:* Güntzelstr. 3, Wilmersdorf
*Additional information:* Attorney and notary; after the National Socialist seizure of power in 1933 his license as a notary was revoked; he was still working as an attorney in 1936; he died in 1937 at the age of 53; he was buried at Weißensee.
*Sources:* JMBl. 33, p. 208; *li; LAB, Liste 10/15/1933; Liste 36 (Lön); BArch, R 3001 PAK; BG; Friedh.W. Sterbereg.

**Löb, Alexander, Judicial Councillor**
02/11/1868 Elberfeld - no information
*Home address:* Prager Str. 23, W 50
*Law firm address:* Prager Str. 23, W 50
*Additional information:* After the National Socialist seizure of power he was readmitted, he was still working as an attorney until the general occupational ban in 1938. He emigrated to Buenos Aires, Argentina via Belgium on 01/24/1939.
*Sources:* *li; LAB, Liste 10/15/1933; Liste 36; MRRAK; BG: LAB, OFP files

**Loebinger, Günther Dr.**
11/17/1899 Schlesiengrube - 01/11/1944 Auschwitz
*Home address:* Brandenburgische Str. 38, W 15, Wilmersdorf
*Law firm address:* Friedrichstr. 182, W 8
*Additional information:* Attorney at the KG; after the National Socialist seizure of power he was readmitted; he worked as an attorney until the general occupational ban in 1938, thereafter as a "consultant." Date of declaration of property: 06/18/1943; collecting station Große Hamburger Str. 26; transportation on 07/01/1943 to Theresienstadt; from there he was transported on 10/28/1944 to Auschwitz, where he was murdered shortly after arrival.
*Sources:* Br.B. 32; *li; LAB, Liste 10/15/1933; Liste 36; MRRAK; BG; GB II

**Loebinger, Rudolf Dr.**
01/29/1901 Berlin - no information
*Home address:* no information
*Law firm address:* Unter den Linden 39, NW 7

*Additional information:* Attorney at the KG; after the National Socialist seizure of power he was made subject to an occupational ban on 06/10/1933.
*Sources:* Br.B. 32; Liste d. nichtzugel. RA, 04/25/1933; JMBl. 33, p. 209; BArch, R 3001 PAK, PA

**Loeser, Erich Dr.**
01/12/1908 Berlin - no information
*Home address:* no information
*Law firm address:* Konstanzer Str. 64, W 15
*Additional information:* After the National Socialist seizure of power he was made subject to an occupational ban on 06/12/1933.
*Sources:* Liste d. nichtzugel. RA, 04/25/1933; JMBl. 33, p. 267; BArch, R 3001 PAK, PA

**Loevy, Fritz Dr.**
12/26/1895 - no information
*Home address:* Köpenicker Str. 32, SO 16
*Law firm address:* Köpenicker Str. 32, SO 16
*Additional information:* Attorney and notary; after the National Socialist seizure of power he was made subject to a brief occupational ban, he was back in litigation at the end of April, but his license as a notary was revoked; he worked as an attorney until the general occupational ban in 1938. He emigrated to Edgeware, Great Britain (according to the police he fled in 1939), later to Brazil.
*Sources:* Br.B. 32; Liste d. nichtzugel. RA, 04/25/1933 (addendum list); *li; LAB, Liste 10/15/1933; BArch, R 3001 PAK; DJ 36, p. 315; MRRAK; BG

**Loewe, Adolf, Judicial Councillor**
04/25/1860 - 03/01/1937 Berlin
*Home address:* Am Friedrichshain 34, Prenzlauer Berg
*Law firm address:* Am Friedrichshain 34, Prenzlauer Berg
*Additional information:* Attorney and notary; after the National Socialist seizure of power in 1933 his license as a notary was revoked; he was still working as an attorney in 1936; he died in 1937 shortly before his 67th birthday; he was buried at Weißensee.
*Sources:* JMBl. 33, p. 220; *li; LAB, Liste 10/15/1933; Liste 36; BG

**Loewe, Alfons, Judicial Councillor**
12/30/1868 Rogasen - 12/28/1938
*Home address:* Fürstenweg 1, Spandau

*Law firm address:* Potsdamer Str. 40, Spandau
*Additional information:* Attorney and
notary; after the National Socialist seizure
of power in 1933 his license as a notary was
revoked, he still worked as an attorney until
the general occupational ban in 1938; from the
beginning of 1937 he worked in the acquired
practice of an emigrated colleague, but he
had to give up at the end of the year because
of lack of mandates. His wife Katharine was
regarded as non-Jewish. He committed suicide
at the end of 1938. Since February 1999, a
street has been named after him, in the district
Staaken, Spandau.
*Sources:* JMBl. 33, p. 208; *li; LAB, Liste
10/15/1933; Liste 36; MRRAK; BG; GB II;
information Flechtmann

**Loewe, Arthur**
12/27/1886 Berlin -
04/12/1942 Litzmannstadt/
Lodz
*Home address:* Schillerstr.
15, Charlottenburg
*Law firm address:*
Marburger Str. 17, W 50
*Additional information:* Attorney and
notary; after the National Socialist seizure
of power he was readmitted; his license as a
notary was revoked in 1935, he worked as an
attorney until the general occupational ban
in 1938. He had to do forced labor, and was
used as a worker. Transportation from 10/27-
29/1941 to Litzmannstadt/Lodz; there he died
in April 1942.
*Sources:* *li; LAB, Liste 10/15/1933; DJ 36, p.
315; Liste 36; BArch, R 3001 PAK; MRRAK;
Naatz-Album; BG; GB II

**Loewe, Edith, nee Schless**
07/30/1903 Leipzig
*Home address:* Helmstedter Str. 26,
Wilmersdorf
*Law firm address:* Stresemannstr. 12, SW 11
*Additional information:* After the National
Socialist seizure of power he was made subject
to an occupational ban in early 1933. He
emigrated to Neuilly, France on 11/01/1933.
Edith was the wife of Erich, both of them
survived the National Socialist regime; Edith
was still living in Paris in 2000.
*Sources:* Liste d. nichtzugel. RA, 04/25/1933;
BArch, R 3001 PAK; BG; information
attorney Lang, 2000

**Loewe, Erich Dr.**
09/23/1889 Breslau - no information
*Home address:* Helmstedter Str. 26,
Wilmersdorf
*Law firm address:* Stresemannstr. 12, SW 11
*Additional information:* Attorney
and notary; he was made subject to an
occupational ban in early 1933. Emigration to
Neuilly, France, on 11/01/1933. Erich was the
husband of Edith; both of them survived.
*Sources:* Br.B. 32; Liste d. nichtzugel. RA,
04/25/1933; JMBl. 33, p. 220/1; BArch, R
3001 PAK; BG

**Loewe, Ernst Dr.**
12/19/1878 Berlin - no information
*Home address:* Nassauische Str. 64,
Wilmersdorf
*Law firm address:* Kronenstr. 4/5, W 8
*Additional information:* Attorney and notary
in a law partnership with Hans Carl Ladewig
and Max Lichtwitz; after the National Socialist
seizure of power in 1933 he was readmitted; his
license as a notary was revoked in 1935; he was
still working as an attorney until the general
occupational ban in 1938; in 1939 he was still
living in Berlin. He emigrated to Argentina.
*Sources:* *li; LAB, Liste 10/15/1933; DJ 36, p.
315; Liste 36; MRRAK; BG: LAB, OFP files,
L., Dorothea files; VZ 39

**Loewe, Fritz**
12/03/1873 Loslau - 03/07/1941
*Home address:* no information
*Law firm address:* Französische Str. 28, W 8
*Additional information:* Attorney and notary;
after the National Socialist seizure of power
in 1933 his license as a notary was revoked, he
worked as an attorney until the occupational
ban in 1939, he was in a law partnership with
Martin Loewe. Fritz died in 1941 at the age of
78. He was buried at Weißensee.
*Sources:* JMBl. 33, p. 220; *li; LAB, Liste
10/15/1933; Liste 36; MRRAK; BG

**Loewe, Josef Dr.**
09/20/1878 Berlin - no
information
*Home address:* Friedrichstr.
42, SW 68
*Law firm address:*
Friedrichstr. 41/42, SW 68
*Additional information:*
Attorney and notary; after the National

Socialist seizure of power in 1933 his license as a notary was revoked, he was disbarred as an attorney on 05/07/1938. He was regarded as "mixed race."
*Sources:* BR.B. 32, JMBl. 33, p. 208; *li; LAB, Liste Mschl. 36; Naatz-Album; BG

**Loewe, Martin Dr.**
01/31/1881 - 08/11/1938 Berlin
*Home address:* Meinekestr. 16-17, Wilmersdorf
*Law firm address:* Französische Str. 28, W 8
*Additional information:* He worked in a law partnership with Fritz Loewe; after the National Socialist seizure of power in 1933 his license as a notary was revoked, he was still working as an attorney in 1936, he presumably worked as an attorney until his death in August 1938.
*Sources:* *li; LAB, Liste 10/15/1933; Liste 36; BG

**Loewe, Walter**
10/01/1903 Berlin - no information
*Home address:* Lichtensteinallee 2 a, W 35
*Law firm address:* Krausenstr. 15, W 8
*Additional information:* Attorney since 1939; he supported the DVP (Demokratische Volkspartei = Democratic People's Party); after the National Socialist seizure of power he was made subject to an occupational ban on 05/26/1933.
*Sources:* Br.B. 32; Liste d. nichtzugel. RA., 04/25/1933; JMBl. 33, p. 220; BArch, R 3001 PAK, PA; Naatz-Album

**Loewenberg, Albert, Judicial Councillor**
No information
*Home address:* no information
*Law firm address:* no information
*Additional information:* Attorney and notary; after the National Socialist seizure of power in 1933 his license as a notary was revoked; in October 1933 he was not listed in the Berlin directory of attorneys, presumably he had given up his practice.
JMBl. 33, p. 208

**Loewenberg, Fritz Dr.**
07/13/1898 Bromberg - no information
*Home address:* Nestorstr. 3, Wilmersdorf
*Law firm address:* Taubenstr. 21, W 8
*Additional information:* After the National Socialist seizure of power in 1933 he was readmitted; he was still working as an

attorney in 1936. Emigration to Buenos Aires, Argentina, on 07/04/1938.
*Sources:* *li; LAB, Liste 10/15/1933; Liste 36; BArch, R 3001 PAK; BG

**Loewenberg, Georg**
07/28/1891 - no information
*Home address:* Helmstedter Str. 30, Wilmersdorf
*Law firm address:* Mohrenstr. 48, W 8
*Additional information:* Attorney and notary; after the National Socialist seizure of power he was made subject to an occupational ban in early 1933. He emigrated to Palestine in October 1933.
*Sources:* Br.B. 32; Liste d. nichtzugel. RA., 04/25/1933; JMBl. 33, p. 221; BG

**Loewenberg, Hermann Dr.**
09/04/1903 - no information
*Home address:* no information
*Law firm address:* Steglitzer Str. 27
*Additional information:* After the National Socialist seizure of power he waas made subject to an occupational ban in early 1933. He emigrated to Portland, Oregon, USA.
*Sources:* Br.B. 32; Liste d. nichtzugel. RA, 04/25/1933; JMBl. 33, p. 220; BArch, R 3001 PAK; BG

**Loewenberg, Julius, Judicial Councillor**
10/09/1870 Straßburg/ West Prussia - 1934
*Home address:* Podbielskiallee 8, Zehlendorf
*Law firm address:* Habsburger Str. 12, W 30
*Additional information:* He. resigned from the Jewish Synagogue in 1919; after the National Socialist seizure of power in 1933 his license as a notary was revoked, he was readmitted as an attorney, in the same year he emigrated to Karlsbad, Czechoslovakia; he died in 1934.
*Sources:* Br.B. 32; JMBl. 33, p. 208; *li; LAB, Liste 10/15/1933; BG; Wolf, BFS

**Loewenberg, Kurt**
04/14/1907 - no information
*Home address:* no information
*Law firm address:* Steglitzer Str. 27, W 35
*Additional information:* After the National Socialist seizure of power he was made subject to an occupational ban on 06/09/1933. He emigrated in August 1933 to Palestine.
*Sources:* Liste d. nichtzugel. RA, 04/25/1933; JMBl. 33, p. 234; BArch, R 3001 PAK, PA; BG

**Loewenfeld, Erwin Dr.**
06/18/1888 Berlin - no information
*Home address:* An der Heerstr. 88,
Charlottenburg
*Law firm address:* Rathenower Str. 78,
NW 21
*Additional information:* Attorney and
notary; together with Heinrich Freund and
Udo Rukser they were the founders and
publishers of the journal "Ostrecht [Eastern
European law]"; after the National Socialist
seizure of power in 1933 he was readmitted;
his license as a notary was revoked in 1935,
he worked as an attorney until the general
occupational ban in 1938. He emigrated
together with his brother Günther to London,
Great Britain, on 03/10/1939; there he worked
as a jurist; he became an attorney at the
Supreme Court and a member of the Law
Faculty at Cambridge (1960).
*Sources:* *li; LAB, Liste 10/15/1933; DJ
36, p. 315; Liste 36; BG: LAB, OFP files;
Osteuropa-Recht [Law of Eastern Europe],
special edition 1/1960, p. 3

**Loewenfeld, Günther Dr.**
10/10/1885 - no information
*Home address:* no information
*Law firm address:* Rathenower Str. 78,
NW 21
*Additional information:* Attorney and
notary; after the National Socialist seizure of
power in 1933 he was readmitted; his license
as a notary was revoked in 1935; he worked
as an attorney until the general occupational
ban in 1938, he emigrated in 1939 together
with his brother Erwin to Great Britain.
*Sources:* *li; LAB, Liste 10/15/1933; DJ 36, p.
315; Liste 36

**Loewenstein, Arthur**
12/30/1886 Lessen -
transportation 1942
*Home address:* Lessingstr.
7, Tiergarten
*Law firm address:* Neue
Schönhauser Str. 10, N 54
*Additional information:*
Attorney and notary; after the National
Socialist seizure of power in 1933 he was
readmitted; his license as a notary was
revoked at the latest at the end of 1935; he
was still working as an attorney until the
general occupational ban in 1938. Date
of declaration of property: 07/19/1942;

collecting station Große Hamburger Str.
26; transportation on 07/23/1942 to
Theresienstadt; from there he was transported
on 10/01/1944 to Auschwitz.
*Sources:* *li; LAB, Liste 10/15/1933; Liste 36;
BArch, R 3001 PAK; MRRAK; BG; GB II

**Loewenstein, Emil Dr.**
10/30/1878 - 05/06/1933
*Home address:* Wilmersdorfer Str. 93,
Charlottenburg
*Law firm address:* Königstr. 22-24
*Additional information:* He died in May 1933
at the age of 54, he was buried at Weißensee.
*Sources:* Br.B. 32; JMBl. 9.6.33, p. 28; Naatz-
Album; BG

**Loewenstein, Georg Dr.**
02/08/1887 Lessen - October 1941
Litzmannstadt/Lodz
*Home address:* no information
*Law firm address:* An der Spandauer
Brücke 4/5
*Additional information:* Attorney and
notary; after the National Socialist seizure of
power he was made subject to an occupational
ban in early 1933. On 10/18/1941 he was
transported to Litzmannstadt/Lodz; he died
there in October 1941.
*Sources:* Br.B. 32; Liste d. nichtzugel. RA,
04/25/1933; JMBl. 33, p. 209; BArch, R 3001
PAK; BG; GB II

**Löwenstein, Otto**
11/10/1883 Woldenburg - no information
*Home address:* Gasteinerstr. 8, Wilmersdorf
*Law firm address:* Schönhauser Allee 108,
N 113
*Additional information:* Attorney and
notary; after the National Socialist seizure of
power in 1933 he was readmitted; his license
as a notary was revoked in 1935; he worked
as an attorney until the general occupational
ban in 1938. He emigrated to London, Great
Britain, on 05/12/1939.
*Sources:* *li; LAB, Liste 10/15/1933; DJ 36, p.
315; Liste 36; BG

**Löwenstein, Siegfried Dr., Judicial Councillor**
09/08/1867 Emmerich - no information
*Home address:* Siegmundshof 9, NW 87
*Law firm address:* Siegmundshof 1, NW 87
*Additional information:* Attorney and
notary; after the National Socialist seizure
of power in 1933 his license as a notary was

revoked; he applied for readmission as an attorney, which was granted; he was still listed in the attorney business directory in October 1933. He emigrated at the same time, in September 1933, to the USA.
*Sources:* *li; LAB, Liste 10/15/1933; BG

**Löwenthal, Fritz Dr.**
09/15/1888 Munich - 08/28/1956 Valdorf, Westphalia
*Home address:* no information
*Law firm address:* Lützowplatz 14, W 62
*Additional information:* Studied law and political science in Berlin and Munich; 1914 he was a court counsellor; 1918 he was a council assessor and legal counsel of a trade board in Bamberg; in the same year he established himself as an attorney in Nuremberg; 1922 he was legal counsel in Stuttgart; since 1927 he was an attorney in Berlin. 1928 he became a member of the KPD and at the same time a member of the International Law Association; as an attorney he was involved in the legal protection order of the "Rote Hilfe" (Red Aid); 1930-32 he was the KPD delegate in the Reichstag; 1930-31 he was the editor of "Revue der Internationalen Juristischen Vereinigung [Revue of the International Law Association]" (published in 1931).
After the seizure of power by the National Socialists in May 1933, the board of the RAK reported to the Prussian Ministry of Justice that he had been a defender in the Felseneck trial and had represented the "Rote Hilfe" in other criminal proceedings and that he was non-Aryan. A little later he was made subject to an occupational ban. He immediately emigrated via France to the USSR. After the end of the war he returned to Germany, in 1946, he became head of the Judiciary Department of the Central Administration for Justice in the Soviet Occupied Zone, although he had built a clear distance to Ulbricht during his Moscow exile. The conditions in the Soviet-occupied zones did not emulate his understanding of a socialist constitutional state. He expressed his critical stance in the book "Der neue Geist von Potsdam" [The new spirit of Potsdam]. In May 1947 he went to West Germany; there he became a member of the SPD. The distribution of his book was stopped by the British occupation zone, the circumstances are unknown. He became a member of the Parliamentary Council. In May 1949 he was expelled after public attacks from

the SPD faction. He died in 1956 at the age of 66 in Westphalia.
*Publications:* Der Neue Geist von Potsdam [The new spirit of Potsdam], Hamburg 1948
*Sources:* GHStA, Rep. 84a, Nr. 20363; Liste d. nichtzugel. RA, 04/25/1933 (addendum); BG; BArch, R 3001, PAK; BHdE vol. 1, pages 457/58; Schneider, Schwarz, Schwarz, pages 205/06; information Flechtmann, 7/00

**Löwenthal, Georg Dr.**
04/22/1898 Brandenburg - no information
*Home address:* no information
*Law firm address:* Stresemannstr. 163, SW 11
*Additional information:* After the National Socialist seizure of power he was made subject to an occupational ban in early 1933.
*Sources:* Liste d. nichtzugel. RA, 04/25/1933 (addendum); JMBl. 33, page 209 (Loewenthal); BArch, R 3001 PAK

**Loewenthal, Max Dr.**
01/28/1880 Berlin - no information
*Home address:* Bayreuther Str. 42, W 62
*Law firm address:* Bayreuther Str. 42, W 62
*Additional information:* Attorney and notary; after the National Socialist seizure of power in 1933 he was readmitted; his license as a notary was revoked in 1935; he was still working as an attorney in 1936. He emigrated to London, Great Britain.
*Sources:* *li; LAB, Liste 10/15/1933; DJ 36, p. 315; Liste 36; BG

**Loewenthal-Landeck, Carl Dr.**
No information
*Home address:* no information
*Law firm address:* Bülowstr. 100, W 57
*Additional information:* Attorney and notary; after the National Socialist seizure of power he was made subject to an occupational ban in 1933.
*Sources:* Br.B. 32; Liste d. nichtzugel. RA, 04/25/1933; JMBl. 08/21/1933, p. 267

**Loewy, James Dr.**
05/13/1873 Moschin - 01/19/1943 Theresienstadt
*Home address:* Nordweg 64, Oranienburg-Eden
*Law firm address:* Luitpoldstr. 30, W 30
*Additional information:* Attorney and notary; after the National Socialist seizure of power in 1933 he was readmitted; his license as a notary was revoked in 1935; in 1936 he was still working as an attorney. He last resided in

Radinkendorf at Beeskow, southeast of Berlin; transportation from Berlin to Theresienstadt on 10/28/1942, he died there three months later.
*Sources:* *li; LAB, Liste 10/15/1933; DJ 36, p. 315; Liste 36; BG; ThG; GB II

**Loewy, Käthe Dr.**
02/07/1905 Silesia - July 1994 Hamburg
*Home address:* no information
*Law firm address:* Berchtesgadener Str. 5, W 30
*Additional information:* She grew up in Berlin, she studied in Berlin, Bonn and Freiburg; she was admitted as an attorney in March 1933; a little later she was made subject to an occupational ban early in the year. She adhered to Zionistic, romantic, lyrical ideals; 1938 she emigrated to Palestine; she married attorney Fritz Manasse, who in 1935 had emigrated to South Africa and who now followed his wife to Palestine; there she headed "Hillachut olej germania," the self-help work of former Germans, she worked in a women's organization for the protection of oriental Jews and so on.
1949 the couple returned to Germany; in Hamburg she was appointed a judge. She (nee Loewy) was active in the Society for Christian-Jewish Cooperation, she always sought understanding; Prussian virtues, a pronounced sense of justice and a good sense of humor accompanied her her whole life long. Her husband worked as an attorney until an advanced age.
*Sources:* Liste d. nichtzugel. RA, 04/25/1933; JMBl. 33, p. 220; BArch, R 3001 PAK; Information Witwer, HH; Board of the Society for Christian-Jewish Cooperation in Hamburg: Annäherungen. 50 Jahre christlich-jüdische Zusammenarbeit in Hamburg [Approaches. 50 years of Christian-Jewish cooperation in Hamburg], Hamburg 2002

**Loewy, Siegbert, Judicial Councillor**
05/27/1876 Berlin - 08/08/1942
*Home address:* Mommsenstr. 7, Charlottenburg
Law firm: Friedrichstr. 106, N 24
*Additional information:* Attorney (since 1903) and notary (since 1919); member of the SPD. In 1921 the town council elected him deputy member of the Prussian Council of State; end of the 1920s he was used as a notary in the completion of land transactions; in addition he was also an arbitrator in expropriation proceedings. After the seizure of power by the National Socialists in 1933, he was elected a city councillor. In the same year his license as a notary was revoked, he was readmitted as an attorney. He was besieged by National Socialist State Commissioner Lippert to make payments to the city; afraid of being arrested, he fled with his wife and three children and a search was launched for the couple. He emigrated in 1936 to Italy. The German Attorney and Notary Insurance reported to the Chief Finance President that he had died abroad in 1942.
*Sources:* *li; LAB, Liste 10/15/1933; Pr.J. 33, p. 466; Liste 36; BG; Verfolgte Stadtverordn.u.Mag.mitgl., p. 277; Wolf, BFS

**Lomnitz, Arthur**
08/27/1876 Berlin - 05/23/1941 Berlin
*Home address:* Gervinusstr. 20, Charlottenburg
*Law firm address:* Alexanderstr. 56, O 27
*Additional information:* Attorney and notary; after the National Socialist seizure of power in 1933 his license as a notary was revoked; in 1936 he was still working as an attorney. In May 1941 he died at the Jewish Hospital in Berlin at the age of 64.
*Sources:* JMBl. 33, p. 208; *li; LAB, Liste 10/15/1933; Liste 36; BG

**Looser, Günther**
04/11/1904 - July 1984
*Home address:* no information
*Law firm address:* Konstanzer Str. 64, W 15
*Additional information:* After the National Socialist seizure of power he was made subject to an occupational ban in early 1933. He emigrated to the USA, he last lived in Los Angeles.
*Sources:* Liste d. nichtzugel. RA, 04/25/1933; JMBl. 08/21/1933, p. 267; BArch, R 3001 PAK; SSDI

**Lorch, Herbert Dr.**
01/20/1902 - no information
*Home address:* no information
*Law firm address:* Motzstr. 51, Wilmersdorf

*Additional information:* After the National Socialist seizure of power he was made subject to an occupational ban in early 1933. He emigrated to Great Britain in November 1933. *Sources:* Liste d. nichtzugel. RA, 04/25/1933; JMBl. 33, p. 220; BArch, R 3001 PAK; BG

**Löwenfeld, Otto**
10/25/1898 - no information
*Home address:* no information
*Law firm address:* Passauer Str. 36, W 50
*Additional information:* After the National Socialist seizure of power he was made subject to an occupational ban in early 1933.
*Sources:* Liste d. nichtzugel. RA, 04/25/1933; JMBl. 08/21/1933; p. 267; BArch, R 3001 PAK

**Löwy, Adolf Dr.**
No information
*Home address:* no information
*Law firm address:* Zimmerstr. 92/93, SW 68
*Additional information:* Attorney and notary; after the National Socialist seizure of power in 1933 his license as a notary was revoked, he was still working as an attorney until the general occupational ban in 1938.
*Sources:* JMBl. 33, p. 208; *li; LAB, Liste 10/15/1933; Liste 36; MRRAK

**Lubinski, Georg Dr.**
03/22/1902 Berlin - 01/01/1974 Jerusalem
*Home address:* Niebuhrstr. 11a, Charlottenburg
*Law firm address:* no information
*Additional information:* He completed his legal studies in Berlin and Frankfurt a. M.; 1927 he received his doctorate; he established himself as an attorney in Berlin, he was last admitted at the LG I-III and AG Berlin-Mitte; in addition to his legal activity, he was Director of the Zionist youth movement in Germany and Secretary General of the Reich Committee of Jewish Youth Organizations. After the National Socialist seizure of power he was made subject to an occupational ban in early 1933; 1933-38 head of the department for vocational training of the Reich Representation, thus also responsible for emigration assistance; he was a member among others of Hechaluz and Poale Zion; 1938 he emigrated to Palestine, he now called himself Giora Lotan; he was active in charitable organizations; he was engaged in social policy after the founding of the State of Israel, 1959-60 he was Minister of Social Welfare and 1969 he was Minister of Labor; he died 1974 in Jerusalem.
*Sources:* TK 33; Liste d. nichtzugel. RA, 04/25/1933; JMBl. 33, p. 220; BArch, R 3001 PAK; BG; BHdE, vol. 1, p. 461; Walk, p. 248

**Lublinsky, Eugen**
12/10/1882 - 10/10/1934
*Home address:* Grolmanstr. 36, Charlottenburg
*Law firm address:* Grolmanstr. 36, Charlottenburg
*Additional information:* Attorney and notary; after the National Socialist seizure of power in 1933 his license as a notary was revoked, he was readmitted as an attorney. He died in 1934 at the age of 51, he was buried at Weißensee.
*Sources:* JMBl. 33, p. 208; *li; LAB, Liste 10/15/1933; BG

**Lubszynski, Julius Dr., Judicial Councillor**
11/04/1869 Posen - 10/24/1939
*Home address:* Admiral-von-Schröder-Str. 8, W 35
*Law firm address:* Königin-Augusta. Str. 23, W 35
*Additional information:* Attorney and notary; after the National Socialist seizure of power in 1933 he was readmitted; his license as a notary was revoked in 1935; he was still working as an attorney until the general occupational ban in 1938. He emigrated to New York, USA, where he died soon after.
*Sources:* *li; LAB, Liste 10/15/1933; DJ 36, p. 315; Liste 36; MRRAK; BG

**Luft, Gerhard Dr.**
02/28/1889 Leobschütz - no information
*Home address:* Grunewaldstr. 46, Schöneberg
*Law firm address:* Forststr. 33, Steglitz
*Additional information:* After the National Socialist seizure of power he was readmitted, he was still working as an attorney until the the general occupational ban in 1938 (later under the address Ritterstr. 54, SW 68); he was baptized, he was a member of the Reich Association of Non-Aryan Christians.
*Sources:* *li; LAB, Liste 10/15/1933; Liste 36; BArch, R 3001, PAK; MRRAK; BG; Mitt. bl. Reichsverband nicht-arischer Christen, 12/06/1934

**Lüpschütz, Alfons, Dr.**
07/24/1881 Berlin - transportation 1942
*Home address:* Bülowstr. 28, W 57
*Law firm address:* Bülowstr. 28, W 57
*Additional information:* Attorney and
notary; after the National Socialist seizure of
power in 1933 he was readmitted; his license
as a notary was revoked in 1935; he was
still working as as attorney until the general
occupational ban in 1938. He emigrated
to France; transportation from Drancy to
Auschwitz on 08/14/1942.
*Sources:* Br.B. 32; *li; LAB, Liste 10/15/1933;
DJ 36, p. 315; Liste 36; MRRAK; BG; GB II

**Lurje, Max**
05/18/1882 Stettin - transportation 1943
*Home address:* Hektorstr. 12, Wilmersdorf
*Law firm address:* no information
*Additional information:* After the National
Socialist seizure of power he was made
subject to an occupational ban in 1933.
Transportation on 02/19/1943 to Auschwitz.
*Sources:* BArch, R 3001 PAK; BG; GB II

**Lustig, Max Dr.**
07/31/1881 Berlin -
03/11/1971 Berlin
*Home address:* Ulricistr. 21,
Zehlendorf
*Law firm address:*
Budapester Str. 33, W 62
*Additional information:*
Attorney (since 1909) and notary (since 1919);
he had fought in the First World War. In the
elections in November 1932, he chose the
DVP. He was a Protestant, his wife Käthe
was of non-Jewish origins. After the National
Socialist seizure of power in 1933 he was
readmitted. The approvals were withdrawn,
according to his own information, in 1935
by a court of honor procedure with reference
to his "racial descent." He then worked until
1944 as legal counsel. In the same year he was
forced to do civil engineering work in the labor
camp Jena. He survived the National Socialist
regime. In April 1947 he was again admitted as
an attorney, but then committed to a judgeship.
After retirement, when he reached retirement
age, he again applied to be admitted as an
attorney, which was approved. Until his death
at age 89 he worked as an attorney.
*Sources:* *li; LAB, Liste 10/15/1933; BG;
Verz. zugel. Anw. 45; LAB, RAK, PA

**Lutz, Hans Dr.**
No information
*Home address:* Eichenallee 66,
Charlottenburg
*Law firm address:* Behrenstr. 23, W 8
*Additional information:* Attorney and
notary; after the National Socialist seizure
of power in 1933 his license as a notary was
revoked, he still worked as an attorney until
the general occupational ban in 1938. (He
was one of the cases in which the National
Socialists in 1938 only with difficulty
managed to use the term "Jew.") He survived
and was admitted after 1945 as an attorney
and notary.
*Sources:* JMBl. 33, p. 208; *li; LAB, Liste
10/15/1933; Liste 36; BArch, R 3001
PAK, PA, Bl. 30; Schreiben des RMJ an
KG-Präsidenten [Letter of the Reich Ministry
of Justice to the President of the Court of
Appeals], see BArch, R 3001/62210, p. 30;
MRRAK; Verz. zugel. Anw. 45

# M

**Maass, Ernst**
01/23/1887 Stettin - 11/10/1963 Berlin
*Home address:* Pfalzburger Str. 82, W 15
*Law firm address:* Wallstr. 1, Mitte
*Additional information:* He fought in the
First World War and awarded the EK II.
K. Attorney (since 1919) and notary (since
1928). After the National Socialist seizure of
power he was readmitted; 1935 his license as
a notary was revoked; he still worked until as an
attorney until the general occupational ban in
1938. In 1942 he was arrested and accused of
espionage because he wanted to get a visa for
Switzerland. He was released again. In 1943
he was arrested again and taken into "Jewish
custody." In the same year he was forcibly
conscripted as a demolition worker. His wife
Margaret was considered non-Jewish, thus he
lived in a "mixed marriage." He survived the
camp assignment and lived after 1945 at the
address listed above.
*Sources:* Br.B. 32; LAB, Liste 10/15/1933;
DJ 36, p. 315; Liste 36; BArch, R 3001
PAK; MRRAK; Verz. zugel. Anw. 45; BG;
information of the son

**Machol, Kurt Dr.**
02/19/1904 Heme - transportation 1942
*Home address:* Yorckstr. 88, SW 61,
Kreuzberg
*Law firm address:* Kaiser-Wilhelm-Str. 4,
Niederschönhausen
*Additional information:* He was Protestant;
after the National Socialist seizure of power
in April 1933 he was made subject to an
occupational ban; he was readmitted upon
request; he still worked as an attorney until the
general occupational ban in 1938, thereafter as
a "consultant." Date of declaration of property:
9/24/1942, transportation on 09/24-26/1942 to
Raasiku at Reval/Tallinn.
*Sources:* *li; LAB, Liste 10/15/1933; Liste
36; BArch, R 3001 PAK; MRRAK; BG; BdE;
GB II

**Magnus, Julius Dr., Judicial Councillor**
09/061867 Berlin - 05/15/1944 Theresienstadt
*Home address:* Blumeshof 13, W 35
*Law firm address:* lMaaßenstr. 27, W 62
*Additional information:* Attorney at the KG
(since 1898), later also a notary. He specialized
in copyright and patent law, competition law,
intellectual property law and international
law, he had numerous publications. In
addition, he was editor of the "Juristischen
Wochenschrift (JW)"[Legal Weekly Journal],
published by the German Bar Association,
for more than 18 years. He had developed the
JW to internationally recognized magnitude.
Here legal discussion was offered a forum for
central questions, thus the writing contributed
substantially to the legal development of the
Weimar Republic.
After the seizure of power by the National
Socialists he had to give up his position as
editor of the JW immediately. His license as a
notary was revoked in 1933; he worked as an
attorney until the general occupational ban
in 1938. Victor Klemperer noted in his diary
on October 9, 1936 that judicial councillor
Magnus gave a eulogy for a mutual friend,
attorney James Breit (a Protestant of Jewish
descent), in Dresden-Tolkewitz. On August
25, 1939, Magnus fled to Holland, but was
caught there by his persecutors. In the summer
of 1943 he was transported to the Westerbork
concentration camp, on 01/25/1944 he was
transported from there via Bergen-Belsen to
Theresienstadt. There he presumably died of
starvation. The last known information about

Julius Magnus came from judicial councillor
Georg Siegmann, who was in Theresienstadt
at the same time. Siegmann wrote to the
attorney Willi Naatz.
*Publications i.a.:* Die Höchsten Gerichte der
Welt [The supreme courts of the world], 1929;
Die Notlage der Anwaltschaft [The plight of
the attorney], 1930; Zivilprozessrecht [Civil
litigation], 1931; editor of the JW.
*Sources:* JMBl. 33, p. 208; *li; LAB, Liste
10/15/1933; Liste 36; MRRAK; postcard
from Siegmann to Naatz; BG; GB II; Göpp.,
p. 253; Ausst. AoR

**Mainzer, Max Dr.**
01/10/1902 Berlin - 09/16/1987 Los Angeles
*Home address:* Lützowplatz 3, W 62
*Law firm address:* Wichmannstr. 10, W 9
*Additional information:* After the National
Socialist seizure of power in early 1933 he
was made subject to an occupational ban. He
emigrated to the USA; he died in 1987 at the
age of 85.
TK 33; p. 49; Br.B.32; BArch, R 3001 PAK;
JMBl. 33, p. 220; BG; SSDI

**Mainzer, Otto Dr.**
11/26/1903 - 06/28/1995 New York
*Home address:* no information
*Law firm address:* Wormser Str. 4, W 8
*Additional information:* He had, among
others, studied in Frankfurt with Prof. Dr. med.
Hugo Sinzheimer, he married his daughter
Gertrud, who was also an attorney. Attorney at
the KG; after the National Socialist seizure of
power he was made subject to an occupational
ban in early 1933. He emigrated to the USA, he
worked as an attorney again; he lived in New
York, where he died at the age of 91.
*Sources:* Liste d. nichtzugel. RA, 04/25/1933;
JMBl. 33, p. 203; BArch, R 3001 PAK; SLW,
unpublished Fraenkl biography

**Makower, Felix, Judicial Councillor**
1863 Berlin - 01/31/1933 Berlin
*Home address:* no information
*Law firm address:* Potsdamer Str. 131
*Additional information:* Attorney
and notary; active in numerous Jewish
organizations alongside his law practice:
co-founder of the Association of German
Jews; board member of the CV; 1924-27
board member of the Jewish Synagogue Berlin
and head of the Jewish Boys' Orphanage

Pankow; he died at the time of the National Socialist seizure of power.
*Sources:* Br.B. 32; JMBl. 02/24/1933; Walk, p. 252

**Malinowski, Wolf**
06/13/1882 Pleschen - transportation 1943
*Home address:* Rolandstr. 4/Am Schlachtensee 38, Zehlendorf
*Law firm address:* Kurfürstenstr. 15/16
*Additional information:* After the National Socialist seizure of power in 1933 he was made subject to an occupational ban. He was last conscripted as a forced laborer; transportation on 05/17/1943 to Auschwitz.
*Sources:* Br.B. 32; JMBl. 33, p. 209; BG; GB II

**Mamlok, Gerhard Dr.**
08/11/1897 Greifswald - transportation 1942
*Home address:* Kantstr. 49, Charlottenburg
*Law firm address:* Alexanderstr. 5, C 25
*Additional information:* Attorney at the KG; after the National Socialist seizure of power he was readmitted, he worked as an attorney until the general occupational ban in 1938, thereafter he was admitted as a "consultant." Date of declaration of property: 08/29/1942, transportation on 09/05/1942 to Riga.
*Sources:* *li; LAB, Liste 10/15/1933; Liste 36; Liste der Kons. v. 04/15/1939; MRRAK; BG; BdE; GB II

**Manasse, Martin Dr.**
11/09/1881 Breslau - December 1970
*Home address:* Xantener Str. 1, W 15
*Law firm address:* Kronenstr. 3, W 8
*Additional information:* Attorney and notary; after the National Socialist seizure of power in 1933 his license as a notary was revoked, he was readmitted as an attorney until his disbarment on 05/01/1937. He emigrated on 05/12/1937 to the USA; he last lived in San Francisco, California.
*Sources:* Br.B. 32; JMBl. 33, p. 208; *li; LAB, Liste 10/15/1933; Liste 36; BG; SSDI

**Manasse, Sally, Judicial Councillor**
04/25/1863 Filehne - 01/10/1941 Berlin
*Home address:* Berkaer Str. 32-35, Wilmersdorf
*Law firm address:* Klosterstr. 10
*Additional information:* Attorney and notary; after the National Socialist seizure

of power in 1933 his license as a notary was revoked, he was readmitted as an attorney until his disbarment on 05/01/1937. He died at the beginning of 1941 in the Jewish retirement home in Wilmersdorf, he was buried at Weißensee.
*Sources:* JMBl. 33, p. 208; *li; LAB, Liste 10/15/1933; Liste 36; BG

**Manheim, Siegfried**
07/13/1879 - no information
*Home address:* Keithstr. 14 a
*Law firm address:* Fasanenstr. 28, W 15
*Additional information:* Attorney and notary; after the National Socialist seizure of power in 1933 his license as a notary was revoked; he applied for his readmission as an attorney, which was approved, but then gave up his job. He emigrated to Tel Aviv, Palestine.
*Sources:* TK 33; JMBl. 33, p. 208; *li; Pr.J. 33, p. 598; BG

**Mann, Fritz Alexander**
08/11/1907 Frankenthal - 1992 (?)
*Home address:* no information
*Law firm address:* Bamberger Str. 44, Schöneberg; Lützowplatz 3, W 35
*Additional information:* 1926-28 he completed his legal studies in Geneva, Munich and Berlin; 1930 he received his doctorate at Berlin University; he established himself as an attorney with admittance to the LG I-III, at the same time he was an assistant of Martin Wolff at the Law Faculty of Berlin University. After the National Socialist seizure of power he was made subject to an occupational ban in 1933. He emigrated to London, Great Britain, in May 1933; he changed his first name to Frederick, he studied and obtained a second doctorate; he established himself as an attorney; he held important positions and became involved in Jewish organizations; he became prominent with numerous specialized publications; he received many awards, amongst others the German Federal Cross of Merit and the honorary doctorate of the University of Kiel; he was an honorary professor at the University of Bonn; in 1975 he was living in London; he died at the end of 1991/beginning 1992. The University of Bonn held a funeral for him on February 8, 1992.
*Sources:* TK 33; JMBl. 33, p. 253; BG: LAB, OFP files; BHdE vol. 2, 2, p. 769; information E. Proskauer

**Mannheimer, Carl Dr., Judicial Councillor**
06/14/1861 Beuthen - no information
*Home address:* Holsteinische Str. 37, Steglitz
*Law firm address:* Bamberger Str. 44, W 30
*Additional information:* Attorney and
notary; after the National Socialist seizure
of power in 1933 his license as a notary was
revoked, he was still working in 1936.
*Sources:* TK 33; JMBl. 33, p. 208 (Karl M.);
*li; LAB, Liste 10/15/1933; Liste 36; BG

**Mannheimer, Friedrich Dr.**
No information
*Home address:* no information
*Law firm address:* Tauentzienstr. 12, W 50
*Additional information:* After the National
Socialist seizure of power he was made subject
to an occupational ban in early 1933.
*Sources:* Br.B. 32; Liste d. nichtzugel. RA,
04/25/1933

**Mannheimer, Ludwig Dr.**
08/27/1887 Oranienburg - no information
*Home address:* Bechstedter Weg 1,
Wilmersdorf
*Law firm address:* Friedrichstr. 11, SW 68
*Additional information:* Attorney and
notary, law partner of Kurt Maschke, he
took over the defense of the Aachen editor
Sattler, who had published a speech by Ernst
Thalmann; he was active in the context of
"Rote Hilfe;" after the National Socialist
seizure of power in 1933 he was readmitted;
his license as a notary was revoked in 1935;
he still worked as an attorney until the general
occupational ban in 1938; he emigrated to
Shanghai, China in 1939.
*Sources:* *li; DJ 36, p. 315; Liste 36;
MRRAK; BG; Schneider, Schwarz, Schwarz,
pages 209/10

**Marba, Theodor, Judicial Councillor**
11/21/1862 Berlin - 03/21/1941 Croatia
*Home address:* Wittelsbacher Str. 18,
Wilmersdorf
*Law firm address:* Oberwallstr. 20 a, W 8
*Additional information:* After the National
Socialist seizure of power in 1933 he was
readmitted as an attorney. He emigrated to
Yugoslavia; he died there in 1941.
*Sources:* TK 33; *li; LAB, Liste 10/15/1933;
Liste 36; BG: LAB, OFP files

**Marcus, Alfred Dr.**
06/09/1876 Posen - 01/29/1944
Theresienstadt
*Home address:* Mommsenstr. 50/Wielandstr.
10, Charlottenburg
*Law firm address:* Kantstr. 49,
Charlottenburg 4
*Additional information:* After the National
Socialist seizure of power in 1933 he was
readmitted, he still worked as an attorney
until the general occupational ban in 1938;
long-standing employee of the Jewish Cultural
Affairs Administration. Date of declaration
of property: 05/10/1943, transportation on
05/19/1943 to Theresienstadt; he died at the
beginning of 1944.
*Sources:* TK 33; *li; LAB, Liste 10/15/1933;
Liste 36; MRRAK; BG; ThG; GB II

**Marcus, Eduard, Judicial Councillor**
04/15/1868 Berlin - 06/24/1940 Berlin
*Home address:* Hubertusallee 27, Grunewald
*Law firm address:* Joachimsthaler Str. 43/44,
Charlottenburg
*Additional information:* Attorney and
notary; after the National Socialist seizure
of power in 1933 his license as a notary was
revoked, he was readmitted as an attorney
until disbarment on 11/19/1937. He died
in 1940 at the age of 72 and was buried at
Weißensee.
*Sources:* Br.B. 32; *li; LAB, Liste 10/15/1933;
Liste 36; BG

**Marcus, John Dr.**
12/26/1896 - no information
*Home address:* no information
*Law firm address:* Lietzenburger Str. 45, W 15
*Additional information:* He had participated
in the First World War, however, not in
combat; he was an attorney since 1929; after
the National Socialist seizure of power he
was made subject to an occupational ban in
1933, his time served in the military was not
regarded as "frontline fighting." He emigrated
to Palestine in September 1933.
*Sources:* Br.B. 32; Liste d. nichtzugel. RA,
04/25/1933; JMBl. 33, p. 209; BArch, R 3001
PAK, PA; BG

**Marcus, Ludwig Dr.**
03/04/1901 - no information
*Home address:* no information
*Law firm address:* Marktstr. 1, Reinickendorf

*Additional information:* After the National Socialist seizure of power he was made subject to an occupational ban in early 1933.
*Sources:* Br.B. 32; Liste d. nichtzugel. RA, 04/25/1933; JMBl. 08/21/1933, S. 267; BArch, R 3001 PAK

**Marcus, Paul**
No information - 01/12/1935
*Home address:* no information
*Law firm address:* Kurfürstendamm 155a, Wilmersdorf
*Additional information:* After the National Socialist seizure of power in 1933 he was readmitted as an attorney.
*Sources:* TK 33; *li; LAB, Liste 10/15/1933

**Marcuse, Erich Dr.**
02/12/1885 - 11/30/1941 Riga
*Home address:* no information
*Law firm address:* Nestorstr. 43, Halensee
*Additional information:* After the National Socialist seizure of power he was made subject to an occupational ban in early 1933. Transportation on 11/27/1941 to Riga, there he was murdered the day after arrival.
*Sources:* Br.B. 32; Liste d. nichtzugel. RA, 04/25/1933; JMBl. 33, p. 221; BArch, R 3001 PAK; BG; BdE; GB II

**Marcuse, Hans Dr.**
04/19/1898 Berlin - no information
*Home address:* Kurfürstendamm 185, W 15
*Law firm address:* Schöneberger Ufer 34, W 35
*Additional information:* After the National Socialist seizure of power in 1933 he was readmitted, he was still working as an attorney until 1936. He emigrated to Brussels, Belgium, 1936.
*Sources:* *li; LAB, Liste 10/15/1933; Liste 36; BArch, R 3001 PAK; BG

**Marcuse, Martin Dr.**
No information - before May 1961
*Home address:* Von-der-Heydt-Str. 16, W 10
*Law firm address:* Budapester Str. 29, W 62
*Additional information:* Attorney and notary; after the National Socialist seizure of power in 1933 his license as a notary was revoked. He emigrated to Palestine in May 1933; he had apparently applied for readmission, he was still listed in the directory of October 1933; however, he remained abroad permanently.

*Sources:* JMBl. 33, p. 208; *li; LAB, Liste 10/15/1933; BG

**Marcuse, Paul Dr.**
No information
*Home address:* no information
*Law firm address:* Leipziger Str. 115/116, W 8
*Additional information:* Specialized in tax law. He was still a board member of the RAK in 1932. After the National Socialist seizure of power he was readmitted until disbarment on 03/20/1936.
*Sources:* TK 33; *li; LAB, Liste 10/15/1933; Liste 36; Philo-Lexikon, p. 604

**Marcuse, Richard Dr.**
07/03/1893 Berlin - 02/28/1944 Theresienstadt
*Home address:* Kleiststr. 13, W 62/Potsdamer Str. 111, W 35, Schöneberg
*Law firm address:* Bellevuestr. 11 a, W 8
*Additional information:* Attorney and notary; after the National Socialist seizure of power in 1933 he was made subject to an occupational ban; he was readmitted; his license as a notary was revoked in 1935; he worked as an attorney until the general occupational ban in 1938; thereafter he worked as a "consultant." Date of declaration of property: 10/03/1942, transportation on 10/03/1942 to Theresienstadt, he died in February 1944.
*Sources:* *li; LAB, Liste 10/15/1933; DJ 36, p. 315; Liste 36; Liste d. Kons., 04/15/1939; MRRAK; BG; ThG; GB II

**Marcuse, Siegmund, Judicial Councillor**
No information - 11/06/1938
*Home address:* Geisbergstr. 41, W 30
*Law firm address:* Geisbergstr. 2, W 30
*Additional information:* Attorney and notary; after the National Socialist seizure of power in 1933 his license as a notary was revoked, he was still working as an attorney in 1936. He died in 1938 under unclear circumstances.
*Sources:* JMBl. 33, p. 208; *li; LAB, Liste 10/15/1933; Liste 36; Naatz-Album; BG

**Marcuse, Theodor, Judicial Councillor**
07/30/1867 - 03/26/1935
*Home address:* Clausewitzstr. 7,
Charlottenburg
*Law firm address:* Schöneberger Ufer 34, W 35
*Additional information:* Attorney and
notary; after the National Socialist seizure
of power in 1933 his license as a notary was
revoked, he was readmitted as an attorney,
he died in 1935 at the age of 67, he was
buried at Weißensee.
*Sources:* JMBl. 33, p. 208; *li; LAB, Liste
10/15/1933; BG

**Maretzki, Ernst Dr.**
08/21/1884 - no information
*Home address:* no information
*Law firm address:* Potsdamer Str. 129/130, W 9
*Additional information:* Attorney at the
KG and notary; after the National Socialist
seizure of power in 1933 he was readmitted;
his license as a notary was revoked in 1935;
he was still working as an attorney in 1936.
*Sources:* *li; DJ 36, p. 315; Liste 36; BArch,
R 3001 PA

**Margolinski, Siegfried**
02/20/1876 Deutsch-Eylau - no information
*Home address:* Würzburger Str. 1, W 50
*Law firm address:* Würzburger Str. 1, W 50
*Additional information:* Attorney and
notary; after the National Socialist seizure
of power in 1933 his license as a notary was
revoked, he was disbarred as an attorney in
1936. He emigrated during the same year.
*Sources:* *li; LAB, Liste 10/15/1933; Liste
36; BG

**Margoninsky, Eduard, Judicial Councillor**
No information
*Home address:* no information
*Law firm address:* Potsdamer Str. 96, W 57
*Additional information:* Attorney and
notary, in a partnership with Helmut
(presumably his brother); after the National
Socialist seizure of power in 1933 his license
as a notary was revoked, he was still working
as an attorney until March 1938.
*Sources:* JMBl. 33, p. 208; *li; LAB, Liste
10/15/1933; Liste 36

**Margoninsky, Helmut Dr.**
05/22/1899 - no information
*Home address:* no information
*Law firm address:* Potsdamer Str. 96, W 57

*Additional information:* Attorney at the
KG, in a law partnership with Eduard
(presumably the brother); after the National
Socialist seizure of power in 1933 he was
readmitted; he was still working as an
attorney in 1936.
*Sources:* *li; LAB, Liste 10/15/1933; Liste 36;
BArch, R 3001 PAK

**Markson, Hans Dr.**
08/27/1901 Gera - no information
*Home address:* Nikolsburger Platz 1,
Wilmersdorf
*Law firm address:* no information
*Additional information:* After the National
Socialist seizure of power he was made
subject to an occupational ban in 1933. He
emigrated to Tel Aviv, Palestine, 1935.
*Sources:* JMBl. 33, p. 220; BArch, R 3001
PAK; BG: BLHA, OFP files (Marksohn)

**Markus, Alfred Dr.**
01/06/1906 Berlin - 1979
*Home address:* no information
*Law firm address:* Scheffelstr. 5, Lichtenberg
*Additional information:* 1932 he was
admitted as an attorney, he defended members
of the "Reichsbanner" organization; he
was a member of the Zionist Association
for Germany. After the National Socialist
seizure of power he was made subject to an
occupational ban on 06/12/1933; to prepare
for emigration he was a volunteer at a
plumbing business; he emigrated to the USA;
he lived from support payments of his family
and worked i.a. as a salesman and accountant;
in 1947 he passed the exam to be a state-
approved auditor; 1948-70 he worked as an
auditor in his own company, he worked as a
consultant in the area of reparation affairs and
in Jewish organizations; in 1978 he was living
in Pittsburgh.
*Sources:* Liste d. nichtzugel. RA, 04/25/1933;
JMBl. 33, p. 220; BArch, R 3001 PAK, PA;
BG: BHdE vol. 1, p. 478; Walk, p. 256

**Markuse, Max**
05/10/1883 - no information
*Home address:* no information
*Law firm address:* Prager Platz 6,
Wilmersdorf
*Additional information:* After the National
Socialist seizure of power in 1933 he was
readmitted, he worked as an attorney until
the general occupational ban in 1938.

*Sources:* \*li; LAB, Liste 10/15/1933; Liste 36; BArch, R 3001 PAK; MRRAK

**Markwald, Alexander, Judicial Councillor**
01/31/1857 - 02/09/1935 Berlin
*Home address:* Kurfürstenstr. 21/22, W 57
*Law firm address:* Kurfürstenstr. 21/22, W 57
*Additional information:* Attorney and notary; after the National Socialist seizure of power in 1933 he was readmitted; he died in 1935 in Berlin at the age of 78, he was buried at Weißensee.
*Sources:* \*li; LAB, Liste 10/15/1933; Liste 36; BG

**Markwald, Richard Dr.**
03/20/1880 Berlin - no information
*Home address:* Nachodstr. 24, Wilmersdorf
*Law firm address:* Motzstr. 53, W 30
*Additional information:* Attorney at the KG and notary; after the National Socialist seizure of power in 1933 his license as a notary was revoked, he worked as an attorney until the general occupational ban in 1938. He emigrated to Buenos Aires, Argentina on 11/20/1939.
*Sources:* JMBl. 33, p. 208; \*li; LAB, Liste 10/15/1933; MRRAK; BG

**Marwitz, Bruno Dr., Judicial Councillor**
06/16/1870 Angermünde - December 1940 Berlin
*Home address:* Fregestr. 59, Schöneberg
*Law firm address:* Friedrich-Ebert-Str. 7, W 9
*Additional information:* Attorney and notary; after the National Socialist seizure of power in 1933 (or 1935, differing information) his license as a notary was revoked; he worked as an attorney until 01/30/1938; from the end of 1938 he worked at the firm of attorney Dr. Schönberg, who was admitted as a "consultant." "He died of a broken heart. The attorney Dr. Margarete von Erffa . . . participated in his funeral and had the opportunity to converse for a lengthy period of time with Dr. Schönberg; a cemetery was one of the few locations where one was not pursued by sergeants or curious individuals. His wife was later arrested during an attempted flight to Switzerland and was transported to a concentration camp." (Göpp.)
*Publications:* Commentary on copyright law
*Sources:* JMBl. 33, p. 208; \*li; LAB,

Liste 10/15/1933; DJ 36, p. 315; Liste 36; MRRAK; BG; Göpp., p. 226

**Marx, Arthur Dr.**
04/11/1879 Cologne - transportation 1943
*Home address:* Dahlmannstr. 30
*Law firm address:* Friedrichstr. 81, W 8
*Additional information:* After the National Socialist seizure of power in 1933 he was readmitted, he worked as an attorney until the general occupational ban in 1938. Transportation on 01/29/1943 to Auschwitz.
*Sources:* \*li; LAB, Liste 10/15/1933; Liste 36; MRRAK; BG; GB II

**Marx, Hans Dr.**
01/15/1898 - no information
*Home address:* no information
*Law firm address:* Jägerstr. 62 a, W 8
*Additional information:* After the National Socialist seizure of power he was readmitted, he was still working as an attorney until October 1937.
*Sources:* \*li; LAB, Liste 10/15/1933; Liste 36; BArch, R 3001 PAK

**Maschke, Kurt Dr.**
01/05/1894 Konitz - no information
*Home address:* Lietzenburger Str. 17, W 15
*Law firm address:* Friedrichstr. 11, SW 48
*Additional information:* Attorney at the KG and notary; he was in addition to Ludwig Mannheimer a defender in a lawsuit against the editor Sattler, who had published a speech by Ernst Thalmanns in the "Aachener Volkszeitung." After the National Socialist seizure of power in 1933 he was readmitted; his license as a notary was revoked in 1935; he worked as an attorney until the general occupational ban in 1938.
*Sources:* \*li; LAB, Liste 10/15/1933; Liste 36; BArch, R 3001 PAK; MRRAK; BG; Schneider, Schwarz, Schwarz, p. 212

**Masur, Oskar Dr.**
07/12/1882 Breslau - no information
*Home address:* Nassauische Str. 64 at Grünwald, Wilmersdorf
*Law firm address:* Potsdamer Str. 78, W 57
Attorney at the KG and notary; after the National Socialist seizure of power in 1933 he was readmitted; his license as a notary was revoked in 1935; he still worked as an attorney until the general occupational ban in

1938. He emigrated to Cambridge, Great Britain.
*Sources:* *li; LAB, Liste 10/15/1933; DJ 36, p. 315; Liste 36; MRRAK; BG

**Mathias, Georg Dr.**
01/01/1893 - no information
*Home address:* Courbièrestr. 16
*Law firm address:* Taubenstr. 35, W 8
*Additional information:* Attorney and notary; after the National Socialist seizure of power in 1933 he was readmitted; his license as a notary was revoked in 1935, he was disbarred in 1938.
*Sources:* *li; LAB, Liste 10/15/1933; DJ 36, p. 315; Liste 36; BArch, R 3001 PAK; BG

**Mathias, Karl**
12/24/1881 Cologne - no information
*Home address:* Württembergallee 25
*Law firm address:* Steinplatz 2, Charlottenburg
*Additional information:* Attorney and notary; after the National Socialist seizure of power in 1933 his license as a notary was revoked; he was still working as an attorney in 1936. He emigrated via Italy to Uruguay, Montevideo in September 1936.
*Sources:* JMBl. 33, p. 208; *li; LAB, Liste 10/15/1933; Liste 36; BG

**Mathis, Emil Albert Paul Dr.**
06/20/1884 Rittergut Bruse, Kr. Glogau - no information
*Home address:* Bozener Str. 3, Schöneberg
*Law firm address:* Bozener Str. 3, Schöneberg
*Additional information:* After the National Socialist seizure of power he closed his law firm in early 1933. He emigrated to Paris, France on 06/30/1934.
*Sources:* Br.B. 32; JMBl. 33, 5.5.33; p. 137; BArch, R 3001 PAK; BG

**Mattersdorf, Franz August, Judicial Councillor**
09/29/1863 Breslau - 10/04/1942 Theresienstadt
*Home address:* Droysenstr. 18/Mommsenstr. 26, Charlottenburg
*Law firm address:* Lützowplatz 5, W 62
*Additional information:* Attorney and notary; after the National Socialist seizure of power in 1933 his license as a notary was revoked, he worked as an attorney

until the general occupational ban in 1938. Transportation on 09/24/1942 to Theresienstadt, he died there only a few days after arrival.
*Sources:* JMBl. 33, p. 208; *li; LAB, Liste 10/15/1933; Liste 36; BG; ThG; GB II

**Mautner, Richard Dr.**
No information
*Home address:* Giesebrechtstr. 9
*Law firm address:* Brunnenstr. 25, N 31
*Additional information:* Attorney at the KG; commissioned by the legal protection unit of "Rote Hilfe," in 1932 he took over the defense of clients who had been charged mostly for violent breaches of the peace and insurrection after clashes with National Socialists. These activities did not go by unnoticed; after the National Socialist seizure of power the RAK board reported in May 1933 to the Prussian Ministry of Justice that, according to the SS Section III, he had received payments from "Rote Hilfe." He was subsequently not listed in any legal business directory.
*Sources:* Jüd.Adr.B.; TK 33; GHStA, Rep. 84a, No. 20363; Schneider, Schwarz, Schwarz, p. 213

**May, Bruno Dr.**
07/08/1883 Ratibor - no information
*Home address:* Meinekestr. 2, Charlottenburg, W 15
*Law firm address:* Meinekestr. 2, Charlottenburg, W 15
*Additional information:* Attorney and notary; after the National Socialist seizure of power in 1933 his license as a notary was revoked, he worked as an attorney until the general occupational ban in 1938.
*Sources:* JMBl. 33, p. 208; *li; LAB, Liste 10/15/1933; Liste 36; BArch, R 3001 PAK; MRRAK; BG

**May, Max Dr.**
07/13/1883 Meiningen - 04/26/1943
*Home address:* Auguststr. 14-15, N 4, Mitte; Bamberger Str. 36, W 15; Bayerische Str. 2 (law firm address as from May 1942), Schöneberg
*Law firm address:* Kronenstr. 64/65, W 8
*Additional information:* Attorney and notary; after the National Socialist seizure of power he was readmitted; 1935 his license as a notary was revoked, he worked as an

attorney until the general occupational ban in 1938, he still worked as a "consultant," he died in 1943 at the age of 60.
*Sources:* *li; LAB, Liste 10/15/1933; DJ 36, p. 315; Liste 36; MRRAK; Liste d. Kons. v. 04/15/1939; BG

**Mayer, Jacques Dr.**
10/19/1898 Frankfurt/M. - no information
*Home address:* Freisinger Str. 7, Schöneberg
*Law firm address:* Kurfürstendamm 233, W 50
*Additional information:* After the National Socialist seizure of power he was readmitted, he worked as an attorney until the general occupational ban in 1938.
*Sources:* *li; LAB, Liste 10/15/1933; Liste 36; BArch, R 3001 PAK; MRRAK (J.Meyer); BG

**Mayer, Ludwig**
12/24/1880 Neidenstein - 08/27/1943 Shanghai
*Home address:* Nollendorfstr. 16, Schöneberg
*Law firm address:* Nollendorfplatz 6, W 30
*Additional information:* Attorney at the KG and notary; after the National Socialist seizure of power in 1933 his license as a notary was revoked, he still worked as an attorney until the general occupational ban in 1938. He emigrated to Shanghai, China, on 05/04/1939, he died there in 1943.
*Sources:* Jüd.Adr.B; JMBl. 33, p. 208; *li; LAB, Liste 10/15/1933; Liste 36; MRRAK; BG

**Mayer, Ludwig Dr.**
No information
*Home address:* Fritz-Eitel-Str. 12, Zehlendorf
*Law firm address:* Anhalter Str. 3
*Additional information:* Attorney and notary; after the National Socialist seizure of power in 1933 he was made subject to an occupational ban. He survived and after 1945 he was readmitted as an attorney and notary.
*Sources:* Jüd.Adr.B.; Br.B. 32; JMBl. 33, p. 282; Verz. zugel. Anw. 45

**Mayer, Max Dr.**
02/04/1897 Straßbourg - no information
*Home address:* Martin-Luther-Str. 55, Schöneberg
*Law firm address:* Andreasstr. 32, O 27
*Additional information:* Attorney and notary; after the National Socialist seizure of power occupational ban in early 1933; immediately afterwards he emigrated to France.

*Sources:* Jüd.Adr.B; ; Br.B. 32; Liste d. nichtzugel. RA, 04/25/1933; JMBl. 33, 06/17/1933; BG

**Mayer-Mahr, Robert**
05/16/1904 Berlin - transportation 1942
*Home address:* no information
*Law firm address:* Schweinfurthstr. 62, Dahlem
*Additional information:* After the National Socialist seizure of power he was made subject to an occupational ban in July 1933. He emigrated to France. On 09/04/1942 he was transported from Auschwitz to Drancy.
*Sources:* Liste d. nichtzugel. RA, 04/25/1933; JMBl. 07/28/1933, p. 234; BArch, R 3001 PAK; VZ 39; BG; GB II

**Mehlich, Martin Dr.**
12/31/1876 Nagradowice - 08/18/1942 Riga
*Home address:* Sächsische Str. 5, Wilmersdorf
*Law firm address:* Fasanenstr. 22, W 15
*Additional information:* Attorney and notary, he was also a legal advisor to the German Arms and Ammunition Factory. After the National Socialist seizure of power in 1933 his license as a notary was revoked, he was still working as an attorney in 1936. He was conscripted as a forced laborer and last used as a factory worker; date of declaration of property: 08/14/1942; transportation on 08/15/1942 to Riga; he was murdered there on the day of his arrival.
*Sources:* *li; LAB, Liste 10/15/1933; Liste 36; BG; BdE; GB II

**Meinhardt, Peter Dr.**
03/14/1903 Berlin - no information
*Home address:* Rauchstr. 11, W 35
*Law firm address:* Margaretenstr. 8, W 10
*Additional information:* After the National Socialist seizure of power he was made subject to an occupational ban in early 1933. He emigrated to London, Great Britain.
*Sources:* Br.B. 32; Liste d. nichtzugel. RA, 04/25/1933; BArch, R 3001 PAK; BG

**Meinhardt, William Dr.**
08/28/1872 Schwedt - 05/31/1955 London
*Home address:* Rauchstr. 11, W 35
*Law firm address:* Krausstr. 16, Grunewald
*Additional information:* 1914 he was a member of the management board of Deutsche Gasglühlicht AG (Auer-

Gesellschaft); 1919 he was the managing chairman of Osram GmbH KG; he was a board member of the Reich Association of German Industry. He was a law specialist; he was a board member of the Osram Society and a member of the International Chamber of Commerce. He was admitted as an attorney and a notary at the same time. After the National Socialist seizure of power in 1933 his license as a notary was revoked; he worked as an attorney until the general occupational ban in 1938. He emigrated to Great Britain on 11/24/1938.
*Sources:* Br.B. 32; JMBl. 33, p. 220; *li; LAB, Liste 10/15/1933; Liste 36; MRRAK; BG; Göpp., p. 303; Walk, p. 261; information Strauß, 06/01

**Meissner, Salomon**
03/24/1882 Schildberg - transportation 1943
*Home address:* Bamberger Str.31, W 30
*Law firm address:* Lindenstr. 15, SW 68
*Additional information:* Attorney and notary; after the National Socialist seizure of power in 1933 his license as a notary was revoked, he worked as an attorney until the general occupational ban in 1938. Transportation on 03/04 to Auschwitz.
JMBl. 33, p. 208; *li; LAB, Liste 10/15/1933; Liste 36; MRRAK (Salo M.); BG; GB II

**Memelsdorf, Wilhelm Dr.**
01/20/1895 - no information
*Home address:* no information
*Law firm address:* Taubenstr. 32, W 8
*Additional information:* Attorney and notary; after the National Socialist seizure of power in 1933 he was readmitted; his license as a notary was revoked in 1935; he was still working as an attorney until October 1937; he presumably emigrated.
*Sources:* *li; LAB, Liste 10/15/1933; DJ 36, p. 315; Liste 36; BArch, R 3001 PAK, PA

**Mendel, Sidney Dr.**
1885 - 1967 New York
*Home address:* no information
*Law firm address:* Potsdamer Str. 96, W 57
After the National Socialist seizure of power he was readmitted; he was still working as an attorney until the general occupational ban in 1938; he campaigned for the release of internees. He emigrated via Belgium to the USA.
*Sources:* *li; LAB, Liste 10/15/1933; Liste 36; MRRAK; Walk, p. 263

**Mendelsohn, Bruno Dr.**
11/13/1888 Königsberg - 12/01/1942 Berlin
*Home address:* Tharandter Str. 5, Wilmersdorf
*Law firm address:* Mittelstr. 63, NW
*Additional information:* Attorney (since 1919) and notary (since 1929); after the National Socialist seizure of power he was made subject to an occupational ban on 06/08/1933; then he was an employee of the Jewish Synagogue (Economic Aid). He was one of several hostages shot dead in 1942 in retaliation for members of the synagogue administration who escaped.
*Sources:* Br.B. 32; JMBl. 33, p. 234; BArch, R 3001 PAK, PA; BG; GB II; Göpp., p. 255

**Mendelsohn, Conrad Dr.**
01/05/1881 - 02/22/1933
*Home address:* Lützowufer 13, Tiergarten
*Law firm address:* Lützowufer 13, Tiergarten
*Additional information:* Attorney and notary; died shortly after the National Socialist seizure of power at the age of 52; he was buried at Weißensee.
*Sources:* Br.B. 32; JMBl. 03/10/1933; BG

**Menke, Walter**
02/21/1902 Berlin - no information
*Home address:* Sächsische Str. 8, Wilmersdorf
*Law firm address:* Friedrichstr. 85
*Additional information:* Attorney at the KG; after the National Socialist seizure of power he was made subject to an occupational ban in 1933. He emigrated to New York, USA on 11/05/1936.
*Sources:* JMBl. 06/30/1933, p. 203; BArch, R 3001 PAK; BG

**Meschelsohn, Max, Judicial Councillor**
No information - 1934
*Home address:* no information
*Law firm address:* Französische Str. 21, W 8
*Additional information:* Attorney and notary; he was also the legal advisor for A. Wertheim AG. After the National Socialist seizure of power in 1933 he was readmitted; he died in 1934.
*Sources:* *li; LAB, Liste 10/15/1933

**Meseritz, Johannes Dr.**
03/31/1884 Berlin - no information
*Home address:* Klopstockstr. 29, NW 87
*Law firm address:* Reinickendorfer Str. 2, N 65
*Additional information:* Attorney and notary; at the beginning of the 1930s he operated a

legal protection order for "Rote Hilfe." After the National Socialist seizure of power he was made subject to an occupational ban. He emigrated to Palestine.
*Sources:* JMBl. 33, p. 220/1; BArch, R 3001 PAK; BG; Schneider, Schwarz, Schwarz, p. 217

**Messow, Kurt**
12/09/1888 Berlin - no information
*Home address:* Prenzlauer Str. 17, C 2
*Law firm address:* Jerusalemer Str. 13, SW 19
*Additional information:* Attorney and notary; after the National Socialist seizure of power in 1933 he was readmitted; his license as a notary was revoked in 1935; he worked as an attorney until the general occupational ban, thereafter he was still admitted as a "consultant." He survived the National Socialist regime and in December 1945 he was living in Berlin.
*Sources:* *li; LAB, Liste 10/15/1933; DJ 36, p. 315; Liste 36; BArch, R 3001 PAK; BG

**Metz, Hans**
09/21/1875 Minden - 08/12/1943 Theresienstadt
*Home address:* Joachim-Friedrich-Str. 16, Wilmersdorf; Pestalozzistr. 54 a, Schillerstr. 57, Charlottenburg
*Law firm address:* Bismarckstr. 66, Charlottenburg
*Additional information:* Attorney and notary; after the National Socialist seizure of power in 1933 his license as a notary was revoked; he still worked as an attorney until the general occupational ban in 1938; he took over the absence trusteeship for attorney Ernst Kalischer and other trusteeships. Date of declaration of property: 03/14/1943; collecting station Große Hamburger Str. 26; transportation on 03/17/1943 to Theresienstadt; he died there barely half a year later.
*Sources:* JMBl. 33, p. 208; *li; LAB, Liste 10/15/1933; Liste 36; BG; ThG, GB II

**Meumann, Richard Dr.**
12/16/1880 Berlin - transportation 1942
*Home address:* Gieselerstr. 23/Bayerische Str. 9, Wilmersdorf
*Law firm address:* Schönhauser Allee 6/7, N 54
*Additional information:* Attorney and notary; after the National Socialist seizure of power in 1933 he was readmitted; his license as a notary was revoked in 1935; he was still working as an attorney until the

general occupational ban in 1938; last as an "assistant consultant." He was arrested on 09/24/1942; transportation by transport from Frankfurt/M. via Berlin on 09/24-26/1942 to Raasiku near Reval/Tallinn.
*Sources:* *li; DJ 36, p. 315; Liste 36; MRRAK; BG; BdE; GB II

**Meyer, Edmund Dr.**
11/15/1882 Lodz - 07/04/1939 Berlin
*Home address:* Treuchtlinger Str. 10, Schöneberg
*Law firm address:* Blücherstr. 4, SW 61
*Additional information:* Attorney and notary; after the National Socialist seizure of power in 1933 his license as a notary was revoked; he was still working as an attorney in 1936; his wife Elsa was regarded as non-Jewish. He died in 1939 at the age of 56, he was buried at Weißensee.
*Sources:* TK 33; JMBl. 33, p. 208 (Eduard M.); *li; LAB, Liste 10/15/1933; Liste 36; BArch, R 3001 PAK; Naatz-Album; BG

**Meyer, Erich**
05/16/1888 Berlin - 11/22/1943 Berlin
*Home address:* Bismarckstr. 107, Charlottenburg
*Law firm address:* Eichbornstr. 48, Reinickendorf
*Additional information:* Attorney and notary (since 1930); he was a member of the dueling fraternity Pomerania-Silesia. He fought in the First World War, he was captured by the French, but managed to escape. He was awarded the EK II and decorated for his wounds (WOUNDED BADGE IN BLACK). He was a German nationalist and in 1932 he supported an SA troop in his neighborhood in both word and deed.
After the National Socialist seizure of power it was immediately known that he was "non-Aryan," he was Protestant. Since his father was Jewish he was regarded as "mixed race first degree." He was readmitted in 1933, because he had been a "frontline fighter." In 1935 he was admitted as a notary; his fraternity excluded him because of a general "non-Aryan decision." In March 1936 the RAK inquired

about the "race affiliation" of his wife; the couple had been married in 1924 and got divorced in 1937 (his ex-wife was probably later killed in the context of "euthanasia").
The general occupational ban in 1938 did not apply to him, because he was regarded as "mixed race." In 1939, he resigned from the Protestant religious community. He met a woman he wanted to marry and in 1940 he applied for a "marriage permit" with the "Aryan" Miss P. This was denied with reference to his "mixed race status." In the same year their daughter was born; a little later a neighbor denounced the couple. The Gestapo then demanded their separation. Miss P. moved to Falkensee with their daughter and the couple continued to meet there secretly. In 1943 their son was born. In November 1943, he died in an air raid on Berlin, his reference files were stored in Falkensee and survived the time. His marriage with Miss P. was recognized after 1945. His daughter was adopted as a child by a Norwegian couple and lives in Norway.
*Sources:* *li; TK 36; Liste 36; Adr.B. 38; BG; information and documents Steinar Bugge (grandchild) 1/99 and 6/99

**Meyer, Erich Dr.**
08/14/1897 Berlin -
01/25/1972 Berlin
*Home address:* Frankfurter Allee 68, O 112
*Law firm address:*
Frankfurter Allee 68, O 112
*Additional information:*
He had fought for three years in the First World War; he was deployed at the Western Front; he was an attorney since 1925. After the National Socialist seizure of power he was recognized as a "frontline fighter" and he could once again work as an attorney after 1933 until the general occupational ban in 1938. In 1936, he was denounced and arrested and released for lack of evidence; he was arrested again in 1938 for "insulting the Führer"; he was released after an amnesty; after the occupational ban in 1938 he still worked as an "assistant consultant;" August 1941 to February 1943 he was subjected to forced labor as a transport worker at Weber & Co., Berlin-Treptow. After February 1943 he went underground and lived close to Potsdam. Once he met a former colleague

who approached him inconspicuously and said, "Glad that you are still alive!" Such experiences kept him going, however, the time of persecution and constant threats wore him out physically. After the end of National Socialism he was admitted to Allied military courts as an attorney. On 06/05/1947 he obtained general admission as an attorney.
*Sources:* *li; LAB, Liste 10/15/1933; MRRAK; BG: LAB, OFP files; BAP, 15.09 RSA; LAB, RAK, PA; Verz. zugel. Anw. 45; information son Albert Meyer

**Meyer, Ernst Dr.**
09/07/1889 Berlin - 11/28/1940 Chelm
*Home address:* Landesheilanstalt Eberswalde/ Orber Str. 9, Wilmersdorf/Wilhelmsaue 136 (until 10/25/1935)/Karlsruher Str. 7, Wilmersdorf
*Law firm address:* Bamberger Str. 59, W 62
*Additional information:* Attorney and notary; after the National Socialist seizure of power in 1933 he was readmitted; his license as an attorney was revoked in 1935; he was disbarred on 10/15/1936. He was transported to Chelm near Lublin in the summer of 1940, where he died in late November 1940.
*Sources:* *li; LAB, Liste 10/15/1933; DJ 36, p. 315; Liste 36; BArch, R 3001 PAK; BG; GB II

**Meyer, Fedor**
No information - 03/02/1936
*Home address:* no information
*Law firm address:* Wilmersdorfer Str. 51, Charlottenburg
*Additional information:* Attorney and notary; after the National Socialist seizure of power in 1933 his license as a notary was revoked; he worked as an attorney until his death in 1936.
*Sources:* JMBl. 33, p. 208; *li; LAB, Liste 10/15/1933; Liste 36

**Meyer, Georg, Judicial Councillor**
No information
*Home address:* Friedrich-Wilhelm-Str. 37, Zehlendorf
*Law firm address:* Wittenbergplatz 2, W 62
*Additional information:* Attorney and notary; after the National Socialist seizure of power in 1933 he was readmitted, but moved his office; his license as a notary was revoked; he was still working as an attorney in 1936.
*Sources:* Adr.B. 32; *li; DJ 36, p. 315; Liste 36

**Meyer, Georg Dr.**
07/01/1892 Berlin - no information
*Home address:* Grolmanstr. 40,
Charlottenburg
*Law firm address:* Mauerstr. 94, W 8
*Additional information:* He was made
subject to an occupational ban in early 1933;
he emigrated on 09/07/1933 to Paris, France.
*Sources:* Br.B. 32; Liste d. nichtzugel. RA,
04/25/1933; JMBl. 33, p. 282; BArch, R 3001
PAK; BG

**Meyer, Hans Adalbert Dr.**
11/13/1881 Berlin - no information
*Home address:* Kurfürstendamm 216,
Charlottenburg
*Law firm address:* Kurfürstendamm 216,
Charlottenburg
*Additional information:* Attorney at the
KG and notary; after the National Socialist
seizure of power in 1933 his license as a
notary was revoked; he was still working
as an attorney in 1936. He emigrated to
Antwerp, Belgium, in November 1938 (or on
01/02/1939); he survived the Nazi regime.
*Sources:* *li; LAB, Liste 10/15/1933; Liste
36; BG

**Meyer, Hans Martin**
05/22/1876 Berlin - 02/03/1943
Theresienstadt
*Home address:* Tempelhofer Ufer 34, SW 11,
Kreuzberg
*Law firm address:* Tempelhofer Ufer 34, SW
11, Kreuzberg
*Additional information:* After the National
Socialist seizure of power he was readmitted;
he was still working as an attorney until
the general occupational ban in 1938. Date
of declaration of property: 10/07/1942;
collecting station Große Hamburger Str.
26; transportation on 10/29/1942 to
Theresienstadt; there he died three months
later at the beginning of February 1943.
*Sources:* *li; LAB, Liste 10/15/1933; Liste 36;
MRRAK; BG; ThG; GB II

**Meyer, Hermann**
02/01/1901 Berlin - 1972 Jerusalem
*Home address:* no information
*Law firm address:* Neue Friedrichstr. 4, C 2
*Additional information:* Member of the
Zionist youth organization; 1924-37 he
was founder and director of the Soncino

Society of Friends of the Jewish Book; he as
an attorney at the LG Berlin; he was made
subject to an occupational ban in early 1933;
he emigrated to Palestine in 1937; he worked
there as a publisher, especially in the field
of cartography, as a bookseller and as an
antiquarian; he died in 1972 in Jerusalem.
*Sources:* Liste d. nichtzugel. RA, 04/25/1933
(addendum); JMBl. 33, p. 253; BArch, R 3001
PAK; BG; BHdE, vol. 1, p. 497

**Meyer, Hugo Dr.**
12/09/1877 Dramburg - transportation 1942
*Home address:* Meierottostr. 6, W 15,
Wilmersdorf
*Law firm address:* Leipziger Str. 110, W 8
*Additional information:* Attorney and notary;
after the National Socialist seizure of power
in 1933 he was readmitted; his license as
a notary was revoked in 1935; he was still
working as an attorney until the general
occupational ban in 1938. He was conscripted
for forced labor, last as a factory worker;
transportation on 09/05/1942 to Riga.
*Sources:* *li; LAB, Liste 10/15/1933; DJ 36, p.
315; Liste 36; MRRAK; BG; BdE; GB II

**Meyer, Julius Dr.**
03/01/1873 Berlin - transportation 1943
*Home address:* Schlüterstr. 45, W 15,
Charlottenburg
*Law firm address:* Kurfürstendamm 23 (and/
or 65), W 15
*Additional information:* Attorney and
notary; after the National Socialist seizure
of power in 1933 his license as a notary was
revoked, he was temporarily made subject
to an occupational ban; however, later he
was readmitted again, he worked until the
general occupational ban in 1938. 1943
transportation to Auschwitz.
*Sources:* Br.B. 32; Liste d. nichtzugel. RA,
04/25/1933; JMBl. 33, p. 208; *li; LAB, Liste
10/15/1933; Liste 36; MRRAK; BG; GB II

**Meyer, Julius Lyonel Dr.**
07/121901 - July 1968
*Home address:* no information
*Law firm address:* Frankfurter Allee 14, O 34
*Additional information:* After the National
Socialist seizure of power he was made subject
to a representation ban in April 1933, then an
occupational ban. He emigrated to the USA; he
applied for a scholarship there, his application

was rejected because the impression he made did not correspond to what the donors were looking for; he died in 1968.
*Sources:* TK 33; Liste d. nichtzugel. RA, 04/25/1933; JMBl. 33, p. 209; BArch, R 3001 PAK; NY Publ. Lib.(Am.Com.) Meyer, Julius L.; SSDI

**Meyer, Kurt Dr.**
09/04/1894 Stargard - no information
*Home address:* Zimmerstr. 3/4, SW 68
*Law firm address:* Zimmerstr. 3/4 SW 68
*Additional information:* Attorney and notary; after the National Socialist seizure of power in 1933 he was readmitted; his license as a notary was revoked in 1935; he was admitted to work as an attorney until 11/08/1937. He emigrated to London, Great Britain.
*Sources:* *li; LAB, Liste 10/15/1933; DJ 36, p. 315; Liste 36; BG

**Meyer, Leopold**
05/30/1873 Konitz - 02/25/1941
*Home address:* Waitzstr. 16, Charlottenburg
*Law firm address:* Waitzstr. 16, Charlottenburg
*Additional information:* Attorney and notary; after the National Socialist seizure of power in 1933 his license as a notary was revoked; he was still working as an attorney until the general occupational ban in 1938; he died in 1941 at the age of 67, he was buried at Weißensee.
*Sources:* Br.B. 32; JMBl. 33, p. 208; *li; LAB, Liste 10/15/1933; Liste 36; MRRAK; BG

**Meyer, Manfred Dr.**
11/29/1898 - no information
*Home address:* no information
*Law firm address:* Oranienstr. 61, S 42
*Additional information:* After the National Socialist seizure of power he was first made subject to a representation ban, then an occupational ban in early 1933.
*Sources:* Br.B. 32; Liste d. nichtzugel. RA, 05/24/1933; JMBl. 33, p. 234; BArch, R 3001 PAK

**Meyer, Max Dr., Judicial Councillor**
04/14/1863 Stavenhagen - 01/01/1943 Theresienstadt
*Home address:* Passauer Str. 8-9, W 50
*Law firm address:* Oranienstr. 61, S 42
*Additional information:* Attorney and notary; after the National Socialist seizure

of power in 1933 his license as a notary was revoked, he worked as an attorney until the general occupational ban in 1938. Date of declaration of property: 08/31/1942; collecting station Artilleriestr. 31; transportation on 09/14/1942 to Theresienstadt, he died there.
*Sources:* JMBl. 33, p. 208; *li; LAB, Liste 10/15/1933; Liste 36; MRRAK; BG; ThG; GB II

**Meyer, Michael Dr.**
ca. 1871 Blankenburg - 1956 Berlin
*Home address:* Niebuhrstr. 6, Charlottenburg
*Law firm address:* Niebuhrstr. 6, Charlottenburg
*Additional information:* He grew up in a traditional religious family in the Harz Mountains; he studied law after his high school examination. During his legal traineeship, a friend, Arthur Ruppin, introduced him to the ideas of Zionism. He established himself as an attorney in Berlin in 1909 and specialized in commercial, property and tenancy law; he was also appointed as a notary; he fought in the First World War. After the National Socialist seizure of power in 1933 his license as a notary was revoked; he was readmitted as an attorney, because he had been recognized as a "frontline fighter" and an "elderly attorney; he worked as an attorney until the general occupational ban in 1938; as from 1939 he worked as a volunteer at the Palestine Office in Berlin, which led to the emigration to Palestine. He arrived in Palestine in August 1940 with one of the last transports. He survived the explosion of the *Patria* in the harbor of Haifa; he became an official of the mandate government; as from 1952 he worked as a compensation attorney. He died on a business trip to Berlin and was buried in Israel.
*Sources:* TK 33; *li; LAB, Liste 10/15/1933; Liste 36; MRRAK; BG; Richarz, Monika: Jüdisches Leben in Deutschland [Jewish life in Germany], Stuttgart 1982, p. 367

**Meyer, Paul, Judicial Councillor**
No information
*Home address:* no information
*Law firm address:* Magdeburger Str. 34, W 35
*Additional information:* After the National Socialist seizure of power in 1993 he was readmitted, on 07/20/1937 his admission was "deleted upon request."
*Sources:* TK 33; *li; LAB, Liste 10/15/1933

**Meyer, Robert Dr.**
09/27/1884 Berlin - 11/25/1938
Sachsenhausen
*Home address:* Prager Platz 6, Wilmersdorf
*Law firm address:* Prager Platz 6,
Wilmersdorf
*Additional information:* Attorney and notary;
after the National Socialist seizure of power
in 1933 his license as a notary was revoked,
he still worked as an attorney until the general
occupational ban in 1938. He was arrested
in the mass arrest wave after the Night of the
Broken Glass in November 1938; he died in
the Sachsenhausen concentration camp.
*Sources:* JMBl. 33, p. 208; *li; LAB, Liste
10/15/1933; Liste 36; BArch, R 3001 PAK;
MRRAK; BG; GB Sachsenhausen; GB II

**Meyer, Siegfried Dr.**
01/17/1872 Bernburg - 09/19/1942
Theresienstadt
*Home address:* Leibnizstr. 73,
Charlottenburg; Münchener Str. 34,
Schöneberg
*Law firm address:* Grunewaldstr. 446,
Schöneberg
*Additional information:* Attorney and
notary; after the National Socialist seizure
of power in 1933 his license as a notary
was revoked, in 1936 he was still working
as an attorney. Date of declaration of
property: 07/08/1942; collecting station
Große Hamburger Str. 26; transportation on
07/16/1942 to Theresienstadt; he died there
two months later.
*Sources:* JMBl. 33, p. 208; *li; LAB, Liste
10/15/1933; Liste 36; BG; ThG; GB II

**Meyer, Werner Dr.**
07/31/1899 Delmenhorst - January 1979
*Home address:* no information
*Law firm address:* Hermannstr. 226,
Neukölln
*Additional information:* Attorney
(since 1929); after the National Socialist
seizure of power he was readmitted. After
emigration to the USA he established
himself in Harrisburg, Pennsylvania; he
applied for a scholarship with American
Committee, however, he withdrew the
application because he considered himself
only an "average attorney" and had already
exceeded the age limit for application.
From his application it becomes apparent

how urgently he would have needed the
scholarship. He died in 1979 at the age
of 79.
*Sources:* *li; LAB, Liste 10/15/1933; Liste
36; BArch, R 3001 PAK; NY Publ.Lib. (Am.
Com.) Meyer, Werner; SSDI

**Meyerheim, Rolf**
02/11/1902 - no information
*Home address:* no information
*Law firm address:* Hardenbergstr. 13,
Charlottenburg
*Additional information:* After the National
Socialist seizure of power he was made subject
to an occupational ban in early 1933.
*Sources:* Br.B. 32; Liste d. nichzugel. RA,
04/25/1933; JMBl. 33, p. 209; BArch,
R 3001 PAK

**Meyerstein, Eduard**
03/26/1871 Berlin - 07/06/1942 Jerusalem
*Home address:* no information
*Law firm address:* Wannseestr. 12,
Neubabelsberg
*Additional information:* He was the son
of the woman on whom the literary figure
"Jettchen Gebert" from the novel of Georg
Herrmann was based. He specialized in
commercial law, he was admitted at the KG
and was also a notary. Since 1908 he was
the legal counsel of the Berlin Chamber of
Industry and Commerce. After the National
Socialist seizure of power in 1933 his license
as a notary was revoked. Previously, the
Chamber of Industry and Commerce had
sent a "request" to Jewish notaries seeking
to "waive the right of admission as a notary
to avoid the discharge of public anger." This
was cancelled by the enforced dismissal.
He still worked as an attorney until the
general occupational ban in 1938. In an
anecdote it was reported that when a SA
man approached him in 1937 for a donation,
he replied that he could not give anything,
"since I am a Jew." The SA man replied:
"Anyone can claim that."
He emigrated to Palestine in December 1938.
His wife and children had already emigrated
there; he died in 1942 in Jerusalem.
*Sources:* JMBl. 33, p. 208; *li; Liste
36; MRRAK; BG; information Ruth U.
Liebstaedter; David Arad, conference 06/1999
and information 08/2006

**Meyners, Felix Dr., Judicial Councillor**
No information
*Home address:* no information
*Law firm address:* Pariser Str. 21/22, W 15
*Additional information:* Attorney and notary; after the National Socialist seizure of power in 1933 his license as a notary was revoked, he was still working as an attorney in 1936.
*Sources:* Br.B. 32; JMBl. 33, p. 208; *li; Liste 36

**Michaeli, Wilhelm Dr.**
03/10/1889 - no information
*Home address:* Johann-Sigismund-Str. 20, Wilmersdorf
*Law firm address:* Bellevuestr. 6a, W 9
*Additional information:* Attorney at the KG and notary; after the National Socialist seizure of power he was made subject to an occupational ban in 1933. He emigrated to Stockholm, Sweden, on 12/16/1933.
*Sources:* Adr.B. 33; TK 33; JMBl. 33, p. 203; BG

**Michaelis, Alfred Dr.**
11/23/1898 Neustettin - no information
*Home address:* Apostel-Paulus-Str. 26 (1929), Schöneberg
*Law firm address:* Kantstr. 49, Charlottenburg
*Additional information:* After the National Socialist seizure of power in April 1933 he was made subject to an occupational ban; later he was readmitted. He worked as an attorney until he was made subject to an occupational ban in 1938.
*Sources:* Liste d. nichtzugel. RA, 04/25/1933; *li; LAB, Liste 10/15/1933; Liste 36; BArch, R 3001 PAK; DJ 38, p. 1901; MRRAK; BG

**Michaelis, Alfred Dr.**
01/15/1903 - no information
*Home address:* no information
*Law firm address:* Wichmannstr. 28, W 62
*Additional information:* After the National Socialist seizure of power he was first made subject to a representation ban, then an occupational ban in early 1933. Emigration.
*Sources:* Liste d. nichtzugel. RA, 04/25/1933; JMBl. 33, p. 253; BArch, R 3001 PAK; information E. Proskauer

**Michaelis, Hans Dr.**
12/11/1875 Berlin - 08/12/1942
*Home address:* Joachim-Friedrich-Str. 43, Wilmersdorf
*Law firm address:* Kleine Präsidentenstr. 3, C 2

*Additional information:* Attorney and notary; after the National Socialist seizure of power in 1933 his license as a notary was revoked, he still worked as an attorney until the general occupational ban in 1938. He committed suicide in 1942 by poison in the face of imminent deportation.
*Sources:* JMBl. 33, p. 208; *li; LAB, Liste 10/15/1933; Liste 36; BArch, R 3001 PAK; MRRAK; BG; GB II; Göpp., p. 235

**Michaelis, Max Dr., Judicial Councillor**
10/23/1865 Meseritz - transportation 1942
*Home address:* Kantstr. 120-121, Charlottenburg
*Law firm address:* Jägerstr. 18, W 8
*Additional information:* Attorney and notary; after the National Socialist seizure of power in 1933 his license as a notary was revoked, he still worked as an attorney until the general occupational ban in 1938. Transportation on 07/30/1942 to Theresienstadt; from there he was transported on 09/26/1942 to Treblinka.
*Sources:* JMBl. 33, p. 208; *li; LAB, Liste 10/15/1933; Liste 36; MRRAK; BG; GB II

**Michaelis, Max**
10/08/1885 Berlin - transportation 1942
*Home address:* Pariser Str. 30/31, W 15
*Law firm address:* Pariser Str. 30/31, W 15
*Additional information:* Attorney at the KG and notary; after the National Socialist seizure of power he was readmitted; his license as a notary was revoked in 1935, he worked as an attorney until the general occupational ban in 1938, thereafter he worked as a "consultant." Date of declaration of property: 06/20/1942; transportation on 06/24-26/1942 to Minsk.
*Sources:* *li; LAB, Liste 04/14/1933; DJ 36, p. 315; Liste 36; MRRAK; Liste d. Kons. v. 10/15/1939; BG; GB II

**Michaelis, Paul**
10/22/1889 - no information
*Home address:* Magdeburger Str. 26, W 35
*Law firm address:* Kurfürstendamm 14/15, W 50
*Additional information:* After the National Socialist seizure of power he was made subject to an occupational ban in 1933. He emigrated to Palestine in June 1934.
*Sources:* Adr.B. 33; Liste d. nichtzugel. RA, 04/25/1933; JMBl. 33, p. 253; BG

**Michalski, Julius Dr.**
04/11/1890 - no information
*Home address:* Kurfürstendamm 23, W 15
*Law firm address:* Französische Str. 49, W 8
*Additional information:* Attorney and notary; after the National Socialist seizure of power he was readmitted; in 1935 his license as an attorney was revoked; he was still working as an attorney in 1936. He emigrated to South Africa on 05/16/1937.
*Sources:* *li; LAB, Liste 10/15/1933; DJ 36, p. 315; Liste 36; BArch, R 3001 PAK; BG

**Michel, Alfred Dr.**
07/18/1903 - 09/05/1933 Berlin
*Home address:* Lindenallee 25, Charlottenburg
*Law firm address:* Schlüterstr. 22/23, Charlottenburg
*Additional information:* After the National Socialist seizure of power he was made subject to an occupational ban in summer 1933; he died in September 1933 at the age of 30; he was buried at Weißensee.
*Sources:* JMBl. 07/28/1933, p. 234; BArch, R 3001 PAK; BG

**Michelsohn, Felix Dr.**
04/20/1878 Königsberg - no information
*Home address:* Levetzowstr. 13 a, NW 87
*Law firm address:* Friedrichstr. 65 a, W 8
*Additional information:* Attorney and notary; after the National Socialist seizure of power in 1933 he was readmitted; in 1935 his license as a notary was revoked; he worked as an attorney until the general occupational ban in 1938.
*Sources:* *li; LAB, Liste 10/15/1933; DJ 36, p. 315; Liste 36; MRRAK; BG

**Milchner, Erich Dr., Judicial Councillor**
No information - 1937
*Home address:* no information
*Law firm address:* Bahnhofstr. 5, Zossen
*Additional information:* Attorney and notary; after the National Socialist seizure of power in 1933 he was readmitted; his license as a notary was revoked at the latest at the end of 1933; until his death in 1937 he worked as an attorney.
*Sources:* *li; LAB, Liste 10/15/1933; Liste 36

**Miodowski, Martin**
08/23/1889 - no information
*Home address:* no information
*Law firm address:* Potsdamer Str. 123 a, W 35
*Additional information:* Attorney at the KG

and notary; after the National Socialist seizure of power in 1933 he was readmitted; his license as a notary was revoked in 1935; he worked as an attorney until the general occupational ban in 1938. His wife was regarded as non-Jewish; he emigrated to Australia in 1939.
*Sources:* *li; LAB, Liste 10/15/1933; DJ 36, p. 315; Liste 36; BArch, R 3001 PAK; MRRAK; BG

**Mittwoch, Felix Dr.**
1887 Schrimm - 1959 Haifa
*Home address:* no information
*Law firm address:* Mohrenstr. 16, W 8
*Additional information:* He was an active Zionist; attorney and notary; after the National Socialist seizure of power he was made subject to an occupational ban in 1933; thereafter he worked in the area of emigration counseling. 1938 emigration to the Netherlands; 1940 in Westerbork, later he was interned in Bergen-Belsen; he was freed in 1944 in the course of an exchange program to relocate to Palestine.
*Sources:* Br.B. 32; Liste d. nichtzugel. RA, 04/25/1933; JMBl. 33, p. 209; Walk, p. 269

**Moral, Reinhard Dr.**
07/05/1894 Berlin - 04/30/1958 Berlin
*Home address:* Schmargendorfer Str. 12, Friedenau
*Law firm address:* Schmargendorfer Str. 12, Friedenau
*Additional information:* He was Protestant, he fought in the First World War; he was an attorney and notary. After the National Socialist seizure of power he was regarded as "mixed race first degree" (his father was a Jew). Formally, he was allowed to exercise his activities as an attorney and notary until the end of the war, but the mandates and revenues were already significantly reduced from 1933. Therefore, he tried i.a. to secure a living with legal revisions. In 1935 this activity was forbidden by the Gestapo. He then advised Jewish emigrants. In 1944 he was conscripted by the Todt organization, which was not possible because of his poor health. Nevertheless, he was used for construction and sewerage work. After the end of the Nazi regime he was again admitted as an attorney and notary. He acquired a high reputation in the city and founded the Association of Berlin Defense Attorneys.
*Sources:* *li; LAB, Liste 10/15/1933; Tel.B. 41; Verz. zugel. Anw. 45; LAB, RAK, PA; BG

**Morgenroth, Max Dr.**
No information
*Home address:* no information
*Law firm address:* Burgstr. 26, C 2
*Additional information:* After the National
Socialist seizure of power he was readmitted,
he was still working as an attorney until the
general occupational ban in 1938.
*Sources:* *li; LAB, Liste 10/15/1933; Liste 36;
MRRAK

**Mosczytz, Siegfried**
10/01/1899 Berlin - no information
*Home address:* Landsberger Str. 59, C 25
*Law firm address:* Potsdamer Str. 32 a, W 35
*Additional information:* Attorney (since
1930); after the National Socialist seizure of
power he was made subject to an occupational
ban in summer 1933. Emigration.
*Sources:* Jüd.Adr.B.; LAB, Liste nichtzugel.
RA, 04/25/1933; JMBl. 07/28/1933, p. 234;
BArch, R 3001 PAK; BG; information
Werner Wolff

**Moser, Franz Dr.**
06/16/1899 - July 1959
*Home address:* Mauerstr. 80, W 8
*Law firm address:* Mauerstr. 80, W 8
*Additional information:* After the National
Socialist seizure of power he was readmitted;
he was still working as an attorney until
the general occupational ban in 1938. He
emigrated to the USA, he changed his first
name to Frank.
*Sources:* *li; LAB, Liste 10/15/1933; Liste 36;
MRRAK; BArch, R 3001, PAK, PA; SSDI

**Moser, Werner Dr.**
10/21/1879 Neustadt at Danzig - no
information
*Home address:* Achenbachstr. 6, W 50
*Law firm address:* Ludwigkirchplatz 2, W 15
*Additional information:* He was a Protestant,
attorney and notary. After the National
Socialist seizure of power he was readmitted.
He emigrated to Zurich, Switzerland, on
05/30/1938.
*Sources:* *li; LAB, Liste 10/15/1933;
Liste 36; BG

**Moses, Fritz Dr.**
09/02/1897 Berlin - no information
*Home address:* Holsteiner Ufer 11, NW 87
*Law firm address:* Klosterstr. 70, C

*Additional information:* He was an attorney,
from 1925 to 02/25/1933 he was admitted
at the AG Berlin-Mitte and the LG I-III; he
was disbarred because of a move to Belgard
(Pomerania); he was briefly admitted there as
an attorney. Later he emigrated to Palestine.
*Sources:* Br.B. 32; JMBl. 10.3.33; BArch, R
3001 PAK; BG

**Moses, Gustav Dr.**
12/24/1871 Witkowo - 02/08/1944
Theresienstadt
*Home address:* Krausnickstr. 18, Mitte
*Law firm address:* Friedrichstr. 131, N 24
*Additional information:* Attorney and notary;
after the National Socialist seizure of power
in 1933 he was readmitted; 1935 his license
as a notary was revoked; he still worked as an
attorney until the general occupational ban
in 1938. Transportation to Theresienstadt on
01/13/1943, he died there a year later.
*Sources:* *li; LAB, Liste 10/15/1933; DJ 36, p.
315; Liste 36; MRRAK; BG; ThG; GB II

**Moses, Siegfried Dr.**
05/03/1887 Lautenburg -
01/14/1974 Tel Aviv
*Home address:* no
information
*Law firm address:*
Kurfürstendamm 234, W 50
*Additional information:*
Attorney at the KG; he supported Zionism
since his youth; 1931-36 he was a member
of the representative assembly of the Jewish
Synagogue Berlin. After the National Socialist
seizure of power in 1933 his license as a
notary was revoked. 1933-37 he was chairman
of the Zionist Association for Germany, also
vice president of the Reich Representation. He
gave up his job in 1936 in the face of steadily
declining revenue and decided in September
1937 to emigrate to Palestine. There he
established himself in Tel Aviv. The house,
in which two other Berlin attorneys lived,
had been designed by a Bauhaus architect.
1937-38 he was a managing director of the
Havaara transfer agreement; 1939-49 he
was a public auditor, auditor and income tax
specialist. Even during the war, he thought
about the legal clarification of the claims of
the Jews against the German state. He later
became head of the Israeli Court of Auditors.
He was chairman of the Council of Jews

from Germany and the Leo Baeck Institute in 1956-74.
*Sources:* JMBl. 33, p. 208; *li; LAB, Liste 10/15/1933; Liste 36; BHdE vol. 1, p. 509; Göpp., p. 304; information Dr. G. Meyer; Tramer, H.: In zwei Welten. Siegfried Moses zum 75. Geburtstag [In two worlds. Siegfried Moses on his 75th birthday], Tel Aviv 1962

**Moses, Wilhelm**
03/01/1882 - after 1946
*Home address:* Kottbusser Damm 76 (1929), Neukölln
*Law firm address:* Kottbusser Damm 24, S 59
*Additional information:* Attorney and notary; after the National Socialist seizure of power he was readmitted in 1933; his license as a notary was revoked in 1935; disbarment as an attorney upon emigration to the Netherlands on 01/01/1938. His wife was regarded as non-Jewish. He lived in 1946 in Amsterdam.
*Sources:* *li; LAB, Liste 10/15/1933; DJ 36, p. 315; Liste 36; BG

**Mosheim, Rudolf Dr.**
04/28/1889 - no information
*Home address:* no information
*Law firm address:* Behrenstr. 35/37, W 8
*Additional information:* After the National Socialist seizure of power he was readmitted, he was still working as an attorney until the general occupational ban in 1938.
*Sources:* *li; LAB, Liste 10/15/1933; Liste 36; BArch, R 3001 PAK; MRRAK

**Mosler, Alfred Dr.**
02/05/1883 Gleiwitz - July 1963
*Home address:* Leistikowstr. 2, Charlottenburg
*Law firm address:* Schinkelplatz 1/4, W 56
*Additional information:* After the National Socialist seizure of power he was readmitted, he was still working as an attorney until the general occupational ban in 1938. He emigrated to Great Britain in March 1939, later to Beverly Hills, USA.
*Sources:* *li; LAB, Liste 10/15/1933; Liste 36; MRRAK; BG; SSDI

**Mosse, Walter**
09/26/1886 - October 1973
*Home address:* no information
*Law firm address:* Siegmundstr. 6, W 10

*Additional information:* After the National Socialist seizure of power he was made subject to an occupational ban in early 1933. He emigrated to the USA; he last lived in New York.
*Sources:* Br.B. 32; Liste d. nichtzugel. RA, 04/25/1933; JMBl. 33, p. 209; BArch, R 3001 PAK; SSDI

**Moszkowski, Richard Dr.**
105/10/1885 Berlin - 1959 Chicago
*Home address:* Caspar-Theyss-Str. 5, Grune-wald
*Law firm address:* Französische Str. 55/56, W 8
*Additional information:* Attorney at the KG; since 1920 he was simultaneously an advisor and appraiser of the Reichskreditgesellschaft. After the National Socialist seizure of power he was readmitted, he worked as an attorney until the general occupational ban in 1938. He emigrated to the USA; he applied for a scholarship in 1940; he was presumably rejected. He died in 1959 at the age of 74.
*Sources:* TK 33; *li; LAB, Liste 10/15/1933; Liste 36; MRRAK; BG; BHdE 1933 vol. 2,2, p. 836 (Steven A. Moszkowski); NY Publ.Lib. (Am.Com.)

**Mühsam-Werther, Georg Dr., Judicial Councillor**
No informaton - 1936
*Home address:* no information
*Law firm address:* Dorotheenstr. 42, NW 7
*Additional information:* Attorney and notary; after the National Socialist seizure of power in 1933 he was readmitted; his license as a notary was revoked in 1935; he presumably worked as an attorney until his death in 1936.
*Sources:* *li; LAB, Liste 10/15/1933; DJ 36, p. 315; Liste 36

**Müller, Georg Dr.**
05/06/1885 Berlinchen - no information
*Home address:* Neue Ansbacher Str. 7a, Schöneberg
*Law firm address:* Neue Ansbacher Str. 7a, W 50
*Additional information:* Attorney at the KG; after the National Socialist seizure of power in 1933 he was readmitted. He emigrated to New York, USA.
*Sources:* *li; LAB, Liste 10/15/1933; BG

**Müller, Johannes Dr.**
11/06/1893 Berlin - no information
*Home address:* Waltraudstr. 27, Zehlendorf
*Law firm address:* Waltraudstr. 27,
Zehlendorf
*Additional information:* After the National
Socialist seizure of power in 1933 he was
readmitted. 1934 he emigrated to Neuilly-
sur-Seine, France. An arrest warrant for tax
code violations was issued against him. His
wife Edith was transported from France and
murdered in Auschwitz.
*Sources:* *li; LAB, Liste 10/15/1933; BArch, R
3001 PAK; BG; Wolf, BFS

**Müller, Josef Dr.**
09/18/1881 Nuremberg - 10/09/1934
*Home address:* Brandenburgische Str. 28,
W 15
*Law firm address:* Potsdamer Str. 134 a, W 9
*Additional information:* After the National
Socialist seizure of power his license as a
notary was revoked, he gave up his law firm.
He died in October 1934 at the age of 53.
*Sources:* Br.B. 32; Pr.J. 33, p. 466; LAB, Liste
10/15/1933

**Müller, Siegbert Dr.**
07/11/1895 Hirschberg - October 1975
*Home address:* Kurfürstendamm 184, W 15
*Law firm address:* Kurfürstendamm 184,
W 15
*Additional information:* Attorney at the
KG and notary; after the National Socialist
seizure of power in April 1933 he was made
subject to a representation ban; subsequently
he was readmitted; his license as a notary
was revoked in 1935; he worked until the
general occupational ban in 1938, thereafter
he worked as a "consultant," he was pictured
as such in a case of foreign exchange offense
in the "Volkischer Beobachter" (01/28/1939).
He emigrated to Baltimore, USA, on
11/22/1939. His abandoned property
was auctioned. He last lived in Queens,
New York.
TK 33; Liste d. nichtzugel. RA, 04/25/1933;
*Sources:* *li; LAB, Liste 10/15/1933; DJ 36, p.
315; Liste 36; VB 01/28/1939; MRRAK; BG;
Information Grischa Worner, 11/20/2000;;
SSDI (Bert Muller); information Grischa
Worner, 11/00

**Munk, Richard Dr.**
12/04/1881 Posen - no information
*Home address:* Schorlemerallee 19,
Zehlendorf
*Law firm address:* Friedrich-Ebert-Str. 7, W 9
*Additional information:* He was still a
board member of the RAK in 1932. After
the National Socialist seizure of power in
1933 his license as a notary was revoked,
he worked as an attorney until the general
occupational ban in 1938. He emigrated to
Chile on 06/14/1939.
*Sources:* TK 33; JMBl. 33, p. 208; *li; LAB,
Liste 10/15/1933; Liste 36; MRRAK; BG

**Munk, Walter Dr.**
12/29/1873 Berlin - no information
*Home address:* Viktoria-Luise-Platz 9,
Schöneberg
*Law firm address:* Taubenstr. 8/9, W 8
*Additional information:* After the National
Socialist seizure of power he was readmitted.
He emigrated to Haifa, Palestine, on
01/12/1939, he was disbarred at the same time.
*Sources:* *li; Liste 36; BG

**Munter, Hans Dr.**
01/08/1902 - March 1956
*Home address:* no information
*Law firm address:* Alexanderstr. 38, C 25
*Additional information:* Attorney; close
cooperation with Dr. Siegfried Benjamin and
Martin Freund. After the National Socialist
seizure of power he was made subject to an
occupational ban in early 1933. He emigrated
to the USA, he died there at the age of 54.
*Sources:* Br.B. 32, Liste d. nichtzugel. RA,
04/25/1933; JMBl. 33, p. 209; BArch, R
3001, PAK; SSDI

**Münz, Josef Dr.**
12/19/1876 Kempen - no information
*Home address:* Dahlmannstr. 13,
Charlottenburg
*Law firm address:* Schlüterstr. 39,
Charlottenburg
Attorney and notary; after the National
Socialist seizure of power in 1933 his license
as a notary was revoked, he was still working
as an attorney until the general occupational
ban in 1938. He emigrated to Jerusalem,
Palestine, on 12/06/1938.
*Sources:* JMBl. 33, p. 208; *li; LAB, Liste
10/15/1933; Liste 36; MRRAK; BG

**Münzer, Felix Dr.**
11/13/1868 Tschepplau - no information
*Home address:* Bleibtreustr. 24,
Charlottenburg
*Law firm address:* Meinekestr. 21, W 15
*Additional information:* Attorney and
notary; after the National Socialist seizure
of power in 1933 his license as a notary was
revoked, he was disbarred as an attorney
on 11/05/1937. He emigrated to Pasadena,
California, USA.
*Sources:* JMBl. 33, p. 208; *li; LAB, Liste
10/15/1933; Liste 36; BG

**Münzer, Hans**
05/10/1901 - no information
*Home address:* no information
*Law firm address:* Tauentzienstr. 9, W 50
*Additional information:* Attorney at the
KG; after the National Socialist seizure of
power he was disbarred on 06/09/1933. He
still worked as an attorney in Beuthen (Upper
Silesia) until 1937. He survived and was again
admitted as an attorney in Berlin in 1947.
*Sources:* Liste d. nichtzugel. RA, 04/25/1933;
JMBl. 33, p. 203; BArch, R 3001 PAK; Verz.
zugel. Anw. 45; LAB, RAK, PA Werthauer

# N

**Nachum, Gerhard**
09/30/1904 - 02/04/1943 Auschwitz
*Home address:* Bayernallee 19, Charlottenburg
*Law firm address:* Potsdamer Str. 106, W 35
*Additional information:* After the National
Socialist seizure of power he was made subject
to an occupational ban in early 1933; he then
worked as a metal dealer for the company
Schlesinger & Nachum. On 01/12/1943 he
was transported to Auschwitz, where he was
murdered three weeks after arrival.
*Sources:* Br.B. 32; Liste d. nichtzugel. RA,
04/25/1933; JMBl. 08/21/1933, p. 267;
BArch, R 3001 PAK; BG; GB II

**Nagel, Karl Heinz Dr.**
10/17/1904 Berlin - no information
*Home address:* Neue Königstr. 70, Mitte
*Law firm address:* Kleiststr. 15, W 62
*Additional information:* After the National
Socialist seizure of power he was made subject
to an occupational ban in early 1933. He
emigrated to Palestine in August 1933.

*Sources:* Liste nichtzugel. RA, 04/25/1933;
JMBl. 08/04/1933, p. 253; BArch, R 3001
PAK; LAB; BG

**Narewczewitz, Albert Dr.**
12/22/1894 Eschwege - transportation 1943
*Home address:* Innsbrucker Str. 1, Schöneberg
*Law firm address:* Friedrichstr. 49 a, GW 68
*Additional information:* After the National
Socialist seizure of power in 1933 he was
readmitted; he worked as an attorney until
the general occupational ban in 1938; he last
worked at the Reich Association of Jews in
Germany. Transportation to Auschwitz on
03/12/1943.
*Sources:* *li; LAB, Liste 10/15/1933; Liste 36;
BArch, R 3001 PAK; MRRAK; BG; GB II

**Nast, Leo Dr.**
10/18/1879 Marienburg - 02/21/1943
Theresienstadt
*Home address:* Meinekestr. 26, W 15
*Law firm address:* Suarezstr. 5,
Charlottenburg
*Additional information:* Attorney and
notary; after the National Socialist seizure of
power in 1933 he was readmitted; his license
as a notary was revoked in 1935; he worked
as an attorney until the general occupational
ban in 1938; later he was employed at the
Jewish Culture Administration. Collecting
station Gerlachstr. 18-21; transportation to
Theresienstadt on 11/20/1942, he died there
there two months later.
*Sources:* *li; LAB, Liste 10/15/1933; DJ 36, p.
315; Liste 36; MRRAK; BG; ThG; GB II

**Nathansohn, Bruno Dr.**
12/11/1891 Berlin - 10/29/1942 Riga
*Home address:* Rykestr. 10, NO 55
*Law firm address:* Zimmerstr. 79/80, SW 68
*Additional information:* Attorney and
notary; after the National Socialist seizure
of power he was made subject to an
occupational ban in early 1933; he was
last employed in the Jewish hospital as a
forced laborer. Transportation to Riga on
10/26/1942; he was murdered there on the
day of his arrival.
*Sources:* Br.B. 32; Liste d. nichtzugel. RA,
04/25/1933; JMBl. 08/21/1933, p. 267; BG;
BdE; GB II

**Nauenberg, Hans Dr.**
01/27/1894 Berlin - no information
*Home address:* Sybelstr. 11, Charlottenburg
*Law firm address:* Grolmanstr. 51,
Charlottenburg
*Additional information:* Attorney and
notary; after the National Socialist seizure of
power in 1933 he was readmitted; his license
as a notary was revoked in 1935; he worked
as an attorney until the general occupational
ban in 1938. He emigrated to Argentina.
*Sources:* *li; LAB, Liste 10/15/1933; DJ 36, p.
315; Liste 36; MRRAK; BG

**Naumann, Alfred Dr., Judicial Councillor**
04/21/1865 - 07/11/1938
*Home address:* Prinzregentenstr. 91,
Wilmersdorf
*Law firm address:* Lessingstr. 50, NW 87
*Additional information:* Attorney and
notary; after the National Socialist seizure
of power in 1933 his license as a notary was
revoked; he was still working as an attorney
in 1936; he died in 1938 at the age of 73; he
was buried at Weißensee.
*Sources:* Br.B. 32; Pr.J. 33, p. 390; *li; LAB,
Liste 10/15/1933; Liste 36; BG: LAB, OFP
files; Friedh.W.Sterbereg.

**Naumann, Max Dr.**
01/12/1875 Berlin - 1939 Berlin
*Home address:* no information
*Law firm address:* Französische Str., W 8
*Additional information:* He fought in the
First World War, he held the rank of major,
he was awarded with the EK 1st Kl. for his
special achievements; he was co-founder of the
Association of National German Jews, from
1921 he was the president of the association
(until its ban in 1935); he was a member of the
Reformed Jewish Synagogue Berlin. He was
an attorney and notary; after the National
Socialist seizure of power in 1933 he was
readmitted, since he had been recognized as
a "frontline fighter;" in 1935 his license as a
notary was revoked; he was admitted as an
attorney until the general occupational ban in
1938; he was temporarily imprisoned in 1935;
He died in 1939 at the age of 64.
*Publications:* Publisher of the journal
"Der nationaldeutsche Jude" [The national
German Jew];
*Sources:* *li; DJ 36, p. 315; Liste 36;
MRRAK; BG; Göpp., p. 227; Krach,

p. 434; SLW: Freiheit und Bindung, p. 163-
166, 182

**Neimann, Kurt Dr.**
12/28/1877 Neidenburg - 03/12/1944
Theresienstadt
*Home address:* Parkstr. 22, Weißensee
*Law firm address:* Wilmersdorfer Str.
143/144, Charlottenburg
*Additional information:* Attorney and
notary; after the National Socialist seizure
of power in 1933 his license as a notary
was revoked; he was still working as an
attorney until the general occupational ban
in 1938. Transportation to Theresienstadt on
09/14/1942, he died there in March 1944. .
*Sources:* JMBl. 33, p. 220; *li; LAB, Liste
10/15/1933; Liste 36; MRRAK; BG; ThG
(Neumann); GB II

**Nelson, Erich Dr.**
03/26/1881 Berlin - 08/16/1961 Berlin
*Home address:* Meraner Str. 19, Schöneberg
*Law firm address:* Lützowstr. 82, W 35
*Additional information:* Attorney (since
1911) and notary (since 1921); he was a
specialist in traffic law, in particular liability,
hereto he had numerous publications; from
1930-1933 he was a member of the board
of the Berlin Bar Association and chairman
of the Conciliation Committee. He had
revenues of RM 30-40,000 p.a., which were
due to large mandates for Reichskredit AG
and other banks and insurance companies.
After the National Socialist seizure of power
in 1933 his license as a notary was revoked;
he worked as an attorney until the general
occupational ban in 1938, thereafter the
worked for three months as a "consultant."
In 1939, revenues had fallen to a third of that
of 1933.
After the Night of the Broken Glass he was
arrested on 11/11/1938 and taken to the
Sachsenhausen concentration camp near
Oranienburg. When he was released in
December 1938, he had to sign a letter of
commitment to emigrate. A Protestant, he
went with his wife, who was non-Jewish,
to London, Great Britain. There he studied
English civil law and prepared for the
Bachelor of Law examination. In 1946 he
returned to Germany and was again admitted
as an attorney. In the meantime, he had
worked for the British military government.

Sources: JMBl. 33, p. 208; *li; LAB, Liste 10/15/1933; Liste 36; MRRAK; BG; LAB, RAK PA

**Nesselroth, Fritz Dr.**
07/01/1895 - no information
*Home address:* Luitpoldstr. 23, Schöneberg
*Law firm address:* Hardenbergstr. 24, Charlottenburg
*Additional information:* Attorney and notary; after the National Socialist seizure of power in 1933 he was readmitted; his license as a notary was revoked in 1935; he was still working as an attorney in 1936; he presumably emigrated.
*Sources:* Br.B. 32; *li; DJ 36, p. 315; Liste 36; BG

**Netter, Oscar Dr.**
05/11/1878 - 1937 Palestine
*Home address:* Freiherr-vom-Stein-Str. 10, Schöneberg
*Law firm address:* Kronenstr. 64/65, W 8
*Additional information:* Attorney and notary, he specialized in commercial and antitrust law. After the National Socialist seizure of power in 1933 his license as a notary was revoked, he was still admitted as an attorney until 04/22/1936. He emigrated to Jerusalem, Palestine, he died there at the age of 69.
*Sources:* JMBl. 33, p. 220 (Oskar N.); *li; LAB, Liste 10/15/1933; Adr.B. 34; Liste 36; BG

**Neulaender, Robert Dr.**
10/24/1889 Berlin - no information
*Home address:* Düsseldorfer Str. 58 a, Wilmersdorf
*Law firm address:* Kleiststr. 42, W 62
*Additional information:* After the National Socialist seizure of power in 1933, he was readmitted; he worked as an attorney until the general occupational ban in 1938 (he was one of those for whom the National Socialists in 1938 only with difficulty managed to use the term "Jew"). He presumably emigrated.
*Sources:* *li; LAB, Liste 10/15/1933; Liste 36; letter of the Reich Ministry of Justice to the President of the Court of Appeals in Berlin, see BArch, R 3001/62210, p. 30; MRRAK; BG

**Neumann, Franz Leopold Dr. Ph.D.**
05/23/1900 Kattowitz - 09/02/1954 Visp, Switzerland
*Home address:* Dernburgstr. 32, Charlottenburg
*Law firm address:* Alte Jakobstr. 155
*Additional information:* He had mainly studied in Frankfurt a. M.; he was a member of a circle of socialist students there; he was mentored by Prof. Hugo Sinzheimer and the main focus of his studies were on labor law; he was a member of the SPD; an attorney in Berlin (since 1927), law partner of Ernst Fraenkel; he was at the same time adviser to various German trade unions and lecturer at the Deutsche Hochschule für Politik. After the National Socialist seizure of power he was first made subject to a representation ban, then an occupational ban in early 1933; the office was located in the metalworkers' union building and was stormed by SA troops at the beginning of May; he fled in May 1933 to London, Great Britain; there he obtained a second doctorate on 05/25/1936, this time at the London School of Economics and Political Science with the dissertation "The Governance of the Rule of Law;" in 1936 he went to New York, USA; there he was a member of the International Institute of Social Research. He dealt with National Socialism from a political point of view, the result of this research was the book entitled "Behemoth," which was published in 1942. From 1942-1945 he worked at the Office of Strategic Services (OSS); here he was assigned to the Research & Analysis Branch. In 1948 the complete change to political science occurred: he was at first a visiting professor, then in 1950 a Full Professor of Public Law and Government at Columbia University. In this capacity he also became the teacher of the young Raul Hilberg ["Die Vernichtung der europäischen Juden. Die Gesamtgeschichte des Holocaust" (The annihilation of European Jews. The comprehensive history of the Holocaust)]. He maintained contact with Germany and was instrumental in the establishment of the Free University of Berlin and the development of the independent discipline of political science; in 1954 he died in a car accident.

*Publications:* "Behemoth. Struktur und Praxis des Nationalsozialismus 1933-1944" [Behemoth. Structure and practice of national socialism], New York, 1944; "Die Grundrechte, Handbuch der Theorie und Praxis" [The fundamental rights, handbook of theory and practice]; 1954; "Wirtschaft, Staat, Demokratie. Aufsätze 1930-1954" [Economy, state, democracy. Essays 1930-1954]. Frankfurt a. M.1978.
*Sources:* Adr.B. 33; Liste d. nichtzugel. RA, 04/25/1933; LAB, Liste 10/15/1933; NY Pub. Lib. (Am.Com.) Neumann, F.; BG: BHdE vol. 2,2, p. 856; Söllner, Alfons: Franz L. Neumann – "Skizzen zu einer intellektuellen und politischen Biographie" [Sketches for an intellectual and political biography], in: Franz L. Neumann: "Wirtschaft, Staat, Demokratie, Aufsätze 1930-1954" [Economy, state, democracy, essays 1930-1954, Frankfurt a. M 1978; Raul Hilberg/Alfons Söllner: "Das Schweigen zum Sprechen bringen" [Make the silence speak] contribution in: Diner, Dan (publisher): "Zivilisationsbruch. Denken nach Auschwitz" [Breach of civilization. Thinking about Auschwitz], Frankfurt a. M. 1988, pages 175-200; Göpp. p. 354

**Neumann, Fritz Simon Dr.**
09/08/1891 Berlin - 03/04/1965 Tel Aviv
*Home address:* Wissmannstr. 21
*Law firm address:* Wissmannstr. 21
*Additional information:* After the National Socialist seizure of power in 1933 he was readmitted, on 08/03/1936 he was disbarred. He emigrated to Palestine.
*Sources:* Adr.B. 33; *li; LAB, Liste 10/15/1933; Liste 36

**Neumann, Georg, Judicial Councillor**
No information
*Home address:* no information
*Law firm address:* Charlottenstr. 86, SW 68
*Additional information:* After the National Socialist seizure of power his licenses as an attorney and notary were revoked.
*Sources:* Adr.B. 33; TK 33; JMBl. 33, 06/17/1933, pages 184/5

**Neumann, Heinrich Dr.**
No information
*Home address:* no information
*Law firm address:* Burggrafenstr. 3, Schöneberg
*Additional information:* Attorney and notary; after the National Socialist seizure

of power in 1933 his license as a notary was revoked. On 11/30/1935 his membership to the bar was removed upon request.
*Sources:* *li; JMBl. 33, p. 220; LAB, Liste 10/15/1933; BG

**Neumann, Kurt**
04/14/1888 - no information
*Home address:* no information
Genthiner Str. 29, W 35
*Additional information:* He was at first admitted as an attorney in Königsberg, he moved to Berlin, on 03/17/1932 he was admitted as an attorney in Berlin; after the National Socialist seizure of power in 1911 he was made subject to an occupational ban.
*Sources:* Adr.B. 33; JMBl. 33, 06/17/1933, p. 184; BArch, R 3001 PAK

**Neumann, Oskar Dr.**
09/06/1889 Hamburg - transportation 1944
*Home address:* Clausewitzstr. 5, Charlottenburg
*Law firm address:* Königin-Augusta-Str. 7, W 9
*Additional information:* He was a Catholic. He was an attorney at the KG; after the National Socialist seizure of power in 1933 he was readmitted; he was still working as an attorney until the general occupational ban in 1938; he was a member of the Reich Association of Non-Aryan Christians. Transportation on 08/10/1944 to Auschwitz.
*Sources:* *li; LAB, Liste 10/15/1933; Liste 36; Mitt.bl. Reichsverband nichtarischer Christen, 12/06/1934; MRRAK; BG; GB II

**Neumann, Rudolf**
07/03/1904 Berlin - 10/09/1975 New York
*Home address:* no information
*Law firm address:* Augsburger Str. 46, W 50
*Additional information:* 1923-26 he completed his studies in Berlin; 1927 he received his doctorate in Leipzig; 1927-33 he was an assistant at the Berlin University; he was an attorney at the KG, at the same time a business consultant; he worked closely with his wife Eva. After the National Socialist seizure of power he was made subject to an occupational ban in early 1933; he emigrated in 1933 together with his wife to Switzerland via the Netherlands. In 1939 the couple went to the USA. He changed his name to Randolph Henry Newman. 1939-44 he was an economic consultant, after another legal examination he was readmitted

as an attorney; 1946-48 he was a prosecutor for the U.S. War Department at the Nuremberg war crimes trial; 1950-53 he was at the US High Command in Germany as head of the IG Farben control office; he then practiced as an attorney in New York; he was a specialist for reparation affairs.
*Sources:* Liste d. nichtzugel. RA, 04/25/1933; BG; BHdE vol. 1, p. 532; SSDI; information Dr.Y. Arndt.

**Noah, Albert, Judicial Councillor**
01/28/1863 Moschin - 08/06/1942
*Home address:* Weinmeisterstr. 1, C 54
*Law firm address:* Weinmeisterstr. 1, C 54
*Additional information:* Law partner of Hans, presumably his father; after the National Socialist seizure of power in 1933 his license as a notary was revoked, he worked as an attorney until the general occupational ban in 1938. Albert died in 1942 at the age of 79, he was buried at Weißensee.
*Sources:* JMBl. 33, p. 220; *li; LAB, Liste 10/15/1933; Liste 36; MRRAK; BG

**Noah, Hans Dr.**
04/17/1899 - no information
*Home address:* no information
*Law firm address:* Weinmeisterstr. 1, N 54
*Additional information:* Law partner of Albert (presumably his son); attorney at the KG; after the National Socialist seizure of power he was readmitted, he was still working as an attorney until the general occupational ban in 1938.
*Sources:* Br.B. 32; *li; LAB, Liste 10/15/1933; Liste 36; BArch, R 3001 PAK, PA; MRRAK

**Norden, Erich Dr.**
04/27/1899 - March 1979 New York
*Home address:* no information
*Law firm address:* Potsdamer Str. 96, W 57
*Additional information:* Attorney since 1925, previously during his legal internship i.a in a law office with Fliess. After the National Socialist seizure of power in 1933 he was readmitted, on 09/09/1936 he emigrated to the USA, at the same time he was disbarred. He last lived in Queens, New York.
*Sources:* *li; LAB, Liste 10/15/1933; Liste

36; BArch, R 3001 PA; Naatz-Album; SSDI; information Dorothee Fliess, 01/03/1999

**Nothmann, Rudolf**
05/23/1891 Berlin - no information
*Home address:* Bismarckstr. 97-99, Charlottenburg
*Law firm address:* Wilhelmstr. 44, W 8
*Additional information:* Attorney and notary; after the National Socialist seizure of power in 1933 he was readmitted; his license as a notary was revoked in 1935; he was still working as an attorney until the general occupational ban in 1938. He emigrated to French Indochina, on 01/24/1939; later presumably to Palestine.
*Sources:* *li; LAB, Liste 10/15/1933; DJ 36, p. 315; Liste 36; MRRAK; BG

**Nürnberg, Herbert Dr.**
07/31/1896 Berlin - March 1983
*Home address:* Turmstr. 6, NW 21
*Law firm address:* Turmstr. 6, NW 21
*Additional information:* After the National Socialist seizure of power in 1933 he was readmitted, in 1936 he was still working as an attorney. He emigrated to the USA on 07/01/1938; he changed his name to Nurnberg, he last lived in New York.
*Sources:* *li; LAB, Liste 10/15/1933; Liste 36; BArch, R 3001 PAK; SSDI; BG

**Nussbaum, Arthur Dr.**
01/31/1877 Berlin - 11/22/1964 New York
*Home address:* no information
*Law firm address:* Lützowufer 24, W 62
*Additional information:* As from 1904 he was an attorney, admitted to the KG; as from 1914 he was a lecturer at the Berlin University; he was an official of the CV. After the National Socialist seizure of power in 1933 he was readmitted as an attorney, he was dismissed as university lecturer. 1934 he emigrated to New York, USA; he took up a professorship at Columbia University (until 1950); he was a specialist in international private law and came out with numerous publications that also linked legal and economic aspects; he died in 1964 at the age of 86 in New York.
*Publications i.a.:* "Deutsches internationales Privatrecht" [German international private law], 1932; "Money in the law," 1939; "Principles of private international law,"1942; "Concise history of the law of nations," 1947

*Sources:* *li; LAB, Liste 10/15/1933; Liste 36; BG; BHdE vol. 2,2, p. 869; NY Publ. Lib. (Am.Com.) Kurt Jacobsohn

**Nußbaum, Julius Dr.**
11/20/1874 Berlin - no information
*Home address:* Kaiserallee 26, Wilmersdorf
*Law firm address:* Kaiserallee 26, Wilmersdorf
*Additional information:* Attorney at the KG and notary; after the National Socialist seizure of power in 1933 his license as a notary was revoked, he was still working as an attorney until the general occupational ban in 1938. He emigrated to Stockholm, Sweden, on 09/02/1938.
*Sources:* JMBl. 33, p. 220; *li; LAB, Liste 10/15/1933; Liste 36; MRRAK; BG; information E. Proskauer

# O

**Oborniker, Alfred**
11/25/1885 - 05/07/1936
*Home address:* Duisburger Str. 59, Wilmersdorf
*Law firm address:* Oranienburger Str. 59, N 24
*Additional information:* Attorney at the KG and notary, he also managed mandates in the legal protection order of "Rote Hilfe." After the National Socialist seizure of power in 1933 he was readmitted; his license as a notary was revoked in 1935; he still worked as an attorney until his death in 1936; he died in 1936 at the age of 51; he was buried at Weißensee.
*Sources:* *li; LAB, Liste 10/15/1933; DJ 36, p. 315; Liste 36; BG; Göpp., p. 370; Schneider, Schwarz, Schwarz, p. 227

**Oettinger, Ernst Dr.**
12/08/1881 Marienwerder - 12/03/1953 Berlin
*Home address:* Wehlauer Str. 3, NO 55
*Law firm address:* Rheinstr. 6/7, Friedenau
*Additional information:* He was a Protestant; attorney (since 1912) and notary (since 1919); supporter of the DVP. After the National Socialist seizure of power in 1933 he was readmitted; in 1935 his license as a notary was revoked, he worked as an attorney until the general occupational ban in 1938. His

annual income, which in 1931 amounted to RM 22,400 reduced steadily from 1933 from RM 7,000 (1934) to 2,500 (1938). After the occupational ban his annual income was RM 800. In 1943 he "was recruited for labor, first to clean up homes damaged by planes, later as a metal worker." He was exempted from the deportations, presumably because he was married in a "mixed marriage" with a woman considered to be "Aryan." He survived the National Socialist regime and lived in Schöneberg after 1945. He was immediately readmitted as an attorney and notary.
*Sources:* *li; DJ 36, p. 315; Liste 36; MRRAK; Verz. zugel. Anw. 45; LAB, RAK, PA; BG

**Ohnstein, Max**
07/01/1879 Posen - transportation 1943
*Home address:* Meinekestr. 26, W 15
*Law firm address:* Tauentzienstr. 7 b, W 50
*Additional information:* Attorney and notary; after the National Socialist seizure of power in 1933 his license as a notary was revoked, he worked as an attorney until the general occupational ban in 1938. Transportation on 03/12/1943 to Auschwitz.
*Sources:* JMBl. 33, p. 208; *li; LAB, Liste 10/15/1933; Liste 36; BArch, R 3001 PAK, PA (Elkeles); MRRAK; BG; GB II

**Olden, Rudolf Dr.**
01/14/1885 Stettin - 09/17/1940 Atlantic
*Home address:* no information
*Law firm address:* Joachimsthaler Str. 38
*Additional information:* He was a well-known defense attorney, who was also involved in political trials, he i.a. appeared as defender of Carl von Ossietzky. In addition to practicing law, he was a journalist ("Berliner Tageblatt") and active in the League for Human Rights. He initiated a congress under the title "The Free Word" on 02/19/1933, after a major event of the League he was banned on 02/03/1933. Around 1,000 artists, journalists, politicians and scientists gathered at the Kroll Opera.
After the Reichstag fire he was warned that "you arrest members of the opposition everywhere." The next day he represented a case at the AG. When he learned that "his

home was being watched and the Gestapo was already waiting for him at the District Court, he notified his wife, slept with a friend, drove south the next day, and fled across the border to Czechoslovakia on skis." (Müller, p. 187) In May 1933 he published the first edition of "Hitler the Conqueror" in Prague. In 1934 he and his wife Ika went to Paris. Here he compiled for the Comité des Juives one of the most abundant contemporary descriptions of the Nazi persecution of Jews, the "Black Book on the State of the Jews in Germany." In early 1933 he was made subject to an occupational ban as an attorney in Germany. In December 1936 he was expatriated. He moved his residence from Paris to London. There he published his third great biography, after Stresemann and Hitler, about Hindenburg. He worked intensively as a writer, but his income remained low. Nevertheless, he put all his strength into helping the German PEN club (in his opinion but "an illusion") in exile to help the distressed German writers scattered all over the world by supporting actions, begging in letters and appeals to English and American organizations.

Now stateless, he was declared as an "enemy alien" in 1939 after the beginning of the war in Britain. He came to a detention center. When he received a job offer from the New School of Social Research, New York, Ika and Rudolf boarded the "City of Benares," their two-year-old daughter had already been sent on a separate child transport. During the crossing on the Atlantic, the ship was torpedoed by the German submarine U 48. Ika and Rudolf died together with many others.

**Publications include:** "Der Justizmord an Jakubowsky" [The judicial murder of Jakubowky], Berlin 1928; "Stresemann," Berlin 1929; "Das Wunderbare oder Die Verzauberung. Propheten in deutscher Krise" [The wonderful or the enchantment. Prophets in German crisis], Berlin 1932; Das Schwarzbuch über die Lage der Juden in Deutschland [The black book on the situation of Jews in Germany], Paris 1934; "Hitler der Eroberer" [Hitler the conqueror], Amsterdam edition 1936; "Hindenburg oder der Geist der preußischen Armee" [Hindenburg or the spirit of the Prussian army], Paris 1935.

*Sources:* Liste d. nichtzugel. RA, 04/25/1933; JMBl. 33, p. 266; Müller, Ingo: Beitrag zu [Contribution on] Rudolf Olden, in: Kritische Justiz (Publisher): Streitbare Juristen. Eine andere Tradition. [Controversial attorneys. Another tradition] Baden-Baden 1988, pages 180-192; Göpp., pages 306/7; Krach, p. 435

**Ollendorff, Friedrich Dr.**
03/14/1889 Breslau - no information
*Home address:* Niebuhrstr. 11, Charlottenburg
*Law firm address:* no information
*Additional information:* Attorney at the KG; after the National Socialist seizure of power his license was revoked in the summer of 1933.
*Sources:* TK 33 (Ollendorf); JMBl. 33, p. 266; BG

**Oppenheim, Franz Dr.**
05/30/1891 - 09/29/1942 Sachsenhausen
*Home address:* Lutherstr. 31/32, W 62
*Law firm address:* Jerusalemer Str. 13, SW 19
*Additional information:* Attorney at the KG and notary; after the National Socialist seizure of power in 1933 his license as a notary was revoked, he was readmitted as an attorney; he gave up his activity before 1936. He died in 1942 in the Sachsenhausen concentration camp.
*Sources:* Adr.B. 33; *li; BG; GB Sachsenhausen; GB II

**Oppenheim, Max Dr.**
02/12/1883 Berlin - 08/29/1942 Auschwitz
*Home address:* Pariser Str. 23 (53), Wilmersdorf
*Law firm address:* Königstr. 22/24, C 2
*Additional information:*
Attorney and notary; after the National Socialist seizure of power his license as a notary was revoked in 1933, he was still working as an attorney until the general occupational ban in 1938, 1939 he emigrated to France, transportation from Drancy to Auschwitz on 8/24/1942, there he was murdered in the gas chambers a few days after arrival.
*Sources:* JMBl. 33, p. 208; *li; Liste 36; Naatz-Album; MRRAK; BG; GB II

**Oppenheimer, Ernst**
03/23/1890 Marsberg - September 1978
*Home address:* Nürnberger Str. 16, W 50
*Law firm address:* Nürnberger Str. 16, W 50
*Additional information:* Attorney and
notary; after the National Socialist seizure of
power in 1933 he was readmitted; his license
as a notary was revoked in 1935, he worked as
an attorney until the general occupational ban
in 1938. 1939 he emigrated to the USA, he last
lived in California.
*Sources:* *li; DJ 36, p. 315; Liste 36; MRRAK;
BG; SSDI

**Oppenheimer, Fritz Dr.**
03/10/1898 Berlin - 02/06/1968 Nairobi,
Kenya
*Home address:* Großadmiral-Prinz-Heinrich-
Str. 6, W 35
*Law firm address:* Regentenstr. 2, W 10
*Additional information:* 1915-18 he was
a soldier in the First World War, he was
wounded, he was awarded the EK; after the
end of the war he studied in Berlin, Freiburg
and Breslau; in 1922 he obtained his doctorate
in Breslau; 1924-25 he went on study visits
to Paris and London; as from 1925 he was
an attorney in Berlin, last admitted at the LG
I-III and AG Berlin-Mitte, later also a notary;
he specialized in international law. After the
National Socialist seizure of power in 1933
he was readmitted; his license as a notary was
revoked in 1935, in 1936 he was still working.
Emigration to Great Britain in 1936; 1936-40
he was a legal advisor of the Queen's Counsel
and of the Finance Ministry; 1940 he emigrated
to the USA; from 1940-1943 he worked at
a law firm; he became an American citizen;
1943-46 with the U.S. Army, he became
a lieutenant colonel; 1945-46 with the US
Military Administration in Germany, he was
responsible for legal and judicial reform; in
1946 he wrote the "Law for the liberation of
national socialism and militarism." The Allied
Control Council adopted the law unchanged
as Directive No. 38 and made it binding on all
zones of occupation; from 1947-48 he worked
for the U.S. State Department; from 1948 for a
law firm in New York; he continued to work for
US government agencies, including in 1950 at
the London Debt Conference. He died shortly
before his 70th birthday in Kenya.
*Sources:* TK 33; *li; Liste 36; BG: LAB,
OFP files; BHdE vol. 1, p. 542; Dietmar

Nix: Entnazifizierung [Denazification] (AK
Zeitgeiststudien)

**Oppenheimer, Georg, Judicial Councillor**
04/23/1862 Sprottau - 08/12/1942
Theresienstadt
*Home address:* Iranische Str. 2, N 65 (Jewish
hospital)
*Law firm address:* Grolmanstr. 34/35,
Charlottenburg
*Additional information:* Attorney and
notary; after the National Socialist seizure
of power in 1933 his license as a notary was
revoked, he still worked as an attorney until
the general occupational ban in 1938. On
07/04/1942 he was transported from the
Jewish hospital in Berlin to Theresienstadt;
there he died four weeks later.
*Sources:* Adr.B. 33; JMBl. 33, p. 208; *li;
Liste 36; MRRAK; BG; ThG; GB II

**Oppenheimer, Ludwig Dr.**
No information
*Home address:* Waldseestr. 8, Hermsdorf
*Law firm address:* Wilhelmstr. 44, W 8
*Additional information:* Attorney at the
KG and notary; after the National Socialist
seizure of power in 1933 his license as a
notary was revoked, in 1936 he was still
working as an attorney; he was said to have
emigrated to the Netherlands.
*Sources:* Adr.B. 33; JMBl. 33, p. 208; *li;
Liste 36

**Oppenheimer, Stefan**
03/16/1885 Mainz - May
1964
*Home address:* Kufsteiner
Str. 2, Schöneberg
*Law firm address:* Leipziger
Str. 123a, W 8
*Additional information:*
After the National Socialist seizure of power
in 1933 he was readmitted, he worked as an
attorney until the general occupational ban in
1938. He emigrated to France on 06/26/1939,
later he went to the USA, changed his first
name to Stephen, last lived in New York.
*Sources:* *li; Liste 36; MRRAK; Naatz-Album;
BG; SSDI

**Oppenheimer, Werner Dr.**
11/24/1901 Berlin - no information
*Home address:* Schillstr. 18, W 62

*Law firm address:* Schellingstr. 5, W 9
*Additional information:* After the National Socialist seizure of power he was made subject to an occupational ban in early 1933. Emigration on 06/07/1933 to Copenhagen, Denmark.
*Sources:* Liste d. nichtzugel. RA, 04/25/1933; JMBl. 08/04/1933, p. 253; BG

**Orlipski, Gustav Dr.**
02/04/1997 Bromberg - transportation 1942
*Home address:* Ansbacher Str. 26, Schöneberg
*Law firm address:* Nürnberger Str. 22, W 50
*Additional information:* Attorney and notary; after the National Socialist seizure of power he was made subject to an occupational ban in early 1933; later he was an employee of the Jewish Synagogue. Date of declaration of property: 06/01/1942; collecting station Levetzowstr. 7-8; transportation on 06/13/1942 to Sobibor.
Br.B. 32; Liste d. nichtzugel. RA, 04/25/1933; JMBl. 33, p. 221; BG; GB II

**Ostberg, Ernst Dr.**
02/14/1880 Berlin - 01/22/1943 Theresienstadt
*Home address:* Klopstockstr. 9, NW 87
*Law firm address:* Kottbusser Damm 5, S 59
*Additional information:* Attorney and notary, his wife Elsa was an employee at the law firm; after the National Socialist seizure of power in 1933 he was readmitted, in 1935 his license as a notary was revoked, he worked as an attorney until the general occupational ban in 1938, thereafter as a "consultant." Date of declaration of property: 10/02/1942; transportation on 10/03/1942 to Theresienstadt, he died there in January 1943. His wife was transported from Theresienstadt to Auschwitz in May 1944.
*Sources:* l*li; DJ 36, p. 315; Liste 36; MRRAK; Liste d. Kons. of 04/15/1939; BG; ThG; GB II

# P

**Paechter, Curt**
04/07/1888 Crossen - transportation 1942
*Home address:* Nassauische Str. 61, Wilmersdorf
*Law office address:* Mauerstr. 39, W 8
*Additional information:* After the National Socialist seizure of power in 1933 he was

readmitted, he still worked as an attorney until the general occupational ban in 1938. Transportation on 10/30/1942 to Theresienstadt; from there he was transported on 10/09/1944 to Auschwitz.
*Sources:* *li; Liste 36; MRRAK; BG; GB II

**Pakscher, Benno, Judicial Councillor**
09/06/1859 Posen - no information
*Home address:* Witzlebenplatz 6, Charlottenburg
*Law office address:* Kurfürstendamm 29, W 15
*Additional information:* After the National Socialist seizure of power in 1933 he was readmitted; he was still working as an attorney until the general occupational ban in 1938.
*Sources:* *li; Liste 36; MRRAK; BG

**Pauly, Richard Dr.**
01/10/1883 Berlin - no information
*Home address:* Wielandstr. 41, Charlottenburg
*Law office address:* Warschauer Str. 26, O 34
*Additional information:* Attorney (since 1912) and notary (since 1924); after the National Socialist seizure of power in 1933 his license as a notary was revoked on 07/01/1933, he would have been readmitted as an "elderly attorney," but he discontinued his membership in the Bar on 07/24/1933.
*Sources:* Jüd.Adr.B.; Br.B. 32; JMBl. 33, p. 208; BArch, R 3001 PAK, PA

**Pechner, Hanns Günter**
09/11/1905 Berlin - no information
*Home address:* no information
*Law office address:* Jägerstr. 18, W 8
*Additional information:* 1924-28 he completed his legal studies in Munich and Berlin; as from October 1931 he was an attorney in Berlin, admitted to the KG. He was Protestant. After the National Socialist seizure of power he was made subject to an occupational ban in 1933; he did resistance work in the context of the socialist group "Neu Beginnen"; he was briefly in custody in the penitentiary Luckau; he escaped from imminent concentration camp admission on 03/19/1939 via Switzerland to Paris, France; 1940 he went back to Switzerland; he was active in exile organizations; 1946 he returned to France; until 1953 he was a book printer in Paris; he went to Berlin in March 1954 as an employee of the URO; he then established himself as attorney and notary in Berlin, he

specialized in reparation affairs; in 1977 he lived in West Berlin.
*Sources:* Adr.B. 33; Pr.J. 33, p. 502; BArch, R 3001 PAK; BG; BHdE vol. 1, p. 551

**Peisach, Lothar**
06/06/1888 Glogau - no information
*Home address:* Konstanzer Str. 12 a
*Law office address:* Colditzstr. 2, Tempelhof
*Additional information:* After the National Socialist seizure of power in 1933 he was readmitted, he worked as an attorney until the general occupational ban in 1938, thereafter still as a consultant. His wife was regarded as non-Jewish. He emigrated to the USA after 07/21/1941.
*Sources:* Adr.B. 33; *li; Liste 36; MRRAK; BG

**Peiser, Georg, Judicial Councillor**
03/02/1898 Jarotschin - no information
*Home address:* Zietenstr. 16, Schöneberg
*Law firm address:* Potsdamer Str. 129/ 130
*Additional information:* Attorney and notary; after the National Socialist seizure of power in 1933 his license as a notary was revoked, he was readmitted as an attorney; he was no longer working in 1936. He emigrated to Chile on 12/04/1939.
*Sources:* TK 33; JMBl. 33, p. 220; *li; BG

**Peltason, Walther Dr.**
06/06/1887 Plauen - May 1985
*Home address:* Schopenhauerstr. 44, Nikolassee
*Law firm address:* Motzstr. 72, W 30
*Additional information:* Attorney and notary; after the National Socialist seizure of power in 1933 he was readmitted; his license as a notary was revoked in 1935; he worked as an attorney until the general occupational ban in 1938, thereafter as a "consultant." He emigrated on 03/31/1939, he went to the USA, he last lived in New York state.
*Sources:* *li; DJ 36, p. 315; Liste 36; MRRAK; Liste d. Kons. of 04/15/1939; BArch, R 3001 PAK; BG; SSDI

**Peyser, Walther Dr.**
12/29/1882 Schöneck - 02/25/1953
*Home address:* no information
*Law firm address:* Berliner Str. 141, Charlottenburg

*Additional information:* Attorney (since 1912), later also a notary; after the National Socialist seizure of power in 1933 he was readmitted, since he was regarded as an "elderly attorney," his license as a notary was revoked in 1938; until the general occupational ban in 1938 he worked as an attorney. Before 1933 his income averaged RM 40,000 p.a., from 1933 it dropped to RM 6,000 (1933), 4,000 (1934), 2,000 (1935), and finally 1,000 (1938). His wife was of non-Jewish origins. He was conscripted for forced labor as from 1941 and first used as a worker at the Charlottenburg Motor Works (armor), then at the Deutsche Reichsbahn, later at Friedrich Vogt, bottle wholesale (night watchman). His annual income was maximum RM 1,450. He survived the Nazi regime; he lived in Charlottenburg. On 06/05/1947 he was readmitted as an attorney.
*Sources:* Br.B. 32; *li; DJ 36, p. 315; Liste 36; MRRAK; Verz. zugel. Anw. 45; LAB, RAK, PA; BG

**Pfeffermann, Bruno Dr.**
01/10/1881 Görlitz - no information
*Home address:* Lietzenburger Str. 13
*Law firm address:* Lietzenburger Str. 13
*Additional information:* Attorney and notary; after the National Socialist seizure of power in 1933 his license as a notary was revoked, he was readmitted as an attorney, he was still working as an attorney until the general occupational ban in 1938. He emigrated to Palestine.
*Sources:* JMBl. 33, p. 208; *li; Liste 36; MRRAK; BG

**Philipp, Herbert**
11/10/1890 - 05/06/1934
*Home address:* Sybelstr. 62, Charlottenburg
*Law firm address:* Hardenbergstr. 24, Charlottenburg
*Additional information:* After the National Socialist seizure of power in 1933 he was made subject to an occupational ban as an attorney and notary; he died in 1934 at the age of 53, he was buried at Weißensee.
*Sources:* Br.B. 32; Liste d. nichtzugel. RA, 04/25/1933; JMBl. 33, p. 195; BArch, R 3001 PAK; BG

**Philipp, Richard Dr.**
08/27/1880 Stolp - no information
*Home address:* Rosenheimer Str. 15/Bozener
Str. 9, Schöneberg
*Law firm address:* Bülowstr. 28, W 57
*Additional information:* Attorney at
the KG and notary, law partner of Hans
Beermann and Alfons Lüpschütz. After the
National Socialist seizure of power in 1933
he was readmitted; his license as a notary
was revoked in 1935; he still worked as
an attorney until the general occupational
ban in 1938. He emigrated to the USA on
03/14/1940; he last lived in New York.
*Sources:* *li, Br.B. 32; DJ 36, p. 315 Liste 36;
MRRAK; BG

**Philipp, Rudolf**
03/14/1882 Frankfurt/Oder - transportation
1942
*Home address:* Regensburger Str. 23
*Law firm address:* Regensburger Str. 23
*Additional information:* After the National
Socialist seizure of power his license as an
attorney was revoked at the end of 1933.
He was transported on 01/13/1942 from the
police prison Berlin to Riga.
*Sources:* Adr.B. 33; Pr.J. 33, p. 807; BG;
BdE; GB II

**Philippsborn, Siegfried**
03/11/1887 Quedlinburg - no information
*Home address:* no information
*Law firm address:* Motzstr. 68, W 30
*Additional information:* Attorney since
1919; after the National Socialist seizure of
power he was made subject to an occupational
ban on 06/09/1933. He was used in 1941 as a
worker at Warnecke & Böhm, Weißensee, for
forced labor.
*Sources:* Liste d. nichtzugel. RA, 04/25/1933;
JMBl. 33, p. 234; BArch, R 3001 PAK,
PA ; BG

**Philippson, Arthur**
10/22/1888 Braunschweig - no information
*Home address:* no information
*Law firm address:* Unter den Linden 56,
NW 7
*Additional information:* Attorney (since 1920)
and notary (1930); after the National Socialist
seizure of power in 1933 he was made subject
to an occupational ban in June 1933.
*Sources:* Br.B. 32; JMBl. 33, pages 220/1;
BArch, R 3001 PAK, PA

**Philipsborn, Alexander Dr.**
11/21/1882 Berlin - no information
*Home address:* Markgraf-Albrecht-Str. 14,
Halensee
*Law firm address:* Nikolsburger Str. 8/9,
Wilmersdorf
*Additional information:* Attorney at the
KG and notary; after the National Socialist
seizure of power in 1933 his license as a
notary was revoked, he was still working as
an attorney until the general occupational ban
in 1938. He emigrated to Brussels, Belgium.
*Sources:* JMBl. 33, p. 220; *li; Liste 36; DJ
38, p. 1705; BG

**Philipsborn, Georg**
10/02/1901 Stralsund - no information
*Home address:* no information
*Law firm address:* Tauentzienstr. 10, W 50
*Additional information:* Attorney since 1927
in a joint law firm with Willy Bachwitz; after
the National Socialist seizure of power in
1933 he was made subject to an occupational
ban on 06/09/1933.
*Sources:* Br.B. 32; JMBl. 33, p. 220; BArch, R
3001 PAK, PA

**Pick, Ernst**
11/07/1884 Cosel - no information
*Home address:* no information
*Law firm address:* Kaiser-Wilhelm-Platz 4,
Schöneberg
*Additional information:* Attorney since
1912, notary since 1927, law partner of
Dagobert Auerbach; he had served in the
Navy in the First World War; on 07/08/1933
his license as a notary was revoked; he still
worked as an attorney until the general
occupational ban in 1938.
*Sources:* Br.B. 32; JMBl. 33, p. 220; *li, Liste
36; MRRAK; BArch, R 3001 PAK, PA

**Pick, Felix Dr., Judicial Councillor**
05/13/1871 - no information
*Home address:* Bamberger Str. 59, W 50
*Law firm address:* Bamberger Str. 59, W 50
*Additional information:* He was still a
board member of the RAK in 1932; after
the National Socialist seizure of power in
1933 his license as a notary was revoked;
he worked as an attorney until the general
occupational ban in 1938. He emigrated in
1938 to Switzerland.
*Sources:* JMBl. 33, p. 220; *li; Liste 36;
MRRAK; BG; Krach, p. 435

**Pick, Fritz**
05/27/1887 Lissa - no information
*Home address:* Kurfürstendamm 64, Pension Olympic, Friedrichstr. 221
*Law firm address:* Friedrichstr. 221, SW 48
*Additional information:* Attorney and notary; in addition to in-house counsel for the UFA; after the National Socialist seizure of power in 1933 he was readmitted; his license as a notary was revoked in 1935; he still worked as an attorney until the general occupational ban in 1938. He emigrated to Amsterdam, the Netherlands; he returned to Germany, in 1951 he lived in Munich.
*Sources:* *li; DJ 36, p. 315; Liste 36; BArch, R 3001 PAK; MRRAK; BG; information Werner Wolff, 09/22/1998

**Pick, Max Dr.**
11/27/1879 - 03/21/1937
*Home address:* no information
*Law firm address:* Steglitzer Str. 54, W 35
*Additional information:* Attorney and notary; after the National Socialist seizure of power in 1933 his license as a notary was revoked, he was still working as an attorney in 1936; in 1937 he committed suicide at the age of 58.
*Sources:* JMBl. 33, p. 220; *li; Liste 36; BG

**Pick, Rudolf Dr.**
08/15/1892 Ostrowo - 11/30/1941 Riga
*Home address:* no information
*Law firm address:* Brückenallee 13, NW 87
*Additional information:* Attorney (since 1924), later also notary; after the National Socialist seizure of power he was made subject to an occupational ban in April 1933, he was readmitted, 1935 his license as a notary was revoked, he worked as an attorney until 1936. He was last the head of the Palestine Office; he accompanied a youth transport to Palestine, but returned to his family in Berlin. Transportation on 11/27/1941 to Riga; he was murdered there on the day of his arrival.
*Sources:* Liste d. nichtzugel. RA, 04/25/1933; *li; DJ 36, p. 315; Liste 36; BArch, R 3001 PAK; Naatz-Album; BG; BdE; GB II; Göpp. p. 257; Walk, p. 295

**Pick, Walter Dr.**
08/02/1901 - no information
*Home address:* Bamberger Str. 59, W 50
*Law firm address:* Belle-Alliance-Platz 4, SW 61
*Additional information:* After the National Socialist seizure of power he was made subject to an occupational ban in early 1933. He emigrated to London, Great Britain.
*Sources:* Br.B. 32; Liste d. nichtzugel. RA, 04/25/1933; JMBl. 33, p. 253; BArch, R 3001 PAK; BG

**Pickardt, Ludwig Dr.**
No information
*Home address:* no information
*Law firm address:* Uhlandstr. 24, Charlottenburg
*Additional information:* Attorney and notary; after the National Socialist seizure of power in 1933 his license as a notary was revoked, thereupon he gave up his law practice. Presumably he emigrated to Paris, France.
*Sources:* Br.B. 32; JMBl. 33, p. 209; Pr.J. 33, p. 679; Naatz-Album

**Pincus, Alfred Dr.**
07/08/1892 Dortmund - 01/15/1945 Bergen-Belsen
*Home address:* Xantenerstraße 10, W 15
*Law firm address:* Gontardstr. 5, C 25
*Additional information:* Attorney and notary; after the seizure of power by the National Socialists in May 1933, the board of the RAK reported to the Prussian Ministry of Justice that he had taken over the defense in the Felseneck trial, at the same time emphasizing that he was "non-Aryan." Soon after he was made subject to an occupational ban. He emigrated 1936 to Holland. An arrest warrant for tax evasion was issued against him. He died at the beginning of 1945 in the Bergen-Belsen concentration camp. His wife and son survived the Nazi regime and went to the United States.
*Sources:* Br.B. 32; GHStA, Rep. 84a, Nr. 20363; Liste d. nichtzugel. RA, 04/25/1933; JMBl. 33, p. 209; BG; GB II; Wolf, BFS

**Pincus, Dagobert Dr.**
06/18/1886 Lötzen -
08/23/1958 Berlin
*Home address:*
Zähringerstr. 38 a,
Wilmersdorf
*Law firm address:*
Kurfürstendamm 229,
W 50

*Additional information:* Attorney (since 1913) and notary (since 1924); he fought in the First World War. After the National Socialist seizure of power he applied to be readmitted, but was not recognized as a "frontline fighter." Since he had established himself as an attorney before 1914, he was allowed to continue practicing, but his license as a notary was revoked. In 1938 he was made subject to the general occupational ban for Jewish attorneys.
He was arrested on November 10, 1938 and went to the Sachsenhausen concentation camp. On 12/07/1938 he was released again, after signing a commitment to emigrate. His wife was non-Jewish and accompanied him to France on 06/12/1939. The couple lived there until 10/19/1948. In France he was a member of the Union des Immigrés Allemands Antinazis, a recognized Résistance group. Under the Vichy government he was imprisoned twice at the Camp de la Braconne (1939 and 1940). His mother, Julie Pincus, nee Glass, was transported from Berlin to Theresienstadt and died there. In October 1948 he returned to Berlin. His acquaintances could not understand why he wanted to go to this city, which many people would have preferred to leave immediately. Nevertheless, he worked hard and with the support of colleagues for his readmission as an attorney, which was granted to him on 12/07/1948. The first practice that he established in Köpenick he gave up because of the onset of political pressure and settled in 1950 in Halensee; later he lived in Charlottenburg.
*Sources:* Br.B. 32; JMBl. 33, p. 209; *li; Liste 36; BArch, R 3001 PAK; BG; LAB, RAK, PA

**Pincus, Ernst Dr.**
02/02/1904 Posen - no information
*Home address:* Aschaffenburger Str. 13, W 30
*Law firm address:* Budapester Str. 29, W 62
*Additional information:* Attorney at the KG since 1930; after the National Socialist

seizure of power he was made subject to an occupational ban on 06/09/1933. He emigrated to Denmark in August 1933.
*Sources:* Br.B. 32; Liste d. nichtzugel. RA, 04/25/1933; JMBl. 33, p. 203; BArch, R 3001 PAK, PA; BG

**Pincus, Harry Dr.**
07/03/1883 Königsberg -
04/02/1950 Berlin
*Home address:* Rathenower
Str. 4, NW 40
*Law firm address:*
Rathenower Str. 4, NW 40
*Additional information:*
He left the Jewish religious community in 1920 and joined the Roman Catholic Church. His wife was of non-Jewish origins and she was a Christian, he was a member of the Centre Party. He specialized in legal issues in connection with the newly emerging medium of broadcasting and was active in an advisory capacity for the Reich Broadcasting Corporation. After the seizure of power by the National Socialists in 1933 these mandates were canceled and his revenues were reduced by an average of RM 18,000 p.a. (1931, 1932) to 550 (1935), 250 (1936), 150 (1937) and 280 (1938). Above all, the revocation of the notaryship in 1933 caused his main loss of revenue. He worked as an attorney until the general occupational ban in 1938.
He was a member of the Reich Association of Non-Aryan Christians. After 1938 he was conscripted to work as warehouse and/ or factory laborer. After the liberation, he became a department head at the Berliner Rundfunk. On 04/02/1948 he was readmitted as an attorney. Until his death in 1950 he lived in Charlottenburg.
He had numerous publications on radio broadcasting law as from 1928.
*Sources:* JMBl. 33, p. 209; *li; Liste 36; BArch, R 3001 PAK; Mitt.bl.Reichsverband nichtarischer Christen, 12/06/1934; MRRAK; Verz. zugel. Anw. 45; LAB, RAK, PA; BG

**Pincus, Ludwig Dr.**
No information
*Home address:* Müllerstr. 177, N 65
*Law firm address:* Badstr. 61, N 20
*Additional information:* Attorney and notary; after the National Socialist seizure

of power in 1933 his license as a notary was revoked, he was still working as an attorney until the general occupational ban in 1938; he presumably emigrated.
*Sources:* JMBl. 33, p. 209; *li; Liste 36; DJ 38, p. 1705; BG

**Pincuß, Leo**
07/07/1889 Berlin - no information
*Home address:* Invalidenstr. 113, Mitte
*Law firm address:* Chausseestr. 111/112, N 4
*Additional information:* Attorney and notary; after the National Socialist seizure of power in 1933 he was readmitted; his license as a notary was revoked in 1935; he was still working as an attorney until the general occupational ban in 1938; he presumably emigrated.
*Sources:* *li; DJ 36, p. 315; Liste 36; BArch, R 3001 PAK; MRRAK; BG

**Pindar, Kurt Dr.**
02/02/1885 Königsberg - no information
*Home address:* no information
*Law firm address:* Unter den Linden 15, W 8
*Additional information:* Attorney (since 1913) and notary (since 1929); in the 1933 business directory his hours of operation are listed: weekdays 11-12 and 4-6, Sundays from 11-12 only. After the National Socialist seizure of power in 1933 his license as a notary was revoked, he was readmitted as an attorney, because he was recognized as an "elderly attorney," he still worked as an attorney until 06/10/1938. He had changed his name in 1922 from the former "Pincus," which was mentioned on several occasions. In particular, he was quoted in a dispute against Jewish attorneys [see Lippert, Julius: Im Strom der Zeit (In the stream of time), Berlin 1942, pp. 86-89, here: 88].
*Sources:* Adr.B. 33; JMBl. 33, p. 220; *li; Liste 36; BArch R 3001 PAK; PA; information Flechtmann

**Pinkus, Martin**
No information
*Home address:* no information
*Law firm address:* Markstr. 1 (today Residenzstr.), Reinickendorf
*Additional information:* Attorney and notary; after the National Socialist seizure of power in 1933 he was readmitted; his

license as a notary was revoked in 1935; he still worked as an attorney until the general occupational ban in 1938.
*Sources:* *li; DJ 36, p. 315 (Pincus); Liste 36; MRRAK

**Pinn, Georg, Judicial Councillor**
10/19/1867 - no information
*Home address:* Bülowstr. 18, Schöneberg
*Law firm address:* Bülowstr. 19, W 57
*Additional information:* Attorney and notary; after the National Socialist seizure of power in 1933 his license as a notary was revoked, he was still admitted as an attorney until the general occupational ban in 1938; emigration.
*Sources:* JMBl. 33, p. 220; *li; Liste 36; MRRAK; BG

**Pinner, Albert Dr., Judicial Councillor**
1857 Berlin - 1933
*Home address:* no information
*Law firm address:* Markgrafenstr. 46
*Additional information:* Attorney at the LG I-III and notary; board member of the Berlin Bar Association and the DAV, officially recognized as the last Jewish jurist in a commemorative publication in 1932; he died in 1933 at the age of 76 years while emigrating.
Various publications on commercial law.
*Sources:* Br.B. 32; TK 33; BG; BHdE vol. 1, S 562 (Heinz Albert Pinner); Krach, p. 435

**Pinner, Ernst**
07/24/1889 Kosten - 08/20/1947 Israel
*Home address:* no information
*Law firm address:* Linkstr. 19, W 9
*Additional information:* Attorney and notary; after the National Socialist seizure of power in 1933 he was readmitted; his license as a notary was revoked in 1935; he was still working as an attorney until the general occupational ban in 1938. He emigrated on 08/28/1939 to Tel Aviv, Palestine; there he died in 1947 at the age of 58.
*Sources:* *li; DJ 36, p. 315; Liste 36; BArch, R 3001 PAK; MRRAK; BG

**Pinner, Heinz Dr.**
02/20/1893 Berlin - September 1986
*Home address:* Eichenallee 24, Charlottenburg
*Law firm address:* Markgrafenstr. 46, W 8

*Additional information:* 1914-18 he fought in the First World War; 1919 he received his doctorate in Greifswald; attorney and notary; he was a Protestant and was married to an Ullstein daughter; until 1933 he was a member of the supervisory board of Ullstein AG. After the National Socialist seizure of power in 1933 he was readmitted; his license as a notary was revoked in 1935; he was still working as an attorney until the general occupational ban in 1938. In June 1939 he emigrated with his wife and children to Switzerland; in December 1941 to Los Angeles, USA; he studied auditing and became a tax specialist partner of a public accountancy firm; he was exempted from the residence requirement and admitted to the Higher Regional Court of Düsseldorf from 1947 as an attorney, he was a specialist in reparation affairs; in 1978 he lived in Los Angeles. 1979 he was an honorary member of the DAV.
*Publications:* Aktienrechts-Kommentar [Stock corporation law comment], Staub/Pinner
*Sources:* TK 33; *li; DJ 36, p. 315; Liste 36; MRRAK; SSDI; BG; BHdE vol. 1, p. 562 (with first names Heinz Albert); BAP, 15.09 RSA; Jewish Immigrants . . . in the U.S.A., Oral History, p. 96; information Liselotte K.

**Pinner, Leo David**
12/24/1861 - 05/23/1938
*Home address:* Güntzelstr. 2, Wilmersdorf
*Law firm address:* Kronprinzenufer 11, NW 40
*Additional information:* Attorney and notary; after the National Socialist seizure of power in 1933 he was readmitted, in 1935 his license as a notary was revoked, he was still working as an attorney in 1936; he died in 1938 at the age of 77; he was buried at Weißensee.
*Sources:* Adr.B. 33; *li; DJ 36, p. 315; Liste 36; BG

**Pinner, Paul**
04/28/1884 Erfurt - 11/01/1941
*Home address:* Helmstedter Str. 23, Wilmersdorf
*Law firm address:* Martin-Luther-Str. 79, W 30
*Additional information:* Attorney at the KG and notary; after the National Socialist seizure of power in 1933 his license as a

notary was revoked, he was still working as an attorney until the general occupational ban in 1938; he died in 1941 at the age of 58; he was buried at Weißensee.
*Sources:* JMBl. 33, p. 220; *li; Liste 36; MRRAK; BG

**Pinner, Sally**
12/05/1880 Graudenz - 08/20/1939
*Home address:* Wallnertheaterstr. 7, C 2
*Law firm address:* An der Spandauer Brücke 1 b, C 2
*Additional information:* After the National Socialist seizure of power in 1933 he was readmitted, he still worked as an attorney until the general occupational ban in 1938; he died in 1939 at the age of 59; he was buried at Weißensee.
*Sources:* TK 33; *li; Liste 36; MRRAK; BG

**Pinner, Sigismund, Judicial Councillor**
No information
*Home address:* no information
*Law firm address:* Alexanderstr. 14a, O 27
*Additional information:* Attorney and notary; after the National Socialist seizure of power in 1933 he was readmitted; his license as a notary was revoked in 1935; in 1936 he was still working as an attorney.
*Sources:* Br.B 32; *li; DJ 36, p. 315; Liste 36

**Pinthus, Heinrich Dr.**
10/25/1884 Berlin - 07/24/1938
*Home address:* Waitzstr. 13, Charlottenburg
*Law firm address:* Waitzstr. 13
*Additional information:* Attorney at the KG and notary; after the National Socialist seizure of power in 1933 his license as a notary was revoked; he was still working as an attorney in 1936; he died in 1938 at the age of 53; he was buried at Weißensee.
*Sources:* JMBl. 33, p. 220; *li; Liste 36; BArch, R 3001 PAK; BG

**Pitsch, Erich**
02/10/1883 Berlin - 11/02/1939 Berlin
*Home address:* Bleibtreustr. 47
*Law firm address:* Alexanderufer 1, NW 40
*Additional information:* Attorney (since 1911) and notary (since 1923); he was Protestant. After the National Socialist seizure of power in 1933 his license as a notary was revoked, he was regarded as an "elderly attorney," therefore he was readmitted as an attorney. He was regarded

as "mixed race," his wife as non-Jewish, for this reason he remained admitted despite the general occupational ban. He died in 1939 at the age of 56 in Berlin.
*Sources:* JMBl. 33, p. 209; *li; Liste Mschlg. 36; BArch, R 3001 PAK, PA; BG

**Placzek, Michaelis, Judicial Councillor**
12/25/1860 Schwersenz - no information
*Home address:* Joachimsthaler Str. 21 at Wolff, W 15
*Law firm address:* Joachimsthaler Str. 13, W 15
*Additional information:* Attorney and notary; after the National Socialist seizure of power in 1933 he was readmitted; in 1935 his license as a notary was revoked; he was still working as an attorney until the general occupational ban in 1938. He emigrated on 08/13/1941 with his family to Uruguay.
*Sources:* *li; DJ 36, p. 315; Liste 36; BG

**Platz, Alfred Dr.**
06/26/1890 Cologne - no information
*Home address:* Oldenburgallee 61, Charlottenburg
*Law firm address:* Behrenstr. 20, W 8
*Additional information:* Attorney and notary; after the National Socialist seizure of power in 1933 his license as a notary was revoked, he was readmitted as an attorney. He emigrated to Amsterdam, the Netherlands, on 05/02/1934; he returned to Germany.
*Sources:* JMBl. 33, p. 220; *li; BArch, R 3001 PAK; BG

**Plaut, Leo Dr.**
04/29/1900 Willingshausen - no information
*Home address:* no information
*Law firm address:* Potsdamer Str. 76, W 57
*Additional information:* Attorney since 1926; he was a participant in the Felseneck trial (it was about the events in an allotment garden, in which there had been a violent conflict between right wing and left wing groups). In his personal file there is the indication that he was "energetically opposed" to communist attorneys in this trial. Apparently he made no secret of his conservative attitude. Despite his political stance, in May 1933 the board of the RAK reported to the Prussian Ministry of Justice that he was active as a communist, according to a "notice of the head of the

Ortsgruppe Märzhausen of N.S.D.A.P.," at the same time emphasizing that he was "non-Aryan." On 05/31/1933 he was made subject to an occupational ban.
*Sources:* Br.B. 32; GHStA, Rep. 84a, Nr. 20363; Liste d. nichtzugel. RA, 04/25/1933; JMBl. 33, p. 209; BArch, R 3001 PAK, PA

**Pleuss, Wilhelm Dr.**
11/25/1905 Lüneburg - no information
*Home address:* no information
*Law firm address:* Nymphenburger Str. 11, Schöneberg
*Additional information:* He was an attorney at the KG; after the National Socialist seizure of power his origins do not appear to have been known; he was Protestant; in 1936 he was regarded as "mixed race," due to this status, he was allowed to continue practicing law until at least 1941.
*Sources:* Adr.B. 32; Liste Mschlg. 36; Tel.B. 41; BG

**Plonski, Herbert Dr.**
06/05/1878 Zirke - transportation 1942
*Home address:* Elisabethufer 1 (heute Hoffmanndamm), SO 36
*Law firm address:* Elisabethufer 34, SO 36
*Additional information:* Attorney and notary; after the National Socialist seizure of power in 1933 his license as a notary was revoked, he still worked as an attorney until the general occupational ban in 1938. He was arrested on 12/19/1941; on 01/25/1942 he was transported to Riga.
*Sources:* JMBl. 33, p. 209; *li; Liste 36; MRRAK; BG; BdE; GB II

**Plonski, Hugo, Judicial Councillor**
01/03/1858 Neustadt - 11/21/1942 Berlin
*Home address:* Stühlinger Str. 11 b, Karlshorst
*Law firm address:* Stühlinger Str. 11 b, Karlshorst
*Additional information:* Attorney and notary; after the National Socialist seizure of power in 1933 his license as a notary was revoked, he was readmitted as an attorney, he gave up his legal activity before 1936. He died at the end of 1942 in the Berlin-Alexanderplatz police prison.
*Sources:* JMBl. 33, p. 220; *li; BG; GB II

**Polke, Albert Dr.**
07/09/1889 Berlin - no information
*Home address:* Laubacher Str. 56,
Wilmersdorf
*Law firm address:* Potsdamer Str. 22 b, W 9
*Additional information:* Attorney and
notary; after the National Socialist seizure
of power he was made subject to an
occupational ban in early 1933, subsequently
he was readmitted; 1935 his license as a
notary was revoked; he worked as an attorney
until the general occupational ban in 1938.
He emigrated to New York, USA; in 1952 he
was working as a public accountant.
*Sources:* Br.B. 32; Liste d. nichtzugel. RA,
04/25/1933; *li; Liste 36; BArch, R 3001
PAK; BG

**Pollack, Erich Dr.**
10/27/1882 Köslin -
10/11/1956 Berlin
*Home address:* no
information
*Law firm address:*
Kurfürstendamm 13, W 50
*Additional information:*
Attorney (since 1911), in addition, he is said
to have worked as a legal advisor. After the
seizure of power by the National Socialists
he was arrested in 1933, after he was noticed
when representing a client residing abroad,
a "general manager Scheuer from the grain
industry." He was personally persecuted by
two state police officers. He was taken to the
police prison on Alexanderplatz, where he
was crammed into a dark, damp basement
room with numerous other prisoners. Later
he was transferred to the military prison
in Spandau and/or the old penitentiary in
Brandenburg/Havel. Only through the efforts
of his wife Hildegard, who was non-Jewish
and had become known under the stage
name Ingrid Lindstroem as an opera and
operetta singer, he was released from custody
again. In 1936 his admission as an attorney
was revoked. His wife was expelled from
the Reichskulturkammer because of her
commitment to her husband, which amounted
to a ban on performing. In 1943 and 1944, a
Protestant, he was arrested again, once "off
the street" for alleged "star offense," the other
time after denunciation of a woman from
Bonin, to whose local group district the couple
had been sent after bombardment. He was
conscripted to work as a laborer, he survived

the persecution and lived in Charlottenburg
after the persecution. Materially, he had made
a living as a tutor after 1933. In May 1947
he applied for readmission as an attorney.
After more than two and a half years of
examination, he was re-admitted as an
attorney on 01/10/1950.
*Sources:* Br.B. 32; TK 33; *li; Liste 36; BG;
LAB, RAK, PA

**Pommer, Martin Dr.**
06/22/1888 - August 1982
*Home address:* no information
*Law firm address:* Lindenstr. 7, SW 68
*Additional information:* Attorney and
notary; after the National Socialist seizure of
power in 1933 he was readmitted; his license
as a notary was revoked in 1935, he was
still working as an attorney until the general
occupational ban in 1938. He emigrated to
the USA, he last lived in the state of Ohio.
*Sources:* *li; DJ 36, p. 315; Liste 36; BArch, R
3001 PAK; MRRAK; BG; SSDI

**Posener, Erwin**
01/17/1904 Berlin - no information
*Home address:* no information
*Law firm address:* Nollendorfplatz 7, W 30
*Additional information:* After the National
Socialist seizure of power he was made subject
to an occupational ban in early 1933.
*Sources:* Liste d. nichtzugel. RA, 04/25/1933;
JMBl. 28.7.33, p. 234; BArch, R 3001 PAK

**Posener, Paul Dr.**
No information
*Home address:* no information
*Law firm address:* Prager Platz 4,
Wilmersdorf
*Additional information:* Attorney and
notary; after the National Socialist seizure
of power in 1933 his license as a notary was
revoked, then his admission as an attorney
was also revoked.
*Sources:* Adr.B. 33; JMBl. 33, p. 220 and
p. 234

**Präger, Alfred Dr.**
02/11/1902 Neustadt a.d.Orla - 12/19/1993
*Home address:* Am Karlsbad 1 a, W 35
*Law firm address:* Kaiserstr. 38, C 25
*Additional information:* Studied in Berlin;
1926 he received his doctorate in Leipzig;
1927-30 he worked at the Prussian Ministry
of Justice; he was an attorney (since 1931);

since 1914 he was a member of the Zionist Association for Germany; he was a SPD member and attorney of the party. After the National Socialist seizure of power in 1933 he went underground; he was made subject to an occupational ban in early 1933; he emigrated to the USA in May 1933; 1933-35 he renewed his legal studies, in addition he worked in a jewelry grinding shop; 1937 he took the bar examination; 1938 he was an attorney in New York; he was entrusted with numerous municipal (honorary) offices; he was a close associate of the journal "Aufbau;" he died in 1993 at the age of 91.
*Sources:* TK 33; Liste d. nichtzugel. RA, 04/25/1933; JMBl. 28.7.33, p. 234; BArch R 3001 PAK, PA 71128; BG; BHdE vol. 1, p. 574; SSDI

**Prager, Arthur, Judicial Councillor**
No information
*Home address:* no information
*Law firm address:* Südwestkorso 2, Friedenau
*Additional information:* After the National Socialist seizure of power he was disbarred as an attorney in early 1933.
*Sources:* Adr.B. 33; TK 33; JMBl. 33, 05/05/1933

**Prasse, Herbert Dr.**
10/21/1894 Danzig - transportation 1944
*Home address:* Kaiserdamm 85, Charlottenburg
*Law firm address:* Kaiserdamm 85, Charlottenburg
*Additional information:* After the National Socialist seizure of power in 1933 he was readmitted, he was still working as an attorney in 1936. He emigrated, probably to the Netherlands. He went to the Westerbork concentration camp; from there he was transported to Theresienstadt on 09/04/1944; on 10/16/1944 he was transported to Auschwitz.
TK 33; *li; Liste 36; BG; GB II

**Preis, Siegfried**
05/19/1872 Königshütte - no information
*Home address:* Bissingzeile 17, Tiergarten
*Law firm address:* Potsdamer Str. 32 a, W 35
*Additional information:* Attorney and notary; after the National Socialist seizure of power in 1933 his license as a notary was revoked, he still worked as an attorney until the general occupational ban in 1938.

*Sources:* Br.B. 32; JMBl. 33, p. 209; *li; Liste 36; BArch, R 3001 PAK; MRRAK; BG

**Preuß, Hans**
06/11/1900 Berlin - August 1978
*Home address:* Frankfurter Allee 285
*Law firm address:* no information
*Additional information:* After the National Socialist seizure of power he was made subject at first to a representation ban, then an occupational ban on 05/05/1933. He emigrated to the USA, last lived in San Francisco.
*Sources:* Liste d. nichtzugel. RA, 04/25/1933; Br.B. 32; JMBl. 33, p. 163; BArch, R 3001 PAK; BG; SSDI

**Preuß, Hans Helmuth**
12/19/1901 Berlin - 12/04/1983 Paris
*Home address:* Landgrafenstr. 10, W 62
*Law firm address:* Herwarthstr. 4
*Additional information:* He left the Jewish Synagogue at the end of 1932; after the National Socialist seizure of power he was made subject to an occupational ban on 07/06/1933; he went to Paris, where he completed supplementary studies; 1939 naturalization; in 1940 he fled to southern France together with his mother Else, nee Liebermann, the widow of the jurist and politician Hugo Preuss; then illegally went to Switzerland; at the end of the war he returned to Paris, he worked there as an attorney; he died in 1983 in Paris.
*Sources:* Br.B. 32; JMBl. 33, p. 234; BArch, R 3001 PAK; BG; information Prof. Christoph Müller, Hugo-Preuß-Gesellschaft; website of the Hugo-Preuß-Gesellschaft

**Preuss, Julius**
06/24/1887 Deutsch Krone - no information
*Home address:* no information
*Law firm address:* Chausseestr. 118, N 4
*Additional information:* Attorney and notary; after the National Socialist seizure of power he was made subject to an occupational ban in summer 1933.
*Sources:* Br.B.32; Liste d. nichtzugel. RA, 04/25/1933; JMBl. 08/21/1933, p. 266; BArch, R 3001 PAK

**Priebatsch, Ludwig Dr.**
08/18/1899 Berlin - 12/15/1987
*Home address:* no information
*Law firm address:* Tauentzienstr. 14, W 50
*Additional information:* Attorney since 1924; after the National Socialist seizure of power

he was made subject to an occupational ban on 06/09/1933. He emigrated to the USA, he changed his name to Priebat, last lived in California.
*Sources:* Adr.B. 32; Liste d. nichtzugel. RA, 04/25/1933; JMBl. 08/04/1933, p. 253; BArch, R 3001 PAK; SSDI

**Priester, Harry, Judicial Councillor**
06/26/1865 Memel - 01/06/1943
*Home address:* Hohenstaufenstr. 36, Schöneberg
*Law firm address:* Zimmerstr. 21, SW 68
*Additional information:* Attorney and notary; after the National Socialist seizure of power in 1933 his license as a notary was revoked; he worked as an attorney until the general occupational ban in 1938; he died in 1943 at the age of 77, he was buried at Weißensee.
*Sources:* JMBl. 33, p. 220; *li; Liste 36; MRRAK; BG

**Priester, Siegfried Dr.**
10/29/1898 Landsberg - no information
*Home address:* Wielandstr. 22, Schöneberg
*Law firm address:* Leonhardstr. 6, Charlottenburg
*Additional information:* Attorney at the KG; after the National Socialist seizure of power in 1933 he was readmitted, he worked as an attorney until the general occupational ban in 1938.
*Sources:* TK 33; *li; Liste 36; BArch, R 3001 PAK; MRRAK

**Pringsheim, Ernst Dr.**
11/20/1901 Oppeln - no information
*Home address:* Hebbelstr. 16, Charlottenburg
*Law firm address:* Schellingstr. 6
*Additional information:* After the National Socialist seizure of power he was made subject to an occupational ban in 1933. He emigrated on 03/12/1938 to South America.
*Sources:* Br.B. 32; Liste der nichtzugel. RA, (8th addendum list of 07/24/1933); Pr.J. 33, p. 532; BArch R 3001 PAK; BG

**Prinz, Arthur**
11/18/1886 Berlin - no information
*Home address:* no information
*Law firm address:* Fasanenstr. 22, W 15
*Additional information:* Attorney at the KG and notary; after the National Socialist seizure of power in 1933 he was readmitted;

1935 his license as a notary was revoked; he still worked as an attorney until the general occupational ban in 1938.
He survived the National Socialist regime and was readmitted as an attorney and notary after 1945.
*Sources:* *li; DJ 36, p. 315; Liste 36; BArch, R 3001 PAK; MRRAK; Verz. zugel. Anw. 45; BG

**Prinz, Heinrich**
10/18/1878 Krotoschin - transportation 1943
*Home address:* Hohenzollerndamm 96, Zehlendorf
*Law firm address:* Pallasstr. 10/11, W 57
*Additional information:* Attorney at the KG and notary; after the National Socialist seizure of power in 1933 his license as a notary was revoked; he worked as an attorney until 1936. He emigrated to Amsterdam, the Netherlands, 1937. According to his daughter, her parents were transported from Amsterdam in 1943.
*Sources:* Br.B. 32; JMBl. 33, p. 220; *li; Liste 36; DJ 38, p. 1705; BG; information of the daughter

**Priwin, Jakob**
04/19/1885 Graudenz - no information
*Home address:* no information
*Law firm address:* Kurfürstendamm 24, W 15
*Additional information:* Attorney and notary; after the National Socialist seizure of power in 1933 he was readmitted, in 1935 his license as a notary was revoked; he was still working as an attorney until the general occupational ban in 1938.
*Sources:* *li; DJ 36, p. 315; Liste 36; BArch, R 3001 PAK; MRRAK

**Pröll, Rudolf**
No information - 02/15/1944
*Home address:* Invalidenstr. 111, N 4
*Law firm address:* Neustädtische Kirchstr. 15, NW 7
*Additional information:* Attorney at the KG and notary; after the National Socialist seizure of power in 1933 he was readmitted; he was regarded as "mixed race second class" and therefore could continue to work as an attorney, even after 1938 until his death in 1944.
*Sources:* *li; Liste Mschlg. 36; BArch, R 3001 PAK

**Proskauer, Max E. Dr.**
12/19/1902 Berlinchen - 06/16/1968 Berlin
*Home address:* no information
*Law firm address:* Schwäbische Str. 3, W 30
*Additional information:* Attorney at the KG;
after the National Socialist seizure of power
he was made subject to an occupational ban in
early 1933. He did not apply for readmission.
He emigrated immediately after the boycott on
April 1, 1933 via Paris to Palestine, together
with his wife Erna, who was also an attorney.
In Palestine, he sought to gain access to the
British-oriented legal system, but never gained
admission to practice as an attorney. His
wife started a laundry business, thus making
a living for the couple. In the 1950s both of
them returned to Berlin. Here he reestablished
himself as an attorney. His wife, who had
separated from him, continued the law
practice after his death in 1968.
*Sources:* kBr.B. 32; Liste d. nichtzugel.
RA, 04/25/1933; JMBl. 33, p. 203; BArch,
R 3001, PAK; Proskauer, Erna, Wege und
Umwege [Paths and detours], Frankfurt a. M.
1996

**Proskauer, Oskar Dr.**
08/03/1879 Bauerwitz, Silesia - no
information
*Home address:* no information
*Law firm address:* Mommsenstr. 21,
Charlottenburg
*Additional information:* Fall 1899 he
completed his school leaving examination at the
St. Maria Magdalena High School in Breslau;
he then completed his one year of "mechanical
engineering studies" at the Königl. He was a
workshop inspector at Breslau IV; he completed
his mechanical engineering studies at the TH
Berlin 1900-1905; 1905/06 at the J.M.Voith
Company in Heidenheim an der Brenz; 1906-
10 he completed his legal studies in Breslau;
he took his first state examination 1910, May
1910 he received his doctorate. Attorney and
notary; after the National Socialist seizure of
power he was made subject to an occupational
ban in early 1933.
*Sources:* Resume in the doctoral thesis of
Oskar Proskauer, Stabi; Br.B. 32; Liste d.
nichtzugel. RA, 04/25/1933; JMBl. 33, pages
220/1

**Prytek, Oskar Dr.**
10/02/1882 Osnabrück - 07/25/1942
Sachsenhausen

*Home address:* Konstanzer Str. 10,
Wilmersdorf
*Law firm address:* Seydelstr. 31, SW 19
*Additional information:* Attorney and
notary; after the National Socialist seizure of
power in 1933 he was readmitted; at the end
of 1935 his license as a notary was revoked.
He died in 1942 in the Sachsenhausen
concentration camp.
*Sources:* *li; Liste 36; BArch, R 3001 PAK;
BG; GB Sachsenhausen; GB II

**Pulvermacher, Ralph Dr.**
04/18/1890 Kempen - no information
*Home address:* Spichernstr. 19, W 50
*Law firm address:* Spichernstr. 19, W 50
*Additional information:* Attorney at the
KG and notary; after the National Socialist
seizure of power he was made subject to an
occupational ban in early 1933; he emigrated
to Tel Aviv, Palestine.
*Sources:* Adr.B. 32; Liste d. nichtzugel. RA,
04/25/1933; JMBl. 33, p. 203; BArch, R 3001
PAK; BG

# Q

**Quaatz, Reinhold Georg Dr.**
05/08/1876Berlin - 08/15/1953 Berlin
*Home address:* no information
*Law firm address:* Dessauer Str. 26
*Additional information:* He was Protestant;
he attended high school in Berlin; 1894
he took his school leaving examination;
he studied economics and law in Jena and
Berlin; after the clerkship from 1904-1913
he was an official at the Prussian state
railways; during the First World War he
was responsible for the organization of
military transports, coordinator of the
critical Ruhr-Mosel traffic and responsible
for coal supply in the west of the German
Reich; he had contacts in important banking
and industrial circles, i.a. to Hugo Stinnes,
Emil Kirdorf, Albert Vögler and Alfred
Hugenberg; 1919 he was Privy Councilor
and Lecturer Council in the Prussian
Ministry of Public Works; 1920 he received
his doctorate at the University of Cologne;
1920-1923 he was First Legal Advisor
of the Essen Chamber of Commerce and
head of several economic associations;
1920-1933 he was a member of the
Reichstag, 1920-1924 he was a member

of the DVP, then because of rejection of the Stresemann communication policy for the DNVP; in the DNVP he supported Alfred Hugenberg's wing. Hugenberg was elected party chairman in 1928 (and in 1933 coalition with Hitler); he was known as a keen, uncompromising debater and author of newspaper articles, who also used racist, anti-Semitic, nationalist slogans; 1924 he was an attorney in Berlin; 1931 he was on the board of Dresdner Bank as a representative of the Reich. After the National Socialist seizure of power, he had to leave the board of the Dresdner Bank, as he was considered by the racist Nazi criteria as "mixed race," despite his nationalist-ethnic spirit and his close contacts in the DNVP. However, he retained his admission as an attorney and could continue to practice after the general occupational ban in 1938. He is listed as an attorney for the last time in the 1939 business directory. In October 1944, the lawyer, who was a close friend of a pastor of the Confessing Church, was interrogated by the Gestapo, but remained otherwise unmolested.

He survived the National Socialist regime. After the invasion of the Red Army he was appointed mayor in Lichtenrade by the local commander, but already dismissed again in mid-June 1945 for political reasons; from now on he was active exclusively in the ecclesiastical field, he was elected chairman of the Evangelical Brotherhood in Lichtenrade and was a member of the Berlin-Brandenburg provincial synod of the Protestant Church; he was instrumental in the reconstruction of the Kirchliche Hochschule Berlin, he also lectured on world view issues and sociological day-to-day issues and was a member of the University Curatorium, as from ca. 1948 he was curator; he was one of the co-founders of the CDU in Berlin, even if he was no longer active in party politics.
*Sources:* Br.B. 32; TK 33; TK 36; Liste Mschlg. 36; Br.B. 39; BG; Walk, p. 304; Hermann Weiß/Paul Hoser, introduction to the edition: Die Deutschnationalen und die Zerstörung der Weimarer Republik. Aus dem Tagebuch von Reinhold Quaatz 1928-1933 [The German nationalists and the destruction of the Weimar Republic. From the diary of Reinhold Quaatz 1928-1933], Munich 1989.

# R

**Rabau, Alfred Dr.**
06/17/1896 Berlin - 1958 Tel Aviv, Israel
*Home address:* Kurfürstendamm 145
*Law firm address:* Klosterstr. 83/85, C 2
*Additional information:* He was a board member of the Jewish Synagogue Berlin; zionist; attorney at the KG and notary; after the National Socialist seizure of power in 1933 he was readmitted; in 1935 his license as a notary was revoked; he worked as an attorney until the general occupational ban in 1938. He emigrated to Amsterdam, the Netherlands, in March 1939, then to Palestine, he worked during the war for the inmates of the Westerbork concentration camp and Bergen-Belsen in the Netherlands; 1945 he returned to Palestine; he died in 1958 in Tel Aviv.
*Sources:* TK 33; *li; Liste 36; DJ 36, p. 315; MRRAK; BArch, R 3001 PAK; BG; BHdE, vol. 2,2, p. 733 (Ernst Mordechai Rabau); Walk

**Rabbinowitz, Julius**
05/12/1886 Königsberg - no information
*Home address:* Budapester Str. 8
*Law firm address:* Friedrich-Ebert-Str. 4; laterr: Kurfürstendamm 175/76
*Additional information:* He was director of a corporation, in addition to his activity at his law practice; he was admitted as an attorney at the LG I-III; after the National Socialist seizure of power in 1933 he was made subject to an occupational ban. He emigrated to Paris, France. An arrest warrant for tax evasion was issued against him.
*Sources:* Br.B. 32; TK 33; JMBl. 33, p. 209; Wolf, BFS

**Radt, Heinrich Dr.**
10/02/1876 - 11/25/1934 Berlin
*Home address:* no information
*Law firm address:* Müllerstr. 6, N 65
*Additional information:* Attorney and notary; after the National Socialist seizure of power in 1933 he was readmitted; he died in 1934 at the age of 58, he was buried at the Jewish cemetery in Weißensee.
*Sources:* *li; BG

**Rahmer, Erwin Dr.**
06/22/1886 Berlin - no information
*Home address:* no information
*Law firm address:* Unter den Linden 48/49

*Additional information:* Attorney and notary; after the National Socialist seizure of power he was made subject to an occupational ban in early 1933.
*Sources:* Br.B. 32; Liste d. nichtzugel. RA, 04/25/1933; JMBl. 08/21/1933; BArch, R 3001 PAK

**Raphael, Max Dr.**
08/29/1899 Posen - no information
*Home address:* no information
*Law firm address:* Burgstr. 28, C 2
*Additional information:* Joint law partnership with Richard Auerbach; after the National Socialist seizure of power he was made subject to an occupational ban in early 1933. He emigrated on 06/12/1939 to La Paz, Bolivia.
*Sources:* Br.B. 32; Liste d. nichtzugel. RA, 04/25/1933; BArch, R 3001 PAK; BG

**Rathe, Heinrich**
06/27/1906 Hamburg - no information
*Home address:* no information
*Law firm address:* Hauptstr. 34/35, Schöneberg
*Additional information:* Attorney since 1931; after the National Socialist seizure of power he was made subject to an occupatonal ban on 05/26/1933. The RAK had reported to the PrMJ on 05/11/1933 that he had scorned the SA in a pleading, stressing that he was "non-Aryan."
*Sources:* TK 33; Liste d. nichtzugel. RA, 04/25/1933; GHStA, Rep. 84a, No. 20363; JMBl. 33, p. 209; BArch, R 3001 PAK

**Rathe, Kurt**
10/06/1892 - no information
*Home address:* no information
*Law firm address:* Behrenstr. 49, W 8
*Additional information:* He took the young Werner Wolff into his office as a partner. The most important client was the Berlin Commerzbank. Moreover, he presumably was to restructure Iduna Insurance. He was a Social Democract. He did not apply for readmission in April 1933, but went into exile in Paris as a political opponent of the National Socialists. He survived the National Socialist regime and established himself in Frankfurt after 1945.
*Sources:* Br.B. 32; BArch, R 3001 PA; Pr.J. 33, p. 502; information Werner Wolff

**Rawitz, Kurt**
09/18/1903 - no information
*Home address:* no information

*Law firm address:* Nürnberger Str. 14/15, W 50
*Additional information:* Attorney since 1928; after the National Socialist seizure of power he was made subject to an occupational ban on 06/08/1933.
*Sources:* Br.B. 32; Liste d. nichtzugel. RA, 04/25/1933; JMBl. 33, p. 267; BArch, R 3001 PAK

**Redlich, Hans Dr.**
10/28/1893 Breslau - no information
*Home address:* Bundesallee 11, Charlottenburg
*Law firm address:* Meinekestr. 26, W 15
*Additional information:* Attorney and notary; after the National Socialist seizure of power in 1933 he was readmitted; his license as a notary was revoked in 1935; he worked as an attorney until the general occupational ban in 1938, then he still worked as a "consultant." He emigrated to Great Britain in April 1939.
*Sources:* *li; DJ 36, p. 315; Liste 36; MRRAK; BArch, R 3001 PAK; Liste d. Kons. 39; Naatz-Album; BG

**Rehfisch, Hans-José Dr.**
04/10/1891 Berlin - 06/09/1960 Schuls, Switzerland
*Home address:* no information
*Law firm address:* Württembergallee 26, Charlottenburg
*Additional information:* He fought in the First World War. Attorney since 1921, at the same time he was a legal advisor of a film company. Already as from 1913 he published different dramas, after the success of the piece "Who weeps around Juckenack?" at the latest, (1925) he devoted himself mainly to writing. He was head of the Association of German Playwrights and Composers, but obviously was still admitted as an attorney. After the National Socialist seizure of power he was made subject to an occupational ban as an attorney on 06/23/1933. He was arrested, but was released, because the SA men mistook him for Erwin Piscator. He went to Vienna and in 1936 to London, where he became president of the Club of German Cultural Creators.

In 1944 he published the history of the German resistance movement from four centuries in the anthology entitled "In Tyrannos" (German first edition 2004). From 1947 to 1949 he was a lecturer at the New School for Social Research in New York, and occasionally had to make a living as a precision grinder. In 1950, he returned to Europe and soon to Germany. He successfully wrote dramas, as well as screenplays. As in the Weimar Republic with the play "The Affair Dreyfus" (1929), he chose socially critical themes, e.g. in the homecoming tragedy "Colonel Chabert," or in "Beyond Fear," a piece that questions the responsibility of scientists in regard to for nuclear fission. This piece was controversial and was partially discontinued in the Federal Republic. He used the following pseudonyms: Georg Turner, René Kestner, Sydney Phillips. In 1956 he was awarded the Federal Cross of Merit First Class. He died in 1960 in Switzerland, he was buried in Berlin at the Dorotheenstadt Cemetery.
*Sources:* Liste d. nichtzugel. RA 04/25/1933; BArch, R 3001 PAK, PA; Munzinger-Archiv; Jens Brüning unbound collection; www.literaturport.de

**Reich, Hans Dr.**
10/27/1890 Berlin - transportation 1942
*Home address:* Wullenweberstr. 3, NW 87
*Law firm address:* Kurfürstendamm 188/189, W 15
*Additional information:* Attorney and notary; after the National Socialist seizure of power in 1933 he was readmitted; 1935 his license as a notary was revoked; he worked as an attorney until the general occupational ban in 1938, thereafter he was still admitted as a "consultant." Transportation on 08/26/1942 to Theresienstadt, from there he was transported to Auschwitz on 09/28/1944.
*Sources:* *li; DJ 36, p. 315; Liste 36; MRRAK; BG; GB II

**Reich, Hellmut**
05/11/1901 - no information
*Home address:* no information
*Law firm address:* Jägerstr. 20, W 8
*Additional information:* After the National Socialist seizure of power he was made subject to an occupational ban in summer 1933

despite a request to be readmitted, it was reportedly lacking sufficient explanations.
*Sources:* Jüd.Adr.B.; Adr.B. 33; TK 33; JMBl. 33, p. 234; BArch, R 3001 PAK, PA

**Reiche, Erwin Dr.**
01/20/1894 Berlin - no information
*Home address:* no information
*Law firm address:* Wichmannstr. 5, W 62
Attorney at the KG and notary; after the National Socialist seizure of power he was made subject to an occupational ban in early 1933.
*Sources:* Br.B. 32; Liste d. nichtzugel. RA, 04/25/1933; JMBl. 33, p. 203; BArch, R 3001 PAK

**Reiche, Martin Dr., Judicial Councillor**
11/29/1859 Berlin - no information
*Home address:* Landhausstr. 42, Wilmersdorf
*Law firm address:* Landhausstr. 42, Wilmersdorf
*Additional information:* After the National Socialist seizure of power in 1933 he was readmitted as an attorney, in 1936 he was no longer working.
*Sources:* TK 33; *li; BG

**Reichmann, Hans Dr.**
03/09/19011 Hohensalza - 05/24/1964 Wiesbaden
*Home address:* Emser Str. 44, W 15
*Law firm address:* Mommsenstr. 45, Charlottenburg
*Additional information:* 1919-22 he completed his legal studies in Berlin, Freiburg and Greifswald; 1924 he received his doctorate; as a student he was a member of the dueling Jewish fraternity the Cartell Convent; from 1926-27 he was an attorney in Hindenburg/Oberschlesien, at the same time he was legal counsel for the Upper Silesia State Association of the CV; as from 1927 he was legal counsel, later director of the CV in Berlin; he constantly pointed out the danger of anti-Semitism; he was married to Dr. Eva, senior staff member of the CV; he was established as an attorney since 1929. After the National Socialist seizure of power on 05/26/1933 he was made subject to an occupational ban; in 1938 he was arrested in November after the Night of the Broken Glass, he was interned at the Sachsenhausen

concentration camp until December 1938; he was released again. He emigrated via the Netherlands in April 1939 to London, Great Britain; after the beginning of the war he was interned for seven months on the Isle of Man, because he was considered an enemy alien; 1946/47 he was the managing director of the HIAS (Hebrew Immigrant Aid Society). As from 1949 he was a staff member of the United Restitution Office (URO), London, as from 03/04/1955 he was General Secretary of the URO; as from 1949 he was also member of the presidium of the Council of Jews from Germany, deputy chairman of the Association of Jewish Refugees (AJR); he had a collaboration at the Leo Baeck Institute, London. He died in 1964 in Germany during a business trip.
*Sources:* TK 33; JMBl. 33, p. 209; BG: LAB, OFP files; BHdE vol. 1, p. 592; BArch, R 3001 PAK; Walk; p. 308; Lowenthal, p. 188; Krach, p. 435; Göpp., pages 309/10

**Reimer, Eduard Dr.**
12/08/1896 Berlin - no information
*Home address:* Theodor-Fritsch-Allee 34, Zehlendorf
*Law firm address:* Maienstr. 2, W 62
*Additional information:* He fought in the First World War. He was an attorney at the KG; after the National Socialist seizure of power he was readmitted, however, he was designated as "non-Aryan," he was regarded as "mixed race," with this status he could also practice as an attorney in 1941. He survived the National Socialist regime.
*Sources:* *li; BG: BAP, 15.09 RSA; Liste Mschlg. 36; BArch, R 3001 PAK; Tel.B. 41

**Reimer, Ernst Dr.**
12/05/1897 Berlin - no information
*Home address:* Theodor-Fritsch-Allee 34, Zehlendorf
*Law firm address:* Mohrenstr. 10, W 8
*Additional information:* He fought during the First World War; after the National Socialist seizure of power in 1933 he was readmitted, but he was designated as "non-Aryan;" He was regarded as "mixed race," he was a Protestant.
*Sources:* *li; Liste Mschlg. 36; BG

**Reis, Theodor Dr.**
12/31/1884 Karlsruhe - 06/11/1950 Berlin
*Home address:* In den Zelten 20, NW 40
*Law firm address:* Jägerstr. 12
*Additional information:* Attorney at the KG; after the National Socialist seizure of power in 1933 occupational ban. His wife Luise was regarded as non-Jewish, he himself as Catholic, the marriage was regarded as a so-called "mixed marriage." In 1938 he was imprisoned for seven weeks in the Sachsenhausen concentration camp; he was released again. In 1942 he was re-imprisoned for a week by the Gestapo. He survived. After a provisional admission he was finally admitted as a laywer in January 1950, he died only a few months later in Berlin.
*Sources:* Br.B. 32; JMBl. 33, p. 203; BArch R 3001, PAK; Verz. zugel. Anw. 45; LAB, RAK, PA

**Reiwald, Paul Dr.**
05/26/1895 Berlin - 08/11/1951 Basel
*Home address:* no information
*Law firm address:* Charlottenstr. 53
*Additional information:* Attorney at the KG and notary; His admission as an attorney was revoked in the fall of 1933. He emigrated in 1933 to Brussels; he went to Palestine for a short time, because of the difficult climate he returned to Brussels; at the outbreak of war he was on vacation in Switzerland, he remained there; amongst others he held lectures on mass psychology; as from 1950 he was based in Basel.
*Publications:* Moabit - Verbrecher und Verteidiger [Moabit - criminal and defender], 1933; Vom Geist der Massen, Handbuch der Massenpsychologie [From the spirit of the masses, handbook of mass psychology], 1946; Die Gesellschaft und ihre Verbrecher [Society and its criminals], 1948 and/or 1973, published by H. Jäger and T. Moser.
*Sources:* Adr.B. 32; Pr.J. 33, p. 502; BArch, R 3001 PAK; Göpp., p. 310

**Remak, Paul Dr.**
08/03/1877 Posen - no information
*Home address:* Am Birkenhügel 8, Zehlendorf
*Law firm address:* Ritterstr. 64, SW 68

*Additional information:* Attorney and notary; after the National Socialist seizure of power in 1933 his license as a notary was revoked in 1933, he worked as an attorney until the general occupational ban in 1938. He emigrated with his wife Gertrud to Shanghai, China on 10/05/1940.
*Sources:* JMBl. 33, S. 220; *li; Liste 36; MRRAK; BG

**Richter, Hans Dr.**
08/10/1876 Berlin -
11/13/1955 Berlin
*Home address:*
Hohenzollernstr. 9, Wannsee
*Law firm address:*
Hohenzollernstr. 9, Wannsee
*Additional information:*
He fought in the First World War. He was an attorney and notary; after the National Socialist seizure of power he was readmitted in 1933. He was now regarded as "mixed race first degree" and was therefore able to practice as an attorney despite the general occupational ban in 1938. His revenue was limited and only increased slightly after 1942. He explains this fact: "Since 1942, when Hitler's retreat began, my professional income increased due to the fact that clients again dared to trust an attorney who was known as a half-Jew and a Nazi opponent." At the beginning of 1945 he was forced to give up his job "because of race." He survived the National Socialist regime and was readmitted as an attorney and a notary after 1945. He died in 1955 at the age of 79.
*Sources:* *li; Tel.B. 41; Verz. zugel. Anw. 45; LAB, RAK, PA; BG

**Richter, Walter**
12/10/1887 Filehne - no information
*Home address:* Kaiserallee 192, Wilmersdorf
*Law firm address:* Schillstr. 9, W 62
*Additional information:* Attorney and notary; after the National Socialist seizure of power in 1933 his license as a notary was revoked, thereupon his license as an attorney was revoked. He emigrated on 08/15/1933.
*Sources:* Adr.B. 33 (Walther R.); JMBl. 33, p. 266; Pr.J. 33, p. 807; BArch, R 3001 PAK; BG

**Riegelhaupt, Manek Dr.**
01/02/1899 Przemysl - December 1978
*Home address:* Prinzregentenstr. 42, Wilmersdorf

*Law firm address:* Friedrichstr. 136, N 24
*Additional information:* He had performed military service in the Austro-Hungarian army from March 1917 to November 1918. In 1920 he was naturalized in Germany. In February 1928 he established himself as an attorney in Berlin. His income was low and he obtained permission to work as a property manager on the side. However, the situation did not improve fundamentally. Nevertheless, he understood his clients' situation and pursued their concerns, even if he did not expect the full fee due to him. As a result of such a case, legal proceedings were brought before him before the Bar Association, because he was charging fees that were too low, thus a violation of the fee schedule. The event was even dealt with in the press. The income of his legal activities remained low. When he was not paid after the assumption of a mandate for a legal aid order for "Rote Hilfe," he sent a reminder in March 1931. However, even "Rote Hilfe" had financial difficulties and referred to its empty coffers. At the end of August 1931, he was then able to receive RM 86.55.
After the National Socialist seizure of power his license as an attorney was revoked on 05/23/1933, in June 1933 his name was removed from the Bar Association list, because of "non-Aryan descent and activity in the communist sense." In the personnel files his further efforts to be admitted can be retraced. However, the occupational ban remained; eventually his naturalization was also revoked. He emigrated to the USA; he died in 1978 at the age of 79.
*Sources:* Br.B. 32; JMBl. 33, p. 209; BArch, R 3001 PAK, PA; SSDI; Schneider, Schwarz, Schwarz, pages 237-239

**Riegner, Heinrich**
01/26/1878 - 12/26/1964 New York
*Home address:* no information
*Law firm address:* Joachimsthaler Str. 41, Charlottenburg (1932)
*Additional information:* Attorney since 1907, "frontline fighter" in the First World War; he was associated with attorney Kurt Rosenfeld; he was still a board member of the RAK in 1932. After the National Socialist seizure of power in 1933 he was made subject to a temporary representation ban, the examination of the application took

some time, he was recognized as a "frontline fighter and an "elderly attorney" and was readmitted, but his license as a notary was revoked. But "in the meantime, he lost his clients," reported his son. He moved his law office to Berna, he was admitted as an attorney until the general occupational ban in 1938. He emigrated with his family to the USA in 1938, where he died in 1964 at the age of 86. His son, a law clerk in 1933, later became a member of the Jewish World Congress. He died in December 2001.
*Sources:* Liste d. nichtzugel. RA, 04/25/1933; Pr.J. 33, p. 633; *li; Liste 36; MRRAK; Krach, p. 436; information of the son Gerhard Riegner, 1998

**Riesenfeld, Friedrich Dr.**
06/23/1888 Königshütte - no information
*Home address:* no information
*Law firm address:* Jägerstr. 18, W 8
*Additional information:* Attorney and notary; after the National Socialist seizure of power he was made subject to an occupational ban in June 1933. He emigrated on 11/08/1933 to Paris, France.
*Sources:* Br.B. 32; Liste d. nichtzugel. RA, 04/25/1933; JMBl. 33, p. 203; BArch, R 3001 PAK; BG

**Riess, Ernst Dr.**
08/19/1879 Breslau - no information
*Home address:* Niebuhrstr. 77, Charlottenburg
*Law firm address:* Mauerstr. 81, W 8
*Additional information:* Attorney and notary; after the National Socialist seizure of power in 1933 his license as a notary was revoked; he worked as an attorney until the general occupational ban in 1938. As to his further fate, there are contradictory statements: according to the database of the Berlin Memorial Book he should have emigrated to Valparaiso, Chile, on 08/14/1939, according to the memory of Dorothee Fliess, he committed suicide.
*Sources:* JMBl. 33, p. 220; *li; Liste 36; MRRAK; BG; Information Dorothee Fliess, 01/03/1999

**Ritter, Ernst Dr.**
06/12/1903 Breslau - no information
*Home address:* no information
*Law firm address:* Dircksenstr. 26/27, C 25

*Additional information:* After the National Socialist seizure of power he was made subject to an occupational ban in June 1933; he presumably emigrated to Haifa, Palestine.
*Sources:* Br.B. 32; Liste d. nichtzugel. RA, 04/25/1933; JMBl. 33, p. 209; BArch, R 3001 PAK; BG

**Ritter, Hans**
05/12/1901 Orzegow/Schlesien - no information
*Home address:* Schwäbische Str. 9, Schöneberg
*Law firm address:* Berliner Allee 238, Weißensee
*Additional information:* Attorney since 1928; after the National Socialist seizure of power he was made subject to an occupational ban in July 1933. He was married and had a child. He emigrated to Palestine in January 1935.
*Sources:* Liste nichtzugel. RA, 04/25/1933; JMBl. 08/04/1933, p. 253; BArch, R 3001 PAK, PA R 22/72425; BG: BLHA, Pr.Br. Rep. 36 A, Dev.st., Nr. A 3506

**Rittler, Wilhelm, Judicial Councillor**
08/30/1867 Tuchel - 11/16/1941 Litzmannstadt/Lodz
*Home address:* Alte Schönhauser Str. 33/34, N 54
*Law firm address:* Alte Schönhauser Str. 33/34, N 54
*Additional information:* Attorney and notary; after the National Socialist seizure of power in 1933 his license as a notary was revoked, he worked as an attorney until the general occupational ban in 1938. Transportation to Litzmannstadt/Lodz on 10/24/1941, he died there three weeks later.
*Sources:* JMBl. 33, p. 220; *li; Liste 36; MRRAK; BG; GB II

**Roetter, Friedrich Dr.**
03/21/1888 Berlin - 10/24/1953 East Orange/ New York, USA
*Home address:* Kaiserallee 74, Wilmersdorf
*Law firm address:* Rankestr. 5, W 50
*Additional information:* Officer during the First World War, awarded the EK I; attorney at the KG and notary; member of the DNVP (Deutschnationale Volkspartei = German National People's Party). After the National Socialist seizure of power in 1933 he was readmitted; he also defended political

opponents of National Socialism (amongst others he was the assigned counsel for Ernst Thälmann). March to June 1935 he was under Gestapo arrest. He was brought to trial before the tribunal. After his release from custody in 1935 he escaped to France; he became prominent with lectures and publications, especially on the Thälmann trial and Nazi justice; as part of the Thälmann campaign he stayed in Zurich, London, Prague and Sweden. A warrant was issued against him for tax code violations. He went to the USA in 1939, to New York. There, on December 29, 1939, he applied for a scholarship from the American Committee for the Guidance of the Professional Personnel to study at an American law school. He was rejected because of his age. His situation was desperate, because he was only able to work partially because of a disability, but at the same time he had to pay for the livelihood of a family of five. He worked from 1940-45 as a radio commentator; from 1942-45 as an employee of the OSS (Office for Strategic Services) for the evaluation of foreign press, besides studying political science; from 1947 he was a lecturer at a college in East Orange, New York. He died in 1953 at the age of 65.
*Sources:* *li; NY Publ.Lib. (Am. Com.) Roetter; BG: BHdE vol. I, p. 609; Wolf, BFS

**Ronau, Kurt**
11/06/1899 Berlin - no information
*Home address:* Konstanzer Str. 59, W 15
*Law firm address:* Konstanzer Str. 59, W 15
*Additional information:* After the National Socialist seizure of power he was readmitted, he worked as an attorney until the general occupational ban in 1938; he presumably emigrated later.
*Sources:* *li; Liste 36; MRRAK; BArch, R 3001 PAK; BG

**Rosenbaum, Berthold Dr.**
07/18/1885 Schneidemühl - no information
*Home address:* Von-der-Heydt-Str. 9, W 35
*Law firm address:* Von-der-Heydt-Str. 5, W 35
*Additional information:* Attorney and notary; after the National Socialist seizure of power in 1933 his license as a notary was revoked, he worked as an attorney until the general occupational ban in 1938. He emigrated to New York, USA on 03/28/1941.
*Sources:* *li; Liste 36; MRRAK; BG

**Rosenbaum, Fritz**
08/25/1897 Berlin - no information
*Home address:* Plantage 10-11, Spandau
*Law firm address:* Potsdamer Str. 35, Spandau
*Additional information:* Soldier during First World War from 1916-1918; attorney since 1927. After the National Socialist seizure of power in 1933 he was readmitted. He emigrated to Palestine. His license as an attorney was revoked in 1935. After 1945 he returned to Berlin, he worked for the URO, later he returned to Israel.
*Sources:* Br.B. 32; *li; BArch, R 3001 PAK, PA; BG; information E. Proskauer

**Rosenbaum, Kurt Dr.**
01/29/1903 Gießen - October 1986
*Home address:* no information
*Law firm address:* Berliner Allee 241, Weißensee
*Additional information:* After the National Socialist seizure of power he was made subject to an occupational ban in early 1933. He emigrated to the USA in April 1934, he last lived in Suffolk, New York.
*Sources:* Br.B. 32; Liste d. nichtzugel. RA, 04/25/1933; JMBl. 08/21/1933; BArch, R 3001 PAK; BG; SSDI

**Rosenberg, Bruno**
08/08/1885 Samotschin - no information
*Home address:* Kurfürstendamm 230, W 50
*Law firm address:* Kurfürstendamm 230, W 50
*Additional information:* Attorney and notary; after the National Socialist seizure of power his license as a notary was revoked in 1933, he was further admitted as as an attorney. He emigrated to London, Great Britain.
*Sources:* JMBl. 33, S. 220; *li; BG

**Rosenberg, Curt Dr.**
08/19/1890 Berlin - no information
*Home address:* no information
*Law firm address:* Badstr. 60, N 20
*Additional information:* Attorney and notary; after the National Socialist seizure of power in 1933 his license as a notary was revoked, in 1936 he was still working as an attorney in the Netherlands.
*Sources:* Pr.J. 33, p. 390; *li; Liste 36; BArch, R 3001 PAK; BG

**Rosenberg, Hugo, Judicial Councillor**
12/30/1874 - no information
*Home address:* no information
*Law firm address:* Nassauische Str. 2,
Wilmersdorf
*Additional information:* Attorney at the
KG and notary; after the National Socialist
seizure of power in 1933 his license as a
notary was revoked, he was readmitted as an
attorney; he was no longer working in 1936.
*Sources:* JMBl. 33, p. 220; *li; BG

**Rosenberg, Kurt Dr.**
05/25/1876 Berlin - 04/20/1964 Edinburgh,
Scotland
*Home address:* Schlüterstr. 32,
Charlottenburg
*Law firm address:* Stresemannstr. 103, SW 11
*Additional information:* He was involved
in the defense of Karl Liebknecht as a
law student intern; he fought as a soldier
in the First World War and was honored
for his combat mission; he was married
and the father of three children; he was
religious, he attended the New Synagogue
in Oranienburger Str.; he was a member of
the SPD and on the board of the Steglizt
construction cooperative. After the National
Socialist seizure of power he was readmitted
as attorney and notary, in 1935 his license as
a notary was revoked, he was still working as
an attorney until the general occupational ban
in 1938. In his identity card of 1939 it states
under occupation: "without."
He emigrated with his wife to Great
Britan, where a son was already living and
established himself in Glasgow, Scotland.
In 1940, like many German refugees, he
was interned on the Isle of Man. He did not
experience that time as stressful, but rather as
intellectually very stimulating, because there
were many academics among the internees.
His experiences were in clear contrast to those
of his son, who was deported to Canada and
confronted with soldiers who did not want
to distinguish between German Nazis and
refugees from Germany who had fled the
Nazis. He published a book on international
matrimonial law and a biography of Disraeli.
He died in 1964 shortly before his 88th
birthday surrounded by his family.
*Sources:* *li; DJ 36, p. 315; Liste 36;
MRRAK; BG; information of the daughter
Miriam Whitfield

**Rosenberg, Ludwig**
08/06/1880 Posen - no information
*Home address:* Kurfürstendamm 146,
Charlottenburg
*Law firm address:* Kurfürstendamm 146,
Charlottenburg
*Additional information:* Attorney and notary;
after the National Socialist seizure of power
in 1933 he was readmitted, in 1935 his license
as a notary was revoked, he still worked as an
attorney until the general occupational ban
in 1938; also until at least 1935 he was the
president of Akiba Eger Loge, which belonged
to B'nai B'rith. He emigrated before September
1939 to Great Britain.
*Sources:* Adr.B. 32; *li; DJ 36, p. 315; Liste
36; MRRAK; BArch, R 3001 PAK, PA (E.
Rosenberg); BG

**Rosenberg, Martin**
11/05/1903 - no information
*Home address:* Bandelstr. 12, NW 12
*Law firm address:* Ritterstr. 80, SW 68
*Additional information:* Attorney since 1931;
after the National Socialist seizure of power he
was made subject to an occupational ban on
06/08/1933. He emigrated in 1933 to Palestine.
*Sources:* Liste d. nichtzugel. RA, 04/25/1933;
JMBl.33, p. 253; BArch, R 3001 PAK, PA; BG

**Rosenberg, Max Dr.**
12/30/1884 Landsberg - no information
*Home address:* no information
*Law firm address:* Alexanderstr. 13, O 27
*Additional information:* Attorney and
notary; after the National Socialist seizure
of power in 1933 he was made subject to an
occupational ban.
*Sources:* Adr.B. 33; TK 33; JMBl. 33, p. 253;
BArch R 3001 PAK

**Rosenberg, Werner Dr.**
06/06/1903 Berlin - 05/03/1957 New York
*Home address:* no information
*Law firm address:* Kurfürstendamm 11, W 50
*Additional information:* He studied in
Würzburg and Berlin; he was active in student
organizations and student self-government,
amongst others in the AStA Berlin; at the same
time he was a member of the board of the CV
and coworker of the CV newspaper; 1930
he received his doctorate in Breslau, as from
1930 he was an attorney, later also a notary in
Berlin. After the National Socialist seizure of

power he was made subject to an occupational ban in early 1933; until 1930 he was one of the directors of the aid organiation that was particularly involved in Jewish emigration; 1938 he was a representative of the aid organization at the refugee conference of Evian; he emigrated to the USA in 1938; after renewed legal studies admitted as an attorney in New York; legal counsel for the German Consulate General in New York; he died there in 1957 at the age of 53.
*Sources:* TK 33; Liste d. nichtzugel. RA, 04/25/1933; JMBl. 33, p. 221; BArch, R 3001 PAK; BG; BHdE vol. I, p. 613

**Rosenberger, Arthur Dr., Judicial Councillor**
03/01/1872 Berlin - 12/19/1942 London
*Home address:* Darmstädter Str. 7, W 15
*Law firm address:* Nikolsburger Platz 2, Wilmersdorf
*Additional information:* Attorney and notary; after the National Socialist seizure of power in 1933 license as a notary was revoked; he worked as an attorney until the general occupational ban in 1938. He emigrated to London, Great Britain.
*Sources:* TK 33; JMBl. 33, p. 220; *li; Liste 36; MRRAK; BG

**Rosendorff, Richard Dr.**
No information
*Home address:* no information
*Law firm address:* Behrenstr. 50/52, W 8
*Additional information:* Attorney and notary; after the National Socialist seizure of power in 1933 his license as a notary was revoked; in 1936 he was no longer working as an attorney, he presumably emigrated to Switzerland, since he still published academic articles there in 1942.
*Publications:* among others Das internationale Steuerrecht des Erdballs [Global international tax law], Basel 1942.
*Sources:* JMBl. 33, S. 220; *li

**Rosenfeld, Georg, Judicial Councillor**
No information - 06/18/1936
*Home address:* Archivstr. 8, Dahlem
*Law firm address:* Paulsborner Str. 13, Halensee
*Additional information:* Attorney and notary; after the National Socialist seizure of power in 1933 his license as a notary was revoked, he worked as an attorney until his death in 1936.

*Sources:* Adr.B. 33; JMBl. 33, p. 220; *li; Liste 36

**Rosenfeld, Hans Dr.**
03/06/1888 Berlin - no information
*Home address:* no information
*Law firm address:* Französische Str. 21, W 8
Attorney and notary; after the National Socialist seizure of power in 1933 he was readmitted.
*Sources:* *li; BArch, R 3001 PAK

**Rosenfeld, Julius Dr.**
08/22/1887 Karlsruhe - no information
*Home address:* no information
*Law firm address:* Kurfürstendamm 136, Wilmersdorf
*Additional information:* Attorney since 1913; he fought in the First World War. He was admitted as notary in February 1933, his admission was deleted upon request in July 1933.
*Sources:* JMBl. 02/10/1933, 08/21/1933; BArch, R 3001 PAK, PA

**Rosenfeld, Kurt Dr.**
02/01/1877 Marienwerder - 09/25/1943 New York
*Home address:* Lärchenweg 28, Berlin-Eichkamp
*Law firm address:* Joachimsthaler Str. 41
*Additional information:* 1896-99 he studied law and economics in Freiburg i. Br. and Berlin; as from 1905 he was an attorney in Berlin; 1914-18 he fought in the First World War; already while studying he was admitted to the SPD; 1910-20 he was a city councilor in Berlin; 1917 he was co-founder of the USPD; November 1918 to January 1919 he was the Prussian Minister of Justice; he was a member of the constituent Prussian State Assembly; 1920-32 he was a member of the Reichstag for the USPD, then for the SPD; he counted in the SPD as left opposition; he was excluded from the SPD and belonged in 1931 to the co-founders of those settled between the SPD and KPD; as attorney he was a prominent defender in political processes (amongst others Rosa Luxemburg, Kurt Eisner, Carl v. Ossietzky); he was a member of the League for Human Rights. He was the brother of Siegfried and the father of the attorney Hilde Kirchheimer. Together with

Hugo Sinzheimer he took on one of the major political processes of the Weimar Republic, the Bullerjahn process, which dealt with the consequences of the Treaty of Versailles. The already imprisoned Bullerjahn was released after the trial was resumed on the initiative of its defense attorneys. He had broken away from the Jewish religion, he was a dissident. After the seizure of power by the National Socialists, he could have asserted his readmission in 1933 as an "elderly attorney." He was made subject to an occupational ban because of participation in Communist activities. In May 1933, the board of the RAK reported him to the Prussian Ministry of Justice as defense counsel for Ossietzky and emphasized that he was "non-Aryan." He emigrated in 1933, first to Czechoslovakia, then to Paris. A warrant was issued against him for tax code violations. In the fall of 1933 in London he was a co-organizer of the counter process to the Reichstag fire process; he arrived in the USA in 1934; he campaigned for the merger of Hitler's opponents in the Popular Front. He died in 1943 at the age of 76 in New York.
*Sources:* JMBl. 08/04/1933, p. 253; GHStA, Rep. 84a, No.. 20363; BG; BHdE vol. 1, p. 614, Göpp., p. 311; Krach, p. 436 (with different information); information Krumeder 10/2001

**Rosenfeld, Siegfried**
03/22/1874 Marienwerder - November 1947
*Home address:* Adolf-Scheidt-Platz. 8, Tempfelhof
*Law firm address:* no information
*Additional information:* Admitted as an attorney in 1904; he participated in the First World War between 1914 and 1919; before 1919 he was also admitted as a notary; 1923 his license was revoked and he was appointed to the council of the KG; later he was appointed as undersecretary and subsequently as head of the section. A Prussian member of parliament for the SPD, he was placed on temporary retirement in November 1932 in the course of political "adjustments." He applied for readmission as an attorney in 1933 with the president of the KG, which took place on March 16, 1933. In April 1933, his license as an attorney was revoked, his application for readmission took a long time to be processed and examined. In October 1933, the district court president came to the

following conclusion: His "entry in the . . . list of attorneys was deleted with regard to his non-Aryan descent." He was not readmitted as an attorney, he was made subject to an occupational ban. Of course it was important that his brother was the politically active Kurt. He was imprisoned in Berlin in 1934. He was released and moved to Icking near Munich. On 04/04/1938 he applied for permission to move to Argentina, where his oldest daughter was already working as a nanny. The Gestapo had no objection against the departure. He emigrated to Great Britain with his two younger children, where he was interned as an "enemy alien" after the war began on the Isle of Man (June-September 1940); he died in 1947; he did not go to Argentina.
*Sources:* BArch, R 3001 PAK, PA; BG; Information Krumeder 2001

**Rosenfeld, Waldemar Dr.**
03/01/1887 Moscow - no information
*Home address:* Heilbronner Str. 26, Schöneberg
*Law firm address:* Prager Str. 23, Wilmersdorf
*Additional information:* After the National Socialist seizure of power he was made subject to an occupational ban in early 1933. He emigrated to London, Great Britain, on 06/01/1939.
*Sources:* Adr.B. 32; Liste d. nichtzugel. RA, 04/25/1933; JMBl. 33, p. 195; BArch, R 3001 PAK; BG

**Rosenthal, Alfred Dr.**
02/13/1875 Moers - no information
*Home address:* no information
*Law firm address:* Sachsallee 30/34, Dahlem
*Additional information:* Attorney at the KG; after the National Socialist seizure of power he was made subject to a representation ban in April 1933, which was abolished. In October 1933 he was readmitted. He emigrated via several stopovers to Mar del Plata, Argentina.
*Sources:* Liste d. nichtzugel. RA, 04/25/1933; *li; BArch, R 3001, PAK; Göpp., p. 312

**Rosenthal, Curt**
06/20/1882 Frankenstein - 03/02/1943 Großbeeren
*Home address:* Prinzregentenstr. 6, Wilmersdorf
*Law firm address:* Potsdamer Str. 24/25, W 35 (Loeser & Wolff-Haus) until the beginning of

1938; Uhlandstr. until the end of 1938
*Additional information:* Attorney at the
KG and notary; fought in the First World
War. After the National Socialist seizure of
power in 1933 his license as a notary was
revoked; he worked as an attorney until the
general occupational ban in 1938. His wife
Katharina was presumably not Jewish. As
part of the wave of arrests after the November
pogrom he was also arrested and went to
the Sachsenhausen concentration camp from
11/10/1938 until 12/16/1938. He was later
arrested again and sent to a "work education
camp." He died in March 1943 at the age of
61 in Großbeeren, presumably at the "work
education camp" there.
*Sources:* *li; Liste 36; MRRAK; BArch, R
3001 PAK, PA; BG; GB II

**Rosenthal, Edwin**
01/20/1884 Berlin - 08/28/1933 Berlin
*Home address:* Hardenbergstr. 1,
Charlottenburg
*Law firm address:* Molkenmarkt 12-13
*Additional information:* Attorney and
notary; he had fought in the First World War,
he was a member of the Reich Association
for Combating Social Democracy and the
German Fleet Association. He died in 1933
at the age of 49, before his application for
readmission could be finalized.
*Sources:* Br.B. 32; BArch, R 3001 PAK, PA;
Pr.J. 33, p. 442; BG

**Rosenthal, Felix**
06/23/1879 Königsberg -
10/27/1964 Berlin
*Home address:* Altonaer Str.
18, NW 87
*Law firm address:*
Klosterstr. 69, C 2
*Additional information:*
Attorney and notary; he was Protestant;
he fought in the First World War and was
honored several times as a soldier; at the last
free elections he voted for the DVP. After
the National Socialist seizure of power in
1933 his license as a notary was revoked,
he worked as an attorney until the general
occupational ban in 1938; he then took up
property management until 1941. In 1942
he was a legal assistant to a "consultant,"
in 1943 he was conscripted to work as a
construction worker for the Schöneberg

District Office. On 01/10/1944 he was
transported to Theresienstadt. He survived;
he returned to Berlin and was readmitted as
an attorney and notary in 1946.
*Sources:* JMBl. 33, p. 209; *li; Liste 36;
MRRAK; Verz. zugel. Anw. 45; LAB, RAK,
PA; BG

**Rosenthal, Fritz**
08/30/1884 Beuthen -
10/29/1968 Berlin
*Home address:*
Kurfürstendamm 93,
Wilmersdorf
*Law firm address:*
Kurfürstendamm 93,
Wilmersdorf
*Additional information:* Attorney and
notary; he was Protestant; he fought in
the First World War; he was established as
an attorney since 1924, he was previously
employed in industry; he voted for the DVP
during the last free elections. After the
National Socialist seizure of power in 1933
he was readmitted; his license as a notary was
revoked in 1935, he worked as an attorney
until the general occupational ban in 1938.
As from 1943 he went underground, he lived
in a basement apartment in Wexstr. 49 in
Wilmersdorf. In 1947 he was readmitted as
an attorney and notary. He died in 1968 at
the age of 84 in Berlin.
*Sources:* *li; DJ 36, p. 315; Liste 36;
MRRAK; Verz. zugel. Anw. 45; BG; LAB,
RAK, PA

**Rosenthal, Hans Bruno Dr.**
12/22/1894 Bernburg - no information
*Home address:* Klosterstr. 43, C 2
*Law firm address:* Klosterstr. 43, C 2
*Additional information:* Attorney and
notary; after the National Socialist seizure of
power he was readmitted in 1933; in 1935 his
license as a notary was revoked, he worked as
an attorney until the general occupational ban
in 1938. He emigrated to La Paz, Bolivia, on
02/27/1939.
*Sources:* *li; DJ 36, p. 315; Liste 36;
MRRAK; BG

**Rosenthal, Hans Dr.**
03/02/1887 Seelow - no information
*Home address:* Kommandantenstr. 51,
SW 19

*Law firm address:* Reinickendorfer Str. 2, N 65

*Additional information:* Attorney and notary; he was Protestant; after the National Socialist seizure of power in 1933 he was readmitted; in 1935 his license as a notary was revoked, he worked as an attorney until the general occupational ban in 1938. His wife was regarded as non-Jewish, the marriage was regarded as privileged. He survived the Nazi regime and was immediately re-admitted as an attorney and notary.

*Sources:* *li; DJ 36, p. 315; Liste 36; MRRAK; BArch, R 3001 PAK; Verz. zugel. Anw. 45; BG

**Rosenthal, Harry Dr.**
03/21/1882 Berlin - no information
*Home address:* no information
*Law firm address:* Unter den Linden 57/58
*Additional information:* Attorney and notary; after the National Socialist seizure of power in 1933 he was readmitted; in 1935 his license as a notary was revoked; he worked as an attorney until the general occupational ban in 1938, later he still worked as a "consultant."

*Sources:* *li; DJ 36, p. 315; Liste 36; MRRAK; Naatz-Album; BG

**Rosenthal, Heinz Dr.**
06/12/1904 Schöneberg - no information
*Home address:* Goethestr. 11, Lichterfelde
*Law firm address:* Potsdamer Str. 114, W 35
*Additional information:* After the National Socialist seizure of power he was made subject to an occupational ban in early 1933.

*Sources:* Liste d. nichtzugel. RA, 04/25/1933 (Nachtrag); BArch, R 3001 PAK; BG

**Rosenthal, James Yaakov**
09/29/1905 Berlin - 09/11/1997 Jerusalem
*Home address:* no information
*Law firm address:* Krausnickstr. 19, N 24
*Additional information:* He studied law in Berlin and Freiburg i.Br.; he had a legal traineeship in the Supreme Court judicial district; on 12/03/1932 he was admitted as an attorney at the LG II; he was involved in the youth and welfare work of the Jewish community. After the National Socialist

seizure of power he was made subject to an occupational ban in early 1933. He was a Zionist; he also loved German culture. 1933 he emigrated to Palestine; 1933-35 he had journalistic retraining; from 1936 he worked as an editor of newspapers and editor; from 1949 he was an editorial member of "Haaretz," until 1970 he was a parliament correspondent and editor for judicial affairs; he died in 1997 in Jerusalem.

*Sources:* Liste d. nichtzugel. RA, 04/25/1933; JMBl. 08/04/1933, p. 253; BArch, R 3001, PAK; BG; BHdE vol. I, p. 617; information of the wife; information Knobloch

**Rosenthal, Ludwig**
No information
*Home address:* no information
*Law firm address:* Helmstedter Str. 20, Wilmersdorf
*Additional information:* Attorney and notary; after the National Socialist seizure of power in 1933 his license as a notary was revoked, he was still working as an attorney in 1936.

*Sources:* JMBl. 33, p. 220; *li; Liste 36

**Rosenthal, Walter**
No information
*Home address:* No information
*Law firm address:* Budapester Str. 29, W 62
*Additional information:* Attorney at the KG and notary; after the National Socialist seizure of power in 1933 his license as a notary was revoked, he was still working as an attorney in 1936.

*Sources:* JMBl. 33, p. 220; *li; Liste 36

**Rosentreter, Isaak**
01/17/1883 Gollantsch - no information
*Home address:* Niebuhrstr. 11, Charlottenburg
*Law firm address:* Alexanderstr. 42, O 27
*Additional information:* Attorney and notary; after the National Socialist seizure of power in 1933 he was readmitted; his license as a notary was revoked in 1935, he was still working as an attorney in 1936. 1936 he emigrated; an arrest warrant for tax evasion was issued against him.

*Sources:* *li; DJ 36, p. 315; Liste 36; BG; BArch, R 3001 PAK; Naatz-Album; Wolf, BFS

**Rosenzweig, Anna Dr., nee Kaiser-Blüth**
01/16/1898 Naumburg - no information
*Home address:* no information
*Law firm address:* Sybelstr. 9, Charlottenburg
*Additional information:* After the National Socialist seizure of power he was made subject to an occupational ban in early 1933. He emigrated to Belgium in 1935; there she was active in the aid committee for Jewish refugees; member of Bnai Brith and vice president of the Women's International Zionist Organization (WIZO).
*Sources:* Liste d. nichtzugel. RA, 04/25/1933; JMBl. 33, p. 234; BArch, R 3001 PAK; BG (R., Aenne): BHdE vol. 1, p. 618 (Arthur Max Moritz Rosenzweig)

**Rosenzweig, Max Dr.**
07/09/1888 Zielenzig - 04/09/1967 Berlin
*Home address:* Fasanenstr. 29, W 15
*Law firm address:* Tauentzienstr. 8, W 50
*Additional information:* Attorney since 1914, later also a notary; he fought in the First World War; he was a member of the Zionist association. After the National Socialist seizure of power in 1933 he was readmitted; in the middle of 1935 his admission was revoked; he emigrated to Tel Aviv, Palestine in 1935; 1942-1945 he was an official at the mandate administration; as from 1948 he was in the Israeli Ministry of Commerce; 1954 he returned to Berlin, he was readmitted as an attorney.
*Sources:* TK 33; *li; DJ 07/05/1935, p. 950; BArch, R 3001 PAK; BG: deleted BHdE vol. 1, p. 618; LAB, RAK, PA

**Rosner, Alfred Dr.**
02/28/1898 Cologne - no information
*Home address:* no information
*Law firm address:* Mauerstr. 80, W 8
*Additional information:* Attorney at the KG; after the National Socialist seizure of power in 1933 he was readmitted, he was still working as an attorney in 1936.
*Sources:* *li; Liste 36; BArch, R 3001 PAK

**Roth, Emil**
No information - before 08/04/1933
*Home address:* no information
*Law firm address:* Hardenbergstr. 1 a, Charlottenburg
*Additional information:* Attorney and notary; after the National Socialist seizure of power in 1933 his license as a notary was revoked, because he was "non-Aryan;" a little later he died.
*Sources:* Adr.B. 33; TK 33; JMBl. 33, p. 209, p. 252

**Rothberg, Alfred Dr.**
12/15/1903 Lemberg - no information
*Home address:* no information
*Law firm address:* Nürnberger Platz 3, W 50
*Additional information:* After the National Socialist seizure of power he was made subject to an occupational ban in early 1933; he survived and worked in the judiciary in North Rhine-Westphalia after 1945.
*Sources:* Liste d. nichtzugel. RA, 04/25/1933; JMBl. 08/04/1933, p. 253; BArch, R 3001 PAK

**Rothe, Friedrich Dr.**
10/18/1873 Guben - 11/27/1956
*Home address:* Fontanestr. 9, Steglitz
*Law firm address:* Französische Str. 47, W 8
*Additional information:* Attorney (since 1901) and notary (since 1912); he fought in the First World War; he was a German national; 1927-1933 he was a member of the board of the Berlin Bar Association, as from 1929 he was vice chairman. After the National Socialist seizure of power in 1933 he was readmitted. He was regarded as "mixed race," for this reason, he was able to practice as an attorney and notary beyond the general occupational ban of 1938. According to his own statements, he generated high revenues, largely due to the mandates of Knorr-Bremse AG, Nederlandse Bankinstelling and two real estate companies. He survived; he gave no details of the exact circumstances in the denazification documents. After 1945, he was again admitted as an attorney and notary and worked until beyond his 80th birthday.
*Sources:* TK 33; *li; Liste Mschlg. 36; BArch, R 3001 PAK; Tel.B. 41; Verz. zugel. Anw. 45; LAB, RAK, PA; BG

**Rothe, Gerhart Dr.**
11/26/1903 Berlin-Schöneberg - no information
*Home address:* Altensteinstr. 58, Dahlem
*Law firm address:* Düsseldorfer Str. 35 a, W 15

*Additional information:* Son of Friedrich; after the National Socialist seizure of power in 1933 he was readmitted. He was regarded as "mixed race second degree," his wife as non-Jewish; because of his status he could practice law despite the general occupational ban in 1938. He survived the National Socialist regime and established himself as an attorney after 1945 in Munich.
*Sources:* *li; Liste Mschlg. 36; BG; Tel.B. 41

**Rothe, Wilhelm Dr., Judicial Councillor**
11/24/1853 - 12/23/1938 Berlin
*Home address:* Hölderlinstr. 11, Mitte
*Law firm address:* Gillstr. 2 a, Grunewald
*Additional information:* Attorney and notary; after the National Socialist seizure of power in 1933 he was readmitted; in 1935 his license as a notary was revoked; in 1936 he was still admitted as an attorney, he died in December 1938 at the age of 84.
*Sources:* *li; DJ 36, p. 315; Liste 36; BG

**Rothenberg, Adolf, Judicial Councillor**
09/01/1861 - 03/02/1935 Berlin
*Home address:* Prager Str. 36, W 50 (1932)
*Law firm address:* Prager Str. 36, W 50
*Additional information:* Attorney and notary; after the National Socialist seizure of power his licenses as an attorney and as a notary were revoked in April 1933 ; he died in 1935 at the age of 73, he was buried at the Jewish cemetery in Weißensee..
*Sources:* Jüd.Adr.B.; JMBl. 04/13/1933; BG

**Rother, Kurt**
03/27/1893 Berlin - no information
*Home address:* Geisbergstr. 37, W 30
*Law firm address:* Werderstr. 3-4
*Additional information:* Attorney and notary; after the National Socialist seizure of power in 1933 he gave up his law office. He emigrated to New York, USA, presumably in 1933.
*Sources:* Adr.B. 32; JMBl. 33, p. 195; BArch, R 3001 PAK; BG

**Rothkugel, Karl Dr.**
07/18/1886 Berlin - transportation 1942
*Home address:* Karl-Schrader-Str. 1, W 30
*Law firm address:* Landsberger Str. 83, C 25
*Additional information:* Attorney and notary; after the National Socialist seizure of power in early 1933 he was made subject to

an occupational ban as an attorney and his license as a notary was revoked; in October 1933 he was readmitted as an attorney; until the general occupational ban in 1938 he worked as an attorney. He was conscripted for forced labor and last used as a laborer for the German Arms and Ammunition Factory or the German Reichsbahn. Date of declaration of property: 10/13/1942; transportation on 10/19/1942 to Riga.
*Sources:* Br.B. 32; Liste d. nichtzugel. RA, 04/25/1933; *li; Liste 36; MRRAK; BArch, R 3001 PAK; BG; BdE; GB II

**Rothkugel, Leon Dr.**
12/04/1883 Berlin - no information
*Home address:* Schwäbische Str. 5, W 30
*Law firm address:* Schwäbische Str. 5, W 30
*Additional information:* Member of the Reformed Jewish Synagogue Berlin; after the National Socialist seizure of power in 1933 he was readmitted; he was not working in 1936.
*Sources:* *li; BArch, R 3001 PAK

**Rothschild, Ernst**
09/27/1883 Berlin - transportation 1943
*Home address:* Mommsenstr. 55, Charlottenburg
*Law firm address:* Potsdamer Str. 49
*Additional information:* Attorney (since 1912) and notary (since 1929); after the National Socialist seizure of power in 1933 his license as a notary was revoked. Bar disciplinary proceedings were carried out against him. In a further proceeding he was declared incompetent and at the same time his license as an attorney was revoked. Collecting station Große Hamburger Str. 26; transportation to Auschwitz on 10/29/1943.
*Sources:* Adr.B. 32; BArch, R 3001 PAK, PA; JMBl. 33, 05/12/1933; BG; GB II

**Rothschild, John**
02/19/1885 Berlin - no information
*Home address:* Salzburger Str. 14, Schöneberg
*Law firm address:* Lützowufer 19 b, W 35
*Additional information:* Attorney at the KG; after the National Socialist seizure of power in 1933 he was readmitted, at the end of 1933 his license as an attorney was revoked. He emigrated to Amsterdam, the Netherlands.
*Sources:* Br.B. 32; JMBl. 33, p. 209; *li; BArch, R 3001 PAK; BG: LAB, OFP files

**Rothschild, Paul**
02/04/1867 Trier - 03/29/1943 Theresienstadt
*Home address:* Prager Str. 35, W 50 (1932)
*Law firm address:* no information
*Additional information:* After the National
Socialist seizure of power he was made subject
to an occupational ban in the middle of 1933.
On 11/05/1942 he was transported from
Berlin to Theresienstadt, where he died at the
end of March 1943.
*Sources:* Jüd.Adr.B.; JMBl. 7.7.33, p. 209; VZ
39; BG; ThG; GB II

**Rothstein, Fritz Dr.**
04/27/1896 Berlin - transportation 1944
*Home address:* no information
*Law firm address:* Klosterstr. 88/90, C 2
*Additional information:* Attorney and
notary; after the National Socialist seizure
of power in 1933 he was readmitted; his
license as a notary was revoked in 1935;
he still worked as an attorney until 1936.
Presumably he emigrated to the Netherlands,
was arrested, imprisoned at Westerbork, on
02/26/1944 transported to Theresienstadt,
from there he was transported on 09/29/1944
to Auschwitz.
*Sources:* *li; DJ 36, P. 315; Liste 36; BArch, R
3001 PAK; BG; GB II

**Ruge, Helmut Dr.**
No information
*Home address:* Heimat 82, Zehlendorf
*Law firm address:* Unter den Linden 10, NW 7
*Additional information:* After the National
Socialist seizure of power he was regarded as
"mixed race," for this reason he was allowed
to practice law throughout the general
occupational ban in 1938; he worked as an
attorney until at least 1941.
*Sources:* TK 33; Liste Mschlg. 36; Tel.B. 41

**Ruhemann, Hans Dr.**
05/09/1900 Berlin - no information
*Home address:* Lietzenburger Str. 31, W 15
Law firm office: Salzburger Str. 31
*Additional information:* After the National
Socialist seizure of power in 1933 he was
made subject to an occupational ban. He
emigrated via the Netherlands to Buenos
Aires, Argentina, in February 1938.
*Sources:* Adr.B. 32; TK 33; JMBl. 33,
05/12/1933; BArch, R 3001 PAK; BG

**Ruhm, Ernst Dr.**
08/20/1876 Königsberg -
no information
*Home address:* Helmstedter
Str. 8, Wilmersdorf
*Law firm address:* Königstr.
49, C 2
*Additional information:*
Attorney and notary; after the National
Socialist seizure of power in 1933 his license
as a notary was revoked, he worked as an
attorney until the general occupational ban
in 1938.
*Sources:* TK 33; JMBl. 33, p. 209; *li; Liste
36; MRRAK; Naatz-Album; BG

**Russ, Georg Dr.**
05/08/1893 Berlin - no information
*Home address:* no information
*Law firm address:* Joachimsthaler Str. 30
and/or 25/26, W 15
*Additional information:* Attorney and
notary; after the National Socialist seizure of
power he was made subject to an occupational
ban on 06/08/1933. He emigrated in
September 1933 to Palestine.
*Sources:* Br.B. 32; Liste d. nichtzugel. RA,
04/25/1933; JMBl. 33, p. 221; BArch, R 3001
PAK, PA; BG

**Rynarzewski, Benno Dr.**
09/04/1893 Labischin - transportation 1942
*Home address:* Sächsische Str. 10-11,
Wilmersdorf
*Law firm address:* Rankestr. 31/32, W 50
*Additional information:* Attorney and
notary; after the National Socialist seizure of
power in 1933 he was readmitted; his license
as a notary was revoked in 1935, he was still
working as an attorney until at least 1936.
He emigrated to Prague, Czechoslovakia,
in 1938; at the beginning of 1941 he was
transported from Prague to Theresienstadt;
from there he was transported on 01/09/1942
to Riga.
*Sources:* *li; DJ 36, p. 315; Liste 36; BArch,
R 3001 PAK; BG (Rynarschweski); GB II

# S

### Saalfeld, Bernhard H. Dr.
11/28/1890 Berlin - no information
*Home address:* Barbarossastr. 23, W 30
*Law firm address:* Barbarossastr. 23, W 30
*Additional information:* After the National Socialist seizure of power in 1933 he was readmitted; he was still working as an attorney in 1936. 1936 he emigrated to Den Haag, the Netherlands.
*Sources:* TK 33; *li; Liste 36; BG

### Sabersky, Fritz Dr.
07/03/1880 Seehof - 1952 Los Angeles
*Home address:* Lützowplatz 5, W 62
*Law firm address:* Bellevuestr. 14, W 9
*Additional information:* He fought in the First World War, he was an attorney at the LG I-III and notary; after the National Socialist seizure of power in 1933 he was readmitted; at the end of 1935 his license as a notary was revoked; he was admitted until at least 1936 as an attorney. He emigrated to Los Angeles, the USA, on 08/25/1938; there he worked for Jewish emigrants; later as an attorney who specialized in reparation affairs.
*Sources:* TK 33; *li; DJ 36, p. 315; Liste 36; BArch, R 3001 PAK; BG: LAB, OFP files; Walk, p. 322

### Sachs, Alfred Dr.
04/23/1891 Berlin - transportation 1943
*Home address:* Münchener Str. 21-22
*Law firm address:* Neue Königstr. 70
*Additional information:* Attorney at the KG and notary; after the National Socialist seizure of power in 1933 he was made subject to an occupational ban. He emigrated to Paris, France. Transportation on 11/20/1943 from Drancy to Auschwitz.
*Sources:* Adr.B. 32; TK 33; JMBl. 08/21/1933, p. 266; BArch, R 3001 PAK; BG; GB II

### Sachs, Benno, Judicial Councillor
02/10/1870 Glatz - 11/09/1943 Theresienstadt
*Home address:* Lützowstr. 42, W 35
*Law firm address:* Lützowstr. 42, W 35
*Additional information:* Attorney and notary; after the National Socialist seizure of power he was temporarily released from notarial duties; in 1935 his license as a notary was revoked. He was arrested on 10/08/1942; collecting station Große Hamburger Str.

26; transportation on 10/29/1942 to Theresienstadt, he died there a few days after arrival.
*Sources:* TK 33; JMBl. 33, p. 209; *li; DJ 36, P. 315; Liste 36; MRRAK; BG; ThG; GB II

### Sachs, Ernst
08/31/1888 Berlin - no information
*Home address:* Duisburger Str. 6/Helmstedter Str. 2 (1939), Wilmersdorf
*Law firm address:* Potsdamer Str. 123 b, W 35
*Additional information:* Attorney at the KG and notary; he was Protestant before, then non-denominational; after the National Socialist seizure of power in 1933 he was readmitted; in 1936 he was still working as an attorney; he was regarded as "mixed race," he presumably emigrated, in 1951 he was living in the USA.
*Sources:* Br.B. 32; TK 33, 1936; *li; BArch, R 3001 PAK; VZ 39; BG

### Sachs, Franz Dr.
05/20/1893 Beuthen - 11/30/1941 Riga
*Home address:* Bechstedter Weg 13 at Joseph, Wilmersdorf
*Law firm address:* Gervinusstr. 11, Charlottenburg
*Additional information:* Attorney and notary; after the National Socialist seizure of power in 1933 he was readmitted; his license as a notary was revoked at the latest at the end of 1935; his license as an attorney was revoked before the general occupational ban in 1938; he tried to flee Germany and transfer part of his assets abroad; he was arrested on 10/01/1938. Proceedings were brought against him, which the *Völkische Beobachter* [National Observer] pleasurably exploited with the title "Winnetou with the mocha cups" (see edition of 01/28/1939 with photo). He was sentenced to two and a half years in prison. He probably was not freed. Date of declaration of property: 11/27/1941; transported on 11/27/1941 to Riga, he was murdered there shortly after arrival.
*Sources:* Br.B. 32; TK 33; *li; BArch, R 3001 PAK; VB 01/28/1938; BG; BdE; GB II

### Sachs, Kurt Dr.
09/06/1890 - no information
*Home address:* no information
*Law firm address:* Leipziger Str. 121, W 8

*Additional information:* Attorney and notary; after the National Socialist seizure of power in 1933 he was readmitted; in 1935 his license as a notary was revoked, until the general occupational ban in 1938 he worked as an attorney, then still as a "consultant" until 01/09/1945; further details of his life are unknown.
*Sources:* TK 33; *li; DJ 36, p. 315; Liste 36; MRRAK; VZ 39; BG

### Sachs, Rudolf
10/02/1902 Berlin - 1978 Berlin
*Home address:* no information
*Law firm address:* Neue Friedrichstr. 69
*Additional information:* He appeared as an attorney in political trials, amongst others he defended Socialists and Communists; he himself belonged to an independent socialist association. After the National Socialist seizure of power in 1933 he was made subject to an occupational ban; he first went to Copenhagen, then to Paris, because he did not foresee a chance to practice in Denmark, because of his lack of language skills. After the beginning of the war, he was interned in a camp in France as an "enemy alien;" during this time he got married; together with his wife he managed to flee to the USA. He arrived there on 06/13/1941. He established himself in New York; he worked as an insurance representative, in the 1950s he worked for the URO, then studied at the New School for Social Research, graduated in 1962; in 1967 he was appointed as a lecturer in sociology at the Manchester Community College; in 1972 he retired; he died in 1978 in Berlin, presumably on a trip.
*Sources:* Adr.B. 32; Liste d. nichtzugel. RA, 04/25/1933; JMBl. 33, p. 203; BArch, R 3001 PAK; LBI, Sachs, Rudolf; BG; Jewish Immigrants . . . in the U.S.A., Oral History, p. 107

### Saenger, Léon Dr.
02/26/1877 Stettin - no information
*Home address:* Prinzregentenstr. 1, Wilmersdorf
*Law firm address:* Budapester Str. 14, W 50
*Additional information:* Attorney and notary; after the National Socialist seizure of power in 1933 his license as a notary was revoked. His wife was regarded as non-Jewish, and he of "mixed race."

*Sources:* TK 33; JMBl. 33, p. 220; *li; LAB, Liste Mschlg. 36; BArch, R 3001 PAK; BG

### Salier, Georg Dr.
12/03/1877 Berlin - 1971 USA
*Home address:* Bundesratufer 7, NW 21
*Law firm address:* Claudiusstr. 11
*Additional information:* Attorney and notary; after the National Socialist seizure of power he was readmitted; in 1935 his license as a notary was revoked; he was probably working as an attorney until his emigration on 12/09/1936; he first went to the Netherlands, then to the USA. An arrest warrant for tax evasion was issued against him. He died in 1971 in the USA.
*Sources:* TK 33; *li; DJ 36, p. 315; Liste 36; BG; Wolf, BFS

### Salinger, Ernst Dr.
05/13/1882 - no information
*Home address:* no information
*Law firm address:* Oranienstr. 2, SO 36
*Additional information:* Attorney and notary; after the National Socialist seizure of power in 1933 he was readmitted. At the end of 1935 his license as a notary was revoked; he worked as an attorney until the general occupational ban in 1938.
*Sources:* Adr.B. 32; TK 33; *li; DJ 36, p. 315; Liste 36; MRRAK; BG

### Salinger, Werner Dr.
04/27/1896 - no information
*Home address:* no information
*Law firm address:* Afrikanische Str. 88
*Additional information:* Attorney at the KG, after the National Socialist seizure of power he gave up practicing as an attorney in 1933 in Berlin. The RAK reported to the Prussian Ministry of Justice that he was in contact with Red Aid, stressing that he was "non-Aryan."
*Sources:* Br.B. 32; Adr.B. 32; GHStA, Rep. 84a, No. 20363; JMBl. 33, p. 282; BArch, R 3001 PAK, PA

### Salomon, Adolf, Geh. Judicial Councillor
12/21/1848 - 11/07/1934 Berlin
*Home address:* Magdeburger Str. 31, W 35
*Law firm address:* Magdeburger Str. 31, W 35
*Additional information:* Attorney and notary; after the National Socialist seizure of power in 1933 he was readmitted; he died

in 1934 at the age of 85; he was buried at the Jewish cemetery in Weißensee.
*Sources:* TK 33; *li; BG

**Salomon, Alfred Dr., Judicial Councillor**
05/04/1863 Czarnikau - 02/11/1940
*Home address:* Ludwig-Hoffmann-Hospital, Pankow
*Law firm address:* Jenaer Str. 8
*Additional information:* Attorney at the KG and notary; after the National Socialist seizure of power in 1933 he was readmittted; he ceased working as an attorney before the end of 1935. He died in 1940 at the age of 76; he was buried at the Jewish cemetery in Weißensee.
*Sources:* Br.B. 32; TK 33; *li; BG

**Salomon, Ernst Dr.**
12/01/1886 Berlin - 11/30/1941 Riga
*Home address:* no information
*Law firm address:* Königsgrätzer Str., 75/75a, SW 11
*Additional information:* Attorney and notary; after the National Socialist seizure of power in 1933 he was readmitted; in 1935 his license as a notary was revoked, he worked as an attorney until the general occupational ban in 1938. He last lived in Kleinmachnow; transportation on 11/27/1941, he was murdered there shortly after arrival.
*Sources:* TK 33; *li; DJ 36, p. 315; Liste 36; BArch, R 3001 PAK; MRRAK; BG; BdE; GB II

**Salomon, Fritz Dr.**
05/22/1891 - no information
*Home address:* Sächsische Str. 5, Wilmersdorf
*Law firm address:* Kurfürstendamm 199, W 15
*Additional information:* Attorney and notary; after the National Socialist seizure of power in 1933 he was readmitted; in 1935 his license as a notary was revoked, he was still working as an attorney until at least 1936. He emigrated to New York, USA.
*Sources:* TK 33; *li; DJ 36, p. 315; Liste 36; TK 1936; BG

**Salomon, Heinrich**
08/17/1883 Tiegenhoff - 11/30/1941 Riga
*Home address:* Barbarossastr. 32 a, Schöneberg
*Law firm address:* Martin-Luther-Str. 19, W 30

*Additional information:* Attorney at the KG and notary; after the National Socialist seizure of power in 1933 his license as a notary was revoked, he worked as an attorney until the general occupational ban in 1938. Transportation on 11/27/1941 to Riga, he was murdered there shortly after his arrival.
*Sources:* TK 33; JMBl. 33, p. 209; *li; Liste 36; MRRAK; BArch, R 3001 PAK; BG; BdE; GB II

**Salomon, Hermann**
10/20/1881 Posen - no information
*Home address:* Prager Str. 33, W 50; Sodener Str. 30, Wilmersdorf (1945)
*Law firm address:* Fasanenstr. 72, W 15
*Additional information:* Attorney at the KG and notary; after the National Socialist seizure of power in 1933 his license as a notary was revoked, he worked as an attorney until the general occupational ban in 1938. He survived by going underground, in December 1945 he was living in Berlin-Wilmersdorf; he was readmitted as an attorney, but he emigrated in 1946 to the USA.
*Sources:* TK 33; JMBl. 33, p. 220; *li; Liste 36; MRRAK; BArch, R 3001 PAK; Verz. zugel. Anw. 45; BG

**Salomon, Kurt**
01/25/1907 Berlin - no information
*Home address:* Barstr. 39, Wilmersdorf
*Law firm address:* no information
*Additional information:* After the National Socialist seizure of power he was made subject to an occupational ban in August 1933. He emigrated on 03/15/1936 to Palestine.
*Sources:* JMBl. 33, p. 282; BArch, R 3001 PAK; BG

**Salomon, Max Dr.**
No information - 1935/1936
*Home address:* Pariser Str. 32, W 15
*Law firm address:* Oranienburger Str. 58, N 24
*Additional information:* Attorney at the LG I-III; until fall 1935 he was listed in the attorney directory; at the end of 1935/ beginning of 1936 he died.
*Sources:* TK 33; *li; TK 36; DJ 36, p. 23

**Salomon, Paul**
02/10/1887 Schivelbein - transportation 1943
*Home address:* Maikowskistr. 107, Charlottenburg
*Law firm address:* Jägerstr. 61, W 8
*Additional information:* Attorney and notary; after the National Socialist seizure of occupation in 1933 he was readmitted; at the end of 1935 his license as a notary was revoked, he worked as an attorney until the general occupational ban in 1938. He was conscripted to do forced labor, he was last used as a laborer. Date of declaration of property; 02/28/1943; collecting station Levetzowstr. 7-8; transportation on 03/02/1943 to Auschwitz.
*Sources:* TK 33; *li; DJ 36, p. 315; Liste 36; MRRAK; BArch, R 3001 PAK; BG; GB II; Naatz-Album

**Salomon, Philipp Dr., Judicial Councillor**
02/10/1867 Landsberg - 04/27/1941
*Home address:* Württembergallee 8, Charlottenburg
*Law firm address:* Lützowstr. 67
*Additional information:* Attorney at the KG and notary; after the National Socialist seizure of power in 1933 his license as a notary was revoked, he worked as an attorney until the general occupational ban in 1938; he died in 1941 at the age of 74, he was buried at the Jewish cemetery in Weißensee.
*Sources:* TK 33; JMBl. 33, p. 220; *li; Liste 36; MRRAK; BG

**Salomon, Richard Dr.**
06/25/1894 Berlin-Charlottenburg - transportation 1942
*Home address:* Gervinustr. 24, Charlottenburg
*Law firm address:* Uhlandstr. 163, W 15
*Additional information:* Attorney at the KG and notary; after the National Socialist seizure of power in 1933 he was readmitted; his license as a notary was revoked in 1935; he worked as an attorney until the general occupational ban in 1938. Transportation on 12/14/1942 to Auschwitz.
*Sources:* TK 33; *li; DJ 36, p. 315; Liste 36; MRRAK; BArch, R 3001 PAK; BG; GB II

**Salomon, Samuel Dr.**
07/27/1884 - no information
*Home address:* no information
*Law firm address:* Friedrichstr. 72, W 8
*Additional information:* Attorney and notary; after the National Socialist seizure of power in 1933 his license as an attorney was revoked; before fall of 1935 he was deleted from the list of attorneys.
*Sources:* TK 33; JMBl. 33, 220; *li; BArch, R 3001 PAK

**Salomon, Wolff Dr.**
03/01/1888 - no information
*Home address:* Kaiserkorso 4, Tempelhof
*Law firm address:* Belle-Alliance-Str. 11
*Additional information:* Attorney at the KG and notary; after the National Socialist seizure of power he was made subject to an occupational ban in early 1933; emigration.
*Sources:* Adr.B. 32; TK 33; Liste d. nichtzugel. RA, 04/25/1933; JMBl. 33, p. 209; BArch, R 3001 PAK; BG

**Salomonski, Georg Dr.**
04/12/1895 Berlin - no information
*Home address:* no information
*Law firm address:* Kufsteiner Str. 20, Schöneberg
*Additional information:* Attorney at the KG and notary; after the National Socialist seizure of power he was made subject to an occupational ban on 06/20/1933. He emigrated to Palestine, there he operated a cafe in the first years in Haifa, later he was an attorney in the Israeli income tax authority.
*Sources:* Br.B. 32; TK 33; Liste d. nichtzugel. RA, 04/25/1933; JMBl. 33, p. 253; BArch, R 3001 PAK, PA; information from attorney Joel Levi, Tel Aviv

**Salz, Benno, Judicial Councillor**
No information
*Home address:* no information
*Law firm address:* Bamberger Str. 48, Schöneberg
*Additional information:* Attorney and notary; after the National Socialist seizure of power in 1933 he was readmitted, before fall of 1935 he was deleted from the list of attorneys.
*Sources:* Br.B. 32; TK 33; *li

**Salz, Walter**
06/06/1897 Berlin - transportation 1942
*Home address:* no information
*Law firm address:* Kaiserdamm 19,
Charlottenburg
*Additional information:* After the National
Socialist seizure of power he was made
subject to an occupational ban in early 1933.
Transportation on 03/28/1942 to Piaski.
*Sources:* Liste d. nichtzugel. RA, 04/25/1933
(addendum); BG; GB II

**Samoje, Ferdinand**
01.19/1875 Ratibor - 04/10/1937 Berlin
*Home address:* no information
*Law firm address:* Berliner Str. 157,
Wilmersdorf
*Additional information:* Attorney since 1906,
last at the KG, and notary; he was a specialist
in labor law; he had fought in the First World
War; in 1932 he was still a board member of
the RAK, since 1929 he was chairman of the
court of honor, member of the main board of
the CV, co-founder of the Reichs Union for
Jewish Front Soldiers (Reichsbund jüdischer
Frontsoldaten = R.j.F.), and representative of
the merger of non-Aryan lawyers. After the
National Socialist seizure of power in 1933 he
was readmitted; at the end of 1935 his license
as a notary was revoked, at the beginning of
1937 he committed suicide.
*Sources:* TK 33; *li; Liste 36; BG:
Friedh.W.Sterbereg.; Wolf, BFS; Göpp., p.
228; information Dorothee Fliess, 01/03/1999

**Samolewitz, Leopold Dr.**
11/23/1883 Berlin - no information
*Home address:* Fasanenstr. 66, W 15
*Law firm address:* Bayreuther Str. 41, W 62
*Additional information:* He fought in the
First World War; attorney at the KG and
notary. After the National Socialist seizure of
power in 1933 he was readmitted; in 1935 his
license as a notary was revoked; he worked as
an attorney until the general occupational ban
in 1938, thereafter still as a "consultant." He
emigrated to Palestine.
*Sources:* TK 33; *li; DJ 36, p. 315; Liste 36;
MRRAK; Liste d. Kons., 12/31/1938; BArch,
R 3001 PAK; BG

**Samter, Albert**
05/11/1902 Berlin - no information
*Home address:* no information

*Law firm address:* Köpenicker Str. 39, SO 16
*Additional information:* He resigned from
the Jewish Synagogue; after the National
Socialist seizure of power he was made subject
to an occupational ban in early 1933.
*Sources:* TK 33; Liste d. nichtzugel. RA,
04/25/1933 (addendum); JMBl. 06/17/1933,
BArch, R 3001 PAK; BG

**Samter, Gottfried Dr.**
10/22/1884 Liegnitz - 02/07/1959 Berlin
*Home address:* Linkstr. 42, W 9
*Law firm address:* Linkstr. 42, W 9
*Additional information:* He fought as a
soldier during the First World War and was
awarded the EK I. Kl.; attorney (since 1914)
and notary (since 1925). After the National
Socialist seizure of power he was readmitted
in 1933; at the end of 1935 his license as
a notary was revoked; he worked as an
attorney until the general occupational ban
in 1938, he worked as a "consultant" until
1939. He emigrated to Palestine; he worked
as a taxi driver in Jerusalem; in 1954 he was
readmitted as an attorney and returned to
Berlin; he was appointed as a notary again in
1955, he died in 1959 in Berlin.
*Sources:* TK 33; *li; DJ 36, p. 315; Liste 36;
MMRAK; Liste d. Kons. v. 12/31/1938;
BArch, R 3001 PAK; BG: LAB, RAK, PA

**Samuel, Felix Dr.**
03/08/1888 - 04/24/1937
*Home address:* Martin-Luther-Str. 42,
Schöneberg
*Law firm address:* Landsberger Str. 92, NO 18
*Additional information:* Attorney and
notary; after the National Socialist seizure
of power in 1933 he was readmitted; at
the end of 1935 his license as a notary was
revoked, he worked until at least 1936 as an
attorney; he died in April 1937 at the age of
49 and was buried at the Jewish cemetery in
Weißensee.
*Sources:* TK 33; *li; DJ 36, p. 315; Liste
36; BG

**Sandak, Alfred Dr.**
No information
*Home address:* no information
*Law firm address:* Schaperstr. 6 a, W 50
*Additional information:* Attorney and
notary; after the National Socialist seizure
of power in 1933 his license as a notary was

revoked, he was still working as an attorney until emigration on 03/11/1936.
*Sources:* Adr.B. 32; TK 33; JMBl. 33, p. 209; * li; Liste 36; DJ 36, p. 454

**Sandberg, Gustav, Judicial Councillor**
02/19/1856 Posen - 12/28/1940 Berlin, Jewish Hospital
*Home address:* no information
*Law firm address:* Kottbusser Str. 6, SO 36
*Additional information:* "[He] had been an attorney in Berlin since 1914. He was on the board of the Jewish Reformation Synagogue, he married into an old established 'mixed-race family,' he remained a liberally conscious Jew and proud German, a very friendly, popular man - generous and cultivated. He never made much money as an attorney, but that was not a problem since his wife had 'brought money.' He especially represented members of the 'lower classes', especially gypsies. They were repeatedly accused of fraud in horse sales (teeth sharpened to make the horses look younger). [He] represented them even if they could not remunerate him. After 1918, the family had lost some of their wealth, but was still very wealthy, living in a beautiful apartment on Kurfürstendamm." This is how his grandson, Prof. Grenville, described him in February 1997.
After the National Socialist seizure of power he was readmitted; in 1935 his license as a notary was revoked, he still worked as an attorney until ca. 1936. The grandson continues: "As a kid, I remember the time after 1933. My grandparents had to move with my parents to a modest apartment on Hohenzollerndamm. My father, who was District Court Director, was forcibly retired in 1933. During this time, former clients showed their loyalty to old Sandberg. When Sinti and Roma came through Berlin, they left a basket of eggs and other food at our door. Every week my grandfather sent my brother to a certain bakery. He should knock on the back door and say, 'I come from Judge Sandberg,' then a basket of baked goods was handed over. My grandfather died before the deportation in 1941 in the Jewish hospital on Iranian road. My grandmother, in her late seventies, was deported and murdered in 1942."
*Sources:* TK 33; *li; DJ, 36, p. 315; Liste 36; BG; information Prof. J.A.S. Grenville, Great Britain

**Sandelowsky, Selmar**
03/16/1888 Nordenburg - no information
*Home address:* no information
*Law firm address:* Motzstr. 37, Wilmersdorf
*Additional information:* Attorney and notary; after the National Socialist seizure of power in 1933 he was readmitted; at the end of 1935 his license as a notary was revoked; he worked as an attorney until at least 1936.
*Sources:* TK 33; *li; DJ 36, p. 315; Liste 36; BArch, R 3001 PAK

**Sander, Eugen Dr., Judicial Councillor**
No information
*Home address:* Vopeliuspfad 5, Zehlendorf
*Law firm address:* Wittenbergplatz 1, W 62
*Additional information:* Attorney at the KG and notary; he was still a board member of the RAK in 1932; after the National Socialist seizure of power in 1933 he was readmitted; at the end of 1935 his license as a notary was revoked, he worked as an attorney until the general occupational ban in 1938, last in his apartment.
*Sources:* TK 33; *li; DJ 36, p. 315; Liste 36; Tel.B. 38; MRRAK

**Sandheim, Heinz Dr.**
08/02/1899 Berlin - no information
*Home address:* Kurfürstendamm 184, W 15
*Law firm address:* Kurfürstendamm 182/183, W 15
*Additional information:* After the National Socialist seizure of power in 1933 he was readmitted, he worked as an attorney until the general occupational ban in 1938. He emigrated to London, Great Britain; in 1952 he lived in Wembley, he changed his first name to Henry.
*Sources:* TK 33; *li; Liste 36; MRRAK; BG

**Sass, Heinrich**
08/04/1891 Gutstadt, Ostpreußen - no information
*Home address:* no information
*Law firm address:* Taubenstr. 21, W 56
*Additional information:* After the National Socialist seizure of power he was made subject to an occupational ban on 06/19/1933. He emigrated on 05/09/1940 to Shanghai, China.
*Sources:* Br.B. 32; TK 33; Liste d. nichtzugel. RA, 04/25/1933; JMBl. 33, p. 234; BArch, R 3001 PAK, PA; BG

**Schachian, Herbert Prof. Dr.**
05/05/1888 Berlin - September 1971
*Home address:* Rauchstr. 8
*Law firm address:* Hinter der Katholischen
Kirche 1, W 56
*Additional information:* Attorney and notary,
at the same time he was an interpreter for
English and French, related to Julius Schachian,
who was his law partner. After the National
Socialist seizure of power in 1933 his license
as a notary was revoked; he was deleted from
the list of attorneys before fall of 1935. He
emigrated to Amsterdam, the Netherlands, later
he went to the USA, he last lived in New York.
*Sources:* Adr.B. 33; TK 33; *li; Pr.J. 33, p. 390;
BArch, R 3001 PAK; BG; SSDI

**Schachian, Julian Dr.**
06/02/1880 Berlin - 10/29/1942 Riga
*Home address:* Schleswiger Ufer 6, Tiergarten
*Law firm address:* Friedrichstr. 63, W 8
*Additional information:* Attorney and
notary; after the National Socialist seizure
of power in 1933 his license as a notary
was revoked, he worked as an attorney
until the general occupational ban in 1938.
Transportation on 10/26/1942 to Riga, he
was murdered there on the day of his arrival.
*Sources:* TK 33; JMBl. 33, p. 220; *li; Liste
36; MRRAK; BArch, R 3001 PAK; BG; BdE;
GB II

**Schachian, Julius, Judicial Councillor**
No information
*Home address:* no information
*Law firm address:* Hinter der Katholischen
Kirche 1, W 56
*Additional information:* Attorney and notary,
in a law partnership with Herbert Sch.; after the
National Socialist seizure of power in 1933 he
was readmitted; he was deleted from the list of
attorneys before fall of 1935.
*Sources:* TK 33; *li

**Schachnow, Julian Dr.**
No information - 1936
*Home address:* no information.
*Law firm address:* Wichmannstr. 28, W 62
*Additional information:* Attorney and
notary; after the National Socialist seizure
of power in 1933 his license as a notary was
revoked; he worked as an attorney until his
death in 1936.
*Sources:* TK 33; JMBl. 33, p. 220; *li; Liste 36

**Schachtel, Ernst Dr.**
06/26/1903 - November 1975
*Home address:* no information
*Law firm address:* Frankfurter Allee 79,
O 112
*Additional information:* After the National
Socialist seizure of power he was made subject
to an occupational ban in early 1933; in his
application for readmission, he emphasizes
that he and his associates did not terminate
the employees. He emigrated to the USA, he
changed his first name to Ernest, he died in
1975 at the age of 72.
*Sources:* Br.B. 32; TK 33; Liste d. nichtzugel.
RA, 04/25/1933; JMBl. 33, p. 253; BArch, R
3001 PAK, PA, esp. p. 6; SSDI; information
E. Proskauer

**Schachtel, Jacob, Judicial Councillor**
10/03/1867 Schmierzycze - no information
*Home address:* Frankfurter Allee 79, O 112
*Law firm address:* Frankfurter Allee 79,
O 112
*Additional information:* Attorney at the
KG and notary; after the National Socialist
seizure of power in 1933 he was readmitted.
1934 he emigrated to Haifa, Palestine.
*Sources:* TK 33; *li; BG; information E.
Proskauer

**Schaefer, Ernst Dr.**
02/15/1891 Berlin - no information
*Home address:* Leonhardstr. 4,
Charlottenburg
*Law firm address:* Ehrenbergstr. 11/14, O 17
*Additional information:* After the National
Socialist seizure of power in 1933 he was
readmitted, he worked as an attorney until the
general occupational ban in 1938. Emigration;
he later became a member of the URO.
*Sources:* TK 33; *li; Liste 36; MRRAK;
BArch, R 3001 PAK; BG; information Werner
Wolff, 09/22/1998

**Schatzky, Georg Dr.**
08/11/1878 Breslau - no information
*Home address:* Niebuhrstr. 4, Charlottenburg
*Law firm address:* Kurfürstenstr. 127, W 62
*Additional information:* Attorney at the
KG and notary; he was a member of the
Republican Association of Judges. After
the National Socialist seizure of power in
1933 his license as an attorney was revoked;
he worked as an attorney until the general

occupational ban in 1938. Emigration to London, Great Britain, in August 1939.
*Sources:* TK 33; MvRRB; JMBl. 33, p. 220; *li; Liste 36; MRRAK; BG

**Schaul, Hans Dr.**
12/13/1905 Hohensalza - 05/10/1988
*Home address:* no information
*Law firm address:* Friedrichstr. 78, W 8
*Additional information:* As from 1915 he was in high school in Frankfurt/Oder; 1925-1928 he studied law and economics in Berlin, Freiburg i. Br. and Heidelberg; he joined the Socialist Student Union; 1932 he was admitted as an attorney; he was made subject to an occupational ban in early 1933; emigration to France in 1933; 1936-1938 he fought in the Spanish Civil War as a soldier in the International Brigades; 1938 he returned to France, in Paris he was active in the Aid Committee for German fighters in Spain; 1939 he changed to the KPD; from September 1939 at the beginning of the war until 1944 he was held in internment camps and employed in labor companies, last in Djelfa in Algeria. He was first married to the children's book author Ruth Rewald, who was arrested in France in 1942 by the Gestapo and was probably murdered in Auschwitz; their daughter Anja was also deported from France to Auschwitz in 1944 and murdered.
He went to the USSR in 1944, there, amongst others, he worked as a political instructor in POW camps and as a teacher at Antifa schools; 1948 he returned to Germany in the SBZ (Sowjetische Besatzungszone = Soviet Occupation Zone); 1948-1951 he was in state economic administration and planning; 1951-1956 he was a professor and vice-rector at the University of Economics; 1956-1972 he was the editor-in-chief of "Einheit" [Unity], the theoretical organ of the SED (Sozialistische Einheitspartei Deutschlands = Socialist Unity Party of Germany), until 1976 he was on the editorial board of the journal, then he volunteered at the Central Committee of the SED, Department of International Relations; he died in 1988, he was buried in Berlin.
*Sources:* Liste d. nichtzugel. RA, 04/25/1933; JMBl. 08/04/1933, S. 253; BArch, R 3001 PAK; BG; BHdE vol. 1, p. 641; Wer war wer in der DDR? [Who was who in the GDR?], Berlin 2000; diverse Internet articles

**Scheer, Hermann Gustav**
06/11/1886 Oldenburg - 11/15/1947 Berlin
*Home address:* Kaiserdamm 18, Charlottenburg
*Law firm address:* Kaiserdamm 18, Charlottenburg
*Additional information:* He fought in the First World War; after the National Socialist seizure of power in 1933 he was readmitted; he was regarded as "mixed race" and was allowed to practice law throughout the general occupational ban in 1938, although limited, since he was not allowed to take on any poverty law cases; he was reported in mid-1943 by the KG president to the employment office as one of the "non-members of the National Socialist Association of Legal Professionals," because his "legal profession" was not assessed as "important to the war." He wrote: "I succeeded in performing my legal duties, in addition to my work as legal counsel for Gebr. Hertling in Berlin-Charlottenburg, to which I was assigned by the employment office." He survived the Nazi regime and was immediately readmitted as an attorney and notary.
*Sources:* TK 33; *li; LAB, Liste Mschlg. 36; BG; LAB, RAK, PA

**Schendel, Kurt Dr.**
02/07/1904 Berlin - no information
*Home address:* no information
*Law firm address:* Potsdamer Str. 114, W 35
*Additional information:* After the National Socialist seizure of power he was made subject to an occupational ban on 06/15/1933.
*Sources:* TK 33; Liste d. nichtzugel. RA, 04/25/1933; JMBl. 08/04/1933, p. 253 (Curt Sch.); BArch, R 3001 PAK, PA

**Scherek, Leo Dr.**
1893 Posen - 1962 Israel
*Home address:* no information
*Law firm address:* Alt-Moabit 86 c
*Additional information:* Attorney since 1920; he was active in numerous Zionist organizations. After the National Socialist seizure of power in 1933 he was made subject to an occupational ban; 1937-1939 he was a member of the representative assembly of the Jewish community; after the Night of the Broken Glass in November 1938 he was interned in a concentration camp. He emigrated to Palestine after his release; there he was

active in the Organization of Immigrants from Central Europe (Irgun Olej Merkas Europa), he died in 1962 in Israel.
*Sources:* Br.B. 32; TK 33; JMBl. 08/04/1933, p. 253; Liste nichtzugel. RA, 04/25/1933; Walk, p. 329

**Schereschewsky, Benno Dr.**
05/17/1907 Königsberg - no information
*Home address:* no information
*Law firm address:* Taubenstr. 23, W 56
*Additional information:* Attorney at the KG; after the National Socialist seizure of power he was made subject to an occupational ban in early 1933.
*Sources:* Liste d. nichtzugel. RA, 04/25/1933; JMBl. 08/21/1933, p. 266; BArch, R 3001 PAK

**Scherman, Georg Dr.**
09/18/1881 Potsdam-Nowawes - 11/01/1952 Berlin
*Home address:* Kurfürstendamm 36, W 15
*Law firm address:* Fredericiastr.13, Charlottenburg
*Additional information:* He was Protestant; he fought in the First World War; he was an attorney at the LG I-III and a notary. After the National Socialist seizure of power in 1933 his license as a notary was removed; he was regarded as "mixed race" and was married to a woman who was regarded as non-Jewish, for this reason he was able to practice law throughout the general occupational ban in 1938; he was later "prosecuted by the Gestapo and after July 20, 1944 he was captured by "Aktion Mitte" (own account in denazification process); he was supposed to be used for clearance work, but was released because of his poor physical condition. His office and apartment were bombed out in 1943 and 1944. He was restrained when talking about his difficult life situation: " During the Nazi period, I was subjected to serious professional injuries and persecution. I was, amongst others, excluded from the representation of all state and municipal authorities, I did not receive any assistance as a pauper, I also could not represent anyone as a guardian." After the war he was only admitted provisionally, from 1947 permanently as an attorney.

*Sources:* TK 33; JMBl. 33, p. 220; *li; BArch, R 3001 PAK; Tel.B. 41; Verz. zugel. Anw. 45; LAB, RAK, PA

**Schey, Oskar**
07/29/1897 Allenstein - no information
*Home address:* Kastanienallee, 23, Charlottenburg
*Law firm address:* Friedrichstr. 131, N 24
*Additional information:* Attorney at the KG and notary; after the National Socialist seizure of power in 1933 he was readmitted; at the end of 1935 his license as a notary was revoked, he worked as an attorney until the general occupational ban in 1938. Emigration.
*Sources:* TK 33; *li; DJ 36, p. 315; Liste 36; MRRAK; BArch, R 3001 PAK; BG

**Schidwigowski, Paul Dr.**
08/27/1895 Gadderbaum/Westphalia - 05/25/1943 Auschwitz
*Home address:* Sächsische Str. 67, W 15, Düsseldorfer Str. 58a (1940)
*Law firm address:* Fasanenstr. 73, W 15,
*Additional information:* He fought in the First World War; he passed both legal and state examinations with "good," he was admitted as an attorney since 1927. After the National Socialist seizure of power in 1933 he was readmitted, he worked as an attorney until the general occupational ban in 1938, from 1938 to 1943 he was admitted as a "consultant," in this function he represented individual family members of the department store company Wertheim, but also former colleagues, such as attorney Hanna Katz, subsequently he was a "consultant aid worker." Date of declaration of property: 01/14/1943; collecting station Große Hamburger Str. 26; transportation on 04/19/1943 to Auschwitz; he was murdered there a month later.
*Sources:* TK 33; *li; Liste 36; MRRAK; BArch, R 3001 PAK, PA; BG; GB II; Ladwig-Winters: Wertheim I; BLHA, OFP files Katz

**Schiffmann, Wolf**
No information
*Home address:* no information
*Law firm address:* Alexanderpl. 1, C 25, Berolina-Haus
*Additional information:*

After the National Socialist seizure of power in 1933 he was readmitted; he worked as an attorney until the general occupational ban in 1938.

*Sources:* TK 33; *li; Liste 36; BArch, R 3001 PAK; Naatz-Album

**Schildberger, Hermann Dr.**
10/04/1899 Berlin - 09/24/1974 Melbourne, Australia
*Home address:* no information
*Law firm address:* Paul-Singer-Str. 6
*Additional information:* From 1917-20 he studied law, philosophy and music in Berlin, Frankfurt a. M., Greifswald and Würzburg; 1920 he received his doctorate in law in Greifswald; then he was a music critic at a local paper in Gleiwitz, Upper Silesia; 1926 he returned to Berlin and began his traineeship; as from 1927 he was the music director of the Jewish Reform Synagogue in Berlin; in this role he was responsible for music recordings of liturgical chants with well-known artists, e.g. Paula Lindberg and Josef Schmidt; as from 1930 after he took the second state examination in law he was an attorney at the LG I-III; he was active in addition to his legal activity as a cultural official of the Prussian State Association of Jewish Communities (until 1938). After the National Socialist seizure of power in 1933 he was made subject to an occupational ban; until 1938 he was in the management of the Jewish Cultural Association. He emigrated with his family in March 1939 to Australia via Great Britain; in July 1939 he arrived in Melbourne; he worked there as a music conductor at the temple of Beth Israel, thereby building up the Australian music culture as a whole. For his services he was awarded the Order of the British Empire.
*Sources:* Br.B. 32; TK 1933; JMBl. 33, p. 220; BArch, R 3001 PAK; BG: BHdE vol. 2,2, p. 1032; Walk, p. 330; Die Musiktradition der Jüdischen Reformgemeinde zu Berlin [The music tradition of the Jewish Reform Synagogue in Berlin], 1998

**Schiller, Robert Dr.**
04/29/1900 - no information
*Home address:* no information
*Law firm address:* Ansbacher Str. 51, W 50

*Additional information:* Attorney at the KG; after the National Socialist seizure of power he was made subject to an occupational ban in early 1933.
*Sources:* Br.B. 32; TK 33; Liste d. nichtzugel. RA, 04/25/1933; JMBl. 33, p. 209; BArch, R 3001 PAK

**Schindler, Arthur, Judicial Councillor**
05/30/1871 Beuthen - 09/21/1942 Theresienstadt
*Home address:* Pestalozzistr. 53, Charlottenburg
*Law firm address:* Zimmerstr. 92, SW 68
*Additional information:* Attorney and notary; after the National Socialist seizure of power in 1933 his license as a notary was revoked, he was readmitted as an attorney. he worked until the general occupational ban in 1938. Transportation on 08/28/1942 to Theresienstadt; he died there three weeks later.
*Sources:* Br.B. 32; TK 33; JMBl. 33, p. 220; *li; Liste 36; MRRAK; BG; ThG; GB II

**Schindler, Ernst Dr.**
03/26/1875 Brieg - 06/12/1950
*Home address:* Potsdamer Str. 14, W 9
*Law firm address:* Bülowstr. 100, W 57
*Additional information:* He fought in the First World War; attorney and notary; he voted for the SPD at the last free elections; he earned an average income of about RM 20,000 per annum before 1933; after the National Socialist seizure of power in 1933 his license as a notary was revoked, he worked as an attorney until the general occupational ban in 1938. His wife was regarded as non-Jewish, he lived in a "mixed marriage." After 1940, he received an annual pension of the Anwaltsruheverein. He was arrested by the Gestapo on November 2, 1943 and remained in detention until April 22, 1945. He survived the National Socialist regime and was readmitted as an attorney in 1947.
*Sources:* TK 33; *li; Liste 36; MRRAK; Verz. zugel. Anw. 45; LAB, RAK, PA; BG

**Schindler, Fritz Dr.**
01/12/1903 - no information
*Home address:* no information
*Law firm address:* Charlottenstr. 60, W 8

*Additional information:* After the National Socialist seizure of power he was made subject to an occupational ban in early 1933.
*Sources:* Br.B. 32; TK 33; Liste d. nichtzugel. RA, 04/25/1933; JMBl. 08/04/1933, p. 253; BArch, R 3001 PAK

**Schindler, Julius Dr.**
02/28/1885 Lautenburg - transportation 1942
*Home address:* Augsburger Str. 21, W 50; Ansbacher Str. 9, W 50
*Law firm address:* Ansbacher Str. 9, W 50
*Additional information:* Attorney and notary; after the National Socialist seizure of power he was readmitted in 1933; at the end of 1935 his license as a notary was revoked, he worked as an attorney until the general occupational ban in 1938, then he was still admitted as a "consultant." Transportation on 09/14/1942 to Theresienstadt, from there he was transported to Auschwitz on 10/23/1944.
*Sources:* *li; DJ 36, p. 315; Liste 36; MRRAK; Liste d. Kons. v. 03/15/1939; BG; GB II

**Schindler, Kurt**
04/13/1885 Antonienhütte - 10//22/1942 Riga
*Home address:* Schillingstr. 1, C 2, Mitte
*Law firm address:* Blumenstr. 94, O 27
*Additional information:* After the National Socialist seizure of power he was readmitted, he worked as an attorney until the general occupational ban in 1938. He was used for forced labor, last used as a worker. Date of declaration of property: 10/16/1942; transportation on 10/19/1942 to Riga, there he was murdered on the day of his arrival.
*Sources:* TK 33; *li; Liste 36; MRRAK; BArch, R 3001 PAK; BG; BdE; GB II

**Schindler, Walter Dr.**
02/01/1897 Rybnik - 1953 Berlin
*Home address:* Carmerstr. 4, Charlottenburg; Pariser Str. 32, Eisenzahnstr. 65, Wilmersdorf
*Law firm address:* Pariser Str. 20, W 15
*Additional information:* Attorney since 1930; he was readmitted after the National Socialist seizure of power in 1933, he worked as an attorney until the general occupational ban in 1938, thereafter as a "consultant" (until 1942); in 1938 after the Night of the Broken Glass he was imprisoned in the Sachsenhausen concentration camp; he was released again and escaped from the Gestapo; he lived under a false name; he worked

until liberation at Flettnerlüfter GmbH, Mariendorf. He lived in Wilmersdorf after 1945; he immediately received admission as an attorney and notary and ran his law office again at the former address.
*Sources:* K 33; *li; Liste 36; MRRAK; BArch, R 3001 PAK; Verz. zugel. Anw. 45; LAB, RAK, PA; BG

**Schitkowski, Walter**
05/08/1898 Berlin - transportation 942
*Home address:* Berchtesgadener Str. 2-3, W 30
*Law firm address:* urfürstendamm 14, W 50
*Additional information:* After the National Socialist seizure of power he was made subject to a representation ban in April 1933, a little later he was readmitted, he worked as an attorney until the general occupational ban in 1938; he last worked as a clerk. Transportation on 06/24-26/1942 to Minsk.
*Sources:* Br.B. 32; TK 33; Liste d. nichtzugel. RA, 04/25/1933; *li; Liste 36; MRRAK; BArch, R 3001 PAK; BG; GB II

**Schlesinger, Alexander Dr.**
12/16/1893 Petersburg - no information
*Home address:* Windscheidstr. 36, Charlottenburg (1932)
*Law firm address:* Hardenbergstr. 27, Charlottenburg
*Additional information:* Attorney since 1926; after the National Socialist seizure of power he was made subject to an occupational ban in June 1933.
*Sources:* Jüd.Adr.B.; TK 33; JMBl. 15.7.33, p. 220; BArch, R 3001 PAK, PA

**Schlesinger, Edgar H. Dr.**
01/01/1904 Berlin - January 1968
*Home address:* no information
*Law firm address:* Wallotstr. 8 a, Grunewald
*Additional information:* He established himself as an attorney in Berlin in 1928; he temporarily also worked in London, from 1930 only in Berlin; after the National Socialist seizure of power he was made subject to an occupational ban in early 1933; thereafter he worked as a property manager; he went to the Netherlands, he studied law again. He emigrated in 1939 to the USA, there he applied for a scholarship from the American Committee for the Guidance of the Professional Personnel; he died in 1968 at the age of 64.

*Sources:* Br.B. 32; TK 33; JMBl. 33, p. 253; BArch, R 3001 PAK; NY Publ. Lib. (Am. Com.) Schlesinger, E.; SSDI

**Schlesinger, Ernst Dr., Judicial Councillor**
12/12/1865 Oberglogau - 09/21/1942 Theresienstadt
*Home address:* Kaiserallee 207, Wilmersdorf
*Law firm address:* Belle-Alliance-Platz 20, SW 61
*Additional information:* Attorney and notary; after the National Socialist seizure of power in 1933 his license as a notary was revoked; he worked as an attorney until the general occupational ban in 1938. Date of declaration of property: 08/12/1942; he was transported on 09/04/1942 to Theresienstadt, there he died after a few days.
*Sources:* TK 33; JMBl. 33, p. 220; *li; Liste 36; MRRAK; BG; ThG; GB II; Göpp., p. 259

**Schlesinger, Hans Georg Dr.**
03/01/1902 Gleiwitz - no information
*Home address:* Badenallee 1, Charlottenburg
*Law firm address:* no information
*Additional information:* After the National Socialist seizure of power he was made subject to an occupational ban in early 1933.
*Sources:* TK 33; JMBl. 33, p. 234; BArch, R 3001 PAK; Naatz-Album; BG (born 02/01/1902)

**Schlesinger, Hans Dr.**
01/30/1883 Berlin - transportation 1942
*Home address:* Niebuhrstr. 76, Charlottenburg
*Law firm address:* Kurfürstenstr. 98
*Additional information:* He was Protestant; attorney at the LG I-III; after the National Socialist seizure of power he was made subject to an occupational ban in early 1933. Date of declaration of property: 12/29/1941; transportation on 01/25/1942 to Riga.
*Sources:* Br.B. 32; Liste d. nichtzugel. RA, 04/25/1933; JMBl. 33, p. 234; BArch, R 3001 PAK; BG; BdE; GB II (Johannes Sch.)

**Schlesinger, Hans Dr.**
02/27/1888 Oppeln - 04/01/1945 Auschwitz
*Home address:* Mommsenstr. 12, Charlottenburg
*Law firm address:* Linkstr. 42, W 9
*Additional information:* He fought in the First World War and was seriously wounded; he was awarded the Iron Cross I. and II. Kl. Attorney at the KG and notary, in the law firm Abrahamsohn, Ludwig, Fürth, Samter and Schlesinger. After the National Socialist seizure of power in 1933 he was readmitted; in 1935 his license as a notary was revoked, he worked as an attorney until the general occupational ban in 1938; then he was still admitted as a "consultant." Transportation together with his wife on 10/03/1942 to Theresienstadt; from there he was transported on 10/06/1944 to Auschwitz; later he was declared as dead. The son of the family was sent to Den Haag, the Netherlands after the Night of the Broken Glass in 1938. After the occupation of the Netherlands he was imprisoned, first in the concentration camp Westerbork, later in Theresienstadt, then in Auschwitz. In October 1944 he came to Dresden for forced labor in the munitions factory HASAG in Meuselwitz, where he was freed by American troops.
*Sources:* TK 33; *li; DJ 36, p. 315; Liste 36; Liste d. Kons. 39; BG; GB II; information son F.G. Schlesinger, 01/13/1999 to 09/20/1999

**Schlesinger, Heinz**
No information
*Home address:* no information
*Law firm address:* Helmstedter Str. 11, Wilmersdorf
*Additional information:* Attorney at the KG; after the National Socialist seizure of power he was made subject to an occupational ban in early 1933.
*Sources:* TK 33; Liste d. nichtzugel. RA, 04/25/1933; JMBl. 08/04/1933, p. 253; BArch, R 3001 PAK

**Schlesinger, Kurt Dr.**
09/03/1900 Berlin - September 1984
*Home address:* Meinekestr. 11, W 15, Charlottenburg
*Law firm address:* Leipziger Str. 105, W 8

*Additional information:* After the National Socialist seizure of power he was made subject to an occupational ban in early 1933, later he was readmitted, he relocated the law firm from Leipziger Straße to the private residence; he worked as an attorney until the general occupational ban in 1938. He emigrated to Johannesburg, South Africa, on 03/08/1939, later he went to the USA, where he died at the age of 84.
*Sources:* Adr.B. 33; TK 33; Liste d. nichtzugel. RA, 04/25/1933; *li; Liste 36; MRRAK; BArch, R 3001 PAK; BG; SSDI

### Schlesinger, Max Dr.
01/04/1900 Görlitz - no information
*Home address:* no information
*Law firm address:* Kottbusser Str. 6, SO 36
*Additional information:* After the National Socialist seizure of power he was made subject to an occupational ban in early 1933. He emigrated to South Africa.
*Sources:* Br.B. 32; TK 33; Liste d. nichtzugel. RA, 04/25/1933; JMBl. 08/04/1933, p. 253; BArch, R 3001, PAK; BG

### Schlesinger, Robert
04/25/1892 Berlin - transportation 1942
*Home address:* Schönhauser Allee 136, N 58
*Law firm address:* Beethovenstr. 2, NW 40
*Additional information:* He was Protestant; after the National Socialist seizure of power in 1933 he was readmitted as attorney, he worked as an attorney until the general occupational ban, then he worked as a "consultant." Date of declaration of property: 09/18/1942, he said goodbye to his closest friends, he went to the collection station Große Hamburger Str. 26; transportation on 09/24/1942 to Theresienstadt, from there he was transported on 12/18/1943 to Auschwitz.
*Sources:* TK 33; *li; Liste 36; MRRAK; Liste d. Kons., 12/31/1938; BG; GB II

### Schlesinger, Selmar Dr., Judicial Councillor
08/23/1869 Landeshut/Silesia - 09/10/1942 (1941?) Berlin
*Home address:* no information
*Law firm address:* Friedrichstr. 39, Friedrichshagen
*Additional information:* Attorney at the LG I-III, at the AG Köpenick and notary; after the National Socialist seizure of power in 1933 he was readmitted, at the end of 1935 his license as a notary was revoked, he worked as an attorney until the general occupational ban in 1938, he died in 1941 or 1942 in Berlin.
*Sources:* TK 1933; *li; Liste 36; MRRAK; BG; BHdE vol. 2,2, p. 1035 (Kurt Schlesinger); Lüdersdorf, Gerd: Es war ihr Zuhause [It was their home], Berlin o.J., p. 56

### Schlesinger, Walter Dr.
01/18/1907 Berlin - no information
*Home address:* no information
*Law firm address:* Hasenheide 72, S 59
*Additional information:* He was admitted in September 1932 and was one of the youngest attorneys in Berlin. After the National Socialist seizure of power he applied for readmission in April 1933. In the personnel file, there is only a red line above, which meant "occupational ban." He emigrated to Rangoon, British India.
*Sources:* BArch R 3001 PAK, PA; JMBl. 33, p. 221; BG

### Schlimmer, Ludwig Dr.
01/15/1887 Obersitzko - 05/31/1941 New York
*Home address:* Westarpstr. 3, W 30
*Law firm address:* Stresemannstr. 30, SW 11
*Additional information:* Attorney and notary; after the National Socialist seizure of power in 1933 his license as a notary was revoked; he worked as an attorney until the general occupational ban in 1938. He emigrated to the USA via Spain on 03/19/1941; according to a letter from his widow, "he died one week after we arrived, from a typhoid illness that he contracted on the Spanish ship *Magellanes*."
*Sources:* TK 33; JMBl. 33, p. 220; *li; Liste 36; MRRAK; BArch, R 3001 PAK; BG

### Schlomann, Benno, Judicial Councillor
02/08/1862 Schirwindt - no information
*Home address:* Parkstr. 96, Zehlendorf
*Law firm address:* Jägerstr. 61, W 8
*Additional information:* Attorney and notary; after the National Socialist seizure of power in 1933 he was readmitted. He emigrated to Italy.
*Sources:* TK 33; *li; BG

### Schloßmann, Georg
No information
*Home address:* no information
*Law firm address:* Hortensienplatz 1, Lichterfelde

*Additional information:* After the National Socialist seizure of power he was readmitted, he was still working as an attorney until at least 1936.
*Sources:* TK 33; *li; Liste 36

**Schmitthoff, Maximilian Dr.**
03/24/1903 Berlin - 1990
*Home address:* Behrenstr. 26 a, W 8
*Law firm address:* no information
*Additional information:* Son of the attorney Hermann Schmulewitz; he changed his name to Schmitthoff; he studied in Berlin and Freiburg i. Br.; 1927 he received his doctorate in Berlin; he was an attorney at the KG; at the same time an assistant to Prof. Martin Wolff at the Law Faculty of the University of Berlin and reporter for the Reichstag Committee on Stock Corporation Law. After the National Socialist seizure of power he was made subject to an occupational ban in 1933; he emigrated to London, Great Britain, in September 1933; he graduated in 1936 with a Master's Degree in Law; he changed his first name to Clive Macmillan; as from 1936 he was admitted as an attorney in London; 1940-45 he was in the service with the British Army; 1948-1971 he was a university lecturer in London; he took on numerous guest professorships, was a consultant to international organizations and received many awards; in 1978 he was still living in London, Great Britain.
*Sources:* Br.B. 32; TK 1933; JMBl. 33, p. 203; BArch, R 3001 PAK; BG; BHdE 1933, vol. I; Göpp., p. 315; Walk, p. 332; Oxford Dictionary of National Biography, Sept. 2004

**Schmoller, Ernst Dr.**
04/08/1892 Frankfurt a. M. - 12/26/1939 Berlin
*Home address:* Niebuhrstr. 77, Charlottenburg
*Law firm address:* Kaiser-Wilhelm-Str. 34
*Additional information:* Attorney and notary; after the National Socialist seizure of power in 1933 he was readmitted; at the end of 1935 his license as a notary was revoked; he worked as an attorney until the general occupational ban in 1938; he died in December 1939 at the age of 47, he was buried in Berlin.
*Sources:* TK 33; *li; DJ 36, p. 315; Liste 36; MRRAK; BArch, R 3001 PAK; BG

**Schmulewitz, Hermann**
07/10/1870 Jutroschin - 1943 Great Britain
*Home address:* Flensburger Str. 23, NW 87
*Law firm address:* Alexanderplatz 10, C 25
*Additional information:* Attorney at the LG I-III and notary; after the National Socialist seizure of power in 1933 his license as a notary was revoked; he worked as an attorney until the general occupational ban in 1938. He emigrated to London, Great Britain, on 02/23/1939; he followed his son Maximilian Schmitthoff into exile, he died in 1943 in Great Britain.
*Sources:* TK 1933; JMBl. 33, p. 220; *li; Liste 36; MRRAK; BG; BHdE 1933, vol. I, p. 656 (Sohn: Schmitthoff, Maximillian)

**Schneidemühl, Fritz**
03/05/1898 Berlin - no information
*Home address:* Bozener Str. 9
*Law firm address:* Hermannplatz 2/3, S 59
*Additional information:* After the National Socialist seizure of power in 1933 he was readmitted, he was still working as an attorney until at least 1936; he emigrated in 1937 to Austria, there he lived in Vienna, later USA.
*Sources:* TK 33; *li; Liste 36; BArch, R 3001 PAK; Wolf, BFS; information Cann

**Schneider, Albert**
03/14/1892 Berlin - no information
*Home address:* Brückenallee 8/Hindersinstr. 14, NW 40
*Law firm address:* Kronprinzenufer 2, NW 40
*Additional information:* Attorney at the KG and notary; after the National Socialist seizure of power in 1933 his license as a notary was revoked; he worked as an attorney until the general occupational ban in 1938; he emigrated to London, Great Britain, in July 1939.
*Sources:* TK 33; Pr.J. 33, p. 466; *li; Liste 36; MRRAK; BArch, R 3001 PAK; BG

**Schneider, Erich Dr.**
03/19/1885 Koschmin - no information
*Home address:* Kantstr. 76, Charlottenburg
*Law firm address:* Kantstr. 76, Charlottenburg
*Additional information:* Attorney and notary; after the National Socialist seizure of power in 1933 his license as a notary was revoked in 1935; he worked as an attorney until the general occupational ban in 1938. He emigrated to Chile.

*Sources:* TK 33; *li; DJ 36, p. 315; Liste 36; MRRAK; BArch, R 3001 PAK; BG

**Schneider, Karl Dr.**
08/17/1882 Koschmin - no information
*Home address:* Kaiser-Wilhelm-Str. 57, C 2
*Law firm address:* Kaiser-Wilhelm-Str. 57, C 2
*Additional information:* He was a dissident; attorney and notary; after the National Socialist seizure of power in 1933 he was readmitted; at the end of 1935 his license as a notary was reovked, he worked as an attorney until the general occupational ban in 1938.
*Sources:* *li; DJ 36, p. 315; Liste 36; BArch, R 3001 PAK; MRRAK; BG: LAB, OFP files; BAP, 15.09 RSA

**Schnitzer, Adolf Dr.**
07/30/1889 Berlin - 01/12/1989 Geneva
*Home address:* no information
*Law firm address:* Mohrenstr. 48, W 8
*Additional information:* Attorney and notary; after the National Socialist seizure of power he was made subject to an occupational ban in early 1933. He emigrated via Switzerland to Annemasse, France, on 10/01/1933. 1948-1959 he was a private lecturer and lecturer at the University of Geneva, University of Luxembourg (Droit comparé de la Famille); from 1946 he was a legal advisor to various organizations in Geneva; 1948-1952 he worked for the International Organization of Refugees, 1953-1973 he was chief of the International Bureau for Declarations of Death of Missing Persons (UN); honorary doctorate from the Universities of Geneva and Uppsala.
*Sources:* Br.B. 32; TK 33; Liste d. nichtzugel. RA, 04/25/1933; JMBl. 33, p. 209; BArch, R 3001 PAK; BG; Göpp. p. 315

**Schocken, Leo Dr.**
03/02/1898 - no information
*Home address:* no information
*Law firm address:* Friedrichstr. 131, N 24
*Additional information:* Attorney at the KG; after the National Socialist seizure of power he was made subject to an occupational ban in early 1933.
*Sources:* TK 33; Liste d. nichtzugel. RA, 04/25/1933; BArch, R 3001 PAK

**Schoenfeld, Julius Dr.**
06/18/1894 Posen - 10/23/1942
*Home address:* Nassauische Str. 5, Wilmersdorf

*Law firm address:* Krausenstr. 9, W 8
*Additional information:* Attorney and notary; after the National Socialist seizure of power he was made subject to an occupational ban in early 1933, then he worked at the Palestine Office of the Jewish Synagogue Berlin; he was an administrative director of the Jewish Hospital Berlin. He committed suicide together with his wife after refusing to name staff for deportation at the Gestapo's request. He was buried at the Jewish Cemetery in Weißensee.
*Sources:* Br.B. 32; Liste d. nichtzugel. RA, 04/25/1933; JMBl. 08/04/1933, p. 253; BArch, R 3001 PAK; BG; g; Göpp. p. 236; Walk, p. 334

**Schoenfeldt, Herbert S. Dr.**
05/26/1895 Landeck - 06/29/1956 Bad Godesberg
*Home address:* Aschaffenburger Str. 16, Schöneberg
*Law firm address:* Behrenstr. 25, W 8
*Additional information:* Volunteer in the First World War, he was wounded on the Western Front in France; attorney and notary; legal counsel for Bankhaus Mendelsohn & Co. After the National Socialist seizure of power in 1933 he was readmitted; at the end of 1935 his license as a notary was revoked; he worked as an attorney until at least the end of 1936. 1938 he emigrated to Switzerland via France, 1940 via Spain and Portugal to the USA; 1946-48 he cooperated in the preparation and execution of war crime trials, 1948-56 he was an attorney and a legal advisor of the JRSO (Jewish Resitution Successor Org.); 1956 in Germany he was the Director of the Conference on Jewish Material Claims against Germany (Claims Conference).
*Sources:* TK 1933; *li; DJ 36, p. 315; Liste 36; BArch, R 3001 PAK; BG; BHdE Bd. 1, p. 663; Göpp. p. 360; Wolf, BFS

**Schoenlank, Bernhard, Judicial Councillor**
03/27/1867 - 08/15/1937 Berlin
*Home address:* no information
*Law firm address:* Jägerstr. 4, W 8
*Additional information:* Attorney and notary; after the National Socialist seizure of power in 1933 his license as a notary was revoked; he worked as an attorney until at least 1936.
*Sources:* TK 33; JMBl. 33, p. 220; *li; Liste 36; BG

**Schoenlank, Hugo**
No information
*Home address:* no information
*Law firm address:* Berliner Str. 6, Tegel
*Additional information:* Attorney and
notary; after the National Socialist seizure of
power in 1933 he was readmitted; he gave up
his law firm before 1936.
*Sources:* TK 33; *li

**Schoeps, Gustav Dr., Judicial Councillor**
No information
*Home address:* no information
*Law firm address:* Alexanderstr. 53, C 25
*Additional information:* Attorney and
notary; after the National Socialist seizure
of power in 1933 his license as a notary was
revoked; he was readmitted as an attorney;
before the fall of 1935 he was deleted from
the list of attorneys.
*Sources:* Br.B. 32; TK 33; JMBl. 33,
p. 220; *li

**Scholle, Sigurd**
03/09/1893 Danzig - Mai 1971
*Home address:* Sybelstr. 11, Charlottenburg
*Law firm address:* Taubenstr. 46, W 8
*Additional information:* Attorney and notary;
after the National Socialist seizure of power
he was made subject to an occupational ban
in early 1933. He emigrated to Paris, France,
later to the USA, he last lived in New York.
*Sources:* Br.B. 32; TK 33; Liste d. nichtzugel.
RA, 04/25/1933; JMBl. 08/04/1933, p. 253;
BArch, R 3001 PAK; BG; SSDI

**Schönbeck, Friedrich (Fritz)**
12/17/1888 Nordhausen - 09/11/1971 London
*Home address:* Bleibtreustr. 27, W 15
*Law firm address:* Stresemannstr. 4, SW 11,
later Kurfürstendamm 186, Charlottenburg
*Additional information:* He studied law in
Berlin and Munich; he fought in the First
World War from 1915-18; he was a member of
the SPD; 1919-20 he was an employee of the
Reich Ministry of Economics; 1920-30 he was
in the Prussian Ministry of Finance 1919-20,
from 1927 he worked for the undersecretary;
he played a leading role as a consultant in
the regulation of property relations between
the state and the House of Hohenzollern;
1931 he was in-house counsel of the Prussian
State Theater; then an attorney at the KG,
at the same time he was legal counsel of the

Deutsche Arbeiterbank (until 1933); he was
a member of the Republican Association of
Judges. After the National Socialist seizure of
power in 1933 he was imprisoned for a short
while; until the general occupational ban in
1938 he was admitted as an attorney, then
still as a "consultant." He emigrated to Great
Britain in August 1939; after 1945 he was an
advisor to the Consulate General in London
and Head of the German Office for Validation
of Securities in London.
*Sources:* TK 1933; MvRRB; *li; Liste 36;
MRRAK; Liste d. Kons. v. 03/15/1939;
BArch, R 3001 PAK; BG; BHdE 1933, vol. 1,
p. 662; Göpp., p. 315; Walk, p. 333; Schreiben
C. Arndt, 08/15/1999; Landesverwaltungsamt
Berlin, 04/19/2000; information H. Jäckel;
information Dr. Y Arndt

**Schönberg, Curt**
01/20/1894 Kreuz/Ostbahn - 11/10/1948
*Home address:* Kaiserdamm 86,
Charlottenburg
*Law firm address:* Brückenallee 9, NW 87
*Additional information:* He fought in the First
World War; attorney since 1922, last at the KG,
and notary (since 1929). Sch.'s average income
was between RM 20-25,000 p.a.; he voted for
the DDP in the last free elections. After the
National Socialist seizure of power in 1933 he
was readmitted, 1935 his license as a notary
was revoked, he worked as an attorney until
the general occupational ban in 1938, then as a
"consultant" and/or until 1945 as an "assistant
consultant." His wife was regarded as non-
Jewish, because of their child their marriage
was regarded as a so-called "privileged mixed
marriage." The substantial income losses did
not occur until 1943. He survived, but was
handicapped after an accident. In 1946 he was
readmitted as an attorney.
*Sources:* TK 33; *li; DJ 36, p. 315 (Kurt Sch.);
MRRAK; Verz. zugel. Anw. 45; LAB, RAK,
PA; BG

**Schönberg, Karl Dr.**
08/20/1893 Berlin - transportation 1943
*Home address:* Mommsenstr. 52,
Charlottenburg; Xantener Str. 16,
Wilmersdorf
*Law firm address:* Friedrich-Ebert-Str.
(Hermann-Göring-Str.) 7, W 9
*Additional information:* Attorney and
notary; after the National Socialist seizure of

power in 1933 he was readmitted; at the end of 1935 his license as a notary was revoked, he worked as an attorney until the general occupational ban in 1938, amongst others for the emigrated author Else Lasker-Schüler; he was still admitted as a "consultant," he had to vacate his practice in 1942 within a short time, because "a company active within the framework of the Four-Year Plan, which had to perform tasks essential to the war, wanted to move in." (OFP files); later he was arrested; collecting station Große Hamburger Str. 26; transportation on 04/19/1943 to Auschwitz.
*Sources:* TK 33; *li; DJ 36, p. 315; Liste 36; MRRAK; Liste d. Kons. v. 03/15/1939; BG: LAB, OFP files; GB II; information Flechtmann, 7/2000

### Schottländer, Erich Dr.
05/20/1898 Halle a.d. Saale - no information
*Home address:* Köpenicker Str. 48/49
*Law firm address:* Köpenicker Str. 48/49
After the National Socialist seizure of power he was made subject to an occupational ban in early 1933. He emigrated to London, Great Britain, on 03/29/1935. His wife was regarded as non-Jewish. He ceased to follow Judaism as a religion.
*Sources:* Br.B. 32; TK 33; Liste d. nichtzugel. RA, 04/25/1933; JMBl. 08/04/1933, p. 253; BArch, R 3001 PAK; BG

### Schreiber, Ernst Dr.
07/20/1898 Leipzig - no information
*Home address:* Bamberger Str. 22 at Kohn, Wilmersdorf
*Law firm address:* Leipziger Str. 108, W 8
*Additional information:* Attorney and notary; after the National Socialist seizure of power in 1933 his license as a notary was revoked, he worked as an attorney until the general occupational ban in 1938; in 1939 he emigrated to Paris, France.
*Sources:* TK 33; Pr.J. 33, p. 243; *li; Liste 36; MRRAK; BArch, R 3001 PAK; BG

### Schreuer, Felix Dr.
10/15/1880 - 05/25/1933
*Home address:* Burggrafenstr. 20, Zehlendorf
*Law firm address:* Potsdamer Str. 126
*Additional information:* Attorney and notary; after the National Socialist seizure of power in 1933 his license as a notary was revoked; he died at the end of May 1933 at the age of 53.

*Sources:* Adr.B. 33; TK 33; JMBl. p. 220, 281; BArch, R 3001 PAK; BG

### Schulenburg, Günther Dr. von
05/27/1893 Berlin - no information
*Home address:* no information
*Law firm address:* Marburger Str. 9, W 50
*Additional information:* He was Protestant; frontline fighter in the First World War, last as a lieutenant colonel; after the National Socialist seizure of power in 1933 he was readmitted as an attorney. He was regarded as "mixed race" and was therefore exempted from the general occupational ban in 1938, in 1941 he was no longer practicing.
*Sources:* TK 33; *li; LAB, Liste Mschlg. 36; BArch, R 3001 PAK

### Schwabach, Hans
08/05/1889 Berlin - before 1942, France
*Home address:* Elßholzstr. 4, W 57
*Law firm address:* Friedrichstr. 79 a
*Additional information:* Attorney and notary; he gave up his law office in 1933; according to RSA: 1938 "unknown deregistered"; he emigrated to France, he died before 1942.
*Sources:* Adr.B. 33; TK 33; BArch, R 3001 PAK; BG: LAB, OFP files

### Schwabe, Walter Dr.
09/07/1882 Göttingen - no information
*Home address:* Brüderstr. 2-3, Lichterfelde
*Law firm address:* Reichstagsufer 9, NW 7
*Additional information:* Attorney at KG, partner of Bankhaus Schwabe & Co. After the National Socialist seizure of power in 1933 he was readmitted, he worked as an attorney until the general occupational ban in 1938. In the same year he emigrated to the Netherlands; he lived in Wimbledon, Great Britain, in 1947.
*Sources:* TK 33; *li; Liste 36; MRRAK; BArch, R 3001 PAK; BG

### Schwarz, Ernst
06/10/1882 Berlin - transportation 1943
*Home address:* Knesebeckstr. 77 at Weinberg, Charlottenburg
*Law firm address:* Kurfürstendamm 14, W 50
*Additional information:* Attorney and notary; after the National Socialist seizure of power in 1933 he was readmitted; at the end of 1935 his license as a notary was

revoked, he worked as an attorney until the general occupational ban in 1938. He was conscripted for forced labor, last as a laborer (nailer) at Paul Gelling & Co., Wood Specialties, Kurfürstendamm 15, W 15; date of declaration of property: 11/19/1942; transported on 03/04/1943 to Auschwitz.
*Sources:* *li; DJ 36, p. 315; MRRAK; BArch, R 3001 PAK; BG; GB II

**Schwarz, Fritz**
02/21/1891 - no information
*Home address:* Wittelsbacherstr. 12, Wilmersdorf
*Law firm address:* Mittelstr. 118, NW 7
*Additional information:* Attorney and notary; after the National Socialist seizuer of power in 1933 he was readmitted; at the end of 1935 his license as a notary was revoked; he worked as an attorney until the general occupational ban in 1938; then as a "consultant." He was arrested for defending a communist. 1939 he emigrated to Great Britain, his mother was interrogated several times after his escape.
*Sources:* Br.B. 32; TK 33; *li; DJ 36, p. 315; Liste 36; MRRAK; Liste d. Kons., Jan.39; BArch, R 3001, PAK, PA; BG

**Schwarz, Walter C. Dr.**
02/11/1906 Berlin-Charlottenburg - 08/17/1988 Zürich
*Home address:* no information
*Law firm address:* Taubenstr. 21, W 56
*Additional information:* He was admitted as an attorney at the KG in May 1932; after the National Socialist seizure of power in 1933 he tried to be readmitted, his father, Benno, also wrote to the Reich Commissioner for the Prussian Ministry of Justice and described the patriotic attitude, which was maintained in the family: even his grandfather had fought in the Battle of Königgrätz. He could not claim any of the legal exceptions; he was made subject to an occupational ban on 06/15/1933, because he "was not of Aryan descent." He emigrated to Palestine at the beginning of 1938; 1940-1944 he was used by the Royal Air Force in Africa; 1944 he was an attorney; together with Siegfried Moses he wrote a commentary on income tax law in Palestine; in 1950 he worked at the Jewish Agency in Munich; 1952 he obtained a doctorate in Heidelberg; 1952-1967 he was an

attorney in Berlin; from 1958 he was an editor and/or employee of the magazine "RzW," 1963-1981 he was the magazine's publisher and/or co-publisher.
*Sources:* Liste d. nichtzugel. RA, 04/25/1933; BArch, R 3001 PAK, PA; Göpp., pages 360/61

**Schwarz, Walter**
02/10/1896 Bonn - no information
*Home address:* no information
*Law firm address:* Badensche Str. 54; Schöneberg
*Additional information:* He had fought in the First World War, like his five brothers, of whom one had perished. Attorney since 1927; after the National Socialist seizure of power in 1933 he was readmitted; he worked as an attorney until the general occupational ban in 1938. He emigrated 1939; he lived in London, Great Britain, in 1952.
*Sources:* Br.B. 32; *li; Liste 36; BArch, R 3001 PAK, PA; BG

**Schwarzbart, Bernhard**
09/13/1902 - no information
*Home address:* no information
*Law firm address:* Friedrichstr. 190, W 8
*Additional information:* After the National Socialist seizure of power he was made subject to an occupational ban in early 1933.
*Sources:* TK 33; Liste d. nichtzugel. RA, 04/25/1933; JMBl. 08/04/1933, p. 253; BArch, R 3001 PAK; Naatz-Album

**Schwarzer, Hans Dr.**
10/06/1900 Wilmersdorf - February 1981
*Home address:* Darmstädter Str. 7, W 15
*Law firm address:* Spichernstr. 24/25, W 50
*Additional information:* After the National Socialist seizure of power he was made subject to an occupational ban in early 1933. He emigrated to the USA, he changed his first name to John, he last lived in Beverly Hills.
*Sources:* Br.B. 32; Jüd.Adr.B.; TK 33; Liste d. nichtzugel. RA, 04/25/1933; JMBl. 07/07/1933, p. 209; BArch, R 3001 PAK, PA; SSDI

**Schweitzer, Ernst Emil Dr.**
05/11/1891 Breslau - no information
*Home address:* no information
*Law firm address:* Neue Winterfeldtstr. 20
*Additional information:* Attorney and notary at the LG I-III and at AG Schöneberg; he was a

member of the League for Human Rights. After the National Socialist seizure of power he was made subject to an occupational ban in early 1933. He escaped to Danzig, 1939 to France. *Sources:* Br.B. 32; TK 33; Liste d. nichtzugel. RA, 04/25/1933; JMBl. 33, p. 209; BArch, R 3001 PAK; Krach, p. 436

### Schwenk, Felix Dr.
10/27/1879 Grottkau - 01/31/1942 Riga
*Home address:* Kurfürstenstr. 34, W 35
*Law firm address:* Potsdamer Str. 27, W 35
*Additional information:* After the National Socialist seizure of power in 1933 he was readmitted, he worked as an attorney until the general occupational ban in 1938. Date of declaration of property: 01/05/1942; transportation to Riga on 01/25/1942, he was murdered there a day after arrival.
*Sources:* TK 33; *li; Liste 36; MRRAK; BG; BdE; GB II

### Schwersenz, Manfred Dr.
10/20/1893 Hohensalza - no information
*Home address:* Zähringerstr. 19/Nürnberger Str. 37 at Cabalcao
*Law firm address:* Uhlandstr. 45
*Additional information:* Attorney at the KG and notary; after the National Socialist seizure of power he was made subject to an occupational ban in early 1933. His wife was regarded as non-Jewish; the couple divorced in 1935. He emigrated to Bolzano, Italy and London, Great Britain, before 11/30/1939.
*Sources:* Br.B. 32; TK 33; Liste d. nichtzugel. RA, 04/25/1933; JMBl. 33, p. 203; BG

### Seegall, Hermann Dr., Judicial Councillor
02/16/1856 Berlin - 07/16/1937 Berlin-Lichterfelde
*Home address:* Marienstr. 5, Lichterfelde
*Law firm address:* Wilhelmstr. 38, SW 68
*Additional information:* Attorney at the KG and notary; after the National Socialist seizure of power in 1933 he was readmitted; at the end of 1935 his license as a notary was revoked; he worked as an attorney until at least the 1936; he died in 1937 in Berlin.
*Sources:* TK 33; *li; DJ 36, p. 315; Liste 36; BG

### Seelig, Ernst Dr.
02/04/1871 Leipzig - no information
*Home address:* Kurfürstenstr. 43, W 35
*Law firm address:* Kurfürstenstr. 43, W 35
*Additional information:* Attorney and notary; after the National Socialist seizure of power in 1933 his license as a notary was revoked, he worked as an attorney until at least 1936.
*Sources:* TK 33; JMBl. 33, p. 220; *li; Liste 36; BG

### Seelig, Ludwig Dr.
*Home address:* no information
*Home address:* no information
*Law firm address:* Marburger Str. 17
*Additional information:* After the National Socialist seizure of power in October 1933 he was readmitted as an attorney.
*Sources:* TK 33; *li

### Seelig, Meinhard Dr.
06/27/1895 Wissek - no information
*Home address:* no information
*Law firm address:* Friedrichstr. 209, SW 68
*Additional information:* After the National Socialist seizure of power he was made subject to an occupational ban on 06/14/1933. He emigrated to London, Great Britain.
*Sources:* Br.B. 32; TK 33; Liste d. nichtzugel. RA, 04/25/1933; JMBl. 08/21/1933, p. 267; BArch, R 3001 PAK; BG

### Seelig, Walter Dr.
11/12/1904 Berlin-Charlottenburg - no information
*Home address:* no information
*Law firm address:* Rosenthaler Str. 44, N 54
*Additional information:* After the National Socialist seizure of power he was made subject to an occupational ban in early 1933. He emigrated to New York, USA.
*Sources:* TK 33; Liste d. nichtzugel. RA, 04/25/1933; JMBl. 08/04/1933, p. 253; BArch, R 3001 PAK; BG

### Seelmann, Ernst
12/13/1894 Aachen - 01/26/1945 Buchenwald
*Home address:* Landshuter Str. 35, Schöneberg
*Law firm address:* Joachimsthaler Str. 21, W 15
*Additional information:* Attorney and notary; after the National Socialist seizure of power in 1933 he was readmitted; at the end of 1935 his license as a notary was revoked, he worked as an attorney until the general occupational ban in 1938. He emigrated to the Netherlands on 10/05/1938.

On 01/18/1944 he was transported from Westerbork to Theresienstadt, from there he was transported to Auschwitz on 09/28/1944. On 01/26/1945 he died at the Buchenwald concentration camp.
*Sources:* TK 33; *li; DJ 36, p. 315; Liste 36; MRRAK; BArch, R 3001 PAK; BG; g; GB II

**Segall, Hellmut Dr.**
03/29/1899 Königs Wusterhausen - no information
*Home address:* Giesebrechtstr. 18, Charlottenburg
*Law firm address:* Kleiststr. 34, W 62
*Additional information:* After the National Socialist seizure of power in 1933 he was readmitted, he worked as an attorney until at least the beginning of 1936. He emigrated to London, Great Britain, in September 1936.
*Sources:* TK 33; *li; Liste 36; BArch, R 3001 PAK; BG

**Segall, Julius Dr.**
03/22/1886 Berlin - no information
*Home address:* Kantstr. 149, Charlottenburg
*Law firm address:* Friedrichstr. 71, W 8
*Additional information:* Attorney and notary; after the National Socialist seizure of power in 1933 he was readmitted; at the end of 1935 his license as a notary was revoked, he worked as an attorney until the general occupational ban in 1938. He emigrated to Sydney, Australia.
*Sources:* TK 33; *li; DJ 36, p. 315; Liste 36; MRRAK; BArch, R 3001 PAK; BG

**Selbiger, Leo Dr.**
04/18/1875 Tuchel - 07/16/1942
*Home address:* Viktoria-Luise-Platz 12 a
*Law firm address:* Viktoria-Luise-Platz 12 a
*Additional information:* Attorney at the KG and notary; after the National Socialist seizure of power in 1933 he was readmitted; at the end of 1935 his license as a notary was revoked, he worked as an attorney until the general occupational ban in 1938; he died in 1942 at the age of 67 and was buried in the Jewish cemetery at Weißensee.
*Sources:* TK 33; *li; DJ 1936, p. 315; Liste 36; MRRAK; BG

**Seligmann, Martin Dr.**
07/10/1900 Berlin - no information
*Home address:* Brahmsstr. 19, Wilmersdorf

*Law firm address:* Potsdamer Str. 32 a, W 35
*Additional information:* After the National Socialist seizure of power in 1933 he was readmitted, he worked as an attorney until the general occupational ban in 1938; he presumably emigrated - Note "signed out on 02/28/1939"
*Sources:* Br.B. 32; TK 33; *li; Liste 36; MRRAK; BArch, R 3001 PAK; BG

**Seligsohn, Arnold Dr., Judicial Councillor**
09/13/1854 Samotschin (Posen) - 02/03/1939 Berlin
*Home address:* no information
*Law firm address:* Knesebeckstr. 45, W 15
*Additional information:* Attorney and notary, in a law partnership with Julius, his son, and Martin, his nephew; he was a specialist in the field of intellectual property and patent law. After the National Socialist seizure of power in 1933 he was readmitted; at the end of 1935 his license as a notary was revoked, he worked as an attorney until the general occupational ban in 1938; he was a member in various nonprofit Jewish associations; he died in 1939 in Berlin.
*Sources:* TK 33; *li; DJ 1936, p. 315; Liste 36; MRRAK; BG: LAB, OFP files; Göpp., p. 228; Walk, p. 340; J. Levi unbound collection

**Seligsohn, Ernst Dr.**
07/04/1903 Berlin - 02/10/1983 Tel Aviv
*Home address:* no information
*Law firm address:* Knesebeckstr. 45, W 15
*Additional information:* Son of Martin, in the third generation of attorneys in the Seligsohn family; together they formed a law firm. In his youth he was a member of the "comrades," a youth organization, which stood as a counterpart to the Zionist "BlauWeiß."
After the National Socialist seizure of power he was made subject to an occupational ban and he joined the "Alija." He managed to persuade his parents to leave Germany and to go to Palestine. He emigrated on 02/26/1934 to Tel Aviv, Palestine; at first he was a patent attorney, since 1940 he was an attorney, he worked as an attorney until the end of his life, he focused on copyright and trademark law.
*Sources:* Br.B. 32; TK 33; Liste d. nichtzugel. RA, 04/25/1933; JMBl. 08/04/1933, p. 253; BArch, R 3001 PAK, PA; Information Arnan Gabrieli, Konf. 6/1999; unbound collection J. Levi

**Seligsohn, Felix, Judicial Councillor**
09/19/1868 Berlin - 07/29/1942
*Home address:* Schönhauser Allee 22, N 54,
Prenzlauer Berg (retirement home of the local
Jewish synagogue)
*Law firm address:* Französische Str. 59, W 8
*Additional information:* Attorney and
notary; after the National Socialist seizure
of power in 1933 his license as a notary was
revoked, he worked as an attorney until
the general occupational ban in 1933. He
committed suicide at the end of July 1942 at
the age of 74, presumably in the face of the
threatening transportation, he was buried at
the Jewish cemetery at Weißensee.
*Sources:* Br.B. 32, TK 33; Pr.J. 33, p. 502; *li;
Liste 36; MRRAK; BG; GB II

**Seligsohn, Franz Dr.**
09/15/1880 Berlin - no information
*Home address:* Fasanenstr. 30, W 15
*Law firm address:* Fasanenstr. 30, W 15
*Additional information:* Attorney at the
KG and notary; after the National Socialist
seizure of power in 1933 he was readmitted;
at the end of 1935 his license as a notary was
revoked, he worked as an attorney until the
general occupational ban in 1938, then he
was admitted as a "consultant." He emigrated
to Valparaiso, Chile, on 03/08/1939; in 1950
he was living in London.
*Sources:* TK 33; *li; LAB, Liste 10/15/1933;
DJ 36, p. 315; Liste 36; MRRAK; BArch, R
3001 PAK; BG

**Seligsohn, Julius Dr.**
05/07/1890 Berlin -
02/28/1942 Sachsenhausen
*Home address:* Meinekestr.
22, Charlottenburg
*Law firm address:*
Knesebeckstr. 45,
Charlottenburg
*Additional information:* He fought in the First
World War and received high war awards;
he later belonged to the Jewish Association
of Frontline Soldiers; he had completed both
state examinations with "good." Attorney and
notary; partner of Arnold (his father), Ernst
and Martin. After the National Socialist seizure
of power in 1933 he was readmitted; in his
application the usual processing notes are to
be found: red line for "non-Aryan," green line
for "frontline fighter," supplemented by a green

cross (recipient of the EK I. and II. Kl.). In the
"Questionnaire on the implementation of the
law on the restoration of the professional civil
service of 04/07/1933" he writes on the question
of "Aryan descent": "I am a Jew and all my
ancestors whom I can trace back were Prussian
Jews." At the end of 1935 his license as a notary
was revoked, he was admitted as a notary until
1938. Member of the Presidential Committee
of the Reich Association, responsible for
emigration counseling. He sent his wife and two
children to a safe foreign country, but remained
in his hometown Berlin. In November 1940 he
was arrested, on 03/18/1941 he was transported
to the Sachsenhausen concentration camp,
there he died at the end of February 1942 from
pneumonia.
*Sources:* TK 33; * li; LAB, Liste 10/15/1933;
DJ 36, p. 315; Liste 36; MRRAK; BArch,
R 3001 PAK, PA; BG; GB Sachsenhausen;
GB II; Juden in Preußen [Jews in Prussia],
4th ed. 1983; Göpp. p. 259; J. Levi unbound
collection

**Seligsohn, Martin, Judicial councillor**
10/27/1868 Berlin - 12/26/1942 Tel Aviv,
Palästina
*Home address:* no information
*Law firm address:* Knesebeckstr. 45, W 15
*Additional information:* Attorney at the
KG and notary; law partner of Arnold,
Ernst and Julius, his son. For more than 40
years, Arnold and his cousins twice removed
were law partners and specialized in patent,
trademark and copyright law. After the
National Socialist seizure of power in 1933
his license as a notary was removed, he was
recognized as an "elderly attorney" and
readmitted. His license as an attorney was
revoked in 1934, when he decided to leave
Germany at the urging of his son Ernst. He
emigrated to Tel Aviv, Palestine, where the
family and other relatives settled in Shivtei
Israel Street (today Ruppin St.). He died in
1942 at the age of 74 in Tel Aviv.
*Sources:* TK 33; LAB, Liste nichtzugel. RA,
04/15/1933; JMBl. 33, p. 220; *li; BG; J. Levi
unbound collection

**Seligsohn-Netter, Julius Dr.**
12/10/1884 Berlin - no information
*Home address:* Ilmenauer Str. 11, Wilmersdorf
*Law firm address:* Oppenstr. 87/97,
Adlers-hof

*Additional information:* After the National Socialist seizure of power in 1933 he was readmitted, he worked as an attorney until at least 1936. He emigrated on 04/14/1938 to Great Britain.
*Sources:* TK 33; *li; LAB, Liste 10/15/1933; Liste 36; BArch, R 3001 PAK; BG; LAB, OFP files

**Selowsky, Karl Dr.**
02/16/1889 Dresden - no information
*Home address:* Cicerostr. 54, Wilmersdorf
*Law firm address:* Behrenstr. 20, W 8
*Additional information:* Attorney and notary; after the National Socialist seizure of power in 1933 he was readmitted; at the end of 1935 his license as a notary was revoked, he worked as an attorney until the general occupational ban in 1938, then as a "consultant." He emigrated to Paris, France, in May 1939. In 1949 he was living in Freiburg.
TK 33; *li; LAB, Liste 10/15/1933; DJ 36, p. 315; Liste 36; MRRAK; Liste d. Kons.v. 03/15/1939; BArch, R 3001 PAK, PA; BG

**Selowsky, Kurt**
ca.1890 - no information
*Home address:* no information
*Law firm address:* Dorotheenstr. 77/78, NW 7
*Additional information:* Represented the Jacob Michael Group as an attorney; after the National Socialist seizure of power in early 1933 he was made subject to a temporary representation ban, he was still readmitted in the same year, on 12/17/1934 the admission was revoked, he emigrated to Australia.
*Sources:* TK 33; Liste d. nichtzugel. RA, 04/25/1933; *li; LAB, Liste 10/15/1933; information Werner Wolff, 09/22/1998

**Selten, Ernst Dr.**
09/25/1885 Berlin - transportation 1942
*Home address:* Kuno-Fischer-Platz 1, Charlottenburg
*Law firm address:* Friedrichstr. 236, SW 68
*Additional information:* Attorney at the KG and notary; after the National Socialist seizure of power in 1933 his license as a notary was revoked. He worked as an attorney until the general occupational ban in 1938. He was transported on 06/24-26/1942 to Minsk.

*Sources:* TK 33; JMBl 33, p. 220; *li; LAB, Liste 10/15/1933; Liste 36; MRRAK; BArch, R 3001 PAK; BG; GB II

**Selten, Franz Dr.**
10/05/1881 Berlin - 02/11/1943 Theresienstadt
*Home address:* Barbarossastr. 52, W 30; Traunsteiner Str. 10, Innsbrucker Str. 44, Schöneberg
*Law firm address:* Schönhauser Allee 6/7, N 54
*Additional information:* Attorney at the KG and notary; after the National Socialist seizure of power in 1933 he was readmitted, in 1935 his license as a notary was revoked, he worked as an attorney until the general occupational ban in 1938, than as a "consultant." Date of declaration of property: 08/12/1942; collecting station Große Hamburger Str. 26; transportation on 08/31/1942 to Theresienstadt, he died there in February 1943.
*Sources:* Br.B. 32; TK 33; *li; LAB, Liste 10/15/1933; DJ 36, p. 315; Liste 36; MRRAK; Liste d. Kons., 03/15/1939; BArch, R 3001 PAK; BG; ThG; GB II

**Selten, Fritz Dr.**
09/04/1875 - 09/27/1942 Theresienstadt
*Home address:* Mommsenstr. 2, Charlottenburg
*Law firm address:* Rankestr. 31/32, W 50
*Additional information:* Attorney and notary; member of the Justice Examination Board; after the National Socialist seizure of power in 1933 his license as a notary was revoked, he worked as an attorney until the general occupational ban in 1938, he last practiced law in his own home. He was transported to Theresienstadt on 07/17/1942; he died there at the end of September 1942.
*Sources:* TK 33; JMBl. 33, p. 220; *li; LAB, Liste 10/15/1933; Liste 36; MRRAK; VZ 39; BG; ThG; GB II

**Semon, Hans M. Dr.**
05/23/1890 - no information
*Home address:* Leonhardtstr. 19, Charlottenburg
*Law firm address:* Berliner Str. 82, Neukölln
*Additional information:* Attorney at the LG Berlin and AG Neukölln; after the National Socialist seizure of power he was made subject

to an occupational ban; he was still included in the 1939 census.
*Sources:* Adr.B. 33; Pr.J. 33, p. 565; VZ 39

**Senff, Adolph, Judicial Councillor**
12/27/1855 - 02/11/1934 Berlin
*Home address:* Kurfürstendamm 46, Charlottenburg
*Law firm address:* Französische Str. 57/58, W 8
*Additional information:* Attorney and notary; after the National Socialist seizure of power in 1933 he was readmitted; he died in 1934 at the age of 79 and was buried in the Jewish cemetery at Weißensee.
*Sources:* TK 33; *li; LAB, Liste 10/15/1933; BG

**Senff, Werner**
06/22/1892 Berlin - 07/03/1943 Auschwitz
*Home address:* no information
*Law firm address:* Französische Str. 57
Attorney at the LG I-III; occupational ban in early 1933. Transported on 04/19/1943 to Auschwitz, he was murdered there.
*Sources:* Br.B. 32; TK 33; Liste d. nichtzugel. RA, 04/25/1933; JMBl. 08/21/1933, p. 267; BArch, R 3001 PAK; BG; g; GB II

**Senger, Hans Dr.**
08/11/1900 Berlin - no information
*Home address:* Augustastr. 65
*Law firm address:* Grolmanstr. 37, Charlottenburg
*Additional information:* He had fought in the First World War for half a year; he was an attorney since 1925; after the National Socialist seizure of power in 1933 he made a request to be readmitted; however, he was not recognized as a "frontline fighter," with the result that he was made subject to an occupational ban.
*Sources:* Jüd.Adr.B.; Adr.B. 33; TK 33; JMBl. 33, p. 282; BArch, R 3001 PAK

**Sieburg, Felix Dr.**
04/02/1884 Posen - no information
*Home address:* Martin-Luther-Str. 26, Schöneberg
*Law firm address:* Potsdamer Str. 71, W 57
*Additional information:* Attorney at the KG and notary; after the National Socialist seizure of power in 1933 his license as a notary was revoked, he worked as an attorney

until the general occupational ban in 1938. He emigrated to Great Britain, in 1951 he lived in Oxford.
*Sources:* TK 33; JMBl. 33, p. 220; *li; LAB, Liste 10/15/1933; Liste 36; MRRAK; BArch, R 3001 PAK; BG

**Siegel, Siegfried Kurt**
11/12/1885 Meiningen - no information
*Home address:* Ahornallee 7, Charlottenburg
*Law firm address:* Prager Platz 6, Wilmersdorf
*Additional information:* After the National Socialist seizure of power in 1933 he was readmitted, he worked as an attorney until at least 1936. He emigrated to Vina del Mar, Chile, on 06/25/1937; he was still living there in 1950.
*Sources:* TK 33; *li; Liste 36; LAB, Liste 10/15/1933; BArch, R 3001 PAK; BG

**Siegel, Walter Dr.**
04/28/1899 Brieg - no information
*Home address:* Duisburger Str. 7, Wilmersdorf
*Law firm address:* Potsdamer Str. 129/130, W 9
*Additional information:* Attorney and notary; after the National Socialist seizure of power in 1933 he was readmitted; at the end of 1935 his license as a notary was revoked, he worked as an attorney until the general occupational ban in 1938. He emigrated to Malmö, Sweden, in May 1940; in 1946 he lived in Stockholm.
*Sources:* TK 33; *li; DJ 36, p. 315; Liste 36; LAB, Liste 10/15/1933; MRRAK; BArch, R 3001 PAK; BG

**Siegmann, Georg Dr., Judicial Councillor**
05/21/1869 Berlin - transportation 1943
*Home address:* Lützowstr. 77, W 35
*Law firm address:* Lindenstr. 112, SW 68
*Additional information:* Judicial councillor he was admitted as an attorney at the LG I-III and the AG Tempelhof, he also worked as a notary. When the National Socialist seizure of power occurred, he was 63 years old. As an "elderly attorney," who had been admitted before 1914, his application for readmission was granted in 1933, however, his license as a notary was revoked in the summer of 1933. He worked until the general occupational ban in 1938.

On 07/02/1942 he signed his declaration of property, at this time he was living in the Jewish retirement home in Lützowstr. 48. Two weeks later, on 07/16/1943, Siegmann and his wife were transported to Theresienstadt. From there, in August 1944, he sent a card to the legal clerk Naatz and informed him of the death of the well-known judicial councillor Julius Magnus. He was deported from Theresienstadt to Auschwitz on 10/28/1944.

*Sources:* Br.B. 32; TK 33; JMBl. 33, p. 220; *li; LAB, Liste 10/15/1933; Liste 36; MRRAK; BG: BAK, GB; BAP, 15.09 RSA, LAB, OFP files; Karte Naatz; GB II; Naatz-Album

**Sieskind, Jacob Dr.**
02/07/1874 St. Petersburg - no information
*Home address:* Kaiserdamm 10, Charlottenburg
*Law firm address:* Friedrichstr. 234, SW 68
*Additional information:* Attorney and notary; after the National Socialist seizure of power he was made subject to a representation ban in early 1933, his licenses as an attorney and notary were revoked; then in the fall of 1933 he was readmitted; at the end of 1935 his license as a notary was revoked, he was admitted as an attorney until the general occupational ban in 1938. He emigrated to Stockholm, Sweden, on 02/13/1940.
*Sources:* TK 33; Liste d. nichtzugel. RA, 04/25/1933; JMBl. 08/21/1933, S. 267; Pr.J. 33, p. 532; LAB, Liste 10/15/1933; Korr. Liste der arischen Anw., 10/15/1933; DJ 36, p. 315 (Jakob S.); Liste 36; MRRAK; Naatz-Album; BG

**Silber, Erwin Dr.**
05/16/1902 Berlin - 09/07/1987
*Home address:* no information
Law firm: Frankfurter Allee 181, Lichtenberg
*Additional information:* After the National Socialist seizure of power he was made subject to an occupational ban in early 1933. He emigrated to the USA, he last lived in Cleveland, Ohio.
*Sources:* TK 33; Liste d. nichtzugel. RA, 04/25/1933; JMBl. 33, p. 209; BArch, R 3001 PAK; SSDI

**Silberberg, Rudolf Dr.**
06/05/1878 - 03/23/1937
*Home address:* Neue Winterfeldtstr. 43, Schöneberg
*Law firm address:* Nürnberger Str. 13, W 50
*Additional information:* After the National Socialist seizure of power in 1933 he was readmitted; he worked as an attorney until at least 1936; he died in 1937 at the age of 59 and was buried in the Jewish cemetery at Weißensee.
*Sources:* TK 33; *li; LAB, Liste 10/15/1933; Liste 36; BG

**Silbermann, David Dr., Judicial Councillor**
No information - 05/01/1937
*Home address:* no information
*Law firm address:* Waitzstr. 7, Charlottenburg
*Additional information:* After the National Socialist seizure of power in 1933 he was readmitted, he worked as an attorney until at least 1936; he died in May 1937.
*Sources:* TK 33; *li; LAB, Liste 10/15/1933; Liste 36

**Silbermann, Fritz Dr.**
05/05/1895 Berlin - 01/28/1943 Theresienstadt
*Home address:* Yorckstr. 65, Kreuzberg
*Law firm address:* Kantstr. 8, Charlottenburg
*Additional information:* After the National Socialist seizure of power he was made subject to a representation ban in April 1933, he was readmitted in the fall, with the general occupational ban at the end of 1938 he was deleted from the list of attorneys. Already in August 1938 he emigrated to Czechoslovakia; he was transported on 08/18/1942 from Prague to Theresienstadt; he died there at the end of January 1943.
*Sources:* TK 33; Nachtragsliste, 04/25/1933; *li; LAB, Liste 10/15/1933; Liste 36; MRRAK; BG; GB II

**Silberschmidt, Ludwig Dr.**
12/08/1883 Bocholt - no information
*Law firm address:* Tauentzienstr. 12 a, W 50
*Additional information:* He had been released in 1931 at his own request as a public notary, during a longer vacation, the attorney Hans Fraustaedter was appointed as a representative. In 1933 he was admitted as an attorney at the AG Charlottenburg. After the National Socialist seizure of power the board of the RAK noted in the summer of 1933 that he, who had listed his religion as "mosaic," was of "non-Aryan

descent" and had moved to an unknown address. His license as an attorney was revoked in October 1933.
*Sources:* Pr.J. 33, p. 633; BArch, R 3001 PAK, PA

**Silberstein, Alfred Dr.**
08/07/1897 Berlin-Charlottenburg - August 1971
*Home address:* Schönhauser Allee 144
*Law firm address:* Burgstr. 29, C 2
*Additional information:* Attorney and notary; after the National Socialist seizure of power he was made subject to a representation ban in April 1933, then he was readmitted; at the end of 1935 his license as a notary was revoked, he worked as an attorney until the general occupational ban in 1938. He emigrated to the USA, he last lived in Philadelphia.
*Sources:* TK 33; *li; LAB, Liste 10/15/1933; DJ, 36, p. 315; Liste 36; MRRAK; BArch, R 3001 PAK; BG; SSDI

**Silberstein, Heinrich**
12/10/1878 - 10/13/1936 Berlin
*Home address:* Weidenweg 35, O 34
*Law firm address:* Weidenweg 35, O 34
*Additional information:* Attorney and notary; after the National Socialist seizure of power in 1933 he was readmitted; at the end of 1935 his license as a notary was revoked; he died in 1936 at the age of 67, he was buried in the Jewish cemetery at Weißensee.
*Sources:* TK 33; *li; LAB, Liste 10/15/1933; DJ 36, p. 315; Liste 36; BG

**Silberstein, Hermann Dr., Judicial Councillor**
07/18/1867 Neuruppin - 01/14/1942 Litzmannstadt/Lodz
*Home address:* Meierottostr. 4, W 15
*Law firm address:* Meierottostr. 4, W 15
*Additional information:* Attorney and notary; after the National Socialist seizure of power in 1933 his license as a notary was revoked, he was admitted as an attorney until 01/15/1938. Transportation on 10/18/1941 to Litzmannstadt/Lodz, there he died in 1942.
*Sources:* TK 33; JMBl. 33, p. 220; *li; LAB, Liste 10/15/1933; Liste 36 (Henry S.); BG; GB II

**Silberstein, Leopold, Judicial Councillor**
08/17/1870 - 01/09/1934 Berlin
*Home address:* Fasanenstr. 60, W 15
*Law firm address:* Fasanenstr. 60, W 15

*Additional information:* He came from a humble background; he befriended the daughter of his landlady, who did general tasks for him for 19 years, until he was established as an attorney and the two could marry. Attorney at the LG I-III and notary. After the National Socialist seizure of power in 1933 his license as a notary was revoked. He died in 1934 at the age of 63. He died when he was waiting on a bench for his wife, while she was at a business. He was buried in the Jewish cemetery at Weißensee.
*Sources:* TK 33; JMBl. 33, p. 220; *li; LAB, Liste 10/15/1933; BG; information E. Proskauer

**Simon, Alfred Ferdinand Dr.**
08/13/1875 Magdeburg - transportation 1942
*Home address:* Kluckstr. 27, W 35
*Law firm address:* Magdeburger Str. 24, W 35
*Additional information:* Attorney at the KG and notary; after the National Socialist seizure of power in 1933 he was readmitted, at the end of 1935 his license as a notary was revoked, he worked as an attorney until at least 1936; he belonged to the Reich Association of Non-Aryan Christians. Transportation on 04/02/1942 to Warsaw.
*Sources:* Br.B. 32; TK 33; *li; LAB, Liste 10/15/1933; DJ 36, p. 315; Liste 36; Mitt. bl. Reichsverband nicht- arischer Christen, 12/06/1934; BG; GB II

**Simon, Erich Dr.**
08/11/1881 Bromberg - no information
*Home address:* no information
*Law firm address:* Königstr. 50, C 2
*Additional information:* Attorney and notary; after the National Socialist seizure of power in 1933 his license as a notary was revoked, he worked as an attorney until the general occupational ban in 1938. He emigrated to Argentina.
*Sources:* TK 33; JMBl. 33, p. 202; *li; LAB, Liste 10/15/1933; Liste 36; BArch, R 3001 PAK

**Simon, Erich Max**
01/20/1885 Jüstrow - February 1974
*Home address:* no information
*Law firm address:* Taubenstr. 35, W 8
*Additional information:* Attorney and notary; after the National Socialist seizure of power in 1933 he was readmitted; at the end of 1935 his license as a notary was revoked; he worked

as a notary until the general occupational ban in 1938, thereafter he still worked as a "consultant." He emigrated to the USA in 1940 (or on 03/26/1941); in 1949 he was living in New York under the name Eric M. Simon.
*Sources:* TK 33; *li; LAB, Liste 10/15/1933; DJ 36, p. 315; Liste 36; MRRAK; BArch, R 3001 PAK; Liste der Kons. v. 02/23/1939; BG; SSDI

**Simon, Fritz Dr.**
01/15/1884 Frankfurt/Oder - 03/22/1935 Berlin
*Home address:* Tauentzienstr. 13, W 50
*Law firm address:* Tauentzienstr. 13, W 50
*Additional information:* Attorney and notary; after the National Socialist seizure of power in 1933 he was readmitted; he died in 1935 at the age of 51, he was buried in the Jewish cemetery at Weißensee.
*Sources:* TK 33; *li; BArch, R 3001 PAK; BG

**Simon, Heinrich Veit Dr.**
08/01/1883 Berlin - 05/18/1942 Berlin
*Home address:* Hindenburgdamm 11, Steglitz
*Law firm address:* Pariser Platz 6, NW 7; 1939: Viktoriastr. 10, W 35
*Additional information:* The Veit Simon family was prominent in Berlin: Hermann Veit Simon (1856 - 1914) was already an attorney, he published "Die Bilanzen der Aktiengesellschaft [The accounts of the stock company]." Heinrich was an attorney and notary, as well as a longtime member of the board of trustees of the University for the Science of Judaism. After the National Socialist seizure of power in 1933 his license as a notary was revoked, he worked as an attorney until the general occupational ban in 1938, then he was admitted as a "consultant." His wife was regarded as "Aryan," the couple had five children. When two of the children were to be sent to England on a child transport, he tried to protect them financially. Because of the procurement of foreign currency, he was arrested, and went to the detention center Berlin-Mitte (Keibelstr.) and was murdered. His deaf and dumb sisters, as well as his mother were transported to Auschwitz and/or Theresienstadt and died there.
*Sources:* TK 33; JMBl. 33, p. 220; *li; LAB, Liste 10/15/1933; Liste 36; MRRAK; Liste d. Kons., 03/15/1939; BG; Lowenthal, p. 232 (Veit-Simon); information attorney Erdmann

**Simon, Herbert Dr.**
01/01/1881 Bromberg - 01/26/1936
*Home address:* no information
*Law firm address:* Joachimsthaler Str. 12, W 15
*Additional information:* Attorney and notary; after the National Socialist seizure of power in 1933 he was readmitted; at the end of 1935 his license as a notary was revoked, he was admitted as an attorney until his death in 1936.
*Sources:* *li; LAB, Liste 10/15/1933; DJ 36, p. 315; BArch, R 3001 PAK, PA

**Simon, Herbert Heinrich Dr.**
04/30/1897 Berlin - April 1969
*Home address:* Sodener Str. 34, Wilmersdorf
*Law firm address:* Beuthstr. 7, SW 19
*Additional information:* Attorney and notary; after the National Socialist seizure of power in 1933 he was readmitted; at the end of 1935 his license as a notary was revoked, he was admitted as an attorney until the general occupational ban in 1938. He emigrated, in 1947; he was living in Kansas City, USA.
*Sources:* *li; Liste 36; LAB, Liste 10/15/1933; DJ 1936, p. 315; MRRAK; BArch, R 3001 PAK; BG: LAB, OFP files; SSDI

**Simon, Manfred**
06/10/1887 Seelow - January 1970
*Home address:* Eisenzahstr. 66, Halensee (1939)
*Law firm address:* Prenzlauer Str. 26/27, C 25; later: Eisenzahnstr. 66, Halensee
*Additional information:* Confessing Jew; he had fought in the First World War; he was married and had two children (born ca. 1930 and 1932); attorney at the LG I-III and notary (as from 1924); 1929-1933 he was a board member of the RAK. After the National Socialist seizure of power in July 1933 his license as a notary was revoked, then he was ordered back to be a notary, until the general occupational ban for Jewish notaries at the end of 1935; he worked as an attorney until the general occupational ban in 1938, then he was admitted as a "consultant," in July 1939 he gave up this activity. He emigrated to the USA, he last lived in Seattle, he died in 1970 at the age of 82.
*Sources:* TK 33; JMBl. 33, p. 220; *li; LAB, Liste 10/15/1933; DJ 36, p. 315; Liste 36; MRRAK; BArch, R 3001 PAK, PA; BG; SSDI

**Simon, Max Dr.**
03/06/1881 Berlin - no
information
*Home address:* no
information
*Law firm address:*
Friedrichstr. 85, W 8
*Additional information:*
Attorney and notary; after the National
Socialist seizure of power in 1933 his license
as a notary was revoked, he worked as an
attorney until the general occupational ban in
1938. He presumably emigrated in 1939.
*Sources:* TK 33; JMBl. 33, p. 220; *li: LAB,
Liste 10/15/1933; Liste 36; MRRAK; BArch,
R 3001 PAK; Naatz-Album; BG

**Simon, Paul Dr.**
02/08/1876 Culm - no information
*Home address:* Tannenbergallee 10-12,
Charlottenburg
*Law firm address:* Königstr. 50, C 2
*Additional information:* Attorney and notary;
after the National Socialist seizure of power
in 1933 his license as a notary was revoked,
he worked as an attorney until the general
occupational ban in 1938. He emigrated to
Buenos Aires, Brazil, on 07/28/1939, in 1946
he was still living in Buenos Aires.
*Sources:* TK 33; JMBl. 33, p. 220; *li; LAB,
Liste 10/15/1933; Liste 36; MRRAK; BG

**Simon, Walter**
10/17/1882 Berlin-Schöneberg -
transportation 1942
*Home address:* Brauner Weg 28,
Friedrichshain
*Law firm address:* Kantstr. 130,
Charlottenburg
*Additional information:* Attorney and
notary; after the National Socialist seizure
of power in 1933 his license as a notary was
revoked, he worked as an attorney until
the general occupational ban in 1938; later
he worked at Palestine & Orient Lloyd,
Meinekestr. 2, W 15. Transportation on
01/19/1942 to Riga.
*Sources:* TK 33; JMBl. 33, p. 220; *li; LAB,
Liste 10/15/1933; Liste 36; MRRAK; BArch,
R 3001 PAK; BG; BdE; GB II

**Simon, Wilhelm Meno**
02/24/1885 Straßburg - no information
*Home address:* no information

*Law firm address:* Brunnenstr. 25, N 54
*Additional information:* Attorney and
notary; after the National Socialist seizure of
power in 1933 he was readmitted; at the end
of 1935 his license as a notary was revoked;
he worked as an attorney until 10/02/1938.
*Sources:* TK 33; *li; LAB, Liste 10/15/1933;
DJ 36, p. 315; Liste 36; BArch, R 3001 PAK

**Simoni, Erich Dr.**
03/30/1896 Berlin
- 12/18/1976
*Home address:* no
information
*Law firm address:*
Köpenicker Str. 110, SO 16
*Additional information:*
Attorney (since 1924) and notary (since
1932); before 1933 he was a member of the
SPD; after the National Socialist seizure
of power in 1933 he was readmitted. The
attorney, whose father was Jewish, was
regarded as "mixed race first degree" and
was allowed to practice law throughout the
general occupational ban in 1938.
In 1944, he was assigned to forced labor by
the OT as part of the "Action Center" and
employed as a construction worker, he was
then taken to Thuringia to a labor camp,
where he contracted a serious illness. He
survived the National Socialist regime and
was readmitted as an attorney and a notary
after 1945. Only then could he marry his wife,
since the marriage had not been approved
before 1945. In 1949 he became a member
of the executive commitee of the Berlin Bar
Association. He died in 1976 at the age of 80.
*Sources:* TK 33; *li; LAB, Liste 10/15/1933;
Liste Mschlg. 36; Tel.B. 41; Verz. zugel. Anw.
45; LAB, RAK, PA; BG

**Simonsohn, Georg Dr.**
08/13/1875 - 06/23/1933 Berlin
*Home address:* no information
*Law firm address:* Keithstr. 21, W 62
*Additional information:* In 1904 he worked
as an attorney for the city council, in 1914
he was elected as a salaried city councillor.
During the First World War he was
responsible for the allocation of bread. He
took care of the fair distribution of rationed
goods, he also ensured that Jews were
provided with matzoh during the Passover
feast, vegetarians with special rations of pasta

products. After the revolution he remained in office until 1920 (last elected with votes from the list of the left). Afterwards he established himself as an attorney, admitted at the LG I-III. After the National Socialist seizure of power in April 1933 he was made subject to a representation ban; he died in June of 1933 at the age of 57 and he was buried in the Jewish cemetery at Weißensee.
*Sources:* Br.B. 32; TK 33; Liste d. nichtzugel. RA, 04/25/1933; JMBl. 07/28/1933, p. 234; BG; Verfolgte Berl.Stadtverordn.u.Mag. mitgl., p. 348

**Simson, Robert von Dr., Judicial Councillor**
07/13/1866 Frankfurt a. M. - 06/11/1938 Berlin
*Home address:* Graf-Spee-Str. (today: Hiroshimastr.) 15, W 35
Law office: Pariser Platz 1, W 8
*Additional information:* Attorney and notary; he was, like the brothers Wolff, the grandson of the Reichsgericht president Eduard von Simson, legal counsel and grandson of Walther, also uncle of Werner; he was Protestant. After the National Socialist seizure of power in 1933 he was readmitted; he was regarded as "mixed race," because he had two Jewish grandparents; the office was moved from Pariser Platz to Matthaikirchplatz 4 before 1938. He died in 1938 at the age of 71 in Berlin.
*Sources:* TK 33; *li; LAB, Liste 10/15/1933; Liste Mschlg. 36; Tel.B. 38, information Horst Rohmer, 02/21/2000

**Simson, Walther von Dr.**
03/18/1899 Charlottenburg - 03/01/1943 Berlin
*Home address:* Boeckelweg 7, Zehlendorf
Law office: Pariser Platz 1, W 8
*Additional information:* He was the nephew of and the legal counsel for Robert; he was Protestant and married; attorney at the KG. After the National Socialist seizure of power in 1933 he was readmitted, he was regarded as "mixed race second degree," because he had Jewish grandparents, because of this reason he could practice law throughout the general occupational ban in 1938. He was killed on March 1, 1943 in an air raid.
*Sources:* TK 33; *li; LAB, Liste 10/15/1933: Liste Mschlg. 36; Tel.B .41; information Horst Rohmer, 02/21/2000

**Simson, Werner von Dr.**
02/21/1908 Kiel - 09/20/1996 Freiburg
*Home address:* Freiherr-von-Stein-Str. 12, Schöneberg
Law office: Pariser Pl. 1, NW 7
*Additional information:*
He was a nephew of Robert; he was also regarded as "mixed race," he was admitted for this reason even after 1933 and was therefore allowed to work througout 1938 as a judge at the Kammergericht. Shortly before the occupation of Poland he left Germany with his wife and went to Great Britain. There he was interned as an "enemy alien" in 1940 on the Isle of Man. After his release two years later, he settled in Birmingham as a legal advisor to a mechanical engineering company. After the war, he was member of a denafizification committee of the Allies from 1946-1948. When the Court of Justice of the European Community was created in 1953, he sought to re-enter legal practice and settled in Luxembourg with his family. Here he dealt at first primarily with legal issues of the European Coal and Steel Community Coal in coal and steel production, later with human rights proceedings. Visiting Professor at the University of Freiburg in 1965 and later he was appointed as a full professor of public law there. 1976 he retired; he received the German Federal Cross of Merit in the 1980s.
*Sources:* LAB, Liste Mschlg. 36; TK 1936; Tel.B. 38; information Horst Rohmer, 02/21/2000; information and unbound collection John v. S., 03/21/2000

**Singer, Harry**
No information
*Home address:* no information
*Law firm address:* Lützowstr. 83, W 35
*Additional information:* Presumably admitted at the turn of the year 1932/33; after the National Socialist seizure of power he was made subject to a representation ban and presumably also an occupational ban in early 1933.
*Sources:* LAB AG Köpenick A Rep 343 (Vertr.V.)

**Singer, Herbert**
03/06/1885 Kreuzburg - September 1964
*Home address:* Reichsstr. 106, Charlottenburg
*Law firm address:* Taubenstr. 25, W 56; later: Friedrichstr. 71

*Additional information:* Attorney and notary; after the National Socialist seizure of power he was readmitted; at the end of 1935 his license as a notary was revoked, he worked as an attorney until the general occupational ban in 1938, then he was admitted as a "consultant." He emigrated on 08/01/1939 to Cleveland, Ohio, USA.
*Sources:* Br.B. 32; TK 33; *li; LAB, Liste 10/15/1933; DJ 36, p. 315; Liste 36; MRRAK; BArch, R 3001, PAK; BG; SSDI

**Sluzewski, Curt Dr.**
12/09/1895 Berlin - no information
*Home address:* Am Erlenbusch 6, Dahlem
*Law firm address:* Wallstr. 3, SW 19
*Additional information:* Attorney at the KG and notary; after the National Socialist seizure of power in 1933 he was readmitted; at the end of 1935 his license as a notary was revoked, he worked as an attorney until the general occupational ban in 1938. He emigrated to London, Great. Britain.
*Sources:* TK 33; *li; LAB, Liste 10/15/1933; DJ 36, p. 315; Liste 36; MRRAK; BArch, R 3001 PAK; BG

**Smoschewer, Julius, Judicial Councillor**
06/07/1862 Krotoschin - 01/29/1941
*Home address:* Passauer Str. 2, W 50
*Law firm address:* Passauer Str. 2, W 50
*Additional information:* Attorney at the KG and notary; after the National Socialist seizure of power in 1933 he was readmitted; at the end of 1935 his license as a notary was revoked, he worked as an attorney until the general occupational ban in 1938, he died at the end of January 1941.
*Sources:* TK 33; *li; LAB, Liste 10/15/1933; DJ 36, p. 315; Liste 36; MRRAK; BG; information E. Proskauer

**Soelling, Erich**
11/26/1882 Bromberg - Myi 1970 USA
*Home address:* no information
*Law firm address:* Grolmanstr. 41, Charlottenburg
*Additional information:* Attorney and notary; after the National Socialist seizure of power his licenses as an attorney and as a notary were revoked. He emigrated in 1933 to Paris, France, later to the USA. An arrest warrant for tax evasion was issued against him.
*Sources:* Br.B. 32; TK 33; BArch, R 3001 PAK; Wolf, BFS

**Sokolowski, Julian (Julius) Dr.**
09/17/1888 Wreschen/Posen - no information
*Home address:* Dahlmannstr. 28, Charlottenburg
*Law firm address:* Alexanderstr. 37 a (1932)
*Additional information:* He was married and had two children, he had studied law in Breslau, he was admitted as an attorney in Berlin at the LG I-III. After the National Socialist seizure of power he was made subject to an occupational ban in early 1933 (admittance withdrawn in June 1933, deleted in July 1933). He emigrated to London, Great Britain, on 07/25/1939.
*Sources:* TK 33; Liste d. nichtzugel. RA, 04/25/1933; JMBl. 08/04/1933, p. 253; BArch, R 3001 PAK, PA 76688; VZ 39; BG

**Solon, Friedrich Dr.**
07/07/1882 Berlin - no information
*Home address:* Wichmannstr. 25, Tiergarten
*Law firm address:* Memhardstr. 4, C 25
*Additional information:* He attended the Gymnasium in Luisenstadt, he fought in the First World War. After his legal studies he established himself as an attorney in Berlin-Mitte, he was admitted at the KG, later also as a notary. After the National Socialist seizure of power in 1933 he was made subject to a representation ban, after a few weeks' trial his application for readmission was approved, he had been recognized as a "frontline fighter." 1935 his license as a notary was revoked; thereupon he moved his law office to his apartment. He worked as an attorney until the general occupational ban, subsequently still as a "consultant." Faced with increasing harassment, he decided to emigrate with his family to London, Great Britain.
On the initiative of Prof. Hartmann, he wrote down his memoirs in 1939 as part of a competition of Harvard University. These memories contain various very personal poems, including the following:
*Conclusion*
*Despite the dull and lacklustre mass*
*And despite all the mockers*
*I stay faithful to my gods*
*My love, my hatred.*
*Sources:* TK 33; *li; LAB, Liste 10/15/1933; DJ 36, p. 315; Liste 36; MRRAK; BArch, R 3001 PAK; LBI Memoirs, F. Solon, Erinnerungen [Memoirs]; BG

**Sommerfeld, Manfred**
06/26/1882 Schneidemühl - 04/20/1942
Litzmannstadt/Lodz
*Home address:* Emser Str. 8, Wilmersdorf,
Wielandstr. 22
*Law firm address:* Weißenburger Str. 1
*Additional information:* Attorney at the KG;
after the National Socialist seizure of power
he was deleted from the list of attorneys in
early 1933. Date of declaration of property
10/16/1941; collecting station Levetzowstr.
7-8; transportation on 10/27-29/1941 to
Litzmannstadt/Lodz, he died there.
*Sources:* Br.B. 32; TK 33; JMBl. 04/17/1933;
BArch, R 3001 PAK; BG; GB II

**Sommerfeld, Max Dr.**
08/09/1895 Magdeburg - transportation 1942
*Home address:* Rankestr. 27 a, W 50,
Charlottenburg
*Law firm address:* Kurfürstendamm 200,
Charlottenburg, W 15
*Additional information:* After the National
Socialist seizure of power he was made
subject to an occupational ban in early 1933.
Transportation on 12/09/1942 to Auschwitz.
*Sources:* Br.B. 32; TK 33; Liste d. nichtzugel.
RA, 04/25/1933; JMBl. 08/04/1933, p. 253;
BArch, R 3001 PAK; BG; GB II

**Sommerfeld, Werner Dr.**
09/25/1904 Berlin-Schöneberg - no
information
*Home address:* no information
*Law firm address:* Uhlandstr. 27, W 15
*Additional information:* Attorney at the KG;
after the National Socialist seizure of power
he was made subject to a representation ban
and on 05/19/1933 an occupational ban,
because he "is of non-Aryan descent,"– the
editor changed the spelling: the word "non-
Aryan" was separated in pencil.
*Sources:* Br.B. 32; TK 33; Liste d. nichtzugel.
RA, 04/25/1933; BArch, R 3001 PAK, PA

**Sonnenfeld, Kurt Dr.**
04/16/1892 Berlin -
10/17/1964 New York
*Home address:*
Klopstockstr. 31, NW 23
*Law firm address:* Berliner
Str. 19, Pankow
*Additional information:*
He studied at Friedrich Wilhelm University,

Berlin, 1919 he completed his doctorate
at Greifswald with a dissertation entitled:
"Der Schutz der weiblichen Arbeiter gegen
gewerbliche Ausbeutung" [The protection
of female workers against commercial
exploitation], 1924 he was admitted as
an attorney. After the National Socialist
seizure of power he was made subject to an
occupational ban in early 1933; his wife
was regarded as non-Jewish, the marriage as
privileged, because they had a daughter, who
took part in religious Christian education;
1933-1938 he was a representative of
Allianz and Stuttgarter Versicherung;
1937 he took his examination to be a
state-certified masseur. Concern about
further developments, especially after the
"annexation" of Austria, caused the family
to leave Germany. Every certificate had to
be paid for dearly, the export possibility
of goods was quite limited. On 05/15/1938
he emigrated to Den Haag, Holland; on
09/29/1938 further to Panama, there he
had a three-month stay; on 01/11/1939 he
arrived in the USA. He and his wife lived
in the Bronx in New York and died there
in 1964.
*Sources:* Br.B. 32; TK 33; Liste d. nichtzugel.
RA, 04/25/1933; BArch, R 3001 PAK;
information of the relatives of Tobias Schell

**Spier, Siegfried Dr.**
No information
*Home address:* Uhlandstr. 28, W 15
*Law firm address:* Behrenstr. 67
*Additional information:* Attorney and
notary; after the National Socialiast
seizure of power he was made subject to a
representation ban in early 1933; his license
as a notary was revoked in the fall of 1933, he
was readmitted as an attorney until 1936; he
presumably emigrated.
*Sources:* Br.B. 32; TK 33; Liste d.
nichtzugel. RA, 04/25/1933; Pr.J. 33, p. 443;
Liste 36; BG

**Spindel, Hermann**
10/21/1902 Hannover - no information
*Home address:* no information
*Law firm address:* Spandauer Str. 27, C 2
*Additional information:* Attorney at the LG
I-III and AG Berlin-Mitte; after the National
Socialist seizure of power he was made subject
to an occupational ban in early 1933.

*Sources:* Br.B. 32; TK 33; Liste d. nichtzugel. RA, 04/25/1933; JMBl. 08/21/1933, p. 267; BArch, R 3001 PAK

**Spiro, Erwin Dr.**
08/01/1901 Düsseldorf - no information
*Home address:* no information
*Law firm address:* Hohenstaufenstr. 37
*Additional information:* 1920-24 he completed his legal studies in Berlin; 1924 he took his first state examination; 1925 he received his doctorate in Breslau; 1927 he took his second state examination; as from 1927 he was an attorney at the KG; after the National Socialist seizure of power he was made subject to an occupational ban on 06/09/1933. He emigrated to South Africa in September 1936; he performed casual labour in Cape Town until 1940; 1940-1946 he was in military service as a paramedic; 1946-47 he renewed his legal studies in Cape Town; from 1948 he was an attorney at the Supreme Court of South Africa; from 1962 at the same time he was a lecturer in law at the University of Cape Town; he was still living there in 1975.
Br.B. 32; TK 33; Liste d. nichtzugel. RA, 04/25/1933; BArch, R 3001 PAK; BG; BHdE vol. 1, p. 716

**Spitzer, Frida Fanny Dr., nee Rosenthal**
05/30/1900 Berlin - no information
*Home address:* Köpenicker Str. 58, SO 16 (1928)
*Law firm address:* Monbijoupl. 4, N 42
*Additional information:* She was admitted as an attorney on 10/21/1932 at the LG III, later also at the other LG and at AG Wedding. On 06/20/1933 her license as an attorney was revoked. She was married to the dentist Dr. Richard Spitzer.
*Sources:* JMBl. 08/04/1933. p. 253; BArch, R 3001 PAK, PA

**Springer, Kurt Dr.**
11/06/1899 Landsberg /W. - Auschwitz
*Home address:* no information
*Law firm address:* Kantstr. 19, Charlottenburg
*Additional information:* After the National Socialist seizure of power he was made subject to an occupational ban in early 1933. Transported to Auschwitz under unknown circumstances; he was murdered there.

*Sources:* TK 33; Liste d. nichtzugel. RA, 04/25/1933 (addendum); JMBl. 08/04/1933, p. 253; BG; GB II

**Sprinz, Wilhelm Dr.**
09/09/1877 Hohensalza - 10/29/1942 Riga
*Home address:* Niebuhrstr. 77, Charlottenburg.
*Law firm address:* Frankfurter Allee 31, O 112
*Additional information:* Attorney and notary; after the National Socialist seizure of power he was readmitted; at the end of 1935 his license as a notary was revoked, he worked as an attorney until the general occupational ban in 1938. Date of declaration of property: 09/14/1942; transportation on 10/26/1942 to Riga, he was murdered there on the day of their arrival.
*Sources:* TK 33; *li; LAB, Liste 10/15/1933; DJ 36, p. 315; Liste 36; MRRAK; BG; BdE; GB II

**Stadthagen, Georg Dr.**
06/10/1884 Berlin - no information
*Home address:* Brettschneiderstr. 11, Charlottenburg
*Law firm address:* Kaiserdamm 9, Charlottenburg
*Additional information:* Attorney and notary; after the National Socialist seizure of power in 1933 his license as a notary was revoked, he worked as an attorney until ca. 1936. He emigrated on 07/01/1938 to London, Great Britain, accordingly, his license was revoked.
TK 33; JMBl. 33, p. 220; *li; LAB, Liste 10/15/1933; Liste 36; BArch, R 3001 PAK; BG

**Stadthagen, Kurt Philipp Dr.**
06/24/1887 Berlin - 1943 transportation
*Home address:* Sybelstr. 54, Charlottenburg
*Law firm address:* Turmstr. 35
*Additional information:* Attorney and notary; after the National Socialist seizure of power his license as a notary was revoked in 1933; he worked as an attorney until the general occupational ban in 1938. He was conscripted for forced labor and last used as a laborer. Date of declaration of property: 02/28/1943, deportation on 03/01/1943 to Auschwitz.
*Sources:* TK 33; JMBl. 33, p. 220; *li; LAB, Liste 10/15/1933; Liste 36; MRRAK; BArch, R 3001 PAK; BG; g; GB II

**Starke, Arthur Dr.**
10/13/1877 - 06/09/1937
*Home address:* Wilhelmstr. 128, SW 68
*Law firm address:* Friedrichstr. 234, SW 68,
last in his own home
*Additional information:* Attorney and notary;
after the National Socialist seizure of power
in 1933 his license as a notary was revoked;
he was admitted as an attorney until at least
1936; he died 1937 at the age of 59 and was
buried in the Jewish cemetery at Weißensee.
*Sources:* TK 33; JMBl. 33, p. 220; *li; LAB,
Liste 10/15/1933; Liste 36; BG

**Staub, Friedrich Dr.**
01/11/1889 Ratibor - 08/29/1942
*Home address:* Kurfürstendamm 90,
Wilmersdorf
*Law firm address:* Kurfürstendamm 90,
Halensee
*Additional information:* Attorney and
notary; after the National Socialist seizure
of power his license as a notary was revoked
at the end of 1935; he worked as an attorney
until the general occupational ban in 1938,
thereafter briefly admitted as a "consultant"
(Nestorstr.1). He committed suicide on
08/29/1942, presumably in the face of
imminent transportation, he was buried in the
Jewish cemetery at Weißensee.
*Sources:* TK 33; *li; LAB, Liste 10/15/1933;
DJ 36, p. 315; Liste 36; MRRAK; Liste d.
Kons. v. 12/31/1938; BArch, R 3001 PAK;
BG; GB II

**Staub, Hugo**
11/18/1885 - no information
*Home address:* Mommsenstr. 23,
Charlottenburg (1932)
*Law firm address:* Friedrich-Ebert-Str. 4
(1932)
*Additional information:* Attorney at the
KG and notary; after the National Socialist
seizure of power he was made subject to an
occupational ban in April 1933.
*Sources:* Jüd.Adr.B.; Br.B. 32; TK 33; JMBl.
04/28/1933; BArch, R 3001 PAK, PA

**Stein, Arthur Dr.**
09/24/1890 Berlin - no information
*Home address:* Derfflinger Str. 8, W 35
*Law firm address:* Behrenstr. 20, W 8
*Additional information:* Attorney and
notary; after the National Socialist seizure of

power he was readmitted in 1933; at the end
of 1935 his license as a notary was revoked,
he worked as an attorney until the general
occupational ban in 1938. He emigrated to
Tel Aviv, Palestine, on 12/31/1938.
*Sources:* TK 33; *li; LAB, Liste 10/15/1933;
DJ 36, p. 315; Liste 36; MRRAK; BG: LAB,
OFP files

**Stein, Hans Dr.**
09/18/1895 Allenstein
- 1980
*Home address:* no
information
*Law firm address:*
Dorotheenstr. 53, NW 7
*Additional information:*
He was Protestant; he fought in the First
World War; he was an attorney and notary.
After the National Socialist seizure of
power, his request for readmission was
reviewed, he was recognized as a "frontline
fighter" and was readmitted. His existing
law firm with the attorneys Drs. Erwin and
Günther Loewenfeld, as well as Karl Siebert
in Rathenower Str. 78 had to be dissolved
because it consisted of "Aryan and non-
Aryan" partners. He established himself
as a solo practitioner in Dorotheenstr. 53.
According to National Socialist guidelines he
was regarded as "mixed race" (two Jewish
grandparents); he was allowed to practice law
throughout the general occupational ban in
1938. He did not seem to have given up his
admission in Berlin, although he emigrated
to the Netherlands on 07/01/1939. There he
tried to raise his three sons without National
Socialist influences. One son also became an
attorney in the Netherlands; the other two
became professors at a Dutch university. He
went back to Berlin after the war and became
a judge at the Reparation Court.
*Sources:* Adr.B. 33; TK 33; *li; LAB, Liste
10/15/1933; Liste Mschlg. 36; Tel.B. 41;
information Prof. Stein, 2001; information R.
Recknagel

**Stein, Leon Dr.**
10/20/1896 - no information
*Home address:* no information
*Law firm address:* Bleibtreustr. 32, W 15
*Additional information:* Attorney and notary;
after the National Socialist seizure of power in
1933 he was readmitted; at the end of 1935 his

license as a notary was revoked; he worked as an attorney until the general occupational ban in 1938. He emigrated to Argentina.
*Sources:* TK 33; *li; LAB, Liste 10/15/1933; DJ 36, p. 315; Liste 36; MRRAK; BArch, R 3001 PAK

**Stein, Ludwig Dr.**
No information
*Home address:* no information
*Law firm address:* Martin-Luther-Str. 113, W 30
*Additional information:* Attorney at the LG; after the National Socialist seizure of power he was readmitted, he still worked as an attorney until 1935.
*Sources:* TK 33; *li; Adr.B. 35

**Stein, Siegbert Dr.**
09/03/1892 Berlin - March 6, 1973, Jerusalem
*Home address:* Offenbacher Str. 24, Wilmersdorf
*Law firm address:* Schinkelplatz 1/2, W 8
*Additional information:*
He passed the first state examination in August 1914; he fought as a soldier from 1914-1918 in the First World War, he was seriously wounded; he was awarded the EK II. Kl. and the Purple Heart; as from 1920 he had a legal traineeship; 1921 he received his doctorate in Würzburg; 1922 he took his second state examination (in shortened form because of his military service), then he was a court assessor with occasional assignments; from 1926 he was a "permanent assistant" (district court judge); as from 1927 he was an attorney in Berlin, with admission for LG I-III and AG Berlin-Mitte. After the National Socialist seizure of power in 1933 he was readmitted, because he was recognized as a "frontline fighter." 1937 he emigrated to Tel Aviv, Palestine, hence he was deleted from the attorneys' list on 07/13/1937 upon his own request. Although he became a convinced citizen of the state of Israel, he remained rooted in German culture throughout his life.
*Sources:* TK 33; *li; LAB, Liste 10/15/1933; Liste 36; BArch, R 3001 PAK, PA

**Steinberg, Erich**
02/25/1892 - no information
*Home address:* Düsseldorfer Str. 41, W 15

*Law firm address:* Frankfurter Allee 79, O 112
*Additional information:* After the National Socialist seizure of power in 1933 he was readmitted, before fall 1935 he was deleted from the list of attorneys. He emigrated to London, Great Britain.
*Sources:* TK 33; *li; BArch, R 3001 PAK; BG

**Steinberg, Wilhelm Dr.**
07/06/1906 Bonn - no information
*Home address:* Kantstr. 47, Charlottenburg
*Law firm address:* Tauentzienstr. 8, W 50
*Additional information:* Attorney at the KG; after the National Socialist seizure of power he was made subject to an occupational ban in early 1933. He emigrated on 07/27/1939 via Holland to Santiago, Chile.
*Sources:* Liste d. nichtzugel. RA, 04/25/1933; JMBl. 33, p. 209; BG

**Steiner, Ludwig, Judicial Councillor**
02/26/1876 - 04/14/1935 Berlin
*Home address:* no information
*Law firm address:* Unter den Linden 57/58, NW 7
*Additional information:* Attorney and notary; after the National Socialist seizure of power in 1933 his licence as a notary was revoked, he was readmitted as an attorney; he died in 1935 at the age of 59 and was buried in the Jewish cemetery at Weißensee.
*Sources:* TK 33; JMBl. 33, p. 220; *li; LAB, Liste 10/15/1933; BG

**Steinfeld, Ernst, Judicial Councillor**
No information
*Home address:* no information
*Law firm address:* Hildegardstr. 31, Wilmersdorf
*Additional information:* Attorney at the KG and notary; after the National Socialist seizure of power in 1933 he was readmitted; at the end of 1935 his license as a notary was revoked; he was admitted as an attorney until at least 1936.
*Sources:* Br.B. 32; *li: DJ 36, p. 315; Liste 36

**Steinfeld, Kurt Dr.**
04/22/1884 Berlin - transportation 1942
*Home address:* Stromstr. 48, Tiergarten
*Law firm address:* Uhlandstr. 90, Wilmersdorf
*Additional information:* He was a Protestant; after the National Socialist seizure of power

in 1933 he was readmitted; he worked as an attorney until the general occupational ban in 1938; then as a "consultant." Date of declaration of property: 08/27/1942; collecting station Große Hamburger Str. 26; transportation on 11/04/1942 to Theresienstadt.
*Sources:* *li; Liste 36; MRRAK; Liste d. Kons. v. 12/31/1938; VZ 39; BG; GB II

**Steinfeld, Rudolf Dr.**
11/21/1886 Berlin - no information
*Home address:* Xantener Str. 10, Wilmersdorf
*Law firm address:* Dörnbergstr. 1, W 10
*Additional information:* After the National Socialist seizure of power in 1933 he was readmitted, he worked as an attorney until the general occupational ban in 1938. He emigrated to the USA, "as from 01/31/1939 he gave notice of departure to New York."
*Sources:* *li; Liste 36; MRRAK; BArch, R 3001 PAK; BG

**Steinhagen, Erich Dr.**
04/17/1902 Berlin - no information
*Home address:* no information
*Law firm address:* Gertraudenstr. 23, C 19
*Additional information:* After the National Socialist seizure of power he was made subject to an occupational ban in early 1933. He emigrated to Brazil.
*Sources:* Br.B. 32; TK 33; Liste d. nichtzugel. RA, 04/25/1933; JMBl. 33, p. 234; BArch, R 3001 PAK; information Werner Wolff, 09/22/1998

**Steinitz, Hans, Judicial Councillor**
No information
*Home address:* no information
*Law firm address:* Badstr. 35/36, N 20
*Additional information:* Attorney at the LG I-III, at the AG Berlin-Mitte and notary; after the National Socialist seizure of power in 1933 his license as a notary was revoked; he was readmitted as an attorney; but he was deleted from the list of attorneys before fall of 1935.
*Sources:* TK 33; JMBl. 33, p. 220; *li

**Steinitz, Hermann Dr.**
11/09/1882 Janowitz - January 1965
*Home address:* Augsburger Str. 70, W 50
*Law firm address:* Kurfürstenstr. 113, W 62
*Additional information:* Attorney at the LG

I-III and AG Berlin-Mitte; after the National Socialist seizure of power in 1933 he was readmitted, he worked as an attorney until the general occupational ban in 1938. He emigrated on 07/18/1941 to the USA; he last lived in New York.
*Sources:* TK 33; *li; Liste 36; MRRAK; BG; SSDI

**Steinitz, Kurt Dr.**
12/18/1894 - no information
*Home address:* Fredericiastr. 5, Charlottenburg
*Law firm address:* Jägerstr. 10, W
*Additional information:* Attorney at the LG I-III and AG Berlin-Mitte; after the National Socialist seizure of power he was made subject to an occupational ban in early 1933.
*Sources:* Br.B. 32; TK 33; Liste d. nichtzugel. RA, 04/25/1933; JMBl. 08/04/1933, p. 253; BArch, R 3001 PAK; BG

**Steinitz, Max Dr.**
08/23/1875 - 12/21/1938
*Home address:* no information
*Law firm address:* Müllerstr. 177, N 65
*Additional information:* Attorney and notary; after the National Socialist seizure of power in 1933 his license as a notary was revoked, he worked as an attorney until the general occupational ban in 1938; he died at the end of December 1938 at the age of 63, he was buried in the Jewish cemetery at Weißensee.
*Sources:* TK 33; JMBl. 33, p. 220; *li; Liste 36; MRRAK; BG

**Steinitz, Werner Dr.**
03/27/1890 Berlin - January 13, 1988
*Home address:* no information
*Law firm address:* Alexanderstr. 21, O 27
*Additional information:* He had fought in the First World War; he was Protestant, like his mother and his siblings; attorney (since 1920) and notary (since 1926); he was married for the second time and had two children (born 1925 and 1929). After the National Socialist seizure of power, he was thoroughy examined for further approval, he was classified as a "frontline fighter." However, the registration office had informed the RAK that he had given notice of departure at the end of April 1933. As a result, the Chamber reported him as an attorney to be deleted to the President of the Kammergericht, who in turn forwarded the

case to the Ministry of Justice. On November 4, 1933, his admittance was deleted, because he had allegedly abandoned his residence in Berlin. In 1938, the Gestapo announced that he ("mixed race first degree") was residing in Havana. The procedure for the revocation of German citizenship was initiated, which also extended to hish family members. A seizure of assets was not requested. Almost all the refugees who came to Cuba actually wanted to enter the USA. He later succeeded in getting there; he last lived in Queens, New York.
*Sources:* BARch R 3001, PAK, PA; SSDI

**Stern, Arthur Dr.**
08/15/1895 Berlin - no information
*Home address:* Uhlandstr. 175, W 15
*Law firm address:* Taubenstr. 35, W 8
*Additional information:* Attorney and notary; after the National Socialist seizure of power in 1933 he was readmitted; at the end of 1935 his license as a notary was revoked, he worked as an attorney until the beginning of 1936. He emigrated to the USA in October 1936.
*Sources:* TK 33; *li; DJ 1936, p. 315; Liste 36; BArch, R 3001 PAK; BG

**Stern, Erich Heinrich Dr.**
05/28/1896 Berlin - transportation 1944
*Home address:* Mackensenstr. 7, Schöneberg
*Law firm address:* Jägerstr. 62 a, W 8
*Additional information:* Attorney and notary; after the National Socialist seizure of power in 1933 he was readmitted; at the end of 1935 his license as a notary was revoked, he was already deleted from the lists before the general occupational ban in 1938. He emigrated to the Netherlands; he was deported from Amsterdam to Theresienstadt on 04/21/1943, from there he was transported to Auschwitz on 09/29/1944.
*Sources:* TK 33; *li; DJ 36, P. 315; Liste 36; BArch, R 3001 PAK; BG; GB II

**Stern, Erich Otto Dr.**
05/26/1902 - October 1958
*Home address:* no information
*Law firm address:* Jägerstr. 10, W 8
*Additional information:* Attorney since 1929; in 1930 he adopted the middle name Otto: after the National Socialist seizure of power in 1933. He requested to be readmitted, but since he was unable to claim any of the exceptions, he was banned from doing so "because he was

not of Aryan descent." He emigrated to the USA. He changed his first name to Eric; he died in 1958 at the age of 56.
*Sources:* Liste d. nichtzugel. RA, 04/25/1933; JMBl 33, p. 203; BArch, R 3001 PAK, PA; SSDI

**Stern, Franz Dr.**
08/16/1894 - no information
*Home address:* Waitzstr. 22, Charlottenburg
*Law firm address:* Friedrichstr. 64, W 8
*Additional information:* Attorney and notary; after the National Socialist seizure of power in 1933 he was readmitted; at the end of 1935 his license as a notary was revoked; he worked as an attorney until at least 1936.
*Sources:* *li; DJ 36, p. 315; Liste 36; BArch, R 3001 PAK

**Stern, Heinrich**
11/01/1883 Berlin - 02/08/1951 London
*Home address:* Corneliusstr. 72, Lankwitz
*Law firm address:* Potsdamer Str. 22 b, W 9
*Additional information:* Attorney (since 1910) and notary (since 1919), married since 1912, he had four children; he fought in the First World War from 1915/1916 and sustained damage to his health. As a result, he was appointed as a notary early; he was temporarily on the board of the RAK; he was an official at the Jewish Synagogue and in Jewish organizations. After the National Socialist seizure of power in 1933, he was readmitted, because he was an "elderly attorney" and "frontline fighter," he moved his law office from Friedrichstraße to Potsdamer Straße. At the end of 1935 his license as a notary was revoked; he was admitted as an attorney until the general occupational ban in 1938. 1938 he emigrated to London, Great Britain; there he worked as a merchant and was still active in Jewish organizations, he died 1951 in London.
*Sources:* Jüd.Adr.B; *li; DJ 36, p. 315; Liste 36; MRRAK; BArch, R 3001 PAK, PA; BG; Göpp., p. 319; Walk, p. 354; Krach, p. 436; Lowenthal, p. 217

**Stern, Heinrich Dr.**
06/16/1882 Berlin - July 1950 London
*Home address:* Prager Str. 9, W 50
*Law firm address:* Prager Str. 9, W 50
*Additional information:* Attorney at the LG 1-III and notary; in 1933 his license as a

notary was revoked; he worked as an attorney until the general occupational ban in 1938, he had to relocate his office several times. He emigrated to Great Britain; he died in 1950 in London.
*Sources:* Jüd.Adr.B.; TK 33; JMBl. 33, p. 220; *li; Liste 36; MMRAK; information of the son, 08/11/2004

**Stern, Leo Dr.**
07/06/1876 Königshütte - 04/15/1943 Auschwitz
*Home address:* Xantener Str. 2, Wilmersdorf
*Law firm address:* Kurfürstenstr. 99 a, W 62
*Additional information:* Attorney and notary; after the National Socialist seizure of power in 1933 his license as a notary was revoked, he was admitted as an attorney until the general occupational ban in 1938. He and his wife were "transferred to the Auschwitz concentration camp on 02/03/1943." His wife was murdered on 02/22/1943, he on 04/15/1943.
*Sources:* TK 33; JMBl. 33, p. 220; *li; Liste 36; MRRAK; BG; GB II

**Stern, Walter Dr.**
No information
*Home address:* no information
*Law firm address:* Friedrichstr. 166, W 8
*Additional information:* Attorney and notary; after the National Socialist seizure of power in 1933 his license as a notary was revoked, he was admitted as an attorney until at least 1936.
*Sources:* JMBl. 07/15/1933, p. 220; *li; Liste 36; BArch, R 3001 PAK

**Stern, Walter Hermann Dr.**
01/04/1888 Berlin - 04/18/1940 Sachsenhausen
*Home address:* no information
*Law firm address:* Berliner Str. 95, Charlottenburg
*Additional information:* Attorney and notary; he was a member of the Republican Association of Judges. After the National Socialist seizure of power in 1933 he was readmitted; at the end of 1935 his license as a notary was revoked, he was admitted as an attorney until at least 1936; he last lived in Brandenburg. On 06/23/1939 he was transported to the Sachsenhausen concentration camp; he died on 04/18/1940.

*Sources:* TK 33; MvRRB; *li; DJ 36, p. 315; Liste 36; BArch, R 3001 PAK; BG; GB II

**Sternberg, Franz Dr.**
07/17/1883 - no information
*Home address:* no information
*Law firm address:* Berliner Str. 30, Charlottenburg
*Additional information:* After the National Socialist seizure of power in 1933 he was readmitted, he worked as an attorney until the general occupational ban in 1938.
*Sources:* *li; Liste 36; MRRAK; BArch, R 3001 PAK

**Sternberg, Fritz Dr.**
07/27/1886 Berlin - ca. 1959 USA
*Home address:* Lennéstr. 6 a, W 9
*Law firm address:* Voßstr. 24/25, W 9
*Additional information:* After the National Socialist seizure of power in 1933 he was readmitted, he worked as an attorney until the general occupational ban in 1938. He emigrated to Great Britain on 12/30/1938, 1942 he was in a detention center in Australia, later he went to the USA via Buenos Aires.
*Sources:* *li; Liste 36; MRRAK; BArch, R 3001 PAK; BG

**Sternberg, Leo Dr.**
11/02/1880 Ostrowo - 06/30/1961 Santiago de Chile
*Home address:* Bleibtreustr. 24, Charlottenburg
*Law firm address:* Kalckreuthstr. 16, W 62
*Additional information:* Attorney at the KG and notary, specializing in land register and notary law; in 1932 he was still a board member of the RAK, the Honorary Court of the RAK and the Great Disciplinary Court at the KG. After the National Socialist seizure of power in 1933 he was readmitted; at the end of 1935 his license as a notary was revoked, he worked as an attorney until the general occupational ban in 1938, then still as a "consultant." He emigrated to Santiago, Chile, on 03/31/1939; there he founded a shoe factory, he died 1961 in Santiago.
*Sources:* TK 33; *li; DJ 36, p. 215; Liste 36; Philo-Lexikon, p. 604; MRRAK; Liste Kons. 39; BG; Göpp., p. 320; Walk, p. 356

**Sternberg, Max Dr.**
10/19/1873 Pasewalk - 11/10/1942
Theresienstadt
*Home address:* Niebuhrstr. 7, Charlottenburg
*Law firm address:* An der Spandauer Brücke
9, C 2
*Additional information:* Attorney and notary;
after the National Socialist seizure of power
in 1933 his license as a notary was revoked, he
was admitted as an attorney until the general
occupational ban in 1938. Transportation on
09/22/1942 to Theresienstadt, he died there
after only a few weeks.
*Sources:* JMBl. 33, p. 220; *li; Liste 36;
MRRAK; BG; ThG; GB II

**Stettner, Emil Dr.**
10/31/1879 Stuttgart - no information
*Home address:* Mommsenstr. 55,
Charlottenburg
*Law firm address:* Reinickendorfer Str. 6,
N 65
*Additional information:* Attorney and
notary; after the National Socialist seizure
of power in 1933 his license as a notary was
revoked, he was admitted as an attorney
until the general occupational ban in 1938.
His wife was regarded as non-Jewish. He
emigrated to Denmark on 01/31/1941; he last
lived in Copenhagen in 1950.
TK 33; JMBl. 33, p. 253; *li; Liste 36;
MRRAK; BG

**Stillschweig, Kurt Dr.**
07/28/1905 Berlin - 08/15/1955 Stockholm
*Home address:* no information
*Law firm address:* Grolmanstr. 30-31,
Charlottenburg
*Additional information:* 1929 he received his
doctorate in Heidelberg; as from 1932 he was
an attorney at LG I-III and AG Berlin-Mitte.
After the National Socialist seizure of power
he was made subject to an occuptional ban
in early 1933; 1933-38 he worked in Jewish
institutions; 1938-39 he was an advisor for
emigration questions at the aid organization
and the Reichsvertretung; he emigrated to
Sweden on 08/27/1939; 1939-50 he was a
board member of the Jewish Synagogue in
Stockholm; 1948-50 he was an administrative
director of a reparation counselling center; he
had a collaboration in 1950-55 in a law firm; he
studied law again and passed the examination
in 1954; he died in 1955 at the age of 50.

*Sources:* TK 1933; Liste d. nichtzugel. RA;
JMBl. 33, p. 203; BArch, R 3001 PAK; BG;
BHdE vol. 1, p. 735

**Stock, Gustav, Judicial Councillor**
12/23/1867 Züllichau - 06/16/1935
*Home address:* no information
*Law firm address:* Berliner Allee 225,
Weißensee
*Additional information:* Attorney at the LG
I-III, at the AG Weißensee and notary. After
the National Socialist seizure of power in
1933 he was readmitted; he died in 1935 at
the age of 67 and was buried at Weißensee.
*Sources:* TK 1933; *li; BG; BHdE vol. 1, p.
736 (Werner Stock)

**Story, Fritz**
11/30/1876 Glogau - no information
*Home address:* Ludwigkirchstr. 10, W 15;
Uhlandstr. 162
*Law firm address:* Potsdamer Str. 78, W 57
*Additional information:* Attorney at the
KG and notary; after the National Socialist
seizure of power in 1933 his license as a
notary was revoked, he worked as an attorney
until the general occupational ban in 1938.
He emigrated to Great Britain on 06/26/1939.
His wife was regarded as non-Jewish.
*Sources:* TK 33; JMBl. 33, p. 220; *li; Liste
36; MRRAK; BG

**Stranz, Martin**
09/05/1890 Berlin - 05/15/1976 London
*Home address:* Berliner Allee 225, Weißensee
*Law firm address:* Berliner Allee 225,
Weißensee
*Additional information:* Attorney and
notary; after the National Socialist seizure
of power in 1933 he was readmitted; at
the end of 1935 his license as a notary was
revoked, he worked as an attorney until the
general occupational ban in 1938. After
the Night of the Broken Glass in 1938 he
was imprisoned from 11/12 to 12/16 in the
Sachsenhausen concentration camp. After
his release he emigrated to London, Great
Britain, on 04/06/1939; there at first he was
a fitter; 1953-1979 he was a legal advisor for
the URO (United Restitution Office).
*Sources:* TK 33; *li; DJ 36, p. 315; Liste 36;
MRRAK; BArch, R 3001 PAK; BG; Göpp.,
p. 320

**Straßner, Alfred Dr.**
04/03/1896 Berlin-Charlottenburg -
transportation 1943
*Home address:* Kleiststr. 62 or 32, W 62;
Uhlandstr. 1, Charlottenburg
*Law firm address:* Unter den Linden 66,
NW 7
*Additional information:* Attorney at the KG;
after the National Socialist seizure of power
in 1933 he was readmitted, he worked as an
attorney until the general occupational ban
in 1938. Transportation on 09/28/1943 to
Auschwitz.
*Sources:* TK 33; *li; Liste 36; MRRAK;
BArch, R 3001 PAK; BG; GB II

**Strauss, Fritz Dr.**
04/23/1892 Geisenheim, Rheingau - no
information
*Home address:* Märkisches Ufer 24, SW 19
*Law firm address:* Große Frankfurter Str.
102, NO 18
*Additional information:* He was used during
the First World War at the Court Martial;
attorney (since 1919) and notary (since 1928).
After the National Socialist seizure of power
he was not readmitted in 1933, his assignment
during the First World War was not regarded
as "frontline fighting," as a consequence he
was made subject to an occupational ban. He
emigrated on 11/30/1935.
*Sources:* Adr.B. 33; TK 33; JMBl. 33, p. 253;
BG

**Strauss, Fritz H. Dr.**
09/05/1894 Berlin - no information
*Home address:* Duisburger Str. 14, W 15
*Law firm address:* Schöneberger Ufer 42,
W 35
*Additional information:* Soldier during the
First World War, he was awarded the EK
II. Kl.; he was an attorney (since 1924) and
notary (since 1930); he was a member of the
SPD since 1929. After the National Socialist
seizure of power he was made subject to an
occupational ban in April 1933, it was lifted
again, because he was a "frontline fighter;"
he requested readmission, however, prior to
the decision of the examination procedure,
its approval was deleted at his own request.
He emigrated to the USA.
*Sources:* Adr.B. 33; TK 33; JMBl. 33, p. 282;
BArch R 3001, PAK, PA; BG; information
Rahel Millo, conference 6/1999

**Strauss, Hans Dr.**
10/19/1904 Marburg - July 1987 New York
*Home address:* Meinekestr. 22, Charlottenburg
*Law firm address:* Mohrenstr. 50/52, W 8
*Additional information:* After the National
Socialist seizure of power he was made subject
to an occupational ban in early 1933. He
emigrated to Czechoslovakia in 1936, in 1937
to New York, USA. A warrant was issued
against him for tax code violations.
*Sources:* TK 33; Liste d. nichtzugel. RA,
04/25/1933; JMBl. 33, p. 209; BArch, R 3001
PAK; Wolf, BFS

**Strauss, Max Dr.**
04/26/1888 - no information
*Home address:* no information
*Law firm address:* Kurfürstendamm 47, W 15
*Additional information:* Attorney at the
KG and notary; after the National Socialist
seizure of power he was made subject to an
occupational ban in 1933.
*Sources:* Br.B. 32; TK 33; Liste d. nichtzugel.
RA, 04/25/1933; Pr.J. 33, p. 443; BArch, R
3001 PAK

**Strauss, Sally**
03/23/1901 Fulda - no information
*Home address:* no information
*Law firm address:* Mohrenstr. 9, W 8
*Additional information:* He was according
to his own information"unaffiliated with any
denomination," he was admitted as an attorney
as from 1929, last at the KG; after the National
Socialist seizure of power he was made subject
to an occupational ban on 06/07/1933.
*Sources:* JMBl. 07/07/1933; p. 209; BArch, R
3001 PAK, PA

**Stulz, Günter Dr.**
07/05/1901 Berlin - no information
*Home address:* Bismarckstr. 100,
Charlottenburg 4
*Law firm address:* Bismarckstr. 100,
Charlottenburg 4
*Additional information:* Attorney since
1929; he did not apply for readmission after
the National Socialist seizure of power, in his
personal file there is a question mark in the
field "religion." The deletion took place on
September 30, 1933 on the grounds that "you
are not of Aryan descent."
*Sources:* Pr.J. 33, p. 532; BArch, R 3001
PAK, PA

**Sturmthal, Leopold Dr.**
06/21/1891 - no information
*Home address:* no information
*Law firm address:* Lietzenburger Str. 4, W 15
Attorney at the LG I-III and AG Berlin-Mitte.
After the National Socialist seizure of power
in 1933 he was readmitted, he worked as an
attorney until at least 1936.
*Sources:* TK 33; *li; Liste 36; BArch, R 3001
PAK

**Sulzberger, Paul Dr.**
10/18/1891 Wiesbaden - 1945 Jerusalem
*Home address:* Landgrafenstr. 18 a,
Wilmersdorf
*Law firm address:* Landgrafenstr. 18 a,
Wilmersdorf
*Additional information:* He completed his
legal studies in Marburg, Munich and Berlin;
1914-19 he fought in the war; 1919-24 he was
an attorney in Wiesbaden; as from 1924 in
Berlin, he was an attorney at the LG I-III and
notary; a committed Zionist since his youth,
he was involved in Zionist and other Jewish
organizations, he traveled to Palestine several
times. After the National Socialist seizure of
power he was made subject to a representation
ban in April 1933, then he was readmitted;
at the end of 1935 his license as a notary was
revoked; he was admitted as an attorney until
at least 1936. He emigrated on 03/04/1939 to
Jerusalem, Palestine; he changed his first name
to Paltiel; he died there in 1945.
*Sources:* Br.B. 32; TK 33; *li; DJ 36, P. 315;
Liste 36; BArch, R 3001 PAK; BG; BHdE,
vol. 1, p. 750 (year of birth)

**Süskind, Siegfried Dr.**
12/23/1885 Herborn - no information
*Home address:* Matthäikirchplatz 5, W 35
*Law firm address:* Mauerstr. 53, W 8
*Additional information:* Attorney and
notary; after the National Socialist seizure
of power in 1933 his license as a notary was
revoked, he was admitted as an attorney until
at least 1936. He emigrated on 04/25/1938 to
London, Great Britain.
TK 33; JMBl. 33, p. 220; *li; Liste 36; BArch,
R 3001 PAK; BG

**Sussmann, Edith Dr.**
07/11/1892 Berlin - no information
*Home address:* Jenaer St. 6, Wilmersdorf
*Law firm address:* Jenaer Str. 6, Wilmersdorf

*Additional information:* Attorney at the LG
I-III; after the National Socialist seizure of
power he was made subject to an occupational
ban on 06/20/1933. He emigrated to Buenos
Aires, Brazil.
*Sources:* Br.B. 32; TK 33; Liste d. nichtzugel.
RA, 04/25/1933; JMBl. 08/04/1933, p. 253;
BArch, R 3001 PAK, PA; BG

**Süßmann, Georg Dr.**
10/14/1887 Liegnitz - 04/14/1959 Jerusalem
*Home address:* Mauerstr. 81, W 8
*Law firm address:* Mauerstr. 81, W 8
*Additional information:* Attorney at the LG
I-III and notary; after the National Socialist
seizure of power in 1933 he was readmitted;
he was deleted from the list of attorneys
before the fall of 1935. He emigrated to
Jerusalem, Palestine.
*Sources:* TK 33; *li; BArch, R 3001 PAK; BG:
LAB, OFP files

**Sußmann, Manfred Dr.**
04/23/1892 Berlin - no
information
*Home address:* no
information
*Law firm address:*
Spandauer Chaussee 50/56,
Charlottenburg
*Additional information:* After the National
Socialist seizure of power in 1933 he was
readmitted, he worked as an attorney until
the general occupational ban in 1938.
*Sources:* TK 33; *li; Liste 36; MRRAK;
BArch, R 3001 PAK; Naatz-Album

**Szkolny, Felix Dr., Judicial
Councillor**
08/31/1870 Berlin - no
information
*Home address:* Olivaer Platz
10, W 15
*Law firm address:*
Charlottenstr. 17, SW 68
*Additional information:* Attorney and
notary; after the National Socialist seizure
of power in 1933 his license as a notary was
revoked, he worked as an attorney until the
general occupational ban in 1938, presumably
he emigrated (file note "unsubscribed").
*Sources:* TK 33; JMBl. 33, p. 220; Korr. Liste
arische Anw., 10/15/1933; Liste 36; MRRAK;
Naatz-Album; BG

# T

**Talbot, Kurt Dr., Dipl.-Ing.**
No information
*Home address:* no information
*Law firm address:* Stresemannstr. 92/102
(Europahaus), SW 11
*Additional information:* After the National
Socialist seizure of power in 1933 he was
readmitted as attorney; he was still listed in
the lists of attorneys in the fall of 1935, he
was also still listed in the 1938 telephone
directory, then he was no longer listed.
*Sources:* JMBl. 02/03/1933, p. 17,
02/17/1933, p. 27; *li; TK 36; Tel.B. 38

**Tarnowski, Georg**
07/31/1884 - no information
*Home address:* no information
*Law firm address:* Tauentzienstr. 10, W 50
*Additional information:* Attorney at the
KG and notary; after the National Socialist
seizure of power in 1933 his license as a
notary was revoked, he still worked as an
attorney until the general occupational ban
in 1938.
*Sources:* Br.B. 32; TK 33; JMBl. 33, p. 220;
*li; Liste 36; MRRAK; BArch, R 3001 PAK

**Tarnowski, Hans Dr.**
04/04/1900 - 08/11/1941
*Home address:* no information
*Law firm address:* Nollendorfplatz 9, W 30
*Additional information:* Attorney at the KG;
after the National Socialist seizure of power
occupational ban in early 1933; he died in
the summer of 1941 at the age of 41 and was
buried in the Jewish cemetery at Weißensee.
*Sources:* Br.B. 32; TK 33; Liste d. nichtzugel.
RA, 04/25/1933; JMBl. 33, p. 203; BArch, R
3001 PAK; BG

**Tasse, Julius**
06/06/1872 Barby - 01/13/1948 Berlin
*Home address:* Motzstr. 72
*Law firm address:* Boddinstr. 66, Neukölln
*Additional information:* He fought in
the First World War, attorney at the LG
I-III and AG Neukölln. After the National
Socialist seizure of power in 1933 he was
readmitted; at the end of 1935 his license as
a notary was revoked, he was admitted as
an attorney until the general occupational
ban in 1938. His wife was regarded as

non-Jewish. He was one of the prisoners
of Rosenstraße (02/27-03/07/1943), but
mentioned this only casually in his resume.
He survived the National Socialist regime
and was readmitted as an attorney; after
1945 he lived in Neukölln.
*Sources:* TK 33; *li; DJ 36, p. 315; Liste 36;
MRRAK; BG; LAB, RAK, PA; Verz. zugel.
Anw. 45

**Tauber, Ernst Dr.**
No information
*Home address:* no information
*Law firm address:* Köthener Str. 28/29, W 9
*Additional information:* Attorney and
notary; after the National Socialist seizure
of power in 1933 his license as a notary was
revoked, he worked as an attorney until at
least 1936.
*Sources:* TK 33; JMBl. 33, p. 220; *li;
Liste 36

**Tell, Martin Dr.**
11/21/1883 Berlin - 01/18/1941 Gurs
*Home address:* no information
*Law firm address:* Uhlandstr. 165/166, W 15
*Additional information:* Attorney (since
1913) and notary (since 1924); after the
seizure of power by the National Socialists
in 1933 he should have been admitted as a
so-called "elderly attorney," nevertheless
his license as a notary was revoked. His
admission as an attorney was also revoked in
the course of the merger of the district courts,
which meant a professional ban. At first he
emigrated to Spain, where he had worked for
the German Embassy in 1914, later apparently
to France, where he was interned after the
occupation and died in the Gurs camp.
*Sources:* Adr.B. 33; JMBl. 33, p. 220; Pr.J. 33,
p. 868; BArch, R 3001 PAK, PA; BG; GB II

**Themal, Ernst**
01/15/1888 - no information
*Home address:* Kaiserallee 18, W 15
*Law firm address:* Meinekestr. 11, W 15
*Additional information:* Attorney at the LG
III and notary; after the National Socialist
seizure of power he was made subject to an
occupational ban in early 1933; presumably
emigrated.
*Sources:* Br.B. 32; TK 33; Liste d. nichtzugel.
RA, 04/25/1933; JMBl. 33, p. 209; BArch, R
3001 PAK; BG

**Themal, Franz Jakob Dr.**
04/04/1892 Berlin - no information
*Home address:* Knesebeckstr. 67,
Charlottenburg
*Law firm address:* Meinekestr. 11, W 15
*Additional information:* Attorney at the LG
I-III; after the National Socialist seizure of
power in 1933 he was readmitted, he worked
as an attorney until the general occupational
ban in 1938. He emigrated to Montevideo,
Uruguay, on 12/17/1938; he changed his name
to Francisco Themal; in 1950 he was still
living in Buenos Aires.
*Sources:* TK 33; *li; Liste 36; MRRAK;
BArch, R 3001 PAK; BG

**Tichauer, Theodor Dr.**
02/18/1891 Berlin - 04/06/1942 Auschwitz
*Home address:* Kantstr. 137, Charlottenburg
*Law firm address:* no information
*Additional information:* Attorney and
notary; after the National Socialist seizure of
power he was made subject to an occupational
ban in 1933. He emigrated to Paris, France,
on 07/26/1933. transportation on 03/27/1942
from Compiègne to Auschwitz, he was
murdered there on 04/06, a few days after his
arrival.
*Sources:* Br.B. 32; TK 33; JMBl. 33, p. 221;
BArch, R 3001 PAK; BG; GB II

**Tietz, Hugo Dr.**
10/13/1889 Breslau - no information
*Home address:* no information
*Law firm address:* Brunnenstr. 144,
Wedding
*Additional information:* He was Catholic,
his mother was Jewish, he was an attorney
at the LG I-III; after the National Socialist
seizure of power he was made subject to an
occupational ban in 1933. He survived the
National Socialist regime and was readmitted
as an attorney in 1947; he lived and practiced
in Wedding.
*Sources:* TK 33; BArch, R 3001 PAK, PA;
BG; LAB, RAK, PA Werthauer

**Tiktin, Peter Paul Dr.**
02/10/1902 Berlin - no information
*Home address:* no information
*Home address:* Werderscher Markt 4 a
*Additional information:* He was Protestant;
he was an attorney at the LG I-III; after the
National Socialist seizure of power he was

made subject to an occupational ban in the
summer of 1933. He emigrated to Uruguay.
*Sources:* Adr.B. 32; TK 33; Liste d.
nichtzugel. RA, 04/25/1933; JMBl. 33, p.
253; BArch, R 3001 PAK, PA

**Tiktin, Robert Dr.**
06/27/1897 Berlin - no
information
*Home address:*
Lietzenburger Str. 39,
Wilmersdorf
*Law firm address:*
Französische Str. 57/58, W 8
*Additional information:* Attorney at the LG
I-III and notary; after the National Socialist
seizure of power in 1933 he was readmitted;
at the end of 1935 his license as a notary
was revoked, he worked as an attorney
until the general occupational ban in 1938,
then he was admitted as a "consultant." He
emigrated on 07/25/1940 to Montevideo,
Uruguay.
*Sources:* TK 33; *li; DJ 36, p. 315; MRRAK;
Liste d. Kons., 03/15/1939; BArch, R 3001
PAK; Naatz-Album; BG

**Tiktin, Willy Dr.**
05/22/1877 Petersburg - no information
*Home address:* Pariser Str. 19, W 15
*Law firm address:* Wilhelmstr. 9, SW 48
*Additional information:* Attorney at the LG
I-III; after the National Socialist seizure of
power in 1933 he was readmitted, he worked
as an attorney until the general occupational
ban in 1938. He emigrated on 03/08/1939 to
Brooklyn, New York, USA.
*Sources:* TK 33; *li; LAB, Liste 04/15/1933;
MRRAK; BG

**Timendorfer, Walter**
05/21/1897 - no information
*Home address:* no
information
*Law firm address:*
Wielandstr. 25/26, W 15
*Additional information:*
After the National Socialist
seizure of power in 1933 he was readmitted,
he worked as an attorney until 11/20/1937.
*Sources:* TK 33; *li; LAB, Liste 10/15/1933;
Liste 36; BArch, R 3001 PAK; Naatz-Album

**Tovote, Hans-Georg Dr.**
09/12/1900 Berlin-Schöneberg - 04/17/1971
*Home address:* Kurfürstendamm 186, Charlottenburg
*Law firm address:* Maaßenstr. 36, W 62
*Additional information:* Attorney at the LG I-III and AG Schöneberg. After the National Socialist seizure of power in 1933 he was readmitted; he was regarded as "mixed race," he could therefore practice law throughout the general occupational ban; he survived the National Socialist regime and was readmitted to practice law on 07/04/1945; he died in 1971 at the age of 70.
*Sources:* TK 33; *li; LAB, List 10/15/1933; Liste Mschlg. 36; Verz. zugel. Anw. 45; BG; information B. Dombek; RAK LAB PA (photo)

**Traube, Alfred Dr.**
05/01/1895 Berlin - November 1972
*Home address:* Sächsische Str. 2, Wilmersdorf
*Law firm address:* Mauerstr. 53, W 8; später: Fasanenstr. 73, W 15
*Additional information:* Attorney at the KG and notary; after the National Socialist seizure of power in 1933 he was readmitted; his license as a notary was revoked at the end of 1935; he worked as an attorney until the general occupational ban in 1938, then he was admitted as a "consultant." He was arrested in November 1938 after the Night of the Broken Glass. To secure his release, he had to pledge to emigrate to a non-European country, he emigrated to New York, USA, on 01/20/1940.
*Sources:* TK 33; *li; LAB, Liste 10/15/1933; DJ 36, p. 315; Liste 36; MRRAK; Liste Kons. 39; BArch, R 3001 PAK, PA; BG; SSDI; information A. Wertheim

**Treftz, Arthur, Judicial Councillor**
No information
*Home address:* Kyllmannstr. 10, Lichterfelde
*Law firm address:* Kyllmannstr. 10, Lichterfelde
*Additional information:* He was Protestant; he was an attorney at the LG I-III and AG Lichterfelde; after the National Socialist seizure of power in 1933 he was readmitted, he was admitted until at least 1936; he was

regarded as "mixed race first degree," it seems that he was no longer practicing in 1938.
*Sources:* TK 33; *li; LAB, Liste 10/15/1933, Liste Mschlg. 36

**Treitel, Erich Dr.**
05/17/1892 Berlin - 08/28/1945 Buenos Aires
*Home address:* no information
*Law firm address:* Tiergartenstr. 12 a/13, W 15
*Additional information:* Attorney and notary; after the National Socialist seizure of power he was made subject to an occupational ban in early 1933. He emigrated to Buenos Aires, Argentina, in 1934. A warrant was issued against him for tax code violations.
*Sources:* Br.B. 32; TK 33; Liste d. nichtzugel. RA, 04/25/1933; BArch, R 3001 PAK; Wolf, BFS; information E. Proskauer

**Treitel, Richard Dr.**
10/27/1879 Betsche - 02/13/1947
*Home address:* Giesebrechtstr. 15, Charlottenburg
*Law firm address:* Unter den Linden 53
*Additional information:* Attorney at the LG I-III, at AG Berlin-Mitte and notary (since 1924); 1920 he was a member of the Kreuzberg district council, he was elected in 1921 as an unpaid city councillor to the Berlin city council; he established a law partnership with Theodor, his brother. After the National Socialist seizure of power in 1933 his license as a notary was revoked, he was admitted as an attorney until the general occupational ban in 1938. He was a volunteer of the RV, Berlin district office, he was arrested on 06/03/1943 and was transported on 06/29/1943 to Theresienstadt. He survived the camp. He died in February 1947 in a camp for "displaced persons" in Deggendorf in the Bavarian forest.
He had publications on film and stage law.
*Sources:* TK 33; JMBl. 33, p. 220; *li; LAB, Liste 10/15/1933; Liste 36; MRRAK; BG; Liste der Theresienstadt-Überlebenden; Verfolgte Berl. Stadtverordnete u. Magistratsmitgl.; Vor die Tür gesetzt [Shown the door], p. 362

**Treitel, Theodor Dr.**
01/03/1885 Betsche - 1974 London
*Home address:* no information
Law firm: Unter den Linden 53

*Additional information:* Attorney at the LG I-III, at AG Berlin-Mitte and notary; law partnership with his brother Richard. After the National Socialist seizure of power in 1933 his license as a notary was revoked, he was admitted as an attorney until the general occupational ban in 1938. 1939 he emigrated with his family to Great Britain.
*Sources:* Br.B. 32; TK 33; JMBl. 33, 220; *li; LAB, Liste 10/15/1933; Liste 36; MMRAK; BArch, R 3001 PAK; BG; BHdE vol. 2,2, p. 1173 (Guenter Heinz Treitel)

**Triebel, Walter Dr.**
No information
*Home address:* no information
*Law firm address:* Altonaer Str. 3, NW 87
*Additional information:* Attorney at the LG I-III and at AG Berlin-Mitte; after the National Socialist seizure of power he was made subject to an occupational ban in early 1933.
*Sources:* Br.B. 32; TK 33; Liste d. nichtzugel. RA, 04/25/1933; Pr.J. 33, p. 839

**Trip, Heinrich**
No information
*Home address:* Pariser Str. 3, W 15
*Law firm address:* Fasanenstr. 41, W 15
*Additional information:* Attorney at the KG; after the National Socialist seizure of power he was made subject to a temporary representation ban in early 1933, then he was readmitted and worked as an attorney until at least 1936.
*Sources:* Br.B. 32; TK 33; Liste d. nichtzugel. RA, 04/25/1933 (addendum); *li; BArch, R 3001 PAK

**Tuch, Georg**
05/02/1880 - 06/14/1935
*Home address:* Grunewaldstr. 27, Schöneberg
*Law firm address:* Grunewaldstr. 27, Schöneberg
*Additional information:* Attorney and notary; after the National Socialist seizure of power in 1933 he was readmitted; he died in 1935 at the age of 55 and was buried in the Jewish cemetery at Weißensee.
*Sources:* TK 33; *li; LAB, Liste 10/15/1933; BG

**Türk, Hans Dr.**
No information
*Home address:* no information
*Law firm address:* Berliner Str. 158, Charlottenburg

*Additional information:* Attorney at the KG, after the National Socialist seizure of power he was made subject to an occupational ban in early 1933.
*Sources:* Br.B. 32; TK 33; Liste d. nichtzugel. RA, 04/25/1933; JMBl. 33, p. 253; BArch, R 3001 PAK

# U

**Ullmann, Friedrich Dr.**
03/16/1892 - no information
*Home address:* no information
*Law firm address:* Charlottenstr. 56, W 8
*Additional information:* He was Protestant. After the National Socialist seizure of power in 1933 he was readmitted; he worked until at least 1936; he was regarded as "mixed race" (two Jewish grandparents); he gave up his law practice before 1938.
*Sources:* *li; LAB, Liste 10/15/1933; Liste Mischlg. 36; BArch, R 3001 PAK

**Unger, Hugo**
No information
*Home address:* no information
*Law firm address:* Chausseestr. 16
*Additional information:* Attorney and notary; after the National Socialist seizure of power in 1933 his license as a notary was revoked, he worked as an attorney until the general occupational ban in 1938.
*Sources:* TK 33; JMBl. 33, p. 220; *li; LAB, Liste 10/15/1933; Liste 36; MRRAK

**Unger, Leopold, Judicial Councillor**
No information - 09/30/1938
*Home address:* no information
*Law firm address:* Dorotheenstr. 27, NW 7
*Additional information:* Attorney at the LG I-III and notary; after the National Socialist seizure of power in 1933 he was dismissed as a notary, but reinstated, at the end of 1935 his license as a notary was finally revoked; he worked as an attorney until at least 1936, presumably until his death in 1938.
TK 33; JMBl. 33, p. 220; *li; DJ 36, p. 315; Liste 36

**Ury, Ludwig Dr., Judicial Councillor**
06/12/1870 Berlin - no information
*Home address:* Kaiserdamm 24, Charlottenburg
*Law firm address:* Alexanderplatz 1, C 25

*Additional information:* Attorney and notary; after the National Socialist seizure of power in 1933 his license as a notary was revoked; he worked as an attorney until at least 1936. He emigrated to London, Great Britain, on 03/03/1939.
*Sources:* TK 33; JMBl. 33, p. 220; *li; LAB, Liste 10/15/1933; Liste 36; BG

# V

**Victor, Hugo**
12/02/1874 Berlin - 03/05/1942
*Home address:* Xantener Str. 23 (until March 1935), Wilmersdorf
*Law firm address:* Potsdamer Str.118, W 35
*Additional information:* Attorney at the KG and notary; after the National Socialist seizure of power in 1933 his license as a notary was revoked, he worked as an attorney until the general occupational ban in 1938. His wife was regarded as non-Jewish. He died in 1942 at the age of 67 and was buried in the Jewish cemetery at Weißensee.
*Sources:* TK 33; JMBl. 33, p. 220; *li; LAB, Liste 10/15/1933; Liste 36; MRRAK; BG

# W

**Wachsmann, Oskar Dr.**
12/29/1878 Breslau - no information
*Home address:* Brandenburgische Str. 16
*Law firm address:* Friedrichstr. 66, W 8
*Additional information:* Attorney and notary; after the National Socialist seizure of power in 1933 he was dismissed as a notary, he worked as an attorney until the general occupational ban in 1938; he was amongst others a client of Anita Eisner. He emigrated to Brussels, Belgium, on 03/29/1939, he was living there in 1952.
*Sources:* TK 33; JMBl. 33, p. 220; *li; Liste 36; MRRAK; BG; information Flechtmann 07/00

**Wachsner, Ernst Dr.**
07/21/1888 Berlin - transportation 1943
*Home address:* Sybelstr. 42, Charlottenburg
*Law firm address:* no information
*Additional information:* Attorney at the KG and notary; after the National Socialist seizure of power in 1933 he was made

subject to an occupational ban. He was used for forced labor; date of declaration of property: 06/25/1943; collecting station Große Hamburger Str. 26; transportation on 06/28/1943 to Auschwitz.
*Sources:* Br.B. 32; TK 33; Liste d. nichtzugel. RA, 04/25/1933; JMBl. 33, p. 203; BArch, R 3001 PAK; BG; GB II

**Wachsner, Fritz Dr.**
10/09/1893 - no information
*Home address:* no information
*Law firm address:* Chausseestr. 95, N 65
*Additional information:* After the National Socialist seizure of power he was made subject to an occupational ban in early 1933.
*Sources:* TK 33; Liste d. nichtzugel. RA, 04/25/1933 (addendum); JMBl. 33, p. 234; BArch, R 3001 PAK

**Wachsner, Josef Dr.**
04/21/1862 - 01/12/1939 Berlin
*Home address:* Starnberger Str. 1, Schöneberg
*Law firm address:* Motzstr. 53, W 30
*Additional information:* Attorney and notary; after the National Socialist seizure of power in 1933 his license as a notary was revoked; he was deleted from the list of attorneys before fall of 1935; he died 1939 at the age of 76 and was buried in the Jewish cemetery at Weißensee.
*Sources:* TK 33; JMBl. 33, p. 220; *li; BG

**Wachsner, Lothar**
06/14/1894 - April 1966
*Home address:* no information
*Law firm address:* Innsbrucker Str. 54, Schöneberg
*Additional information:* Attorney and notary; after the National Socialist seizure of power in 1933 he was readmitted; at the end of 1935 his license as a notary was revoked, he worked as an attorney until the general occupational ban in 1938. He emigrated to the USA, he last lived in New York.
*Sources:* TK 33; *li; DJ 36, p. 315; Liste 36; MRRAK; BArch, R 3001 PAK; SSDI

**Wadler, Arnold Dr.**
No information
*Home address:* Nestorstr. 6, Halensee (1931)
*Law firm address:* Straße 3, Zehlendorf
*Additional information:* He had only been naturalized in Prussia in 1933, but had lived

in Berlin for some time. The RAK reported him to the Prussian Ministry of Justice because he had been "a member of the Bavarian soviet republic" and was "non-Aryan." In early 1933 he was made subject to an occupational ban.
*Sources:* Jüd.Adr.B.; Adr.B. 33; TK 33; GHStA, Rep. 84a, No. 20363; JMBl. 33, p. 267

**Wagener, Wilhelm Dr.**
01/15/1888 - no information
*Home address:* Schlüterstr. 36/ Cramerstr. 15, Charlottenburg
*Law firm address:* Hardenbergstr. 24, Charlottenburg
*Additional information:* Attorney at the KG and notary; after the National Socialist seizure of power he gave up his law office and notaryship in early summer 1933. He emigrated to Amsterdam, the Netherlands.
*Sources:* Br.B. 32; TK 33; JMBl. 33, p. 203; BArch, R 3001 PAK; BG

**Waldeck, Hugo Dr.**
03/21/1876 Berlin - no information
*Home address:* Lützowufer 5 a, W 35
*Law firm address:* Lützowufer 5 a, W 35
*Additional information:* Attorney and notary; after the National Socialist seizure of power his license as a notary was revoked in 1933, he worked as an attorney until the general occupational ban in 1938. He emigrated to Paris, France, on 11/01/1938.
*Sources:* TK 33; JMBl. 33, p. 220; *li; Liste 36; MRRAK; BG

**Wallach, Alfred Dr.**
No information
*Home address:* no information
*Law firm address:* Rankestr. 23, W 50
*Additional information:* After the National Socialist seizure of power in 1933 he was readmitted, he worked as an attorney until at least 1936.
*Sources:* TK 33; *li; Liste 36; Naatz-Album

**Wallbach, Werner Dr.**
No information
*Home address:* no information
*Law firm address:* Markgrafenstr. 61, SW 68
*Additional information:* After the National Socialist seizure of power he was made subject to an occupational ban in early 1933.

*Sources:* Br.B. 32; TK 33; Liste d. nichtzugel. RA, 04/25/1933; JMBl. 08/04/1933, p. 253; BArch, R 3001 PAK

**Waller, Alfred Dr.**
09/13/1881 Cologne - transportation 1944
*Home address:* Bleibtreustr. 10/Mommsenstr. 67, Charlottenburg, Landgrafenstr. 12
*Law firm address:* Landgrafenstr. 12
*Additional information:* He was Protestant; he was an attorney at the LG I-III and notary; after the National Socialist seizure of power he was readmitted in 1933; at the end of 1935 his license as a notary was revoked, he worked as an attorney until 1938. Date of declaration of property: 07/21/1942; collecting station: Große Hamburger Str. 26; transportation on 07/22/1942 to Theresienstadt; from there he was transported on 10/23/1944 to Auschwitz.
*Sources:* TK 33; *li; DJ 36, p. 315; Liste 36; MRRAK; BArch, R 3001 PA H. Simon; BG; GB II

**Walter, Benno Dr.**
11/25/1878 Czarnikau - transportation 1942
*Home address:* Levetzowstr. 11 a, NW 87
*Law firm address:* Zimmerstr. 92/93, SW 68
*Additional information:* Attorney and notary; after the National Socialist seizure of power in 1933 his license as a notary was revoked, he worked as an attorney until the general occupational ban in 1938. He last was a volunteer at the JKV, Division of Welfare; date of declaration of property: 11/24/1942; transportation on 11/19/1942 to Auschwitz.
*Sources:* TK 33; JMBl. 33, p. 220; *li; Liste 36; MRRAK; BG; GB II

**Warschauer, Felix Dr.**
05/14/1879 Posen - transportation 1941
*Home address:* Brandenburgische Str. 42, Wilmersdorf
*Law firm address:* Kurfürstendamm 16, W 50
*Additional information:* Attorney at the KG and notary; attorney at the LG I-III and notary; after the National Socialist seizure of power in 1933 his license as a notary was revoked, he worked as an attorney until at least 1936. Date of declaration of property: 11/10/1941; collecting station Levetzowstr. 7-8; transportation on 11/14/1941 to Minsk.
*Sources:* TK 33; JMBl. 33, p. 220; *li; Liste 36; BG; g; GB II

**Wedell, Siegmund Dr.**
12/17/1875 Stargard - transportation 1943
*Home address:* Sybelstr. 57, Charlottenburg
*Law firm address:* Mommsenstr. 21,
Charlottenburg
*Additional information:* Attorney at the
KG and notary; after the National Socialist
seizure of power in 1933 he was readmitted;
at the end of 1935 his license as a notary was
revoked, he worked as an attorney until the
general occupational ban in 1938. He was
transported to Auschwitz on 01/12/1943.
*Sources:* TK 33; *li; DJ 36, p. 315; Liste 36;
MRRAK; BG; GB II

**Wehlau, Ismar Dr.**
05/01/1885 - no information
*Home address:* no information
*Law firm address:* Lindenstr. 7, SW 68
*Additional information:* Attorney and notary;
after the National Socialist seizure of power in
1933 his license as a notary was revoked, he was
readmitted as an attorney; he was deleted from
the lists of attorneys before September 1935.
*Sources:* TK 33; JMBl. 33, p. 220; *li; BArch,
R 3001 PAK

**Weichmann, Alfred Dr.**
12/05/1882 Eichenau - no information
*Home address:* Schillerstr. 3, Charlottenburg
*Law firm address:* Schillerstr. 3,
Charlottenburg
*Additional information:* Attorney and
notary; after the National Socialist seizure
of power he was deleted from the lists of
attorney in the fall of 1933. He emigrated to
London, Great Britain, on 03/31/1934; he
changed his name to Wykeman, in 1952 he
was living in London.
*Sources:* TK 33; Pr.J. 33, p. 679; *li; BG

**Weigert, Hans Werner Dr.**
04/28/1902 - 10/18/1983 Munich
*Home address:* Wangenheimstr. 30,
Grunewald
*Law firm address:* Hohenzollernstr. 13, W 10
*Additional information:* After the National
Socialist seizure of power in early 1933 he
was made subject to an occupational ban.
He emigrated to the USA in 1938; he taught
at colleges and at the University of Chicago
from 1939, 1947-1951 with the U.S. military
government and the High Commissioner in
Germany; then he was a professor for political

sciences at Georgetown University; he died
1983 in Munich.
*Sources:* TK 33; Liste d. nichtzugel. RA,
04/25/1933; JMBl. 08/04/1933, p. 253;
BArch, R 3001 PAK; BG; Göpp., p. 322

**Weigert, Julius B. Dr.**
03/01/1885 Berlin - no information
*Home address:* no information
*Law firm address:* Potsdamer Str. 71
*Additional information:* Attorney (since
1911) at the KG and notary (1924), he gave
up his U.S. citizenship in order to enter the
German civil service as a notary. After the
National Socialist seizure of power in 1933
his license as a notary was revoked; he gave
up his law office. He emigrated in 1933 to
Paris, France, later to Italy. A warrant was
issued against him for tax code violations. In
1939 he went to New York, USA; he applied
there unsuccessfully for a scholarship of the
American Committee for the Guidance of the
Professional Personnel; in March 1950 he was
still living in New York.
*Sources:* TK 33; JMBl. 33, p. 220; *li; BArch,
R 3001 PAK; NY Publ. Lib.(Am.Com.)
Weigert; Wolf, BFS

**Weil, Bruno Dr.**
04/04/1883 Saarlouis -
11/11/1961 New York
*Home address:* no
information
*Law firm address:*
Landgrafenstr. 1, W 62
*Additional information:*
The German Alsatian settled in 1910 as an
attorney in Strasbourg; he fought in the First
World War; expelled as a German after Alsace
became French again. 1920 he established
himself as an attorney in Berlin, he was
admitted at the KG; later also a notary, since
1922 he was in a law partnership with Ernest
J. Gans, he was a legal advisor to the British
and French Embassies; politically active in the
DDP and as managing director of CV; he was
a representative of the Deutsche Staatspartei
(German State Party) in the Reichstag;
literary work, i.a. a book about the Dreyfus
process that ends with the words, "There is
no freedom without justice!"
After the National Socialist seizure of power
in 1933 he was readmitted, because he was
recognized as a "frontline fighter" and

"elderly attorney;" 1935 he was dismissed as a notary; 1937 he gave up the legal profession and escaped from Germany. 1939 he acquired Argentine citizenship. He and his wife traveled all over the world; during a stay in Paris they were arrested in 1939 and interned. He went to the Le Vernet camp in the Pyrenees and escaped to the USA in 1940, there he was reunited with his wife. The couple traveled tirelessly through the USA to organize help for European refugees. After the end of the war, he campaigned for restitution and the strengthening of democracy in Germany. He died in 1961 at the age of 78. At his funeral, a speaker expressed the feelings of many: "His life was fulfilled. May we console ourselves with the thought that he enjoyed it." (Lowenthal in his eulogy)
*Publications:* "Glück und Elend des General Boulanger" [The happiness and sorrow of General Boulanger], Berlin 1931; "Baracke 37 – Stillgestanden!" [Barrack 37 - Attention!], Buenos Aires, 1941.
*Sources:* TK 33; *li; DJ 36, p. 315; Liste 36; BArch, R 3001 PAK, PA; Bruno Weil Collection LBI; Krach, p. 437; Göpp., p. 323

**Weinberg, Fritz Dr.**
07/23/1889 (? ) - 1943 Palestine
*Home address:* Lietzenburger Str. 32, Wilmersdorf
*Law firm address:* Königstr. 22-24, C 2
*Additional information:* Attorney and notary, he was in a law partnership with attorney Dr. Emil Löwenstein and his oldest son; after the National Socialist seizure of power in 1933 his license as a notary was revoked, he gave up the law office. He emigrated to Paris, France in April 1933; in 1935 he went to Palestine, he died there in 1943.
*Sources:* Br.B. 32; TK 33; JMBl. 33, p. 234; BG; Korr. Lilo Bonwitt; information E. Proskauer

**Weinberg, Hans Dr.**
04/15/1905 Berlin - June 1978
*Home address:* Hohenzollerndamm 156, Wilmersdorf
*Law firm address:* Königstr. 22-24
*Additional information:* Attorney at the KG, he was in a law partnership with his father; after the National Socialist seizure of power occupational ban in 1933. He emigrated on 04/05/1934 to Spain, he later

went to the USA, he last lived in Queens, New York.
*Sources:* Jüd.Adr.B.; Br.B. 32; JMBl. 06/30/1933, p. 203; BG: LAB, OFP files (occupation: merchant); BArch, R 3001 PAK; SSDI

**Weinberg, Herbert**
05/09/1901 Neumark - transportation 1943
*Home address:* Planufer, 26, SW 61
*Law firm address:* Hasenheide 63, S 59
*Additional information:* After the National Socialist seizure of power he was made subject to an occupational ban in early 1933. Transportation on 03/03/1943 to Auschwitz.
*Sources:* Br.B. 32; TK 33; Liste d. nichtzugel. RA, 04/25/1933; JMBl. 33, p. 220; BArch, R 3001, PAK; BG; GB II

**Weinberg, Hugo Dr.**
02/07/1878 Herford - 11/25/1941 Kowno
*Home address:* Kaiserallee 104, Schöneberg-Friedenau
*Law firm address:* Berliner Allee 241, Weißensee
*Additional information:* Attorney at the LG I-III and AG Weißensee; after the National Socialist seizure of power in 1933 he was dismissed as a notary and reinstated as a notary; before 1935 his license as a notary was revoked, he was admitted as an attorney until the general occupational ban in 1938; he last worked as a legal assistant, he was in close association with the attorney Julius Fliess. Collecting station Levetzowstr. 7-8; date of declaration of property: 11/13/1941; transportation on 11/17/1941 to Kowno, he was murdered there a few days after arrival.
*Sources:* Br.B. 32; TK 33; JMBl. 33, p. 220; *li; DJ 36, p. 315; Liste 36; MRRAK; BG; BdE; GB II (Dan W.)

**Weiskam, Godehard Gerhard Dr.**
12/12/1879 Berlin - 07/05/1965
*Home address:* Lutherstr. 21, W 62
*Law firm address:* Lutherstr. 33, W 62
*Additional information:* He fought in the First World War. Attorney at the KG and notary; he voted for the SPD in March 1933. After the National Socialist seizure of power in 1933 he was readmitted; he was regarded as "mixed race first degree" (his mother was Jewish), he could therefore practice law throughout the general occupational ban in

1938. In 1943, like others, the President of the KG reported him to the employment office as not vital to the war effort. He was then used by Teco GmbH, he also still worked part-time as an attorney. During the war he was an air raid warden for the house where he lived. After 1945 he was readmitted as an attorney and as a notary.
*Sources:* TK 33; *li; LAB, Liste Mschlg. 36; Tel.B.41; Verz. zugel. Anw. 45; LAB, RAK, PA; BG

**Weiss, Bernhard Dr.**
07/30/1880 Berlin - 07/29/1951 London
*Home address:* no information
*Law firm address:* Sophie-Charlotte-Platz 1, Charlottenburg
*Additional information:* From 1927 to 1932 he was police vice-president in Berlin; he was constantly insulted and attacked by Nazi members, especially Goebbels (who called him "Isidor"). After the National Socialist seizure of power in early 1933 he was made subject to an occupational ban as an attorney. He emigrated to England; he was expatriated in 1933; he worked as a print shop representative in London.
*Sources:* Liste d. nichtzugel. RA, 04/25/1933; JMBl. 08/04/1933, p. 253; BArch, R 3001 PAK; Göpp., p. 323

**Weißenberg, Curt Dr.**
04/25/1892 Berlin - transportation 1941
*Home address:* Rosenheimer Str. 29 a, Schöneberg
*Law firm address:* Nettelbeckstr. 7/8, W 62
*Additional information:* Attorney at the KG and notary; after the National Socialist seizure of power in 1933 he was readmitted; at the end of 1935 his license as a notary was revoked, he worked as an attorney until the general occupational ban in 1938. Date of declaration of property: 10/26/1941; collecting station Levetzowstr. 7-8; transportation on 11/14/1941 to Minsk.
*Sources:* TK 33; *li; Liste 36; MRRAK; BArch, R 3001 PAK; BG; g; GB II

**Weitzenkorn, Leo Dr.**
02/09/1898 - no information
*Home address:* no information
*Law firm address:* Große Frankfurter Str. 73, NO 18; später Alexanderstr. 21, C 25

*Additional information:* After the National Socialist seizure of power in 1933 he was readmitted, he was still working as an attorney until the general occupational ban in 1938, subsequently he was still admitted as a "consultant."
*Sources:* *li; Liste 36; MRRAK; Liste d. Kons., 12/31/1938; BArch, R 3001 PAK

**Weltmann, Martin Dr.**
10/06/1883 - no information
*Home address:* no information
*Law firm address:* Rosenthaler Str. 26, C 54
*Additional information:* Attorney and notary; after the National Socialist seizure of power in 1933 he was readmitted; in 1935 his license as a notary was revoked, he was still working as an attorney until the general occupational ban in 1938.
*Sources:* *li; DJ 36, p. 315; Liste 36; BArch, R 3001 PAK

**Weltzien, Julius von Dr.**
08/10/1881 Berlin - 11/03/1955
*Home address:* Prinz-Handjery-Str. 3, Zehlendorf
*Law firm address:* Freiherr-von-Stein-Str. 14 a, Schöneberg
*Additional information:* He fought in the First World War, he was awarded the EK 1. and II. Kl.; he was Protestant, while studying he was a corps student. After completing his studies, he worked for various companies, i.e. for a grain trading company. After the seizure of power by the National Socialists in 1933 he had to give up his job, he was able to establish himself as an attorney during the same year; he was regarded as "mixed race second degree." His income was low. In 1936 he accepted a position as legal counsel at the Vereinigung deutscher Eisenofenfabrikanten e.V.; he went to Kassel in this capacity, returned to Berlin in 1943 to establish a branch office; he lived in Berlin until 1945. After the end of National Socialism, he tried to be re-admitted as an attorney, which, however, he was denied initially, without further explanation. In 1948 he was admitted again; he was politically involved in the newly founded CDU (Christian Democractic Union of Germany).
*Sources:* *li; Adr.B.35; LAB, Liste Mschlg. 36; Verz. zugel. Anw.45; LAB, RAK, PA

**Werner, Hans Helmut**
12/20/1904 Berlin - transportation 1942
*Home address:* no information
*Law firm address:* Reinickendorfer Str. 6, N 39
*Additional information:* Attorney at the KG;
after the National Socialist seizure of power
he was made subject to an occupational ban
in early 1933. Transportation on 08/12/1942
from France to Auschwitz.
*Sources:* Liste d. nichtzugel. RA, 04/25/1933;
JMBl. 33, p. 203; BArch, R 3001 PAK, BG;
GB II

**Werner, Isidor, Judicial Councillor**
10/11/1871 - 09/13/1939
*Home address:* Altonaer Str. 4, Tiergarten
*Law firm address:* Nürnberger Str. 24 a, W 50
*Additional information:* Attorney and
notary; after the National Socialist seizure
of power in 1933 he was readmitted; in 1935
his license as a notary was revoked, he was
still working as an attorney in 1936; he died
in 1939 at the age of 77 and was buried in the
Jewish cemetery at Weißensee.
*Sources:* *li; DJ 36, p. 315; Liste 36; BG:
Friedh.W.Sterbereg.

**Werner, Ludwig Dr.**
12/22/1873 Breslau - 12/05/1942
Theresienstadt
*Home address:* Konstanzer Str. 56,
Wilmersdorf
*Law firm address:* Fasanenstr. 69, W 15
*Additional information:* Attorney and
notary; after the National Socialist seizure
of power in 1933 his license as a notary was
revoked, he was still working as an attorney
in 1938. Date of declaration of property:
11/18/1942; on 11/19/1942 he was deported
to Theresienstadt; he died there soon after.
*Sources:* JMBl. 33, p. 220; *li; Liste 36; DJ
38, p. 1705; BG; ThG; GB II

**Werthauer, Heinrich Dr.**
04/20/1894 - no information
*Home address:* no information
*Law firm address:* Brandenburgische Str. 24,
Wilmersdorf
*Additional information:* After the National
Socialist seizure of power he was made subject
to an occupational ban in 1933.
*Sources:* Liste d. nichtzugel. RA, 04/25/1933
(addendum); JMBl. 33, p. 282; BArch,
R 3001 PAK

**Werthauer, Johannes, Judicial Councillor**
01/20/1866 Kassel - 01/31/1938 Paris
*Home address:* Kaiserdamm 77,
Charlottenburg
*Law firm address:* Unter den Linden 66,
NW 7
*Additional information:* He was considered a
prominent defender and criminal justice critic;
in addition he was author of the world stage
(1926). He defended Kurt Tucholsky in legal
proceedings, which the Reichswehr Minister
Noske and the chief of the army Reinhardt
had brought because of the poem "Our
military" (1919). Tucholsky had published the
poem under the pseudonym Kaspar Hauser.
At the same time he was committed to the
Scientific Humanist Committee, which had
established itself around the sexologist.
When the National Socialists came to power
in 1933, he was on a trip to Paris. He never
returned. In August 1933 his license as a
notary was revoked, in October 1933 he was
expatriated, his admission as an attorney
was revoked. Oswald Freisler, the brother
of Roland Freisler, who was later chairman
of the "People's Court," was said to have
taken over the law firm. A warrant was
issued against him for tax code violations. He
received a professorship at the Sorbonne in
Paris, where he died in January 1938.
*Sources:* Br.B. 32; Krach, p. 437; Göpp., p.
371; information H. Bergemann; BG; Wolf,
BFS; photo BPK; information Flechtmann
7/2000; Pariser Tageblatt (Tageszeitung)

**Werthauer, Kurt Dr.**
11/13/1890 Berlin
- 08/24/1965
*Home address:* Grolmanstr.
41, Charlottenburg
*Law firm address:*
Grolmanstr. 41,
Charlottenburg
*Additional information:* Attorney and
notary; he had fought as a "frontline
fighter" in the First World War, he
repeatedly received numerous awards,
before 1933 he was a member of the DDP.
After the National Socialist seizure of
power he was readmitted in 1933; in 1935
his license as a notary was revoked, he
worked as an attorney until the general
occupational ban in 1938; he was then still
admitted as a "consultant;" he moved his

law office premises several times. His wife was regarded as non-Jewish; he survived and was readmitted as an attorney and notary after 1945. He was a member of the board of the Berlin Bar Association until he was admitted as an attorney at the German Federal Supreme Court. Later he was elected to the board of the chamber of attorneys of the German Federal Supreme Court. He was awarded the Grand Cross of Merit.
*Sources:* *li; DJ 36, p. 315; Liste 36; MRRAK; Liste d. Kons. v. 03/15/1939; Verz. zugel. Anw. 45; LAB, RAK, PA; BG; Göpp., p. 367

**Wertheim, Bruno**
10/25/1883 Berlin - no information
*Home address:* Hiddenseer Str. 3, Prenzlauer Berg
*Law firm address:* Alexanderstr. 24, C 25
*Additional information:* Attorney and notary, he was Protestant; after the National Socialist seizure of power he was readmitted in 1933, he remained in office as a notary even beyond 1935 because he was considered as "mixed race" (two Jewish grandparents); he was still practicing in 1941 as an attorney and a notary. He survived and was readmitted immediately after the war.
*Sources:* TK 33; *li; LAB, Liste Mschlg. 36; BArch, R 3001 PAK; RAK; Tel.B. 41; Verz. zugel. Anw. 45; BG

**Wertheim, Fritz**
01/28/1893 - September 1979
*Home address:* no information
*Law firm address:* Hewaldstr. 10, Schöneberg
*Additional information:* After the National Socialist seizure of power in 1933 he was readmitted, he was still working as an attorney until at least 1936. he emigrated to the USA, he last lived in New York, he died in 1979 at the age of 86.
*Sources:* TK 33; *li; TK 36; Liste 36; BArch, R 3001 PAK; SSDI

**Wertheim, John Dr.**
12/13/1884 Rostock - 10/10/1948 Sao Paulo, Brazil
*Home address:* Suarezstr. 29, Charlottenburg
*Law firm address:* Kaiserallee 22, W 15
*Additional information:* After the National Socialist seizure of power he was readmitted in 1933, he worked as an attorney until at least 1936. He emigrated to Brazil, a warrant was issued against him for tax code violations.
*Sources:* *li; Liste 36; BArch, R 3001 PAK; BG: LAB, OFP files; Wolf, BFS (Joel named John W.)

**Wertheim, Julius**
03/19/1886 - 02/08/1950 New York
*Home address:* no information
*Law firm address:* Jüdenstr. 53, C 2
*Additional information:*
Attorney and notary; after the National Socialist seizure of power in 1933 he was readmitted; in 1935 his license as a notary was revoked, he worked as an attorney until at least 1936. He went to Karlsbad, Czechoslovaka, in 1937, later to France, he was arrested there, temporarily interned in the French camp, after his release in 1940 he emigrated to the USA; a warrant was issued against him for tax code violations; he last lived in New York.
*Sources:* li; Liste 36; BArch, R 3001 PAK; Naatz-Album; Wolf, BFS

**Wertheimer, Ernst Dr.**
04/09/1893 Bruchsal - no information
*Home address:* Gustav-Meyer-Str. 8, Zehlendorf
*Law firm address:* Taubenstr. 35, W 8
*Additional information:* Attorney at the KG; after the National Socialist seizure of power in 1933 he was readmitted, he worked as an attorney until at least 1936. He emigrated to London, Great Britain.
*Sources: Sources:* Br.B. 32; *li; Liste 36; BArch, R 3001, PAK; TK 36; BG

**Wieluner, Fritz Dr.**
02/03/1890 Liegnitz - Mai 1944 Theresienstadt
*Home address:* Landshuter Str. 35, W 30
*Law firm address:* Zimmerstr. 21, SW 68
*Additional information:* Attorney and notary; after the National Socialist seizure of power in 1933 he was readmitted; in 1935 his license as a notary was revoked, he still worked as an attorney until the general occupational ban in 1938. Last employed as a clerk at the Reichsvereinigung; date of declaration of property: 05/10/1943;

transportation on 05/18/1943 to Theresienstadt, he died there a year later.
*Sources:* *li; Liste 36; BArch, R 3001 PAK; BG; ThG; GB II

**Wiener, Alfred Dr.**
11/05/1890 Schneidemühl - no information
*Home address:* no information
*Law firm address:* Oranienburger Str. 16, N 24
*Additional information:* Attorney at the KG (since 1918) and notary (since 1928); after the National Socialist seizure of power he was made subject to an occupational ban on 06/30/1933.
*Sources:* Liste d. nichtzugel. RA, 04/25/1933; JMBl. 33, p. 253; BArch, R 3001 PAK

**Wiener, August Dr.**
09/24/1885 - ca. 1939
*Home address:* no information
*Law firm address:* Keithstr. 3, W 62
*Additional information:* After the National Socialist seizure of power he was made subject to an occupational ban in early 1933. In the wake of the Night of the Broken Glass of November 1938, he was arrested, from 11/10/1938 to 12/20/1938 he was detained in a concentration camp, he is said to have died soon after release.
*Sources:* Liste d. nichtzugel. RA, 04/25/1933; JMBl. 33, p. 220; BArch, R 3001 PAK; BG

**Wiener, Hans Dr.**
01/16/1899 - no information
*Home address:* no information
*Law firm address:* Spichernstr. 19, W 50
*Additional information:* Attorney at the KG; member of the Republican Association of Judges; after the National Socialist seizure of power he was made subject to an occupational ban in 1933. He emigrated 1938 to Stockholm, Sweden.
Br.B. 32; TK 33; MvRRB; Liste d. nichtzugel. RA, 04/25/1933; Pr.J. 33, p. 773; BArch, R 3001 PAK; BG

**Wilk, Gerhard Dr.**
09/01/1902 - 08/31/1990
*Home address:* no information
*Law firm address:* Leipziger Str. 123 a
*Additional information:* Attorney since 1929; when, after the seizure of power by the National Socialists in 1933, he campaigned for a detained colleague in the wake of the Reichstag fire,

the prosecutor responsible advised him to give up the mandate and to bring himself to safety. In early 1933 he was made subject to an occupational ban. The RAK had reported him to the Prussian Ministry of Justice, so he was noticed by "propaganda and defense for 'Rote Hilfe' (Red Aid), at the same time it was stressed that he was 'non-Aryan.'" He did not feel threatened at first, but after learning that "some colleagues who were apolitical were beaten up in the Columbia House [the so-called wild concentration camp]," he went to the United States via Yugoslavia. He is said to have never worked as an attorney again, but he expressed his attachment to Germany in the novel "Mulleken." He changed his first name to Gerard, last lived in Queens, New York, and died a day before his 88th birthday.
*Publications:* Mulleken, 1988 GHStA, Rep. 84a, No. 20363; JMBl. 07/07/1933, p. .209; BArch, R 3001 PAK, PA; SSDI; information G. Jungfer; interview through Tillmann Krach

**Wimpfheimer, Heinrich Prof. Dr.**
No information
*Home address:* Viktoriastr. 8, W 35
*Law firm address:* Viktoriastr. 8, W 35
Attorney at the KG and notary; after the National Socialist seizure of power in 1933 his license as a notary was revoked, he was readmitted as an attorney, he presumably gave up his law office before 1936, since he was not listed in any directory.
*Sources:* Adr.B. 33; TK 33, *li

**Windscheid, Werner Dr.**
02/21/1903 Essen - 01/16/1976 Berlin
*Home address:* Fasanenstr. 68, W 15
*Law firm address:* Regentenstr. 14
*Additional information:* He was admitted as an attorney in 1928, he represented a German nationalist attitude, he was a Protestant. After the National Socialist seizure of power he was regarded as "mixed race", he was indeed examined in 1933, however, because of his status he was allowed to practice further; he continued to represent the Wittkowitzer Iironworks and its two subsidiaries (Hoffmann La Roche), so that he could still register an income of over RM 25,000 p.a. after 1940. In 1933 his admission was revoked; he was charged "at the instigation of the Bar Association" before the People's Court for "destruction of military forces and

enemy privileges," he was taken into custody from 08/01/1944 until the liberation on 05/03/1945 (from 04/12/1945 in Dreibergen/ Meckl.). In 1945 he was readmitted as an attorney and notary.
*Sources:* *li; LAB, Liste Mschl.36; BArch, R 3001 PAK; Verz. zugel. Anw. 45; LAB, RAK, PA; BG

**Wisloch, Justus Dr.**
No information
*Home address:* no information
*Law firm address:* Dorotheenstr. 79, NW 7
*Additional information:* Attorney and notary; after the National Socialist seizure of power he was readmitted in 1933, he still worked as an attorney until the general occupational ban in 1938.
*Sources:* *li; LAB, Liste 10/15/1933; DJ 36, p. 315; Liste 36; MRRAK

**Witkowski, Richard**
02/13/1883 - 10/22/1938
*Home address:* Speyerer Str. 9, W 30
*Law firm address:* Landshuter Str. 18, W 30
*Additional information:* Attorney and notary; after the National Socialist seizure of power in 1933 his license as a notary was revoked, he was readmitted as an attorney; he died in 1938 at the age of 65, shortly before the general occupational ban for Jewish attorneys went into effect. He was buried in the Jewish cemetery at Weißensee.
*Sources:* Adr.B. 33; TK 33; JMBl. 33, p. 220; *li; LAB, Liste 10/15/1933; Liste 36; BArch, R 3001 PAK; DJ 38, p. 1811; MRRAK; BG: Friedh.W.Sterbereg.

**Wittenberg, Moritz Dr.**
06/18/1890 Rawitsch - no information
*Home address:* Kurfürstendamm 216, W 15
*Law firm address:* Jägerstr. 6, W 8
*Additional information:* Attorney and notary; after the National Socialist seizure of power in 1933 he was readmitted; in 1935 his license as a notary was revoked, he was still working as an attorney until the general occupational ban in 1938, subsequently he was admitted as a "consultant." He emigrated to Tel Aviv, Palestine.
*Sources:* *li; LAB, Liste 10/15/1933; DJ 36, p. 315; Liste 36; MRRAK; Liste d. Kons. v. 12/31/1938; BArch, R 3001 PAK; BG: LAB, OFP files

**Wittenberg, Paul**
06/07/1882 Kulmsee - no information
*Home address:*
Rosenheimer Str. 27, W 30
*Law firm address:*
Oranienburger Str. 38, N 24
*Additional information:*
Attorney and notary; after the National Socialist seizure of power in 1933 his license as a notary was revoked, he was readmitted as an attorney, he was still working until the general occupational ban in 1938. He emigrated to Great Britain or Chile in June 1939.
*Sources:* JMBl. 33, p. 220; *li; LAB, Liste 10/15/1933; Liste 36; MRRAK; Naatz-Album; BG

**Wittenberg, Victor**
11/16/1877 Berlin - 05/06/1943 Theresienstadt
*Home address:* Helmstedter Str. 24, Wilmersdorf
*Law firm address:* Charlottenstr. 57, W 8
*Additional information:* Attorney and notary; after the National Socialist seizure of power in 1933 his license as a notary was revoked, he was an attorney until the general occupational ban in 1938, subsequently he still worked as a "consultant." Transportation on 10/28/1942 to Theresienstadt, he died there half a year later.
*Sources:* *li; Liste 36; LAB, Liste 10/15/1933; BG; ThG; GB II

**Wittgensteiner, Arno Dr.**
12/06/1883 Krefeld - no information
*Home address:* Podbielskiallee 65, Dahlem
*Law firm address:* Kronenstr. 64, W 8
*Additional information:* Attorney and notary; after the National Socialist seizure of power in 1933 his license as a notary was revoked, thereupon, he also gave up admission as an attorney, although he had been admitted again. He emigrated via Italy to Sydney, Australia.
*Sources:* Br.B. 32; JMBl. 33, p. 220; *li; Pr.J. 33, p. 701; BArch, R 3001 PAK; BG

**Wittkowski, Richard Dr.**
08/27/1877 Berlin - no information
*Home address:* Jerusalemer Str. 10, SW 68
*Law firm address:* Wallstr. 3, C 19

*Additional information:* Attorney and notary; after the National Socialist seizure of power in 1933 his license as a notary was revoked; he was regarded as "mixed race" (he had two Jewish grandparents), he was Protestant, he lived in a "privileged mixed-race marriage," he could practice further, he does not seem to have been working in 1940. He survived and was readmitted after 1945.
*Sources:* JMBl. 33, p. 220; *li; LAB, Liste 10/15/1933; Mitt.bl. Reichsverband nichtarischer Christen, 12/06/1934; LAB, Liste Mschlg. 36; Liste 36; Verz. zugel. Anw. 45; BG

**Wittkowsky, Paul Dr., Judicial Councillor**
No information - 10/16/1934
*Home address:* no information
*Law firm address:* Von-der-Heydt-Str. 7, W 10
*Additional information:* Attorney and notary; after the National Socialist seizure of power in 1933 his license as a notary was revoked. He died in 1934.
*Sources:* JMBl. 33, p. 220; *li; LAB, Liste 10/15/1933

**Wohl, Bruno Dr.**
03/24/1891 Magdeburg - transportation 1942
*Home address:* no information
*Law firm address:* Spandauer Str. 4. Charlottenburg
*Additional information:* After the National Socialist seizure of power he was made subject to an occupational ban in early 1933. He was transported from Frankfurt a. M. via Berlin to Raasiku at Reval/Tallinn.
*Sources:* Br.B. 32; Liste d. nichtzugel. RA, 04/25/1933; JMBl. 33, p. 221; BArch, lR 3001 PAK, BG; BdE; GB II

**Wohl, Erich Dr.**
03/04/1893 Berlin - 08/16/1942 Auschwitz
*Home address:* Tile-Wardenberg-Str. 26 a, NW 87
*Law firm address:* Linkstr. 18, W 9
*Additional information:* He was married, he had two children. On 05/30/1922 he became a freemason in the "Friedrich-Ludwig-Schröder" lodge, in the Freemason Year 1931/32 he held the office of the first overseer. After the National Socialist seizure of power in 1933

he was made subject to an occupational ban. On 07/01/1933 he was granted permission to acquire French francs worth RM 1,000 for emigration to France. The plan was to study and start a business in France. His wife and two sons were to initially stay with the in-laws (Dr. Süßbach in Rosenberg, Upper Silesia), until accommodation in France would be possible. Apparently they followed him later. He was transported from Pithiviers, France, on 07/31/1942 to Auschwitz and murdered a few days after arrival; his sons were also deported to Auschwitz and murdered there: Frank, born in 1927, was transported from Pithiviers on 08/03/1942, Ernst (Erneste), born 1930, was transported on 08/26/1942 from Drancy. There is no information about the further fate of his wife Erna.
*Sources:* Br.B. 32; Liste d. nichtzugel. RA, 04/25/1933; JMBl. 08/04/1933, p. 253; BArch, R 3001, PAK; BG; Naatz-Album; information Knoll (Friedrich-Ludwig-Schröder-Loge); GB II

**Wolff, Bernhard**
09/01/1886 Berlin - 09/25/1966 Karlsruhe
*Home address:* no information
*Law firm address:* Pariser Platz 1, W 8
*Additional information:* Attorney and notary; grandson of the Reichstag President and the first Reichstag President Eduard von Simson; in the Weimar Republic, he was head of the tax office of the Darmstadt Bank and/or or head legal advisor of the Darmstadt and National Bank, Berlin (DANAT Bank), which suffered a deep slump in the global economic crisis. In May 1932 he was readmitted as an attorney in a law partnership with his brother Ernst.
After the National Socialist seizure of power in 1933 he was readmitted; 1935 his license as a notary was revoked; he worked as an attorney until the general occupational ban in 1938. The pogrom in November 1938 throughout the Reich led him to emigrate, on 12/15/1938 he went to Great Britain; there he worked at Epson College; he interned from May 1940 to March 1941; he returned to Germany on 05/26/1946; as from 05/29/1946 he was head of the Legal Department of the Central Office of Economics in the British Zone, moreover, from 04/01/1947 he was at the Administration Office until 02/26/1948 - 10/20/1950. He was in the Legal Division of

the British Control Commission; 10/21/1950 - 09/06/1951 he was a Federal Finance Judge, 09/07/1951 - 08/31/1956 he was a Federal Constitutional Judge (and a member of the second senate); he died in 1966 shortly after his 80th birthday.
*Sources:* *li; LAB, Liste 10/15/1933; DJ 36, p. 315; Liste 36; BArch, R 3001 PAK; MRRAK; Göpp., p. 367; information of J. von Simson

**Wolff, Erich Dr.**
01/02/1903 Bromberg - 02/26/1996
*Home address:* Kurfürstendamm 35, Charlottenburg
*Law firm address:* Stuttgarter Platz 1, Charlottenburg
*Additional information:* After the National Socialist seizure of power he was made subject to an occupational ban in early 1933. He emigrated on 04/06/1938 to New York, USA, he lived there until his death at the age of 93.
*Sources:* Liste d. nichtzugel. RA, 04/25/1933; JMBl. 33, p. 253; BG; SSDI

**Wolff, Ernst Dr.**
11/20/1877 Berlin - 01/11/1959 Tübingen
*Home address:* Böckelweg 9, Zehlendorf
*Law firm address:* Pariser Platz 1, W 8
*Additional information:* He was a grandson of the Reichstag President and later Reichsgericht President Eduard von Simson and brother of Bernhard. After studying, he completed his military service and legal traineeship, he was admitted to the LG I in 1904 as an attorney and from 1905 also to the LG II and III. In 1914 he fought in the Battle of the Marne and was seriously wounded. The hospital he was in was conquered and he was taken prisoner by the French. As part of an exchange, he was assigned as an intern to the German legation in Bern. He always regarded this time of leisure free from work as the most beautiful of his life.
After returning to Berlin, he returned to the office of his uncle August von Simson, which predominantly focused on civil law. 1919 he was admitted as a notary. Through publications on the German-French relationship, he tried to make the bilateral relations objective; in general, he sought a better understanding between nations. In 1932 he was chairman of the RAK and the

Association of the Boards of the German Bar Associations, also a member of the Ständige Deputation des Deutschen Juristentages e.V. [Permanent Deputation of the German Attorneys' Day e.V.]. After the National Socialist seizure of power in 1933 he was recognized as "frontline fighter" and "elderly attorney" and was readmitted; in 1935 his license as a notary was revoked, he worked as an attorney until the general occupational ban. On 02/16/1939 he emigrated to London, Great Britain, with his wife Richardis, who died in a German bombing raid in London. 1948 he returned to Germany, until 1950 he was President of the Supreme Court for the British Zone, 1952-1958 he was a professor at the University of Cologne; he died in 1959 at the age of 81.
*Publications (selection):* "Privatrechtliche Beziehungen zwischen früheren Feinden nach dem Friedensvertrag" [Private law relations between former enemies after the peace treaty], 1921; "Schuldverschreibungen auf Reichs- und Goldmark mit unechter Valutaklausel" [Notes on Reichsmark and gold mark with false value date clause], 1935; The problem of pre-war contracts in peace treaties, 1946.
*Sources:* *li; DJ 36, p. 315; Liste 36; BArch, R 3001 PAK, PA; MRRAK; BG; Krach, p. 437; Göpp., pages 367/68; Maier-Reimer, Georg: Ernst Wolff, in: Heinrichs et al., page 643 ff; information Rohmer, Horst; photo and information of John v. Simson

**Wolff, Ernst Ludwig**
01/19/1994 Berlin - transportation 1944
*Home address:* Ludwigkirchstr. 11 a; Wilmersdorf
*Law firm address:* Charlottenstr. 55, W 8
*Additional information:* Attorney (since 1911) and notary (since 1919); he was a soldier in the First World War from 1914-1916, last as a sergeant, he was a member of the "Odd Fellow" Masonic Lodge, which voluntarily dissolved in the spring of 1933. After the National Socialist seizure of power in 1933 he was readmitted; in 1935 his license as a notary was revoked, he worked as an attorney until the general occupational ban in 1938. He was last employed in the

administration of the JKV; date of declaration of property: 08/26/1942; transportation on 11/06/1942 to Theresienstadt, from there he was transported on 10/09/1944 to Auschwitz. *Sources:* \*li; LAB, Liste 10/15/1933; Liste 36; BArch, R 3001 PAK, PA; Naatz-Album; BG; GB II

**Wolff, Eugen Dr., Judicial Councillor**
10/14/185614.10.1856 Berlin - Theresienstadt
*Home address:* Pariser Str. 32; W 15
*Law firm address:* Fasanenstr. 60
*Additional information:* Attorney at the KG and notary; after the National Socialist seizure of power he was readmitted in 1933; in 1935 his license as a notary was revoked, he worked as an attorney until the general occupational ban in 1938. Date of declaration of property: 01/09/1943; on 01/29/1943 he was transported to Theresienstadt and he died there, neither the date of death nor the circumstances of death are known.
*Sources:* TK 33; \*li; LAB, Liste 10/15/1933; DJ 36, p. 315; Liste 36; MRRAK; BG; ThG; GB II

**Wolff, Felix Dr.**
10/15/1877 Köthen - 02/05/1942 Litzmannstadt/Lodz
*Home address:* Hewaldstr. 6, Schöneberg
*Law firm address:* Kaiser-Wilhelm-Str. 60, C 2
*Additional information:* Attorney and notary; after the National Socialist seizure of power in 1933 his license as a notary was revoked, he was still working as an attorney until the general occupational ban in 1938. Transportation on 10/18/1941 to Litzmannstadt/Lodz, he died there at the beginning of February 1942.
*Sources:* Br.B. 32; JMBl. 33, p. 253; \*li; LAB, Liste 10/15/1933; Liste 36; BG; GB II

**Wolff, Fritz Dr.**
12/19/1884 - 07/13/1936 Berlin
*Home address:* Joachimsthaler Str. 13, W 15
*Law firm address:* Joachimsthaler Str. 13, W 15
*Additional information:* Attorney and notary; after the National Socialist seizure of power in 1933 his license as a notary was revoked, representation ban in April, subsequently he was readmitted and authorized to represent in cases. He died in

1936 at the age of 51 and was buried in the Jewish cemetery at Weißensee.
*Sources:* JMBl. 33, p. 220; \*li; Liste 36; LAB, Liste 10/15/1933; BArch, R 3001 PAK; BG: Friedh.W.Sterbereg.

**Wolff, Hans Alexis**
03/09/1885 Berlin - 05/14/1943 Sobibor
*Home address:* no information
*Law firm address:* Rankestr. 22, W 50
*Additional information:* Attorney since 1919; in early 1933 he was made subject to an occupational ban, his application for readmission was rejected because he was unable to claim any of the exceptions. He presumably emigrated to Holland, he was transported on 05/11/1943 from Westerbork to Sobibor and murdered there after arrival.
*Sources:* Liste d. nichtzugel. RA, 04/25/1933 (W., Hans); BArch, R 3001 PAK, PA; BG; GB II

**Wolff, Harri Dr.**
No information
*Home address:* Potsdamer Str. 138, W 9
*Law firm address:* Potsdamer Str. 138, W 9
*Additional information:* Attorney and notary; after the National Socialist seizure of power in 1933 his license as a notary was revoked, he still worked as an attorney until the general occupational ban in 1938.
*Sources:* JMBl. 33, p. 220; \*li; LAB, Liste 10/15/1933; Liste 36; MRRAK; BG

**Wolff, Otto Dr.**
07/27/1887 Greifenberg - no information
*Home address:* Xantener Str. 16, Wilmersdorf
*Law firm address:* Sybelstr. 40, Charlottenburg
*Additional information:* Attorney and notary; his twin brother Rudolf was at the same time his law partner. After the National Socialist seizure of power in 1933 he was readmitted; in 1935 his license as a notary was revoked, he was still working as an attorney until the general occupational ban in 1938. He was still on duty as a factory worker. Date of declaration of property 07/10/1942; transportation on 07/11/1942 to Auschwitz, he survived the concentration camp according to the files of the Berlin Memorial Book and lived in Schlüterstr. 30, Berlin-Charlottenburg in December 1951.

*Sources:* *li; LAB, Liste 10/15/1933; DJ 36, p. 315; BArch, R 3001 PAK; BG

**Wolff, Reinhold Dr.**
01/31/1899 Grünberg - 07/15/1997
*Home address:* Emser Str. 16, Wilmersdorf
*Law firm address:* Emser Str. 16, Wilmersdorf
*Additional information:* Attorney at the KG; he was Protestant; after the National Socialist seizure of power in 1933 he was readmitted, he was regarded as "mixed race" (first degree), he was married to a Jew, he was therefore regarded as a "Jew of validity," he was still working as a Jew in 1935. He emigrated to the USA in 1936, he last lived in Miami, Florida, he died at the age of 98.
*Sources:* *li; TK 36; LAB, Liste Mschlg. 36; BArch, R 3001 PAK; BG; SSDI

**Wolff, Rudolf Dr.**
07/27/1887 Greifenberg - transportation 1942
*Home address:* Schlüterstr. 50, Charlottenburg (seit 1937)
*Law firm address:* Sybelstr. 40, Charlottenburg
*Additional information:* Attorney and notary; in a law partnership with his twin brother Otto. After the National Socialist seizure of power in 1933 he was readmitted; in 1935 his license as a notary was revoked, he was still working as an attorney until the general occupational ban in 1938. He was last employed as a factory worker; date of declaration of property: 07/10/1942; transportation on 07/11/1942 presumably to Auschwitz.
*Sources:* *li; DJ 36, p. 315; Liste 36; LAB, Liste 10/15/1933; BArch, R 3001 PAK; MRRAK; BG; GB II

**Wolff, Werner**
03/02/1905 Danzig
*Home address:* no information
*Law firm address:* Behrenstr. 49, W 8
*Additional information:* He came in 1913 from Bamberg to Berlin; to complete his studies in Berlin he went to Repetitor Springer, he was a member of the Sprevia association; after his second state examination he was admitted to three district courts in 1932; he formed a

law partnership with attorney Kurt Rathe, their main client was the Commerzbank, in addition they also had a contract to restructure the Iduna. After the National Socialist seizure of power he was made subject to an occupational ban in April 1933. As from June 1933 he attended the retraining center Landwerk Neuendorf near Finsterwalde as an intern, to prepare for emigration to Palestine. 1934 he emigrated to Palestine, he later worked for the URO. He returned to Germany and Berlin in this capacity. In 2002 he was living in Frankfurt a. M.
*Sources:* TK 33; Liste d. nichtzugel. RA, 04/25/1933; JMBl. 08/04/1933, p. 253; BArch, R 3001 PAK; information Werner Wolff 1998, 2000, 2002

**Wolff, Wilhelm**
02/09/1885 - no information
*Home address:* no information
*Law firm address:* Kurfürstendamm 103/104, Halensee
*Additional information:* Attorney and notary; after the National Socialist seizure of power in 1933 his license as a notary was revoked, he worked as an attorney until the general occupational ban in 1938.
*Sources:* Br.B. 32; JMBl. 33, p. 220; *li; Liste 36; BArch, R 3001 PAK; MRRAK

**Wolff, Willy Dr.**
03/21/1884 Berlin - transportation 1943
*Home address:* Mommsenstr. 55, Charlottenburg
*Law firm address:* Grolmanstr. 30/31, Charlottenburg
*Additional information:* Attorney and notary; after the National Socialist seizure of power in 1933 his license as a notary was revoked, he worked as an attorney until the general occupational ban in 1938. He was last conscripted as a laborer at the Siemens-Wernerwerk. Date of declaration of property: 07/24/1943; collecting station Große Hamburger Str. 26; transportation to Auschwitz on 08/04/1943.
*Sources:* JMBl. 33, p. 220; *li; Liste 36; MRRAK; BG; GB II

**Wolffenstein, Emil Dr.**
10/17/1875 Dömnitz - no information
*Home address:* Kurfürstenstr. 43, Tiergarten
*Law firm address:* Kurfürstendamm 43, W 35

*Additional information:* Attorney at the LG I-III and AG Berlin Mitte; after the National Socialist seizure of power in July 1933 his license as a notary was revoked, he was still working as an attorney until the general occupational ban in 1938. Date of declaration of property: 12/18/1941, transportation on 01/13/1942 to Riga.
*Sources:* JMBl. 02/17/1933, p. 27, 07/15/1933, p. 220; *li; LAB, Liste 10/15/1933; Liste 36; MRRAK; BG; BdE;GB II

**Wolffenstein, Siegfried Dr.**
12/05/1883 - 01/22/1936
*Home address:* Bayerische Str. 25, Wilmersdorf
*Law firm address:* Dörnbergstr. 1, W 35
*Additional information:* Attorney and notary; after the National Socialist seizure of power in 1933 his license as a notary was revoked, he worked as an attorney until his death in 1936; he died at the age of 62 and was buried in the Jewish cemetery at Weißensee.
*Sources:* JMBl. 33, p. 220; *li; LAB, Liste 10/15/1933; BArch, R 3001 PAK; BG.

**Wolffram, Ernst Georg**
03/14/1878 Königsberg - transportation 1942
*Home address:* Brandenburgische Str. 10, Wilmersdorf
*Law firm address:* Am Karlsbad 24, W 35
*Additional information:* Attorney and notary; after the National Socialist seizure of power in 1933 he was readmitted; in 1935 his license as a notary was revoked, he was still working as an attorney until the general occupational ban in 1938. Transportation on 10/19/1942 to Riga.
*Sources:* *li; LAB, Liste 10/15/1933; DJ 36, p. 315; Liste 36; MRRAK; BG; BdE; GB II

**Wolfsohn, John Dr.**
02/07/1889 Berlin - 01/26/1936 Jerusalem
*Home address:* Steglitzer Str. 30/31, W 30
*Law firm address:* Wilmersdorfer Str. 15, Charlottenburg
*Additional information:* He was a soldier in the First World War; he obtained his doctorate in 1911; he was admitted as an attorney (since 1919) and notary (since 1931);

he was a specialist in French and Italian law; in his personnal file his religion is stated as "mosaic," he was a widower with two children (born ca. 1922 and 1926). After the National Socialist seizure of power his licenses as an attorney and a notary were revoked in July 1933, in October he was readmitted as an attorney and a notary, because he was recognized as a "frontline fighter." On 07/02/1934 his admission was deleted upon his own request. He emigrated in 1934 to Palestine and married once again, with the birth of a daughter in 1935. He was admitted as an attorney in the mandate area; he died in 1936 at the age of 46 years of a stomach ailment.
*Sources:* Jüd.Adr.B.; JMBl. 08/04/1933; BArch, R 3001 PAK, PA; documents of the daughter

**Wolfsohn, Martin**
11/14/1890 - August 1982
*Home address:* Neue Königstr. 70 (1932)
*Law firm address:* Neue Königstr. 70 (1932)
*Additional information:* Attorney and notary; after the National Socialist seizure of power in 1933 he was made subject to an occupational ban. He emigrated to the USA; he last lived in New York, he died in 1982 at the age of 81.
*Sources:* Jüd.Adr.B.; Br.B. 32; JMBl. 08/04/1933, p. 253; BArch, R 3001 PAK, PA; SSDI

**Wollmann, Ernst Dr.**
10/08/1891 Berlin - 02/11/1967 Berlin
*Home address:* Freiwaldauer Weg 31, Lichterfelde
*Law firm address:* Köthener Str. 38, W 9
*Additional information:* He had studied in Breslau and Freiburg and was admitted as an attorney in Berlin in 1920. After the National Socialist seizure of power in 1933 he was regarded as a "half Jew," since two of his grandparents were Jewish; he himself was Protestant, his wife was regarded as non-Jewish, the marriage was "privileged" because they had children. Because of these circumstances, he was also allowed to practice law throughout the general occupational ban in 1938. In April 1944 his wife, daughter and a domestic worker were killed in a bombing

raid. He was ordered to the Gestapo several times; in December 1944 he received another summons; he was able to postpone this to January 1945. When he appeared there, he was released, completely unexpected for him. His conscripted (non-Jewish) law partners had, in their own interest, advocated for the maintenance of the law firm, which had since been burned down and relocated several times. From 1944 to the end of the war, he practiced from his own home. He was able to escape seizure by the "Volkssturm" and survived. After the war, he was one of the first readmitted attorneys in Berlin.
*Sources:* *li; LAB, Liste 10/15/1933, Liste Mschlg. 36; Verz. zugel. Anw. 45; LAB, RAK, PA; BG

**Wollstein, Heinz**
08/22/1905 - no information
*Home address:* no information
*Law firm address:* Friedrichstr. 23, SW 48
*Additional information:* After the National Socialist seizure of power he was made subject to an occupational ban in early 1933.
*Sources:* Liste d. nichtzugel. RA, 04/25/1933; JMBl. 08/04/1933, p. 253; BArch, R 3001 PAK, PA

**Wolpe, Iwan Dr.**
01/22/1898 - no information
*Home address:* Xantener Str. 9, Wilmersdorf
*Law firm address:* Schellingstr. 2, W 9
*Additional information:* After the National Socialist seizure of power in 1933 he was readmitted, he worked as an attorney until the general occupational ban in 1938, subsequently he was still admitted as a "consultant."
*Sources:* Adr.B. 33; *li; LAB, Liste 10/15/1933; Liste 36; Liste d. Kons. v. 12/31/1938; BArch, R 3001 PAK; BG

**Wronker, Curt**
05/08/1903 Berlin-Wilmersdorf - no information
*Law firm address:* Freisinger Str. 13, W 30
*Additional information:* Attorney since 1930; after the National Socialist seizure of power he was made subject to an occupational ban in June 1933.
*Sources:* Adr.B. 33; TK 33; Liste d nichtzugel. RA, 04/25/1933 (addendum); JMBl. 08/04/1933, p. 253; BArch, R 3001 PAK, PA

**Wronker, Kurt Werner Dr.**
05/24/1893 - no information
*Home address:* Uhlandstr. 173-174, W 15
*Law firm address:* Kurfürstendamm 212, W 15
*Additional information:* Attorney at the KG and notary; 1932 he was in a law partnership with Max, presumably his father. After the National Socialist seizure of power in 1933 he was made subject to a representational ban; it appears that he was readmitted, because in 1935 he was practicing under his former law office address, subsequently he was no longer listed. He emigrated to London, England.
*Sources:* Adr.B. 33; TK 33; Liste d nichtzugel. RA, 04/25/1933; Adr.B. 36; BG: LAB, OFP files; BArch, R 3001 PAK

**Wronker, Max, Judicial Councillor**
07/22/1853 - 12/16/1935
*Home address:* Kurfürstendamm 212, W 15
*Law firm address:* Kurfürstendamm 212, W 15
*Additional information:* Well-known criminal attorney and notary; 1932 he was in a law partnership with Kurt Werner Wronker, presumably his son; after the National Socialist seizure of power in 1933 he was readmitted, he died at the age of 82 shortly after the occupational ban for Jewish notarieswent into effect in late 1935; he was buried in the Jewish cemetery at Weißensee.
*Sources:* Adr.B. 33; TK 33; *li; LAB, Liste 10/15/1933; DJ 36, p. 106; Philo-Lexikon, p. 604; BG: Friedh.W.Sterbereg.

**Wrzeszinski, Richard Dr.**
No information- end of 1933/beginning 1934
*Home address:* Charlottenstr. 55, W 8
*Law firm address:* Charlottenstr. 55, W 8
*Additional information:* He was still a board member of the RAK in 1932. After the National Socialist seizure of power in 1933 his license as a notary was revoked, he was readmitted as an attorney; he is said to have died at the end of 1933/beginning of 1934.
*Sources:* JMBl. 33, p. 220; *li; Naatz-Album; BG: BLHA, Pr.Br. Rep. 36 A, Dev.st., No. A 3267

**Wulff, Ernst Dr.**
02/04/1897 Görlitz - no information
*Home address:* Schützenstr. 68, SW 68
*Law firm address:* Schützenstr. 72, SW 68
*Additional information:* Attorney and
notary; after the National Socialist seizure
of power in 1933 he was readmitted; in
1935 his license as a notary was revoked, he
still worked until the general occupational
ban in 1938. He emigrated to Palestine on
09/02/1938.
*Sources:* *li; LAB, Liste 10/15/1933; DJ 36,
p. 315; Liste 36; MRRAK; BArch, R 3001
PAK; BG

**Wulff, Paul, Judicial Councillor**
No information - 1934
*Home address:* no information
*Law firm address:* Prinzenstr. 48, SW 19
*Additional information:* After the National
Socialist seizure of power he was readmitted
in 1933; he is believed to have died in 1934.
*Sources:* *li, LAB, Liste 10/15/1933;
Adr.B. 34

**Wunderlich, Georg Dr.**
02/02/1883 - no information
*Home address:* no information
*Law firm address:* Linkstr. 13, W 9
*Additional information:* He was still
secretary of the board of the RAK in 1932;
attorney and notary; after the National
Socialist seizure of power in 1933 he was
readmitted; in 1935 his license as a notary
was revoked, he worked as an attorney until
March 1936.
*Sources:* *li; LAB, Liste 10/15/1933; DJ 36, p.
315; Liste 36; BArch, R 3001 PAK

**Wunderlich, Hans**
11/14/1888 Berlin - transportation 1942
*Home address:* Sächsische Str. 40 a,
Wilmersdorf
*Law firm address:* Konstanzer Str. 9,
Wilmersdorf
*Additional information:* After the National
Socialist seizure of power in 1933 he was
made subject to an occupational ban.
Transportation on 03/28/1942 to Piaski.
*Sources:* JMBl. 7.7.33, p. 209; BArch, R 3001
PAK; BG; GB II

**Wunsch, Joseph, Judicial Councillor**
04/06/1864 Schubin - 10/31/1942
Theresienstadt
*Home address:* Bleibtreustr. 33, W 15,
Charlottenburg
*Law firm address:* Bleibtreustr. 33, W 15,
Charlottenburg
*Additional information:* Attorney and
notary; after the National Socialist seizure
of power in 1933 he was readmitted; in
1935 his license as a notary was revoked, he
still worked as an attorney until the general
occupational ban in 1938. Transportation on
10/03/1942 to Theresienstadt, he died there
after a few weeks.
*Sources:* *li; LAB, Liste 10/15/1933; DJ 36, p.
315; Liste 36; MRRAK (Josef W.); BG; ThG;
GB II

**Wurzel, Fritz Isidor Dr.**
03/05/1899 - no information
*Home address:* no information
*Law firm address:* Taubenstr. 32, W 8
*Additional information:* Attorney and
notary; after the National Socialist seizure
of power in 1933 his license as a notary was
revoked, he was still working as an attorney
until the general occupational ban in 1938.
*Sources:* Br.B. 32; JMBl. 33, p. 220 (Isidor
W.); *li; LAB, Liste 10/15/1933; Liste 36;
BArch, R 3001 PAK (Friedrich W.)

**Wurzel, Harold Dr.**
09/19/1901 - March 1974
*Home address:* no information
*Law firm address:* Kurfürstendamm 188/189,
W 15
*Additional information:* After the National
Socialist seizure of power in 1933 he was
made subject to an occupational ban in early
1933. He emigrated to the USA, he last lived
in New York.
*Sources:* Liste d. nichtzugel. RA, 04/25/1933;
JMBl. 33, p. 220; BArch, R 3001 PAK; SSDI

**Wygodzinski, Benno**
12/28/1879 Waldenburg - 08/18/1942 Riga
*Home address:* Sybelstr. 58, Charlottenburg
*Law firm address:* Bismarckstr. 84,
Charlottenburg
*Additional information:* Attorney and
notary; after the National Socialist seizure
of power in 1933 his license as a notary was
revoked, he was still working as an attorney

until the general occupational ban in 1938. Transportation on 08/15/1942 to Riga, there he was murdered on the day of his arrival.
*Sources:* JMBl. 33, p. 253; *li; Liste 36; LAB, Liste 10/15/1933; BG; BdE; GB II

# Z

**Zacharias, James**
08/13/1890 - no information
*Home address:* Innsbrucker Str. 57, Schöneberg
*Law firm address:* Wallstr. 76-79, SW 19
*Additional information:* Attorney and notary; after the National Socialist seizure of power his licenses as an attorney and as a notary were revoked, but obviously he was able to claim exceptions and was readmitted at the end of 1933; in 1935 his license as a notary was finally revoked. He was still working as an attorney until the general occupational ban in 1938.
*Sources:* Pr.J. 33, p. 502; DJ 36, p. 315; Liste 36; BArch, R 3001 PAK; MRRAK; BG

**Zander, Walter Dr.**
06/08/1898 - no information
*Home address:* no information
*Law firm address:* Potsdamer Str. 117, W 35
*Additional information:* Attorney and notary; after the National Socialist seizure of power in 1933 his license as a notary was revoked, he was readmitted as an attorney; he was still working as an attorney in 1936.
*Sources:* *li; Br.B. 32; TK 33; LAB, Liste 10/15/1933; Liste 36; BArch, R 3001 PAK

**Zarinzansky, Kurt Dr.**
01/28/1890 Berlin - 03/11/1945 Mauthausen
*Home address:* Ansbacher Str. 8 a, W 50
*Law firm address:* Ansbacher Str. 8 a, W 50
*Additional information:* Attorney and notary; he was Catholic; after the National Socialist seizure of power in 1933 he was readmitted; in 1935 his license as a notary was revoked, he was still working as an attorney until the general occupational ban in 1938. He last worked as an executor. Date of declaration of property: 03/01/1943; transportation on 03/03/1943 to Auschwitz; he died in March 1945 in Mauthausen.
*Sources:* *li; Liste 36; LAB, Liste 10/15/1933; BArch, R 3001 PAK, PA; BG; GB II

**Zellner, Martin Dr.**
12/13/1893 Berlin - 01/13/1951 Berlin
*Home address:* Grunewaldstr. 10, Steglitz
*Law firm address:* Potsdamer Str. 103a, W 35
*Additional information:* He was a soldier during the First World War; attorney (since 1920) at the KG and notary (since 1930; member of the SPD); he was Protestant. After the National Socialist seizure of power in 1933 he was readmitted; in 1935 his license as a notary was revoked, he was still working as an attorney until the general occupational ban in 1938. Until 1933 he earned an income of about RM 20,000 p.a., after 1938 it was reduced by half. His most important clients before the occupational ban were the Deutsche Glasschutz-Verein, Berlin (legal counsel until 1938), the landowners' association Schönhauser Tor (legal counsel until 1938), as well as Deutsche Auto-Liga, Berlin (legal counsel and expert consultant until 1933). After the Night of the Broken Glass in November 1938 he was arrested, he was imprisoned in the Sachsenhausen concentration camp from 11/11/1938 to 12/16/1938. He was released, subsequently he worked as a construction worker; he lived in a "privileged mixed marriage." His son managed to emigrate to the USA in 1938. He survived the National Socialist regime, after 1945 he lived in Tempelhof and was readmitted as an attorney.
*Sources:* TK 33; *li; DJ 36, p. 315; Liste 36; MRRAK; BArch, R 3001 PAK; BG; LAB, RAK, PA

**Zerba, Fritz Dr.**
04/09/1891 Charlottenburg
*Home address:* no information
*Law firm address:* Roonstr. 13, NW 40
*Additional information:* Attorney since 1936; after the National Socialist seizure of power in early 1933 he was made subject to an occupational ban.
*Sources:* Pr.J. 33, p. 565; BArch, R 3001 PAK, PA

**Zerkowski, Erich Dr.**
06/29/1890 Berlin - no information
*Home address:* no information
*Law firm address:* Budapester Str. 11, W 50
*Additional information:* After the National Socialist seizure of power his status was checked, he was regarded as "non-Aryan," his licenses as an attorney and a notary were revoked.
*Sources:* Pr.J. 33, p. 839; BArch, R 3001 PAK, PA

**Ziegler, Max Dr.**
03/09/1889 Breslau - 10/29/1942 Riga
*Home address:* Wiesener Str. 33, Tempelhof
*Law firm address:* Rosenthaler Str. 34/35,
N 54
*Additional information:* Attorney and
notary; after the National Socialist seizure
of power in 1933 he was readmitted; in
1935 his license as a notary was revoked, he
worked as an attorney until at least 1936.
Date of declaration of property: 10/24/1942;
transportation on 10/26/1942 to Riga, he was
murdered there after arrival.
*Sources:* *li; DJ 36, p. 315; Liste 36; BArch, R
3001, PAK; BG; BdE; GB II

**Zielenziger, Rudolf Dr.**
07/24/1905 - January 1963 New York
*Home address:* no information
*Law firm address:* Sybelstr. 66.
Charlottenburg
*Additional information:* After the National
Socialist seizure of power in 1933 he was
made subject to an occupational ban in early
1933. He emigrated to the USA, he died in
1963 in New York.
*Sources:* Liste d. nichtzugel. RA, 04/25/1933;
JMBl. 33, p. 221; BArch, R 3001 PAK;
information Weißleder

**Zielinski, Gustav Dr.**
07/25/1894 - no information
*Home address:* no information
*Law firm address:* Ansbacher Str. 34, W 50
*Additional information:* Attorney at the KG;
member of the Republican Association of
Judges; after the National Socialist seizure of
power he was made subject to an occupational
ban in early 1933.
*Sources:* Br.B. 32; TK 33; MvRRB; Liste d.
nichtzugel. RA, 04/25/1933; JMBl. 33,
p. 266

**Ziffer, Konrad Dr.**
11/15/1897 Berlin - no information
*Home address:* Cunostr. 49, Schmargendorf
*Law firm address:* Königstr. 34/36, C 2
*Additional information:* Attorney at the
KG and notary; after the National Socialist
seizure of power in 1933 he was readmitted;
in 1935 his license as a notary was revoked,
he worked as an attorney until the general
occupational ban in 1938, then he worked as
a "consultant." He emigrated on 01/06/1940
to Buenos Aires, Argentina.

*Sources:* TK 33; *li; DJ, 36, p. 315; Liste 36;
MRRAK; Liste d. Kons. v. 12/31/1938; BG

**Zimmt, Kurt**
09/24/1900 - no information
*Home address:* no information
*Law firm address:* Friedrichstr. 23, SW 68
*Additional information:* After the National
Socialist seizure of power in 1933 he was
readmitted, he still worked as an attorney
until 1936. In 1936 he emigrated to Sao Paulo,
Brazil; an arrest warrant for tax evasion was
issued against him.
*Sources:* *li; Liste 36; BArch, R 3001 PAK;
Wolf, BFS

**Zippert, Hugo**
No information
*Home address:* Hektorstr. 4, Wilmersdorf
*Law firm address:* Grünstr. 4, Köpenick
*Additional information:* Attorney and
notary; after the National Socialist seizure of
power in 1933 he was readmitted; in 1935 his
license as a notary was revoked, he worked as
an attorney until at least 1936.
*Sources:* *li; Liste 36; BG; Lüdersdorf, Gerd:
Es war ihr Zuhause [It was her home]. Bln,
o.J. , p. 56

**Zippert, Siegbert**
09/05/1875 - 01/08/1939 Berlin
*Home address:* Prenzlauer Str. 28, C 25
*Law firm address:* Prenzlauer Str. 38, C 25
*Additional information:* Attorney and
notary; after the National Socialist seizure
of power in 1933 his license as a notary was
revoked, he was still working as an attorney
until the general occupational ban in 1938; he
died in January 1939 at the age of 63 and was
buried in the Jewish cemetery at Weißensee.
*Sources:* JMBl. 33, p. 220; *li; Liste 36;
MRRAK; BG: Friedh.W.Sterbereg.

**Zirker, Max Dr.**
09/26/1876 Birnbaum - no information
*Home address:* Immelmannstr. 45,
Schöneberg
*Law firm address:* Leipziger Str. 110, W 8
*Additional information:* Attorney and
notary; after the National Socialist seizure of
power in 1933 he was readmitted; in 1935 his
license as a notary was revoked. He emigrated
to Haifa, Palestine, in January 1936, his
license was revoked at the same time.
*Sources:* *li; DJ 36, P. 315; DJ 36, S. 454; BG

**Zolki, Hans Dr.**
09/23/1902 Königsberg - April 1962
*Home address:* no information
*Law firm address:* Potsdamer Platz 1
(Columbushaus), W 9
*Additional information:* After the National
Socialist seizure of power in June 1933 he was
made subject to an occupational ban, this was
preceded by a denunciation. He did not apply
for readmission. He emigrated to the USA, he
changed his first name to Henry, he died in
1962 at the age of 59.
*Sources:* JMBl. 07/15/1933, p. 220; BArch, R
3001 PAK, PA; BG; SSDI

**Zolkowitz, Alexander Dr.**
06/05/1903 - no information
*Home address:* no information
*Law firm address:* Leipziger Str. 119, W 8
*Additional information:* After the National
Socialist seizure of power he was made subject
to an occupational ban in early 1933.
*Sources:* Liste d. nichtzugel. RA, 04/25/1933;
JMBl. 08/04/1933, p. 253; BArch, R 3001
PAK

**Zucker, Ludwig Dr.**
01/02/1882 - no information
*Home address:* Klopstockstr. 9, NW 87
*Law firm address:* Reinickendorfer Str. 2,
N 39
*Additional information:* Board member
of the Israelite Religious Association of the
Oranienburg Suburb, which was responsible
for worship in accordance with Orthodox
rites. After the National Socialist seizure of
power he was readmitted as an attorney. He
emigrated to Jerusalem, Palestine.
*Sources:* Adr.B.; *li; BG: LAB, OFP files

**Zuckermann, Erich Dr.**
01/07/1894 Forst - no information
*Home address:* Soorstr. 28, Charlottenburg
*Law firm address:* Kurfürstenstr. 105, W 62
*Additional information:* Attorney and notary;
he was a member of the Republican Association
of Judges. After the National Socialist seizure
of power in 1933 he was readmitted; in 1935
his license as a notary was revoked, he was
admitted as an attorney until the general
occupational ban in 1938; he emigrated on
08/11/1938 to Bogota, Bolivia.
*Sources:* TK 33; MvRRB; *li; DJ 36, p. 315;
Liste 36; MRRAK; BArch, R 3001 PAK; BG

**Zwirn, Arthur**
12/28/1882 Obornik - transportation 1943
*Home address:* Bergstr. 6, Neukölln
*Law firm address:* Bergstr. 6, Neukölln
*Additional information:* Attorney and
notary; after the National Socialist seizure
of power in 1933 his license as a notary was
revoked, he was still working as an attorney
until the general occupational ban in 1938.
Date of declaration of property: 03/03/1943,
transportation on 03/01/1943 to Auschwitz.
*Sources:* JMBl. 33, p. 253; *li; Liste 36;
MRRAK; BG; GB II

# Abbreviations

Adr.B.    Berliner Adressbuch (mit dem jeweiligen Jahrgang) = Berlin directory (with the respective year)

AG    Amtsgericht = Municipal Court

Am.Com.    American Committee for the Guidance of the Professional Personnel

AoR, Ausst    Wanderausstellung der Bundesrechtsanwaltskammer und des Deutschen Juristentages "Anwalt ohne Recht – Schicksale jüdischer Anwälte nach 1933" = Traveling exhibition of the German Federal Bar Association and the Association of German Jurists entitled "Attorneys without rights - the fate of German attorneys after 1933"

Aufbau    Zeitung der deutschsprachigen jüdischen Emigration, New York = Newspaper of German-speaking Jewish emigrants, New York

Information    Auskunft = Information

AV    Ausführungsvorschrift = Implementation regulation

BArch    Bundesarchiv = German Federal Archive

BAP    Bundesarchiv, die frühere Abt. Potsdam, seit 1996 aufgelöst = German Federal Archive, the former Potsdam branch, has been dissolved since 1996

Ball-Kaduri    Ball-Kaduri, Kurt-Jakob: Das Leben der Juden in Deutschland im Jahre 1933 [The life of Jews in Germany in 1933].

BArch, PAK    Personalkartei des Reichsjustizministeriums im Bestand des Bundesarchiv, R 3001 [Personnel file of the Reich Ministry of Justice in the holdings of the German Federal Archive, R 3001]

BArch, PA    Personalakte des Reichsjustizministeriums, R 3001 [Employee records of the Reich Ministry of Justice, R 3001]

BdE    Buch der Erinnerung = Remembrance Book

BDM    Bund Deutscher Mädel = League of German Girls

Bendix    Bendix, Reinhard: Von Berlin nach Berkeley [From Berlin to Berkeley]

BFS    Biographische Forschungen und Sozialgeschichte e.V., see Wolf, Kerstin and Frank

BG    Gesamtdatei des Gedenkbuchs Berlins, erarbeitet vom Zentralinstitut für sozialwissenschaftliche Forschung der Freien Universität Berlin (aktualisiert) = The complete data of the Berlin Remembrance Book, compiled by the Central Institute for Social Science Research at the Free University of Berlin.

BHdE    Biographisches Handbuch der deutschsprachigen Emigration nach 1933 [Biographical manual of German-speaking emigration after 1933]

Bl.    Blatt = Sheet

Blau, Bruno    Vierzehn Jahre Schrecken und Not, unveröffentl. MS aus dem Jahre 1952, New York [Fourteen years of horror and stress, unpublished manuscript dated 1952, New York]

BLHA    Brandenburgisches Landeshauptarchiv = Brandenburg Central State Archive

BNSDJ    Bund Nationalsozialistischer Deutscher Juristen = Federation of National Socialist German Attorneys

Br.B.    Anhang des Berliner Adressbuchs, Handel- und Gewerbetreibende, Rubrik Rechtsanwälte und Notare = Appendix to the Berlin Address Book, Retailers and Traders, Category Attorneys and Notaries

CJ    Stiftung "Neue Synagoge - Centrum Judaicum Berlin" =

"New Synagogue - Centrum Judaicum Berlin" Foundation

CV      Centralverein deutscher Staatsbürger jüdischen Glaubens = Central Association of German Citizens of Jewish Faith

DAV      Deutscher Anwaltverein = German Bar Association

Dev.Stelle      Devisenstelle = Foreign Exchange Board

DJ      Deutsche Justiz (Amtsblatt d. RJM nach 1935) = Deutsche Justiz (Official Gazette of the Reich Ministry of Justice after 1935)

Dok.      Dokument = Document

EK I/II      Eisernes Kreuz I./II. Klasse = Iron cross I./II. class

Emigr.- u. Sterbedatei

emigration and death data Emigrations- und Sterbedatei, zitiert nach Datei des Gedenkbuchs Berlins = Emigration and death data, cited according to the data of the Berlin Remembrance Book

Entsch.akte      Entschädigungsakte = Compensation Act

Entschädigungsbeh.

Entschädigungsbehörde = Compensation Authority

Friedh.W. Sterbereg. (Friedhof Westerburg Sterberegister) = Westerburg Cemetery Death Register Jüdischer Friedhof Weißensee, Sterberegister = Weißensee Jewish Cemetery, Death Register

g      Gedenkbuch Berlins der jüdischen Opfer des Nationalsozialismus. "Ihre Namen mögen nie vergessen werden!", hg. vom Zentralinstitut für sozialwissenschaftliche Forschung der Freien Universität Berlin im Auftrag des Senators für kulturelle Angelegenheiten, 1995 = Berlin Remembrance Book of Jewish victims of National Socialism.

"Your names must never be forgotten," published by the Central Institute for Social Science Research of the Free University of Berlin by order of the Senator for Cultural Affairs, 1995

GB      Gedenkbuch – Opfer der Verfolgung der Juden unter der nationalsozialistischen Gewaltherrschaft in Deutschland, 1933-1945, hg. vom Bundesarchiv Koblenz, 1986 = Remembrance Book - victims of the persecution of the Jews under the National Socialist regime in Germany, 1933-1945, published by the German Federal Archives Coblenz, 1986

GB II      Gedenkbuch – Bundesarchiv Koblenz, 2. Aufl. 2006 = Remembrance Book - German Federal Archives Coblenz, 2nd edition 2006

Göpp.      Göppinger, Horst: Juristen jüdischer Abstammung im "Dritten Reich". Entrechtung und Verfolgung [Attorneys of Jewish descent in the "Third Reich." Deprivation and persecution]

GStA      Geheimes Staatsarchiv = Secret State Archive

HJ      Hitlerjugend = Hitler Youth

IfZ      Institut für Zeitgeschichte = Institute for Contemporary History

IMT      Internationales Militärtribunal Nürnberg = The International Military Tribunal in Nuremberg

ITS-Transportlisten

ITS transport lists Transportlisten der Gestapo, zitiert nach Datei des Gedenkbuchs Berlins = Transport lists of the Gestapo (Geheime Staatspolizei = Secret State Police), cited in accordance with the data of the Berlin Remembrance Book

Jewish Immigrants . . . in the U.S.A., Oral
History Strauss,
Herbert A.:
Schriftliche Aufzeichnun-
gen von Interviews mit
Jüdischen Einwanderern in
die USA [Written interviews
with Jewish immigrants to
the USA]

Jg. — Jahrgang = Year

JKV — Jüdische Kultusvereinigung
= Jewish Cultural Affairs
Association

JMBl. — Justiz-Ministerialblatt =
Jewish Ministerial Gazette

JR — Justizrat = Judicial
Councillor

Jüd.Adr.B. — Jüdisches Adressbuch für
Gross-Berlin, Ausgabe 1931
(Faks.) = Jewish address
book for Greater Berlin,
1931 edition (facsimile)

Juristinnen — s. Röwekamp, Marion [see
Röwekamp, Marion]

k.A. — keine Angabe = no
information

Kartei d. schulpfl.
Kinder
Kartei der schulpflichtigen
Kinder, BArch, zitiert nach
Datei des Gedenkbuchs
Berlins = Card index of
school-age children, BArch,
cited in accordance with
the data file of the Berlin
Remembrance Book

KG — Kammergericht = Court of
Appeals in Berlin

KJ — Kritische Justiz = Critical
justice (journal)

KK — Kennkarte = identity card

Korr. — Korrespondenz =
Correspondence

Korr. Liste d. arischen Anw.,10/15/1933
Korrektur des vom BNSDJ
herausgegebenen Verzeich-
nisses der arischen Anwälte
vom 5.10.1933 = Correc-
tion of the list of Aryan
attorneys, published by the
BNSDJ on 10/05/1933

Krach — Krach, Tilmann: Jüdische
Rechtsanwälte in Preußen,
s. Literaturverzeichnis =

Krach, Tilmann: Jewish
attorneys in Prussia, see
Bibliography

LAB — Landesarchiv Berlin =
National Archive Berlin

LAB, Liste 10/15/1933
Bearbeitete Liste (ver-
mutlich von Willi Naatz)
der zugelassenen Anwälte
vom Oktober 15.10.1933
= Edited list (presumably
by Willi Naatz) of licensed
attorneys, dated October
10/15/1933

LBI — Leo Baeck Institute, New
York

LG — Landgericht = District
Court

*li — Verzeichnis der im Bezirk
der Anwaltskammer zu
Berlin zugelassenen Rechtsanwälte vom 15. 10. 1933
("Nur für Behörden") =
List of licensed attorneys
registered in the district of
the Berlin Bar Association,
dated 10/15/1933 ("For the
authorities only")

Liste d. Kons.
Liste der Konsulenten, die
in verschiedenen Fassungen
herausgebracht worden ist:
für die endgültig zugelassenen Konsulenten, Stand
15.4.1939
– für die endgültig zugelassenen Konsulenten, Stand
03/15/1939
– für die befristet zugel.
Konsulenten, Stand
31.12.1938 - 31.1.1939
[List of consultants, published in different
versions: for the definitely
approved consultants, version 04/15/1939
- for the definitely approved
consultants, version
03/15/1939
- for the temporarily admitted consultants, version
12/31/1938 - 01/31/1939]

Liste d. nichtzugel. RA, 04/25/1933
Liste der nichtzugelas-
senen Rechtsanwälte

| | |
|---|---|
| | vom 25.4.1933, (früherer Bestand Anwaltszimmer Amtsgericht Tempelhof-Kreuzberg) = list of non-licensed attorneys of 04/25/1933, (former inventory of the Attorneys' Meeting Room of the Tempelhof-Kreuzberg District Court |
| Liste d. nichtzugel. RA, 04/25/1933 (Nachtrag) | Nachtrag zur Liste der nichtzugelassenen Rechtsanwälte vom 25.4.1933 = Addendum to the list of non-licensed attorneys of 04/25/1933 |
| Liste der Theresienstadt-Überlebenden | Unterlagen des Gedenkbuchprojekts Theresienstadt, weitgehend aufgenommen in Theresienstädter Gedenkbuch = Documents of the Theresienstadt Remembrance Book Project, extensively included in the Theresienstadt Remembrance Book |
| LAB, RAK, PA | Personalakten der Rechtsanwaltskammer Berlin (nach 1945) = Personnel records of the Berlin Bar Association |
| Liste 36 | Verzeichnis der jüdischen Rechtsanwälte vom 26. 2. 1936 = Directory of Jewish Attorneys dated 02/26/1936 |
| Liste Mschlg. 36 | Liste der "Mischlinge" vom 26.2.1936, = List of people of "mixed race," dated 02/26/1936, |
| Lodz-TL | Eingangsliste des Ghettos Lodz, zitiert nach Datei des Gedenkbuchs Berlins = Admission list of the Lodz ghetto, quoted from the files of the Berlin Remembrance Book |
| Lowenthal | Lowenthal, Ernst: Juden in Preußen [Jews in Prussia] |
| ME | Memoirs |

| | |
|---|---|
| Mitt.bl. Reichsverband nichtarischer Christen | Mitteilungsblatt des Reichsverbands der nichtarischen Christen e.V. = Newsletter of the Reich Association of non-Aryan Christians |
| MS | Manuscript |
| MRRAK | Mitteilungen der Reichs-Rechtsanwaltskammer = Reports of the Reich Bar Association |
| MvRRB | Mitgliederverzeichnis des Republikanischen Richterbundes = Directory of members of the Republican Association of Judges |
| NJW | Neue Juristische Wochenschrift [New Legal Weekly] |
| NL | Nachlass = Inheritance |
| NSKK | Nationalsozialistisches Kraftfahr-Korps = National Socialist Motor Vehicle Corps |
| NSRB | Nationalsozialistischer Rechtswahrerbund = The National Socialist Association of German Legal Professionals |
| NSV | NS-Volkswohlfahrt e.V. |
| NY Publ.Lib. | New York Public Library, Dep. of Rare Books and Manuscripts: American Committee for the Guidance of the Professional Personnel |
| o.D. | ohne Datum = undated |
| OFP | Oberfinanzpräsident Berlin = Chief Finance President Berlin |
| OKH | Oberkommando des Heeres = Army High Command |
| OSI | Otto-Suhr-Institut Politikwissenschaft am Fachbereich Politik- und Sozialwissenschaften der Freien Universität Berlin = Otto Suhr Institute for Political Science of the Department of Political and Social Sciences of the Free University of Berlin |
| OT | Organisation Todt = the Todt Organization |

Pr.J.  Preußische Justiz, Amtsblatt ab September 1933 = Preußische Justiz [Prussian Justice], official journal from September 1933 onwards

PrMJ  Preußisches Ministerium der Justiz = Prussian Ministry of Justice

RA  Rechtsanwalt = Attorney

RAG  Rechtsanwaltsgesetz – Gesetz über die Zulassung zur Rechtsanwaltschaft = Attorneys' Act - Law on admission to the legal profession

RAK  Rechtsanwaltskammer Berlin = Berlin Bar Association

RAO  Rechtsanwaltsordnung = Attorneys' Act

RGBl.  Reichsgesetzblatt = Reich Law Gazette

RjF  Reichsbund jüdischer Frontsoldaten = Reich Federation of Jewish Front Soldiers

RJM  Reichsjustizministerium = Reich Ministry of Justice

RRAK  Reichs-Rechtsanwaltskammer = Reich Bar Association

RSA  Reichssippenamt = Reich Office of Genealogy

RV  Reichsvereinigung der Juden in Deutschland = Reich's Association of the Jews in Germany

RzW  Rechtsprechung zum Wiedergutmachungsrecht (Zeitschrift) = Jurisdiction on the right of reparation (journal)

SBZ  Sowjetisch-besetzte Zone = Soviet-occupied zone

Schneider, Schwarz, Schwarz  Schneider et al.: Die Rechtsanwälte der Roten Hilfe [The attorneys of the Red Aid]

SenJustArch  Archiv der Senatsverwaltung für Justiz Berlin = Archive of the Senate Administration for Justice in Berlin

SL  Sammellager = collecting station

SLW  Simone Ladwig-Winters

SSDI  Social Security Death Index, frei zugängliche Datenbank von Bürgern der USA = Social Security Death Index, freely accessible database of citizens of the USA

Tel.B. 41  Telefonbuch der Stadt Berlin 1941. 1941 war das letzte Jahr, in dem Juden noch einen Telefonanschluss besitzen durften = Telephone directory of the City of Berlin, 1941. 1941 was the last year in which Jews were allowed to have a telephone connection

ThG  Theresienstädter Gedenkbuch = Theresienstadt Remembrance Book

TK  Terminkalender für Preußische Justizbeamte = Appointment Calendar for Prussian judicial officers

TL  Transportliste = transport list

Trial of A.Eichmann  Eichmann-Prozess-Documentation Vol. VI, = Eichmann trial documentation, vol, VI,

ULAP  Universal Landesausstellungspark Berlin = Universal State Exhibition Park Berlin

URO  United Restitution Office (später Organization) = United Restitution Office (later organization)

VB  Völkischer Beobachter [National observer]

Verfolgte Berl. . . . .  Vor die Tür gesetzt. Im Nationalsozialismus verfolgte Berliner Stadtverordnete und Magistratsmitglieder, s. Quellenverzeichnis = Shown the door. Berlin city councilors and municipal members persecuted under National Socialism, see References

Vertr.V.  Vertretungsverbot = representation prohibition

Verz.  Verzeichnis der arischen Rechtsanwälte für den

Bezirk des Kammergerichts Berlin, hg. vom Bund Nationalsozialistischer Juristen Deutschlands (BNJSD) = Directory of Aryan Attorneys for the District of the Court of Appeals in Berlin, published by the BNJSD (Bund Nationalsozialistischer Juristen Deutschlands = Federation of National Socialist German Attorneys)

Verz.zugel. Anw. 45
Verzeichnis der 1945 wieder zugelassenen Rechtsanwälte = Directory of attorneys readmitted in 1945

VO
Verordnung = Regulation/Ordinance

Vorst.Mitgl.
Vorstandsmitglied = Board member

VZ 39
Volkszählung, 17.5.1939 = Census, 05/17/1939

Walk
Walk, Joseph: Kurzbiographien zur Geschichte der Juden 1918-1945, s. Quellenverzeichnis = Walk, Joseph: Short biographies on the history of the Jews 1918-1945, see Bibliography

Wissenschaftl. Hum.Kom.
Wissenschaftlich-Humanitäres Komitee = Scientific and Humanitarian Committee

WJC
World Jewish Congress

WK I
Erster Weltkrieg = First World War

Wolf, BFS
Wolf, Biographische Forschung und Sozialgeschichte e.V.

WZB
Wissenschaftszentrum Berlin = Berlin Social Science Center

WZO
World Zionist Organization

Yad Vashem
Nationale Gedenkstätte des Staates Israel, Yad Vashem, Archiv, Benno Cohn Collection = National Memorial of the State of Israel, Yad Vashem, Archive, Benno Cohn Collection

# Notes

1    Insofar as the international additions
     in New York, Los Angeles and
     Canada also concerned fate of Berlin
     attorneys, the newly gained insights
     were integrated in the biographical
     list into the short biographies. - The
     supplementary research in Germany
     is published in the following
     publications: Angelika Königseder:
     Recht und nationalsozialistische
     Herrschaft. Berliner Anwälte 1933-
     1945 [Law and National Socialist
     rule. Berlin attorneys 1933-1945]
     (Forschungsprojekt des Berliner
     Anwaltsvereins = Research project
     of the Berlin Bar Association), Bonn
     2001; Anwalt- und Notarverein
     Bochum e.V.: „Zeit ohne Recht". Justiz
     in Bochum nach 1933 ["Time without
     law." Justice in Bochum after 1933],
     Bochum 2002; Hans Bergemann/
     Simone Ladwig-Winters: „Für ihn
     brach die Welt, wie er sie kannte,
     zusammen . . . ". Juristen jüdischer
     Herkunft im Landgerichtsbezirk
     Potsdam ["For him, the world,
     as he knew it, collapsed . . . ."
     Attorneys of Jewish origin in the
     district court region of Potsdam],
     Cologne 2002; Tillmann Krach
     (Editor): Paul Simon (1884-1977),
     Meine Erinnerungen - Das Leben
     des jüdischen Deutschen Paul Simon,
     Rechtsanwalt in Mainz [Paul Simon
     (1884-1977, My memories - the life of
     the German Jew Paul Simon, attorney
     in Mainz], Sonderheft der Mainzer
     Geschichtsblätter [Special issue of the
     Mainz history sheets], Mainz 2003;
     Simone Ladwig-Winters: Gebrochene
     Karrieren und Lebenswege. Zum
     Schicksal jüdischer Anwälte nach
     1933 [Broken careers and life paths.
     On the fate of Jewish attorneys after
     1933], BRAK-Mitteilungen 2003
     [BRAK reports 2003], S. 102; Heinz-
     Jürgen Schneider/Erika Schwarz/
     Josef Schwarz: Die Rechtsanwälte der
     Roten Hilfe. Politische Strafverteidiger
     in der Weimarer Republik [The
     attorneys of the "Rote Hilfe." Political
     defense attorneys in the Weimar
     Republic]. Bonn 2002; Heiko Morisse:
     Jüdische Rechtsanwälte in Hamburg

     – Ausgrenzung und Verfolgung
     im NS-Staat [Jewish attorneys in
     Hamburg - Exclusion and Persecution
     in the Nazi State], Hamburg
     2003; Barbara Dölemeyer: „Dem
     deutschen Volksgenossen der deutsche
     Rechtswahrer! Dem Juden der jüdische
     Konsulent!" [To the German national
     comrade the German attorney! To
     the Jew the Jewish consultant], and
     Simone Ladwig-Winters: Anwalt
     ohne Recht [Attorneys without rights]
     (Frankfurt), both in: "Broschüre zur
     Festveranstaltung zum 125-jährigen
     Bestehen der RAK und des OLG
     Frankfurt am Main am 1. Oktober
     2004" [Brochure on the occasion of
     the 125th anniversary of the RAK
     and the OLG Frankfurt am Main on
     October 1, 2004];
     Edgar Isermann/Michael Schlüter
     (Editors): Justiz und Anwaltschaft
     in Braunschweig 1879-2004,
     Braunschweig 2004 [Justice and the
     legal profession in Braunschweig
     1879-2004, Braunschweig 2004];
     Peter Landau/Rolf Rieß (Editors):
     Recht und Politik in Bayern
     zwischen Prinzregentenzeit und
     Nationalsozialismus. Die Erinnerungen
     von Philipp Loewenfeld [Law and
     politics in Bavaria between Prince
     Regent times and National Socialism.
     The memories of Philipp Loewenfeld],
     Ebelsbach 2004; Peter Landau:
     Justiz und Rechtsanwaltschaft in
     der nationalsozialistischen Diktatur
     [Justice and the legal profession in
     the National Socialist dictatorship],
     BRAK-Mitteilungen 2003 [BRAK
     reports 2003], S. 110;
     Hubert Lang: „Der Führer wünscht
     keine besonderen Maßnahmen." Das
     Ende eines deutschen Rechtsanwalts
     ["The Führer does not want special
     measures."The end of a German
     attorney], BRAK-Mitteilungen 2003
     [BRAK reports 2003], S. 113;
     Klaus Luig: „. . . weil er nicht arischer
     Abstammung ist." Jüdische Juristen
     in Köln während der NS-Zeit [". . .
     Because he is not of Aryan descent."
     Jewish attorneys in Cologne during
     the Nazi era], Cologne 2004; Diemut

Majer: Stufen der Entrechtung jüdischer und politisch missliebiger Anwälte in Deutschland 1933-1945 [Levels of deprivation of Jewish and politically unpopular attorneys in Germany 1933-1945] in: Jahrbuch der Juristischen Zeitgeschichte, Band 5 [Yearbook of Legal History, vol. 5] (2003/2004), edited by Thomas Vormbaum, Berlin 2004, S. 711 ff.; Hinrich Rüping: Rechtsanwälte im Bezirk Celle während des Nationalsozialismus [Attorneys in the Celle district during National Socialism] (Zwischenbericht zum Projekt der Rechtsanwaltskammer Celle = Interim report on the project of the Celle Bar Association), in: Mitteilungen der RAK Celle Mai 2004 [Reports of the Celle RAK], abridged version in AnwBl 2004, S. 300; Cologne Bar Association (Editor): Juristen ohne Recht – Schicksale jüdischer Juristen in Köln, Bonn und Aachen in der NS-Zeit [Attorneys without rights - fates of Jewish attorneys in Cologne, Bonn and Aachen in the Nazi era] (Ausstellungskatalog = exhibition catalog), Köln o.J.; Marion Röwekamp: Juristinnen. Lexikon zu Leben und Werk [Female attorneys. Lexicon on their lives and work]. Baden-Baden 2005; Martina Schröder-Teppe: Wenn Unrecht zu Recht wird … Das Schicksal jüdischer Rechtsanwälte im Bezirk der Rechtsanwaltskammer Kassel nach 1933 [If injustice becomes law . . . The fate of Jewish attorneys in the district of the Kassel Bar Association after 1933], Gudensberg-Gleichen 2006; Reinhard Weber: Das Schicksal der jüdischen Rechtsanwälte in Bayern nach 1933 [The fate of Jewish attorneys in Bavaria after 1933], Munich, 2006. – at this point, the in-depth research on the fate of Jewish judges and prosecutors is mentioned, which in some points allowed conclusions on the situation of attorneys. Hans Bergemann/ Simone Ladwig-Winters: Richter und Staatsanwälte jüdischer Herkunft in Preußen im Nationalsozialismus.

Eine Dokumentation [Judges and prosecutors of Jewish origin in Prussia during National Socialism. A documentation]. Cologne, 2004.

2 Die ergänzenden Informationen, die sich aus den Gesprächen am Rande der Konferenz ergaben, sind in den Kurzbiografien mit „Konf. 99" gekennzeichnet [The supplemental information that emerged from the discussions at the margins of the conference can be found in the short biographies marked with "Conf. 99."]

3 Only in three individual cases did applicants manage to be admitted as attorneys despite the conflicting legal regulations. These three cases were included because the classification as "non-Aryan" was always known here.

4 Simone Ladwig-Winters: „Wer hier photographiert, kommt in Haft . . . ." ["Anyone who photographs here, is imprisoned . . . "], in: Janos Frecot (Editor), Erich Salomon, „Mit Frack und Linse durch Politik und Gesellschaft", Photographien 1928-1938 ["With tailcoat and lens through politics and society,", photographs 1928-1938], Munich 2004.

5 This is especially true for the latest commemorative books: Kárny, Miroslav/Blodigová, Alexandra (Editors): Theresienstädter Gedenkbuch. Die Opfer der Judentransporte aus Deutschland nach Theresienstadt 1942-1945 [Theresienstadt memorial book. The victims of the Jewish transports from Germany to Theresienstadt 1942-1945], Prague 2000; Scheffler, Wolfgang/Schulle, Diana: Buch der Erinnerung. Die ins Baltikum deportierten deutschen, österreichischen und tschechoslowakischen Juden [Book of Remembrance. The German, Austrian and Czechoslovak Jews deported to the Baltics]; edited by Volksbund Deutsche Kriegsgräberfürsorge e.V./Riga-Komitee der deutschen Städte together

with Stiftung Neue Synagoge Berlin – Centrum Judaicum/Gedenkstätte Haus der Wannsee-Konferenz. Munich 2003; Bundesarchiv Koblenz: Gedenkbuch. Opfer der Verfolgung der Juden unter der nationalsozialistischen Gewaltherrschaft in Deutschland 1933-1945 [German Federal Archives Koblenz: Memorial Book. Victim of the persecution of Jews under National Socialist dictatorship in Germany 1933-1945]. 2nd expanded edition, Berlin 2006.

6    Hessisches Staatsarchiv, G 21 A 1098/2, Vorläufige Aufstellung über die Anwälte Preußens, o.D., Kammergerichtsbezirk: Anwälte insgesamt: 3890, „Arier": 1892, „Juden" [Hessian State Archive, G 21 A 1098/2, Preliminary list of the attorneys of Prussia, o.D., Supreme Court district: total attorneys: 3890, "Aryan": 1892, "Jews"]: 1998.

7    Göppinger (1990), footnote 169, referring to Güstrow, Dietrich: Tödlicher Alltag [Deadly daily routine], Berlin 1981, p. 9. This circumstance made the search considerably more difficult because, e.g., in the business directory, these attorneys were often not listed.

8    However, this number cannot be considered certain, but only as an approximation. The examination of the documents relating to ancestry took a long time, without any clear classification being possible in all individual cases. Even in the case of attorneys who died in 1933, it can not be said with certainty whether they were to be considered Jewish or non-Jewish.

9    Report of the board of the Bar Association in Berlin on the financial year 1932, p. 6.

10    Of the major German cities, only Frankfurt a. Main has a comparably high share of 45.8%, s. Dölemeyer (2004), p. 129.

11    Richarz, Monika (1982), p. 17. Accordingly, the Berlin Jewish community was by far the largest in Germany. If one considers the other large cities in the German Reich, then the Frankfurt municipality followed with 26,158 and the Breslauer municipality with 20,202 members. Nonetheless, Berlin, with a percentage of the Jewish minority in the total population of 3.8%, ranked behind Frankfurt with a share of 4.7%.

12    For details, see Grab, Walter (1991), p. 9 ff.

13    Strenge (1996), p. 151 ff.

14    The former training course differed from the later defined two-stage training course (study until the first state examination, legal traineeship up to the second state examination, after passing the qualification as a judge).

15    Strenge, p.155; in addition to this: Fraenkel, Ernst: Zur Soziologie der Klassenjustiz [On the sociology of class justice], Berlin 1927.

16    "In the age of religious anti-Semitism, baptism was seen as a prerequisite for equal rights and advancement." This was the term used in 1936 for the keyword "baptism" in Philo-Lexikon. Handbuch des Jüdischen Wissens [Philo-lexicon. Handbook of Jewish knowledge], Berlin 1936, p. 747.

17    Whereby regional differences, e.g. in comparison to Breslau or Kassel, where the local Gauleitung played a much bigger role, should not be ignored. In Berlin, the Gauleitung, due to the status of the city as a capital of the Reich and its size, did not occupy a position of equal status in 1933. Nevertheless, the demographic peculiarities increased the special status. Thus, the central guidelines on exclusion could not be implemented immediately given the large number of integrated Jewish residents.

18    At that time, the district of the Bar Association in Berlin went beyond the boundaries of the borough of Berlin. It also included parts of the districts of Beeskow-Storkow, Jüterbog, Luckenwalde, Niederbarnim, Oberbarnim, Osthavelland, Westhavelland and Teltow. The municipal court districts outside the borough of Berlin were: Alt-Landsberg, Bernau, Kalkberge, Königs Wusterhausen, Liebenwalde, Mittenwalde, Nauen, Oranienburg, Strausberg, Trebbin and Zossen. The attorneys of Jewish origin settled here were not included in the documentation.

19    The spelling of the terms "non-Jewish" and "non-Aryan" varied within the twelve years of National Socialism. In the following, the presentation adapts to the chronologically different spellings.

20    Reichsgesetzblatt [Reich Law Gazette], 1933, Part 1, p. 195.

21    Part of the documents of the Bar Association, which had its headquarters at Schöneberger Ufer 36 (today No. 67), was destroyed in bomb attacks in 1943. Compare for this purpose: File collection of the Darmstadt Higher Regional Court (OLG), concerning Bar Associations, Az. 3171 E 3, Hess. StA Darmstadt G 28 H No. 976. The surviving or reconstituted part was evacuated shortly before the end of the war to a church. The church burned down in the last days of the war.

22    Listed in the biographical section in each case: lists of representation prohibitions of 04/25/1933 with various supplements; the weekly published „Justiz-Ministerialblätter"(justice ministerial gazettes), which operated as from September 1933 under the names „Preußische Justiz "[Prussian Justice] and later as „Deutsche Justiz" [German Justice], furthermore the so-called list of 10/15/1933 (only

for authorities), in the following indicated with: "li", Brandenburg State Central Archives; List 36: a list listing all Jewish attorneys (with various endorsements); Berlin National Archive; List Mischl.36: a 1936 compiled list of "Mischlinge" (mixed-race persons) with detailed information on their family relationships, their religious affiliation and their service during the First World War, also Berlin National Archive, as well as various lists of consultants and the lists of those who were admitted again after 1945 as attorneys and notaries.

23    Bundesarchiv, Abt. Lichterfelde (BArch); this extensive file includes the index cards of former employees of the Reich Ministry of Justice. Since all attorneys completed a training in a state department during their training and their subsequent establishment also had to be taken note of by the Ministry of Justice, these references to personnel records are handed down here.

24    Representation ban in accordance with § 91 b Paragraphs 2-3 of the RAO, on the basis of § 5 Paragraph 1 of the implementation regulations of 04/25/1933, JMBl. 33, p. 127.

25    The information content of the index cards is very different. On some there is only the name, the indication whether solely admitted as an attorney or as an attorney and notary, sometimes without reference to the city; in other cases, the card provides information about the date of birth and even religious affiliation. In the personnel files of the Reich Ministry of Justice, the master data sheet usually contains information about the date and place of birth, the date of any doctorate, military dates, dates of examinations undertaken and, if necessary, about the deletion. However, personnel files have not been handed down for all persons.

26    Only in the case of multiple occurring names in a court, the first name was inserted in brackets.

27 Wolf, Kerstin/Wolf, Frank: Biographische Forschungen und Sozialgeschichte e.V., now also accessible on the Internet, www.reichsfluchtsteuer.de.

28 This was a project commissioned by the Senator for Cultural Affairs of the Free University of Berlin, whose aim was to include all those who were persecuted in an anti-Semitic fashion in Berlin after 1933. The names of the murdered were published: Memorial Book of Berlin of the Jewish victims of National Socialism. "Your names will never be forgotten!"published by the Central Institute for Social Science Research of the Free University of Berlin on behalf of the Senator for Cultural Affairs (1995). The entire file, which was created as part of the research on the memorial book, contains information on around 170,000 people who have been defined and persecuted as Jews. This file is based on the evaluation of numerous transmissions, e.g. that of the Reich Office of Genealogy, foreign currency documents and other holdings of the Chief Finance President. One copy of the file is in the Landesarchiv (National Archive), another in the Centrum Judaicum. The total file is referred to below as BG.

29 Most of these memoirs were written in connection with a Harvard University competition in 1940, largely initiated by Prof. Hartshore. As enlightening as the presentations were up to that point in time, they were mostly conclusive: they did not provide information about the lives of those persons after 1939.– Another source: Prof. Ernest H. Stiefel, NY, former Mannheim attorney, now deceased, Adjunct Professor of Law at New York Law School. Stiefel repeatedly dealt with the fates of Jewish-German attorneys, see amongst others the same/Mecklenburg, Frank (1991). Otto Sandrock has provided a biographical profile of Stiefel, see Juristen im Porträt: Verlag und Autoren in 4 Jahrzehnten. Festschrift

. zum 225jährigen Jubiläum des Verlages C.H.Beck [Attorneys in profile: publishers and authors in 4 decades. Commemorative publication for the 225th anniversary of the publisher C.H.Beck]. Munich 1988, pages 683-686.

30 So in Jerusalem, where the former Berlin attorney Yaakov Rosenthal lived until September 1997.

31 For the handing over of three albums with writing and photos, I thank the attorney and notary Jürgen Naatz, the grandson of Willy Naatz, very sincerely. The photos are reproduced in the biographical directory of the persons concerned.

32 Der Kurier [The Courier], 04/01/1953.

33 Güstrow (1981), pages 12/13.

34 Klemperer (1947).

35 Interview with Jürgen X., 08/23/1997, Berlin.

36 "Zachor! - Remember!" Title of a study on memory and historiography by Yerushalmi, Yosef Hayim (1988).

37 Der Tagesspiegel, 08/26/1997, in an article related to Alfred Kerr.

38 It remains unclear whether Berlin can be described as a metropolis in comparison to other European capitals. For this discussion, reference is made to other authors: s. et al Alter (1993).

39 Fritz Oliven (05/10/1874 Wrocław - 06/30/1956 Porto Alegre, Brazil), had studied law under pressure from his family, is said to have obtained his doctorate in Leipzig in 1895, but wrote passionately in rhymes. In this way he became a well-known author, published e.g. the "Willi" books, but also the operetta libretto for "Der Vetter aus Dingsda" [The cousin from whatchamacallit] and texts for the Haller-Revue; from Oliven comes

the saying: "Berlin is still Berlin;" in 1926 he became president of the Association of German Songwriters, in the same year board member of GEMA. After the seizure of power by the National Socialists, he lost the position at GEMA, he did not seem to have requested his readmission as an attorney. With the aggravation of the persecution of the Jews, Oliven decided to leave Germany with his family. In 1939 the family traveled to Paris, later to Porto Alegre, where they arrived on 03/02/1939. In 1951 Oliven published his autobiography entitled "A cheerful life." He died in 1956 in Porto Alegre at the age of 82. It now seems undeniable that O. returned his admission as an attorney before 1933, so he is no longer listed in the biographical directory.

40 Schild (1988), p. 125, which refers to a statement made by Emil Julius Gumbel in 1922; probably in: Die Justiz [The Justice].

41 Already in the 1920s Emil Julius Gumbel evaluated numerous methods: Vom Fememord zur Reichskanzlei [From the Fememord to the Reich Chancellery], new edition, Heidelberg 1962, p. 46.

42 Heiber (1996), p. 111.

43 Friedensburg (1946), p. 253.

44 Hannover inter alia (1977), 124 ff. to Scheidemann; S.112 ff. to Rathenau; in contrast to the evaluation of the prosecution: Sabrow (1994) as well as catalog of the exhibition "Die Extreme berühren sich" [The extremes touch] Walther Rathenau 1867-1922, the same, pages 221-235.

45 Heiber (1996), p.. 70 ff. and 113.

46 See each case in the biographical directory.

47 Bosl inter alia (1973).

48 Interview with the son of a former attorney, 1998.

49 Frey (1960).

50 Sling (Paul Schlesinger) (1969), p. 21 ff.

51 After his high school examination the pupil Krantz studied German studies, sociology and education and joined Communist circles. In 1931 he published his novel „Die Mietskaserne" [The tenement]; in 1933 he left Germany and went to France, from there he managed to flee to the United States in 1939. In addition to his journalistic work for the NBC, he worked from 1949-1963 as a professor of literature in Oklahoma and Milwaukee. In 1971 he returned to Germany, he died in 1983. After the trial he had adopted the name Ernst Erich Noth. - The student murder trial served as a model for the film "What is the use of love in thought" (2003).

52 Frey (1960), p. 352.

53 Frey (1960), p. 381.

54 See the detailed profile of Jungfer (1988): Max Alsberg. Verteidigung als ethische Mission [Defense as an ethical mission]; in: Kritische Justiz [Critical Justice] (published)(1988), pages 141-152. Meanwhile, a plaque was attached to Alsberg's former home in Grunewald.

55 Frey (1960), p. 267; although the purport is not clear, this plea was finally held in a courtroom and Alsberg must have most certainly aroused envy due to the recognition he received for his academic achievements.

56 The list of publications is very long, important works were: Justizirrtum und Wiederaufnahme [Miscarriage of justice and recovery](1913); Die Untersuchungshaft [Pretrial detention], commentary with Adolf Lobe (1927); Die Philosophie des Verteidigers [The philosophy of the defender] (1930);

Der Beweisantrag im Strafprozeß [The request for evidence in the criminal case] (1930).

57    Apfel (1931), second semi-annual volume, p. 758.

58    Apfel quoted from Krach (1991), p. 110.

59    Die Weltbühne [The world stage], 1929, 1st volume, p. 407.

60    Krach (1991), p. 136/138 ff.

61    Krach (1991), p. 136.

62    Apfel (1934), p. 166.

63    Gosewinkel (1991), p. 43.

64    Vossische Zeitung, 12/05/1930: „George Grosz freigesprochen" [George Grosz acquitted] (Inquit).

65    Grab (1983), p. 189.

66    For example, the court of honor in 1932 was inter alia staffed with the chairman, attorney Ferdinand Samoje, attorney Paul Marcuse and attorney Ernst Maass, all listed in the following biographical directory; see Personnel file of attorney Walter Paust, BArch R 3001/70431.

67    Gronemann: Tohuwabohu, 2nd edition, p. 129.

68    Toury (1966).

69    Krach (1991), p. 42.

70    Krach (1991), p. 43.

71    Krach (1991), pages 43/44.

72    Ernst Fraenkel: Chronik [Chronicle], 01/09/1933, in: Gesammelte Schriften [Collected works], v.1, published by Hubertus Buchstein, Baden-Baden 1999, pages 606 ff.

73    Since these data could not be systematically recorded, they were

listed, if they were to be taken from the documents, provided that they were remarkably good.

74    The Weimar Constitution, Article 109 RV, stipulated that no such titles should be awarded. This naturally applied to Prussia as well; see Ostler (1971), page 195 f.; for the general development of the office of the attorney and notary see Wiedemann, Wolfgang: Preußische Justizreform und die Entwicklung zum Anwaltsnotariat in Altpreußen (1700-1849) [Prussian legal reform and the development of the office of the attorney and notary in Old Prussia (1700-1849)], Cologne 2003.

75    In the first edition of this book, the number of Jewish attorneys has been specified even higher. In the process personal details were relied upon, which, however, could not be proven by the sources. These women, who were no longer considered, were attorneys who worked in the office of their husbands without being admitted to the Bar.

76    See short biography in the following biographical index.

77    See Schneider, Schwarz, Schwarz (2002), pages 238/9.

78    "Assimilation" is not uncontroversial in literature, it is often supplemented by the concept of acculturation as a developmental precursor. Herbert A. Strauss has dealt extensively with this problem, as has Shulamit Volkov (1983), pages 331-348.

79    So Julius Seligsohn in his personal file, see biographical directory.

80    See: Simone Ladwig-Winters: Freiheit und Bindung. Zur Geschichte der Jüdischen Reformgemeinde zu Berlin [Freedom and attachment. On the history of the Jewish reform community in Berlin], Berlin 2004.

81   See Biographical Directory.

82   Dawidowicz (1979), p. 161.

83   Krach (1991), p. 166.

84   The report of Fritz Ball can be found in a publication of his brother Kurt, who was also an attorney and later called himself Kurt Jacob Ball Kaduri: Das Leben der Juden in Deutschland im Jahre 1933. Ein Zeitbericht [The life of the Jews in Germany in 1933. A time report]. Frankfurt/M. 1963; quoted by Schilde et al. (1996) p. 56 ff.

85   It is now known why the four men of the "Brigade Ehrhardt" had been arrested. The Brigade Ehrhardt had surrendered out of conviction on the side of the "national uprising." Only in 1934 did Ehrhardt quarrel with Hitler and fled to Switzerland.

86   The deletion of the admission of Günther Joachims is published on p. 281 of JMBl. 33.

87   For details: Müller (1988), p. 180 ff, here 189/190.

88   Knobloch (1993), pages 29/30.

89   Hanns Kerrl (1887–12/14/1941).

90   It is often cited in excerpts in secondary literature. Entirely reprinted in the NS publication by Sievert Lorenzen: Juden und die Justiz [Jews and justice], edited on behalf of the Reich Minister of Justice, Berlin, Hamburg, 2nd, partially expanded edition 1943, pages 175-177.

91   Knobloch (1993), pages 31/32.

92   Blau (1952), pages19/20; in the quotes given below, unlike in the original, the umlauts of the German spelling were adjusted.

93   Reference file Erich Meyer: Kerrl letter, transmitted by the president of the Berlin Court of Appeals, 04/06/1933.

94   On the basis of the decree of the RJM dated 04/05/1933, I 6557.

95   Personnel files, see BArch R 3001/68065, pages 10/11 dated 04/08/1933.

96   Blue has, as the photos show, reproduced the events aptly. The processes described in the application for re-admission will not have occurred until after April 6, 1933, because only then were the requirements that the individual had to meet announced. In addition, the references to sources on the photo documents (Süddeutscher Verlag) do not point to April 1, 1933, since otherwise it would probably have been explicitly noted.

97   See Krach (1991), p. 205 ff.

98   Minuth (1983), doc. 93, pt. 8, p. 323.

99   Minuth (1983), footnote 42.

100  Hubatsch (1966), p. 375 (doc. 109).

101  Reichsgesetzblatt [Reich Law Gazette], 1933, part I, p. 195.

102  Reference file Erich Meyer: transcript of Freisler's statement of 04/11/1933.

103  Personnel files, see BArch R 3001, PA 56082, p. 11.

104  In the biographical directory, therefore, the notion that someone successfully passed the re-admission test procedure is taken to be "re-admitted."

105  JMBl. 1933, p. 127.

106  Reference file Erich Meyer: Telefonnotiz, 29.4.1933.

107  This number is to be understood only as an indication, since the lists that were found, once from the stock of AG Köpenick, LAB AG Köpenick A Rep 343, as well as from the stock of AG -Tempelhof-Kreuzberg, see Jungfer unbound collection, significantly differ

108 In these cases addressed directly to the Ministry or the Chamber.

109 Such a card was in the estate of Ernst Fraenkel; copy in the possession of the author.

110 Krach (1991), table 4, p. 418.

111 For example, the brothers Ball, after a brother was released from the "wild" concentration camp in General-Pape-Str., see on the one hand, the personal details in the biographical directory, on the other hand Schilde et al. (1996), pages 55-71. The same applies to the already murdered attorney Günther Joachim.

112 His memoirs have been published with commentary notes by his son: Bendix (1983).

113 Bendix (1983), in the place indicated

114 Bendix (1983), p. 192.

115 Bendix (1983), p. 195.

116 Bendix (1983), p. 193.

117 Steinitz had filed for readmission, could also claim the exemption for "frontline fighters", but the registration office had informed the bar association about his absence. The bar association, in turn, informed the president of the court of appeals, which forwarded the information to the Prussian Ministry of Justice, with the result that the license was not re-issued.

118 Krach (1991), p. 216.

119 Krach (1991), p. 81 with reference to an article of the BZ at noon on 01/16/1933.

*At the top, above 108:*
from one another. Today it is no longer possible to determine all cases in which a prohibition of representation has been issued.

120 GStA Rep. 84a 20155, p. 89 ff.

121 Göppinger (1990), p. 59; also: Jungfer, Gerhard/König, Stefan (as publisher for the Berlin Bar Association): 125 Jahre Rechtsanwaltskammer Berlin – Jubiläumsschrift [125 years Berlin Bar Association - anniversary publication], Berlin 2006, p. 187 ff. as well as p. 224 ff.

122 Krach (1991), p. 223

123 Krach (1991), p. 200 ff.

124 Krach (1991), pages 201/202, with the term "participation" he refers to Oppenhoff, Walter: Erfahrungen eines Kölner Anwalts [Experiences of a Cologne attorney]; in: 100 Jahre Kölner Anwaltverein, Festschrift [100 years Cologne Attorney Association, anniversary], published by von O. Bussenius, M. Hüttemann, G. Schwend, (1987), p. 188.

125 According to an interview with his daughter on 05/04/1998, Berlin.

126 Personnel files, BArch R 3001/ 55127.

127 Personnel files, BArch R 3001/ 50119.

128 See biographical directory.

129 Conversation with Erna Proskauer, April 1997.

130 Hereafter abbreviated as * li.

131 Uhlig (1956), p. 115 ff.; Ladwig-Winters (1997/I), p. 97 ff.

132 The astute analysis by Ernst Fraenkel may be used as proof for this, which speaks of the emergence of a "normative state" and a "state of instrumental measures" in Der Doppelstaat (written 1984-1940 in US exile under the title "The Dual State"). This work, as a contemporary work with enormous analytical precision, exposes the structures and mechanisms of action of National Socialism.

133 Broszat/Frei (1996), p. 88 ff.

134 See communications on labor law decisions in various editions of the newspaper of the Centralverein (CV).

135 The problem of the honorary court proceedings still awaits a closer examination.

136 See Krach (1991), p. 374 ff.

137 LAB, Rep. 68 Acc. 3017, Lenk.

138 LAB, Rep. 68 Acc. 3017, Goldberg.

139 Narrated in Solon's memoirs at the Leo Baeck Institute, NY, Memoirs ME 607.

140 See Bergemann/Ladwig-Winters (2004), as well as Doehring (1988), p. 343, 346.

141 For example, through the creation of trainee training camps, such as the "Hanns Kerrl camp" at Jüterbog.

142 Schmitt, Carl: Staat, Bewegung, Volk [State, movement, nation], 1933, p. 46; quoted from: Müller (1987), p. 80.

143 Doehring (1988), pages 341-349.

144 Doehring (1988), pages 343, 346.

145 Diederichsen (1988), pages 495-510.

146 Göppinger (1990), p. 92.

147 Blau (1952), pages 27/28; see also Göppinger (1990), p. 92.

148 There are no further details about the birth date of Neumann, he mentions that he was a member of the First World War (war volunteer) and was awarded the Iron Cross 1st Class. In 1939 he had to flee to Shanghai.

149 Neumann, Siegfried (1978), p. 89.

150 Broszat/Frei (1996), p. 225.

151 BArch RWM 31.01 P 13862, doc.

497, invitation to the meeting on 08/20/1935; accordingly: Hilberg (1982), p. 31/32.

152 Documented inter alia in the exhibition of the Deutsche Bibliothek Frankfurt in cooperation with the Leo Baeck Institute, New York: Die jüdische Emigration aus Deutschland [1985] [Jewish Emigration from Germany (1985)], catalog, p. 68.

153 Hilberg (1982), p. 56 ff.

154 Lösener is even valued favorably today, see Süddeutsche Zeitung, 06/27/1998.

155 The meticulously differentiated variations are explained in: Meyer, Beate (1999), p. 96 ff.

156 The "racial" definitions related to the religious affiliation of the grandparent generation were therefore not based on the "blood" as always represented in the general principles: see Frei, in: Broszat et al. (1996). pages 124-137, here: p. 128. The illogicality of principles should make the comment of Stuckart-Globke (Globke later became State Secretary in Adenauer's Chancellery) feasible, but that could not succeed in every case, the construction led to "mysterious racial mutations" (Friedländer): "If a wife converted to the Jewish religion reconverted as a widow and had children in a second marriage with an 'Aryan,' they would have a Jewish ancestor in the family tree," see Meyer (199), p. 101.

157 Fraenkel (1984), p. 63.

158 The law is still valid today, albeit in a modified form, see Schorn, Hubert: Rechtberatungsmißbrauchsgesetz [Legal Advice Abuse Act], Darmstadt, Nürnberg 1957.

159 Reifner (1979), p. 33.

160 Krach (1991), p. 336.

161 Göppinger (1990), pages 126/127; in addition to attorneys, members of the so-called legal front included nearly 15,000 judges and prosecutors, 5,800 notaries, over 10,000 administrative attorneys, nearly 400 university teachers and more than 80,000 individual members.

162 Bendix (1985), p. 197 ff.

163 Bendix (1985), p. 203.

164 Göppinger (1991), p. 127.

165 The 2nd Ordinance (VO) on Reich Citizenship Law of 12/20/1935 (RGBl. I, 1524) as well as the decree of the RMdInnern (Reich Ministry of the Interior) of the same day (DJ 1936, p. 98) regulated the departure of Jewish officials from office; in the formal justification for leaving, notaries were not classified as civil servants but as bearers of a public office; see Krach, p. 384 ff.

166 Blau (1952), p. 35.

167 The Reichsnotarordnung (Reich Notary Ordinance) of 02/13/1937 (RGBl. I, 191) stipulated that an official should be dismissed if he was not "German or related blood"; the Jewish notaries had already been deprived of admission at this time.

168 Haase, Berthold, Erinnerungen, Leo Baeck Institute, New York, Memoirs.

169 Ostler (1983), p. 55.

170 Report of the grandson, Prof. Grenville, February 1997, Jerusalem.

171 Report of the son, Prof. Coper, September 1997, Berlin.

172 Blau (1952), p. 30.

173 This is first stated in the decision of the Reichsgericht (Supreme Court of the German Reich) of June 27, 1936; documented by Hofer (1960),

pp. 287-289, with reference to J.A. Seufferts Archiv für Entscheidungen der obersten Gerichte in den deutschen Staaten [Archive for decisions of the highest courts in the German states]. (1937) p.65 ff. Ernst Fraenkel already acknowledged this decision in 1941 in „Der Doppelstaat," p. 126.

174 Broszat et al. (1996), p. 237.

175 Barkai (1986), p. 126.

176 Göppinger (1990), pages 94/95, footnote 186.

177 According to official mention in the communications of the Reich Bar Association of 12/01/1938, p. 218 f.; Göppinger (1990), p. 95, footnote 187, mentions only 671 referring to Ostler.

178 Neumann, Siegfried, Memoirs, Leo Baeck Institute, p. 64.

179 Hilberg (1982), p. 94.

180 Broszat et al. (1996), p. 247, Scheffler (1960), p. 30.

181 Broszat et al. (1996), p. 251.

182 Part of the minutes of this conference has been handed down and used as evidence by the International Military Tribunal (IMT) in Nuremberg; see IMT PS -1816.

183 Blasius (1991), pp. 121-137, here: 122 with comprehensive sources and references.

184 Reference file Erich Meyer, letter of March 20, 1936, President of the RAK to every attorney.

185 General information on this see Gruchmann (1988), p. 188/189.

186 Puhlmann had his office in 1932 at Kaiserplatz 7 (today's Bundesplatz) in Berlin-Wilmersdorf (according to entry in the branch section of the 1933 address book.

187 Jochheim (1993).

188 Communication by Erna Proskauer to the author, 08/03/1997

189 Rumpf (1926), p. 84.

190 Implementation regulation of the Reich Ministry of Justice dated 10/17/1938, DJ 38, p. 1665, I, No. 1

191 The documents for admission as a "consultant" are not part of the personnel files of the RJM. They must have been taken elsewhere, and seemingly got lost.

192 Morisse, Heiko (2003), p. 58.

193 BArch R 3001, PA (Personnel files) Manfred Simon, 76569, p. 57.

194 Implementation regulation of the Reich Ministry of Justice, dated 10/17/1938, DJ 38, p. 1666, III, see also Gruchmann (1988). p. 182.

195 Not a single one of these signs for Berlin have survived.

196 The list of compulsory names was given by the Reich Ministry of the Interior, see Implementing Regulation to the 2nd Regulation on the Implementation of the Act on the Modification of Surnames and First Names of 08/17/1938 (RGBl. I, 1044). Regarding the problem of anti-Semitism, which has long been reflected in the naming, see Bering (1992).

197 Solon, LBI, New York, Memoirs, see 99/100.

198 Implementation provisions to §§ 5 and 14 of the 5th Regulation on the Reich Citizenship Act, Implementation Regulation of the Reich Ministry of Justice dated 10/13/1938, DJ 38, p. 1665.

199 In individual personal files of the Bar Association of those who survived,

there are some clues. So Dr. Hans Friedeberg declared to have earned between RM 18,000 and RM 22,000 in 1933; by 1939 this had been reduced to RM 2,100 p.a.; it also played a role that Friedeberg had been arrested in 1938 in the context of the "November action" and brought to Sachsenhausen and had already suffered loss of revenue for this reason. After his release he was said to have managed to earn more as a "consultant" again, so that he had recorded revenue in the amount of RM 12,000 for the year 1944. In any case, the information about the specified dramatic financial collapse in 1939 seems reliable; please refer to the personnel file of Dr. Hans Friedeberg, LAB RAK Berlin.

200 Implementation regulations of the Reich Ministry of Justice dated 10/17/1938, DJ 38, p. 1666, III, Nos. 1-6.

201 Dr. Katz had changed her name to Hannacha Katz so that the name suffix "Sara" was omitted.

202 LAB, Rep 68 Acc. 3209, no. 68.

203 BLHA, OFP files Günther Wertheim, O 5210 -P II, the last surviving letter is dated 02/04/1942.

204 Whether the remuneration of the services of the "consultant assistants" in Berlin was not to be included in the expenses of the office costs, is not to be indicated by the available documents. In Hamburg this was handled in this way, see Morisse (2003), p. 62 and footnote 133 with reference to an unpublished master's thesis by Andreas Fritzsche: Vom Rechtsanwalt zum „jüdischen Konsulenten." Die institutionalisierte Entrechtung jüdischer Rechtsanwälte im Nationalsozialismus, dargestellt am Beispiel des Oberlandesgerichtsbezirks Hamburg, [From attorney to "Jewish consultant." The institutionalized deprivation of rights of Jewish attorneys under National Socialism,

illustrated by the example of the Higher Regional Court District of Hamburg]. Universität Hamburg 1997.

205    See biographical directory.

206    That must also apply to Dr. med. Kurt Jacobsohn, of whom Bruno Blau writes in his memoirs, he says that he, also a "consultant", let himself be used as an informer by the Gestapo. The threat to his own life, with which Jacobsohn presumably - according to the accusation - had been pressed to perform these services, was concrete: he was murdered in Auschwitz. See Blau (1952), p. 70.

207    Interview with his son, Prof. Coper, 09/09/1997, Berlin.

208    Interview with his son, Prof. Coper, 09/09/1997, Berlin.

209    For this information I thank Prof. Coper, who also provided me with a copy of the poem, which contains 83 stanzas in the original.

210    Zur grundsätzlichen Problematik [The fundamental problem]: Meyer, Beate (1999)

211    LAB, Rep 68 Acc 3209, ( „Liste Mschlg. 36" ["List of mixed race persons 36"]), this is a list that was compiled on 02/26/1936, listing all "mixed race" attorneys, their grandparents, frontline duty, religion and marital status.

212    Meyhöfer (1996), p. 238.

213    The situation was different for children and adolescents who were considered to be "mixed race;" they were as marginalized in schools as were the "full-blooded Jews."

214    Gruner (1996), p. 74.

215    Hilberg (1982), p. 294 ff.

216    Hilberg (1982), p. 302.

217    This post meant the supervision of the lowest department of the Reichsluftschutzbund (Reich Air Protection Corps), colloquially it was equated with the "Blockleiter", a Nazi function, which entailed the supervision and control within a block of apartments. Frequently both posts were combined (Kammer / Bartsch (1992), p. 38). How it was conducted in the present case is unknown. Only the term "block warden" is mentioned in the personnel files.

218    Wistrich (1983), see Todt.

219    LAB, RAK PA Georg Graul.

220    Information Dr. Y. Arndt, Mai 1998.

221    LAB, RAK PA Scheer.

222    The numerous regulations are depicted in: Blau (1958); Walk (1981); Gruner (1996).

223    Based on 1,404 persons, for whom details are available.

224    Meanwhile, advanced research allows more information, since a date of death was only known for 78 of these persons at the time of the first edition of this book.

225    See above for the information on the relevant commemoration books.

226    In some cases there have been multiple deportations, e.g. from Berlin to Theresienstadt and from there to Auschwitz. In these cases, the first date was used. With this information, the presentation of the memorial book, published by the Bundesarchiv [Federal Archive], was taken over. The previously used problematic term "lost" is thus no longer used.

227    Scheffler (1960), p. 93/94.

228    An example of a declaration of property can be found in Heinz Knobloch's book „Meine liebste

Mathilde"["My dearest Mathilde"], 1986, p. 193 ff. The declarations of property of the Upper Finance President Berlin have been given to the Brandenburg State Archives.

229 See biographical directory with further references.

230 Hammerschmidt (1996), p. 155.

231 See biographical directory with further references.

232 This postcard was found by the author in the estate of Willy Naatz.

233 See biographical directory.

234 See biographical directory.

235 See biographical directory.

236 Litten (1947), p. 13.

237 Litten, (1947) p. 253 ff. The largest part of Litten's estate has been given to the Federal Archives in Lichterfelde.

238 Biography of Georg Hamburger by Hartmut Ludwig in: "'Ihr Ende schaut an . . .' "[Your end is watching . . . ] Evangelische Märtyrer des 20. Jahrhunderts [Protestant martyrs of the 20th century], published by Harald Schultze/ Andreas Kurschat, Leipzig 2006.

239 Interview with Erna Proskauer on 04/10/1997, Berlin.

240 Interview with Prof. John A.S. Grenville, today inter alia Head of the English Dependence [sic] of the Leo Baeck Institute in February 1997, Jerusalem.

241 Göppinger (1990), p. 226.

242 Wolf Gruner (1995) arrives at a more differentiated evaluation, pages 229-266, here: p. 253

243 Gruner (1996), p. 14.

244 LAB, RAK, PA Werner Windscheid.

245 Information Ms. Inge Cohn-Lempert, 05/11/1998, Berlin.

246 Hans Globke was formerly responsible for International Law in the Reich Ministry of the Interior and was largely responsible for the introduction of compulsory names for Jews (1938), after 1945 he was the first city treasurer in Aachen, then ministerial director in the Federal Chancellery and from 1953 he was state secretary under Adenauer; see Hilberg, p. 53, 740;

247 LAB, RAK, PA Anita Eisner.

248 II thank Frank Flechtmann for the conveyance of the letters of Anita Eisner to Fray Hugel, which her son had stored in Riquewihr.

249 See here inter alia Michael Traub (1936).

250 Blau (1952), p. 17.

251 This generational aspect is gaining increasing attention in the literature on questions of Jewish assimilation, see inter alia: Die Extreme berühren sich [The extremes are touching] (1994); here the contribution of Shulamit Volkov: Ich bin ein Deutscher jüdischen Stammes [I am a German of the Jewish people], pages 129-138.

252 Neumann, Siegfried, Leo Baeck Institute, New York, Memoirs, p. 82; incidentally, he himself fled to Shanghai on 03/29/1939.

253 This conference took place from 07/06 - 07/15/1938 in Evian on Lake Geneva; Germany did not participate. The climate of the conference was marked by a dismissive attitude towards Jewish organizations; see Die jüdische Emigration aus Deutschland 1933-1941 [Jewish emigration from Germany 1933-1941], (1985), p. 205.

254 Solon, Memoirs, Leo Baeck Institute, New York.

255 Under the pressure of the National Socialists, a union of all German Jews came about, which was to experience various name changes in the course of time; s. et al Hilberg (1982), p. 133.

256 Strauß (1980); p. 313 f., also p. 320.

257 For example, the husband of attorney Chodziesner was also brought to Australia. The son of attorney Kallmann was also transported to Canada.

258 Ladwig-Winters (1997, I), p. 446; here one of the former co-owners and managing directors of Hermann Tietz applied for a residence permit for Switzerland and the Netherlands. For him there only one country in question, "from which one could look at Germany."

259 This also happened to Bruno Blau, who was arrested in Prague. In the end, Blau survived because he was diagnosed with a serious illness and therefore went to the Jewish Hospital in Berlin. A total of eleven attorneys who had gone abroad were assigned to the "perished" in the evaluation carried out here, because they were sometimes killed in the local camps, partially in one of the known concentration camps.

260 Meyer (1993).

261 Conversation with the daughter, Ruth Arons, 11/18/1997, Frankfurt a.M.

262 Information Ernest Stiefel, December 1996, New York.

263 New York Public Library, Dept. of Rare Books and Manuscripts; I owe the reference to Dr. Frank Mecklenburg from the Leo Baeck Institute, New York.

264 This evaluation criterion obviously flowed into the evaluation, as can be seen from the internal correspondence.

265 Am. Com. Werner Meyer file.

266 Am. Com. Fred Levy file.

267 Published in 1941 under the title "The Dual State" in New York; 1949 in German version.

268 Control Council Act No. 46 of 02/25/1947.

269 This impression is shared by the son of Dr. Coper, who reports of many refugees who could no longer live in their hometown. Prof. Coper is of the opinion that "these people lack their own experience." (Interview 9.9.1997, Berlin)

270 Davidowicz (1979), p. 161.

271 The agreement concluded on August 28, 1933 between the Jewish Agency and the Reich Ministry of Economics (RWM) regulating emigration assets. It envisaged that an emigrant acquired a house or a citrus plantation for RM 50,000 from a parent organization, e.g. Hanotea, and was then allowed to carry a showcase fee of RM 15,000. The Jewish Agency undertook in return to accept German goods in the value of the deposit amounts; see catalog of the exhibition: Die jüdische Emigration [The Jewish Emigration], p. 164.

272 In addition, the haunting description of Erna Proskauer (1996), p. 55 ff.

273 Conversation with Mr. Shimon Ullmann, attorney, February 1997, Jerusalem.

274 LAB, RAK, PA Gottfried Samter.

275 Basically, for this purpose: Kühne, NJW 1996, p. 2968 ff.

276 Felix Rosenblüth, 1887 - 1953; R. is not listed in the following biographical directory, since he went to Palestine in 1931, see. Walk (1988), p. 314.

277 Information Shimon Ullmann, February 1997, Jerusalem.

278  Sopade (1980), pages 938-940.

279  In 1997, an exhibition of the Jewish
     Museum in Martin-Gropius-Bau and a
     conference at Haus der Wannsee dealt
     with the theme, on these occasions, the
     conditions of refuge in Shanghai were
     described in detail.

280  Irmtrud Wojak dealt with aspects of
     exile in South America in 1995.

281  Alterthum, Willy, Leo Baeck Institute,
     New York, Memoirs.

282  Blasius (1991), p. 121.

283  For example, Verband Deutscher
     Waren- und Kaufhäuser e.V., see
     Ladwig-Winters (1997,I), p. 116.

284  Neumann, Leo Baeck Institute, New
     York, Memoirs, p. 63.

285  Eckert (1993), pages 34-50.

286  Hoven (1990).

287  Vogel (1995), pages 15-31, p. 27.

288  Arndt (1965), pages 176-196; p. 176.

# Sources

Bundesarchiv [Federal Archive]
R 3001, Reichsjustizministerium
Personalakten [Reich Ministry of Justice,
personnel files]
R 3001, Reichsjustizministerium,
Personalkartei [Reich Ministry of
Justice, personnel card index]
Census documents from 05/17/1939

Brandenburgisches Landeshauptarchiv,
Bornim [Brandenburg State Archives,
Bornim]
Pr Br Rep. 36 A Chief Finance President
Berlin-Brandenburg 4510, also currency
exchange

Geheimes Staatsarchiv Berlin [Secret State
Archive Berlin]
Rep. 84 a, Rep. 84a 20155

Hessisches Staatsarchiv Darmstadt [Hessian
State Archive Darmstadt]
Collection files Higher Regional Court (OLG)
Darmstadt, concerning bar associations,
Az. 3171 E 3, G 28 H No. 976

Jüdisches Museum Berlin [Jewish Museum
Berlin]
LBI, Bruno Weil, Doc. 93/3/44; Doc. Julius
Fliess

Landesarchiv Berlin [National Archive Berlin]
Complete file to the Berlin memorial book
with evaluated sources of the input lists
of the Lodz ghetto, the file of the school-
age children, the transport lists of the
Gestapo,
B Rep. 68 – Inventory of the Berlin Bar
Association
Rep. 68 Acc. 3017
Rep. 68 Acc. 3209
A Rep. 343, AG Köpenick, Vertr.V.
(Vertretungsverbote = representation
bans)
Restitution files of the former restitution
offices of Berlin

Leo Baeck Institute, New York
Alterthum, Willy, Collection; Haase,
Berthold, Erinnerungen (memoirs);
Neumann, Siegfried, Memoirs, Solon;
Bruno Weill Collection

New York Public Library
American Committee for the Guidance of
Personnel Professionel

Senatsverwaltung für Justiz, Berlin (Archiv)
[Archive of the Senate Administration for
Justice in Berlin]
Personnel files
Printed Sources
Directories
Berlin directory 1926, 1933, 1934, 1936,
1938, 1939, 1941 (with the respective
appendices, business section)
Jewish address book for Greater Berlin, 1931
edition. Reprint, Berlin 1994.

Staff and member directories

Appointment Calendar for Prussian Judicial
Officers 1933, Part 2, Berlin.
Calendar for Reich Judicial Officers for the
year 1936, 2nd part, Berlin.
Member directory of the Republican
Association of Judges

Law and regulation sheets
Judicial ministerial gazette for Prussian
legislature 1933
Preußische Justiz [Prussian Justice], from
September 1933
Deutsche Justiz [German Justice] 1935,1936,
1938
Reichsgesetzblatt [Reich Law Gazette], 1933,
1934, 1935, 1936, 1938, 1939

Commemorative books, dictionaries,
directories
Benz, Wolfgang/Graml, Hermann (Editors):
Biographisches Lexikon zur Weimarer
Republik [Biographical lexicon on the
Weimar Republic], Munich, 1988.
Biographisches Handbuch der
deutschsprachigen Emigration
[Biographical manual of German-
speaking emigration], edited by Werner
Röder and Herbert A. Strauß, vol. 1:
Politics, Economy, Public life, Munich
1980; Vol. 2: The Arts, Sciences and
Literature, Munich 1983; Vol. 3:
Complete index, Munich 1983.
Bundesarchiv Koblenz [Federal Archive
Coblenz] (Editor): Gedenkbuch – Opfer
der Verfolgung der Juden unter der
nationalsozialistischen Gewaltherrschaft

in Deutschland, 1933-1945 [Memorial
Book - Victims of the Persecution of the
Jews under National Socialist Tyranny in
Germany, 1933-1945]. 1986.

Bundesarchiv Koblenz [Federal Archive
Coblenz] (Editor): Gedenkbuch.
Opfer der Verfolgung der Juden
unter der nationalsozialistischen
Gewaltherrschaft in Deutschland 1933-
1945 [Memorial Book. Victims of the
persecution of the Jews under National
Socialist dictatorship in Germany
1933-194545]. 2nd expanded edition
Berlin 2006.

Kárny, Miroslav/Blodigová, Alexandra
(Editors): Theresienstädter Gedenkbuch.
Die Opfer der Judentransporte aus
Deutschland nach Theresienstadt 1942-
1945 [Theresienstadt memorial book.
The victims of the Jewish transports
from Germany to Theresienstadt 1942-
1945]. Prague 2000.

Lowenthal, Ernst G.: Juden in Preußen [Jews
in Prussia]. Berlin 1981.

Philo-Lexikon. Handbuch des jüdischen
Wissens [Philo lexicon. Handbook of
Jewish knowledge]. Berlin 1936.

Scheffler, Wolfgang/Schulle, Diana: Buch
der Erinnerung. Die ins Baltikum
deportierten deutschen, österreichischen
und tschechoslowakischen Juden [Book
of Remembrance. The German, Austrian
and Czechoslovakian Jews deported to
the Baltics]; edited by the Volksbund
Deutsche Kriegsgräberfürsorge
e.V. / Riga-Komitee der deutschen
Städte together with Stiftung Neue
Synagoge Berlin - Centrum Judaicum/
Gedenkstätte Haus der Wannsee-
Konferenz. Munich 2003.

Schultze, Harald/Kurschat, Andreas (Editors):
„Ihr Ende schaut an. . . "] Evangelische
Märtyrer des 20. Jahrhunderts [Your
end is watching. Evangelical martyrs of
the 20th century]. Leipzig 2006.

Schumacher, Martin: M.d.R. Die
Reichstagsabgeordneten der
Weimarer Republik in der Zeit des
Nationalsozialismus. Politische
Verfolgung, Emigration und
Ausbürgerung 1933-1945 [M.d.R.
The Reichstag delegates of the Weimar
Republic in the time of National
Socialism. Political persecution,

emigration and expatriation 1933-1945].
Düsseldorf 1991.

Stockhorst, Erich: 5000 Köpfe. Wer war wer
im 3. Reich [Who was who in the 3rd
Reich]. 2nd ed. Kiel 1985.

Vor die Tür gesetzt. Im Nationalsozialismus
verfolgte Berliner Stadtverordnete
und Magistratsmitglieder 1933-1945.
Katalog zur gleichnamigen Ausstellung,
30.9.-30.11.2005 [Shown the door.
Berlin city councilors and magistrates
persecuted during National Socialism,
1933-1945. Catalog for the exhibition
of the same name, 09/30/2005 -
11/30/2005]. Berlin 2006.

Walk, Joseph: Kurzbiographien zur
Geschichte der Juden 1918-1945 [Short
biographies on the history of the Jews].
Munich/New York 1988.

Wistrich, Robert: Wer war wer im Dritten
Reich? [Who was who in the Third
Reich?] Munich 1983.

**Other printed sources**

Die Ausbürgerung deutscher
Staatsangehöriger 1933-45 nach den im
Reichsanzeigerveröffentlichten Listen
[The expatriation of German citizens
1933-45, according to the lists published
in the 'Reichsanzeiger'], edited by
Michael Hepp, Vols. 1-3, Munich 1985.

Barbara Dölemeyer: „Dem deutschen
Volksgenossen der deutsche
Rechtswahrer! Dem Juden der jüdische
Konsulent!" [To the German national
comrades the German attorney!
To the Jew the Jewish consultant!];
Simone Ladwig-Winters: Anwalt
ohne Recht [Attorneys without rights]
(Frankfurt a.M.),both in: Broschüre zur
Festveranstaltung zum 125-jährigen
Bestehen der RAK und des OLG
[Brochure on the occasion of the 125th
anniversary of the RAK and the OLG]
Frankfurt am Main on October 1, 2004.

Internationales Militär Tribunal
[International Military Tribunal],
Nuremberg, PS -1816.

Konrad Redeker: Ansprache anlässlich der
Eröffnung der Ausstellung „Anwalt ohne
Recht" [Speech on the occasion of the
opening of the exhibition "Attorneys
without rights." see U 1-9; in: Deutscher
Juristentag: Verhandlungen des 63.

Deutschen Juristentages [German Attorneys' Day: proceedings of the 63rd German Attorneys' Day. Leipzig 2000, Vol. II/1.

J.A. Seufferts Archiv für Entscheidungen der obersten Gerichte in den deutschen Staaten [Archive for decisions of the supreme courts in the German states. Munich/Berlin 1937, vol. 91

Strauss, Herbert A. (Editor): Jewish Immigrants of the Nazi Period in the U.S.A. An Oral History Record. Munich/London/New York/Paris 1986.

**Speeches, magazines, newspaper articles**

Die Ausbürgerung deutscher Staatsangehöriger 1933-45 nach den im Reichsanzeiger veröffentlichten Listen [The expatriation of German citizens 1933-45, according to the lists published in the 'Reichsanzeiger'], edited by Michael Hepp, vols. 1-3, Munich 1985.

Report of the board of the Berlin Bar Association on the 1932 financial year. Berlin 1933.

Comité des Délégations Juives (Editor): Das Schwarzbuch [The black book]. Paris 1934. Eichmann-Prozess-Documentation [Eichmann trial documentation] vol. VI, Yad Vashem Archives.

Rechtsanwaltskammer Köln [Cologne Bar Association] (Editor): Juristen ohne Recht – Schicksale jüdischer Juristen in Köln, Bonn und Aachen in der NS-Zeit [Attorneys without rights - the fates of Jewish attorneys in Cologne, Bonn and Aachen in the Nazi era (exhibition catalog). Cologne [no year]

Schmitt, Carl: Staat, Bewegung, Volk [State, movement, people]. Hamburg 1933.

Sozialdemokratische Partei Deutschlands - SoPaDe [Social Democratic Party of Germany] (Editor): Deutschland-Berichte 1939 [German reports 1939]. Reprint Nördlingen 1980.

Traub, Michael: Die jüdische Auswanderung aus Deutschland [Jewish emigration from Germany]. Berlin 1936.

**Other sources**

Blau, Bruno: Vierzehn Jahre Not und Schrecken [Fourteen years of distress and horror]. MS. 120 S. New York 1952, YIVO.

Willy Naatz Estate

**Other materials**

Handakte Erich Meyer [Erich Meyer reference files], Bugge, Oslo

Konvolut RA Gerhard Jungfer [Attorney Gerhard Jungfer unbound collection], Berlin

Konvolut RA Joel Levi [Attorney Joel Levi unbound collection], Tel Aviv

**Interviews / information (unless they concern individuals)**

Rita Meyhöfer (deceased.), former employee of the Berlin Memorial Book, September 1996; Kerstin and Frank Wolf, Biographische Forschung und Sozialgeschichte e.V. (BFS), August 1998; attorney Abesser, Berlin 1996; attorney Achelis, Berlin 1997; Dr. Y. Arndt (deceased), Berlin 1998; Ruth Arons; Frankfurt a. M. 1997; Steinar Bugge, Oslo,1999; Inge Cohn-Lempert; Berlin 1998; Prof. Coper; Berlin 1997; attorney Erdmann, Berlin; Frank Flechtmann, 2000/2002; Ms. Dorothee Fliess, Switzerland, 1998; Mr. Gorski; Prof. Grenvile; Jerusalem 1997; Ms. Frau Anne Halle; Berlin 1998; Ms. Maria Haendcke-Hoppe-Arndt, 1998; André Hugel, Riquewihr 2001; Prof. Dr. Helmut Jäckel, Berlin 1998; Heinz Knobloch, Berlin 1997 (deceased); attorney Susanne Kossack, Berlin; attorney Tillmann Krach, Mainz; Mr. Krumeder, Munich; attorney Hubert Lang, Leipzig; attorney Joel Levi, Tel Aviv, Berlin, 1998 – 2007; Andreas Liedtke, Berlin, 1998/1999/2007; Dr. Lomski, Berlin 1998/2000/2004; Simon May, London 2007; Prof. Christoph Müller, Hugo-Preuß-Gesellschaft; Erna Proskauer (deceased), Berlin 1997; Mr. Rohmer; attorney Shimon Ullmann; Jerusalem 1997; E.W. (deceased); Berlin 1998; Dr. Wolfgang Weißleder, Babelsberg; Werner Wolff, Frankfurt/Main 1998/2000/2001; attorney Grischa Worner, 11/20/2000; Jürgen X., 08/23/1997, Berlin.

# Bibliography

1933 – Wege zur Diktatur, Beiträge der Vortragsreihe zur Ausstellung gleichen Titels [Paths to dictatorship, contributions to the lecture series on the exhibition of the same title]. Berlin 1983.

ALTER, Peter (Editor): Im Banne der Metropolen. Berlin und London in den zwanziger Jahren [In the bane of the metropolises. Berlin and London in the twenties]. Göttingen/Zürich 1993.

ANWALT- UND NOTARVEREIN BOCHUM E.V.: "Zeit ohne Recht." Justiz in Bochum nach 1933 ["Time without rights." Justice in Bochum after 1933], Bochum 2002.

APFEL, Alfred: Les dessous de la justice allemande. Paris 1934.

BADINTER, Robert: Un antisémitisme ordinaire. Vichy et les avocats juifs (1940-1944). Paris 1997.

BALL-KADURI, Kurt-Jacob: Das Leben der Juden in Deutschland im Jahre 1933. Ein Zeitbericht. [The life of the Jews in Germany in 1933. A time report]. Frankfurt a.M. 1963.

BARKAI, Avraham: Vom Boykott zur "Entjudung." Der wirtschaftliche Existenzkampf der Juden im Dritten Reich 1933-1943. [From boycott to "elimination of Jewish influence." [The economic struggle for existence of the Jews in the Third Reich 1933-1943]. Frankfurt a.M. 1986.

BAUMGARTNER, Gabriele/HEBIG, Dieter, (Editor): Biografisches Handbuch der SBZ und der DDR. Bd. 1 u. 2 [Biographical handbook of the Soviet Occupation Zone (SBZ) and the General Democratic Republic (DDR). Volumes 1 and 2, Munich 1996/97.

BENDIX, Reinhold: Von Berlin nach Berkeley: Deutsch-jüdische Identitäten [From Berlin to Berkeley: German-Jewish identities]. Frankfurt a. M. 1985.

BERGEMANN, Hans/LADWIG-WINTERS, Simone: Richter und Staatsanwälte jüdischer Herkunft in Preußen im Nationalsozialismus. Eine Dokumentation. [Judges and prosecutors of Jewish origin in Prussia during National Socialism. A documentation]. Cologne, 2004.

BERGEMANN, Hans/LADWIG-WINTERS, Simone: "Für ihn brach die Welt, wie er sie kannte, zusammen . . . " Juristen jüdischer Herkunft im Landgerichtsbezirk Potsdam ["For him, the world, as he knew it, collapsed . . . " Jurists of Jewish origin in the District Court district of Potsdam] Cologne, 2002.k

BERING, Dietz: Der Name als Stigma. Antisemitismus im Deutschen Alltag 1812-1933. [The name as a stigma. Anti-Semitism in German everyday life 1812-1933]. Stuttgart 1992.

BETH HATEFUSOTH, The Nahum Goldmann Museum of the Jewish Diaspora (Editor): Die Musiktradition der jüdischen Reformgemeinde zu Berlin [The music tradition of the Jewish reform community in Berlin], Tel Aviv 1998.

BLASIUS, Dirk/DINER, Dan (Editor): Zerbrochene Geschichte. Leben und Selbstverständnis der Juden in Deutschland [Broken story. Life and self-understanding of the Jews in Germany]. Frankfurt a. M. 1991.

BLASIUS, Dirk: Zwischen Rechtsvertrauen und Rechtsstörung [Between legal certainty and legal arbitrariness]; in: BLASIUS, Dirk/DINER, Dan (Editor): Zerbrochene Geschichte [Broken story], pages 121-137.

BLAU, Bruno: Das Ausnahmerecht für die Juden in Deutschland 1933-1945 [The special legal regime for Jews in Germany 1933-1945]. 2nd edition Düsseldorf 1954.

BOSL, Karl/FRANZ, Günther/HOFMANN, Hans Hubert: Biographisches Wörterbuch zur Deutschen Geschichte [Biographical dictionary of German history]. 2nd edition Munich 1973, vol. 1.

BROSZAT, Martin/FREI, Norbert (Editor): Das Dritte Reich im Überblick. Chronik, Ereignisse, Zusammenhänge [The Third Reich at a glance. Timeline, events, context]. 5th edition Munich 1996.

BUSSENIUS, O./HÜTTEMANN, M./ SCHWEND, G: Erfahrungen eines Kölner Anwalts [Experiences of a Cologne attorney]; in: 100 Jahre

Kölner Anwaltverein, Festschrift [100 years Cologne Attorneys' Association. Commemorative publication]. Cologne 1987.

C.H.BECK VERLAG (Editor): Juristen im Porträt. Verlag und Autoren in 4 Jahrzehnten, zum 225-jährigen Verlagsjubiläum [Attorneys in portrait. Publisher and authors in 4 decades, for the 225th anniversary of the publishing house]. Munich 1988.

DAWIDOWICZ, Lucy: Der Krieg gegen die Juden 1933-1945 [The war against the Jews]. Munich 1979.

DIE EXTREME BERÜHREN SICH. Walther Rathenau 1867-1922. Katalog zur Ausstellung des Deutschen Historischen Museum in Zusammenarbeit mit dem Leo-Baeck-Institute [THE EXTREMES TOUCH. Walther Rathenau 1867-1922. Catalog of the exhibition of the German Historical Museum in cooperation with the Leo-Baeck-Institute], New York, Berlin 1994.

DIE JÜDISCHE EMIGRATION AUS DEUTSCHLAND. Katalog der Ausstellung der Deutschen Bibliothek Frankfurt a.M. in Zusammenarbeit mit dem Leo-Baeck-Institute [THE JEWISH EMIGRATION FROM GERMANY. Catalog of the exhibition of the Deutsche Bibliothek Frankfurt a.M. in cooperation with the Leo-Baeck-Institute], New York, Frankfurt a.M. 1985.

DIEDERICHSEN, Uwe: Karl Larenz, in: C.H.Beck Verlag (1988). Pages 495-510.

DOEHRING, Karl: Ernst Forsthoff, in: C.H.Beck Verlag (1988). Pages 341-350.

DOUMA, Eva: Deutsche Anwälte zwischen Demokratie und Diktatur 1930-1955 [German attorneys between democracy and dictatorship 1930-1955]. Frankfurt a.M. 1998.

EBEL, Friedrich/RANDELZHOFER, Albrecht (Editor): Rechtsentwicklungen in Berlin [Legal developments in Berlin]. Berlin, New York 1988.

ECKERT, Joachim/TENS, Antonia: Hitler und die Juristen. Äußerungen und tatsächliche Politik [Hitler and the attorneys. Utterances and actual politics]; in: Recht und Politik [Law and politics] 1/1993, pages 34-50.

ENGELMANN, Bernt: Die unfreiwilligen Reisen des Putti Eichelbaum [The involuntary journeys of Putti Eichelbaum]. Göttingen 1996.

FRAENKEL, Ernst: Gesammelte Schriften. Bd. 1-4 [Collected words. Volumes 1-4], Baden-Baden 1999-2004.

FRAENKEL, Ernst: Der Doppelstaat (German edition of the original edition "The Dual State"). Frankfurt a.M. 1984.

FRAENKEL, Ernst: Zur Soziologie der Klassenjustiz [On the sociology of class justice]. Berlin 1927.

FREY, Erich: Ich beantrage Freispruch [I demand acquittal]. Hamburg 1960.

FRIEDENSBURG, Ferdinand: Die Weimarer Republik [The Weimar Republic]. Berlin 1946.

GALL, Lothar/FELDMAN, Gerald D./ JAMES, Harold/HOLTFRETERICH, Carl-Ludwig/BÜSCHGEN, Hans E.: Die Deutsche Bank: 1870-1995 [Deutsche Bank: 1870-1995]. Munich 1995.

GÖPPINGER, Horst: Juristen jüdischer Abstammung [Attorneys of Jewish descent] in "Dritten Reich." Entrechtung und Verfolgung [Third Reich. Disenfranchisement and persecution]. 2nd edition Munich 1990.

GOSEWINKEL, Dieter: Adolf Arndt. Wiederbegründung des Rechtsstaates aus dem Geist der Sozialdemokratie (1945-1961) [Adolf Arndt. Reestablishment of the constitutional state from the spirit of social democracy (1945-1961)]. Bonn 1991.

GRAB, Walter: Der Deutsche Weg der Judenemanzipation [The German way of Jewish emancipation]. Munich 1991.

GRAB, Walter: Reflexionen zum Scheitern der Judenemanzipation in Deutschland [Reflections on the failure of Jewish emancipation in Germany]; in: 1933 – Wege zur Diktatur [1933 - Paths to dictatorship]. (1983), pages 179-190.

GRONEMANN, Sammy: Tohuwabohu [Hullabaloo]. 2nd edition Leipzig 2001.

GRUCHMANN, Lothar: Justiz im Dritten Reich 1933-1940. Anpassung und

Unterwerfung in der Ära Gürtner
[Justice in the Third Reich 1933-1940.
Adaptation and subjugation in the
Gürtner era]. Munich 1988.

GRUNER, Wolf: Die Reichshauptstadt und
die Verfolgung der Berliner Juden
1933-1945 [The Reich capital and
the persecution of Berlin Jews 1933-
1945]; in: Topographie des Terrors
[Topography of terror] (1995), pages
229-266.

GRUNER, Wolf: Judenverfolgung in
Berlin 1933-1945. Eine Chronologie
der Behördenmaßnahmen in der
Reichshauptstadt [Jewish persecution
in Berlin 1933-1945. A chronology of
the official measures in the imperial
capital]. Berlin 1996.

GUMBEL, Emil Julius: Vom Fememord zur
Reichskanzlei [From the "Fememord"
murders to the Reich Chancellery].
Heidelberg 1962.

HAMMERSCHMIDT, Wolfgang:
Spurensuche. Zur Geschichte der
jüdischen Familie Hammerschmidt
in Cottbus [Search for clues. On
the history of the Jewish family
Hammerschmidt in Cottbus]. Gießen
1996.

HANNOVER, Heinrich/HANNOVER-
DRÜCK, Elisabeth: Politische Justiz
1918-1933 [Political justice 1918-
1933]. Hamburg 1977.

HEIBER, Helmut: Die Republik von Weimar
[The Republic of Weimar]. 22nd ed.
Nördlingen 1996.

HEINRICHS, Helmut/FRANZKI, Harald/
SCHMALZ, Klaus/STOLLEIS,
Michael (Editors): Deutsche Juristen
jüdischer Herkunft [German attorneys
of Jewish origin]. Munich 1993.

HILBERG, Raul: Die Vernichtung
der europäischen Juden. Die
Gesamtgeschichte des Holocaust [The
destruction of European Jews. The
complete history of the Holocaust].
Frankfurt a.M. 1982.

HOFER, Walther (Editor): Der
Nationalsozialismus. Dokumente
1933-1945 [National Socialism.
Documents 1933-1945]. Frankfurt
a.M. 1960.

HOVEN, Herbert (Editor): Der
unaufhaltsame Selbstmord des Botho
Laserstein [The unstoppable suicide
of Botho Laserstein], Frankfurt
a.M.1990

HUBATSCH, Walter: Hindenburg und der
Staat [Hindenburg and the state].
Göttingen 1966.

ISAY, Rudolf: Aus meinem Leben [From my
life]. Weinheim 1960.

ISERMANN, Edgar/SCHLÜTER, Michael
(Editors): Justiz und Anwaltschaft
in Braunschweig 1879-2004
[Justice and the legal profession
in Braunschweig 1879-2004],
Braunschweig 2004.

JOCHHEIM, Gernot: Frauenprotest in
der Rosenstraße. "Gebt uns unsere
Männer wieder" [Women protest
in Rosenstraße. "Give us our men
again"]. Berlin 1993.

JUNGFER, Gerhard: Julius Magnus. Mentor
und Mahner der freien Advokatur
[Julius Magnus. Mentor and
admonisher of the free law practice;
in: HEINRICHS (1993), pages
517-530.

JUNGFER, Gerhard: Max Alsberg.
Verteidigung als ethische Mission
[Defense as an ethical mission]; in:
Kritische Justiz [Critical justice]
(1988). Pages 141-152.

JUNGFER, Gerhard/KÖNIG, Stefan: 125
Jahre Rechtsanwaltskammer Berlin,
Jubiläumsschrift [125 years Berlin
Bar Association Berlin, Anniversary
publication], edited by the Berlin Bar
Association. Berlin 2006.

KAMMER, Hilde/BARTSCH, Elisabeth:
Nationalsozialismus. Begriffe aus der
Zeit der Gewaltherrschaft 1933-1945
[National Socialism. Terms from the
time of tyranny, 1933-1945]. Reinbek
1992.

KERR, Judith: Warten bis der Frieden kommt
[Wait until peace comes]. Ravensburg
1975.

KLARSFELD, Serge: Vichy, Auschwitz, le
rôle de Vichy dans la solution finale
de la question juive en France, Paris
1985.

KLEIN, Adolf/RENNEN, Günter (Editor):
Justitia Coloniensis. Landgericht
und Amtsgericht Köln erzählen ihre
Geschichte(n) [Justitia Coloniensis.
The Cologne District Court and

Cologne Municipal Court tell their story (stories)]. Cologne 1981.

KLEMPERER, Victor: LTI. Notizbuch eines Philologen [LTI. Notebook of a philologist]. Berlin 1947.

KNOBEL, M.: L' élimination des juristes juifs en Europe à partir de 1933. Cahiers Bernard Lazare, 1990, numéros 125-126.

KNOBLOCH, Heinz: Der beherzte Reviervorsteher [ The courageous district chief]. 2nd edition Berlin 1993.

KNOBLOCH, Heinz: "Meine liebste Mathilde." Das unauffällige Leben der Mathilde Jacob ["My dearest Mathilde." The inconspicuous life of Mathilde Jacob]. 2nd edition Berlin 1986.

KÖNIG, Stefan: Vom Dienst am Recht. Rechtsanwälte als Strafverteidiger im Nationalsozialismus [In the service of justice. Attorneys as defense attorneys during National Socialism] Berlin 1987.

KÖNIGSEDER, Angelika: Recht und nationalsozialistische Herrschaft. Berliner Anwälte 1933-1945 [Law and National Socialist rule. Berlin attorneys 1933-1945] Bonn 2001.

KRACH, Tillmann: Jüdische Rechtsanwälte in Preußen. Bedeutung der freien Advokatur und ihre Zerstörung durch den Nationalsozialismus [Jewish attorneys in Prussia. Importance of the free law practice and its destruction by National Socialism] Munich 1991.

KRACH, Tillmann (Editor): Paul Simon (1884-1977), Meine Erinnerungen – Das Leben des jüdischen Deutschen Paul Simon, Rechtsanwalt in Mainz, Sonderheft der Mainzer Geschichtsblätter [Paul Simon (1884-1977), My memories - The life of the Jewish German Paul Simon, attorney in Mainz, special edition of the Mainzer Geschichtsblätter], Mainz 2003.

KRITISCHE JUSTIZ( Editor): Streitbare Juristen. Eine andere Tradition [Controversial attorneys. Another tradition]. Baden-Baden 1988.

LADWIG-WINTERS, Simone I: Wertheim – ein Warenhausunternehmen und seine Eigentümer. Ein Beispiel der Entwicklung der Berliner Warenhäuser bis zur "Arisierung" [Wertheim - a department store company and its owners. An example of the development of the Berlin department stores until "Aryanization."]. Münster 1997.

LADWIG-WINTERS, Simone II: Wertheim. Geschichte eines Warenhauses [Wertheim. History of a department store]. Berlin 1997.

LADWIG-WINTERS, Simone: Freiheit und Bindung. Zur Geschichte der Jüdischen Reformgemeinde zu Berlin von den Anfängen bis zu ihrem Ende 1939 [Freedom and attachment. On the history of the Jewish Reform Synagogue in Berlin from its beginnings until its end in 1939]; edited by Peter Galliner. Berlin 2004.

LANDAU, Peter/RIESS, Rolf (Editor): Recht und Politik in Bayern zwischen Prinzregentenzeit und Nationalsozialismus. Die Erinnerungen von Philipp Loewenfeld. [Law and politics in Bavaria between the Regency era and National Socialism. The memoirs of Philipp Loewenfeld] Ebelsbach 2004.

LITTEN, Irmgard: Eine Mutter kämpft [A mother is fighting]. Rudolstadt presumably 1947.

LUIG, Klaus: ". . . weil er nicht arischer Abstammung ist." Jüdische Juristen in Köln während der NS-Zeit [". . . because he is not of Aryan descent." Jewish attorneys in Cologne during the National Socialist era] Cologne 2004.

MARX, Alfred: Das Schicksal der jüdischen Juristen in Württemberg und Hohenzollern [The fate of the Jewish attorneys in Württemberg and Hohenzollern]. 1965, Sonderdruck des Amtsblatts des bad.-württ. Justizministeriums, Die Justiz [Special edition of the official journal of the Baden-Wuerttemberg Ministry of Justice, Die Justiz (The Justice), 1965].

MECKLENBURG, Frank/STIEFEL, Ernest: Deutsche Juristen im amerikanischen Exil [German attorneys in American exile]. Tübingen 1991.

MEYER, Winfried: Unternehmen Sieben. Eine Rettungsaktion für vom Holocaust Bedrohte aus dem Amt Ausland [Company Seven. A rescue operation for those threatened by the Holocaust from the Foreign Office]/ Abwehr im Oberkommando der Wehrmacht Frankfurt a.M. (Defense in the High Command of the Armed Forces Frankfurt a.M.) 1993.

MEYHÖFER, Rita: Gäste in Berlin? Jüdisches Schülerleben in der Weimarer Republik und im Nationalsozialismus [Guests in Berlin? Jewish student life in the Weimar Republic and under National Socialism]. Hamburg 1996.

MINUTH, Karl-Heinz: Die Regierung Hitler. Bd.1 [The government of Hitler, vol. 1]. , Boppard a.Rh. 1983.

MORISSE, Heiko: Jüdische Rechtsanwälte in Hamburg – Ausgrenzung und Verfolgung im NS-Staat [Jewish attorneys in Hamburg - exclusion and persecution in the Nazi State]. Hamburg 2003.

MÜLLER, Ingo: Furchtbare Juristen. Die unbewältigte Vergangenheit unserer Justiz [Terrible attorneys. The unresolved past of our justice]. Munich 1987.

MÜLLER, Ingo: Rudolf Olden (1885-1940), Journalist und Anwalt der Republik [Journalist and attorney of the republic]; in: Kritische Justiz [Critical justice](1988), p. 180 ff.

NEUMANN, Franz: Behemoth. Struktur und Praxis des Nationalsozialismus 1933-1944 Frankfurt a.M. 1993 (originally published in 1944 in the USA under the title: Behemoth. The structure and practice of National Socialism 1933-1944).

OSTLER, Fritz: Die deutschen Rechtsanwälte 1871-1971 [The German attorneys 1871-1971]. Essen 1971.

PROSKAUER, Erna: Wege und Umwege. Erinnerungen einer Berliner Rechtsanwältin [Paths and detours. Memoirs of a Berlin attorney]. Frankfurt a.M. 1996.

RASEHORN, Theo: Der Untergang der deutschen linksbürgerlichen Kultur - beschrieben nach den Lebensläufen jüdischer Juristen [The collapse of German left-wing middle-class culture - presented through the lives of Jewish jurists]. Baden-Baden 1988.

RICHARZ, Monika: Jüdisches Leben in Deutschland. Selbstzeugnisse zur Sozialgeschichte 1918-1945 [Jewish life in Germany. Personal testimonials on social history 1918-1945]. Stuttgart 1982.

RÖWEKAMP, Marion: Juristinnen. Lexikon zu Leben und Werk [Female attorneys. Encyclopedia on their lives and work]. Baden-Baden 2005.

RUMPF, Max: Anwalt und Anwaltstand. Eine rechtswissenschaftliche und rechtssoziologische Untersuchung [Attorneys and the legal profession. A jurisprudential and sociological investigation]; published by the Deutsches Anwaltverein. Leipzig 1926.

RÜRUP, Reinhard: Die Emanzipation der Juden und die verzögerte Öffnung der juristischen Berufe [The emancipation of the Jews and the delayed opening of the legal professions]; in: HEINRICHS (1993), pages 1-25.

RÜRUP, Reinhard (Editor): Topographie des Terrors. Gestapo, SS und Reichssicherheitshauptamt auf dem "Prinz-Albrecht-Gelände." Eine Dokumentation. [Topography of terror. Gestapo, SS and the Reich Security Main Office on the "Prinz Albrecht premises." A documentation]. Berlin 1987.

SABROW, Martin: Der Rathenaumord. Rekonstruktion einer Verschwörung gegen die Republik von Weimar [The Rathenau murder. Reconstruction of a conspiracy against the Republic of Weimar]. Munich, 1994.

SCHEFFLER, Wolfgang: Judenverfolgung im Dritten Reich 1933-1945 [Jewish persecution in the Third Reich 1933-1945]. Berlin 1960.

SCHILD, Wolfgang: Berühmte Berliner Kriminalprozesse der Zwanziger Jahre [Famous Berlin criminal trials of the twenties]; in: EBEL, Friedrich/ RANDELZHOFER, Albrecht (Editors): Rechtsentwicklungen in Berlin [Legal developments in Berlin].

Berlin, New York (1988), pages 121-191.

SCHILDE, Kurt/SCHULTZ, Rolf/ WALLECZECK, Silvia: SA-Gefängnis Papestraße. Spuren und Zeugnisse [SA prison Papestrasse. Traces and testimonies]. Berlin 1996.

SCHNEIDER, Heinz-Jürger/SCHWARZ, Erika/SCHWARZ, Josef: Die Rechtsanwälte der Roten Hilfe. Politische Strafverteidiger in der Weimarer Republik [The attorneys of the Red Aid. Political defense attorneys in the Weimar Republic]. Bonn 2002.

SCHORN, Hubert: Rechtberatungsmissbrauchsgesetz [Law for the prevention of the abuse of the provision of legal counsel]. Darmstadt, Nürnberg 1957.

SCHRÖDER-TEPPE, Martina: Wenn Unrecht zu Recht wird ... Das Schicksal jüdischer Rechtsanwälte im Bezirk der Rechtsanwaltskammer Kassel nach 1933 [If injustice becomes law . . . The fate of Jewish attorneys in the district of the Kassel Bar Association after 1933]. Gudensberg-Gleichen 2006.

SLING (Pseudonym für Paul Schlesinger): Richter und Gerichtete [Judges and the judged]. Munich 1969.

STRAUSS, Herbert A.: Jewish Emigration from Germany. Nazi Policies and Jewish Responses (I); in: Yearbook Leo Baeck Institute 1980.

STRENGE, Barbara: Juden im Preußischen Justizdienst 1812-1918. Der Zugang zu den juristischen Berufen als Indikator der gesellschaftlichen Emanzipation [Jews in the Prussian Justice Service 1812-1918. Access to the legal professions as an indicator of social emancipation]. Munich/New Providence/London/Paris 1996.

TERGIT, Gabriele: Blüten der Zwanziger Jahre [Flowers of the twenties]. Berlin 1984.

TOPOGRAPHIE DES TERRORS (Publisher): Jüdische Geschichte in Berlin. Essays und Studien [[Jewish history in Berlin. Essays and studies]. Berlin 1995.

TOURY, Jacob: Die politischen Orientierungen der Juden in Deutschland von Jena bis Weimar [The political orientations of the Jews in Germany from Jena to Weimar]. Tübingen 1966.

UHLIG, Heinrich: Die Warenhäuser im Dritten Reich [The department stores in the Third Reich]. Cologne/Opladen 1956.

VOLKOV, Shulamit: Ich bin ein Deutscher jüdischen Stammes [I am a German of the Jewish people]; in: Die Extreme berühren sich. Walther Rathenau 1867-1922. Katalog. zur Ausstellung im Jahr 1994 [The extremes touch. Walther Rathenau 1867-1922. Catalog of the exhibition in 1994], published by the German Historical Museum, Berlin 1994, pages 129-138.

WALK, Joseph (Editor): Das Sonderrecht für die Juden im NS-Staat. Eine Sammlung der gesetzlichen Maßnahmen und Richtlinien – Inhalt und Bedeutung [The special legal regime for Jews in the National Socialist state. A collection of legal measures and guidelines - content and meaning]. Heidelberg/Karlsruhe 1981.

WEBER, Reinhard: Das Schicksal der jüdischen Rechtsanwälte in Bayern nach 1933 [The fate of Jewish attorneys in Bavaria after 1933]. Munich 2006.

WEISS, Hermann/HOSER, Paul: Einleitung zur Edition: Die Deutschnationalen und die Zerstörung der Weimarer Republik. Aus dem Tagebuch von Reinhold Quaatz 1928-1933 [Introduction to the edition: The German Nationals and the Destruction of the Weimar Republic. From the diary of Reinhold Quaatz 1928-1933]. Munich 1989.

WOLF, Kerstin/WOLF, Frank: Reichsfluchtsteuer und Steuersteckbriefe 1932-1942 [Reich flight tax and warrants issued for tax code violations]; edited by Biographische Forschungen und Sozialgeschichte e.V. Berlin 1997.

YERUSHALMI, Yosef Hayim: Zachor! – Erinnere Dich! [Yosef Hayim: Zachor! - Remember!] Berlin 1988.

## Photo Credits

Archive of the author: Pages 21, 30, 31, 40, 63, 64, 67, 102, 231, 285

Archiv für Kunst und Geschichte [Archive for art and history]: p. 36

Archiv Pisarek [Pisarek Archive]: pages 130, 135, 196, 257, 263

Berlinische Galerie [Berlin Gallery]: Title background

Bildarchiv Preußischer Kulturbesitz [Prussian Cultural Heritage Image Archive]: p. 84

Bundesarchiv [Federal Archive]: pages 52/53, 213

Deutsches Literaturarchiv Marbach [German Literature Archive Marbach]: pages 98, 119, 134

Forschungsstelle für Zeitgeschichte, Hamburg [The Research Centre for Contemporary History, Hamburg]: p. 37

Jüdisches Museum Berlin [Jewish Museum Berlin]: pages 151, 279

Konvolut Bugge [Bugge unbound collection]: p. 224

Landesarchiv Berlin, Landesbildstelle/ Wiedergutmachungsakten/Akten RAK Berlin [Berlin National Archive, National Photographic Service/Compensation files/ Berlin RAK files]: pages 11, 29, 43, 75, 88, 106, 121, 123, 131, 145, 161, 164, 176, 191, 192, 193, 194, 199, 225, 233, 236, 237, 238, 240, 244, 245, 249, 250, 256, 257, 276, 281, 286

Naatz album: pages 17, 79, 83, 120, 124, 130, 131, 135, 136, 137, 139, 142, 143, 148, 150, 157, 159, 162, 164, 170, 175, 179, 181, 184, 188, 192, 200, 201, 203, 208, 209, 211, 215, 216, 221, 224, 234, 235, 237, 243, 249, 250, 251, 253, 257, 262, 265, 267, 274, 275, 276, 278, 282, 283, 285, 287

Neue Justiz, 1959: p. 195

Arndt private collection: p. 77, 109

Arons private collection: p. 110

Bendix private collection: p. 54, 118

Bileski private collection: p. 124

Cohn-Lempert private collection: pages 88, 138

Coper private collection: pages 74, 139

Dobler private collection: p. 151

Eger private collection: p. 143

Engelmann private collection: p. 144

Fliess private collection: p. 151

Fontheim private collection: p. 151

Friedlaender private collection: p. 156

Galliner private collection: p. 158

Goldsmith private collection: p. 93

Grossmann private collection: p. 166

Grunfeld private collection: pages 136, 271

Haas private collection: p. 139

Hammersmith private collection: p. 82

Hepner private collection: p. 173

Kallmann private collection: p. 190

Kuhlmann private collection: p. 146

Levi private collection: p. 208

Lomski private collection: p. 96

Manasse private file collection: p. 216 (Photo Loewy)

May private file collection: p. 212

Müller private file collection: p. 95

Meyer private file collection: p. 225

Numann private file collection: p. 206

Proskaue private file collection: p. 102, 111

Schale private file collection: p. 196

Schlesinger private file collection: p. 258

Schlör private file collection: p. 166

Sholeq private file collection: p. 166

Simson private file collection: p. 284

Sonderstandesamt Arolsen, Abt. Sachsenhausen: p. 81

Sonnenfeld private file collection: p. 269

Stein private file collection: p. 270

Simon private file collection: p. 186

Thaler private file collection: p. 89

Wattenberg private file collection: p. 189

Wolfsohn private file collection: p. 286

Stiftung Akademie der Künste [Academy of Arts Foundation]: p. 14

SV-Bilderdienst: p. 35, 44, 46, 47

Tramer, Hans (Editor): In Zwei Welten [In two worlds]. Tel Aviv 1962: p.229

Ullstein Bild: p. 22, 25, 40, 41, 107

Verfolgte Berliner Stadtverordnete [Persecuted Berlin city councillors]: p. 106

# Author Acknowledgments

The biographical index would not have been achieved without the support of numerous persons and institutions; information ranging from individuals to individual fates, but also to additional sources, was an invaluable help. I would particularly like to single out the support of the attorneys Crash, Mainz; Erdmann, Kossack, Jungfer and Naatz, Berlin; Joel Levi, Tel Aviv. Due to the special support of archivists, who always cooperated, this edition could be expanded considerably, in particular Andreas Grunwald, BArch, and Prof. Dr. Dettmer und Bianca Welzing, LAB, have been reliable partners over the years. I do not want to diminish my thanks to the following people:

Prof. Barkai, Israel; Prof. Atina Grossmann, Dr. Frank Mecklenburg, Prof. Stiefel (deceased) and Prof. Haac (deceased), New York; Mr. Friedlaender, New York; Director Peter Galliner, (deceased.), Berlin; Prof. Grenville, Great Britain; Attorney Shimon Ullmann, Jerusalem; Inge Cohn-Lempert, Berlin; Prof. Dr. Coper, Berlin; Dr. Gabriele Meyer, Hamburg; Ruth Recknagel, Director of the Wiedergutmachungsämter Berlin [Restitution Offices Berlin] (out of service); Dr. Hermann Simon, Centrum Judaicum, Berlin; the Berlin Attorneys Dr. Dombek, Proskauer (deceased), Setsevits, Achelis, Abesser and Lüth; Prof. Dr. Rottleuthner, Department of Law, Free University of Berlin; Verein Biographische Forschungen und Sozialgeschichte [Association of Biographical Research and Social History]; as well as Gabriele Dietz, Marga Richter, Edith Winner, Anna Winters, Laura Winters and Fabian Winters—and especially Hans Bergemann.

—Simone Ladwig-Winters

# LAWYERS WITHOUT RIGHTS
## The Fate of Jewish Lawyers in Berlin after 1933

When the rule of law is corrupted, justice is denied. Each day the ABA Center for Human Rights works to advance the rule of law around the world and ensure access to justice to those who are most disenfranchised.

**Lawyers Without Rights** In partnership with the German Federal Bar, the Lawyers Without Rights project includes an exhibition and book, with ancillary programming. These materials document the plight of Jewish lawyers in Germany during the Third Reich, revealing how the rule of law was manipulated, redefined and distorted during this era and how Jewish lawyers were stripped of their power to protect it. The Nazis employed laws to deny German Jews their freedom and their lives. But more than a focus on a historic moment, the Lawyers Without Rights project eulogizes individual lawyers, preserving stories of their legal contributions, courage and resolve.

## DONATE TO THE PROJECT

Charitable support makes this Center project possible. To continue these critical efforts to protect human rights, please donate to the Center for Human Rights and the Lawyers Without Rights project. Your tax-deductible donation can be made:

Online: **donate.americanbar.org/lawyerswithoutrights**

Over the phone: **312-988-5421**

Mail your contribution, made payable to the
ABA Fund for Justice and Education, to:

**ABA Fund for Justice and Education**
**321 N. Clark St.**
**Chicago, IL 60654**

To learn more about the project, please visit: **lawyerswithoutrights.com**